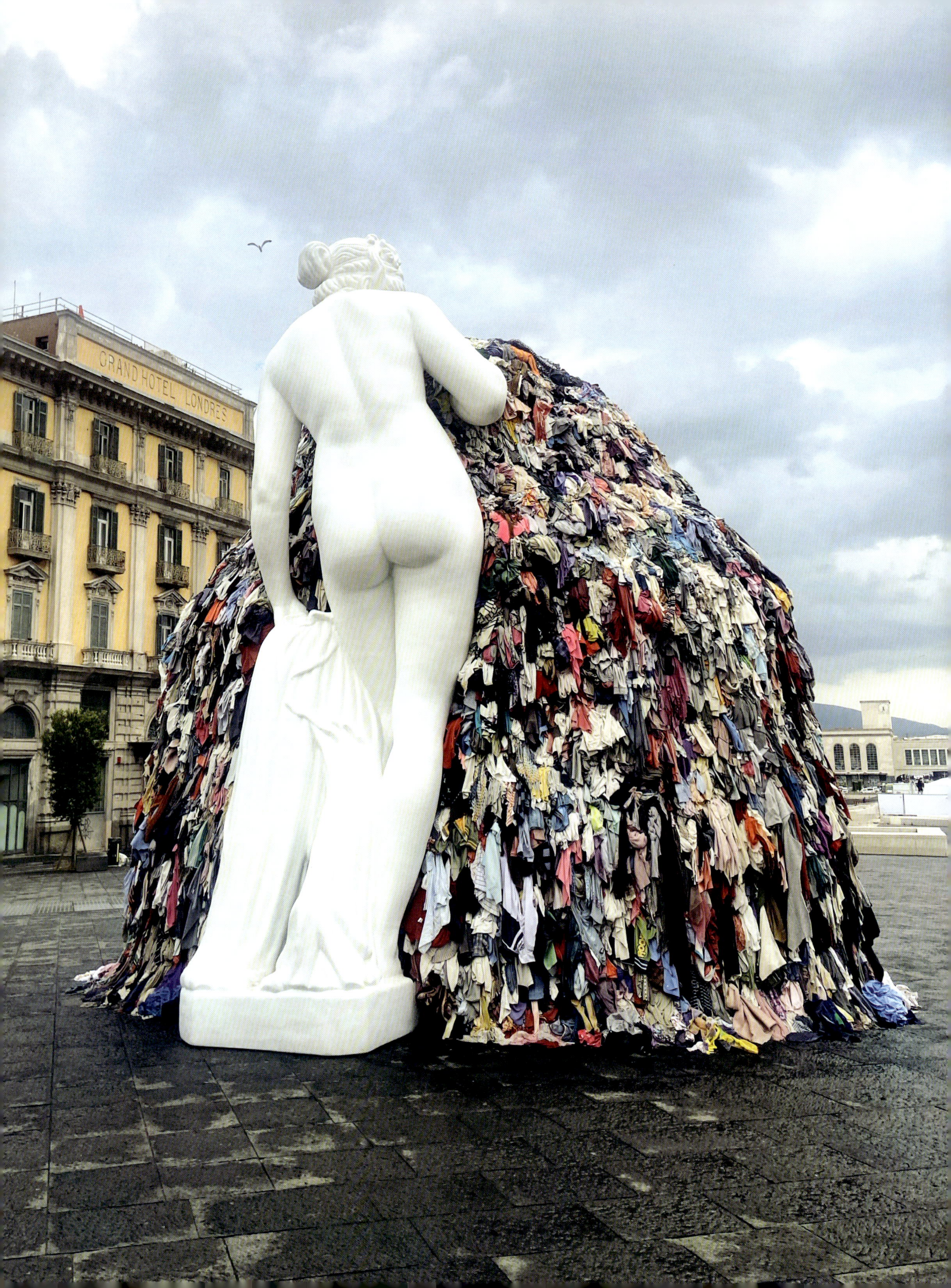
GRAND HOTEL LONDRES

Michelangelo Pistoletto

FIGURATION AND CULTURAL POLITICS

TENLEY BICK

Yale University Press New Haven and London

Published with assistance from The New Foundation for Art History

yalebooks.com/art

Designed by Leslie Fitch and Julie Allred
Cover designed by Jeff Wincapaw
Set in Crimson and Source Sans Pro type by BW&A Books, Inc.
Printed in Singapore by Pristone Pte. Ltd.

Library of Congress Control Number: 2024942631
ISBN 978-0-300-27834-7

A catalogue record for this book is available from the British Library.

This paper meets the requirements of ANSI/NISO Z39.48–1992 (Permanence of Paper).

10 9 8 7 6 5 4 3 2 1

Jacket illustrations: (*front*) fig. 2 detail; (*back*) fig. 21.
Frontispiece: Michelangelo Pistoletto, *Venere degli stracci* (Venus of the Rags), 2023–24. Mixed media, monumental version, approx. 33 ft. (10 m) high. Piazza Municipio, Naples, Italy. Photo: © Tenley Bick

For Sofia

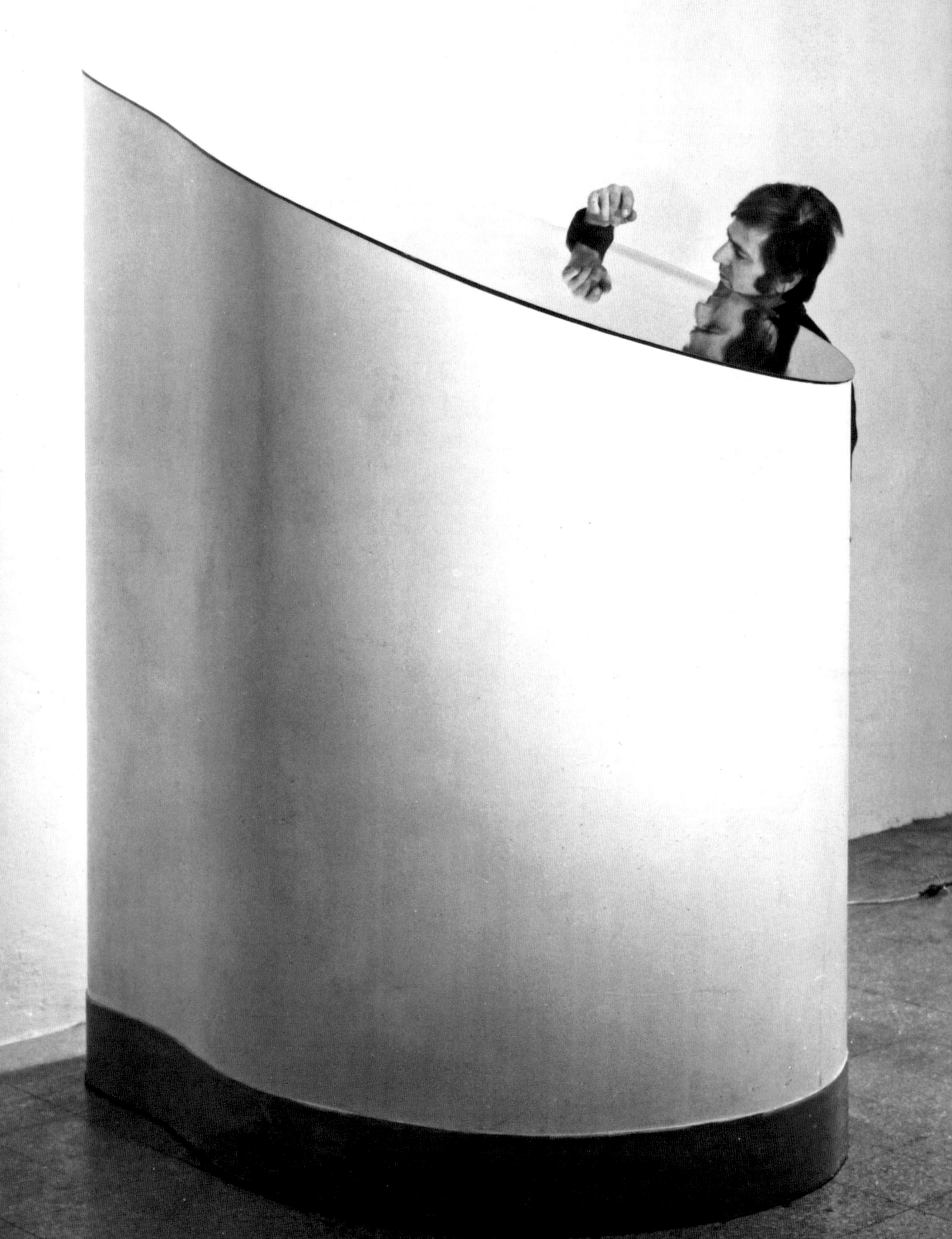

Contents

Fig. 106 detail

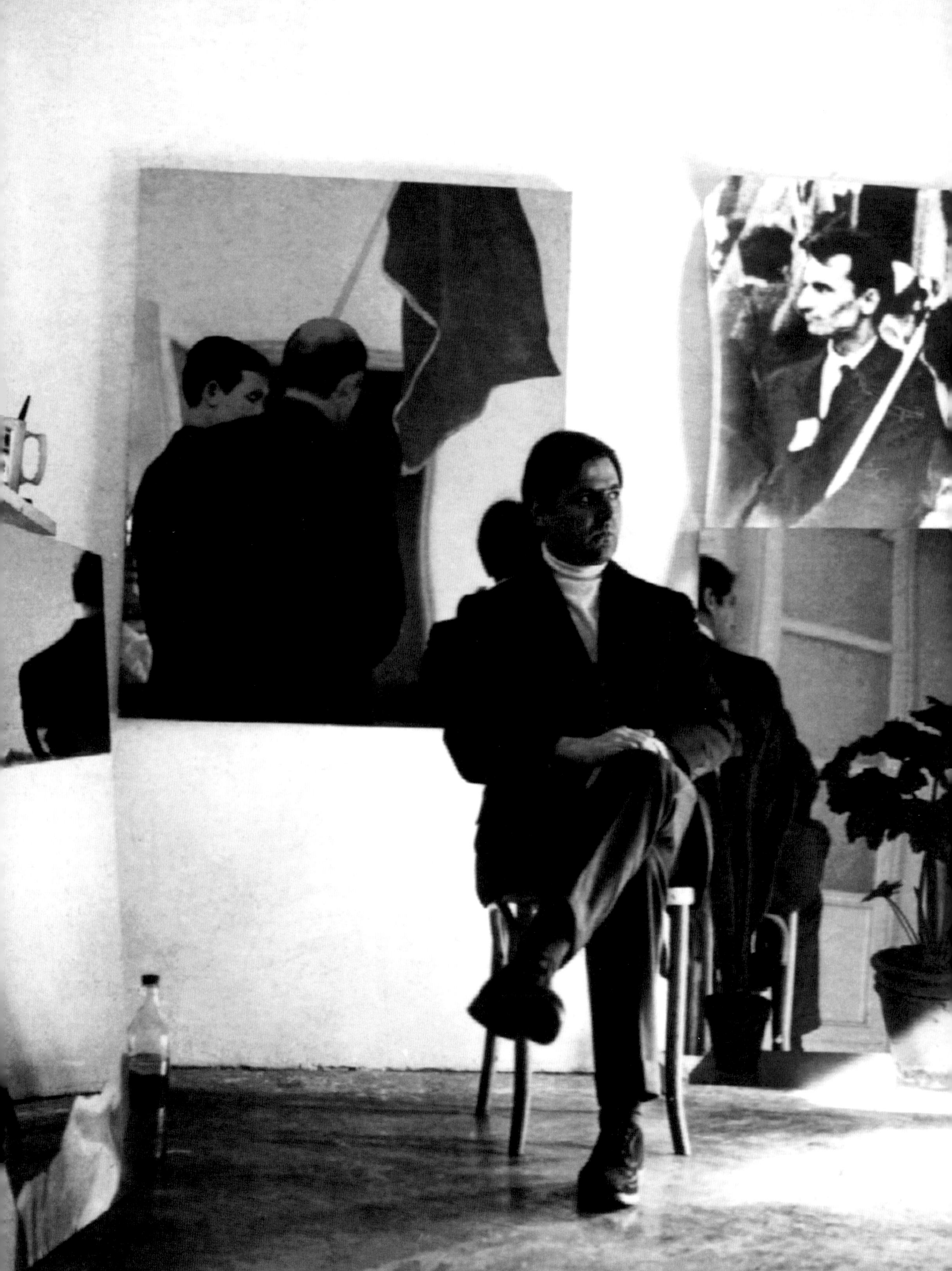

Acknowledgments

Any acknowledgments for this book begin with those due to Michelangelo Pistoletto, the artist whose endlessly compelling practice I have attempted to grapple with here. Michelangelo, thank you for your generous interviews over the years, for answering my questions large and small, and for sharing the history of your work with me. Thank you for your intellectual provocations, artistic convictions, and humor. I thank you and Maria for your hospitality and support, and for providing me with images and reproductions permissions for this book, without which it wouldn't have been possible. While I have long admired your boundless creative energy, I especially admire, and thank you for, your gracious humility and humanity. You made approaching the dauntingly complex and prolific expanse of your work, even in the earliest days of my career, somehow feasible. It has been one of the honors of my life to know you and your work. *Grazie infinite.*

This book would also not have been possible without the generous assistance of Pistoletto's longtime archivist, Marco Farano, whose deep knowledge, conversation, and support, including fact-checking of the final manuscript, aided me throughout this project. I extend my thanks to him, to Alessandro Lacirasella, and to the rest of the collegial team at Cittadellarte–Fondazione Pistoletto, who provided images, assistance, workspace, and a warm welcome whenever I was there.

My immense gratitude also goes to my editor, Amy Canonico, for championing this project and shepherding this book into existence, and to Yale University Press. Amy, your expert editorial stewardship has been invaluable to me as a writer and scholar. This book would not be what it is without your guidance, advice, and support. Thank you. I would also like to thank my manuscript editor, Laura Jones Dooley, for her careful work on the text, as well as interior designer Julie Allred, associate design and production manager Rachel Faulise, assistant managing editor Alison Hagge, editorial assistants Elizabeth Searcy and Owen Silverman, indexer Krister Swartz, cover designer Jeff Wincapaw, and proofreader Kati Woock for their help. I also thank the anonymous readers who provided helpful feedback during peer review.

I am indebted to the institutions that provided subvention grants in support of this project, including the New Foundation for Art History and the Florida State University Council on Research and Creativity. The Florida State University College of Fine Arts and Department of Art History provided essential image and additional subvention funds. I thank my dean, James Frazier, as well as Michael Carrasco, Rachel Collins, and Shelby Heitmuller for support.

This book was made possible through the generous time and assistance of many people, museums, and organizations beyond these key individuals. Critical research and writing support in its advanced stages was provided by Magazzino Italian Art Foundation in Cold Spring, New York, where I was scholar-in-residence from 2019 to 2020. I thank Magazzino's cofounders Giorgio Spanu and Nancy Olnick, as well as former director Vittorio Calabrese, for support. Other funding was provided by the Institute of International Education (IIE) in the form of a Graduate Dissertation Fellowship in International Study (for Italy); by the University of

Fig. 62 detail

California, Los Angeles, Department of Art History, in the form of a Patricia McCarron McGinn Award and Edward A. Dickson Fellowships; and from UCLA's Graduate Division in the form of a Dissertation Year Fellowship. The Italian Art Society, Bibliotheca Hertziana, and University of Louisiana at Lafayette provided other funding for conferences and guest lectures, where I was able to share parts of the project with colleagues and students. The American Association for Italian Studies, Center for Italian Modern Art, and Magazzino Italian Art Foundation provided stimulating panel and conference opportunities at various points in the project, through which I was able to share and receive helpful feedback on some of this work.

This work was also facilitated by archivists and librarians at many institutions, including the Castello di Rivoli, the Archivio di Stato di Torino, the DAMS library at UNITO, the Biblioteca Musicale Andrea della Corte (Turin), the Archivio Rai, the Galleria d'Arte Moderna (GAM) Torino, the Fondazione Merz, the Fondazione Nespolo, and the Smithsonian Archives of American Art in Washington, DC, and New York. Artwork visitations were generously organized by the Walker Art Center and the Herbert F. Johnson Museum of Art at Cornell. The Menil and Des Moines Art Center provided object photography during research. Finally, the National Gallery of Art in Washington graciously provided interview space during Pistoletto's visit in 2017 while I was a visiting assistant professor at Washington College.

I am indebted to the many artists, archives, auction houses, galleries, and institutions who provided images and/or reproduction rights for this book gratis. They are: Aste Bolaffi (Turin); the CSC Archivio Nazionale Cinema Impresa; the Detroit Institute of Arts; Dorotheum (Vienna); the Archivio Elisabetta Catalano; Farsettiarte (Prato); the Galleria d'Arte Moderna, Milan; the Galleria de' Foscherari; the Getty Research Institute; the Galleria Giorgio Persano; the Fondazione Istituto piemontese Antonio Gramsci; the Archivio Fotografico A. Guidetti e G. Ricci; Studio Hiro; Studio Mauri; the Menil Collection; Museum Ludwig, Cologne; the Fondazione Morra for Vettor Pisani; Studio Nespolo; the New York Public Library; the Fondazione Giulio e Anna Paolini; the Fondazione Sandro Penna; the Archivio Penone; Phillips; Gianni Piacentino; the Archivio Gio Ponti; Sotheby's (New York and Milan); the Archivio Testa and heirs of Armando Testa; and the Walker Art Center. Special thanks are due to Jill Vuchetich at the Walker Archives for generous assistance during a visit in 2019, which included finding the Walker's original floor plans for me, and preparation of photography thereafter. I also thank Paolo Mussat Sartor, Luca Carrà, the Fondazione Merz (especially Luisa Borio), the Fondazione Alighiero e Boetti, the Fondazione Olivetti, Paula Cooper Gallery, Luhring Augustine, and the Galleria Sabauda for other images and assistance.

I thank the artists and, in some cases, former collaborators of Pistoletto's, for interviews given in support of this project. In-person interviews were held with Ugo Nespolo, Gianni Piacentino, and Gabriele Oriani. Franco Giachino Nichot spoke with me by video, and Alvin Curran spoke with me at length by phone and email. Email correspondence was provided by Luigi Gambarini and Antonella and Virgilio Bari. Additional discussion with Gianfranco Benedetti was also of assistance, as was email correspondence with Gemma De Angelis Testa. I thank Norman Diekman and Peggy Weil for telephone and email correspondence regarding provenance.

I am also grateful to the distinctly collegial group of scholars on modern and contemporary Italian art whose inspiring work, conversations, and discourse have enriched my thinking and this project. They include Marica Antonucci, Christopher Bennett, Silvia Bottinelli, Maria Bremer, Fabio Cafagna, Adrian Duran, Ross Elfline, Antje Gamble, Francesco Guzzetti, Teresa Kittler, Elizabeth Mangini, Ara Merjian, Laura Moure Cecchini, Jonathan Mullins, Marin Sullivan, and Denis Viva. I also thank the Transnational Italian Studies Working Group, cofounded by Serena Bassi and Giulia Riccò, of which I am a part, for reading and providing feedback on an article related to the manuscript, which informed my work on chapter 1.

The arc of this project has often alerted me to the importance of timing—not of the historical period of a subject of study, but of the lived experience of a researcher, of doing the intellectual and physical work required by such a sustained project. I began researching Pistoletto's work and Arte Povera when I was a graduate student at UCLA in the late 2000s and early 2010s. At UCLA I benefited from studying under scholars whose mentorship and teaching were foundational to my ability to do this work. Primary among them is George Baker, my former doctoral adviser, who first encouraged me to pursue work on Pistoletto, and to whom I will therefore always be grateful. He championed a dissertation on the artist at a time when Arte Povera projects tended to focus on a wider selection of artists, while modeling unflagging rigor, inspiring curiosity, and artist-centered art historical work, to which I still aspire. George, thank you so much. Miwon Kwon also helped me see the potential importance of focusing on a single artist's work and, importantly, encouraged my thinking about artistic process, as did Steven Nelson, whose scholarship, teaching, and mentorship made me a better researcher, writer, and critical thinker. Michelle Clayton's instruction and early input as a committee member helped me to think about multidisciplinary histories of modernism, including performance and literature. To them, I extend my gratitude.

My doctoral research also coincided with others' curatorial projects, which aided my ability to do this work. Most notable was Carlos Basualdo's important retrospective of Pistoletto's work at the Philadelphia Museum of Art and MAXXI in Rome, which I attended in the fall of 2010. It was where I first saw many of the works that appear in this book. Next was a series of major exhibitions in Italy on Arte Povera curated by Germano Celant in 2011 and 2012, on occasion of the country's 150th anniversary of unification; I was able to see his shows at the Castello di Rivoli and Triennale di Milano, along with other important programs of the period, like Andrea Bellini's retrospective on Piero Gilardi, also at the Castello di Rivoli, in 2012. Thanks to their work, I was able to amass a visual library and personal familiarity with artworks in and surrounding this book.

I have been fortunate to have the support and camaraderie of friends and colleagues at two institutions during my early career. I thank the Department of Art and Art History at Washington College, where I was visiting assistant professor from 2017 to 2018, and the Department of Art History at Florida State University, where I have been on faculty since. At FSU, I thank my students and colleagues, especially in art history, Mora Beauchamp-Byrd, Kristin Dowell, Jean Hudson, Lynn Jones, Erika Loic, Sheri Patton, and Lorenzo Pericolo (who also provided helpful comments). Anneliese Hardman provided research assistance in the fall of 2021. Also at FSU, I thank friends and colleagues Michael Franklin, Daniel Luedtke, Meredith Lynn (a great friend and frequent interlocutor on practice), Dave Rodriguez (who shared his digital media expertise), Kris Salata, Aaron Thomas, and Silvia Valisa.

To my other dear friends, family, and loved ones: Eva Rigamonti and Paolo Saguato, Giulio and Dalia, Katie Charles, Omar and his family, Londa and my father, Stewart, Carsten and Caitlin, and Hunter and Deidre. Your love and support were integral to various stages of this project. Special thanks are due to Chari Arespacochaga, whose love, humor, and friendship sustained me along the way. I especially thank my mother, Lisa, who has been a source of constant support and without whom I would not be an art historian.

Finally, I thank those who have made home what it is, wherever we are: Mia and Sofia, the latter now gone, who sat beside me while I wrote so much of this book and made sure I still got out in the world. Thank you, for everything.

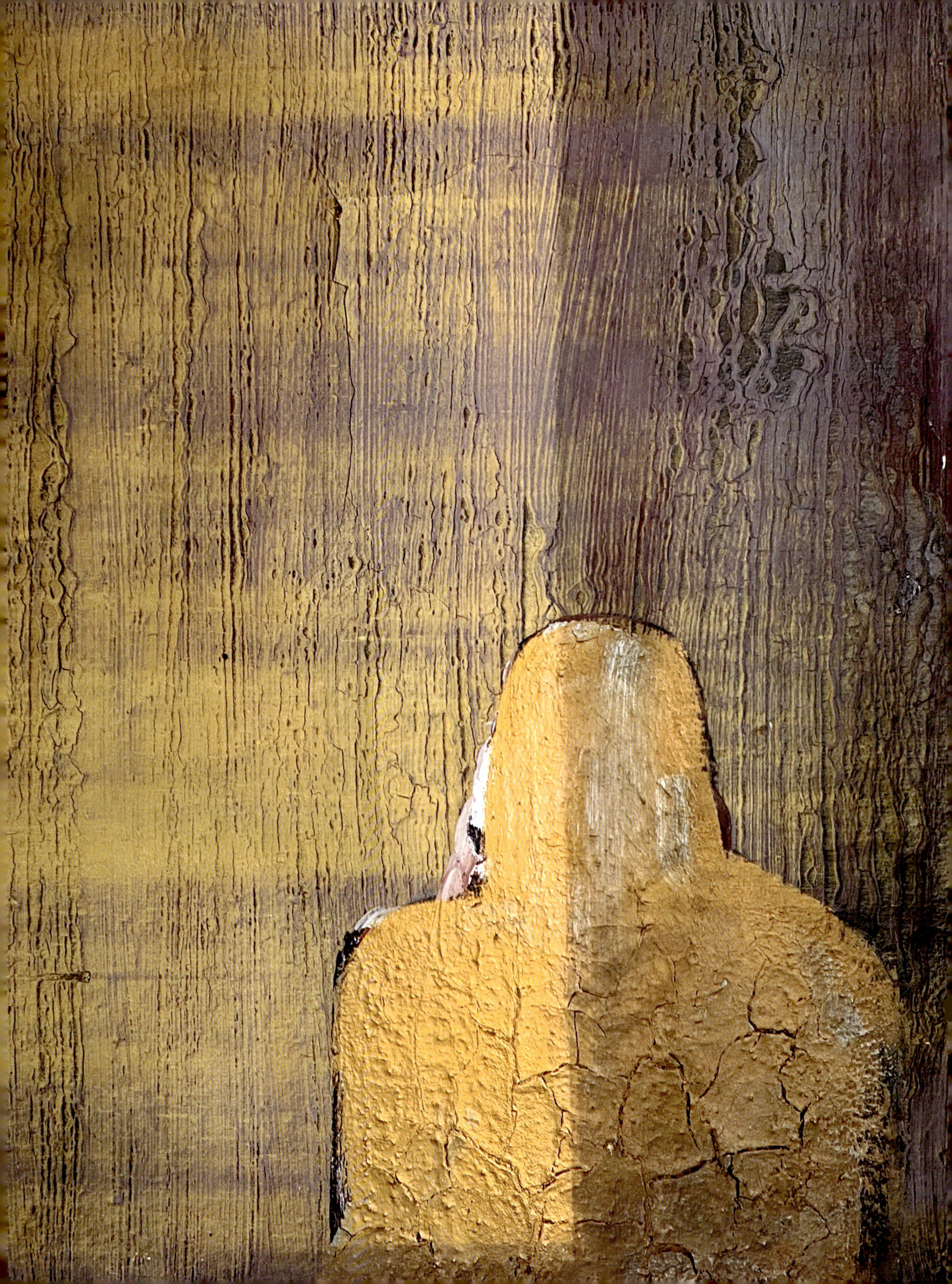

Introduction

A Contradictory Corpus

In the winter of 1965–66, in the northwestern Italian city of Turin, the young Italian artist Michelangelo Pistoletto (b. 1933, Biella) made a series of twenty-five heterogeneous sculptural objects, design-inspired artworks, and furniture items, filling his live-work space with a new body of work. Collectively named the *Oggetti in meno,* or Minus Objects, as the title is regularly translated, the works were markedly different than the ones for which Pistoletto was known. He had recently attained international prominence for his *quadri specchianti,* or mirror paintings (1962–): the ongoing series of highly polished, and later mirrorized, reflective stainless-steel panels, collaged with life-size quasi-photographic cut-outs (and, later, serigraphic prints) of human figures and the occasional object. But that winter in his studio, in the working-class neighborhood of Lingotto, visitors (mostly friends and fellow artists) encountered something else: an eclectic set of works including a lumpy "sphere" of newspaper, a freestanding metal railing, a paper "well," a multicolored plastic grid, a burnt cardboard rose, and a giant photograph of Jasper Johns, cropped short on both sides. These works did not look like Pistoletto's. They did not look like the work of any one artist at all.

This is not the first telling of this story. Long recounted in histories of postwar and contemporary art, in Italy and elsewhere, the history of the Minus Objects is fundamental to narratives on Pistoletto and Arte Povera ("poor" or "impoverished" art)—the loose, primarily Italian avant-garde movement of the late 1960s and early 1970s with which the artist remains best associated. Indeed, not long after the Minus Objects' debut, the young Italian critic and curator Germano Celant (1940–2020) coined the term for the movement, most famously in his essay "Arte Povera: Appunti per una guerriglia" (Arte Povera: Notes for a Guerrilla War), published in the November 1967 issue of *Flash Art.* Celant, who had seen the Minus Objects on their initial showing, when he also met the artist, positioned Pistoletto and the Minus Objects as paradigmatic of Arte Povera. For Celant, the series' unconventional material repertoire, refusal of unifying logic, and semblance as works not of individual, signature authorship but rather of pluralist manufacture gave them a liberated status, unencumbered by artistic convention. They rejected established forms of artmaking (such as mimesis), attendant systems of value, and the so-called

Fig. 19 detail

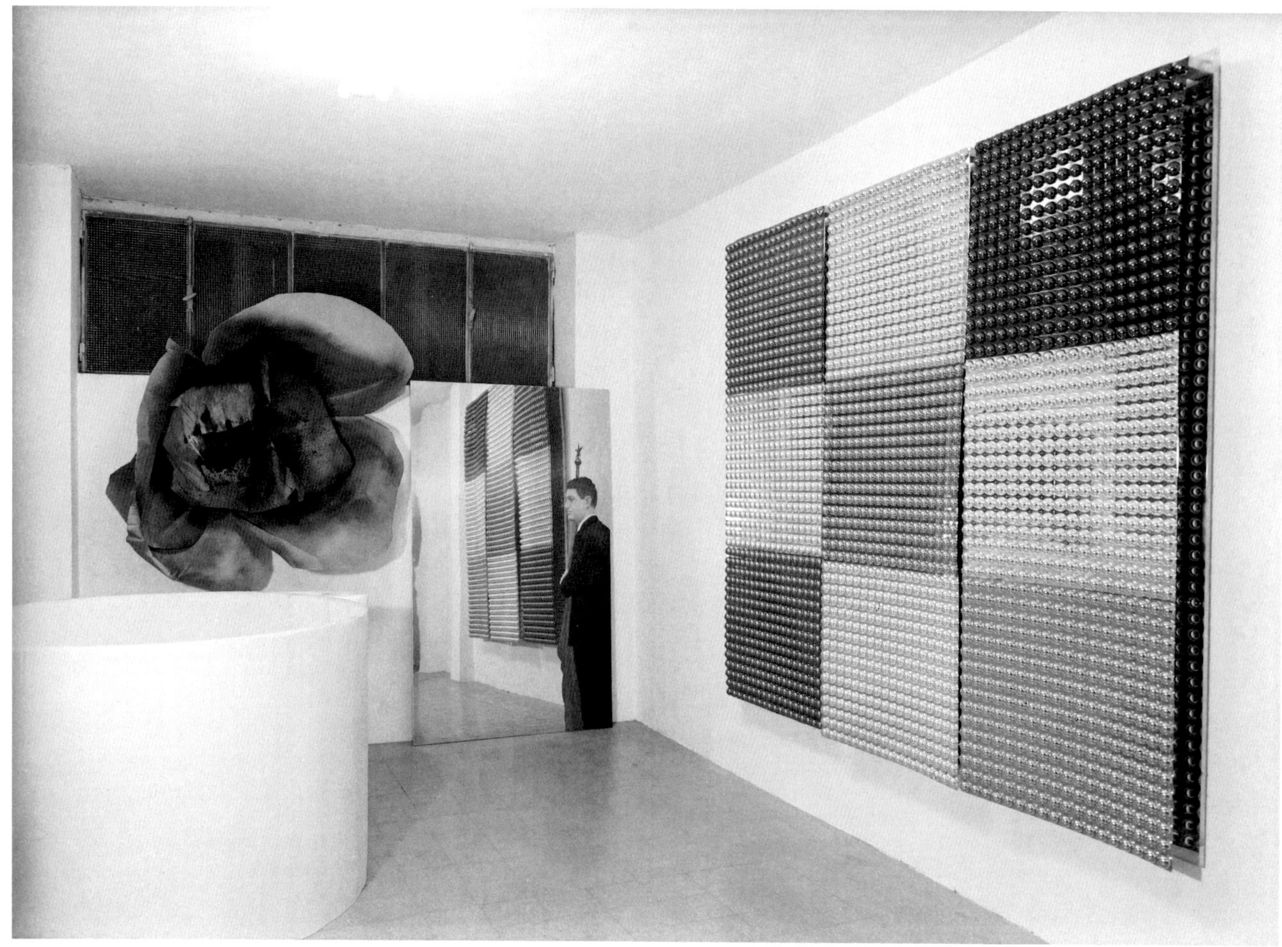

FIG. 1. Michelangelo Pistoletto's *Uomo con bandiera rossa* (Man with Red Flag, 1965–66), collection unknown, with his *Oggetti in meno* (Minus Objects, 1965–66) in his studio, Turin, late 1966. Photo by Paolo Bressano. Archivio Pistoletto, Cittadellarte–Fondazione Pistoletto, Biella.

rich practices (for Celant) of pop and minimalism, then associated with capitalism and US cultural imperialism. The Minus Objects were "opere estremamente 'povere,'" extremely "poor" works.[1]

The prolific scholarship on Pistoletto and the Minus Objects within the discourse on Arte Povera speaks to their importance in the primary framing of the movement, which largely persists in secondary scholarship. The works have also been discussed outside the Italian context, where they have been cited as examples of the broader reaches of postminimalism, conceptual art, process art, and experiments in "object" aesthetics. They are now canonical within postwar and contemporary art history. Indeed, as Anthony White has argued, they "occupy a position of singular importance within the postwar history of modern art."[2] These examples of the works' reception—one primary (Celant), one secondary (White)—speak to the enduring primacy of this scene within the scholarship on Pistoletto, in and outside discourse on Arte Povera, for postwar and global contemporary art.

But consideration of a little-known photograph of the Minus Objects and the as-yet unexplored presence of a work *that doesn't belong*—or, perhaps, always did—in narratives on Pistoletto, Arte Povera, or postwar art history tells a different story. Taken in the artist's studio later in 1966, the photograph reveals an apparent outlier, a contradictory corpus: on the rear wall of the studio, among the Minus Objects, we find one of the artist's mirror paintings, one of his trademark works (fig. 1).

The work was *Uomo con bandiera rossa* (Man with Red Flag, 1965–66), a six-and-a-half-foot-tall mirror painting featuring a life-size silhouette of a young man.[3] Standing in profile, the man holds a scarlet-red flag, a sign widely connected to Soviet communist movements in Italy and elsewhere, in this case, belonging to the Italian

Communist Party (Partito Comunista Italiano, PCI). The presence of the mirror painting and the photograph—both are important here—poses new questions for our consideration, as does their absence from existing histories. Who is this figure? Why is he there? One answer might be that the photograph contains an uncited precursor to Celant's often-ignored description of Arte Povera's subject, the Marxian "'real' man" (*uomo "reale"*).[4] Is this Celant's revolutionary figure? Is this his guerrilla subject? Perhaps. But Celant never included Pistoletto in his discussion of the guerrilla thread of the movement, notably composed of all other artists in his framing. *Man with Red Flag* has appeared nowhere—he has not figured, in view or valence—in histories of Pistoletto's work or of Arte Povera. His absence, and that of the photograph, haunt readings of Pistoletto's work that have, to me, depoliticized the artist's practice and, perhaps more important, not yet identified the major problem that the artist's work poses for existing narratives of postwar and contemporary art history: experimental figuration as a critical strategy. Those movements and periods have been upheld, with rare exception, as anti-mimetic (Arte Povera), as an age characterized by the rise of autonomous abstraction (postwar modernism, from abstract expressionism to concrete art), and as the site of artistic resurrections of historical avant-garde strategies (the postwar period as the time of the so-called neo-avant-garde).[5] By contrast, Pistoletto *held onto the figure*—insisted on it—and did so for the more than six decades of his career, which continues today.

The missing presence of this photograph and the artwork it captures in the discourse on Pistoletto (and beyond) cannot be attributed to any obscurity. The photograph was published soon after it was taken, in the catalog accompanying the first gallery exhibition of the Minus Objects, at the Galleria La Bertesca in Genoa in the winter of 1966, where the first exhibition of Arte Povera, curated by Celant, opened the following year.[6] Nor can the missing presence of this evidence be attributed to any dismissal of its importance on the part of the artist, which may have otherwise led to such inattention to it in his oeuvre. On the contrary, it is very much in line with the artist's conceptualization of his practice. As Pistoletto later told Celant, his work has always "derived from the centrality of the human figure."[7] The photograph of *Man with Red Flag* and the artwork it captures are not only important, then, but have also been there from the outset. They constitute key primary evidence of an artistic timeline that repositions Pistoletto's most canonical works as connected to experiments in figuration—a connection that Celant's framing of Arte Povera ignores.

Indeed, inquiry into this photograph reveals other photographs still of the artwork among the Minus Objects—if previously unpublished—now with Pistoletto in the picture (fig. 2).[8] Draped in the decorative plastic sheeting of the *Decorative Semispheres,* the artist's body, at least on the side that faces the camera, is covered. His legs seem to sprout from the Minus Object. We see the artist's body (and the "figure" of the artist) primarily as an image in the scene; he is reflected in the mirror painting, next to the subject of *Man with Red Flag.* Pistoletto is now also the subject of the painting. His pose, suggesting attention, seems to telegraph awareness of his multiple positions to the viewer. He holds his arms at his side; his feet, easily visible in white Chelsea boots, are pressed together at the heels.

Closer study reveals that *Man with Red Flag* was no outlier: it was one of *fifteen* mirror paintings featuring political subjects, sourced from photographs of antiwar protests and leftist political rallies in northern Italy, that the artist made between the summer of 1965 and the summer of 1966, including the time of the Minus Objects' production. This was the largest subset of mirror paintings the artist had made to date—the largest he would *ever* make using the mirror paintings' original hand-coloring process. While the *Comizi,* or Rallies, as the works featuring political subjects are generally known, have been exhibited and discussed more in recent years, they have yet to be the subject of dedicated art historical study.

As the first English-language monograph on Pistoletto's work, this book seeks to tell this as-yet untold story: to see and recognize this figure as a figurative red flag in the historiography on the artist. In form and metaphoric valence, a red flag is a warning sign that urges a rethinking of existing knowledge—in this case, regarding one of Arte Povera's key protagonists, arguably *the* protagonist of the movement. Often difficult to attend to, this red flag—that is, this figure—nevertheless merits a rethinking of Pistoletto's work as well as Arte Povera's history and its legacies. More specifically, it calls for additional exploration of figuration in his work and in Arte Povera. This book therefore investigates

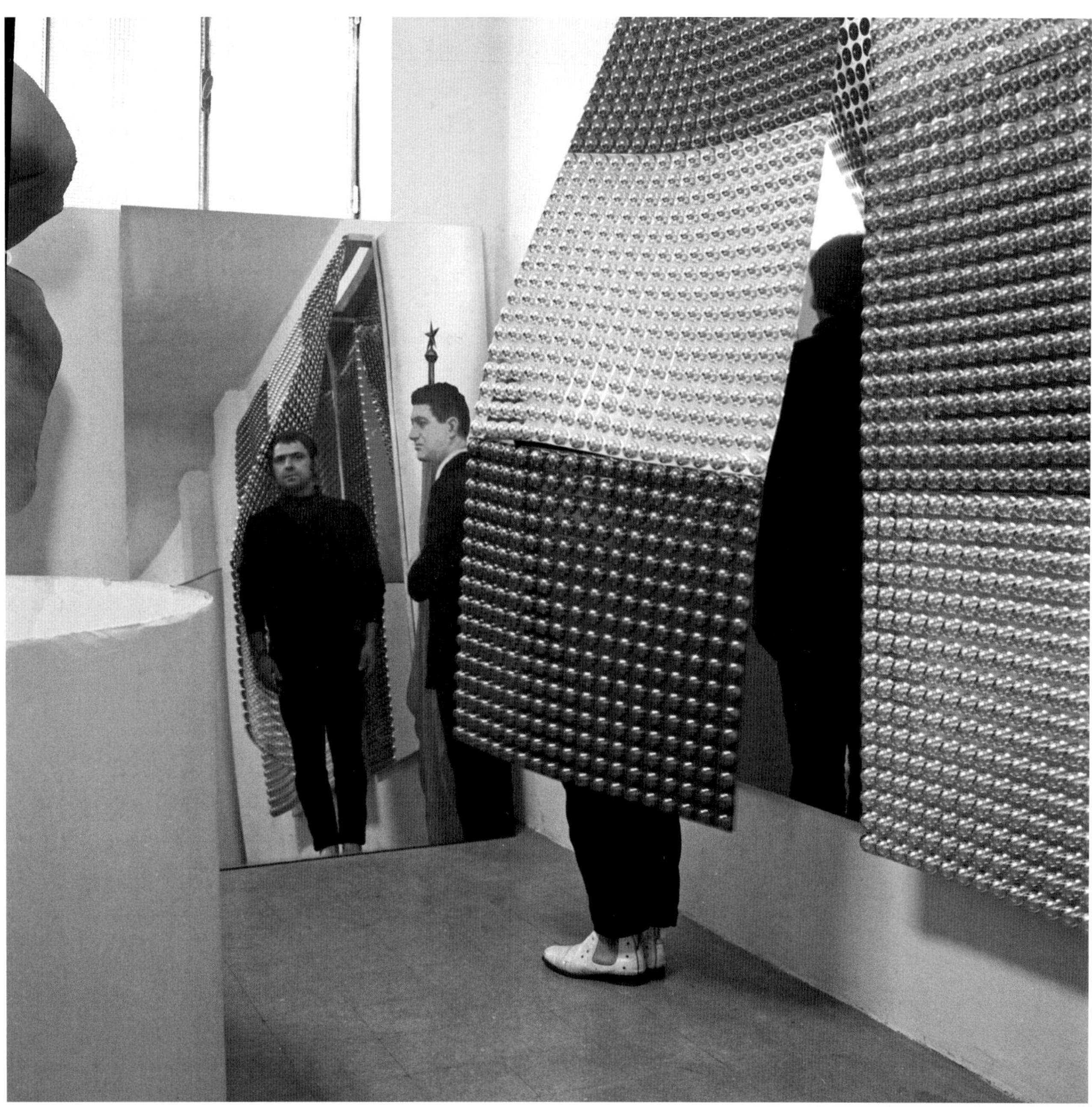

FIG. 2. Michelangelo Pistoletto with *Uomo con bandiera rossa* (Man with Red Flag) and the *Oggetti in meno* (Minus Objects), all 1965–66, in his studio, Turin, late 1966. Photo by Paolo Bressano. Archivio Pistoletto, Biella.

Pistoletto as central figure and outlier within Arte Povera.[9] Last, given Pistoletto's continued work and importance for contemporary art, such revisionist study of his practice also merits rethinking of postwar and global contemporary art in turn.

Michelangelo Pistoletto holds a distinctive and prominent position in the field of contemporary art. This stature has endured for more than six decades, a longevity fueled by the engaging, interactive quality of his work. The scope of his career is quickly telegraphed by his exhibition history. Curatorial attempts to showcase his prolific work began early. Major retrospectives were held at the Walker Art Center in Minneapolis (1966), when he was only thirty-two years old, and at Palazzo Grassi in Venice (1976, in association with the Biennale). He has participated in twelve Venice Biennales—the first in 1966—including receipt of the prestigious career-long Golden Lion in 2003; four São Paulo Bienals; and four iterations of the contemporary art quintennial Documenta.[10] More recent landmark events suggest his continued importance. Major retrospectives in the past two decades have renewed attention to histories of the artist's work, in and out of Arte Povera. Most important among them have been the exhibitions held at the Philadelphia Museum of Art and the Italian national contemporary art museum, MAXXI, in Rome (2010–11, curated by Carlos Basualdo) and at the Louvre in 2013 (curated by Marie-Laure Bernadac), where he was the first contemporary artist to show in the historic institution. The Philadelphia Museum of Art and MAXXI exhibition was accompanied by an extensive exhibition catalog, featuring essays by art historians on different areas of Pistoletto's work. To this bibliography we can add publications of the artist's own extensive writings, some in English translation, as in the volumes printed in the 1980s by independent publisher hopefulmonster (itself connected to Arte Povera via the Merz family) and a book by the artist published in 2022, and in translation in 2023, from Cittadellarte Editions. Other major sources include invaluable compendia of archival documents (especially on Pistoletto's action-based work), supported and in part executed by the artist's longtime archivist Marco Farano; extended interview projects by Andrea Bellini, Alain Elkann, and Basualdo; and gallery catalogs—especially those of Luxembourg Dayan (2013) and Luhring Augustine (2018)—with new critical essays by Robert Lumley and Anthony White on isolated bodies of the artist's work. Incredibly, only one monograph, in the scholarly sense, has been written on Pistoletto: Bruno Corà's short but important book (in Italian) of the mid-1980s, which provides a chronological overview of the artist's practice until that time, with texts on individual groups of artworks. It includes wonderful details from Corà's interviews and collaborative relationship with the artist. This exhibition history and bibliography are only one metric of Pistoletto's significance, but they make the lack of an English-language monograph on the artist's work, or any monograph in the forty years since Corà's, more striking.

In taking on Pistoletto's staggeringly prolific and distinctly heterogeneous career, I find that Pistoletto's work has been unified by a persistent exploration of figuration. It is the throughline of his work, across painting, photomontage, sculpture, installation, experimental film, action-based work, theater, and social practice. More specifically, as I seek to demonstrate in the following chapters, his works have transformed figurative representation into figural forms that have changed our understanding of art and the human condition.

We might therefore begin by asking: Why figuration? Why would Pistoletto, an artist who became (and is still regarded as) a leader of the Italian avant-garde of the 1960s, be interested in figuration in the first place? Major theories of artistic modernism and modernity have questioned and, at times, condemned figuration. As a system of representation, figuration has been historically associated with narrative, allegory, genre, realism, and expressionism, among other conventions that modernism (especially US formalist modernism, whose primacy in the postwar decades went hand in hand with the rise of American cultural imperialism) has denigrated in its move to expunge these conventions from artistic practice, especially from painting.[11] Indeed, figuration has long been associated with *anti*modernism. As art historian Benjamin Buchloh once argued in his discussion of modernism's dedication to the destruction of cultural memory, conventions that were not unique to painting—that is, "historical narrativity, figural representation, [and] theatrical enactment"—have been the "declared enemies" of the entirety of (Euro-American) modernism's various trajectories in the twentieth century.[12]

Discussion of figuration in the discourse on Arte Povera is rare. Claire Gilman and Mark Godfrey have shown that Arte Povera did not reject figuration. In her study of Pino Pascali's sculptural practice from the mid- to late 1960s, Gilman has argued that Pascali's work was driven by an interest in figuration.[13] For Gilman, the figurative drive of Pascali's sculpture (and some of Alighiero Boetti's work) is its privileging of the viewer's perception of the work's semiotic function in advance of its material constitution; we see what the work *is* before we see what it is *made of*.[14] Godfrey has discussed the figure in Arte Povera in different terms, as a form of self-effacement and multiplication of self-representation. Like Gilman, he sees the figure in Arte Povera as a challenge to Romantic conceptualizations of self-mastered subjectivity and of the artist as hero.[15] Although my argument differs from these readings, I share in these scholars' corroboration of a larger point: Arte Povera did not, counter to existing narratives, wholly reject figuration as a convention of artistic practice.

Complicating this discursive terrain surrounding figuration, both primary and secondary, was the crisis of representation and aesthetics that came with viewing the cataclysmic events of World War II as the horrific culmination of Enlightenment thinking and its attendant myths of progress. Writing after the Holocaust, Frankfurt School thinkers Theodor Adorno and Max Horkheimer challenged Hegelian dialectics; if the Enlightenment had "always aimed at liberating human beings from fear and installing them as masters," it had only served to disenchant humanity. After the war, they wrote, "[The] wholly enlightened earth is radiant with triumphant calamity."[16] How could art, as it had been, continue in the wake of such catastrophe? Images and art would have to renounce mimesis; the arts could no longer seek to imitate the world.[17] To revive prewar cultural forms would mean playing accomplice to its evils. Adorno would continue to contemplate these questions, most famously, perhaps, in his declaration in 1949 that "to write poetry after Auschwitz is barbaric."[18] This statement, often misinterpreted as a condemnation of any symbolic expression or as a call to reject all culture, was instead Adorno's outlining of a new categorical imperative (than that of Immanuel Kant): an entire reorganization of human thought and behavior necessitated by the suffering instilled by the war and the exigency to confirm that suffering so as not repeat it.[19] Importantly, this new imperative, Adorno explained in *Negative Dialectics* (1966), could not be addressed discursively. Instead, it would impose on us "a bodily sensation" of morality, by which we physically reject the agonizing violence incurred by man.[20] Artists, including Pistoletto, also ruminated on the consequences of the war. Many turned to figuration to contemplate the human trauma and existential duress incurred by the war. But the politics of postwar culture nevertheless fomented some urgency to reconceptualize figuration as a visual and representational language that had accompanied (and promulgated) the history of "Western" art.

The problems of figuration mounted in postwar art theory were not unique to Anglophone art criticism or questions of the Frankfurt School. They were also contested in postwar Italy. In the years of Pistoletto's formation, Italian art and art discourse were largely defined by politicized cultural debates that set realism (primarily manifest in figurative painting) in conflict with abstraction, often defined as a rejection of figuration (apophatically, as what figuration was not); the result was that figuration and abstraction were at war as viable creative strategies for the postwar period.[21] The stakes of these debates were not small. In some cases, figuration was defined as a historical art form that ended with humanism.[22] Other critics condemned its historical association with communism in Soviet socialist realism. Others still criticized it as an atavistic return to neoclassical ideals, populist subject matter, and figurative allegories favored under fascism.

Furthermore, figuration and abstraction alike held political associations that complicated this terrain with the onset of the Cold War. Figuration's association with communism grew after 1949, when the Italian Communist Party under Palmiro Togliatti officially endorsed realism as the moral duty of the communist artist.[23] Abstraction, however, both geometric and gestural, was also politically contentious, due to nationalistic associations with modernisms in countries other than Italy and with pursuits of "Europeanism" and internationalism. It was therefore criticized by some as thinly veiled Francophilia, echoing French art informel, or as a form of capitalist culture associated with American abstract expressionism.[24] Lyrical forms of abstraction especially functioned as signs of internationalism and capitalism, shoring up an extranational, non-Italian model of modernism and modernity for which postwar Italy strived, to "catch up" to other European nations.[25] Indeed, those who favored the internationalization of Italian art championed abstraction, as did the Forma I group (Rome, 1947–52), who argued against leftist cultural politics that limited artists (especially after Togliatti's declaration) to prescribed, realist practices.[26] Finally, other groups, such as Lionello Venturi's "nonfigurative" Gruppo degli Otto (Group of Eight, 1952–54) of concrete abstractionists, positioned themselves as attempts to "get out of this antinomy" of abstraction and realism.[27] Artist Mario Ballocco of the Rome-based Gruppo Origine (Origin Group, 1950–51) similarly eschewed the decorative associations of abstraction *and* the referentiality of figuration. The new moral, more-valid center of expression, Gruppo Origine argued, was nonfigurative concrete art, composed of elementary marks and pure (nonassociative) lines.[28]

Despite these conflicts, abstraction (unlike realism) gained traction over the 1950s. It emerged as the dominant form of vanguard Italian art after postwar reconstruction with the Informale and Movimento Spaziale (spatialism), further buttressed by movements in concrete art and geometric abstraction that opposed and eventually superseded their gestural counterparts.[29] By the mid-1950s, realism in Italian art had fallen out of favor and, by decade's end, had largely petered out.[30] This was the context in which Pistoletto became an artist. Pistoletto recalled the conflict this way: "But effectively, what was clear in that moment was this tension between abstraction and figuration. There were those who deemed that if a work was abstract, it was modern; if it was figurative, it wasn't modern. And there were those who couldn't stand abstraction and those who couldn't stand figuration."[31]

True to this politicized history, scholarship in art history has often focused on the importance of abstraction in postwar and contemporary Italian art—a history dominated, especially in Anglophone scholarship, by outsized attention to the abstract works of the Italian "neo-avant-garde" of Alberto Burri, Lucio Fontana, and Piero Manzoni.[32] Little consideration has been given to the continued history and significance of figuration for the same period, leaving it largely unattended from the end of neorealism in the mid-1950s to the moment of its "reemergence" in the late 1970s in the work of the neoexpressionist Transavanguardia, where it was criticized as revivalist fascist aesthetics: as "figures of authority, ciphers of regression."[33] By the 1980s, the "return" of figuration was regarded as propagandistic, antimodernist, and even invalid as a strategy for progressive, forward-thinking creative practice in the twentieth century. At the time, figuration still recalled Soviet socialist realism and fascist culture; this was not an eccentric reading, then, but one indicative of Cold War fears at the time.

Revisionist scholarship in postwar art history has since begun to reconsider this critique of figuration, as have those who initially mounted it. In his work on Philip Guston, Robert Slifkin has argued that unconventional models of figuration are a blind spot for art history, which has instead emphasized the "morphological definition" of figuration conventionally used in the discipline. That version of figuration has precluded our attention from being turned to identify other models, "analogical and temporal."[34] Citing figuration's perilous position within the postwar period as a historical threat to modernism (joining Buchloh) and American culture in the Cold War, Slifkin has mounted a call for revisionist scholarship on the role of figuration in postwar art history as a historiographic as well as political problem for the field.[35]

So, why figuration? One reason is biographical: Pistoletto's connection to figurative painting since childhood.[36] Another is art historical: the connection between figuration and histories of Italian art. Remarking in 2009 on his own early work in figuration, Pistoletto said that he "thought it was essential to begin [his] development of the work from the Italian tradition, which has always been figurative, from the classical Greek and Roman images through the Byzantine icons to Renaissance and Baroque [art]."[37] Such remarks reveal that the figure for Pistoletto is fundamental to artistic *italianità* (Italian-ness). They also reveal that "Italian" art was forged through cultural exchange, pluralism, and artistic internationalism. It is the simultaneously national and transnational historicity of the figure that Pistoletto mined and leveraged to think the world anew.

Pistoletto's career took shape within the turbulent sociopolitical climate of 1960s Italy, a period characterized by mass protests, high levels of unemployment, frequent workers' strikes, and the rise of the Italian New Left, galvanized by antiauthoritarian questioning of traditional leftist organizational forms.[38] The neo- and post-Marxist formation of intellectuals and activists, as well as Italy's workers' movement known as *operaismo,* gained traction after the fallout of the so-called *miracolo economico* (economic miracle), Italy's postwar economic boom (1958–63). Widely regarded as Italy's industrial

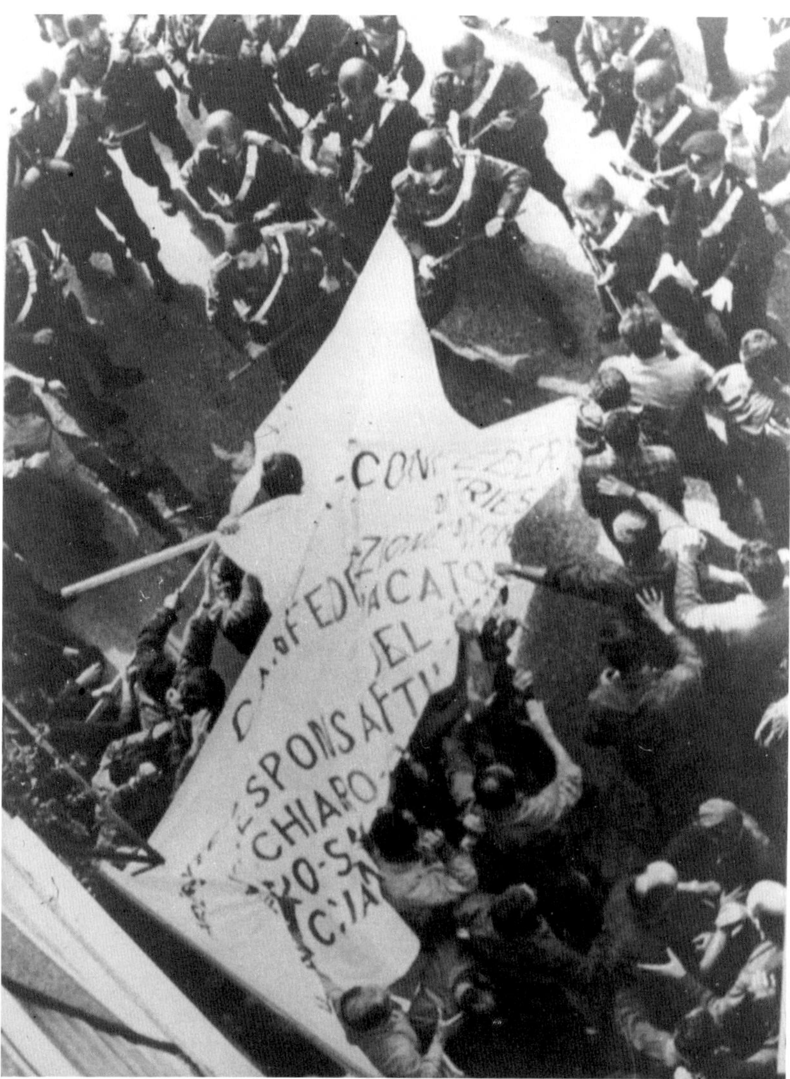

FIG. 3. Protestors and police in conflict as demonstrations erupted in riots in Piazza Statuto, Turin, July 1962. Black-and-white photograph, 24 × 18 in. (61 × 45.7 cm). Fondazione Istituto piemontese Antonio Gramsci–Archivio Storico, Turin.

capital, Turin itself in the postwar decades was a major intellectual, social, and industrial hub—a role that has earned it the moniker of "national laboratory" for experimental Italian culture and nation building.[39] Events in the city, as a major industrial center and historic cradle of modern Italian leftist politics and philosophy, were particularly important to the timeline of the New Left. In the summer of 1962, the largest workers' strike and most violent riots in Italian history took place in Piazza Statuto, just steps from Pistoletto's home and studio then on Via Cibrario (fig. 3). Involving six to seven thousand workers, the riots began a trajectory that reached its zenith in 1968 and the so-called Italian *autunno caldo* (hot autumn) of 1969, when worker and student protests erupted across Italian cities.[40]

With this context in mind, my key concern is Pistoletto's persistent exploration of figuration as an embattled platform for rethinking art and the world in the tumultuous years of the late 1950s through the 1980s, and into today. Through investigation of his work in the formative decades of his career, contextualized within raging cultural debates on politics and art's capacity (if any) to change the world, I find that Pistoletto's exploration of the figure beyond conventional models is a practice through which he sought to transform art and reality.[41] Works studied include those that have been largely unknown (his work with the Gruppo d'Arte "l'Arlecchino" or "Harlequin" Art Group of the late 1950s), understudied (his plexiglass structures of 1964), or little understood (his collaborations with the somewhat esoteric Italian artist Vettor Pisani in the early 1970s).[42] I also explore works that have been relatively unattended but are signature (mirror paintings with political subjects) or well known but underexamined (performance works from the late 1960s through the late 1980s) and conclude with some discussion of his present social practice. By examining these works' navigation of Italian cultural politics, as well as the cultural geopolitics of art of the 1960s, I find that Pistoletto's work consolidates a new model of figuration for postwar and contemporary art, specifically from the *figurative* (symbolic, allegorical, representational) to the *figural* (sensed as present, even when delivered in imagistic form).

Central to my argument are existing theories of the figural as advanced in poststructuralist theory. Drawing on the early writings of French philosopher Jean-François Lyotard, published not long after Pistoletto's work in this area, by "figural" I mean the character of perceived visual form, most often in the form of the human body, that registers as real and concrete—as having a body—even as it necessarily retains some symbolic function (as all images do). Lyotard defined the figural as the space of sensory (as opposed to figurative or linguistic) meaning. The figure is a sensed spatial manifestation or form that registers as a seen "image of presence." The figural (and figure) for Lyotard is importantly imbricated with structures of discourse; it can only be accessed through discourse—through language—but is unable to be neatly accommodated into it without *changing* it, "without [discourse] being shaken," being *ébranlé:* unsettled, disturbed, rattled.[43] Existing on the horizon line of discourse as well as its calm "eye" as cyclone, in Lyotard's metaphor, the figural is therefore endowed with the special capacity to exceed and transgress discursive structures and to therefore change them. The Lyotardian figural is ultimately grounded in the potential of the visual to exceed thought without separating from it. Figural forms, like visual art, are sensed instead of read. They therefore have the power to transform discourse: to challenge and change what we think and what we know.[44] And so did Pistoletto's works; his figural forms reconceptualized painting, the work of art, and, through an integration of the real space of display, the world and our position in it.

My usage of this term also draws on the concept of the "Figure," writ large, from French philosopher Gilles Deleuze, who in the early 1980s expanded Lyotard's definition after a decade of collaboration with French philosopher and psychoanalyst Félix Guattari.[45] In his writings on Francis Bacon, an artist of great importance for Pistoletto, Deleuze defined the "Figure" as the human body in visual form; like the "figural" for Lyotard, the Deleuzian Figure is sensed. It is not representational but rather "is." We perceive it to be material, concrete, and present, as opposed to immaterial, symbolic, and represented (qualities associated with figurative images).[46] The "figure" addressed in this book aligns at various points with Lyotard's and Deleuze's definitions. I seek to track Pistoletto's undoing of and experimentation with representation in favor of creating alternative realities, to be explored and experienced in real time and space.

By invoking these concepts, my study aligns itself with recent discussions in art history, as in Alexander Nagel and Christopher S. Wood's work on early modern European art, that have aimed to reconsider figuration within artistic and cultural practice and within art history methodology by drawing on earlier twentieth-century philosophy on the figural.[47] Fundamental to this recent scholarship is the work of German philosopher Erich Auerbach. In the mid-1940s, most famously in his key text *Mimesis: The Representation of Reality in Western Literature* (1946), Auerbach defined the figural as the condition and position that allows symbolic representation to retain a sense of being real. Auerbach also proposed a model of figural interpretation: a "supratemporal" method through which two chronologically distanced events can be understood to be connected, one prefiguring the other, revealing extra significance than the real alone. Auerbach's "figural schema" positions the figural as a site of potential to be fulfilled elsewhere.[48] The figure (as image, representation, symbol, or allegory) can paradoxically be perceived as something that is (or has been) real and concrete; as in religious texts, mimesis positioned representation as reality to corroborate belief systems. As an interpretive structure and existential position, the figural connects two points (the real and divine, historic and present) otherwise separated in time and space.[49] Auerbach's framework is also invoked in this book's chapters, to elucidate Pistoletto's experiments with the relation between reality and representation, historical and present, on the site of the figure.

Beyond these theoretical engagements, my focus on the individual figure of Pistoletto is in line with the recent turn in Arte Povera scholarship, as found in Mark Godfrey's book on Alighiero Boetti (2011) and Elizabeth Mangini's book on Giuseppe Penone (2021).[50]

This focus on individual artists fosters understanding of their practices and consideration of their work before and after the brief period of Germano Celant's official framing. This approach therefore allows us to move beyond dominant narratives on Arte Povera that often subsume these artists' works under broader, formally analogous, canonical frameworks of postminimalism and process art. What other histories did these artists figure?

My concentration on an individual artist is also grounded in attending to the critical importance of context to histories of postwar Italian art. Regional contexts were widely divergent, as were the interests of individual artists in different cities and the world visions that emerged from them. Last, my approach takes certain cues from the artist. As Pistoletto wrote in his conceptual text-based work *Cento mostre nel mese di ottobre* (One Hundred Exhibitions in the Month of October; 1976), the approach of my book aims to give a "global view of the world" that he and his work inhabited, while "attract[ing] attention to minimal details."[51] Both are important here.

Although this is not a book on Arte Povera, my approach can nevertheless shed light on new reasons for why individual Arte Povera artists—in this case, Pistoletto—matter as part of Arte Povera today. Innumerable art students and artists, all over the world, name Arte Povera as a key influence. It is one of the most frequently cited historical influences in contemporary art. The work of Arte Povera—that is, its efflorescence of creative energy, radical reconceptualization of what counts as a legitimate work of art, rethinking of individual subjectivity and autonomy in favor of relationality and contingency—gives us insights into how creative activity can be a powerful means not just of making do with whatever is ready at hand but of rethinking the world entirely. Arte Povera harnessed creative work—however seemingly humble, informal, casual, and anti-Romantically "intentionally weak," as it is often characterized—as a means of serious sociopolitical devising, as a means of creating, testing, and *doing* different kinds of living and being in the world.[52] Whereas such references are most often made in homage to Arte Povera's experiments with material, form, and process, there are other influences to be accounted for. Here, I argue for Pistoletto's experimentation with figuration and briefly map what I refer to as conceptual figuration in Arte Povera and a figural history of Italian modernism. I believe that Pistoletto's figures can show us how Arte Povera was a site of revolutionary praxis, to borrow Herbert Marcuse's contemporaneous use of the term.[53] His experiments with figuration were about cultivating new ways of being and doing for humankind, based on a rethinking of our representation.

This point brings us to the next reason to consider Pistoletto anew today. As much as this book is a study of the work of Pistoletto, it is also a study of the "long" 1960s and what Kristin Ross and James Meyer have discussed as the decade's "afterlives," legacies, and returns.[54] The 1960s were the tumultuous decade in which Pistoletto's artistic experiments revolutionized artistic practice in and out of Italy, expansions of which we find in his ongoing and equally urgent work today. The 1960s were also the moment in which Italy itself was becoming internationalized, extending a process begun in the 1950s, and when Italian art (and exports) began circulating in earnest around the world. Finally, the 1960s are arguably the twentieth-century decade whose concerns resonate most with our current moment. On all these counts, contemplating the human experience and thinking about global community were and remain imperatives for Pistoletto and for us.

My frequent discussion in this book of the world and our relation to it, as reconfigured by Pistoletto's work, is grounded in part in rapidly shifting perspectives on this topic in technological and cultural artistic theory of the 1960s. The 1960s have often been situated, perhaps more than any other decade, as the first global decade of the twentieth century. In his book *Understanding Media: The Extensions of Man* (1964), Marshall McLuhan theorized the new "electrically contracted" world as a technologically "global village." Translated into Italian in 1967 and cited by Celant that year in his *Flash Art* essay on Arte Povera, McLuhan's book offered a new understanding and "dramatic reversal" of humankind in the advent of the electric (as opposed to mechanical) age. Using technology as an extension of ourselves, humankind is now compressed together, transcending geographical distance, while eliminating social divisions and hierarchies, creating a potentially more democratic world. At the same time, this connectivity inculcated a new "human awareness of responsibility to an intense degree," mandating "commitment and participation" while ushering in the "Age of Anxiety."[55]

These theorizations of "the global" can also be found in Celant's own writings of the period. Less frequently discussed in his writings on Arte Povera is what Celant called Pistoletto's and Arte Povera's *visione globale:* its "global vision" that facilitated a relationship between the work of art and the world. Arte Povera's related *rapporto globale* (global relationship) was its distinguishing characteristic, as was its "perpetually behavioral nomadism."[56] Readily apparent in cartographic, cosmic, and planetary references as well as organic, earth-based materials found in the work of many Arte Povera artists, this global vision was initially theorized by Celant within a fraught sociopolitical context locally, nationally, and internationally. This global vision fueled Celant's curatorial agenda for the movement, as well as important exhibitions before his own.[57] Celant focused on Arte Povera's connection to the global to articulate an artwork's "relationship" with the world. From 1968 to 1970, in large exhibitions and publications that included US and non-Italian European artists alongside Arte Povera's Italian contingency, Celant internationalized Arte Povera. Arte Povera has nevertheless been predominantly regarded as a national, Italian phenomenon, largely due to curatorial work that followed in the 1980s and 1990s that renationalized the movement, much of it belonging to Celant.

Beyond McLuhan and Celant, this opening of the artwork to the world (and destabilization of centered authorship that came with it) was also being addressed in poststructuralist theory of the period, within Italy and elsewhere. From Umberto Eco's concept of the "open work" to Roland Barthes "death of the Author," the work of art could no longer be a site of modernist autonomy or work of the Romantic myth of the artist as genius and Cartesian subject.[58]

My study finds in Pistoletto's work a forging of a previously unnoted creative model for shifting worldviews of the 1960s: the persistent exploration of the figure, against national and international cultural politics of the time, as an embattled site of resistance and new humanism in the postwar decades, beyond the Romantic individualism of the age of abstraction. In Pistoletto's work, the position of the figure and the work of art in the world navigated all of these ideas: of commitment, anxiety, connectivity and alienation, as man (and his image) navigated humanity's new relationship to itself and to the world.

A brief overview of the artist's biography provides more context for the questions I ask in this book. Born in 1933 in the small alpine town of Biella in the northwestern Italian province of Piedmont, Pistoletto spent most of his childhood and early adult life in the nearby industrial and historic city of Turin, living there from 1934 until 1972, except for a brief period during World War II.[59] Having come of age during war, at a time when Italy itself had become transnational in its diasporic formations, of émigrés and colonist repatriates, Pistoletto has always been attuned to the world, to conflicts therein, and to the potential for art to change it. The childhood experience of wartime violence was formative for the artist, who remembers seeing his home country attacked by US soldiers. Following decades of emigration from Italy, most in-country Italians had family in the United States. Although liberation was wholly welcomed, it was also like being attacked, he later told me, "by our cousins."[60]

In his youth and early adulthood after the war, from 1947 to the late 1950s, Pistoletto worked as an assistant to his artist father, Ettore Olivero Pistoletto, in his business conserving and restoring medieval and Renaissance art, especially painting. During this period, in 1953, at his mother's encouragement, Pistoletto also studied graphic and televisual design for two years at the newly established Scuola Testa of designer and future advertising magnate Armando Testa.[61] Although Pistoletto briefly had his own advertising design business, he soon gave up this work and directed his attention fully to painting, for which he quickly earned early career accolades in regional juried exhibitions across northern Italy.

His first paintings in the mid-1950s were primarily dedicated to materialist self-portraiture and exploration of Italo-Byzantine and Renaissance painting, with particular interest in the relation between figure and ground, initiating a career-long interest in man's place in the lived space of the world. In 1958, he gained representation at Turin's Galleria Galatea, where he was inspired by the harrowing existentialist paintings of Francis Bacon. Ultimately finding Bacon's work to be charged with too much anxiety and drama, Pistoletto redirected his work toward creating a model of figuration and painting that would be as objective as possible. This simultaneously antiexpressionist and humanist turn was a pivotal moment for the artist and, as argued in this

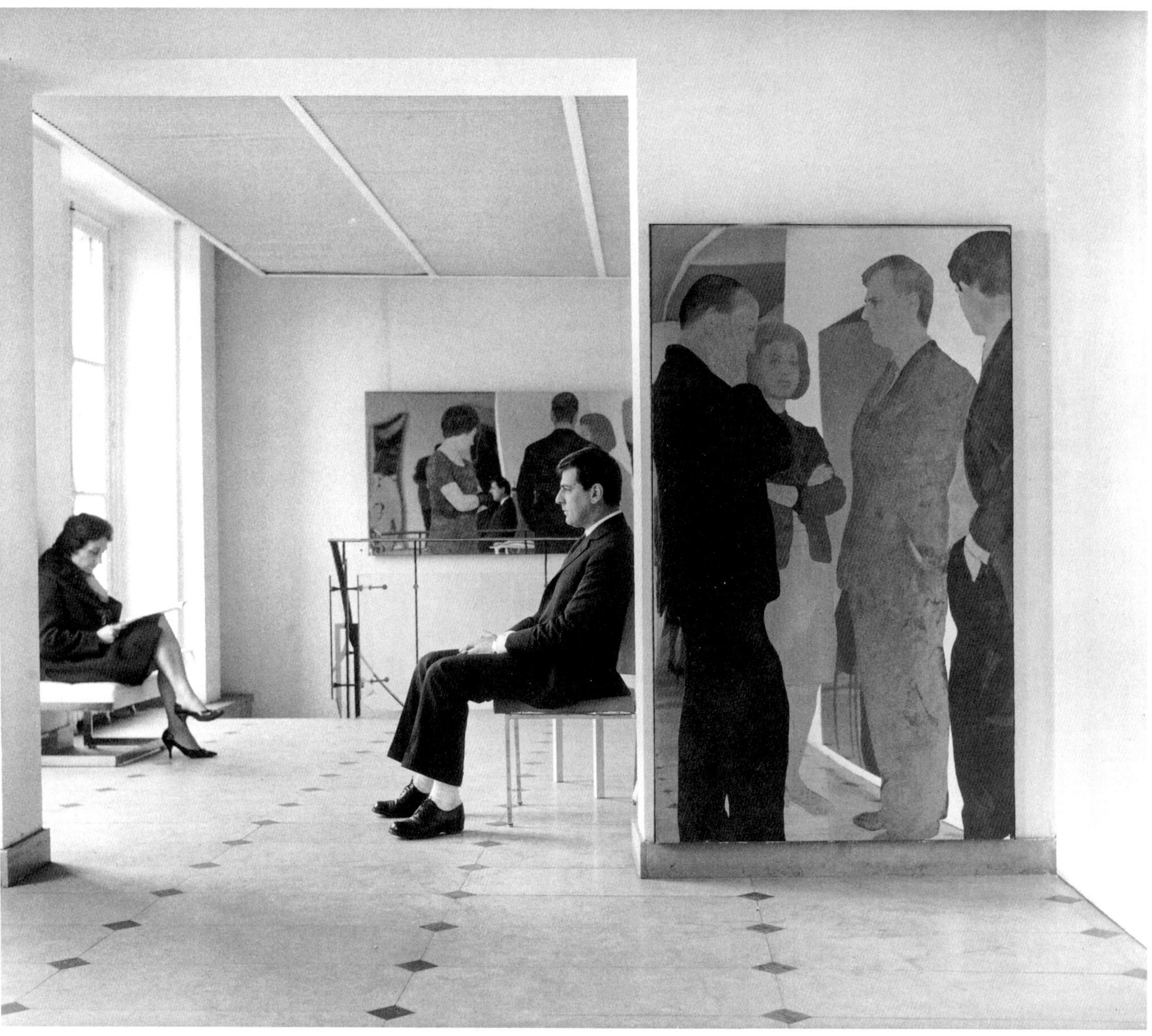

FIG. 4. Harry Shunk and János Kender, Michelangelo Pistoletto exhibition, Galerie Ileana Sonnabend, Paris, opened March 4, 1964. Getty Research Institute, Los Angeles (2014.R.20). Collection: Harry Shunk and Shunk-Kender photographs, 1957–1987.

book, for postwar painting. It led to his lesser-known experiments in photomontage, the well-known mirror paintings, and a series of collaged plexiglass structures. The mirror paintings launched Pistoletto as an artist from a regional to an international platform, earning him a Paris debut at the Galerie Ileana Sonnabend; he was the only Italian artist in the prestigious stable of pop art (fig. 4). Soon came the Minus Objects, rag works, and experiments in performance. In the late 1960s, he expanded his action-based work and conducted living activities as artistic research, performing with his theater group, Lo Zoo (the Zoo, 1968–70), whose members also included Pistoletto's romantic partner (and now spouse) Maria Pioppi. Not long after the end of the Zoo's activities, amid the rise of paramilitary movements and urban terror during the so-called *anni di piombo,* or years of lead, as the tumultuous period of the late 1960s to early 1980s in Italian history are called, Pistoletto left Turin, moving to the Susa Valley, and Arte Povera was over.

The above framing is often where historical studies of Pistoletto's work end, leaving opportunity to consider the artist's continued prolific practice in the following decades. In the 1970s, he experimented with installation and conceptual art. In the 1980s, he pursued large-scale figurative sculpture and revitalized his work with the Zoo in his "world theater" and *Continenti di tempo*

(Continents of Time) series. Those multilocational, durational works continued into the early 1990s—as in *Tartaruga felice* (Happy Turtle), a metaphor for the artist-as-nomad, for Documenta IX in 1992. In 1998 he opened his foundation, Cittadellarte, an experimental institution and cultural laboratory housed in a formerly abandoned textile mill in Biella, where he continues to live and work today. A portmanteau of *cittadella,* or "fortress," and *città dell'arte,* meaning "art city," such that the title means both Art City and Art Citadel, Cittadellarte is an international arts residency center, home of the "seat" of the Third Paradise (his ongoing site-specific practice established in 2003) as well as a center for arts research, site of the artist's archives, and exhibition space.

Since 2003, he has largely pursued social practice under the framework of the Third Paradise, and in mirror paintings that address current subjects of global capitalism, migration, climate change, and technology's effects on human existence. Based on the expansion of the infinity symbol, in which a third space opens between the natural, untouched world and the artificial world dominated by humankind, the Third Paradise is a symbol of environmental and collective social activism, connected for Pistoletto to universal ideas of the "formula of creation," through which we might build a new society.[62] It is a model that uses art—the foundation of symbolic thought, for Pistoletto—to change the world through a call to personal responsibility within global community.

Despite these shifts and ruptures in the artist's practice—a quality for which Pistoletto is well known—study of his continuous reinvention registers a persistent exploration of figuration, as this book discusses across its chapters and conclusion. In the conclusion, instead of focusing only on the most obvious candidates for this history, such as his polystyrene and marble figurative sculptures of the 1980s, composed of multiple figures and figurative styles, or on his *Segno Arte* (Art Sign) of the 1990s and 2000s, which uses forms based on the artist's body, I balance discussion of his more recent practice with attention to works that, at face value, seem to reject the figure (as in his abstract sculptural paintings of the 1980s); those works therefore seem to be the least likely candidates for this history or even counterpoints to it. Even in them, however, this book reveals fundamental connections to the figure as the throughline of Pistoletto's practice and social criticality.

Although I cannot afford to dedicate great space to these later works here, it is my hope this overview will give readers an opportunity to contextualize Pistoletto's historical work in relation to his ongoing work today and to contemplate the special role figuration has had in this artist's practice. Indeed, to attend to all Pistoletto's works (and still-growing oeuvre) would require a different project—one that would necessarily limit in-depth study of the artist's practice and the frameworks it offers art, art history, and society.

This book therefore does not attempt a comprehensive account of Pistoletto's work. What I have sought to offer is an in-depth art historical study of Pistoletto's work in its formative decades, with attention to that period's resonance in his current work. My aim has been to document and elucidate the contributions of one of contemporary art's most important figures and one of the greatest living artists of the 1960s, to grapple with and theorize his contributions to art history, and to consider what study of his work means for today. This book is also the story of how this artist—from his earliest experiments with young friends in Turin to the world stage on which he operates today—never abandoned the figure, that historical site of Italian and humanist concerns. Rather, he saw in it a locus through which to contemplate art's capacity to figure, and reconfigure, the world.

Consider, for example, the *Azione manifesta* (Manifest Action) from 2020: a two-paneled mirror painting with a row of figures engaged in a political demonstration, wearing sanitary masks that situate their action within the global pandemic (fig. 5). Carrying signs that bear the symbol of the Third Paradise alongside others that call for gender equality and climate protection, the figures call for action. "The political dimension of art is necessary," reads one sign, at far right. Conjuring *Man with Red Flag,* Pistoletto's figures here telegraph the history of his practice and the valence of figuration as a sign for social change. His work, then, offers us a different trajectory for art of the twentieth century: neither the rise of autonomous modernist abstraction nor the vanguard tradition of art's turn to life, but the revision of the figure from representation to *something else,* to find a way forward, a way out, of discursive and sociocultural impasses.

◆◆◆

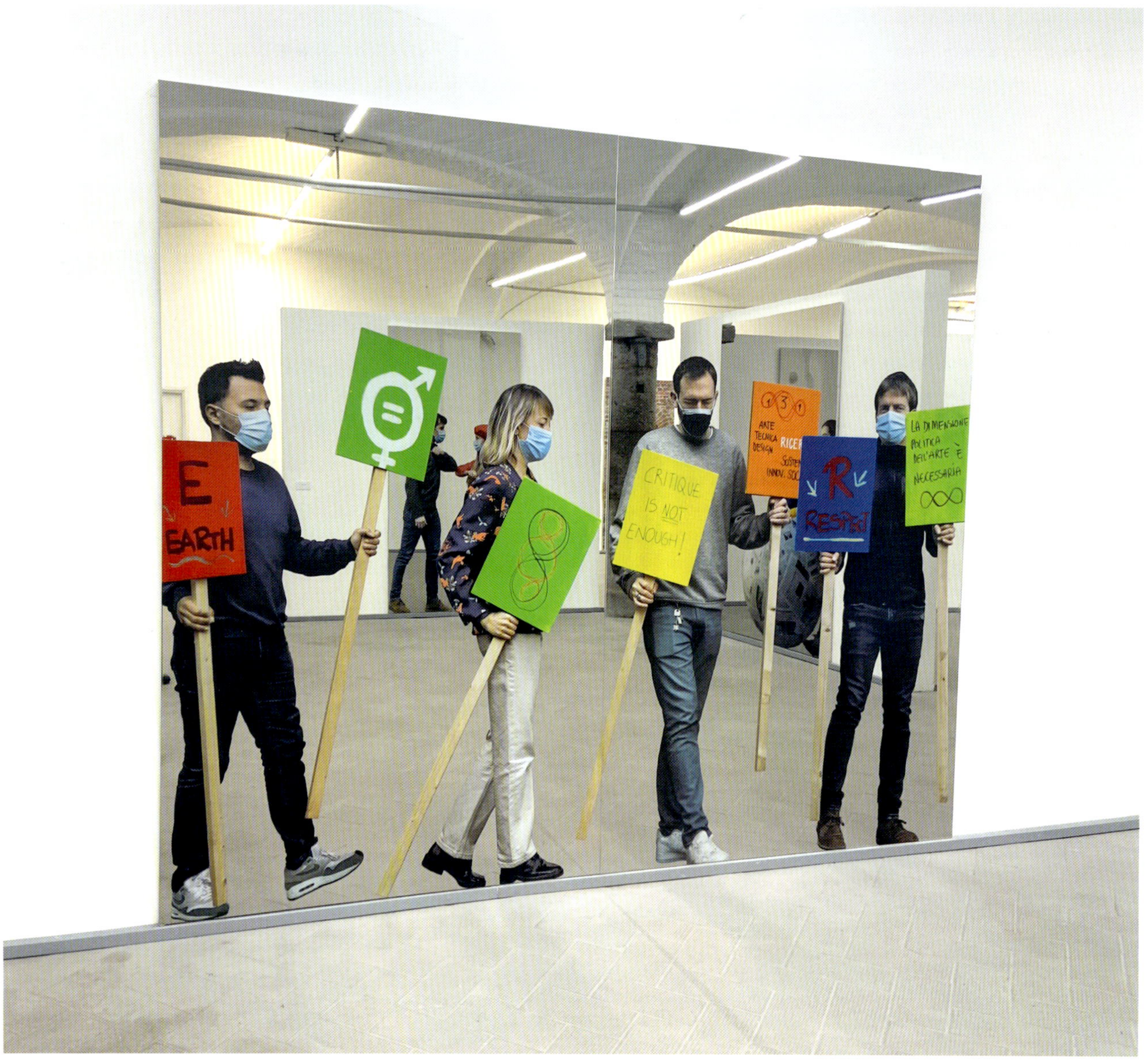

FIG. 5. Michelangelo Pistoletto, *Azione manifesta* (Manifest Action), 2020. Serigraph on mirrorized stainless steel, 8 ft. 2⅜ in. × 9 ft. 10 in. (250 × 300 cm). Cittadellarte–Fondazione Pistoletto, Biella.

Chapter 1, "Formative Figures: Artmaking in Postwar Turin," investigates the artist's early work—from his materialist figurative paintings of the mid- to late 1950s to his little-known photo-collages made in the wake of the Piazza Statuto riots—in relation to the development of an increasingly global worldview in 1950s and early 1960s Turin. Attending to Pistoletto's earliest activities, including his previously little known work with the interdisciplinary Harlequin Art Group and their publication *Presenze* (meaning Presences, or Attendees, 1957–60), I offer a new early history of Pistoletto's work in relation to Turin's emergence as a postwar experimental artistic capital and in relation to the national and international politics surrounding figurative art after World War II. Pistoletto's early work offers examples of what I call "meta-figures": figurative paintings whose inclusion of framing devices, experimentation with figure-ground relations, and reflective materials can be understood as visual and conceptual explorations of figuration as an image system and site of social being.

Chapter 2, "Fragments of Figuration: Mirror Paintings, Plexiglass Structures," investigates the role and significance of the model of the figure that Pistoletto subsequently explored in the early mirror paintings and in an understudied series of photo-collaged plexiglass structures from 1964. Situating this work within the fraught context of the early to mid-1960s Italy, I highlight the different visual experience offered by the artist's two bodies of work at that time. I also examine how those works relate to two problems that were formative to the period: sociopolitical conflicts in the early decline of the economic miracle and the anticapitalist cultural politics of artistic practice in Italy and broader Europe. Close study of the artist's writing associated with the plexiglass works reveals they were made in concert with a reconceptualization of the figure that registers images as real material forms in the space of the gallery.

Chapter 3, "Figures of Protest: Pop and Politics in the Mirror Paintings," brings these questions to bear through the first sustained study of the artist's subset of mirror paintings that include political subjects, made after the plexiglass structures during the ascension of American pop in Europe. In this chapter, I examine the international reception of Pistoletto's work in the United States at his debut exhibition, *Michelangelo Pistoletto: A Reflected World,* curated by Martin Friedman at the Walker Art Center (April 1966), where seven of the fifteen Rallies debuted. I next explore the mirror paintings' navigation of politics and reception at a time of expansion of Italian art in the global context. By examining the Rallies' distinctly figural navigation of Italian labor politics and the cultural geopolitics of the Cold War, I argue that these works consolidated a new model of figuration for art of the 1960s, repositioning our understanding of the mirror paintings and of shifts in the relation between art and politics in the postwar period.

Chapter 4, "Extremely Poor Figures: A World Minus Objects, Minus Men," considers these questions in relation to the Minus Objects and related performances that followed. Drawing attention to Pistoletto's early design work—before this study, only one example was known to have survived—I examine the Minus Objects in relation to the body in Italian mass culture of the 1960s and what I call the "figural turn" in postwar Italian advertising design: a shift from conventional figurative representation to figural imagery, in which products are made bodily. This chapter brings a new perspective to the Minus Objects as "figural objects" that stage an undoing of capitalist subjectivities and symbolic orders.

Chapter 5, "The Real and Performed Figure: Lived and Staged Action in and after the Zoo," addresses Pistoletto's understudied theatrical activities as embodied experiments in real and representational living with his theater group and sometimes commune, the Zoo, and later works. Here I focus especially on then radical subject positions explored by Pistoletto as a site of antiauthoritarian practice beginning with the group's debut performance in Turin, through the late 1960s, 1970s, and 1980s. These positions include queer positions in theatrical "marital unions"; the "master" figure of *L'Uomo nero,* or Minus Man, as the artist translates the term; and a series of collaborative portraits and photo-actions with Vettor Pisani made in the context of the Caso Braibanti, a famous legal case adjudicated against the queer communist philosopher Aldo Braibanti and a key debate for the Italian cultural and political left in those years. Underscoring the connection between Italian New (nonnarrative) Theater and antiauthoritarian social upheaval that emerged in Italy in the late 1960s, I find that the figure in multidisciplinary theatrical activity—"direct, lived action," as Pistoletto described it—could be an agent of transgressive world-staging, in which actors (in theatrical roles, in which their bodies become symbols as well as real presences) occupied new subject positions as radical modes of existence. Coinciding with reexaminations of Italian identity by the cultural left, these discoveries and investigations offer a different story of Pistoletto in and out of theater.

The Conclusion explores the continuation of these lived actions by actual bodies around the world—that is, by people participating in Pistoletto's social practice (without assigned theatrical roles) to which the artist has dedicated his work since the 1990s. My examination of the artist's project of the Third Paradise highlights the global figural vision that connects Pistoletto's works, past and present, and underscores the artist's sustained dedication to using the figure to plumb the possibility of a postwar and now contemporary humanism, concerned with the Anthropocene and posthumanist turn. The connections between these works and those that have been understudied or omitted from former narratives of Pistoletto's practice but model a different world lie at the heart of this book.

As a scholarly study of Pistoletto's work, set against the politicized background of the global artistic context of his work's conceptualization and circulation from the 1950s through the 1970s, 1980s, 1990s, and into today, this book also grapples with difficult questions surrounding Arte Povera and its legacies—its at-times Orientalist and reinscriptive primitivist lens and the politics of Italian culture these works engaged and, on occasion, confronted. Finding great value in context, I begin each chapter with a specific historical moment—or moments, as in chapter 3 both famous and lesser known, that constellate key moments in the artist's exploration of figuration, often coinciding with important moments in Italy's history, that unify his work in the 1960s as the fundamental decade for Pistoletto's career. This modeling of the history of the artist's work, underscoring the importance of the 1960s, also aligns with the artist's view of his practice. The artist dates, for example, all mirror paintings from the origin date of the series' conceptualization in 1962, though preceded by experiments in 1961, to the date of the specific mirror painting's production. I hope that this organization will invite readers into this history through clearly illustrated points of access, details of which often radically change our understanding of the artist's work and elucidate his deep engagement with context. True to Pistoletto's experimentation with temporality, as other scholars of Pistoletto have noted, these moments do not always follow chronological order. Readers might be surprised, for example, that most of this book's discussion of the mirror paintings—dedicated to the works' international reception and to one subset (the Rallies), in particular—comes after the chapter that introduces the early mirror paintings as an entry point to the understudied plexiglass works from 1964. The chapter on the Minus Objects comes after the chapter on the Rallies series, even though the Rallies were begun in the months leading up to the Minus Objects and continued after them. These choices were purposeful. Sometimes they were made to highlight key exhibitions that may have postdated the creation of the works. At other times these choices were made to support the different narrative of Pistoletto's work that emerges in this book. Close study of the plexiglass structures, for example, revises our understanding of the mirror paintings, while investigation of the historically underexamined Rallies provides new histories of the mirror paintings as a whole.

By thinking through Pistoletto's body of work in this way, I mine the historical period of the artist's work—when Pistoletto became Pistoletto—and find its continued resonance in his contemporary practice and in art more broadly. So much of Pistoletto's work has been about self-consciously inhabiting the world and about insisting on our ability to change it. The focus and depth of study that went into this book, and the extensive archival work, site visits, oral histories, and primary research that ground it, are intended to offer readers a chance to inhabit the world that Pistoletto has and continues to live and create. It is my hope that it gives us a clearer picture of Pistoletto's figures, including himself, and how they *figure* in art history—in view and valence. This is the history of how they came to be, what the worlds they fashioned were like, and why they matter.

1 Formative Figures

Artmaking in Postwar Turin

In the spring of 1960, at the age of twenty-six, Pistoletto had his first solo exhibition, held at the Galleria Galatea, a relatively new venue in Turin dedicated to international contemporary art.[1] No photographs of the exhibition exist, but consideration of context and the artworks displayed helps re-create the scene. Pistoletto's debut was composed of twenty artworks, eleven of which included depictions of the human figure.[2] Visitors saw several still lifes, landscapes, and architectural paintings, mainly of Turin's built environment. The large number of figurative paintings, however, relayed that the foundation of the artist's practice was figuration. In an essay for the small catalog, curator Luigi Carluccio introduced Pistoletto's work and the "figure of man" therein as rare and untimely examples of figurative painting.[3] Echoing contemporaneous discourses in phenomenology and existentialism, two influential branches of philosophy for postwar art and theory, Carluccio also cautioned that the work might be met with "diffidence" by viewers. As he stated, "It is dominated in an almost obsessive way by the presence of the image of man."[4] In addition to illustrating Pistoletto's foundational work in figuration, the exhibition also telegraphed the stakes of the imagistic human figure and modernist figuration at the time, both in Italy and elsewhere. Examined through this lens, the exhibition asked a key question: Was a postwar humanism possible in an era increasingly dominated by artistic abstraction?

A POTENTIAL POSTWAR HUMANISM? THE FIGURE AS IMAGE AND SOCIAL BEING

Consider the exemplary *Acrobata azzurro* (Blue Acrobat, 1960), an approximately four-by-two-foot painting that was included in the exhibition and reproduced on the catalog cover. It depicts a male acrobat gripping a high bar as he kicks his legs up into a handstand (fig. 6). The painting's material qualities complicate the image. The figure's facture, or visible quality of the artist's handling of the medium, posits the image of the human body as a negotiation of matter, realized through experimental additive and subtractive processes. Built up in acrylic and then oil paint (an atypical combination of media, as demonstrated by the crawling of white and blue pigment on the figure's lower leg), Pistoletto's acrobat is also marked by incised lines scratched into the surface of his body and of the image. The resulting figure, as corporeal

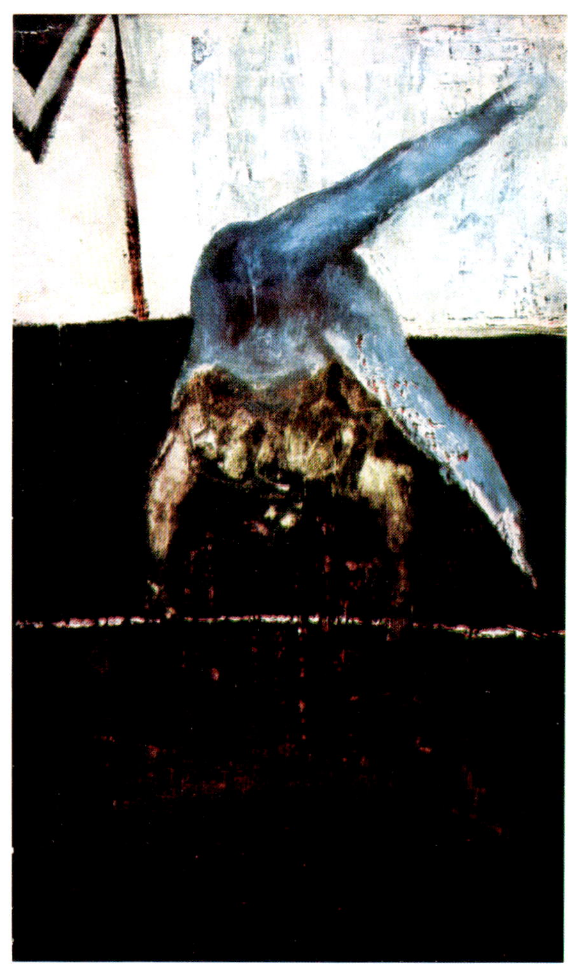

FIG. 6. Cover of the exhibition catalog *Pistoletto* (Turin: Galleria Galatea, 1960). Archivio Pistoletto, Biella. The cover features Michelangelo Pistoletto's *Acrobata azzurro* (Blue Acrobat), 1960. Oil on board, 43¼ × 27½ in. (110 × 70 cm). Collection (of artwork) unknown.

matter and image, draws our attention to its tangible presence even as we register simultaneously its position as symbolic representational form.

This materialist quality was not new in postwar painting. But Pistoletto's figure exceeded analogous experiments in Italy and other contexts (as in art brut, art informel, and Italy's Informale) insofar as it offered a new logic of spectatorship for postwar publics. In combination with his experiments in materialist figuration and the stakes they carried in postwar Italy, this model cannot yet be accounted for with existing narratives of postwar art and culture. Behind Pistoletto's figure, in the upper-left quadrant of the picture, a color-blocked chevron pattern extends beyond the edge. It tells us that the scene takes place under a big top, as does the crowd below, suggested by a dark field in the lower register. Our view of the figure, who is depicted straight on, is not that seen by the crowd below. Instead, Pistoletto gives us a view of the acrobat as captured more characteristically by a camera.[5] *Blue Acrobat* was one of three works in the show that featured performing figures (acrobats and athletes) in motion. The figure's actions are distinguished by spectacularity. His is a feat of human strength and movement designed to be admired by viewing publics.

The suggested presence of the camera in Pistoletto's work points to the confluence of personal and cultural historical factors that framed his emergence as an artist. More specifically, it registers the historic moment of major technological and social change in Italy and broader postreconstruction Europe. The background of his development was Italy's postwar boom, a period characterized by rapid commercialization and media development that ushered in the advent of television.[6] The boom reconnected postwar Italy after reconstruction to the techno-industrial world, which itself was becoming connected in ways never before seen or imagined. Pistoletto was also part of this phenomenon. The expansion of Italy's global commercial exports during this period was further aided by design-focused production as well as print and televisual advertising, in which Pistoletto trained and worked in the 1950s.[7]

In form, content, and suggested technological mediation of human perception, the painting therefore calls to mind theories on image culture, media, and spectacle then circulating the cultural left around the world. In the late 1950s and the 1960s in Italy and western Europe, situationist Guy Debord theorized spectacle culture as a key contributor to the alienating condition (building on Marx) of modern capitalist society with rampant commodity production and the growth of mass media. In *The Society of the Spectacle* (1967), Debord famously declared that contemporary social relations were conditioned and mediated by images; life was no longer "directly lived" but was instead "mere representation."[8] Decrying spectacle as a tool of control, Debord railed against the conditioning of people under spectacle.

In Pistoletto's case, however, Debord's model, widely invoked in histories of postwar art, doesn't hold. Via the suggestion of the camera, the artist's image of the human figure might seem to exist as an index of a real-world subject (as photographs are).[9] This suggested photographic logic of indexicality positions the painted figure as a visual trace of a real subject, more specifically of a subject (and body) who is no longer present.[10] The figure's form is visually prominent, however. Its corporeality and dimensional presence are manifest in the thick material of the painting. The work of art offers us a "real" yet absent subject. In so doing, Pistoletto's figure reworks photography's logic and that of symbolic representation. Both the absent subject of photography and the absent referent that is the precondition of symbolic representation retain some presence.[11] Pistoletto gives us an image that captures a human presence under the condition of spectacle—an impossibility, in Debord's logic. This is a figural form, as Lyotard may have defined it; it insists on offering the viewer an image that is nevertheless tangible, real, and bodily.

Within the context of postwar Italy, the expansion of mass media, and growing capitalism of the boom, the painting positions this kind of figure as an avenue for a potential postwar humanism, despite (or perhaps in response to) shifting symbolic orders of the time. *Blue Acrobat* also implied a redress to fascist spectacle, itself a key component of fascist representation.[12] It reversed the distanced perception or "sensory alienation," as one scholar aptly called it, of spectacle culture under fascism that "flooded the senses" with stimulating but tyrannical visual culture, dominated by the image of Benito Mussolini and popular rituals. The result was, as Simonetta Falasca-Zamponi has put it, "the negation of human nature, the depersonalization of the 'masses,' [and] the deindividualization of the body politic."[13] *Blue Acrobat* therefore posits key art historical questions that prompt reconsideration of this period of Pistoletto's work and postwar art more broadly.

What were the stakes of figuration in postwar Italy? At the time, Pistoletto and younger Italian artists of the postwar generations were trying to find a way forward or "way out," as the artist often puts it, of cultural debates that had settled Italian art discourse into opposing politicized camps of abstraction (then strongly associated with non-Italian, international modernist abstraction) and figuration (championed by the Italian Communist Party). Figuration was also closely associated with existentialist non-Italian European painting by artists such as Francis Bacon, Jean Dubuffet, Alberto Giacometti, and Balthus, all of whom showed at the Galatea and contributed to Turin's increasingly international artistic scene.

Figuration was the critical framework through which the artist contemplated his work in Turin and soon thereafter on the world stage. Pistoletto's persistent exploration of figuration situates questions about histories of modernism and the possibility of postwar humanist culture on the site of the figure as image and as social being. It also demonstrates how these experiments foreshadowed the work ahead.

FIGURATION IN POSTWAR ITALY

Figuration was an embattled field in late 1950s Italy. It often complicated cultural politics of postwar art in Italy and elsewhere that called art's capacity for neohumanist expression into question. In the history of Italian modernism, the figure held great importance. It communicated historicity and classical heritage in the Novecento Italiano, the interwar artistic movement whose tendency toward classical tropes found favor during the *ventennio fascista,* the twenty years, from October 1922 to September 1943, of Mussolini's regime and the rule over the Kingdom of Italy by the National Fascist Party (Partito Nazionale Fascista; PNF). The works of Mario Sironi, Arturo Martini, and the Novecentisti depicted maternal or strong masculine figures that embodied state-serving fascist values in the style of "modern classicism."[14]

Even earlier, in first-wave futurism, the figure relayed humanity's experience of new techno-industrial modernity, illustrated by the dynamic, expansive bodies of Umberto Boccioni and Carlo Carrà. The figure had also been a symbol of estrangement, as in Giorgio de Chirico's metaphysical Italian cityscapes of the 1910s, which were inspired by the artist's visit to Turin. After World War II, postfascist debates led many artists in the cultural left to question political restrictions of what could count as "leftist" progressive form. The political left limited progressive form to figurative realism, which led some leftist artists to move away from figuration as a form of political control. Other artists such as Pistoletto, who were grounded in Italian tradition and the history of painting, viewed figuration as essential to any new development of Italian art after the war. For Pistoletto, the figure, if changed, might offer a visual model of humanism for postwar publics.

In postwar Turin, this problematic legacy of figuration was also a local issue, due to the strong presence of the work of Italian painter Felice Casorati (1883–1963), the *scuola casoratiana,* and the leftist artistic Gruppo di Sei (Group of Six) who coalesced around him in the late 1920s.[15] As part of the Group of Six, Casorati called for the use of creative practice as an antifascist strategy.[16] For the cultural left, Casorati's figures embodied the existential strain of life after World War I caused by the deleterious effects of war and the mounting oppression of Mussolini's regime. Known for his modern figurative style and updated classical motifs, Casorati was also associated with artists of the Novecento, whose champions appreciated the stark, ordered, somewhat-plastic figures in his paintings. To them, his figures seemed to embody the tenets of fascist ideology that newly valued well-proportioned, idealized depictions of the human figure.[17] By the postwar period, the Casoratian nude was a standard within the figurative arts in Turin and much of Italy.[18] The problems of this legacy can be understood in part by Pistoletto's own remarks on Casorati; he rejects any association with the artist or Piedmontese artistic traditions.[19]

In the 1950s, Turin's somewhat conservative artistic climate began to diversify beyond the mostly regional exhibitions and representational styles of Piedmont, opening to abstraction, especially in the style of the rising Informale. This rise was paralleled by the ascendancy of neo-Dada, American pop, and nouveau réalisme. The work of those movements, while not abstract, shared abstraction's aim to do away with mimetic representation, in their case by using everyday materials, popular imagery, and processes of mechanical reproduction. In Turin, a thriving avant-garde and institutional network that championed abstraction as *the* direction of contemporary art joined what was then mainstream figurative painting. International exhibitions in Turin proliferated across the decade. They included the biennial exhibitions *Pittori d'oggi: Francia-Italia* (Today's Painters: France-Italy, 1951–61), which played a key role in the internationalization of Turin's artistic context. By the late 1950s, the exhibitions were composed almost entirely of abstract painting. The major international exhibition *Arte nuova* (billed in English as *Art Today*) at the Artists' Circle Club positioned Turin as an international artistic nexus of unprecedented scale.[20] It was where the artistic Japanese group Gutai made their debut in Europe, held concurrently with their exhibition at Turin's Figurative Arts Association. Curated by Michel Tapié, the French critic and curator who coined art informel, with the important local gallerist Luciano Pistoi in 1959, the exhibition also included US abstract expressionism and art informel.[21] The internationalization of Turin's artistic context was also supported by the presence of non-Italian European artists in Piedmont, including Karel Appel, Constant, and Asger Jorn. In the mid-1950s, those artists coalesced around the nearby town of Alba, an hour from Turin, where they met at the international studio of the artist Giuseppe (Pinot) Gallizio. Gallizio's studio (the Experimental Laboratory) hosted important international artistic formations and events, including the international Imaginist Bauhaus and First World Congress of Free Artists in 1956, which preceded the formation of the Situationist International by Gallizio and Debord the following year. The congress convened with a focus on "free artists and industrial activities" as well as "human society and artistic progress." Gallizio's studio was part of the internationalization of 1950s Piedmont and part of the art discourse on humanity and the changing world. It was another avant-garde site near Turin that influenced the young Pistoletto and art in the coming decade.[22]

While realism was part of the so-called return to figuration in postwar Europe, Italian artists faced a different set of circumstances than their European counterparts. For young artists like Pistoletto, the problem of creating a valid, progressive artistic practice for postwar Italy was complicated by the unique historical legacy of art and culture under fascism. By the late 1930s, Italian futurism had come to be associated with the regime, even though many futurists were, as Günter Berghaus has demonstrated, a-fascist or antifascist. The connection resulted in the denigration and reframing of futurism after World War II. The case was similar for the conservative (if updated) neoclassicism and mythic realism of the Novecento.[23] The cultural politics of metaphysical painting were also problematic. Many of its practitioners had been based in Paris and were associated with surrealism, making any potential legacy somewhat international in kind, while its classicist visual languages positioned it too closely to "return to order" movements.[24] Nor did modernist abstraction provide a suitable reference; most of it would not be seen in Italy until after 1945, following the end of fascism. The modernist abstraction that was available was primarily associated with Russian suprematism, French cubism, and other European artistic movements situated outside Italy.[25]

Figuration in Italy by the 1960s was instead tied to the history of postwar Italian realism and its emergence from antifascist groups, such as the Milan-based Corrente (Current, 1938–43).[26] Rather than align postwar figuration with regressive provincialism, and abstraction with progressive transnationalism, Italian postwar realism was invigorated by renewed access to culture outside of Italy. Realists especially found inspiration in Pablo Picasso's *Guernica* (1937), which they heralded for its disposal of self-aggrandizing artistic practice and realization of an image that captured the collective experience of fascist oppression.[27] After the war, former members of Corrente (Ennio Morlotti and Emilio Vedova) laid out new terms for realism that positioned reality as an objective entity of which "man is a part."[28] Painting and sculpture would be a form of "participation in the total reality of man." In this humanist model of realism, the individual would be repositioned as one of many.[29]

By the 1960s, a second wave of figurative artwork referred to as "new figuration" arose in the wake of neorealism in Italy and elsewhere. In Italy, it was known as Nuova Figurazione: a widely discredited, Florence-centered movement that emerged in 1962 and included artists as varied as Enrico Baj, Roberto Crippa, and Antonio Recalcati.[30] Denigrated by champions of neo-Dada and pop, the movement was nevertheless defended by some, whose positions provide insight into the still-embattled terrain of Italy's artistic context in the early 1960s. In a catalog essay for an international exhibition held in the summer of 1963 in Florence, for example, Florentine art critic and poet Mario Bèrgomi defended the figurative practices that had come under fire as a provincial, regressive, and even treasonous revivalist enterprise.[31] Bèrgomi argued that these artists could, rather than use the "remains" of figuration seen in the work of the Informale, "render the figure coherent unto itself." In Nuova Figurazione, Bèrgomi continued, the artist should be able to "participate or adhere to reality," "to express his own relationship with the world" and "have his own autonomy."[32] The movement's stated effort was to move on from the frenetic, fragmented forms associated with expressionism and the Informale. The response of Nuova Figurazione was not to question these movements but to progress from what was regarded as academic and passé practices to a new figuration.[33]

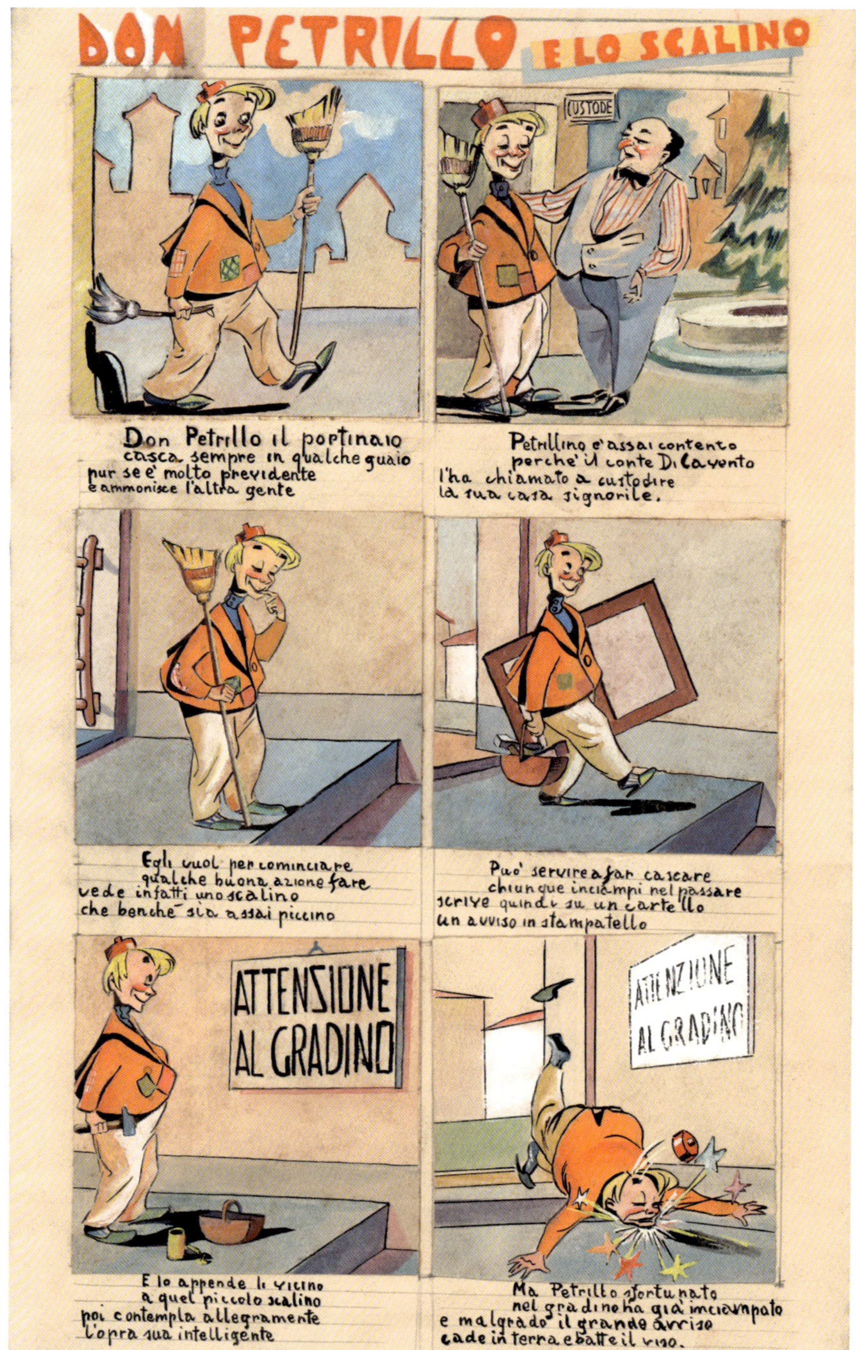

FIG. 7. Michelangelo Pistoletto, *Don Petrillo e lo scalino* (Don Petrillo and the Little Step), 1946–49. Mixed media on paper, 16⅞ × 10⅝ in. (43 × 27 cm). Archivio Pistoletto, Biella.

Although Pistoletto did not ascribe to realism, to Nuova Figurazione, or to new figuration in an international context, he shared certain interests and positioned his formative artistic inquiries in relation to these movements and with the reconceptualization of figuration in mind. He shared an interest in neohumanism and in "adhering" to reality, a phrase used often in his writings. He sought to reclaim agency, if not autonomy, in the world. But Pistoletto went still another way than these art historical interlocutors.

THE EARLY FIGURES

Pistoletto's early figures reveal how the artist forged a distinctive path out of postwar Italian modernism and a postwar artistic and social terrain that had arrived at a politicized impasse. Drawings, caricatures (including a few of Italian and foreign statesmen), cartoons, and comic strips, dating to as early as 1946, survive from the artist's teen years, predominantly featuring figures typical of mass-cultural sources of the period (such as bandits and pin-up girls or class archetypes of the impoverished and well-to-do) (fig. 7). Pistoletto's first formal figurative works, however, were made on the inception of his artistic practice in 1955, when he commenced making his own paintings regularly, beginning with experiments in self-portraiture.[34] His earliest surviving self-portrait, a narrow panel painting from that year, exemplifies his formative artistic interest in the figure-ground relation that would be central to the experimental works that followed and that comprised the beginning of the artist's career (fig. 8). The upper register of the painting is ultramarine in color; it shifts to dappled yellow, green, and purple that frame the subject's head. The figure's jacket is similarly multicolored, its palette glimmering with muted green, white, and mauve. The visual echo connects painted figure and ground.

Pistoletto explored similarly constitutive elements of figurative painting in other early works, as in a self-portrait from 1956 (fig. 9). Colored vermilion and ocher, the painting has a scabrous surface that recalls bodily material; the figure is surrounded by a field of red paint that overlaps and subsumes its edges. The self-portrait reflects the artist's experimentation with bold gesture and *pittura materica,* or "matter painting," found in some postwar painting, especially French art informel, the Italian Informale, and arte nucleare (nuclear art), the latter of keen interest to the artist, then recently established in nearby Milan.[35] The apocalyptic aesthetic and at-times regressive informalism of these movements relayed postwar existential duress through fraught visual languages of inchoate form, material density, and obsessively worked surfaces. Figurative painting, however abstracted, acquired an unprecedented and often unsettling visceral corporeity, also found in Pistoletto's early work. In an oversized, abstracted self-portrait from 1957, for example (as in *Blue Acrobat*), thick impasto and deep sgraffito give the imagistic figure a material presence (fig. 10). The painting exceeds the mimetic conventions of self-portraiture and the genre's representational function while fleshing out a subject in front of the viewer. The effect is bolstered by the scale of the work. Measuring six and a half feet in height, it approximates the scale of the viewer.

This influence of informalist and matterist practices can be attributed in part to the proximity of these movements to Turin. Michel Tapié arrived in 1957, collaborating with Luciano Pistoi's Galleria Notizie and its journal *Notizie Arti Figurative* (Figurative Art News).[36] In 1960, Tapié established his International Center for Aesthetic Research, where he held exhibitions featuring artists from the United States (Willem de Kooning), Italy and Europe (Alberto Burri, Jean Fautrier), and Japan (Yoshihara Jiro). Serving as a hub for Tapié's internationalization of art informel, the center most often featured artists who explored matter painting and the body. By Pistoletto's solo debut in 1960, Turin was a new cosmopolitan center for contemporary art. It was also a surprising nexus of international artistic experimentation in matter-focused figuration and in abstraction that conjured a bodily presence.[37]

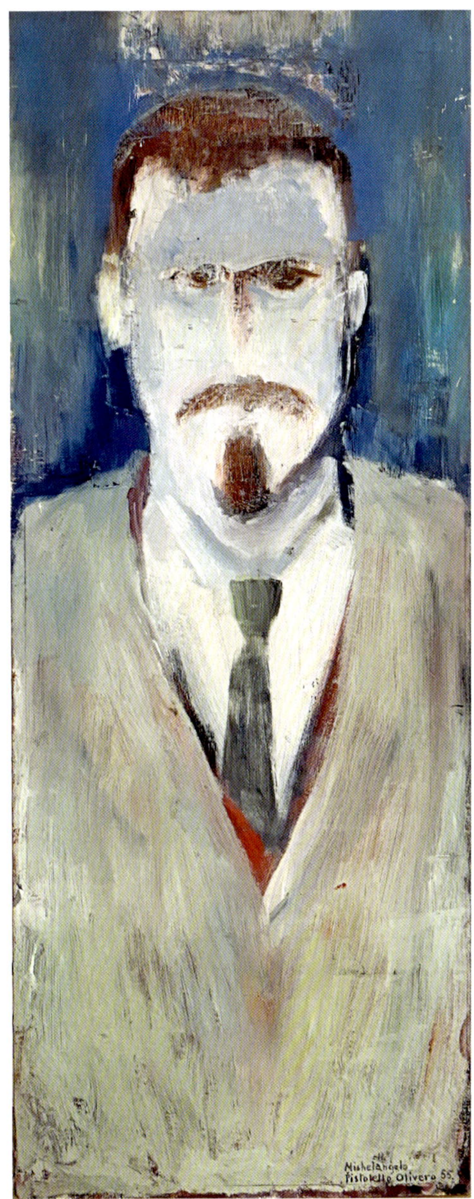

FIG. 8. Michelangelo Pistoletto, *Autoritratto* (Self-Portrait), 1955. Oil on panel, 25⅝ × 9¾ in. (65 × 25 cm). Cittadellarte–Fondazione Pistoletto, Biella.

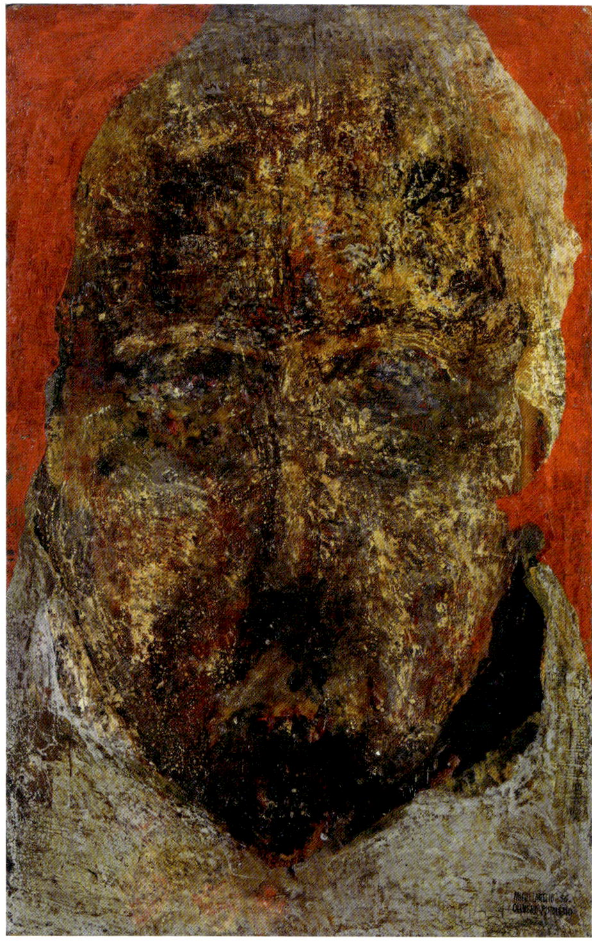

FIG. 9. Michelangelo Pistoletto, *Autoritratto* (Self-Portrait), 1956. Oil and acrylic on canvas, 55 × 35½ in. (140 × 90 cm). Cittadellarte–Fondazione Pistoletto, Biella.

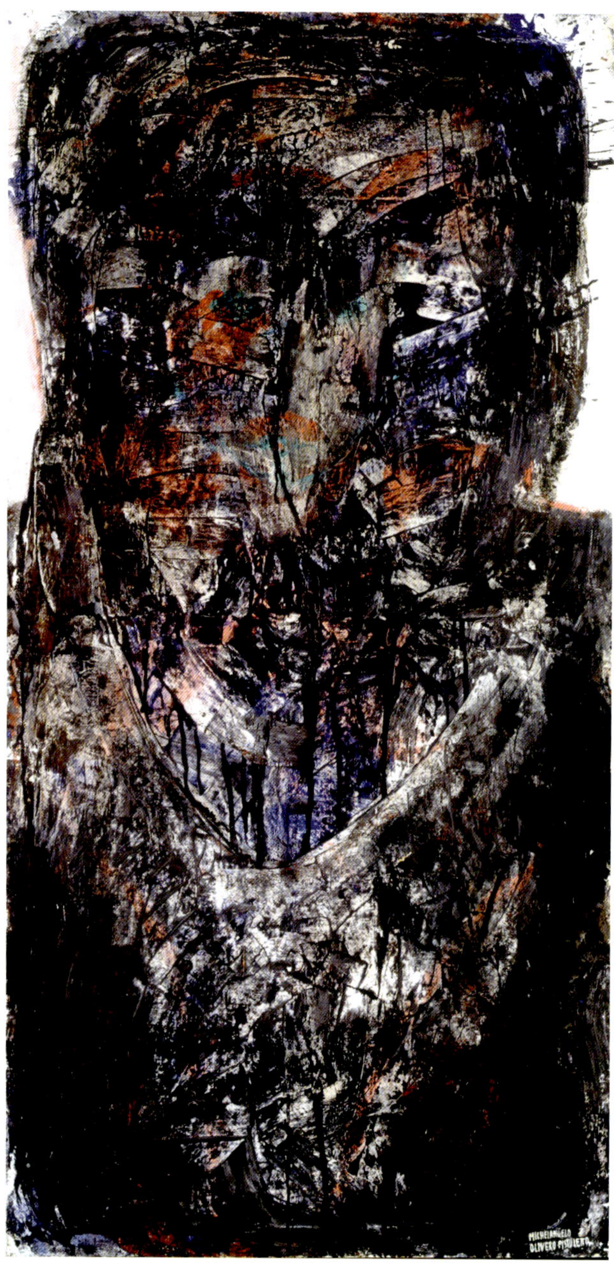

FIG. 10. Michelangelo Pistoletto, *Autoritratto* (Self-Portrait), 1957. Oil and acrylic on canvas, 78¾ × 39⅜ in. (200 × 100 cm). Cittadellarte–Fondazione Pistoletto, Biella.

Pistoletto was especially interested in the work of Francis Bacon, whose work had been shown in a solo show (1958), in group exhibitions (1960, 1960/61, 1961) at the Galatea, and in a group exhibition at the European- and US-focused Galleria Notizie (1961).[38] Pistoletto's active figures and their abstracted grounds echo Bacon's paintings and figure studies of the period, some of whom crouch in grass or stand in athletic poses.[39] Ultimately for Pistoletto, however, Bacon's figurative paintings surpassed everything he had been striving for in his work; any effort to capture existential drama could not exceed Bacon's achievement. Facing a comparable "existential predicament" in American abstract expressionism, he had to find another way forward.

Although Pistoletto's early works recall the scratched figures and thickened facture of international modernist figurative painting, his works also find ready comparisons (in color, material aesthetic, and figure-dominant composition) in late medieval Italian icon painting. This is especially the case with Italo-Byzantine art: painting in the *buona maniera greca antica,* or "good ancient Greek style," as Giorgio Vasari distinguished it in the Cinquecento.[40] These modernist and medieval references might also be attributed to the artist's training. His first instruction was under his artist father, Ettore Olivero Pistoletto, who had a business in the conservation and restoration of medieval and Renaissance art. Michelangelo began assisting him at the age of fourteen;

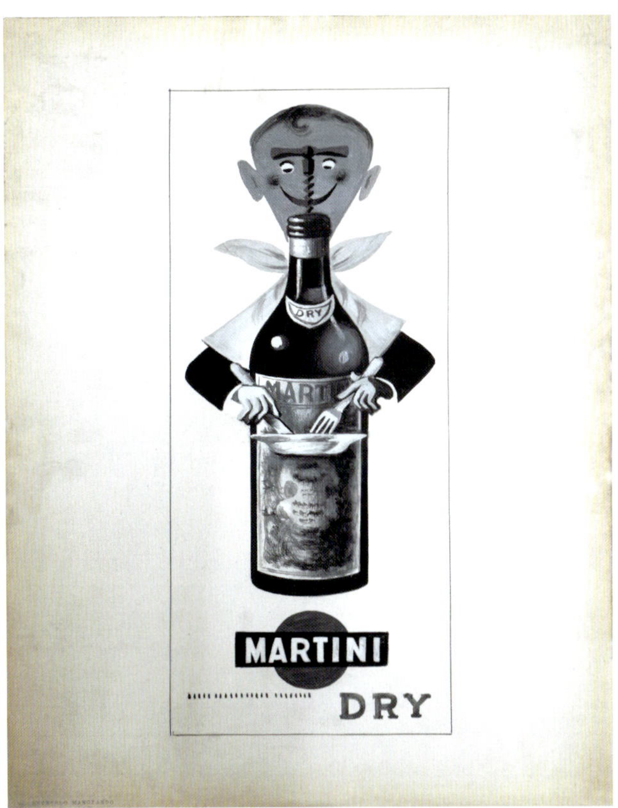

FIG. 11. Michelangelo Pistoletto, "Bevetelo mangiando" (Drink It While Eating), unpublished mock advertisement for Martini dry vermouth, ca. 1953. Acrylic and ink on board, 19½ × 13¾ in. (49.6 × 34.8 cm). Archivio Pistoletto, Biella.

it is where he learned to draw and paint. Pistoletto's only formal artistic training, however, was in graphic and televisual advertising at the Turin school of Armando Testa, whom the artist credits with introducing him to modernism. If Pistoletto's father introduced him to the history of art, Testa gave him an ability to think about art in relation to the present—"the present not only of art but of the world," as the artist described it.[41] Pistoletto's earliest professional artistic work was done through his own advertising design agency; that early design work, discussed in detail in chapter 4, reveals another site in which he explored the figure in his formative practice.[42] Of importance for now is that his advertising images of Italian products often rendered objects as figures, or figures as objects, as in a practice advertisement for Martini dry vermouth, executed while he was at the Scuola Testa. In the advertisement the bottle is at once object and figure; it makes up the body of the consumer depicted in the ad (fig. 11).

Beyond these biographical connections, the historical and contemporary references in Pistoletto's early work position his initial investigation of figuration (and the question of its potential advancement) as an Italian and internationally situated historicist practice. Using new artistic strategies associated with philosophical discourses on existentialism and phenomenology that influenced European figurative painting during postwar reconstruction, Pistoletto remade the historical icon (itself a figure that embodied the history of painting) into a site of postwar humanist contemplation. In his work from the late 1950s, we find the phenomenological encounter intended for the Byzantine and medieval icon commingling with the phenomenological viewership explored in postwar modernist figuration.[43] Indeed, Pistoletto's early works register the phenomenological and existential conditions of aftermath that characterized postwar Europe—conditions artists often rendered as bodily afflictions.

For Luigi Carluccio, a figural humanism united Pistoletto's early paintings, which were distinguished by their immersion in the real world. Pistoletto treated "the figure of man" in his work with "a measure of convincing dignity, by dint of its formal and poetic values." As Carluccio wrote: "Even the artist's few landscapes and rare still lifes reclaim the presence of man; they reflect man's febrile touch, worried gaze."[44] Echoing contemporaneous discourses in phenomenology and existentialism, which also deeply informed art writing of the postwar period, Carluccio contemplated the kind of person we encounter in Pistoletto's paintings. The relevance of the passage merits its quotation in full:

> It seems to me that Man in Olivero Pistoletto's paintings is a man who feels his fragility and at the same time his capacity for resistance, who knows himself and at the same time spies on himself, even when in the form of an acrobat or gymnast, vaulting through a deserted space and leaning against the void, almost to better verify his own weight. He is above all a man "alone," and conscious of the terrible fact that solitude threatens him and encloses him in a trap. This image of Man has something in common with the other images evoked by the artists' names I listed above [Dubuffet, Bacon, Balthus, Giacometti]: the kind of relationships with the surrounding world, that are knowing and existential relationships in the same measure, separate, isolated, stabilizing, refuting

> the help of every element that can connect the mind to the idea of the superfluous; the continual instinctive attitude to put himself in relationship with the corner of the room, with the area of shadow, to painfully sustain the gaze before eluding it.[45]

Ultimately, Carluccio homed in on Pistoletto's work as the site of an unlikely and admirable inquiry on the part of a young artist, to be contemplated within figurative works (that include images of the human figure) and in figural ones (that evoke the body and human experience but might not literally represent a human subject). Pistoletto could sustain the existential pain of humankind in the postwar period and nevertheless hold onto the importance of man's existence. As Carluccio declared, Pistoletto's work "gathers as an indication of his present presentness itself as the condition of [a] hunted beast." He "affronts the problem of figuration from a point of view he thinks is probable: that of also positively considering in the end the existence of man within the values of representation."[46]

Supported by Carluccio, Pistoletto's debut was favorably received by local critics, who heralded the artist's ability to restore art's capacity to relay the poetics of human existence. In his review, for example, *La Stampa* art critic Marziano Bernardi called the exhibition an effort to reconcile painting with the "human image," finding in Pistoletto's images not a simple "antihistorical 'return'" to the visible world but a "recapture" of the themes and motives that allow art to relay "the poetic communication of the truths of aesthetic reason and morality of human existence."[47] In Pistoletto's works, Bernardi observed "a certain fear of abandoning himself with total freedom to the idea that happily inspires him, his restraint to more fully take on the new hypothesis." This "hesitation," Bernardi offered, likely stemmed from Pistoletto's knowledge that he would soon have to change his work, to dissolve himself (*sciogliersi*), so that he might "better collaborate with an endeavor of aesthetic renovation that is as laudable as it is needed and urgent." Ultimately, although Pistoletto was noted early for his training in the difficult work of restoration, critics saw that training as giving him his "love of pictorial materials" while he forged a "cautious but free, anti-academic brushstroke."[48]

This critical prompt for the artist to "abandon" or "dissolve himself" paralleled Pistoletto's effort toward decentered authorship, specifically to move toward a form of figuration that would be as objective as possible. Indeed, in contrast to Carluccio's existentialist reading of Pistoletto's work, the artist was trying to move away from the agita of figurative painting and "drama," as he put it, of Bacon and other contemporary figurative painters whom he admired. He was seeking to find a "way out" of the broader "impasse" of art in the 1950s, to "gain his freedom" from it.[49] As he later recounted: "You had to use art's autonomy to create another world—moving from the subjective level of the artist, where you are the center of the universe, to an external level that involves art in changing the world."[50] During that time, he revised historically religious compositional formats, such as the icon, substituting sacred subjects with secular figures of the new Italy.

The early works thereby also addressed the potential destabilization of the system of representation itself in the shadow of World War II. Pistoletto's oversized self-portraits are difficult to discern as such. The figures' faces, not to mention likenesses, are impossible to make out. In those works, an aesthetic approaching iconoclasm paradoxically becomes the focus of the artist's exploration of representation, precisely as representation began to shift from narrative depiction to material presentation of a body. Pistoletto would explore this tension in other works of the period and across his career.

The artist was also contemplating these issues in lesser-known areas of his early work.[51] In 1957, Pistoletto joined a newly formed interdisciplinary group of artists in Turin called the Gruppo d'Arte l'Arlecchino, or Harlequin Art Group. As part of the group, he contributed to their journal, *Presenze* (1957–60), a publication dedicated to art and thought in and out of Italy. It would be a formative site for Pistoletto's early work in visual arts and in writing, a practice he has continued ever since.[52] Close examination of Pistoletto's and his contemporaries' work in *Presenze* reveals nascent reconceptualizations of Italian avant-gardism heading into the 1960s in Turin that hinged in part on the journal's concern with internationalism and universal humanism.

PISTOLETTO, *PRESENZE*, AND THE HARLEQUIN ART GROUP

At the time of his first involvement in the Harlequin Art Group, Pistoletto, then only twenty-three years old, began publishing his work in the group's journal. *Presenze* featured some of his earliest artistic and creative activities. Pistoletto published short essays on abstraction and contributed reproductions of his early paintings. (Some are now known only through those images.) All those works measured over six and a half feet in height and were vertically oriented, centered compositions, featuring isolated figures or architectural plans. Pistoletto's artworks reproduced in *Presenze* direct us to the previously noted connection between representation and religious history, as well as to the tensions between representation and abstraction in postwar Italy. One work, *Chiesa* (Church), was destroyed by the artist following its appearance in the journal. Like another work, *Il Tempio* (The Temple), it featured religious iconography and architecture that echo the forms of the religious figures he was also painting at the time.[53] Other works, as in the figure in *Sacerdote* (Priest), who is distinguished by stepped shoulders, recall these architectural pictures, as well as paintings by fellow artists that appeared in the first issue of the journal, as in a painting of a local church by Aldo Conti, with whom Pistoletto had at one point shared a studio. With *Il Santo* (The Saint, 1957), *Church* and *Priest* were printed consecutively across the pages of a single issue, conjuring the religious format of a triptych despite their existence as separate works (fig. 12). The juxtaposition of images underscores their shared compositional logic.

In these early paintings, Pistoletto was working out problems concerning representation and abstraction and of "iconophilia" and iconoclasm, as he put it.[54] He was also addressing these questions in his writings, published in *Presenze*.[55] In his first essay, he situated abstraction as part of modernism's logical progression, rather than the cause of its devolution. In a late 1950s essay on abstraction ("Astrattismo"), Pistoletto addressed then popular criticism of modernist abstraction as a conceptually empty, formalist enterprise. Offering a counterview, Pistoletto urged readers to evaluate abstraction by different criteria: to respect the "abstract experience" such paintings offered. For Pistoletto, this experience was "born of an intellectual and spiritual opening destined to expand [*dilatare*] the rational capacities of humanity."[56] Abstraction in Pistoletto's view was far from conceptually vacuous; it was a humanist enterprise.

Pistoletto nevertheless cautioned young artists of the Italian avant-garde against fashioning their work in the *existing* terms of modernist abstraction. The essay mounts a kind of call of artistic duty, echoing the Harlequin Art Group's original directive. He urged young Italian artists to seek *new* creative means for themselves that would be better suited to the new conditions of the contemporary world and the changing condition of humanity. He wrote: "Abstractionist ideology, modern art's latest proposition, cannot repeat itself without degenerating into rhetoric, given that the creative impulse in which it originated has died down. The social function of art must ensure that the new artist seeks out, in the experiences of every modern trend and abstract symbolism, which are built on rationality and simplicity, the means to establish communications of a human reality that is of an increasingly interior and spiritual nature, and to realize expressions of increasingly subtle and as-yet undisclosed feelings."[57] In this passage, Pistoletto called on "the new artist" to relay "human reality," underscoring the social function of art. Compounding the depletion of abstraction was its fundamental incompatibility with the complex social and existential terrain contemporary artists now confronted. The problem with abstraction was not abstraction itself but the reductive, hermetic character of its current logic.

Pistoletto's disavowal of modernist abstraction, tied to a devolution into rhetoric, was not incidental. Language was a primary site of cultural debate and had become the central platform for new creative activity in experimental poetry (especially visual poetry) and the literary neoavanguardia.[58] Writers and poets such as the 1950s group I Novissimi, including Edoardo Sanguineti, who would write on Pistoletto's *spolvero* figure drawings, discussed below, often regarded rhetoric with disdain and criticized it as a meaningless pursuit associated with fascism and totalitarian propaganda.[59] The persuasive, expressive function of the linguistic art form depends on the speaker's ability to leverage, manipulate, and even exploit the words and figures of speech at their disposal. Considering these remarks, we might regard Pistoletto's early work as an effort to conceptualize a new form of figuration, divested of the negative political connotations associated with figurative expression—both linguistic and visual.[60] To do so would require shifting the figure from the rhetorical and representational (the symbolic) to a different order that would communicate the new condition of "human reality."

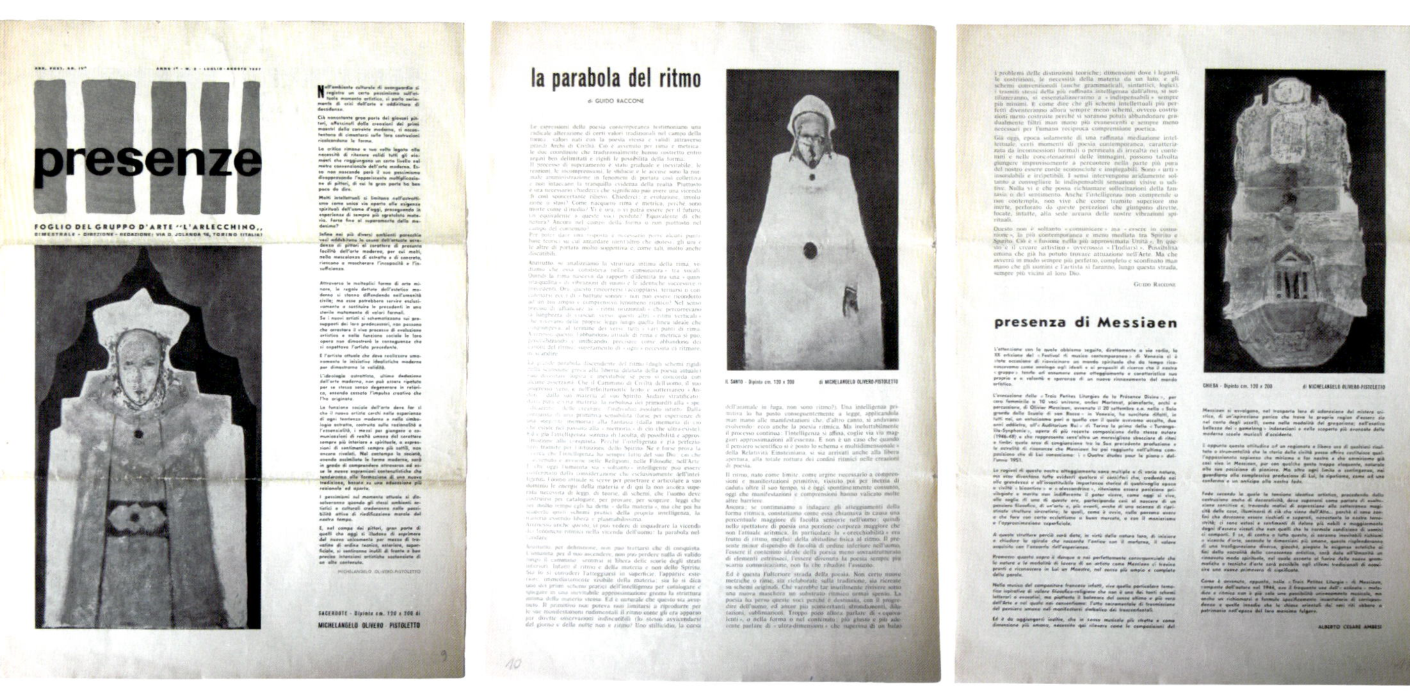

presenze

FOGLIO DEL GRUPPO D'ARTE "L'ARLECCHINO"

SACERDOTE - Dipinto cm. 130 x 200

MICHELANGELO OLIVERO - PISTOLETTO

la parabola del ritmo

di GUIDO RACCONE

presenza di Messiaen

ALBERTO CESARE AMBESI

FIG. 12. Michelangelo Pistoletto, *Sacerdote* (Priest), *Il Santo* (The Saint), and *Chiesa* (Church; destroyed by the artist), all 1957, in *Presenze* 1, no. 2 (July–August 1957), 1–3. Biblioteca Musicale Andrea della Corte, Turin.

For Pistoletto, *Presenze* was also a space for creative inquiry to connect with the broader world. The journal was conceived as a platform for artists and thinkers whose work would lead to the renewal of art and thought as a matter of duty in late 1950s Italy. The idea of renewal was not uncommon in artist-run journals in postwar Italy or as a topic in postwar European art discourse. Vanguard art magazines and literary journals were sites where Italian artists could "catch up" after the restrictions of fascism by participating in aesthetic constructions of international and global modernisms.[61] Proliferating at a high rate in Italy's postwar decades, sometimes referred to as "the journal years," these vanguard art serials recalled the integral role of artist-generated journals in the historical avant-garde and in antifascist artistic circles.[62] This historical trajectory of vanguard activism was especially strong in Turin; socialist and workers' presses, as well as the secret presses of the antifascist partisan resistance, comprised a large part of the city's print culture. Mainstays in Turin since the late nineteenth century, these journals proliferated again in the post–World War II period, continuing themes of exchange and contemporaneity alongside the national project of cultural and social renewal.[63]

Within this context, the Harlequin Art Group espoused a belief "in the new civilization [that] Mankind is making himself encounter." A second objective was an "affirmation of the exigencies of renovation," most often pursued through the group's juxtaposition of local and foreign-situated international cultural topics.[64] The group used editorial and design strategies that set up visual and symbolic correspondences between young (mostly unestablished) Turinese artists and non-Italian artists and creative practitioners, as well as non-Italian "Western" and "non-Western" sources.[65] In one example, readers encountered one of Pistoletto's figurative paintings featuring a man seated on a sofa, which, without explanation, accompanied an essay on Indian art.[66] Images were often put in dialogue with text through visual juxtaposition, without any apparent relation except for the shared space of the page.

The layout of *Presenze* in this regard ultimately works as a collage, despite the seamlessness of the material page. This disjuncture between image content and adjacent text recategorizes would-be illustrations as standalone works. In so doing, the layout constellates new relations between word and image, moving beyond denotative description. It is a repository for the arrangement of visual and textual information that catalyzes rapports among cultures, art forms, and periods that might otherwise seem marked by historical constructions of difference.[67] Its logic is not difference for difference's sake. Rather, it is an expression of pluralist cosmopolitanism, of being connected to the world. The format of the journal ultimately functions as a tabular space that repositions the individual as a distinctive subject and as one of many, across time and place. Moving beyond the restrictive structures of European supremacy and Enlightenment-era thought to which humanism had been historically linked, the shared space asserts an equivalence in value and pluralist presence that relays a new form of humanism for the postwar world.

The artists' conceptualization of this project is further elucidated by their formation as a group. While the name "Harlequin" was dropped after the first two issues of *Presenze* in favor of a more general descriptor, the group's initial selection of the commedia dell'arte figure conjures its function as a symbol of revolutionary collective creative identity, by this time popular and Italian in nature, that had specifically international origins (in the French Harlequin).[68] In the early twentieth century and interwar period in Italy, Arlecchino (among other stock characters) populated futurist paintings and works of metaphysical painting and the Novecento, styles that enjoyed support under fascism. Commedia dell'arte was engaged as a sign of *italianità:* of "Italianness" and popular tradition.[69] In postwar Italy, the *povero diavolo,* or "poor devil" character, as Arlecchino is sometimes referred to, was associated with social revolution and unbridled freedom of expression.[70] He was also associated with postwar reconstruction, healing, and models of creativity that invited audience participation.[71] True to these connotations, the Harlequin Art Group dedicated themselves to fostering a groundswell of experimental creative activity that would attend to the human experience of the postwar world within the context of shifting Italian identity after fascism.[72] As Pistoletto later recalled, that although they didn't succeed in sustaining their effort, *Presenze* was "a little magazine, a little newspaper, made in actuality really to bring our voices together, to connect our voices."[73] Arlecchino related to the constituency of the group and the possibilities they envisioned for themselves: "We called it 'Harlequin' because we knew there wasn't any practical relationship with the Harlequin, which means all colors. We're doing something where there's everything, *everything* is possible, *everyone* can say something. This thing was based on meeting, and by way of different opinions, different backgrounds, because then, at that time, we all already had different backgrounds."[74] Pistoletto's words position *Presenze* as the progenitor of revolutionary ideas that shaped the left in 1960s Italy. The Harlequin Art Group sought new possibilities and rethought existing systems, as would Arte Povera, which sought to break with the restrictions of existing artistic conventions and symbolic orders.[75]

The figure of Arlecchino embodied contemporary interests in Turin and broader Italy. At the time, Italians were visualizing the world and connecting with it through travel and the lens of universal humanism. The development of portable camera technology sparked new possibilities in world photography and adventure reporting.[76] Nationally these interests were best represented by the work of alpinist Walter Bonatti. Internationally renowned for his extensive explorations and writings, Bonatti published extensively in the 1960s, perhaps most famously in the Italian weekly *L'Epoca.* These interests marked a distinctive departure from other forms of global attention in Italian history, such as missionary work and colonial expeditions, founded in proselytization and empire.[77]

Presenze was an important site for Pistoletto to work out problems of figuration and of Turin's and Italy's place in the world at a time of shifting humanisms and worldviews. Pistoletto and fellow artists imagined correspondences, affinities, and resonances between Turin and other locales, in Italy and elsewhere. Bringing together valuable new directions in art and thought, they reconceptualized the international contemporary field into terrain that could accommodate all subjectivities, themselves included. The group ended their activities in 1960. Pistoletto had already moved on and was beginning to gain recognition as an artist.

FIGURES AND FIELDS: ICONS OLD AND NEW

Paintings of isolated figures on monochromatic fields of gold and silver followed the Galatea exhibition (preceding Andy Warhol's better-known experiments begun in 1962). In them, Pistoletto depicted the new modern subject of a booming postwar Italian economy—singular businessmen—as new icons.[78] He also depicted these figures on grounds composed of trompe l'oeil

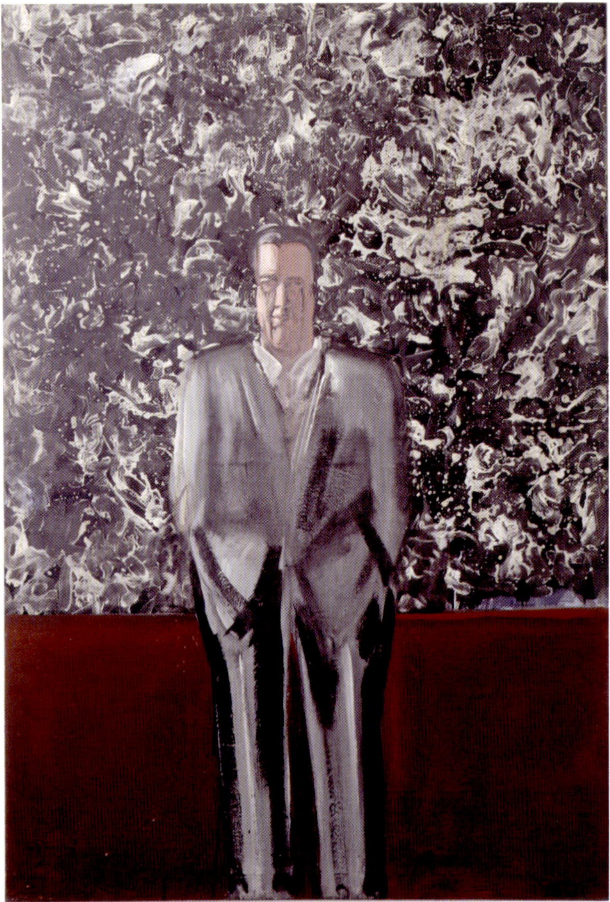

FIG. 13. Michelangelo Pistoletto, *Autoritratto linoleum* (Linoleum Self-Portrait), 1959. Oil and acrylic on canvas, 78¾ × 59 in. (200 × 150 cm). Goetz Collection, Munich.

representations of newly popular industrial materials. At the Galatea, he showed *Autoritratto linoleum* (Linoleum Self-Portrait) from 1959 (fig. 13). Its marbled, faux-granite background frames a quickly rendered figure: the artist as a sharply dressed, on-the-go businessman, occupying the role of the New Man who was then populating Italian mass culture in advertisements for companies ranging from Fiat to mass-produced clothing pioneer Facis, as well as Pistoletto's paintings.[79] Precedents to this work can be found in the history of European modernism, which depicted new modern subjects while undoing mimetic representation, offering new social and formal terms. Pistoletto exceeded such precedents, however, by remaking the space of painting from a figurative, representational space to a figural one.[80]

Three strategies enact this reconceptualization of figurative painting. First, the flat material ground of the painting is emphasized by the flat background composed of two horizontal registers, divided at chair-rail height: a smaller field of monochromatic deep red below and a larger field of mottled "all-over" gray-and-white pattern above. Next, the painted pattern "tricks the eye" and reads as faux-stone-patterned linoleum. Finally, it is also a play on fictive marble—the faux depiction of marble as actual material in medieval and early modern architecture, painting, and manuscript production—here updated to a doubly fictive one.[81] (Marbled linoleum already fakes the veining of marble, making Pistoletto's fictive marble a double entendre, referring to the actual material of linoleum and the representation of it in his painting.)

In medieval painting, fictive marbles sometimes operated to provide viewers with an expanded sense of time, a "lithic-induced perspective on the universe" that goes beyond the short range of human life, to connect viewers to devotional themes such as the afterlife that transcend life on earth, as Robert Mills has argued.[82] In frescoes, sometimes paintings of fictive marbles would frame spiritual imagery. They served, as Herbert Kessler has demonstrated, as an embodied, material example of what the spiritual image depicts; if art could "rematerialize matter," the spiritual image could stand in as the *real* version of the spiritual.[83]

In Pistoletto's work, the spiritual is replaced with the secular New Man of postwar Italy; the fictive "marble" in the painting is of a modern material (linoleum) that is already a fictive marble in the real world. The prompt is not, then, to see the universe in geological time but to consider man in the modern world *as it is now* and to consider that the real is now always a semblance. This is as much a painting of a figure as it is a real scene of man in the world. The ground behind the figure does not recede; there is minimal perspectival space. The painted ground instead emphasizes the flat expanse of the picture plane *and* of the real wall on which the physical painting hangs. The result is that the painted figure appears to stand in front of a depicted and "real" ground that we perceive as spatially congruent with the actual wall on which the painting hangs, in the real space of display. This transgression of the division between representation and reality is bolstered by three other formal choices, all converging on the figure. He is life-size. He is also cropped at the ankles, creating a visual suggestion that he is standing on the same floor as the viewer. His eye level is positioned with ours, since the painting hangs a few inches above the floor. Centered in the pictorial field, he appears to confront the viewer while standing in and outside of the painting, mirroring our position in a space that commingles the depicted and the real.

Let us return to the Galatea exhibition. Alongside the smaller *Blue Acrobat,* many of the artist's paintings (and drawings) on display in his debut exhibition showed figures at home and at rest, in various states of contemplation and repose, but in life-size, constituting another strategy that positioned the represented figure closer to the perceived "real" presence of the figural.[84] In a vertically oriented example from the group, *Uomo sul sofà* (Man on Sofa, 1958), we see a solitary figure seated below an elaborate octagonal window; its outer blue panes frame a pale pink oval at center (fig. 14). Divided into two registers, the composition situates the figure, dressed in a blue suit, and the illuminated window as visual analogues. The suited man was a frequent motif in the artist's work at this time, as noted above, when his figures were almost always business professionals.[85] The figure's head echoes the shape and color of the oval window, while his blue suit echoes the form and shade of the glowing azure panes that frame his shoulders. The figure faces us as viewers, but he is nearly eclipsed by the enormous window.

The painting enacts an inversion of the conventional figure-ground relationship, in which a depicted figure is imposed on the painted ground. This inversion is amplified by the visible facture of the artist's brushstrokes, which follow the contours of the figure's head and shoulders, while his legs extend beyond the bottom edge of the picture. The figure's feet, we imagine, would be where ours are: level with the floor of the gallery.

These exchanges—of figure and ground and of pictorial and physical space—would be pushed even further in Pistoletto's paintings of singular figures depicted on metallic fields of silver and gold. The use of silver paint was inspired in part by process, the artist later recounted, in which he used a mirror to assist his work in self-portraiture and attempt to "reproduce the mirror on the canvas."[86] Other factors, including the process of applying silver, bronze, or gold leaf to a painting, to create a reflective ground that would envelop the figure (as opposed to visually presenting as a background behind it) recalled the practice in the creation of icons, and in late medieval and Renaissance painting more broadly, of gold-grounding: of depicting figures, especially sacred ones such as saints, surrounded by fields of *doratura,* of gilt. Recalling such icons in the autobiographical sections of his recent extended text, *La formula della creazione* (The Formula of Creation, 2022), Pistoletto underscored the impact of these works: "Those human images set against a gold ground lodged themselves in my mind, where I found them again when I started to create my own art."[87]

Such experiments can be traced to 1957, when Pistoletto made two paintings in which he deployed the figure as archetype and icon. In the closely cropped compositions of *The Saint,* painted with a red background, and *Priest,* in gold, we see a monolithic figure positioned centrally within the image field, which he also dominates (fig. 15). Each is dressed in his respective vestments, rendered in reductive, geometric form, pared down to the minimum of detail required to signify their liturgical status. In *Priest,* an architectural black frame (or void) immediately surrounds the figure—or appears to. The figure is painted white; it is therefore difficult to separate him from the white architectural form that also surrounds him and with which he seems to be, at least in part, contiguous. Returning to the black frame, its apex extends to the top edge of the physical panel; its edges cascade down the figure's shoulders before attenuating into vertical black lines on either side of the figure, where they run parallel to the right and left edges of the panel. The black frame operates as a figural boundary as well as an imagistic suggestion. It specifically recalls the carved niches often found in medieval icons, where they enshrine painted sacred figures with a three-dimensional frame and hence suggest the real, bodily presence of the icon's subject (as in this example from Barnaba da Modena, in Turin's Galleria Sabauda, which Pistoletto often visited, especially as a child with his father; fig. 16).[88]

It was through this investigation of historic figurative painting and of the figure more specifically as an image and depicted body that Pistoletto explored structures of signification between iconicity and symbolic representation, which continued in his works that followed. In *Autoritratto su fondo argento* (Self-Portrait on Silver Ground) from 1960, for example, we see a similar strategy of painting the surface of the canvas with brushstrokes that trace the outline of the figure's body. Rather than block out the ground and complete the underpainting (on which to develop the painted figure), Pistoletto painted around the figure, leaving brushstrokes visible,

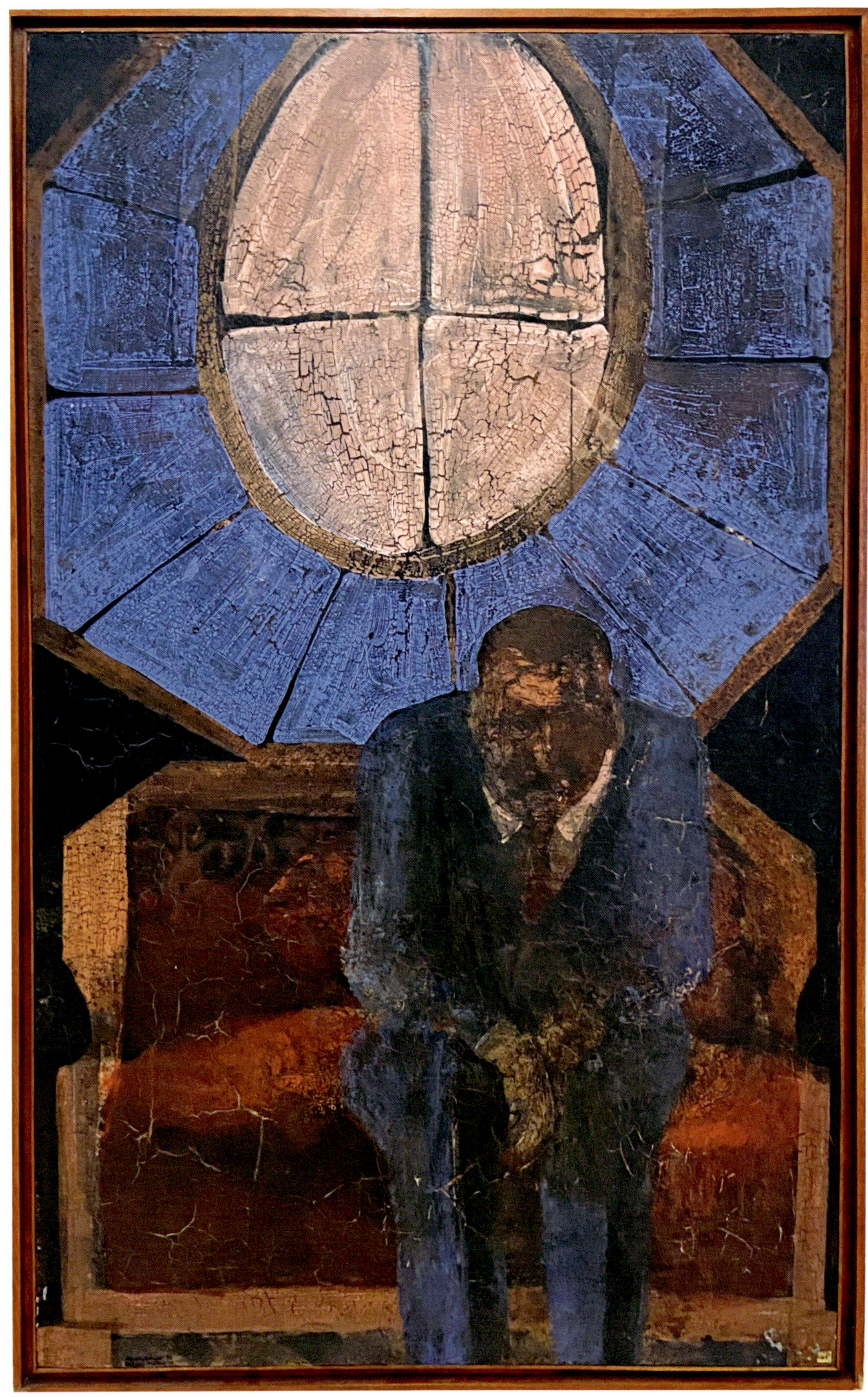

FIG. 14. Michelangelo Pistoletto, *Uomo sul sofà* (Man on Sofa), 1958. Oil and acrylic on canvas, 78¾ × 47¼ in. (200 × 120 cm). Cittadellarte–Fondazione Pistoletto, Biella.

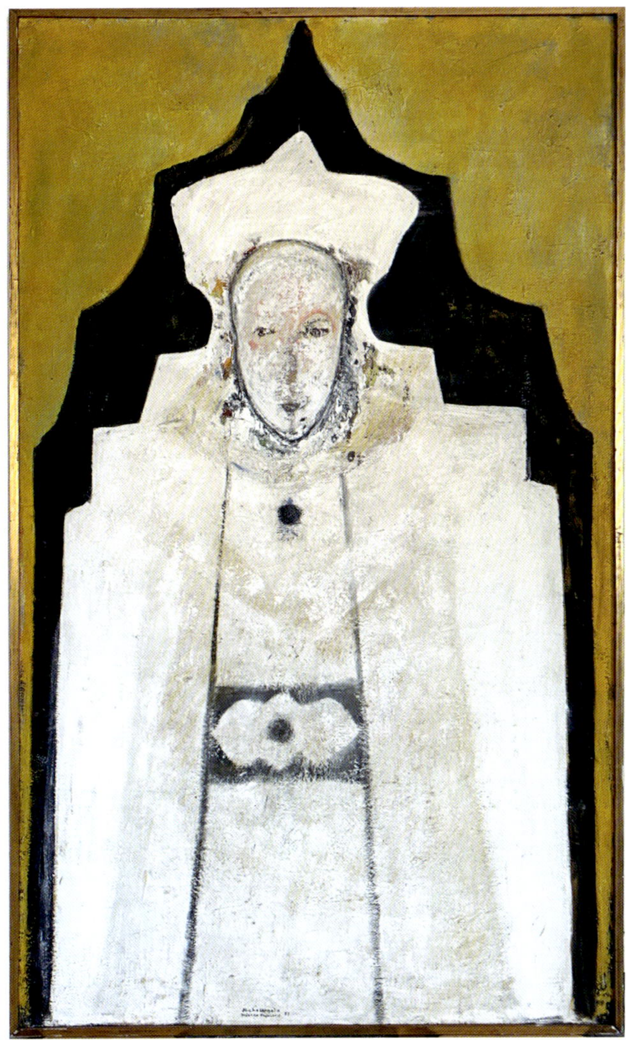

FIG. 15. Michelangelo Pistoletto, *Sacerdote* (Priest), 1957. Oil on canvas, 78¾ × 39⅜ in. (200 × 100 cm). Cittadellarte–Fondazione Pistoletto, Biella.

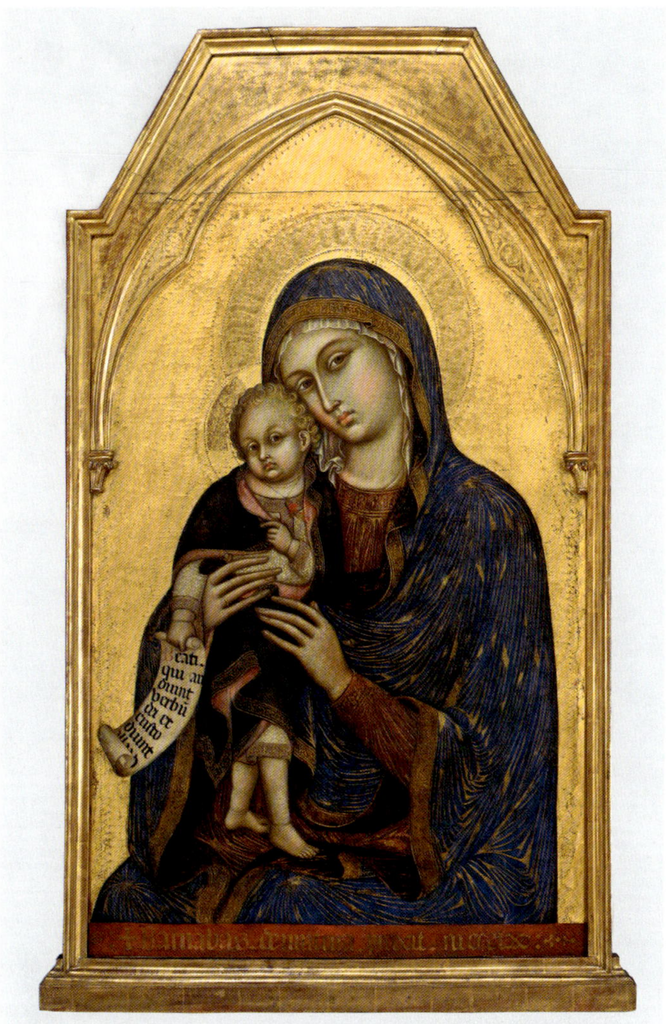

FIG. 16. Agocchiari Barnaba, called Barnaba da Modena, *Madonna con bambino* (Madonna with Child), 1370. Tempera and gilt painting on wood panel, 51½ × 32½ × 2 in. (130.7 × 82.3 × 4.8 cm). Galleria Sabauda, Musei Reali, Turin.

thereby imposing figure on ground (as in early modern painting). The artist leaves a visible trace of built-up paint that encompasses and helps to create the boundaries of the figure (figs. 17, 18). Indeed, close analysis of the edges of the figure reveals a lack of contour line; instead, short brushstrokes of burnt sienna, dove gray, carnelian, and black together register the artist's reassertion of the figure's presence through quick marks of paint around its edges. The result is an oscillation at the site of the would-be suture between figure and ground: between the visual and material prominence of the silver ground, when the figure seems sunken in, and the figure's presence as such, as image and body on a ground. Pistoletto was grappling with the suture as the boundary of the figure itself: a critical, delimiting site of major importance to the history of painting that might allow for a rethinking of the entire endeavor.

For Pistoletto, this exploration between the figure and its subsumption into the abstract revived questions of iconicity and iconoclasm that were fundamental to the history of art and religion. There were other stakes at play, however. To him, a turn to abstraction would be atavistic. Abstraction's real history, represented by the works of Paul Klee and Piet Mondrian, each of great interest to him, was already past. Abstraction was also exhausted in the contemporary field, especially in Turin, where it had become mere imitation (in his view) of American action painting. Pistoletto identified a great need for new subject matter, to be found only in figuration.[89]

In a work preceding *Self-Portrait on Silver Ground,* we find the body nearly subsumed by the metallic field around it. In *Figura oro* (Gold Figure, 1959–60), a bust of a figure in the lower-right-hand corner of the image field is at once brought forward and effaced by gold paint (fig. 19). Imposed over the nearly monochromatic wash of gold and mauve paint, the figure is blocked out in gold; only the edges of the figure underneath are visible. Pink and white brushstrokes peek out from behind the gold silhouette, where the neck meets the shoulder, as a black contour line marks the outline of the arm (at left) and head. The gesture of applying a gold silhouette on top of a depicted figure recalls iconoclastic actions that sought to obscure or erase the faces of sacred figures. Here, we don't see a body: the flat gold shape on the equally flat gold background reads as presence and absence—as a figure without a body and a body without a figure. This negotiation is complicated by the division

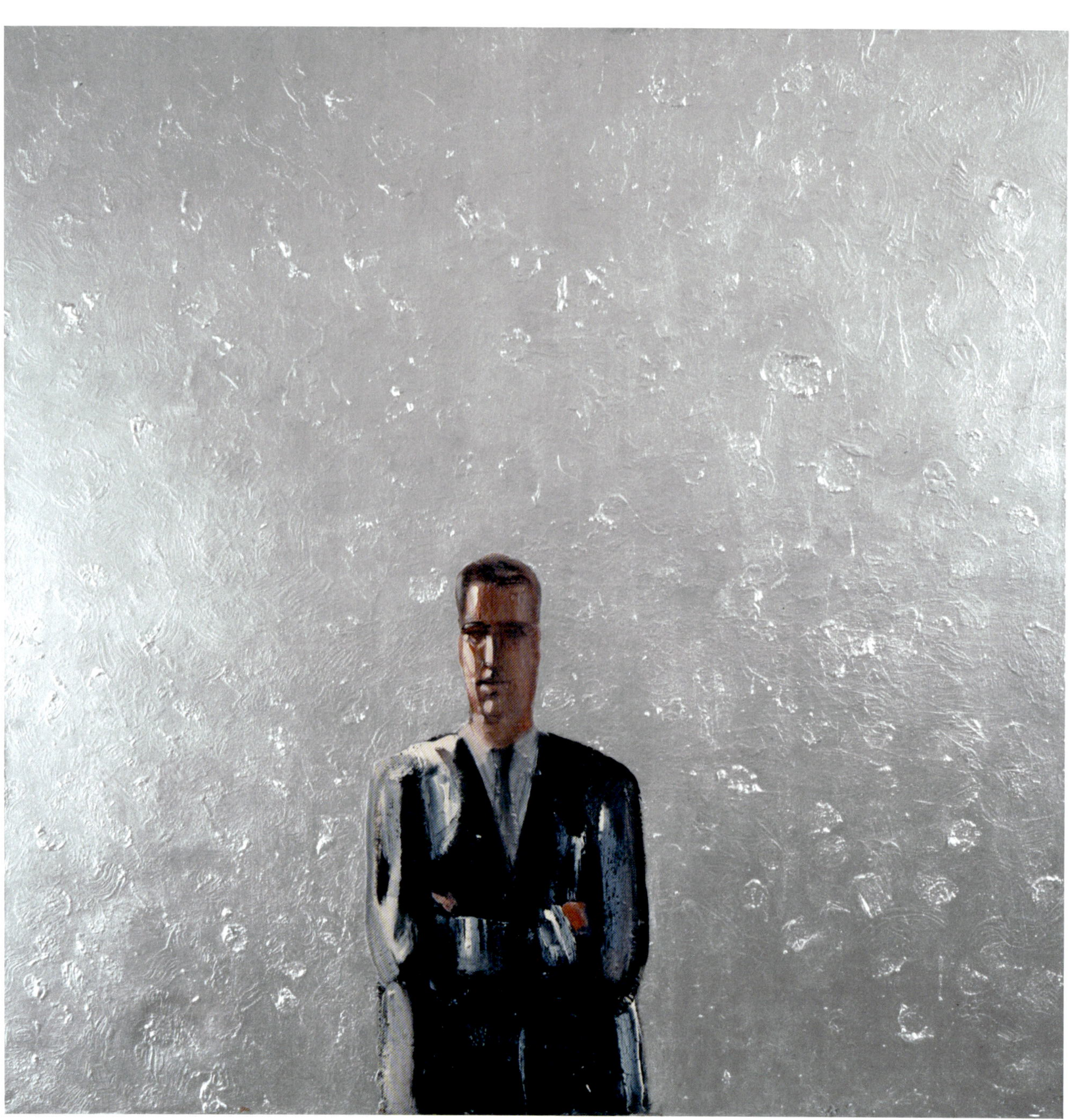

FIG. 17. Michelangelo Pistoletto, *Autoritratto su fondo argento* (Self-Portrait on Silver Ground), 1960. Acrylic, silver, and gesso on canvas, 59 × 59 in. (150 × 150 cm). Cittadellarte–Fondazione Pistoletto, Biella.

of the ground into two vertical registers, one slightly darker, which suggests that a shadow is being cast from the real space of display onto the depicted figure. The division between the registers also bisects the figure, creating a visual relay among the figure, the field, and the real space of display. It suggests a figure at once in the painting and in the real world of the viewer.

A similar inquiry was mounted by his assemblage of the same year: *Esperimento* (Experiment, 1959), in which mounted strings and wooden dowels cast real shadows over the depicted shadow of a portrait bust, painted in silhouette. In that work, the portrait bust is itself a shadow of a figure, but in its absence, the silhouette suggests that it is our own cast shadow, reflected at us from the silver-painted ground (fig. 20). Indeed, Pistoletto would later comment that he had "cut any sense of action or expression" from his early figures; the works with reflective grounds aimed "to discover new space for [his] figures, not narrate their goings-on."[90]

To that end, he revisited this motif in 1960, with *Autoritratto oro* (Gold Self-Portrait), in which a depiction of a life-size standing figure faces us from his position at the center of the gold image field (fig. 21). Like *Gold Figure,* however, this figure—this self-portrait—has no face. While his silhouette is partially rendered in opaque color, his presence fades at the upper and lower boundaries of the body. The gold ground shines through his legs, merging figure and ground at the left knee; his neck fades into a head whose stippled jawline and crown suggests the visual semblance of a poorly executed print. The gold head merges with the ground at the center of the face, where we find only a blank gold field that suggests presence and absence at once. As in *Man on Sofa* and *Linoleum Self-Portrait,* his legs are cropped at the ankles, such that we imagine his feet to be where ours are. The expansion of the figure in this case is underscored not only by compositional cropping but also by the visual dissimulation of the figure into the surrounding field.

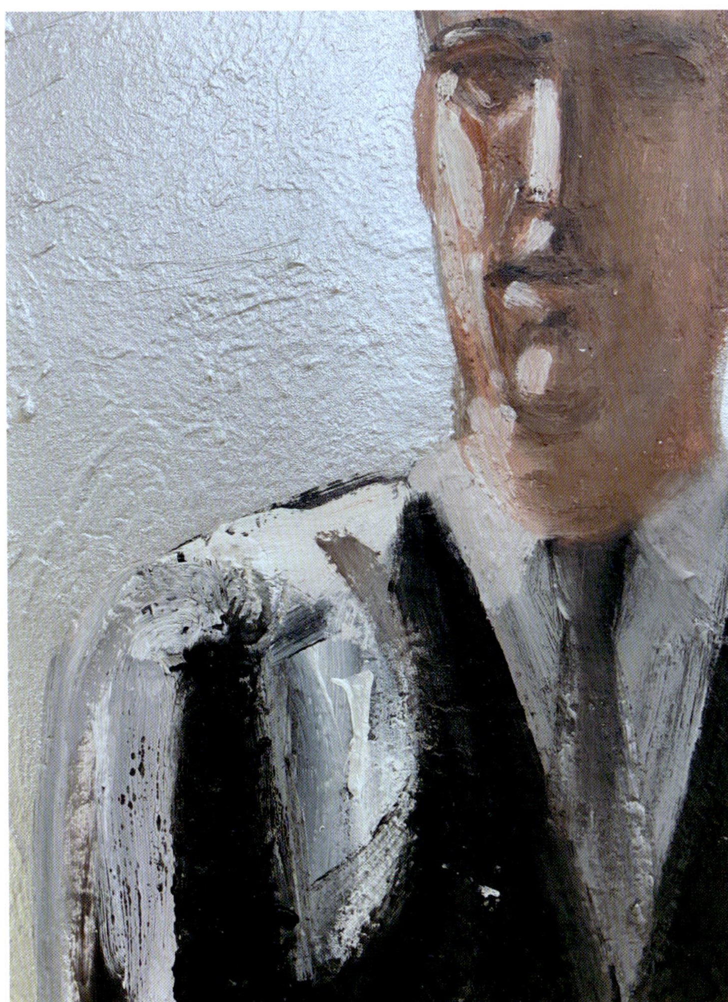

FIG. 18. Michelangelo Pistoletto, *Autoritratto su fondo argento* (Self-Portrait on Silver Ground) (detail), 1960. Cittadellarte–Fondazione Pistoletto, Biella.

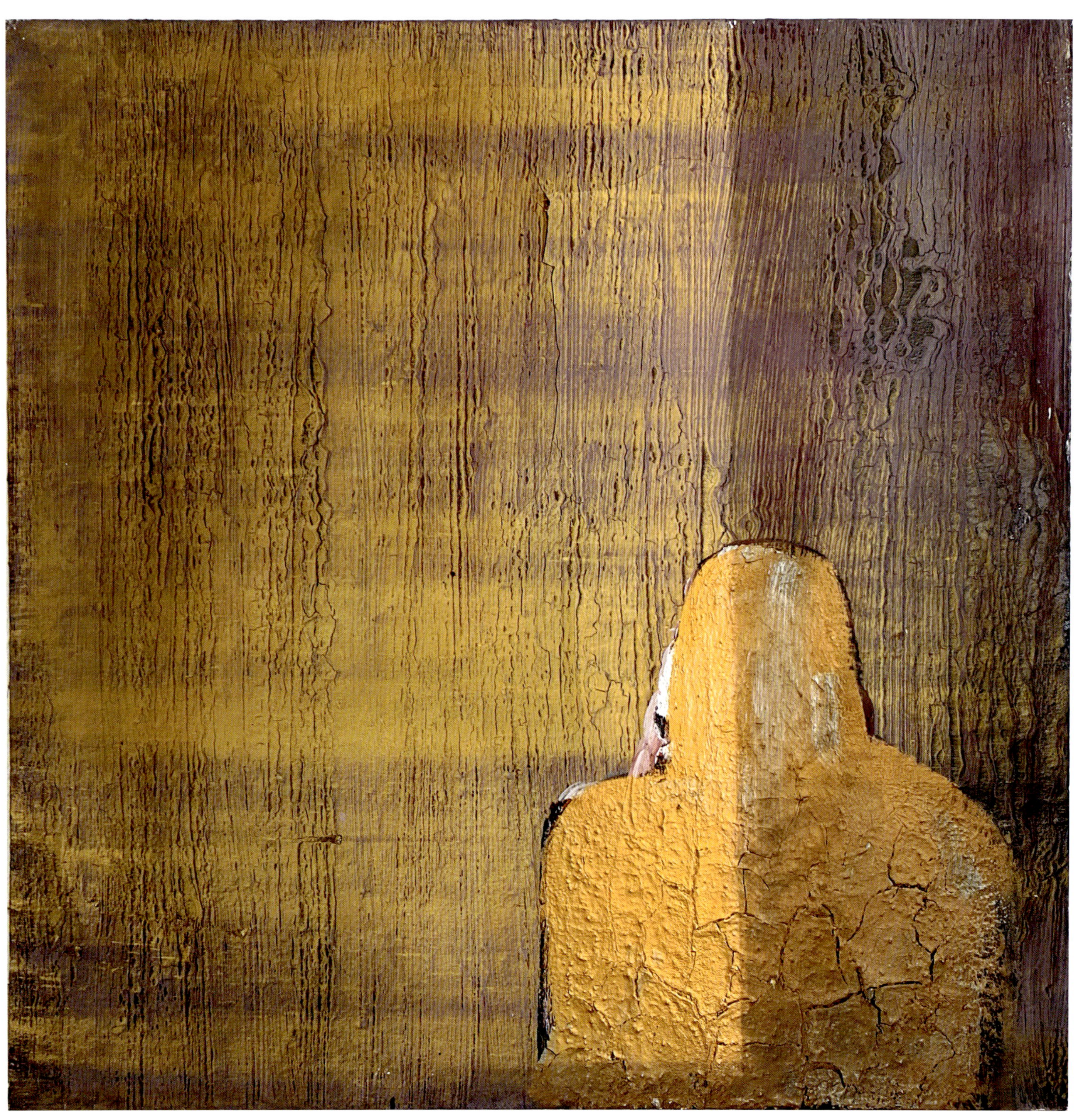

FIG. 19. Michelangelo Pistoletto, *Figura oro* (Gold Figure), 1959–60. Mixed media, 39⅜ × 39⅜ in. (100 × 100 cm). Cittadellarte–Fondazione Pistoletto, Biella.

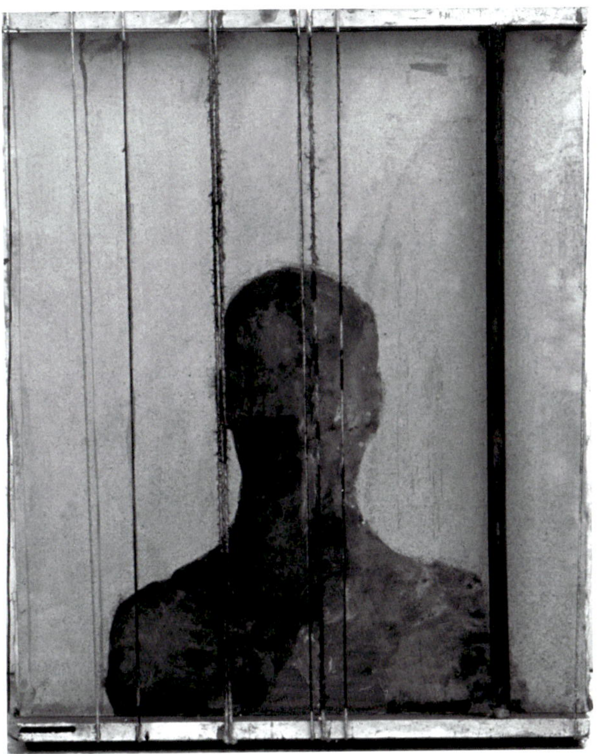

FIG. 20. Michelangelo Pistoletto, *Esperimento* (Experiment), 1959. Acrylic, silver, rope, wood, canvas, 29⅛ × 23⅝ in. (74 × 60 cm). Cittadellarte–Fondazione Pistoletto, Biella.

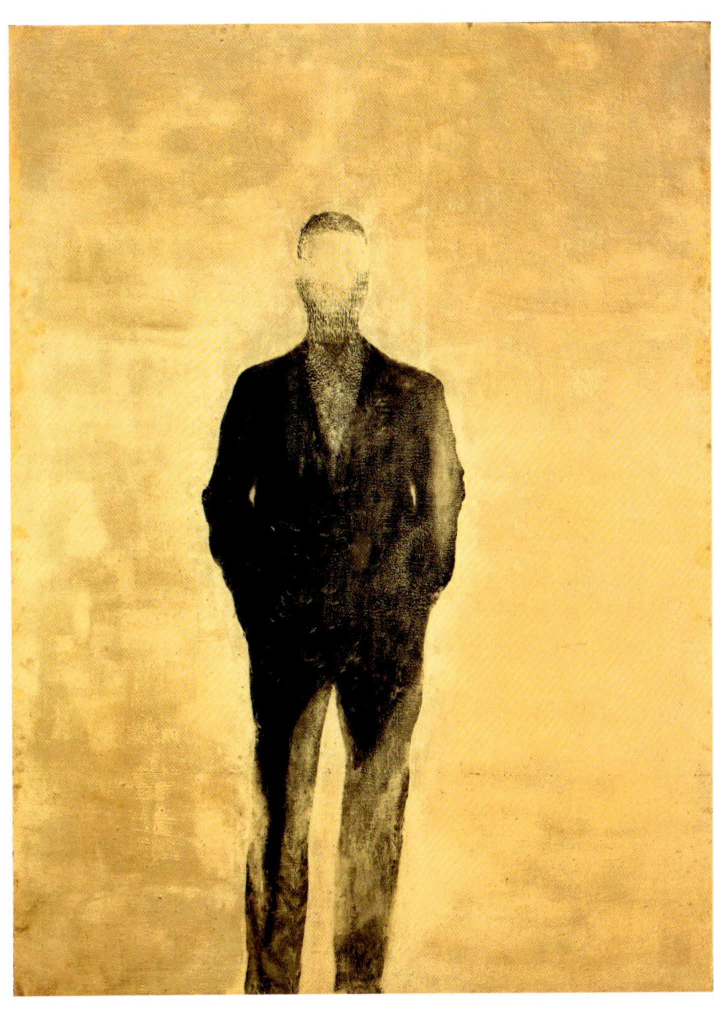

FIG. 21. Michelangelo Pistoletto, *Autoritratto oro* (Gold Self-Portrait), 1960. Oil, acrylic, and gold on canvas, 78¾ × 59 in. (200 × 150 cm). Cittadellarte–Fondazione Pistoletto, Biella.

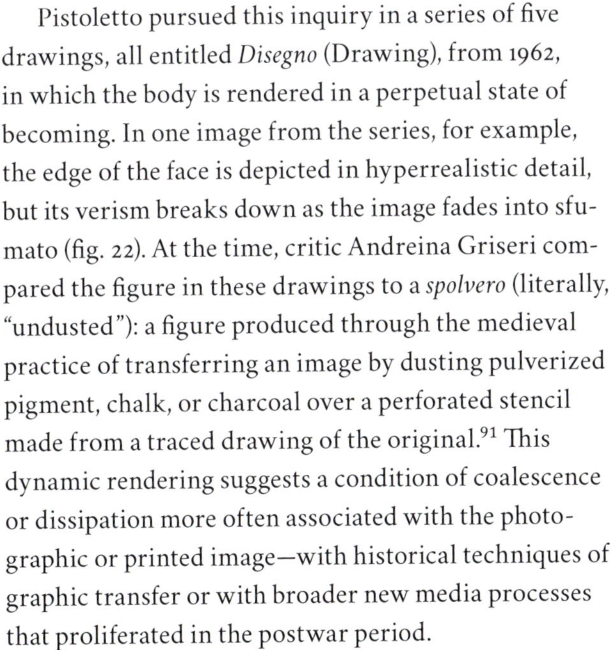

Pistoletto pursued this inquiry in a series of five drawings, all entitled *Disegno* (Drawing), from 1962, in which the body is rendered in a perpetual state of becoming. In one image from the series, for example, the edge of the face is depicted in hyperrealistic detail, but its verism breaks down as the image fades into sfumato (fig. 22). At the time, critic Andreina Griseri compared the figure in these drawings to a *spolvero* (literally, "undusted"): a figure produced through the medieval practice of transferring an image by dusting pulverized pigment, chalk, or charcoal over a perforated stencil made from a traced drawing of the original.[91] This dynamic rendering suggests a condition of coalescence or dissipation more often associated with the photographic or printed image—with historical techniques of graphic transfer or with broader new media processes that proliferated in the postwar period.

In these early works, we see Pistoletto's first experiments with the trope of the posed figure, and with the motif of the expansive figure, who exceeds the limits of the pictorial field through compositional cropping, life-size scale, and dissimulation, strategies he continued to use in the mirror paintings. If *Blue Acrobat* and Pistoletto's spectacular subjects give us insight into an early moment of a career-long fascination with the human figure, and his self-portraits reflect a deep engagement with historical and contemporary forms of figuration, we might say that Pistoletto's early paintings confronted viewers with images that captured the distinctly human experiences of being seen and of seeing ourselves see others. They also captured an awareness of the increasing mediation of those experiences in the postwar technological world.[92] The figures at rest register the respite of privacy in the increasingly media-saturated world of postwar Italy, as well as a condition of disenchantment for the bourgeois worker faced with the increasing systemization of life enacted by the rise of postwar capitalism. Ultimately, the paintings also

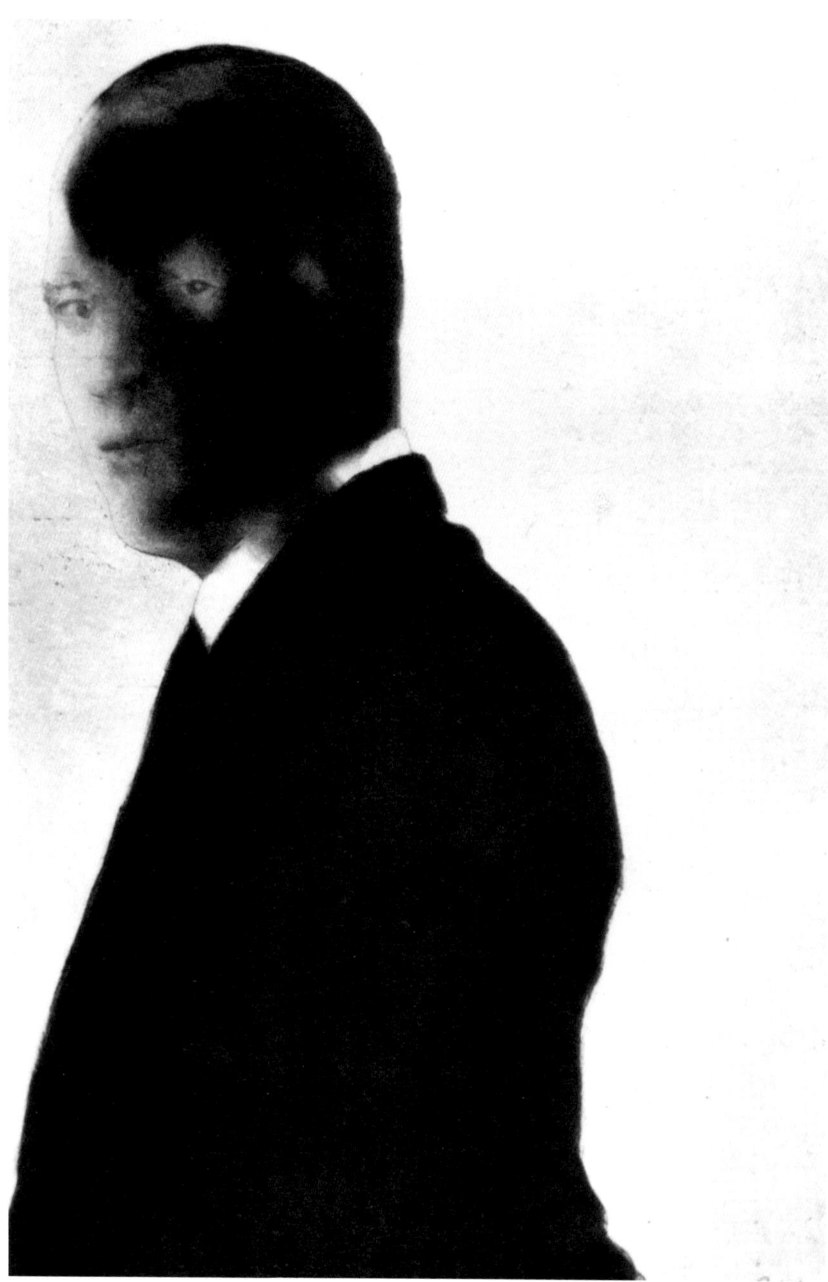

FIG. 22. Michelangelo Pistoletto, *Disegno* (Drawing), 1962. Pencil on paper, 26½ × 19 in. (67 × 48 cm). Private collection.

seriously contemplate the figure's newly precarious position within the history of art: as a representation of the human figure, as an image on a ground, and, via icon painting, as a subject in the world.[93]

PISTOLETTO'S META-FIGURES

Examination of other early works reveals additional strategies that Pistoletto used in this reconceptualization of figuration. Consider a rare still life from 1959 to 1960, made as part of Pistoletto's satisfaction of his contract at the Galatea (fig. 23).[94] Here we find figurative themes connected to Italian modernism and framing devices that conjure historical artistic contexts in which representations of the figure were intended to present viewers in real time and space with a body to be encountered. Framing the scene is an archway depicted in gold paint; it is an elaboration on a motif found elsewhere in Pistoletto's works of the time.

Natura morta (Still Life) appears to depict a tabletop, with a few jars, bottles, and vessels on its surface, in the lower register—the foreground of the scene inside the painting—and a moonlit architectural scene in the background. Between the two—the archway (recalling the carved, frequently arched, gilt frames in icon paintings) and the interior scene of its framing—we find a black rectangular outline. It appears to us at first as a window, framing a view of Turin's many baroque palazzi, but we do not see a wall. Instead, the nighttime scene is in full view, even beyond the perimeter of the window frame. The tabletop scene oscillates then between a setting of objects and a theatrical scene of people on a stage (a *teatrino,* or "little theater," a major motif of Italian modernism). It is a strange nighttime scene of a few figures in an empty piazza, framed by the arch of one of Turin's famous arcades—a redux of Giorgio de Chirico's metaphysical paintings, which were largely inspired by a visit to Turin. It is also an unoccupied icon, waiting for a figure to appear. On closer inspection, we see that the black rectangle is free-floating; it traverses the interior space of the scene to the architectural (and pictorial) frame of the golden arch. Neither part of the interior or diegetic space of the painting nor part of the framing device of the archway, it serves as a *parergon.*

The strange position of this device—and its waiting for a figure—merits further clarification. Jacques Derrida's poststructuralist theorization of the parergon is a device, at once outside of but connected to the accomplished work (*ergon*). It is secondary, "extra, *exterior to the specific field*"; therefore, "it is that which *should not* become, by distinguishing itself, the principal subject."[95] Through analysis of Kant's use of the term, Derrida offered a formal and critical structure for the parergon. As it "rubs" up against the work to which it is connected, the parergon intervenes when there is something missing and when the work is itself missing.[96] In Pistoletto's still life, it would seem to point to the absence of the figure, but its appearance in other paintings of the period, in which figures are depicted, suggests that the absence might be something else. It calls our attention to the exhaustion of figurative painting as it had been, and to the urgency to find and make the human *present,* in a context of increased alienation and capitalist symbolic orders, through new figural forms.

This point about the intervention of Pistoletto's frame in the history of figurative painting is elucidated by further examination of the work. Returning to the still life, the frame finds visual echoes in the right-hand vertical register of the pictorial field, where a black contour line is sketched in paint for the full length of the image—a trope we also see in a portrait painted by the artist in the same year (fig. 24). Similar black lines

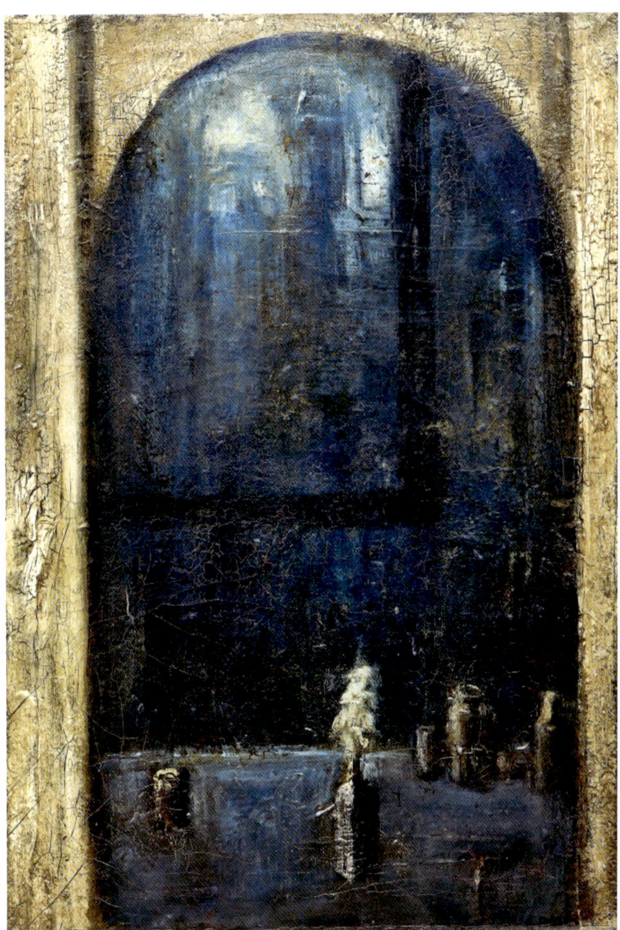

FIG. 23. Michelangelo Pistoletto, *Natura morta* (Still Life), 1959–60. Mixed media on canvas, 39⅜ × 27½ in. (100 × 70 cm). Private collection.

mark the vertical section of the image, where another black rectangle frames our view. The black box also reads as a compositional notation—a pictorial frame not unlike a fresco giornata or a comic-strip panel or publishers' marks on photography.[97] It is a painting-within-the-painting, an abstract painting, for that matter: a metapicture. The trope of the metapicture dates to early modern painting, as do many of Pistoletto's historical influences, when artists began to paint images of paintings within painted scenes, offering imagistic allegories on the work of the artist and visual directives to the viewer, calling attention to certain moral lessons or devotional imagery.[98] The framing, as a device of picture making and abstraction, gets to the core of histories of painting, of art and humanism, and of systems of representation that would occupy much of Pistoletto's artistic inquiries for decades to come.[99] In Pistoletto's case, the framing device is closely connected

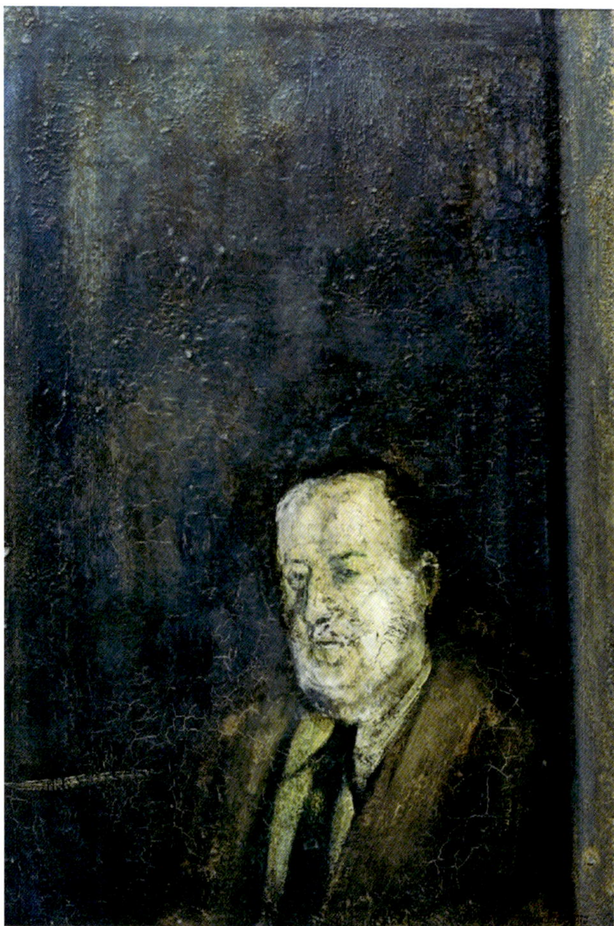

FIG. 24. Michelangelo Pistoletto, *Ritratto* (Portrait), 1960. Mixed media on canvas, 39⅜ × 27½ in. (100 × 70 cm). Private collection.

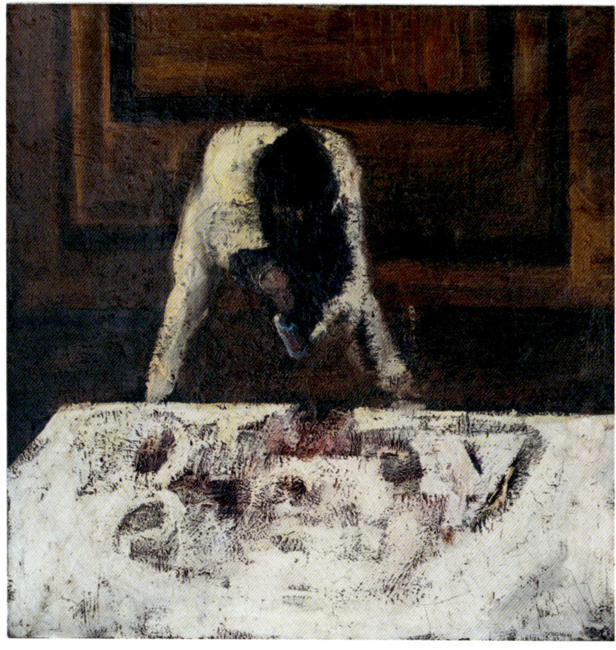

FIG. 25. Michelangelo Pistoletto, *Il pittore* (The Painter), 1959. Oil on canvas, 47¼ × 47¼ in. (120 × 120 cm). Private collection.

to his exploration of figuration. Frames often surround a figure, creating a second image, often a figurative one, within the figurative image. These are what we might call meta-figures.

Compare *Still Life* to the appearance of a similar motif in the work *Il pittore* (The Painter) of the same year, Pistoletto's depiction of an artist painting a canvas on the floor—an image indubitably influenced by Hans Namuth's by then widely circulated, iconic photographs of Jackson Pollock, published in *ARTnews* in May 1951 (fig. 25). Pollock interested Pistoletto. The National Gallery of Modern Art in Rome presented a solo exhibition of his work in 1958, following the artist's untimely death, events that contextualize Pistoletto's depiction as a kind of homage.[100] Pistoletto's *Painter* features two nested rectangles, simply sketched in black paint, spanning the rear wall of the depicted interior setting, where they read as architectural paneling; truncated by the edge of the actual canvas, the rectangles mirror the form of the quadrilateral canvas depicted in the lower register and the perpendicular lines that the represented artist—a mirroring of Pistoletto, actually painting the picture—has made on its surface.

In Pistoletto's early paintings, the use of the meta-figure corresponds to the artist's imminent expansion of painting; with these framings, he blocked off abstract fields, sometimes interrupted by a figure. We see them in the expressionist *Figura umana* (Human Figure, 1957), as well as in the somber *Uomo dietro il tavolo* (Man behind the Table, 1960), in which a single figure sits alone in darkness, dwarfed by the large empty table before him and the great void of vaulted space above (fig. 26), and in a poetic sketch of a figure looking out of a window, in an undated pastel sketch likely made in the same period (fig. 27). Given that Pistoletto was still exploring the image of the human figure in the space of figuration, the parergon as meta-figure operates as a question. It asks for more from figurative painting. It speaks to its limits, to the need for intervention.

In that work, the black frame is sketched and resketched in the upper register of the image. A strong horizontal line denotes the ledge of a balcony, behind which the figure is seated. Diagonal hatching in greens and warm taupe signify that our view of the ledge is from an angle; we are meant to see that it juts out into space. The sketched quality of the black line, however, makes it oscillate between a depiction of a frame

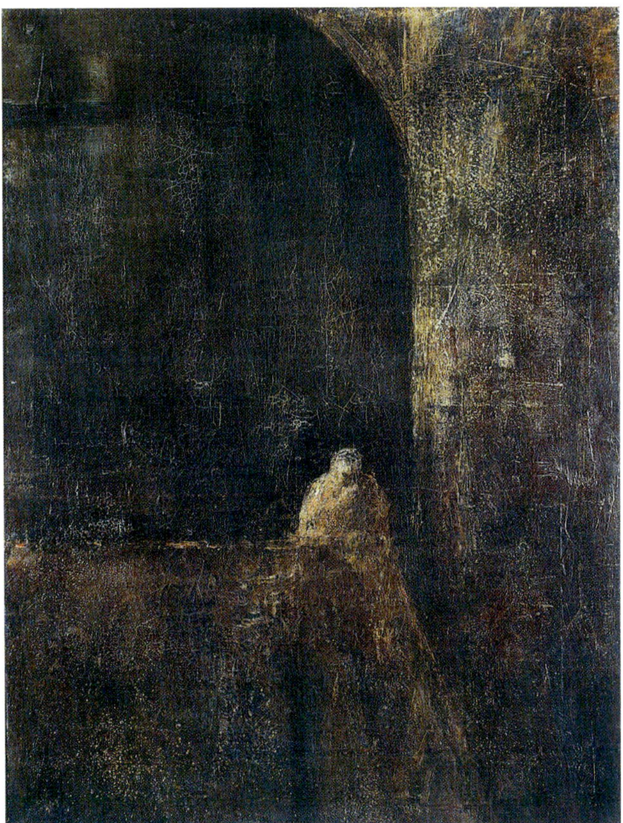

FIG. 26. Michelangelo Pistoletto, *Uomo dietro il tavolo* (Man behind the Table), 1960. Oil on canvas, 57½ × 44½ in. (146 × 113 cm). Archivio Pistoletto, Biella.

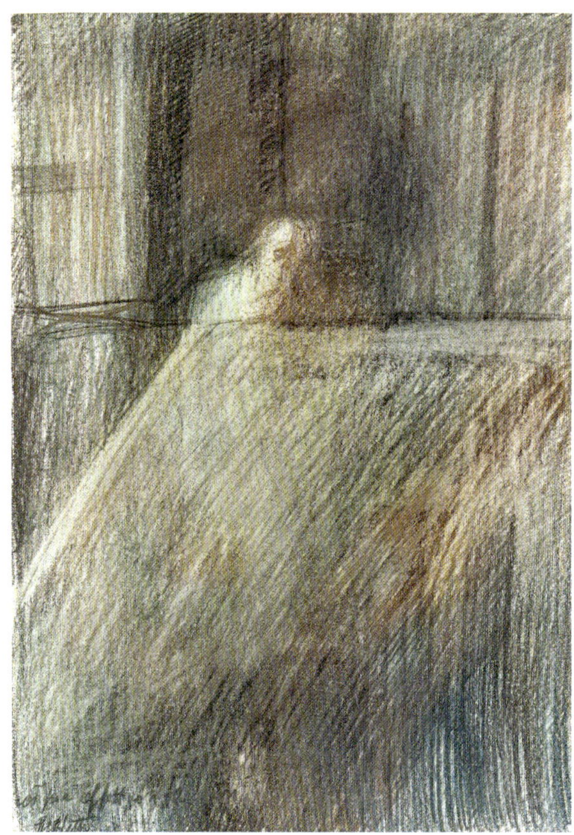

FIG. 27. Michelangelo Pistoletto, untitled sketch, ca. 1960. Pastel on paper, 13¾ × 9⅞ in. (35 × 25 cm). Private collection.

(around the illusionistic three-dimensional space of the figure) and a material mark on the flat sheet of paper. Vertical dark lines extend this frame in different directions. They denote a windowpane, behind the figure, or a box around the ledge, window, and edge of the paper to his right, framing the figure in his own image field. They denote yet another frame, which bisects the figure and extends to his left, up to the end of the sheet. This oscillation between, on one hand, representational framing of the figure (and the illusionistic space of picture making) and the material concreteness of media on a flat piece of paper, on the other, is supported by the abandonment of spatial illusion in the work's lower register. There, diagonal hatching merges with vertical hatching in teal and burnt umber, making up two-thirds of the sheet. Below the figure, the built environment drops out as we become more attuned to the artist's application of flat layers of color on the page. These little-known works evidence Pistoletto's early, sustained exploration of the figure between illusion and material form, between representation and presence.

RECONFIGURING ITALIAN MODERNISM: THE EARLY PHOTOMONTAGES

Recalling the previous discussion of *Blue Acrobat,* the suggested camera view in the painting provides an early clue to one of the defining features of Pistoletto's oeuvre at that point in his practice: a turn to new versions and uses of the figure, especially in an age of increased mediation and social alienation, that would connect it to the real world, as opposed to the illusionist world of painting alone. Soon after his debut at the Galatea, in 1961 and 1962, Pistoletto began using photography as a fundamental medium in his painting practice. It is a strategy for which he remains well known today.

This turn was catalyzed by his little-known experiments in photomontage, namely in two untitled works from fall 1962. Reproduced as illustrations for writer Carlo Montella's short story, "Compito in classe" (Classwork) in the Turin newspaper *La Gazzetta del Popolo,* these works were published just two months after the Piazza Statuto riots in Turin that signaled the sociopolitical unrest that shaped the rest of the decade (fig. 28).[101]

Domenica 16 Settembre 1962 Gazzetta del Popolo Pagina 3

COMPITO IN CLASSE

RACCONTO DI CARLO MONTELLA

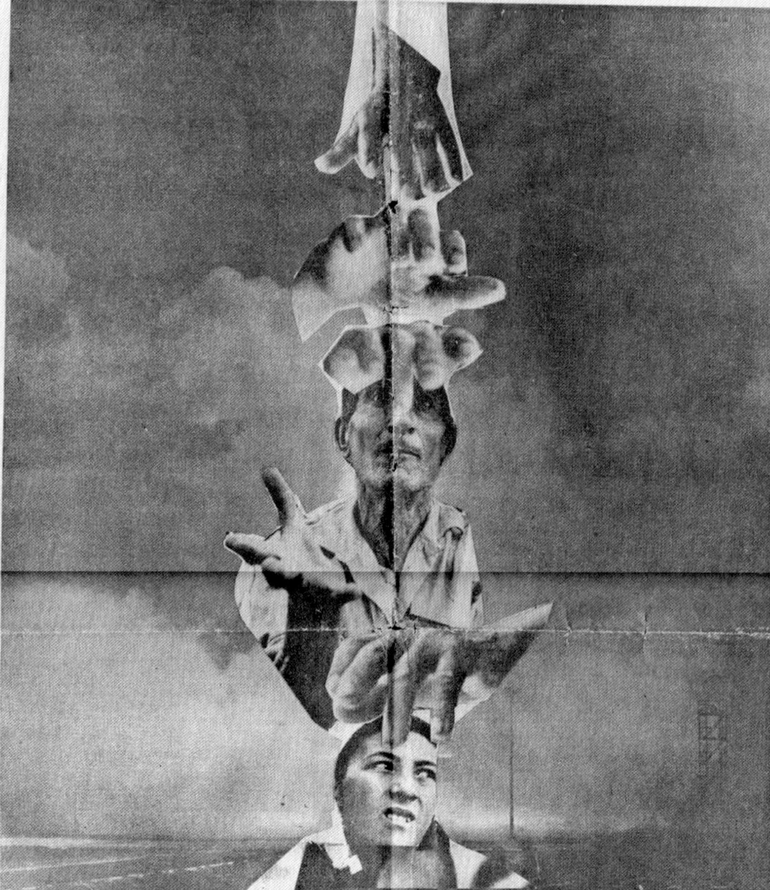

ERA sabato, e il sabato, giorno in cui lavorava solo la mattina, Agenore Cipolli non si portava dietro la sportina col mangiare rifreddo, che consumava poi accoccolato in terra, fra i mucchi di sabbia e di mattoni del cantiere, insieme con gli altri muratori, ma desinava regolarmente a casa, con la moglie e col figlio.

Quel giorno, dopo desinato, arrotolatasi una sigaretta e accesala, più per un senso di dovere che per un reale interessamento alle vicende scolastiche di suo figlio Paolo, che frequentava il secondo anno dell'istituto di avviamento professionale, gli domandò cosa avesse fatto a scuola la mattina.

— Niente —, rispose tranquillamente il ragazzo, seguitando a stuzzicare il vermiciattolo che aveva trovato in una mela, senza nemmeno alzar la testa e mostrando di non far caso della domanda rivoltagli.

— Come, niente! — alzò la voce il padre, già perdendo subito la pazienza. — In tutta la mattina non avete fatto niente? E che ci vai a fare a scuola, allora? Niente!...

Il ragazzo alzò la testa, questa volta, prudentemente, pur non perdendo d'occhio il vermiciattolo che cercava di svignarsela, galoppando sulla tovaglia. In verità anche per lui erano piuttosto misteriose le ragioni per cui lo mandavano a scuola, ma non ritenne di esprimere, in quel momento, la sua perplessità, e si limitò a rispondere, scrollando le spalle:

— Non ci sono ancora tutti i professori. Quando viene un supplente, quando un altro...

— E questi supplenti che fanno? Qualcosa faranno! —, ribattè Agenore Cipolli sempre alterato.

— Ma... Spiegano un po' di italiano, un po' di matematica, e poi se ne vanno.

— Dove se ne vanno?

— Se ne vanno.

Agenore Cipolli posò la sigaretta sull'orlo del piatto: gesto che avrebbe dovuto preludere a un manrovescio. Lo mandava in bestia quel modo di rispondere del ragazzo. Ma si dominò: per non guastarsi subito la giornata, e perchè in fondo, pensò, poteva benissimo darsi che le cose stessero come diceva suo figlio. Che ne sapeva lui? Si rimproverava solo d'aver cominciato a parlar di scuola. Andava sempre a finire così, tutte le volte; il ragazzo rispondeva infastidito, come a dire: — Che vuoi capirne, tu, di queste cose? — ed egli ne prendeva una rabbia che lo lasciava poi d'umor nero per tutto il giorno. Perchè si rendeva conto di non poter capire, in realtà, quello che suo figlio, scrollando le spalle e di malavoglia gli raccontava; e per reazione, alla fine, lo invadeva un risentimento, un rancore verso tutti quelli che andavano a scuola e che diventavano poi dottori, avvocati, professori: gente che non sapeva cosa significasse lavorare col sudore della fronte e che se la passava bene nella vita, alle spalle dei veri lavoratori. E mugugnava allora, dentro di sè: alla vanga! Tutti alla vanga! Verrà il giorno che ci sarà giustizia!

D'altra parte, mandava a scuola suo figlio proprio per riscattarlo dalle durezze, dalla precarietà, dall'indigenza della condizione operaia; e, come tutti i padri, per spirito di rivalsa, s'immaginano che i figli possano un giorno occupare il posto di quelli la cui autorità e la cui forza li soggioga, così egli, muratore, s'immaginava che il suo ragazzo potesse, un giorno, diventare perito edile. Non avvocato, o medico, o professore, no: perito edile. Solo, un dubbio tenace suscitavano in lui proprio gli studi che avrebbero dovuto portare il figlio a quel traguardo; e quando sentiva parlare di italiano, storia, geografia, educazione civica, aveva l'impressione che fosse tutta una turlupinatura. Perchè a scuola non insegnavano a suo figlio l'impasto del cemento, l'uso della livella, l'allineamento e il filo d'una parete? E come sarebbe poi diventato perito edile se non conosceva queste cose?

★

Era questo dubbio, cui si mescolava il sospetto d'esser vittima d'un imbroglio, che lo induceva a domandare ogni tanto al figlio cosa facesse a scuola. E tutte le volte ci capiva sempre meno, e alla fine cambiava discorso per non guastarsi il sangue. E anche quella volta sarebbe andata così se a un tratto il ragazzo, ricordandosi d'una cosa e con l'idea di far contento il padre, non avesse esclamato: — L'altro giorno facemmo un compito in classe. Io ho preso sei meno. Vuoi vedere?

C'era quel «meno», è vero, ma era sempre un sei ed egli pensava già di farsi dare, poi, cento lire per andare al cinema. Cercò nella sua borsa, fra i libri, e tirò fuori un foglio piegato.

— Vediamo —, disse Agenore Cipolli. E preso il foglio dalle mani del ragazzo.

Controllò prima il voto scritto col lapis rosso, e lesse il giudizio dell'insegnante: «Svolgimento vivace. La forma lascia a desiderare. Ancora errori d'ortografia!». Poi lesse la traccia del componimento: «Una buffa scenetta in famiglia». Che voleva dire? Mah!... Per semplice curiosità, ed anche per non restituire subito il compito al figlio, cominciò a leggere, con sforzo e aggrottando la fronte, lo svolgimento. Così concepito:

Scenette buffe nella mia famiglia ne succedono molte e sempre per causa di mio nonno che gli piace molto il vino. Quando mio nonno la sera torna a casa e ha bevuto parecchi «tubi», succedono sempre delle scenette buffe, perchè canta e fa discorsi strampalati. Io rido molto, ma mia mamma si arrabbia, però ora mio nonno l'abbiamo messo all'ospizio, così io ho perduto questo divertimento. Ma voglio raccontare lo stesso la scenetta più buffa di tutte, che successe l'anno scorso, una sera era tardi e mio nonno ancora non si vedeva e mia mamma disse: «Questa volta l'ha presa buona, chi sa che non è caduto nel fosso». Allora mio padre disse: «Vado a vedere» ed io dissi che volevo andare con lui. Così uscimmo insieme e andammo all'osteria dove mio nonno c'era sempre e c'erano anche degli altri uomini e tutti avevano la sbornia. Allora mio padre disse: «Venite a casa, non vi vergognate?» e prese il nonno per il braccio e lo portò fuori, ma lui ad ogni passo stava per cadere e non voleva venire a casa ma si fermava a cantare anche per la strada. Io ridevo perchè era una scena molto buffa e pensavo a quando saremmo arrivati a casa...

Agenore Cipolli alzò gli occhi dal foglio, senza proseguire nella lettura. Guardò un istante il figlio, ch'era rimasto accanto a lui — e che non ebbe il tempo di presagire quanto gli s'apparecchiava — e gli lasciò andare un manrovescio che lo mandò a ruzzolare in terra, col sangue che gli usciva dal naso.

— Figlio d'un cane! — urlò stravolto. E avrebbe massacrato il ragazzo, se questi non fosse stato lesto a mettersi in salvo, piangente e sanguinante.

— Pezzo di carogna! — seguitò a urlare bestemmiando il muratore, fuori di sè. — Delinquente! Questo vi insegnano a scuola: a insultare chi s'è ammazzato di fatica tutta la vita! I piedi dovrebbero baciare a tuo nonno questi cialtroni, che credono di poter sputare addosso a un lavoratore perchè sono andati a scuola, all'università, loro! Professori dei miei stivali! Voglio venire a prenderli per il collo, io, e dirgli: o cacastecchi, che bevete il vino annacquato perchè non sapete cos'è il sudore della fatica e avete le mani lisce come le signorine, venite che v'insegno io che vuol dire lavorare! Alla vanga, cialtroni! E tu, figlio d'un cane, dovresti inginocchiarti davanti a tuo nonno, che per quarant'anni ha curvato la schiena come un forzato per portare il pane alla famiglia! Questo dovevi scrivere nel compito, ingrato!

E come, intanto, s'era intromessa sua moglie domandando cos'era successo e cercando di placarlo, s'avventò anche a lei:

— Silenzio tu, strega! Tu sei stata a non voler più in casa mio padre! Tu hai voluto metterlo all'ospizio! Levati dai piedi o ti striglio anche te, megera!

A questo punto, non volendo porre in atto la minaccia e sentendo tuttavia, come una forza irresistibile, il bisogno di sfogarsi in qualche modo, abbrancò l'orlo del tavolo e rovesciò questo con quanto v'era sopra di piatti e bicchieri e fiaschi e caraffe, con spaventoso rovinio. Del cui effetto pago pel momento, uscì di casa sbattendo l'uscio.

★

Un proposito, nel volger di quella scenata, era maturato nella sua mente; ed egli s'avviò concitato verso l'ospizio, l'animo gonfio d'un rimorso che scaturiva violento dall'ira ancora implacata.

— Padre, perdono! — invocava fra sè, andando. — Perdono, padre! Voi sapete come io vi ho sempre rispettato e amato: tornate nella nostra casa, ch'è prima di tutto la vostra, e sarete onorato come un patriarca! La moglie e il figlio vi baceranno le mani e s'inchineranno davanti a voi: e se non lo faranno li batterò nella strada! Tornate con noi, padre! Vedete, io mi inginocchio davanti a voi per pregarvi...

Arrivato quindi all'ospizio e chiesto del genitore, lo trovò nel cortile, che prendeva il sole in compagnia d'altri cinque o sei vegliardi. E senza preamboli gli intimò:

— Babbo, mettete tutte le vostre cose nella cassetta, alla svelta, chè ho deciso di riportarvi a casa.

Il vecchio s'allarmò: — Che è successo? E' successo qualcosa? Perchè devo tornare a casa?

— Ora non cominciamo con le domande — disse Agenore Cipolli. — V'ho detto di sbrigarvi, chè ho già il fottuto: non me lo fate venire di più!

— Ma che ti piglia? Che sei venuto a fare, che vuoi? — il vecchio s'impermalì. — Perchè devo tornare? Io non torno! Non voglio rivedere quella vipera di tua moglie! Sto bene qui...

— Ah! — fece Agenore Cipolli, movendogli le mani sulla faccia. — State state bene? Lo sapete che vi pago la retta e che voi non vi tengono per elemosina come gli altri?

— Non vuoi pagarmi più la retta! — sbraitò il vecchio. — Sputalo! Non vuoi più pagarmela? Per questo mi vuoi riportare a casa. Ma io non ci vengo, io resto qui, hai inteso?

— O vecchio testardo! — gridò il muratore, sentendosi vittima. — Ecco la vostra gratitudine! Non avete capito mai niente e seguiterete sempre a non capir niente. Siete buono solo a trincare!

E lì stettero per un pezzo a inveire l'uno contro l'altro; finchè Agenore Cipolli se ne tornò via inferocito, essendo fallita la sua missione.

★

Passò la sera con gli amici, senza riuscire a smaltire la rabbia che aveva dentro.

Quando rincasò, per la cena, sua moglie aveva già fatto sparire a letto il ragazzo. Ma non v'era pericolo che si ripetessero scenate. Il muratore non ce l'aveva più col figlio. Solo, al fondo dell'ira, gli rimaneva un rancore, uno sdegno verso tutti coloro che andavano a scuola, che, avendo un titolo di studio, contavano più d'un semplice lavoratore come lui nella società. E quel rancore, quello sdegno, nascevano dal bruciore d'una offesa arrecata a lui, lavoratore, da quella gente ch'egli identificava col mondo dei padroni, dei ricchi, degli sfruttatori. E l'ingenua colpa del figlio, nel raccontare con poco rispetto la storia del nonno ubriaco, si trasformava, nel suo crudo risentimento, in un insulto che tutta la società, di cui egli per eredità di generazioni temeva i soprusi e aborriva le ingiustizie, avesse recato a lui.

Per tutta la notte continuò a rimuginare queste cose, pieno d'umiliazione e d'offesa. Sentendo il respiro del figlio, che dormiva nel letto accanto, si pentì quasi d'averlo picchiato.

Ma quando la mattina s'alzarono insieme per andare, lui al cantiere e il ragazzo a scuola — e tutto quel ch'era successo il giorno avanti pareva ormai passato e dimenticato — a vedere il figlio preparar la borsa coi libri, un furore improvviso, incontenibile, si ridestò in lui. Avventatosi sul ragazzo, gli strappò la borsa con tutte le sue cose di scuola e le sbattè in terra, prendendola poi a calci, facendone schizzar fuori e volare per la stanza libri e quaderni, in miserando scempio.

— Alla vanga! — urlava inferocito. — Tutti alla vanga! Basta con le ingiustizie! E tu, che sei figlio mio, non passerai dall'altra parte! Sarai un lavoratore, come tuo padre e tuo nonno, anche tu! Un lavoratore con le mani dure e la coscienza pulita! Hai le spalle buone per cominciare a portare la paiolina del muratore. E subito devi cominciare! Prendi la bicicletta e vieni in cantiere con me!

E così fu deciso il destino del giovanetto Paolo Cipolli. Che da quella mattina non andò più a scuola e, dopo una settimana, si arrampicava già, col cappellone di carta in testa, su per le impalcature della costruzione dove lavorava suo padre. Soddisfatto del mutamento improvviso della sua vita, orgoglioso del mestiere che avrebbe col tempo imparato, e anche lui convinto, nella sua semplicità ignara, che quel mestiere fosse una cosa più seria e onorata di tutte le insulsaggini ch'era costretto a imparare a scuola.

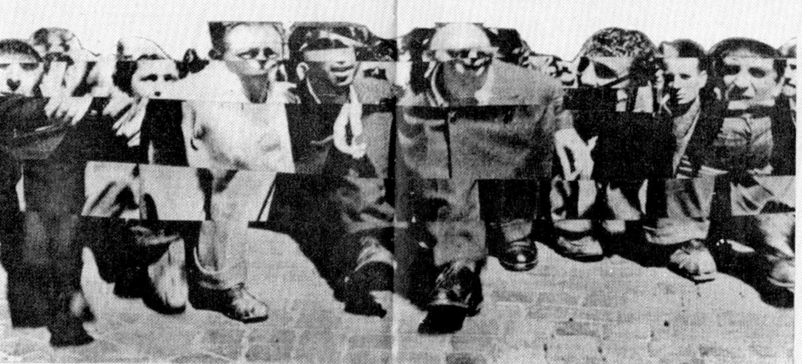

(Composizione di PISTOLETTO)

FIG. 28. Michelangelo Pistoletto, untitled photomontages, published as illustrations for Carlo Montella's short story, "Compito in classe" (Classwork), *La Gazzetta del Popolo,* September 16, 1962. Archivio Pistoletto, Biella.

In the smaller of the two photomontages (as reproduced on the page), we see a bloc of figures, some in business dress, others in workers' clothes, as suggested by baggy pants and scuffed shoes. They stride toward the viewer across the cobblestone pavement in the foreground and lower register of the image. As images of human figures, they are disjointed representationally, in perspective and bodily coherence. First, with regard to perspective, some of the collaged sections, namely the middle register, capture the subject in closer proximity to the camera (and to us) than others; the result is that some figures, when they are discernible as individual subjects, such as the man at center (with outsized hands and a smaller head), have body parts whose scale is disproportionate to other parts of their bodies. Fragmented heads and shoulders rest on mismatched torsos, held up in turn by foreign ankles and orphaned feet that seem to belong to other people than the figures of their compositional alignment.

Despite the figures' fragmentation on the level of representation and process, they nevertheless seem unified due to mechanical and compositional strategies that join the figures together and to the space of the street.[102] First, as a collaged image, the figures' material disjuncture has been mechanically eliminated by dint of the reproduction of Pistoletto's photomontage on the newspaper page. Next, in a strategy we find in the artist's paintings of the late 1950s and in the mirror paintings thereafter, the material construction of the crowd privileges the figures; the urban background that we imagine surrounds them has been excised from the top of the image. The photomontage is composed of a series of horizontal strips, six in total; in the lower registers of the image, the strips span the entire horizontal image-field. At the top of the image-field, however, the strip is irregularly cut; the photographic material has been cut to follow the upper contours of the figures closest to the viewer. Finally, the majority of the figures do not appear to us as individual whole bodies; instead, we get a glimpse of a face, or pairs of busy feet, hands, and tops of heads, belonging to individuals lost in the crowd.

An important precursor for these experiments may have come from the Harlequin Art Group, more specifically from the work of Renato Rinaldi, whom Pistoletto had befriended when the two were students at the Scuola Testa, and from the broader function of collage in *Presenze*. Rinaldi published two untitled photomontages in the journal. They feature details of the human body in relation to the built environment (and one in relation to religious architecture), a concern he shared with Pistoletto. The first, published in 1957, illustrates Rinaldi's short story about class and religion, focused on the reconstruction of a church.[103] A photograph of a seated clerical figure is framed by a series of nested arches that compose a cupola. The second arch is a crowd of people—the bricklayers in Rinaldi's story. The collage is ultimately composed of different kinds of images of figures: photographs of actual people, and photographs of depictions of people, both two- and three-dimensional, as in the carved figurative decoration flanking the central figure. These categories of figurative imagery are then followed by what appears to be an arch composed of a photo of organs of a human body—intestinal in design, the innards of the human body are now the interior of the church, following Rinaldi's own anthropomorphic treatment of the building in the story.

The second photomontage (1957–58) explores similar relationships (fig. 29). Accompanying Rinaldi's essay on the new artistic expression made possible by cinema in an age of televisual media, it reads as human figure and architectural column. It features photographs of a decorative architectural capital, a man's face, and a vertically oriented, rectangular segment of what appears to be a close-up view of skin. Once again, the body is merged with the built environment. The face is framed by two empty spaces; all together, between negative space and positive image, they compose an eye. In the essay, Rinaldi speaks to a number of issues that Pistoletto, as we've seen, was also exploring: the need for the arts to be not closed off but open to more universal concerns and the need for a new art to identify the problems of the time, countering the risk that discourse is "losing itself" in the "obscure feelings" of postwar man, isolated in a rapidly changing, increasingly technological postwar world, still haunted by the "miseries of the war."[104] The use of photography is important for Pistoletto's own subsequent turn to photomontage, particularly in his use of the medium to contemplate the figure as a form and social being.

Unlike Rinaldi's photomontages, however, Pistoletto's works build on modernist and avant-garde precedents connected by an investigation of the figure and figuration. Returning to his photomontage of a crowd of people on the street, the work recalls the history of Dada, but also that of cubism, in the work of

Georges Braque and Pablo Picasso. Pistoletto's photomontage shares their fragmentation of form and exploration of structures of signification, as well as their use of legible body parts as signs that cue the viewer to the figural context of the fragmented planes and geometric shapes of the abstracted image. As an image of a crowd, whose figures occupy most of the image-field and horizontally oriented composition, the work also draws on divergent histories of socialist pictures in modern Italian painting: the "humanitarian" realism of the post-Macchiaioli generation of Italian divisionism. It recalls the iconic *Il quarto stato* (The Fourth Estate, 1901), from a series of paintings on Italy's labor movement by Piedmontese artist Giuseppe Pellizza da Volpedo,

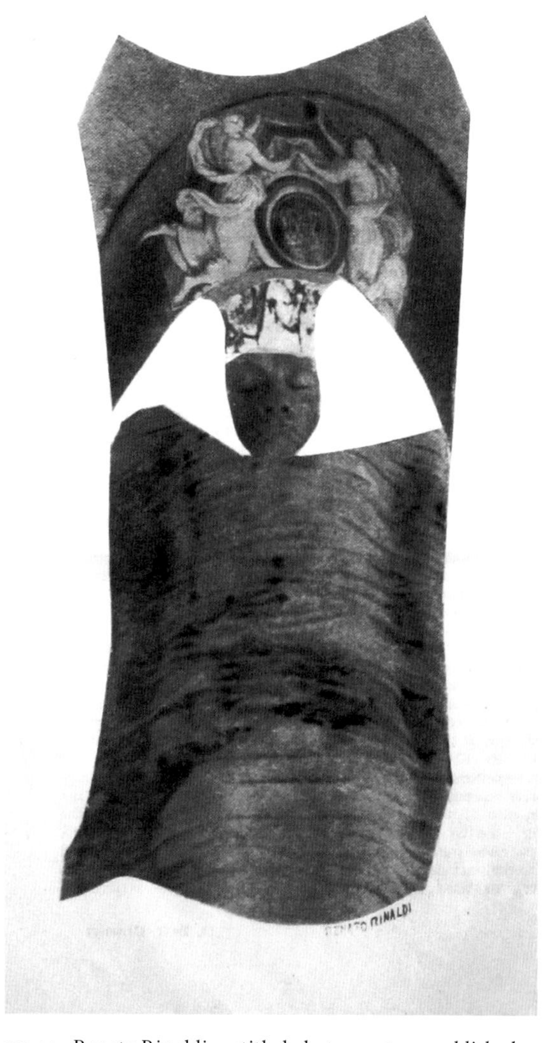

FIG. 29. Renato Rinaldi, untitled photomontage, published alongside his essay "Le nostre speranze al cinema" (Our Hopes at the Cinema), *Presenze* 1, nos. 3–4 (December 1957–January 1958). Biblioteca Musicale Andrea della Corte, Turin.

as well as the fragmented centered figures of futurism (fig. 30). The latter is perhaps best captured by Umberto Boccioni's pictures of around 1912, as in *Materia* (Matter), where the figure's outsized hands (the artist's mother) loom large in the fractured composition of the figure (fig. 31).[105] Both strains of Italian modernism depicted the crowd and the dynamic figure as a symbol of mass collectivity with revolutionary potential.[106] With neither the bristling dynamism of its futurist precedents nor the large-scale visual assertions of class solidarity found in the horizontal mass of workers in Pellizza da Volpedo's *Fourth Estate*, however, Pistoletto's photomontage offers an early and irresolute example of the artist's exploration of figuration as a central, if embattled, motif in Italian modernism.[107] Pistoletto's fragmentation of the figures suggests neither incoherence nor illogic. Instead, it offers an image of bodily movement en masse: a commingling of bodies and subjects in collective action. In her writings on street demonstrations, Judith Butler has referred to such figures as "bodies in alliance": socially minded, corporeal phenomena, who visually register for others as a bodily appearance in public space. In such formations, the human is not ratified as an individual but rather is "a relational and social being," as is Pistoletto's "figure of man."[108] Pistoletto's image positions bodies in a fraught or potential alliance. The arrangement of their bodies in misaligned registers (horizontal and of degrees of spatial depth) makes us contemplate the strangeness of their figural logic (as images and as bodies). Haunted by photographs of Mussolini and his Blackshirts during the March on Rome, which often captured the authoritarian figures in similarly frontal, shoulder-to-shoulder configurations, as well as the strange oscillations between figures and depth of field offered by the socially concerned "humanist photography" of Mario Giacomelli in his late 1950s images of the Italian town of Scanno, Pistoletto's photomontage is a palimpsest of the figure in Italian modernism and modernity.[109] The image presses up against histories of Italian modernism and their fracturing after World War II, as the socialist potential with which it developed, ultimately, in some strains, had contorted into fascism. The photomontage presents us with an unsettling question: are humanitarian realist pictures still possible—after the war, after fascism?

We also find this aesthetic and subject model in the larger of the two photomontages that accompany Montella's story. There again we find disproportional,

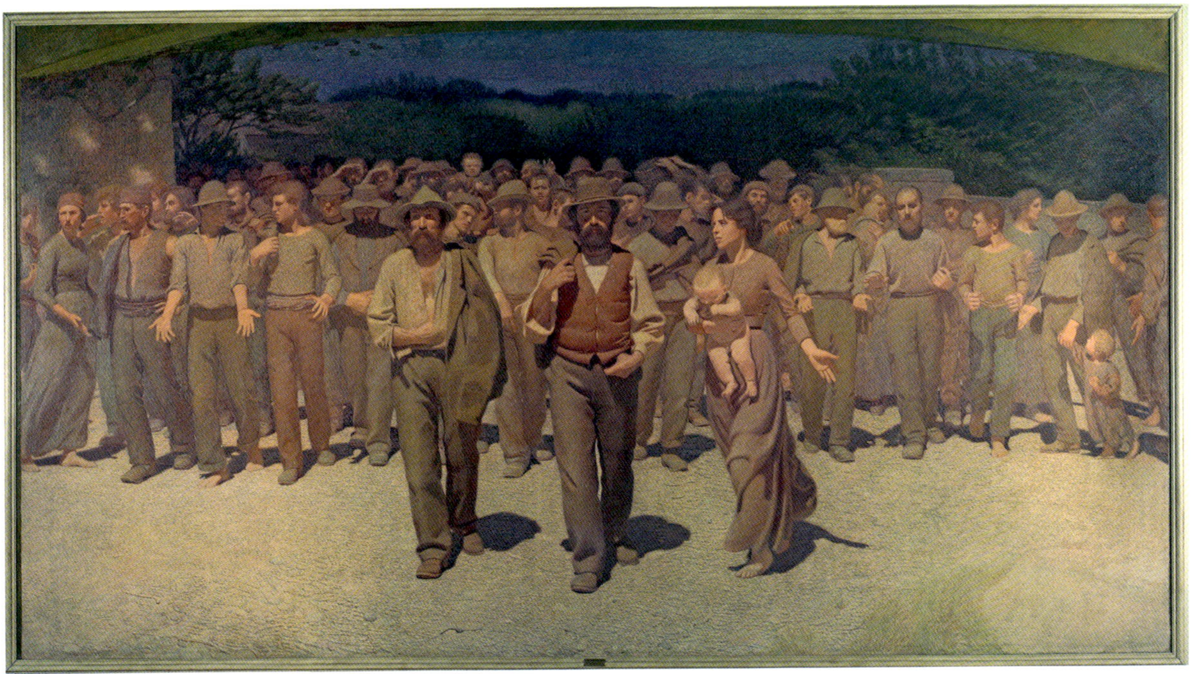

FIG. 30. Giuseppe Pellizza da Volpedo, *Il quarto stato* (The Fourth Estate), 1898–1901. Oil on canvas, 115⅜ × 214½ in. (293 × 545 cm). Inv. GAM 1649, Galleria d'Arte Moderna, Milan.

fragmented figures whose organization dominates the composition but to a different effect. Centered on the newspaper page, we see a stack of body parts—it is a composition the artist would revisit across the 1980s, in his monumental sculptures of partial bodies. In this early version, the figure stack traverses the middle of the image field from top to bottom, in the immediate foreground of the image. This stack reads like a figurative monument, literally: it is composed of parts of bodies, precariously arranged one on top of the other. The vertical form is composed of five unpaired hands, held in various gestures, and the busts of two figures—a wizened old man, who appears near the middle of the column, and a younger fellow at its base, whose sloping shoulders give the stack an approximately pyramidal structure. Several disproportionally large hands reach out toward us viewers, some menacingly, as gestures of interaction. Others reach down as if to grasp something; two are positioned immediately over the much smaller heads of the two figures, as if they are about to pick them up or push them down. The gesture is echoed by all three hands that compose the top of the form. The effect is one of inevitable oppression and fixity; the young boy at bottom seems destined to the fate of the old man, who looks out at us from his position in the middle of the column, hand extended as if asking for help. This amalgamation

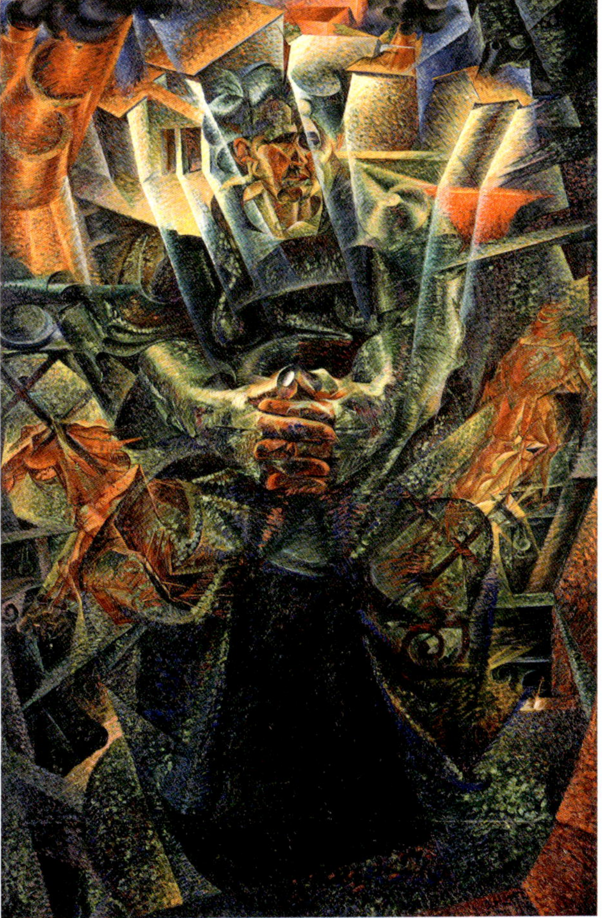

FIG. 31. Umberto Boccioni, *Materia* (Matter), 1912. Oil on canvas, 88⅝ × 59 in. (225 × 150 cm). Private collection.

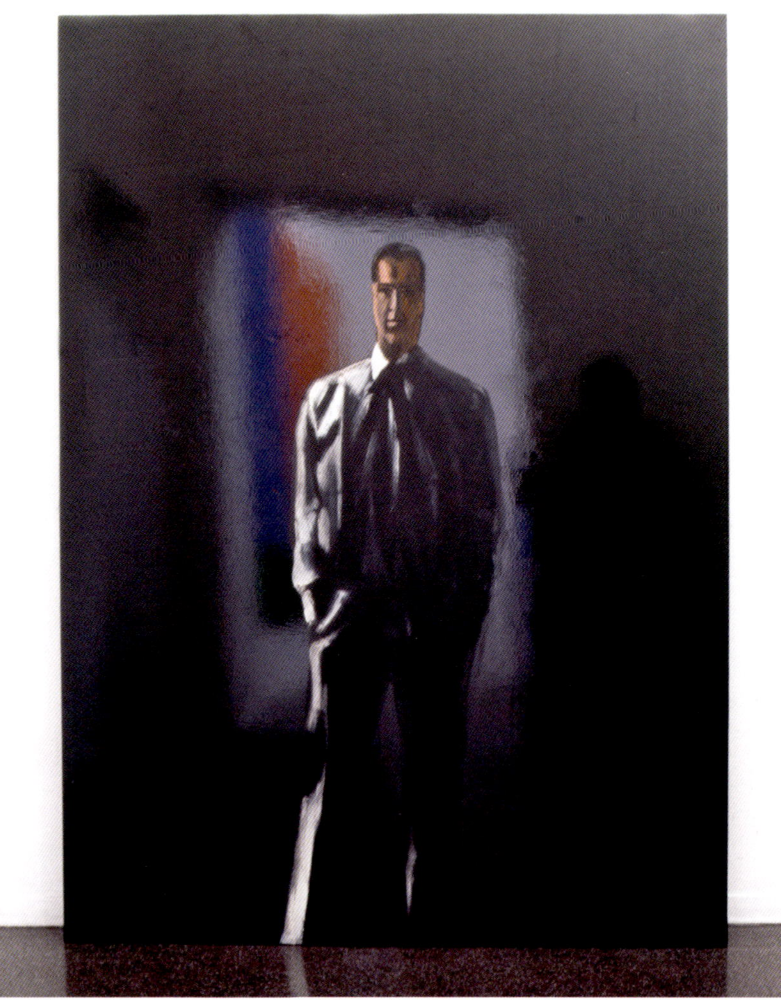

FIG. 32. Michelangelo Pistoletto, *Il presente—Autoritratto in camicia* (The Present—Self-Portrait in Button-Down Shirt), 1961. Acrylic and plastic varnish on canvas, 78¾ × 59 in. (200 × 150 cm). Cittadellarte–Fondazione Pistoletto, Biella.

of structurally precarious hands and figures is set against a photographic background of an empty roadway—a *tangenziale,* perhaps—that occupies the very bottom register and a cloudy sky that makes up most of the image-field, positing a mysterious ambient for the scene. A light pole and a watchtower, to which the young man at the base of the pillar seems to look, disconcertingly, are the only other forms on the horizon line. Given the timing and subject of the work, which accompanies a story about class issues and the intergenerational hardships faced by a low-skilled laborer, the works speak to the tumultuous sociopolitical climate and cultural politics of their production. The photomontages insist upon the figure after Italian modernism, as image and social being; in so doing, the ontology of the photograph, long theorized as a site of memory and afterlife, is repositioned as a site of urgent reconfiguration for the present. Humanist culture must, in an age of spectacle, be forged in the space of mediation, specifically in the space of mediation that is nevertheless connected to the real.

PAINTING AS UNIVERSE

Pistoletto's experiments in figuration in the late 1950s drew on his formative experiences. *Presenze*'s framework for revising figuration in the age of abstraction spanned universal humanism and spiritual philosophies, through which people were seeking to understand the changing world. The journal's dedication to attending to the present, and to being present, now seems connected to some of Pistoletto's most important early experiments.

Consider his creation in 1961 of the painting *Il presente* (The Present), first exhibited at Turin's Società Promotrice delle Belle Arti (Fine Arts Society) in March 1962. Pistoletto would later describe this work as the first mirror painting.[110] Ultimately made in many versions, the first was made with the figure facing the viewer (*Il presente—Autoritratto in camicia,* or "The Present—Self-Portrait in Button-Down Shirt"); it is regarded by the artist as the immediate catalyst for the mirror paintings that followed (fig. 32). Made in succession with his paintings of single figures on metallic backgrounds, this

FIG. 33. Michelangelo Pistoletto, *Il presente—Uomo di schiena* (The Present—Man from Behind), 1961. Acrylic and plastic varnish on canvas, 78¾ × 59 in. (200 × 150 cm). Cittadellarte-Fondazione Pistoletto, Biella.

painting was distinguished by a reflective black background, this time achieved with black plastic varnish. The effect was that the ground registered the artist's reflection on the surface of the painting, alongside the depicted solitary figure at the center of the image. As the artist later recalled: "At that moment, I realized that the universe had plummeted into the work of art—the entire universe, not just the space surrounding me. . . . The outside world, society, the viewer had become part of the picture. This was the passage to an objectivity that accommodated everyone's subjectivity."[111] One version of the painting, *Il presente—Uomo di schiena* (The Present—Man from Behind) from 1961, depicts a life-size figure in a blue business suit, centered on the same black reflective monochromatic field but this time turned away from the viewer (fig. 33). With a compositional logic of metaphysical painting, the work shifts the strange and enigmatic space of that strain of Italian modernism into the real, specifically by reconceptualizing the depicted figure as having a shared ground with the real one: the viewer. Both the depicted figure and real figure of the viewer register on the dark painterly ground, the first via representation, the second via reflection on the material surface of the representational field. Despite this division, the effect is that both figures are materially present. The work therefore visualizes this plummeting of the universe into the work of art: the "inside" and "outside" of the painting are one and the same. In the history of art, painting, and more specifically European modernist abstract painting, had been espoused as a universal language; it could be understood anywhere.[112] Rather than uphold abstraction as a universal language, here Pistoletto reconceptualized figurative painting *as universe:* the world we live in and the world in painting are now merged. Through the meeting of a depicted figure and the reflection of the real figure of the viewer, the figural space of painting could now figure more than what had been given to it through representation. By figuring more, it would now also be a place for everyone, rather than for one person unto themselves.

2 Fragments of Figuration

Mirror Paintings, Plexiglass Structures

Pistoletto's second solo exhibition was held in May 1963. Like his first, it was also held at the Galleria Galatea in Turin. It was where he publicly debuted his mirror paintings: his highly polished, stainless-steel panels, collaged with life-size quasi-photographic cutouts of human figures. Galvanized by the artist's prior experiments with reflective media and photomontage, the mirror paintings opened painting to the external world by using stainless steel instead of canvas as a material support and image ground.[1] No photographs exist of the exhibition. The accompanying catalog included a well-known series of four photographs, all of the same artwork: *Persona seduta* (Seated Person, 1962), which featured an image of a man, seated in profile. Each photograph shows the same figure (Renato Rinaldi was the model) on the surface of the artwork but with a different background in the picture, composed not of paint, as in conventional painting, but of dynamic reflections of the space of the work's display. While photographs in the exhibition catalog demonstrated to readers that Pistoletto's mirror paintings change with their surrounds, they didn't relay the experience of encountering many mirror paintings at once, in real time and space.[2] Nineteen of the twenty works on display included representations of figures; the mirror painting figures now approximated the size of the viewer, who, when reflected in the work, now also figured in the composition.

In the absence of exhibition photographs, curatorial and critical responses to the show shed light on the dizzying and apparently transgressive scene at the Galatea. *La Stampa* critic Marziano Bernardi called the works a "drastic" attempt in the much-discussed "recuperation of the human figure" in art of the period, achieved "with the help of photography." Invoking the absurdist, metatheatrical work of Italian playwright Luigi Pirandello, Bernardi called the exhibition "a kind of Pirandellian exchange between fiction and reality, a hallucinatory, almost surrealist game of images."[3] Luigi Carluccio, who returned to curate this show as he had Pistoletto's first, suggested that the artist had gone too far with the "disconcerting" new works. Carluccio questioned whether calling them "paintings" was even still the right term. He also found other problems: "In fact, the recuperation of the human figure appears to have been actualized beyond every limit of prudence and caution, with a flaw of excess, you could say."[4]

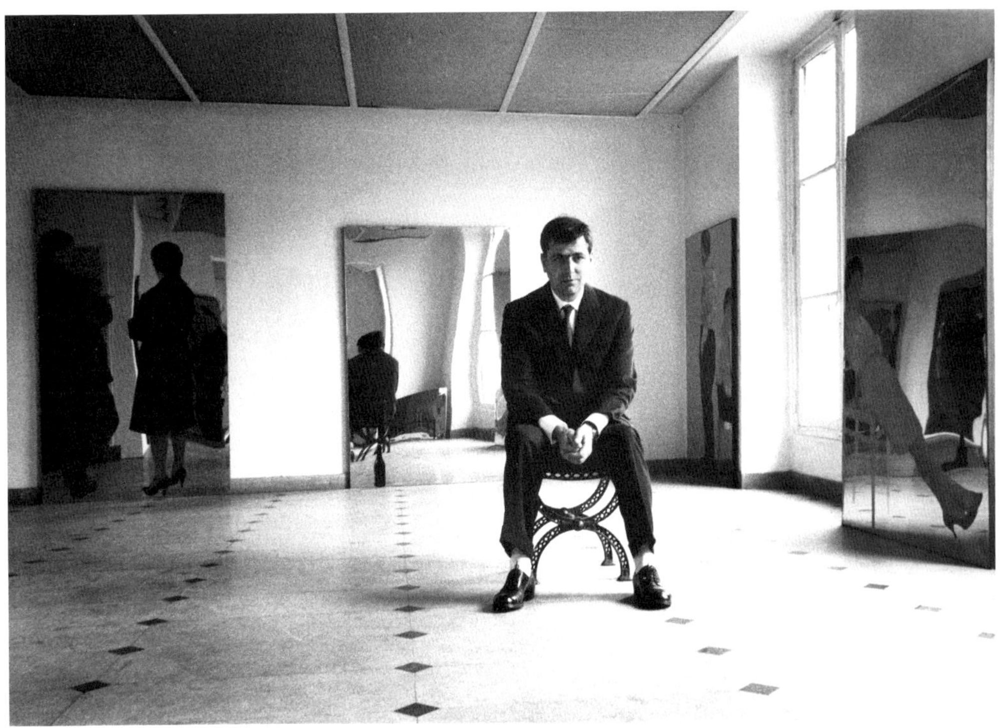

FIG. 34. Harry Shunk and János Kender, photograph of Michelangelo Pistoletto at his eponymous exhibition, Galerie Ileana Sonnabend, Paris, March–May 1964. Getty Research Institute, Los Angeles (2014.R.20). Collection: Harry Shunk and Shunk-Kender photographs, 1957–1987.

With subjects traced from photographic enlargements on tissue paper, which the artist hand-shaded and colored, the early mirror paintings had a quasi-photographic visual quality that bridged mechanical and painterly directions of postwar art, as well as figuration and abstraction. At the time, a broader international field of artists, including Gerhard Richter, Andy Warhol, and Martial Raysse, were experimenting with figuration while drawing on photography and photographic aesthetics. Pistoletto's figures within this context were distinguished by their life-size scale and handmade yet photographic qualities. Henry Martin referred to the latter quality in the black-and-white mirror paintings as a kind of "haziness of pictures published in the newspapers."[5] These characteristics, of scale and visual quality, were linked for the artist. Pistoletto said that they were "painted in a way to suggest life-size photographic reproduction . . . [like a] 'cinemascope.'"[6] Unlike the work of others working in painterly and photographic experimentation, Pistoletto's early mirror paintings by contrast positioned the image of the human body as a visibly symbolic representation and "real" substantive body to be encountered, if hewing closer to the former. The mirror paintings gained reality effects from their procedural and aesthetic connections to photography while existing legibly as constructions; their handmade quality prevented them from seamlessly integrating into the visual field of the gallery. Adding to their dual position as real and imagistic figures was the fact that the reflected surfaces of the panels did not yet function as precise mirrors; their distorted reflections meant that the mirror painting figures resided in space that was clearly distinctive from the real world. The fields they occupied weren't seamlessly connected to the undistorted world around them.

Not long after the mirror paintings' debut, the prestigious Paris-based art dealer Ileana Sonnabend visited Pistoletto's exhibition at his invitation. To the relief of the Galatea, Sonnabend bought out the entire show and, with it, the artist's contract. Less than a year later, in March 1964, Pistoletto had his solo debut in Paris (fig. 34).[7] Photographs of the Sonnabend exhibition, which included many works that had been shown at the Galatea, give better insights into what the debut of the mirror paintings at the Galatea may have been like. Groups of figures populated many of the mirror paintings; some even included full-length self-portraits of the artist. Other works presented single figures. The mirror paintings (and thus the galleries) were predominantly occupied by groups of figures standing in profile or with their backs turned to the viewers. In this regard, the works recalled the painted figures of early Trecento painting, especially the work of the late medieval Florentine painter Giotto. Often noted for their turned backs and convincing modeling, Giotto's figures are often credited with initiating the turn to naturalistic depictions of human figures associated with the Renaissance and values of early modern humanism. Like Giotto's sculptural bodies, Pistoletto's figures remind us of the history of painting in which artists sought to give two-dimensional depicted figures a semblance of having real bodies—of occupying real space.

Perhaps with this historical reference in mind, scholarly discussions surrounding the mirror paintings have focused largely on their engagement with the traditional conventions of painting, seeing therein an ending of painting as it had been. Pistoletto's use of industrial materials, mechanical reproduction, and reflectivity to open painting to its environment were all strategies that defied modernist conventions of the medium. This postmodernist reading of the mirror paintings as the end of painting and medium specificity has led to their categorization as conceptual painting or, as one critic argued in the mid-1980s (at the height of postmodernist theory), a "formal deconstruction of pictorial representation itself."[8] Although Pistoletto displaced painting's traditional media and techniques, he continued to explore what might be called its "syntactical structure": the structure by which painting exists, creates signs, and articulates.[9] Finding ready comparisons in this sense in conceptual art, they are "critical non-painting paintings," to borrow Douglas Crimp's phrase. Following

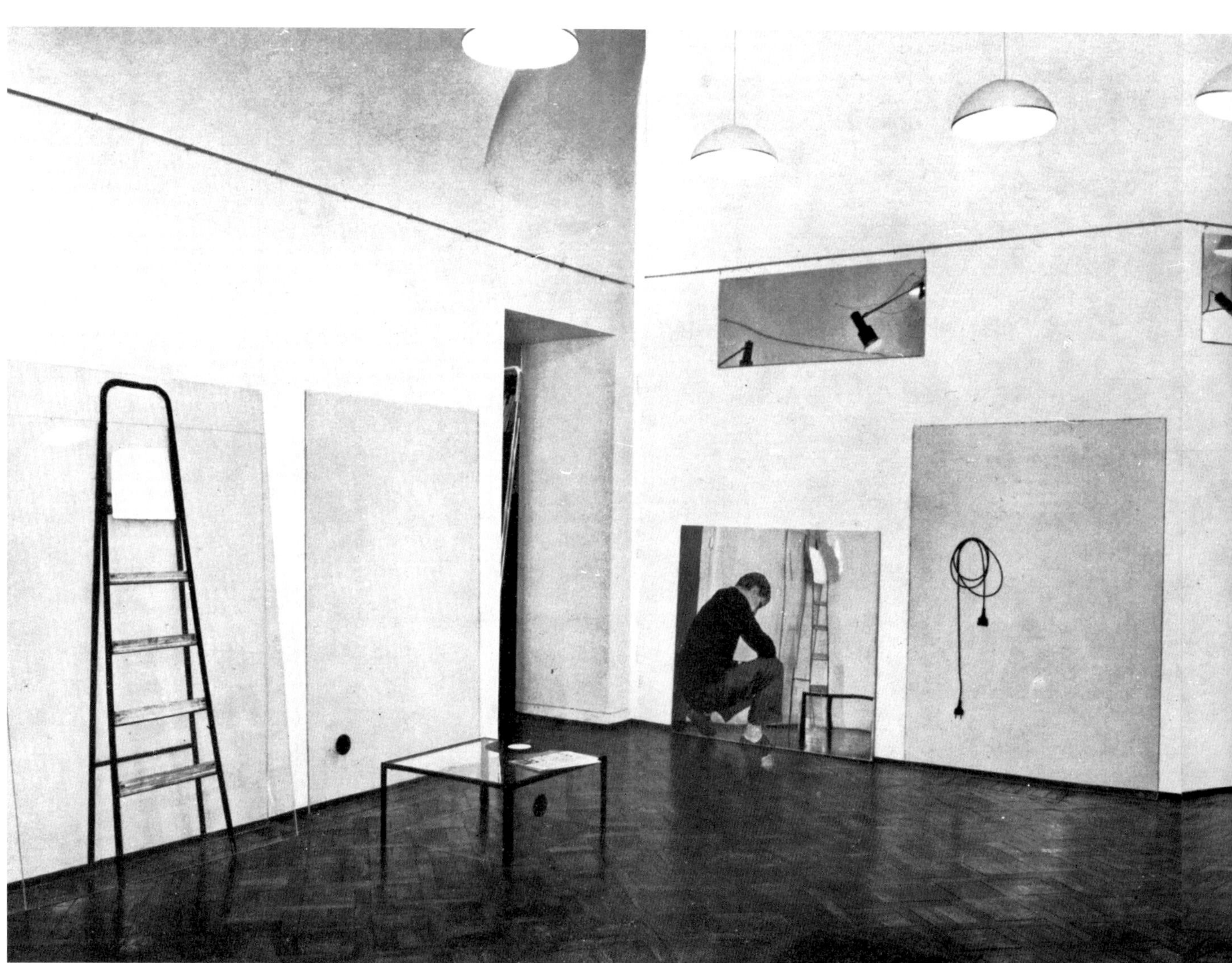

FIG. 35. Installation view, *Michelangelo Pistoletto: I plexiglass* (The Plexiglasses), Galleria Gian Enzo Sperone, Turin, opened October 2, 1964. Photo by Paolo Bressano. Archivio Pistoletto, Biella.

Kaja Silverman, they constitute a kind of painting by other means.[10]

In the primary context, in her review of the Sonnabend exhibition for *Art International* in 1964, critic Annette Michelson addressed the liminality of Pistoletto's mirror subjects. Michelson wrote: "The figure's presence on the surface marks the moment of passage between two worlds, and it stands, poised like a conceptual limit between one's self and one's mobile, slightly distorted reflection, between an experience and an image, between *reality felt and reality seen.*"[11] This new figure type, as a sensed being and seen image, constituted a change to discourse, of art and reality; more specifically, it constituted a transgression or something *in excess,* recalling Carluccio's words. It had the potential to be the artist's "way out" of the politicized impasse between figuration and abstraction. But that change wouldn't be fully realized in these mirror paintings. Instead, it would be figured by a different, lesser-known series of works.

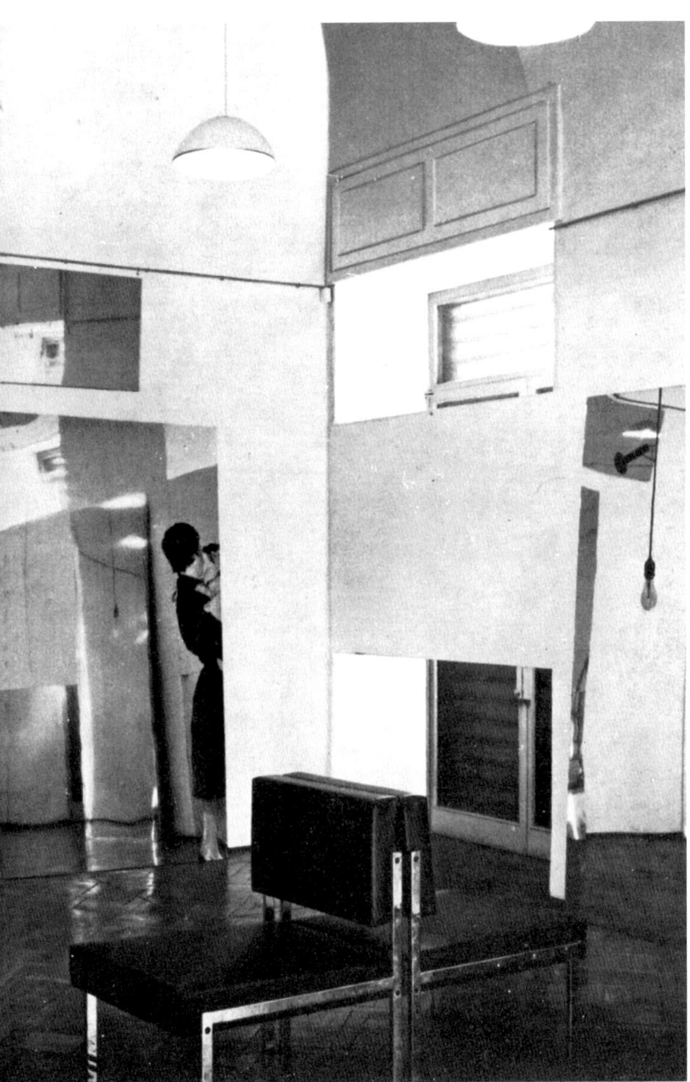

Six months after the Sonnabend exhibition, in October 1964, Pistoletto had a solo exhibition at Gian Enzo Sperone's new eponymous gallery of contemporary art in Turin. Although he showed a few mirror paintings, the show was largely dedicated to a new series of works, collectively entitled *I plexiglass,* or the Plexiglasses (using the word for the generic material), after which the exhibition was also named (fig. 35).[12] Made of clear acrylic plastic, the seven works (four panels, three structures) were well suited to the sleek exhibition space, which had opened only a few months earlier in the historic Piazza Carlo Alberto.[13] Propped up against the white gallery walls or staged freestanding on the floor, underneath high vaulted ceilings (still in place today), the small group of works realized a strange scene made even more peculiar by their composition. On the surfaces of these works—except one, *Il muro* (The Wall, 1964), a nearly six-foot-tall panel, left bare—Pistoletto had collaged and painted a range of imagistic material objects. These included everyday objects (a folded newspaper and a stack of vinyl records), furniture items (a small coffee table), implements (black electrical cords, a sturdy stepladder), and signs (a small red circle or "signal," as he called it). Using what was on hand at home or in the studio as subject matter, Pistoletto had created what seemed to be a mundane setting of everyday objects and necessities.[14] The scene prompts us to ask, as Roland Barthes once asked of seemingly unremarkable descriptive details in literature, what is, ultimately, the significance of these objects' insignificance?[15]

◆◆◆

Closer examination of this grouping of objects reveals that they staged a strange tableau. The items of the Plexiglasses' collective presentation (and representation) that at first seem to be tangible, readymade objects are revealed to be illusionistic, imagistic ones. What looks like a table with a clear glass top and iron legs—*Tavolino con disco e giornale* (Small Table with Record and Newspaper, 1964)—turns out to be a square plexiglass prism with painted "legs" (fig. 36). The newspaper and vinyl record on its surface are life-size photographic cut-outs of the objects, affixed to plexiglass that the artist also cut to the size of the photographs. The viewer's encounter with the structures and objects reveals the illusionistic methods of their production; we realize that what at first appeared to be a real environment is largely fabricated, composed of life-size, artificial stand-ins, two-dimensional photographic reproductions, and imagistic reconstructions that, unlike their referents, have little to no potential utility.

On the viewer's inevitable realization that most of the setting's objects are mediated, the Plexiglasses stage an effective withdrawal of what the series originally seems to offer. The series presents the viewer with something ultimately out of reach, lost, or not what it seems to be. The experience is one of disillusionment—if not displacement—of the reality the Plexiglasses initially appear to constitute. In this regard, the Plexiglasses materialize an experience of visual consumption in a mediated world, as a series of windows or items on display. While this might seem to be a somewhat neutral action, geared perhaps toward creating a dynamic spatiovisual experience of the series that changes in real time, closer examination of the Plexiglasses, specifically in relation to the context of their production, endows this action and the series with further meaning.

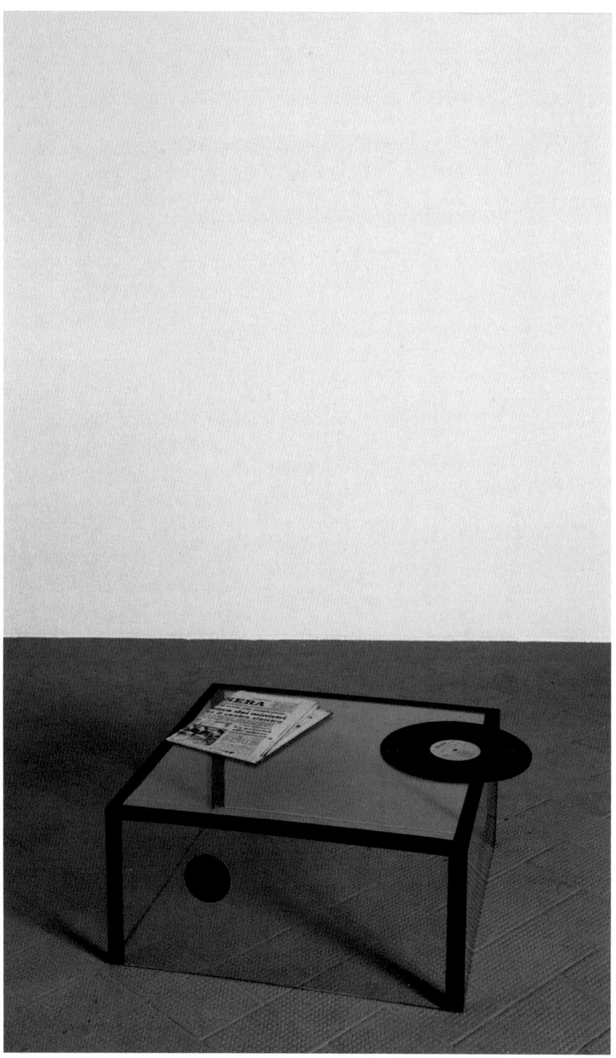

FIG. 36. Michelangelo Pistoletto, *Tavolino con disco e giornale* (Small Table with Record and Newspaper), 1964. Painted plexiglass and photographs on plexiglass, 13¾ × 23⅝ × 23⅝ in. (35 × 60 × 60 cm). Cittadellarte–Fondazione Pistoletto, Biella.

Given the series' logic of reconstruction and reproduction, their precedents in the history of art are the constructions and cubist collages of Braque and Picasso of 1912 and 1913, in which the artists used printed images of real objects to create reality effects and "real" still lifes. Pistoletto's plexiglass structures similarly use collage techniques—here, in the form of photomontage—and signs of the everyday but expand the collage support into three dimensions and into real space. They recall Picasso's use of a printed reproduction of chair caning (1912), the reproduced "folded" newspaper that juts over the "table" surface in Braque's corner still-life construction, and the real still life in Picasso's *Construction with Guitar Player* (both 1913). Their precedents are works that navigated long-held anxieties about art's objecthood.[16] Pistoletto's objects appear to be waiting to be enjoyed but are only imagistic objects. A long black extension cord in *Filo elettrico appeso al muro* (Electric Cord Hanging on the Wall, 1964) hangs ready-at-hand on the wall at elbow height, neatly coiled around its metal pin (fig. 37). A second cord, *Filo elettrico caduto* (Fallen Electric Cord, 1964), needs tidying; it lies on the gallery floor in a tangle (fig. 38). Neither cord, however, is *really* there. Instead of actual material objects, we find life-size photographic cutouts, each mounted on a plexiglass support. Elsewhere, on one of the gallery's small white Laccio tables, a stack of vinyl records—*Pila di dischi* (Stack of Records, 1964)—invites a viewer to look through them. Indeed, their haphazard alignment suggests frequent use. Like the record on the table, however, the records in the pile are also fakes, composed of eleven photographs collaged onto eleven squares of clear plexiglass, all the same size, stacked one on top of the other. Elsewhere, a large stepladder, *Scala doppia appoggiata al muro* (Double Ladder Leaning against the

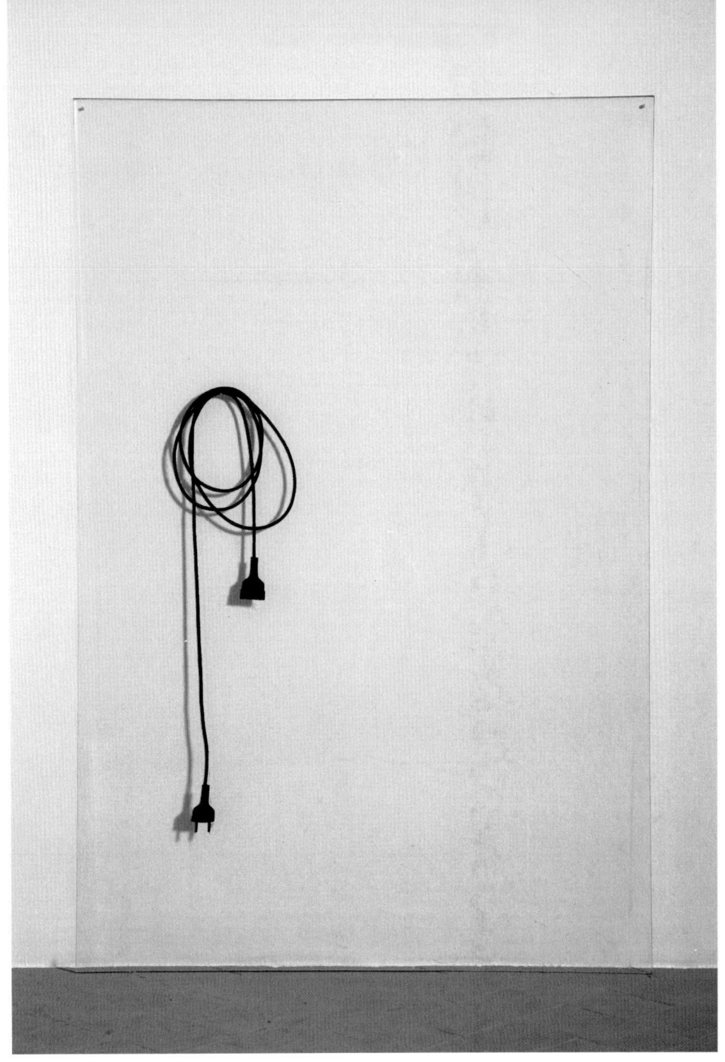

FIG. 37. Michelangelo Pistoletto, *Filo elettrico appeso al muro* (Electric Cord Hanging on the Wall), 1964. Photograph on plexiglass, 70⅞ × 47¼ in. (180 × 120 cm). Cittadellarte–Fondazione Pistoletto, Biella.

FIG. 38. Michelangelo Pistoletto, *Filo elettrico caduto* (Fallen Electric Cord) [alt. *Filo elettrico caduto per terra* (Electric Cord on the Ground)], 1964. Photograph on plexiglass, 70⅞ × 47¼ in. (180 × 120 cm) (panel), ca. 7⅞ × 19⅝ in. (20 × 50 cm) (floor piece). Cittadellarte–Fondazione Pistoletto, Biella.

Wall, using the Italian term for a double-front or "trestle" ladder), is propped against the wall; slightly open, it appears to have been temporarily abandoned by its user (fig. 39). Its rungs face outward; its empty orange shelf—a platform for tools and cans of paint—tilts downward toward the floor. Like the table, records, and power cords, the ladder is also a fiction: a life-size photographic reconstruction—a ladder *double,* as suggested by the polysemic title, which also means "Ladder Double Leaning against the Wall"—of the real material apparatus, supported by two sheets of plexiglass, similarly propped against the wall. One sheet, measuring approximately five feet in height, leans against a slightly larger one that measures one foot taller. As a series of structures, the Plexiglasses ultimately staged a somewhat duplicitous world: a world punctuated by illusions of things, mirages to encounter. The scene, we might say, was one of reality as realism.

How did the Plexiglasses engage with figurative expression and reality in Pistoletto's terms, and to what end? More complexly, why might such a task have been of import to the Italian artist in 1964? This chapter investigates Pistoletto's understudied series of photo-collaged structures from 1964 within the conflicted artistic and sociopolitical context of mid-1960s Italy, focusing on the model of the figure proposed by two linked objects of research: the Plexiglasses and the artist's text that accompanied the series. Consideration of this figure, in conjunction with the series' various references to contemporary art, culture, and economy, reveals a context of disillusionment intersecting art and society.

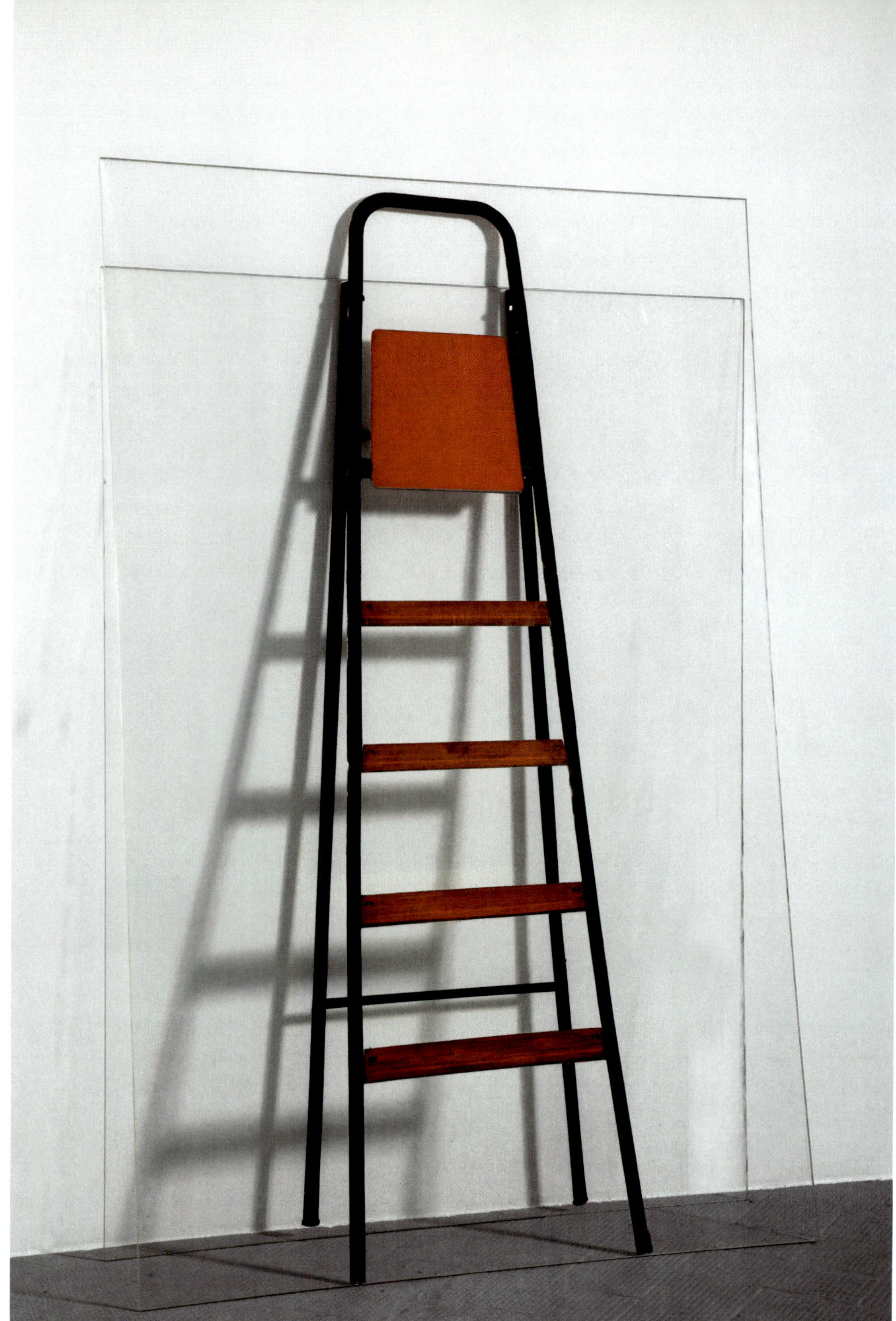

FIG. 39. Michelangelo Pistoletto, *Scala doppia appoggiata al muro* (Double Ladder Leaning against the Wall; *and* Ladder Double Leaning against the Wall), 1964. Photograph on plexiglass (two panels), 70⅞ × 47¼ in. (180 × 120 cm) and 59 × 47¼ in. (150 × 120 cm). Cittadellarte–Fondazione Pistoletto, Biella.

ENCOUNTERING THE PLEXIGLASSES

There is a dissonance to this scene. After we realize that the figures (images) the Plexiglasses present to us are photographs of objects and not the objects themselves, we know that they are images; but the Plexiglasses-as-figures still register less as symbolic and more as concrete real things. This was a key shift from the early mirror paintings. When we discover that the world the Plexiglasses construct is an illusion, our experience of reality—what we perceive to be the material world—is transmuted into a paradoxical experience of reality and realism, simultaneously. We are aware that the real world around us is a veristic illusion but nevertheless engage with these illusions, not as referential images, but as the referents they initially pose and present to us as viewers.

Rounding out the collection was an outlier: *Segnale rosso su plexiglass, sul muro* (Red Signal on Plexiglass, on the Wall, 1964; fig. 40). The work consists of a bare sheet of clear plexiglass, with a translucent, red plexiglass disc mounted on its lower-left-hand corner. Propped against the north wall of the gallery, this work set up a visual and spatial correspondence between itself and an identical red circle painted on one side of *Small Table*, positioned on the floor directly in front of the wall-sited work. Within the context of the exhibition, the red signal calls attention to the material presence of its transparent support as well as the presence of *Small Table*. As a result, the signal undermines the illusion of the rectangular plexiglass prism as table. As a double of the red circle on the table, the red disc is the only object in the collection that initially registers as a sign: a piece of plexiglass that points us to the illusions the plexiglass creates. In this case, however, our encounter with the sign parallels our encounter with it in reality. Red circles are frequently placed on clear glass doors in Italian buildings for safety reasons, to alert people to the material presence of the door. We encounter sign as sign, here.

By leveraging the physical, formal, and spatial properties of the plexiglass panels and structures—their material transparency, visual lightness, and large flat surfaces—Pistoletto was able to use them as inconspicuous structural supports on which to mount mediated objects. By extension, the artist was able to emplace image-objects in the three-dimensional space of the viewer. He thereby constructed what seems to be a real setting, furnished with real objects made available to us. Consequently, Pistoletto displaced the conventionally illusionistic, diegetic, or otherwise separate space of visual representation (photographic and painted, documentary and narrative) with the real space of the gallery.

As a form of introduction to the works, Pistoletto prepared a short artist's statement, dated September 1964, which was printed in the small trifold catalog that accompanied the exhibition. Toward the end of the statement, Pistoletto laid out the terms for a specific worldview in which reality is constituted by figurative expression—that is, in which reality is restaged as something more like realism: "A 'thing' isn't art. The idea *expressed* by the same 'thing' can be. . . . At the moment, the 'thing' for me is the structure of figurative expression, which I've accepted as reality. The picture's physical invasion of the environment, carrying the representations of the mirror with it, allows me to introduce myself among the broken-down elements of figuration."[17] The Plexiglasses thus announced not only a transition in the artist's conception of his practice from painting (if by other means) to sculpture but also a shift from his interest in the virtual space of representation to the environmental space of lived experience.

The "thing" to which Pistoletto refers in this statement should be understood in ways other than the figurative sense, as meaning a task at hand or point of preoccupation. Pistoletto is also making the point that the structure of figurative expression is not art, but the idea expressed by the structure can be. Going further, if Pistoletto has accepted the structure of figurative expression as reality, then similarly, reality cannot be art, but the idea expressed by reality can be. By "invading" the environment of display, the Plexiglasses would intervene in the real world as well as in the space

FIG. 40. Michelangelo Pistoletto, *Segnale rosso su plexiglass, sul muro* (Red Signal on Plexiglass, on the Wall), 1964. Red plexiglass disc on plexiglass sheet, 70⅞ × 47¼ in. (180 × 120 cm). Cittadellarte–Fondazione Pistoletto, Biella.

of figurative expression—spaces that are, somewhat paradoxically, one and the same for Pistoletto. The Plexiglasses are transmimetic in their intervention in reality. They deconstruct representation, and yet these "broken-down elements" of figuration continue to constitute reality. They are what Pistoletto has "accepted."

These transitions to sculpture and to the environmental space of lived experience were enacted in large part by the relation between figure and ground constellated in the Plexiglasses. The works' material properties—namely, transparency, achromatism, and minimal planar depth—endow them with a visual lightness of structure and surface. Propped against walls or staged freestanding directly on the floor, the somewhat ghostly works articulate themselves not through overt material presence or physicality but through the quiet demarcation of their contours and occasional refractions of light on their clear surfaces. Signaled by thin gray edge shadows, the structural contours trace meager, linear silhouettes and frame brief flashes of light in the room, depending on the viewer's position. If material and surface in the mirror paintings were leveraged for their optical function, here they are used for place-holding, both spatial and syntactic. If because of the Plexiglasses' visual lightness we tend to visually privilege the environmental context of their display, Pistoletto's placement of illusionistic found objects on their horizontal surfaces (the rectangle of plexiglass collaged with a life-size photograph of a folded newspaper on the tabletop of *Small Table,* for example) draws attention to the physical presence of the material support we might otherwise overlook.

Unlike contemporaneous experiments with similar materials in American minimalism and the Light and Space movement—Larry Bell's glass boxes (1962–63) and Douglas Wheeler's illuminated, painted plexiglass works (begun in 1964), especially, come to mind—Pistoletto's work with plexiglass was invested in its material and optical properties only as secondary tools to support his primary inquiry into figurative representation. The works are closer to but still distinct from Robert Rauschenberg's use of plexiglass as mediating surface, also begun in 1964, for lithographic printing of found images from newspapers and magazines. In *Shades* (1964), Rauschenberg's first artist book, plexiglass plates are stacked like interchangeable "pages" in a lightbox. Rauschenberg would continue to use plexiglass as a support for screenprinting throughout the 1960s, as would Warhol. Although Pistoletto's investigation of mediation puts him on common ground with the American artist, his interest in inhabited, real space maintains some connection to the aforementioned artists in American minimalism. For the minimalists, however, his use of figurative images and imagistic material would be anathema. Once again, Pistoletto was an outlier.

Pistoletto's application of images in the Plexiglasses, however—images that, as life-size photographic copies or hyperrealist depictions painted in trompe l'oeil, might be perceived as the material, real thing they depict—uses these properties to different ends. In the collaged plexiglass panel *Electric Cord Hanging on the Wall,* for example, a life-size photographic cutout of a coiled, black extension cord hanging on a nail has been glued to the left-hand vertical registry of the transparent panel, several feet above its lower edge. This placement of the collage element on a clear panel leaning against the wall corresponds to the position an actual cord might occupy if hung on a real nail on the real wall. An illusion is thereby created that the photographic cord is the physical, material object of its depiction, hanging in real space. In this regard, the works recall Marcel Duchamp's glass panel sculptures, especially *The Bride Stripped Bare by Her Bachelors, Even* (1915–23), commonly known as *The Large Glass.*[18]

Indeed, Duchamp was in the air in Italy in 1964, when Milan-based gallerist Arturo Schwarz was "reproducing" some of the historical readymades with permission of the artist, who also visited that year. The works were shown at the gallery in June, July, and September. Like Duchamp's glass works, Pistoletto's Plexiglasses also constituted an experiment with montage and transparent material supports to explore structures of signification. However, the distinctively strange images in Duchamp's works engage a personalized, idiosyncratic visual lexicon connected to the artist's previous work—which required consultation of Duchamp's extensive accompanying notes to be understood; they are not easy to read. Pistoletto's Plexiglasses, by contrast, favored readily legible subject matter and structures of signification. Ordinary subject matter was presented to the viewer in an image format that optimized their natural ability to be read for their material referents. By formatting the images in full-scale, cutting them out along the perimeter of each object, and then positioning them where they might be positioned in real space, Pistoletto presented his imagistic elements as natural symbols for their referents—so much so we initially perceive them to be those referents: real concrete things in real space.

In *Fallen Electric Cord,* a photographic cutout once again functions as an illusionist stand-in for the corresponding material object (see fig. 38). This time, the photographic cord is on the floor, where it lies in unordered loops and twists. Mounted on an irregular piece of cutout plexiglass placed on the floor against the base of a larger blank plexiglass panel above it, the cord snakes around the middle of its plexiglass support, looping twice over its edge out onto the real floor. In this case, the efficacy of the illusion is supported by placing the flat image on a structural support that elevated it slightly above the floor. We perceive the photograph as a real as opposed to an imagistic object. Its material is manipulated structurally in real space, on a clear support that endows the image-structure with illusionistic three-dimensionality, placing it in the same position a three-dimensional cord would occupy if it had fallen on the ground.

In an interview with Germano Celant in 1971, Pistoletto explained that the mirror paintings and the Plexiglasses were differentiated by their respective modes of imagistic engagement with reality. In these series, for Pistoletto, the image is a "fiction," a stand-in for the real thing it depicts. In the mirror paintings, Pistoletto's imagistic subjects appear to occupy real space because of their placement on the surfaces of steel mirror panels, which reflect the environment of display. The specular images of the environment they create, however, look like extensions of real space rather than reflections thereof. Because of this illusion of continuity and extension, the cutouts in the mirror paintings appear to be three-dimensional figures that stand within the real space of the gallery. The imagistic forms of the Plexiglasses, however, *commingle* with reality by virtue of their placement within the ambient space of the gallery, which Pistoletto achieved by moving the plexiglass sheets away from the wall. Both strategies create the illusion that a two-dimensional image is a real, three-dimensional entity. As Pistoletto told Celant: "In the mirror paintings, fiction adheres to reality by staying on the surface of the mirror. . . . But with the 'plexiglasses,' fiction adheres to reality by moving itself into visible space, and the experiment is unequivocal. By detaching itself gradually from the mirror according to the requirements of different subjects, the plexiglass surface, in its transparency, is only represented as a support, and carries the subject (the image of the object) to the exact place the object would occupy in reality."[19] For Pistoletto, then, the illusion achieved by the Plexiglasses allowed fiction to stand in for reality: imagistic representation for objective, physical presence.

The success of this illusion, however, is constantly pressured by the visible border of the plexiglass panels. Their edges function as frames, repeatedly cuing the viewer to the images' constructed nature as images articulated on a flat surface. In this sense, Pistoletto's emplacement of figurative elements (representations) within the real, such that they are encountered as real objects (the real thing out in the world they represent and pose as), is always intentionally tenuous, and further compounded by the occasional glare on a clear surface, or the gray shadow of a panel cast on a wall. The Plexiglasses serve as empty bracketed fields and platforms that allow for the articulation of alternative realities or injunction of new elements into the existing world.

The portability, iterability, and standardized format of the panels—the transparent, flat, quadrilateral structural support for a single, cutout, isolated photographic or trompe l'oeil image—call to mind historical moving-image practices, animation techniques, and the pressures of Fordist capitalism, which gave rise to the technology. They draw on early animation's use of cels for elements that would be repeated in a scene, rather than tediously paint or print the image for every frame; this technique allowed for the reuse of the cel, greatly decreasing production time for animation film. Within the context of the postwar period, these characteristics of the Plexiglasses parallel concurrent explorations of the technique in experimental cinema and animation.[20] German American experimental filmmaker Oskar Fischinger began painting plexiglass panels in his animated films in the 1940s, as did filmmakers associated with New American Cinema, who also used direct-to-film and stop-motion material photographic collage (as opposed to Xeroxed or screenprinted images) for background imagery in their animated films in the late 1950s and early 1960s.[21] Exceeding these precedents, the Plexiglasses expanded and reconfigured the diegetic space of cinema into real space, disrupting the sequential logic and duration of film with a constellation of

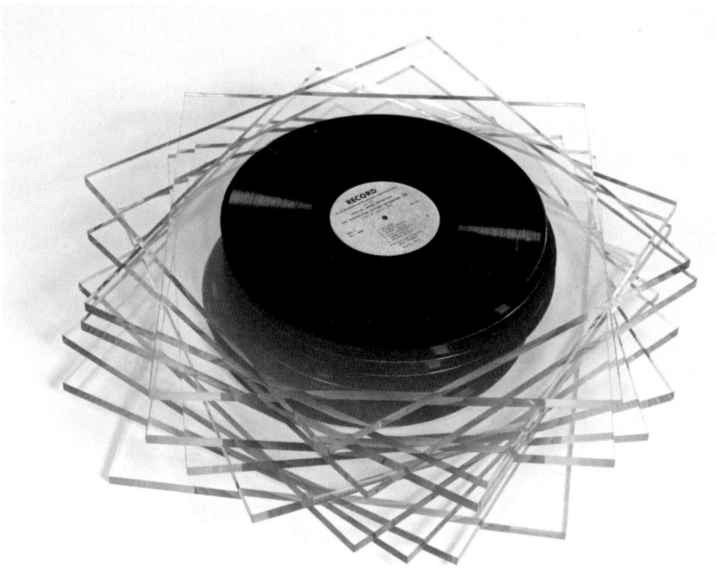

FIG. 41. Michelangelo Pistoletto, *Pila di dischi* (Stack of Records), 1964. Photograph on plexiglass (11 elements), each 15¾ × 15¾ in. (40 × 40 cm). Cittadellarte–Fondazione Pistoletto, Biella.

still frames in a single scene. Often screening images that double as real things emplaced in real space, the separateness of diegetic space is undone.[22] In this sense, the Plexiglasses variously acted as frame, screen, and prop within the context of their display, which discreetly subvert the illusion of the world they simultaneously construct.

A WORKADAY SCENE

What might have merited this reconfiguration, and what kind of world did the Plexiglasses implicate? Returning to their production begins to answer these questions. Though unified by a workaday iconographic repertoire under the theme of the "everyday," specifically one belonging to members of the working classes, the individual elements of the series were differentiated in material constitution and mediating function.

As previously discussed, the works were products of photocollage and assemblage. The plexiglass panels served as a ground on which Pistoletto collaged life-size photographic cutouts of various items—black electric cords in *Electric Cord Hanging on the Wall* and *Fallen Electric Cord,* for example—in the studio. For the former, Pistoletto photographed an electric cord that was already hanging on the wall, coiled around a metal pin. He printed an enlargement from the film negative, such that the size of the cord in the image corresponded to the size of the real cord in real space, and then cut and collaged the photographic cord onto the surface of the plexiglass panel. Propped closely against the wall, the panel held the photographic cord one or two inches out from the wall and three or four feet up from the floor—that is, in the same position as the real cord in the studio. For *Fallen Electric Cord,* Pistoletto's process was similar; he photographed the power cord in its eventual position, as it would appear in the plexiglass structure, lying entangled on a piece of plain white paper on the floor. He subsequently collaged the photographic image of the cord onto an irregularly shaped piece of plexiglass, which had been cut to line up with the exterior edges of the image mounted on its surface. Once the image was mounted on its plexiglass support, it was placed horizontally on the floor, in front of a second panel (left bare), propped up against the wall. The fallen cord was positioned just left of center, like the hanging cord, producing a correspondence between the two. Both works possess reality effects: the first casts a shadow onto the wall, as would a real cord; the second presents with some dimension, gained from the thickness of the horizontal plexiglass support.

Other works, namely *Double Ladder Leaning against the Wall* and *Stack of Records,* incorporated the same techniques of enlargement and photomontage into works of structural assemblage (see fig. 39; fig. 41). Pistoletto once again applied photographic reproductions of objects (in this case, a work ladder and vinyl records) to sheets of plexiglass. This time, however, the artist collaged the images onto more than one panel, either dividing the photographic reproduction of the object across more than one sheet, as in *Double Ladder* (in which two photographic cutouts were made, from two separate images, one for each of the ladder's two legs, then glued to two separate sheets of plexiglass, propped against the wall, one in front of the other), or by printing the same image in multiple, as in *Stack of Records* (in which he collaged eleven photographic reproductions of the same vinyl record onto eleven identical squares of plexiglass, as mentioned previously, then stacked them). In *Double Ladder,* then, the photographic reproduction is also a structural reconstruction of its subject; in *Stack of Records,* it is also an allegorical one. In its display of multiple photographic copies (imagistic records) of the actual vinyl record, the work shows us *records* of records. The photograph, like the object, is both a mechanical reproduction and a document of its subject. The work ultimately underscores the mechanical reproducibility and documentary function of its subject and medium; in its arrangement of these images, one on top of the other in a serial compositional format, it also underscores the commercial logic of its terms.

Other Plexiglasses still included painted representations of their subjects, as opposed to photographic ones. In *Small Table,* life-size photographic objects (a newspaper and a black record) rest on the surface of a plexiglass parallelepiped. The horizontal surface of the form is bordered by a precise, one-inch-wide outline of black paint, which also runs down all four vertices to the floor. The table of *Small Table* is both the material clear plexiglass cube supporting the mediated newspaper and record and the structural image of lines painted on its surfaces, which create a three-dimensional image of a black, metal table with four legs and a clear glass top.

Within the spatial environment of the works' display, these material and semiotic differentiations (between presentation and representation, readymade and image, signified and signifier) are less clear. In the context of the finished work, photographic images applied to the indiscernible, transparent surfaces of plexiglass structures are positioned in real, three-dimensional space. They cast shadows in the space around them and appear to be the three-dimensional material objects to which they refer. By situating the plexiglass work in the space of the gallery, Pistoletto spatially aligns the photographic image of an object with the location the corollary material object might occupy. The works create the optical illusion that the photographic image glued to a flat superficial ground is in fact its photographic subject.

The structural supports of the images highlight the materiality of the clear plexiglass.[23] In this case, the semiotic function of *Small Table* is multiple. It is at once an illusion of a structural object (the black table we see) and an axonometric model thereof (the structural representation of the black table in plexiglass and paint), in addition to being the structural object it substantiates (a rectangular cube with a tabular surface). As if to call attention to the conflict of this multiplicity—*Small Table* cannot at once be all three successfully—a small, painted, opaque red circle no more than three inches in diameter marks one of its lateral panels. By pointing out the physical presence of its transparent ground, the sign simultaneously undermines the object's pretentions for illusion (the field it marks is not, in fact, empty space) and shores up its anti-mimetic one, validating the tangible form of the real, material object (the plexiglass box) for the viewer who encounters it. The same sign appears in *Red Signal,* in the form of a red plexiglass disk.

The red plexiglass disk also operates as an iconographic sign, in which capacity it does more than alert Pistoletto's viewer to the physical presence of the clear plexiglass support. It calls to mind red traffic lights and road signs, specifically those that regulate space and prohibit movement. *Divieto di accesso* (access prohibited), *vietato l'ingresso* (do not enter), and *zona limitata* (restricted area) are all *segnali rossi.* As a public, sometimes-authoritarian sign as well as a cautionary one, as in its function to alert people to the material presence of a glass door, the red disk codifies the spatial environment of the works' display as one of institutionalized, systemic control and bodily regulation. As part of a popular lexicon, it evokes a social space that is determined by structures and systems of capital (such as privatization), in which access is limited, and places the viewer in a position of disciplined movement and spectatorship—a point that would be of much interest in the artist's works to follow.

These operations gain further significance with closer examination of the Plexiglasses, which uncovers additional details that have never been identified or discussed within the vast literature on Pistoletto. In *Small Table,* for example, the photographic copy of the newspaper is an issue of *Stampa Sera,* the evening edition of Turin's daily newspaper *La Stampa.* On the upper corner of the newspaper, we find the publication date in fine print: Monday, July 20–Tuesday, July 21, 1964, approximately ten weeks before the Plexiglasses' debut. Although the specific date is unimportant other than as a familiar sign of the everyday, it helps to identify chronologically the period of work in which Pistoletto was developing the series. When considered in relation to the Italian and European artistic context of 1964, it also situates the works within a key moment in Italian politics and art history.

The life-size photograph of the paper captures the newspaper's front-page upper-right quadrant; the form further supports the convincing illusion that a newspaper is resting on the table, folded in half twice, after having been or waiting to be read. Although only part of the main headline and cover stories are in view, the visible portion includes leading phrases: "headed toward a conclusion," "list of ministers . . . the center left," "Decided socialists' governor's extension of the movement," "[Mariano] Rumor [secretary of the Christian Democratic Party] in all phases of the crisis," and, the headline in best view, on the right-hand side of the page, "The text of the agreement: Priority [goes] to remedial economic measures."[24] For Pistoletto's viewer in the fall of 1964, these headlines may have functioned, like the printed date, as part of the newspaper's signification of the everyday. At the same time, however, that everyday readily recalled the tumultuous political events of that summer, including a monthlong governmental shutdown that resulted from conflicts over economic policy measures. Interpartisan, intragovernmental conflicts between representatives of the antileftist Christian Democratic Party and the center-left Italian Democratic Socialist Party led to the fracture of the Italian government and resignation of the newly elected prime minister, Aldo Moro, in late July, less than one week after the publication of this issue. Pistoletto's selection of this paper hence cued Italian viewers to recent crises and failures of conservative government, economy, and politics. By October 1964, the appearance of this issue in Pistoletto's work conjured the damaging effects of antileftist politics in Italy, as the economic crisis continued without improvement. Although the paper functions as a politicized, anticapitalist sign of economic struggle and social critique, the anticapitalist associations of the newspaper in *Small Table* are amplified by the similarly embattled artistic context the work evokes.

THE CULTURAL POLITICS OF NEO-DADA IN ITALY

The paper Pistoletto selected was published one month after the opening of the Thirty-Second Venice Biennale in June 1964. On Sunday, June 20, it had been announced that Robert Rauschenberg had been awarded the prestigious international grand prize in painting for his Combines; the controversial decision incited outrage across Europe that lasted for months, well beyond the closure of the exhibition that November. Italian critics and institutions, as well as those from broader Europe, lambasted Rauschenberg and his fellow American representatives; French and Italian critics labeled them "impotent by nature" and discredited their work as a "grotesque plagiarism of Dada" that amounted to "mental infantilism."[25] *La Stampa* critic Bernardi argued that the continued celebration of such work would amount to "suicide" for the Biennale.[26] Communists and conservative Catholics found common ground on this point; for them, as *New Republic* critic Tullia Zevi observed in her report on the controversy from Venice, "It is pop-art *vs.* the soul."[27] Giulio Carlo Argan was reported to have "sensed in [pop] the demoniacal," per Giorgio De Marchis.[28] Art critic Annette Michelson cited the backlash in Europe in the opening lines of her Biennale report for the fall 1964 issue of *Art International*, written several months after Rauschenberg's award. As Michelson wrote: "As everyone knows by now, this year's affair has had a violently hostile press in Europe."[29] Such vitriol points to the intensity of cultural geopolitics of the period. The Biennale of 1964 was perceived as an American invasion of Europe that declared the official arrival of pop art.

This American victory was reviled in part because of American claims for the formal qualities of the work displayed. Rauschenberg's Combines were largely ridiculed by European critics for their hodgepodge assemblage aesthetic, whereas they were upheld by American critics as representative of American artistic superiority relative to European practices. The controversy also stemmed from the unprecedented arrangement of the American installation. The high volume of American artwork that was to be shown at the Biennale exceeded the space available in the official exhibition site, leading to an agreement to install the work in two locations.[30] Works by Kenneth Noland, Morris Louis, Claes Oldenburg, and John Chamberlain would be installed in the US Pavilion, along with a few works by other artists, including two smaller Combines.[31] The rest of the work, including twenty-two pieces by Rauschenberg, would be exhibited in an auxiliary space outside the Giardini, rendering them ineligible for prizes.[32] When Rauschenberg emerged as the favored award candidate, dissenting jurists posed questions concerning his eligibility. Heated debates with the American team followed. Alan Solomon, curator of the US Pavilion and associated spaces, threatened to withdraw the American exhibitions; rumors circulated through Venice that the United States would withdraw all funding from the financially ailing Biennale. Still other rumors held that Americans were flying in paintings on fighter jets and sending ships to Venice to secure Rauschenberg's win by way of military intervention.[33] Even more troubling to the Europeans was that for the first time the US Pavilion was sponsored, not by a private institution, as was tradition, but by the US Information Agency, the governmental foreign-programs organization dedicated to promoting American interests abroad. Ultimately, the jury agreed to let Solomon move three Combines to the pavilion, thereby satisfying the award requirements. When Italian photographer Ugo Mulas encountered the early morning transfer of Rauschenberg's works by gondola, subsequently documenting the event in images later disseminated widely by the European press, public perception was that the Americans had made an underhanded agreement with the Biennale administration to ensure Rauschenberg's win.[34] It did not go over well.

The controversy led to widespread characterization in Europe of the rise of American pop as a cultural apocalypse and militant act of artistic imperialism. One French critic forewarned of an American takeover and subsequent "murder" of art: "The Rauschenbergs will proliferate and invade us, they will murder the pictorial idiom with their childish gadgets."[35] In Italian media, the headline of Milan-based political weekly *ABC* lamented, "All Is Lost, Even Shame," highlighting the vulgarity and perversion many Europeans associated with the work.[36] The Vatican vetoed the Biennale on these grounds, asserting that the "moral disorder" of the US Pavilion was evidenced by the "disintegration of the human image" in their work.[37]

Although Pistoletto later noted the importance of Rauschenberg's presence in Italy, examination of the photographic vinyl record in the Plexiglasses discloses other details that corroborate the artist's engagement of pop and cultural geopolitics suggested by the newspaper. In *Small Table,* the photographic record rests on the plexiglass surface, A-side up. Its label presents a list of artists associated with American pop: Jim Dine, Jasper Johns, Roy Lichtenstein, and others. If we read the fine print, we discover that the tracks on the record are Billy Klüver's artist interviews produced for *The Popular Image,* an exhibition of pop, neo-Dada, and new realist art held in Washington, DC, in spring 1963, a year and a half before the Plexiglasses' debut.[38] Regardless of the firmly international origins of the movements included in the show, *The Popular Image* exclusively featured works by American artists, including Rauschenberg, James Rosenquist, Warhol, and Tom Wesselmann, to name a few. Underscoring the nationalist cultural politics of *The Popular Image* exhibition (and the discourse on American pop) was the image featured on the record sleeve and catalog cover. Designed by Dine, it centered on the Washington Monument, Statue of Liberty, and Americana. Indirectly or otherwise, curator Alice Denney and the American dealers who advised her attributed international art movements of the 1950s and 1960s to innovations by American artists.[39]

The recordings themselves provide insight into the conceptual interests shared by Pistoletto and some of the artists associated with American pop. The interview with Rauschenberg, who acquired Pistoletto's lightbulb mirror painting (*Lampadina,* 1963), is particularly telling in this regard. A decade before, Rauschenberg recalled, he had added real lightbulbs to his red paintings (of 1953 and 1954); the artist explained that they were intended to provide the paintings with their own light source to highlight their real material constitution. The goal was to make the artwork "more related to the room that it was in." For Rauschenberg, this was a strategy of "getting the room into the picture," since he had "always felt a little strange about the fixedness of a painting."[40] Rauschenberg's reconceptualization of painting as dynamic and connected to the real world—this "getting the room into the picture"—was of great interest to Pistoletto. The stakes of their shared conceptual interests, however, were different.

Consider the reception of Pistoletto's early 1960s practice, specifically in the mirror paintings, as part of pop and new realism. The mirror paintings' popularity continued the year after the Plexiglasses exhibition, in

1965, when the artist was included in such canonical exhibitions as *Beyond Realism* at the Pace Gallery (New York) and *Pop* at the Galleria Sperone. In those exhibitions, he was again the only Italian artist, alongside a slate of American pop artists. That summer he attracted the attention of Martin Friedman, the director of the Walker Art Center in Minneapolis, who, after seeing Pistoletto's work at the Galerie Sonnabend in Paris, gave the young Italian artist a solo exhibition to be framed as an early career retrospective, held the following spring (discussed in the next chapter).[41]

Pistoletto was conflicted about the reception of his mirror paintings as part of pop and new realism for artistic and political reasons. Although such associations had brought him career success, Pistoletto's chagrin was linked to a broader distrust, shared by many Italian artists in the mid-1960s, of American capitalism and the commoditization of artistic practice. These years were the height of what was regarded as American cultural imperialism. Advertisements for the Castelli Gallery that ran in the summer 1964 issue of *Art International* in concurrence with the Venice Biennale showcased a map of Europe; its major art cities were also marked with the names of American pop artists.[42] American neo-Dada and pop had great success in Paris, London, and Kassel. For the exhibition *Amerikansk pop-konst* (American Pop Art) at Stockholm's Moderna Museet, Lichtenstein designed an exhibition poster (also used for the catalog cover) that featured an image of Uncle Sam's finger, pointing out at the viewer, aligning icons of American military recruitment with American pop.[43] In addition to the many shows of pop that were held at museums in Paris, solo shows for Warhol, Chamberlain, Rauschenberg, and Rosenquist were held at Sonnabend in Paris in the early months of 1964.[44] The year 1964 was pivotal in American-European cultural debates, fueled by Rauschenberg's controversial receipt of the top prize for international (non-Italian) painting at the Venice Biennale, discussed above—the "first time" an American won the Gran Premio, it was often reported, though Mark Tobey won in 1958—and Solomon's role in bending Biennale rules, which incited outrage in the Italian and other European presses. Comment on Rauschenberg's receipt of the prize was not limited to Europe; French and Italian presses, however, were particularly clear that views of the win were driven by cultural imperialism.[45] One article in the newspaper serial *Arts* by Pierre Cabanne summarized such perceptions: "In Venice, America Proclaims the End of the School of Paris and Launches Pop Art to Colonize Europe."[46] Rauschenberg then opened the fall season at Sperone with an exhibition. The solo show immediately preceded Pistoletto's Plexiglasses exhibition.

While American pop had, of course, its own political critiques, Italian perception of pop art as the cultural arm of American capitalist imperialism stemmed from broader histories and conflicts dating to the pre- and postwar periods alike. One major antecedent underpinning this reception was Italy's great history of sociocommunist thought and cultural activism, much of which was centered in Turin. Beginning in the 1910s, the work of Antonio Gramsci (1891–1937), Piero Gobetti (1901–1926), and Carlo Rosselli (1899–1937), along with the postwar writings of Norberto Bobbio (1909–2004), cultivated a strong legacy of leftist thought within Italian culture, in relation to and in excess of shifting partisan concerns, as did the widely distributed leftist publications these thinkers helped establish.[47] Following the fracturing and increased pluralism of Italy's political left in the 1920s, namely with the formation of the Italian Communist Party (PCI) after the historical compromise of 1923, Italy's *intellectual* left became central to the antifascist resistance in the interwar period. Later, as Italy grappled with the aftermath of World War II, this legacy provided postwar Italians with an alternative national history and cultural identity after fascism, leading to a popular political and cultural resurgence of leftist politics in the postwar period.

Other contributions to the growth of anti-American sentiment in Italy included the United States' political and economic interventions in Italy in the immediate postwar years with the onset of the Cold War. Fearing that Italy might become communist, the US government tied critical Marshall Plan aid to an anticommunist political agenda; the United States threatened to rescind all forms of aid (foodstuffs, goods, medicine, business loans and grants, and so on) and to even intervene with military force should the PCI rise to power.[48] The United States famously provided extensive financial support to the moderate Christian Democrats (DC) during the elections of 1948, guaranteeing a DC win of a parliamentary majority—a tactic since identified as a key fire-starter of the Cold War. Although most Italians identified with the political left, these intrusions into Italian politics allowed the United States to exert political control by proxy, wresting political agency and representation from the Italian populace. These interventions laid the groundwork for widespread anti-American sentiment across Italy in the postwar period.[49]

Of particular importance was the Marshall Plan's impact on Italian labor organization and workers' rights. Business loans extended to Italian industry under the plan—the overwhelming majority of which were taken by the automobile industry, centered in Turin, with Fiat taking the largest share—were contingent on the institutionalization of specific changes in management, infrastructure, labor organization, and performance that would improve Italian commercial production and ensure loan repayment.[50] Time limits were imposed for various work tasks, and conservative workplace conditions were ushered in, which included the elimination of workers' rights to discuss politics and religion in the workplace. Most important, factory and trade unions were no longer allowed to negotiate with or interfere in company management.[51] These institutional changes in Italian industry inculcated through the Marshall Plan radically changed Italian labor conditions, resulting in stricter and more demanding work environments that could no longer be contested by a workforce largely divested of its collective bargaining power. These conditions endured for decades beyond the end of Marshall Plan aid, cementing the association between anticapitalism and anti-Americanism in the postwar Italian popular imaginary. The long-term connection of workers' rights and class polarization with Cold War politics in Italy—especially in Turin, Italy's postwar industrial capital and historic cradle of Italian communism and the political left—grew in importance in the 1950s. Matters came to a head in the early 1960s with militant protests, protracted strikes, and riots that marked the beginning of Italian *operaismo.*

With these points in mind, let us return to Pistoletto's inclusion of images of the *Popular Image* record and of the July 1964 issue of *La Stampa* in the Plexiglasses. Their inclusion gains significance beyond the depicted objects' function as signs of the everyday, or even of capitalist modern life as mass-produced industrial commodities. Attribution of the paper to its date and the record to the American nationalist pop exhibition redoubles Pistoletto's imagistic readymades as signs and products associated in Italy with the tumultuous context of American cultural imperialism and Cold War culture.

AN UNCLIMBABLE LADDER: IMAGINARY LABOR AND EMBODIED VIEWERSHIP

Other signs of the everyday in the series gain further valence situationally, in relation to one another. Within the context of the series, the imagistic paper and record contrast with the imagistic work ladder and the laboring subject it elicits. This position for the artist is removed from Romantic conceptualizations of authorship, as it is from the similarly Romantic hypermasculine depictions of agrarian and factory workers that populated fascist imagery during the *ventennio.* Within the increasingly industrialized context of postwar Italy, the work ladder connotes reconstruction as well as the struggle of the lower classes in a time of mass poverty and unemployment. In the context of the artist's studio, it is also an implement for artistic labor. Pistoletto's application of the photographs to the vertical panels of plexiglass duplicates practices of gluing posters to walls—a procedural echo that underscores the position of the artist as laborer and, less directly, as protestor.

Double Ladder recalls unskilled labor and the motif of the menial worker established in Italian neorealist cinema. The ladder conjures, for example, a scene from Vittorio De Sica's masterpiece, *Ladri di biciclette* (Bicycle Thieves, 1948).[52] De Sica's film follows a day in the life of Antonio Ricci (Lamberto Maggiorani), an unemployed father who struggles to support his family in the context of widespread poverty in postwar Rome. He finds a job for the day plastering movie posters around the city, the only requirement for which is possession of a bicycle. Supplied with a wooden ladder and bucket of adhesive, Antonio sets off on his bicycle, one of the family's few possessions. Cycling alongside other workers, each carrying his own ladder through city traffic, Antonio arrives at his post. In the iconic scene, Antonio enthusiastically climbs the ladder with his supplies in tow, cheered by the security of a day's pay ahead of him. In a matter of seconds, however, a young man steals Antonio's bicycle and escapes into city-center traffic. Antonio runs after the thief, abandoning the ladder behind him. Unable to complete his work without the bicycle, he spends the rest of the day trying to find his bicycle without success. Having lost the bicycle and the

Boccioni's proposal drew on the futurist strategy of interpenetration in painting, in which dynamic, intersecting planes and geometries formed images of a world in which subjects, objects, and spaces are interconnected by confluent plasticity. Futurist sculptors would likewise incorporate environmental space into the sculptural "plastic block," making the material artwork coextensive with its immaterial spatial environment. Three-dimensional interpenetration allowed bodies and objects to be modeled in a wide range of materials ("transparent planes, windowpanes, sheets of metal, electric cords, electric outdoor and indoor lights")—an uncannily familiar list of materials, when we consider the futurist practice in relation to Pistoletto's. It would also allow lines to intersect naturally separate forms. Last, it would allow a "new reality" to take shape, in which "the figure and things" could "live . . . outside the logic of physiognomy."[75] Sculptural interpenetration and dynamic line would establish a harmonic interconnection between the figure and its environment, creating a material or "plastic rhythm" between the two; the figure would be expanded in turn. Its parts were made free to move around and become part of the environment around it, reconfiguring reality.

Implicit to these tasks, then, was the remaking of the figure. It had surprisingly endured as a motif despite futurism's condemnation of conventional figuration and its associated academicism and historicity. While calling for the "destruction of the systematic nude," Boccioni articulated a pathway that would allow the futurists to dispose of figuration without excommunicating the figure and therefore the body (a subject of great interest to the group).[76] The solution was an opening of the body and incorporation of its environment. As Boccioni urged his fellow futurists: "Let's overturn everything, then, and proclaim the *absolute and complete abolition of finite line and closed statuary. Let's open the figure wide, and enclose the environment therein.*"[77]

Boccioni's desire to expand the figure to an environmental scale also implied an opening to such a degree that the subject reaches a corporeal and psychic breaking point, threatening destruction of the figure even as its domain is expanded.[78] As Boccioni envisioned it: "Your head can cross the street while your lamp ties its web of rays of gesso between one house and another." On one hand, what we might call the figural imaginary of Boccioni's futurism models a liberated subject position, characterized by expanded spatial and bodily agency. Boccioni imagined a physical world in which figures can occupy disconnected spaces simultaneously. On the other, it envisions this expansion as a breaking apart or dismemberment of the figure that would seem to simultaneously destroy the subject. (If our "head[s] can cross the street," in Boccioni's futurist environment, so must our bodies be left headless, literally and figuratively.)

Illustrative examples of this "environmental" or "ambient figure" include Boccioni's sculptural experiments of the early 1910s. Consider the well-known *Testa + luce + casa* (Head + Light + House, 1912) and *Fusione di una testa e di una finestra* (Fusion of a Head and a Window, 1912–13; fig. 48). In these gesso sculptures, Boccioni remade the conventional sculptural portrait bust, refashioning the masterfully crafted, idealized, aristocratic, and typically historical subject of its depiction into an inelegant figure of, at times, undignified bricolage. The convoluted, agitated figures expand and become disfigured at once. They push through ornate iron balustrades, blocks of wood, panes of glass, and other structural barriers that cross through them. Rejecting traditional media of marble or bronze, as well as the neoclassical dictum of Beaux-Arts style, Boccioni employed an expanded, diverse material repertoire that included prefabricated industrial items (store-bought window frames), media associated with the applied arts (porcelain, gesso), and personal accoutrements—specifically compensatory and prosthetic items (a hairpiece, painted glass eyes). While this democratic material strategy associated (if not emplaced) the work of art within the increasingly industrialized spaces of urban Italy, as scholars have often noted, its relation to the body provides a different reading. In *Fusion of a Head and a Window*, this material selection (especially the hairpiece and the glass eyes) also associated Boccioni's figure with the ugly and prosthetic, with bodies that might be regarded as marked by lack, as opposed to the classical ideals of symmetry, beauty, able-bodiedness, and bodily autonomy.[79]

What I am naming environmental disfiguration should not be confused with or taken as a precursor to other models of disfiguration that emerge in the postwar period: the "défigurations" of Asger Jorn; the "creaturely" or therianthropic model of CoBrA's primal, bestial, and crude subjects; or the "distorted and depleted" figurative aesthetic of Georg Baselitz and German neoexpressionism in the 1960s, 1970s, and 1980s.[80] On the contrary,

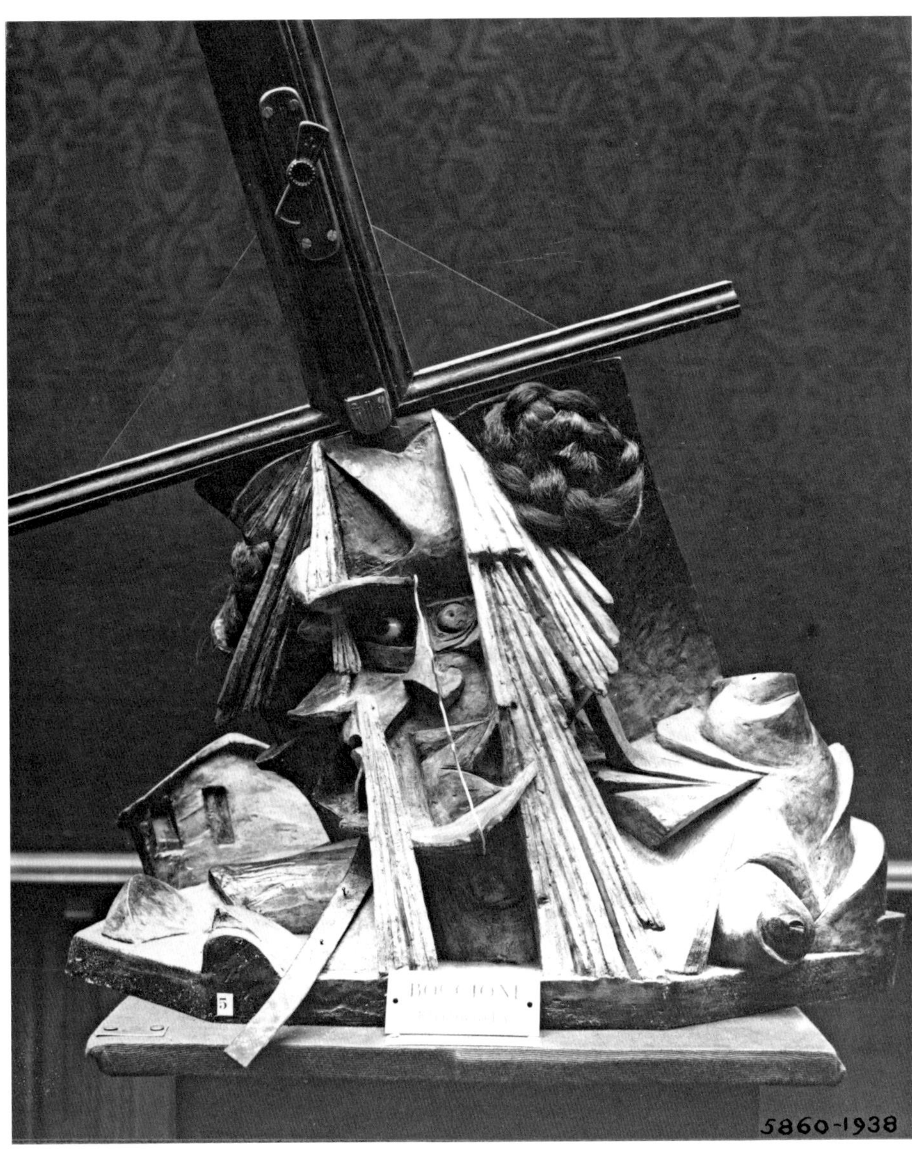

FIG. 48. Umberto Boccioni, *Fusione di una testa e di una finestra* (Fusion of a Head and a Window), 1912–13. Mixed media (plaster, glass eye, window catch, glass, and human hair), dimensions unknown. Destroyed.

the figure in Boccioni's *Fusion of a Head and a Window* is materially and spatially of the world. As opposed to the virile, technocratic futurist subject envisioned by Filippo Marinetti, proposed by the high-speed, superhuman, "machinic" body we readily associate with the Italian historical avant-garde, Boccioni's futurist subject seems less empowered and self-possessed than vulnerable and decentered. Boccioni's conceptualization of a receptive and inclusive body was part of a new "harmony" for the modern world: as this body expands spatially, it incorporates objects, structures, and other forms that may have otherwise constrained or dictated its movement but now are "embedded" in it.

This history also aligns Pistoletto with the interests of the Informale, especially with Lucio Fontana's spatialism. In the late 1940s, the self-titled Artisti spaziali (Spatial Artists) called for painting and sculpture to migrate out into space and to produce *arte aerea* (aerial art), building on the "aero" genres of 1930s second-wave futurism.[81] Of particular interest is a passage from the group's second manifesto (1948). Although the text is better known for its celebration of modern technology, it is also where Fontana and his fellow artists called for painting and sculpture to "go out" (*esca*) from their respective conventional positions of the frame and the glass-enclosed pedestal. They wrote: "We want painting to go out of its frame and sculpture to go out of its bell-jar. [Today], we, Spatial Artists, have escaped our cities, have broken out of our shell, our physical cortex, and we see ourselves from above, photographing the earth from rockets in the air. With that. . . , we want to recuperate our real face, our real image: a change awaited by all of creation, anxiously. The spirit spreads its light, in the freedom that we had been given."[82] Informed by existing ideas circulating among the Argentine artistic avant-garde, Fontana (an Argentine-born, Italian artist) and his fellow artists declared a desire to "recuperate our real face, our real image," by breaking out of their physical form and earthbound environment.[83] Ultimately, Fontana conceived of a spatialized subject as a kind of unbounded light, freed from the limits of the physical body to move as it likes. While spatial environments formally register as experiments in abstraction, they should also be regarded as experiments in figuration.

Examination of Fontana's writings in this respect uncovers new points of contact between spatialism and Pistoletto. Like the Artisti spaziali, who wanted "to recuperate [their] real nature, [their] real image," as previously noted, Pistoletto wanted to "find" and "introduce himself" beyond the mirror. This shared anxiety about securing and restoring control over one's own image, body, and self was worked out by the spatialists and Pistoletto through a spatial reconceptualization of figuration. In 1950, the spatialists declared that they "no longer imposed a figurative theme on the viewer, but rather placed him in the condition of creating himself by himself, through his fantasy and the emotions he experiences."[84]

Pistoletto echoed the spatialists' rhetoric more than a decade later in his Plexiglass statement, when he declared that to examine the structure of art, he "must make the painting *go out* into reality." If for Pistoletto this turn to ambient space resulted in a "break-down" of figuration, in which its constitutive elements are dispersed across a spatial field, then this point of connection between Pistoletto's spatial interests and those of the Spatial Movement prompts new examination of the latter with concern to figuration. Fontana made his spatial artworks—the *Buchi* (Holes), *Tagli* (Cuts), *Concetti spaziali* (Spatial Concepts), and spatial environments for which he is best known—alongside his figurative practice. He made hundreds of figurative drawings over his career. Scholars in recent years—especially Anthony White and Yve-Alain Bois—have brought his early figurative work into dialogue with his abstraction, emphasizing that Fontana explored space not only as artistic "medium" but as something that surrounds the body.[85] From this perspective, Fontana's spatial work, even when abstract, emerges as inextricably tied to his thinking about, and rethinking of, the figure and the body. As Fontana experimented with figuration, playing with incomplete contour and expanded, disconnected forms to define the body, so, too, did the artist's reconceptualization of painting and sculpture take the shape of an experimentation with processes of opening and spatial expansion. The spatial works are not representations of the human figure; instead, they are bodily, figural forms presented in the space of the viewer (rather than in representational, figurative space).

Pistoletto, for his part, imagined introducing himself in an expanded spatial and symbolic field of disassembled figuration.[86] Only by "making the painting go out in reality," he wrote, would he be able to find and introduce himself: "[I] have to make the painting *go out* into reality, creating the fiction of *finding myself* beyond the mirror. . . . The physical invasion of the painting into the real environment . . . allows me to introduce myself among the broken-down elements of figuration."[87] For Pistoletto, then, the spatial recontextualization of the work of art provided a solution to a problem of access and spatial agency. In the mirror paintings, Pistoletto wrote, he was able to "find himself in the painting." The illusionist three-dimensional space of the mirror is an extension of real space through the wall on which the mirror hangs rather than a specular reflection of real space in front of it. While this phenomenological model of self-discovery, retrieval, or reunification allowed the viewer to see their own reflection and to identify it as their image-self, thereby giving them an experience of self-integration into an empowered, self-possessed, whole subject, it was nevertheless limited by its disallowance of the viewer to *physically* enter the world and access his reflection as a tangible body rather than image in front of them.

As the Plexiglasses' spatial interests were invested in a reconceptualization of figuration, they also negotiated the spatialists' formative interest in the history and transformation of figuration. In the *White Manifesto* (1946), a proto-manifesto for spatialism published by Fontana and his students in Buenos Aires, where the artist relocated during the years surrounding World War II (1940–47), he declared that they create a "greater" "four-dimensional" art: an art of new media, technology, and dimensions that would move beyond the obsolete traditional arts to instead engage light, sound, time, and space. The group framed their work as a response to the "new spirit" of modern man as a subject of the new, "mechanical age": a period of technological advancement, scientific discovery, and industrial expansion that had fundamentally changed the nature and condition of man, as well as the organization of the world in which he lives.[88] Attendant to this call was the authors' narration of a history of the arts focused on the representation of "space and depth," which they viewed as the origin point and measure of progress in modern artistic practice. Within this context, a short passage on the baroque is particularly noteworthy. For Fontana and his students, from their perspective in 1946, the expanded representation of space in the baroque period remained unparalleled within the history of art. What is important for this study is the proto-spatialists' description of this achievement in terms of figuration. The "breadth" and "grandeur" of spatial representation achieved by baroque artists was not positioned as a function of scale, or one gained by advances in the representation of perspectival space, or even a result of the characteristic dynamism of baroque imagery. Instead, Fontana and his students attributed this expansion of space to a transformation of the conventional terms and conditions of figuration, writing: "The figures seem to leave [*abandoner*] the plane and carry the represented movements into space."[89] Indeed, the early spatialists qualified the new magnitude of space in the baroque as a function of the period's reconceptualization of the spatial purview of figuration: from a discrete, two-dimensional "plane" or surface (on which an image was conventionally rendered or painted) to an unbound, three-dimensional, ambient environment, freeing the figure from the limiting conventions of traditional media and mimesis and allowing representational, figurative space to move out into real space, in turn.

A FIGURAL SCHEMA

Pistoletto's deconstructionist and, in this case, ambient figuration composes new art historical genealogies that engage conceptual exploration of the figure as a model for creative practice. Pistoletto's work can be positioned as part of a figural schema, recalling Erich Auerbach, in which Pistoletto constellates a figural history of the Italian avant-garde introduced by futurism that continued through spatialism, intersecting with its international areas of practice, and the avant-garde of the 1960s. In so doing, Pistoletto has emerged as the catalyst of vanguard spatialized or ambient figuration: a model that cuts through the intersection between the anti-mimetic turn to real space (anti-diegesis), as well as the anti-mimetic turn to the body. As his figuration opens a new historical genealogy of the Italian avant-garde, so, too, does it open a space for a new trajectory ahead.

To that end, Pistoletto's work is also a figural precursor to that of artists such as Robert Whitman and James Coleman. Coleman's projected images of the 1970s, 1980s, and early 1990s—one of which, incidentally, used photographs of Italian public space as its source image—have been discussed as a kind of "refiguration" of figuration.[90] Ultimately, Pistoletto's work enacted the potential of the figural as theorized by Lyotard: to abut and then transgress discourse, thereby changing it. In art across the 1970s and 1980s, the figural potential of photography—its ability to be image and real presence—would be a key site of inquiry. As such, we might consider Pistoletto's conceptual figuration as a kind of figure itself: a means to open alternative histories and prospective futures of modernisms and avant-gardes.

3 Figures of Protest

Pop and Politics in the Mirror Paintings

For his first-ever solo museum exhibition and solo debut in the United States, curated by Martin Friedman at the Walker Art Center in Minneapolis for the spring 1966 season, Pistoletto showed thirty-three of his recent mirror paintings, dating from 1963 forward (fig. 49). Dedicated to scenes and subjects of everyday life, the works featured ordinary figures lost in routine and leisure activities—"entirely meditative" subjects, artist-critic Sidney Simon called them in his exhibition review for *Art International*.[1] That Pistoletto's solo debut in any museum happened in the United States speaks to the remarkable ascendancy of his work in the global art system. Photographs of the mirror paintings had appeared in international media two years earlier, in a series of fashion photographs for the March 1964 issue of *Harper's Bazaar*, published during his exhibition at the Galerie Sonnabend in Paris (fig. 50).[2] With Ileana Sonnabend's support and that of her connections in American galleries, including Leo Castelli (Sonnabend's former spouse), Pistoletto had become increasingly well known in a short time. His mirror paintings were included in major exhibitions in 1964 of pop and new realism across Europe.[3] The works quickly elevated Pistoletto from a regionally recognized artist to an internationally known one—an exception for postwar generations of Italian artists. American institutions, including the prestigious Museum of Modern Art, New York, were quick to follow with acquisitions.[4]

Ordinary in appearance, Pistoletto's mirror figures, with their unexpressive countenances and relaxed poses, invoked a sense of anonymity and banality. Interspersed among the mirror paintings with human figures were those that featured generic furnishings and common objects—a hanging lightbulb, a wine bottle, a potted plant—creating scenes of everyday life whose context might have just as easily been American as Italian. Readily translatable to any location, they could belong anywhere. Viewers could see their own reflections and the context of display register on the same surface as Pistoletto's photographic figures. The effect was that viewers saw themselves and the real space around them become part of the tableaux before them, reflected back to them as if they were "inside" the painting. This interactive model of spectatorship was referred to by many as a kind of game; one review of the Walker exhibition billed the visitor's experience

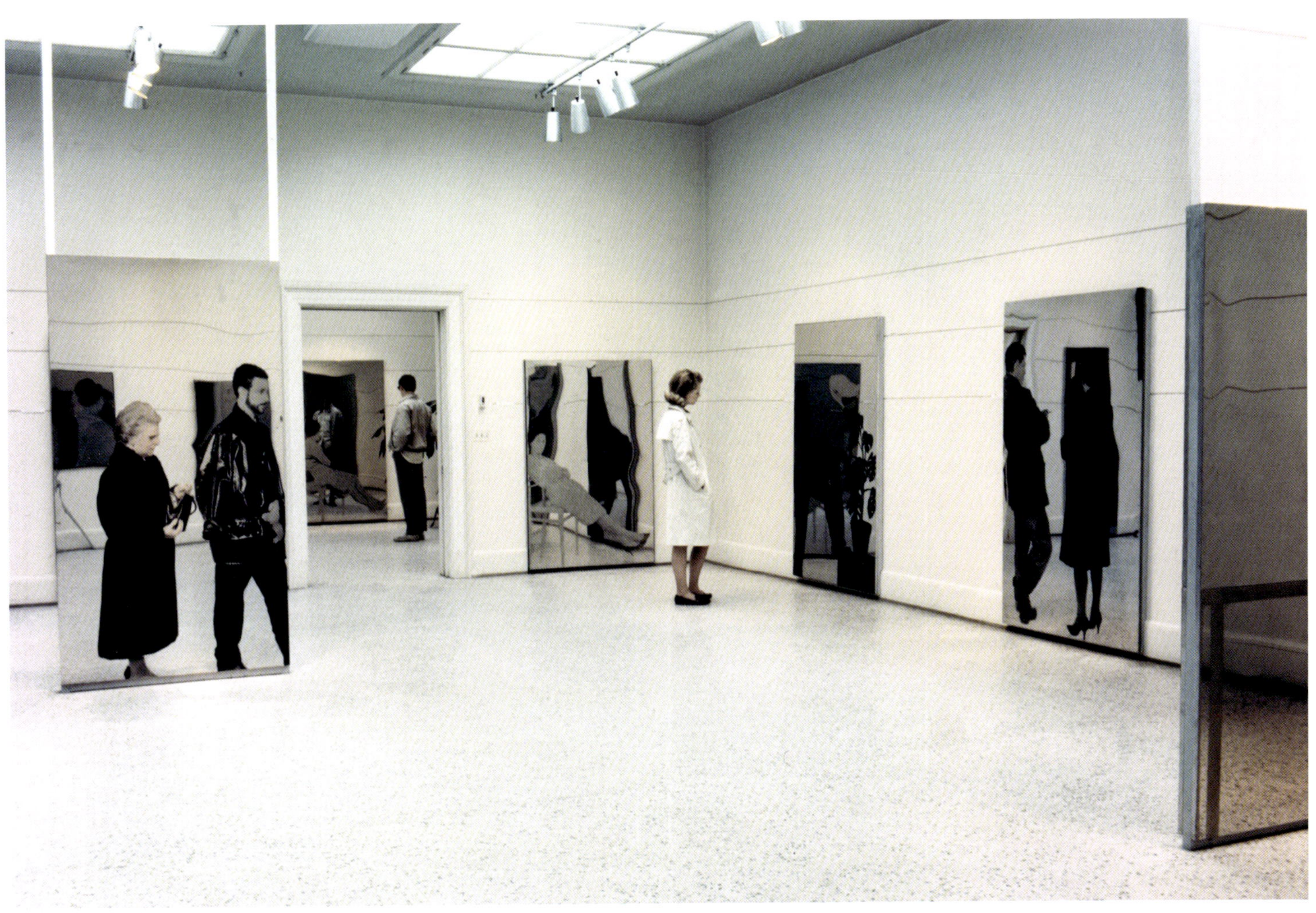

FIG. 49. Exhibition view, gallery 1, *Michelangelo Pistoletto: A Reflected World,* Walker Art Center, Minneapolis, April 4–May 8, 1966. Photo by Eric Sutherland. Walker Art Center Archives, Minneapolis.

in advertorial terms, telling readers: "Now you can put yourself in the picture."[5] By moving around in front of the work, viewers could navigate, "enter," and "exit" the painting in real space and time as they desired, interacting with Pistoletto's figures along the way. Criticism of the mirror paintings in the international context also differentiated from their local reception in Turin. What had been seen as dizzying and transgressive—but also, perhaps, *not painting*—was now often reviewed as gimmicky, a critique that likely resulted, at least in part, from the contextualization of Pistoletto's works within American pop art.

Despite mixed reviews, *Michelangelo Pistoletto: A Reflected World* (April 4–May 8, 1966) was engaging. Local news footage and exhibition photography show visitors interacting with the mirror paintings, delighting in seeing their own reflections register on the mirror paintings' highly polished surfaces alongside the banal, life-size, quasi-photographic cutouts affixed to them. Smiling, laughing, and moving in relation to Pistoletto's subjects, viewers encountered a man standing in a doorframe; another man (a self-portrait of Pistoletto) tying his loose shoelace by a potted plant; others still leaning against a balcony railing, waiting in line, or resting languidly in chairs.[6]

The literature on the mirror paintings has registered a pervasive interest in Pistoletto's figures. Variously referred to as "silhouettes," "characters," "personages," and "subjects" in primary and secondary sources alike, the figures in the mirror paintings have been frequently noted for their characteristically apathetic demeanor. Existing scholarship notes their listless countenances, casual postures, and tendency to be turned away from the viewer in *profils perdus,* as if they are looking toward some distant horizon.[7] Some have compared this alienated, detached quality to developments of the

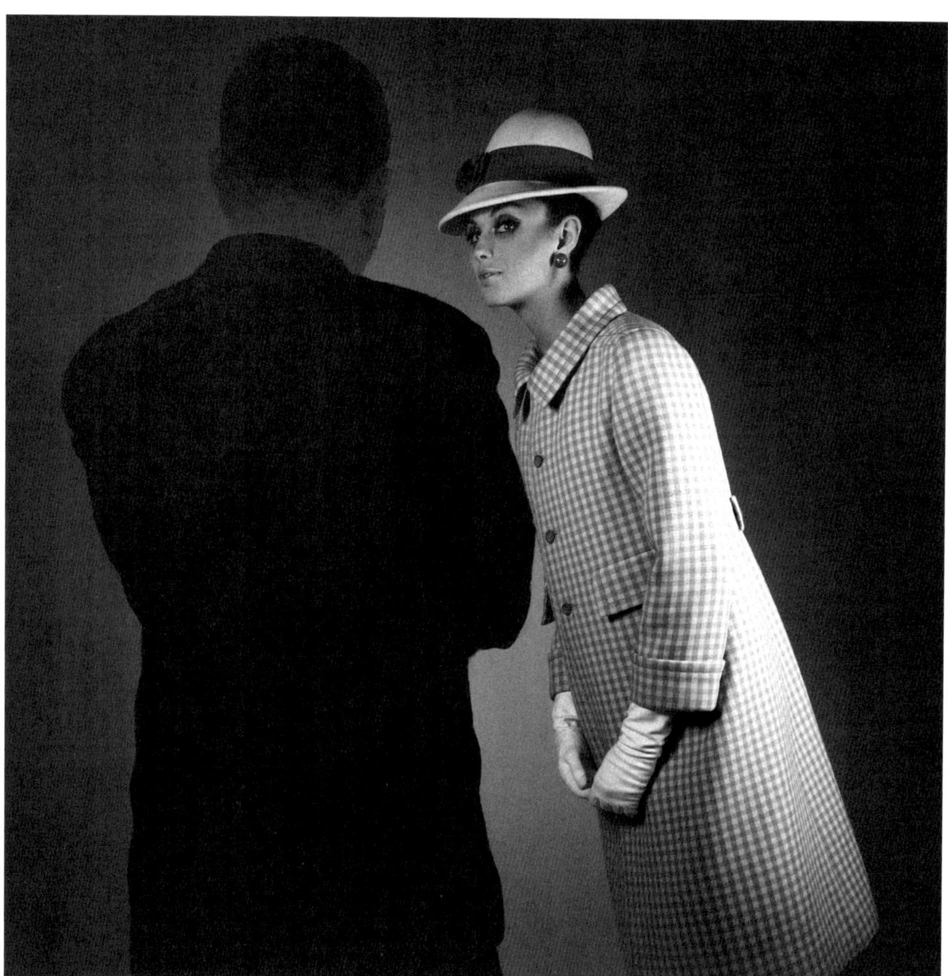

FIG. 50. Hiro (Yasuhiro Wakabayashi), *Venet and Pistoletto, Paris, 1964*. In "International [Spring] Collections," *Harper's Bazaar*, March 1964, 174.

same time in Italian neorealist cinema, arguing that Pistoletto's figures share a sense of modern existentialist ennui associated with the characters of Michelangelo Antonioni's dystopic films of the early 1960s.[8] In these readings, Pistoletto's "disaffected" figures embody the alienated condition of modern life and thereby serve as a social commentary on industrialization and commercialization in early 1960s Italy.[9] Others have focused on the semiotic function of these same enigmatic qualities, finding in Pistoletto's subjects a disquieting emptying out of meaning or unmooring of signification. Pistoletto's figures are "cipher-like," writes Nicholas Cullinan; they are stand-ins or placeholders.[10] This interpretation finds its closest antecedent in a description by French writer and avant-garde associate Alain Jouffroy in March 1964. In his essay for the catalog of Pistoletto's solo exhibition at the Galerie Sonnabend, Jouffroy characterized the mirror subjects as "flat, [like] the figures in playing cards," whose wan coloring and shadowy appearance made them look like "twilight reflections."[11] More recently, Claire Gilman has interpreted Pistoletto's subjects in the mirror paintings as theatrical characters; for Gilman, they have a "theatrical sensibility" and are positioned as "staged" characters in meticulously composed "theatrical tableaux."[12] Despite their differences in theoretical interests, such formalist, social art historical and poststructuralist readings of Pistoletto's mirror subjects promote an interpretation of the figures in terms of a postmodern condition, whether in articulation or in affect.

Whereas the first two galleries of the exhibition were filled with mirror paintings that predominantly featured everyday anonymous subjects and the occasional object, the third and final gallery staged a departure: it was filled with works in a new subset of the mirror paintings, all featuring political subjects—figures from protests, workers' strikes, leftist electoral rallies, and anti-American and antiwar demonstrations then taking place in northern Italy (fig. 51). The figures were, as the artist stated later that year, "more

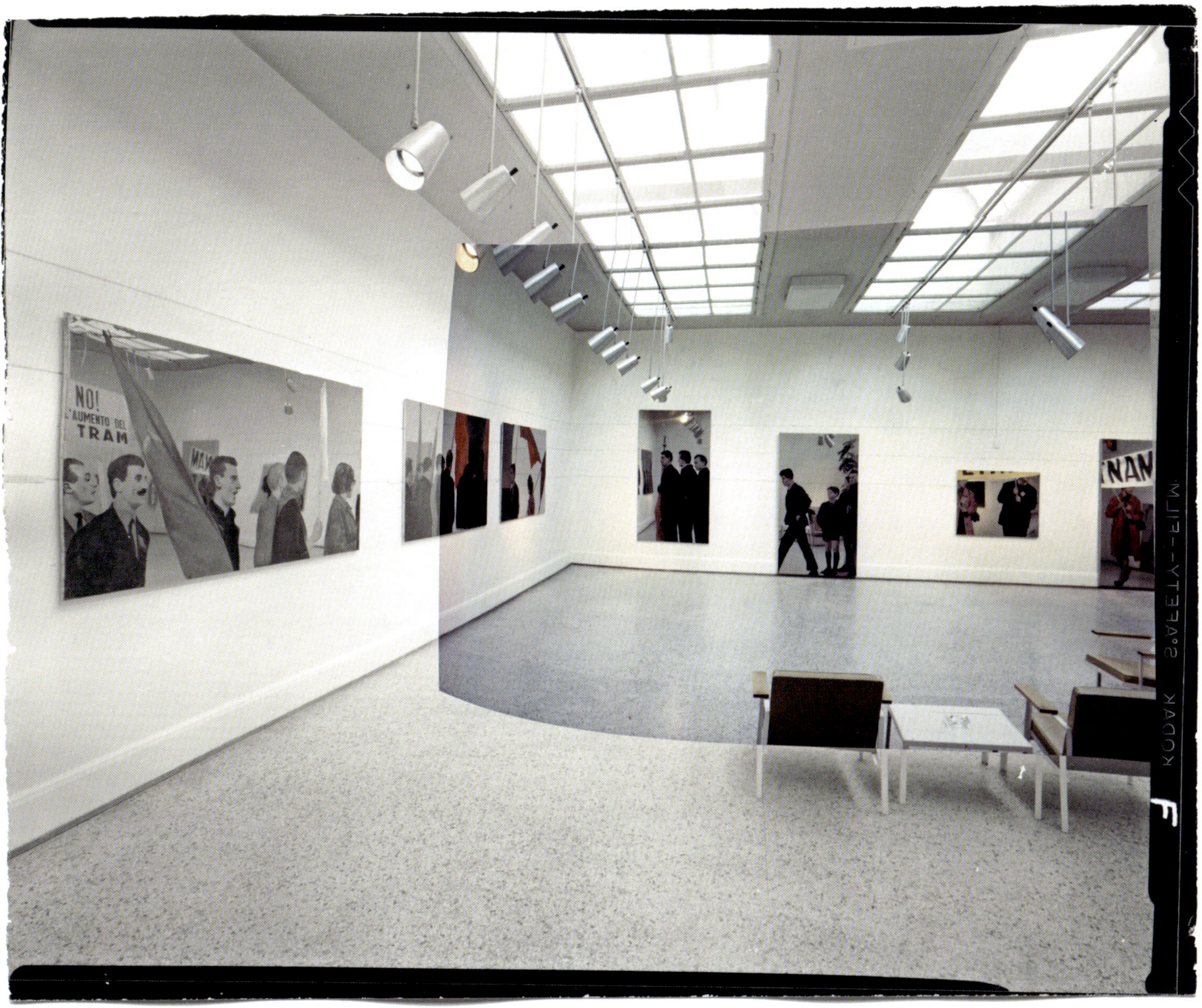

FIG. 51. Digital reconstruction of exhibition view, gallery 3, *Michelangelo Pistoletto: A Reflected World*, Walker Art Center, Minneapolis, April 8–May 4, 1966. Photos by Eric Sutherland. Digital reconstruction mine. Walker Art Center Archives, Minneapolis.

complex and more dynamic" in form and meaning.[13] Seven works from the series (of fifteen), known as the *Comizi* or "Rallies," were shown at the Walker, six in their debut.[14] As viewers approached the final gallery, they saw *Vietnam* (1965); after turning into the room, viewers encountered similar images, which spanned the two main walls of the Walker gallery, staging their own procession. On the left wall of the gallery, figures carry large red communist flags. Visitors confronted images oriented horizontally, staged at eye level, in a more traditionally pictorial composition Pistoletto had experimented with only occasionally before 1965 but debuted as a more standard format with this series. These works bring together what Albright-Knox curator Robert Murdock would later call a "frieze-like composition, that suggests marching."[15] The adjoining wall featured works oriented mostly vertically. In two visually paired works—*Vietnam* and *Striscione arancio* (Orange Banner, 1965)—people march with long banners bearing messages in hand-painted, boldfaced, sans serif capitals.[16] Closer examination of the only seemingly banal work, *Ragazzo* (Boy), reveals a clearly visible detail of a different flag—a black star in a field of green—draped to his side (fig. 52). The flag belongs to the National Association of Italian Partisans (known as ANPI in Italy), begun by members of Italy's antifascist resistance; it is a reference American viewers would likely not have recognized.[17] Although scholars have noted difficulty in dating these photographs, architectural details of the source images, organizations' signage, and the presence of party cards worn by the marchers tell us that these photographs were taken on two important dates—Workers' Day and, less often, Liberation Day—in Milan (not Turin), in the Piazza del Duomo.[18] (The source photograph for *Boy* was taken during Liberation Day [Festa della liberazione d'Italia], a holiday commemorating Lombardy's contribution to the largely communist antifascist *partigiani* resistance of World War II.)[19] Pistoletto's boy appeared again in the well-known multipaneled mirror painting *Biennale 66,* which debuted shortly thereafter at the artist's first showing at the 1966 Venice Biennale.

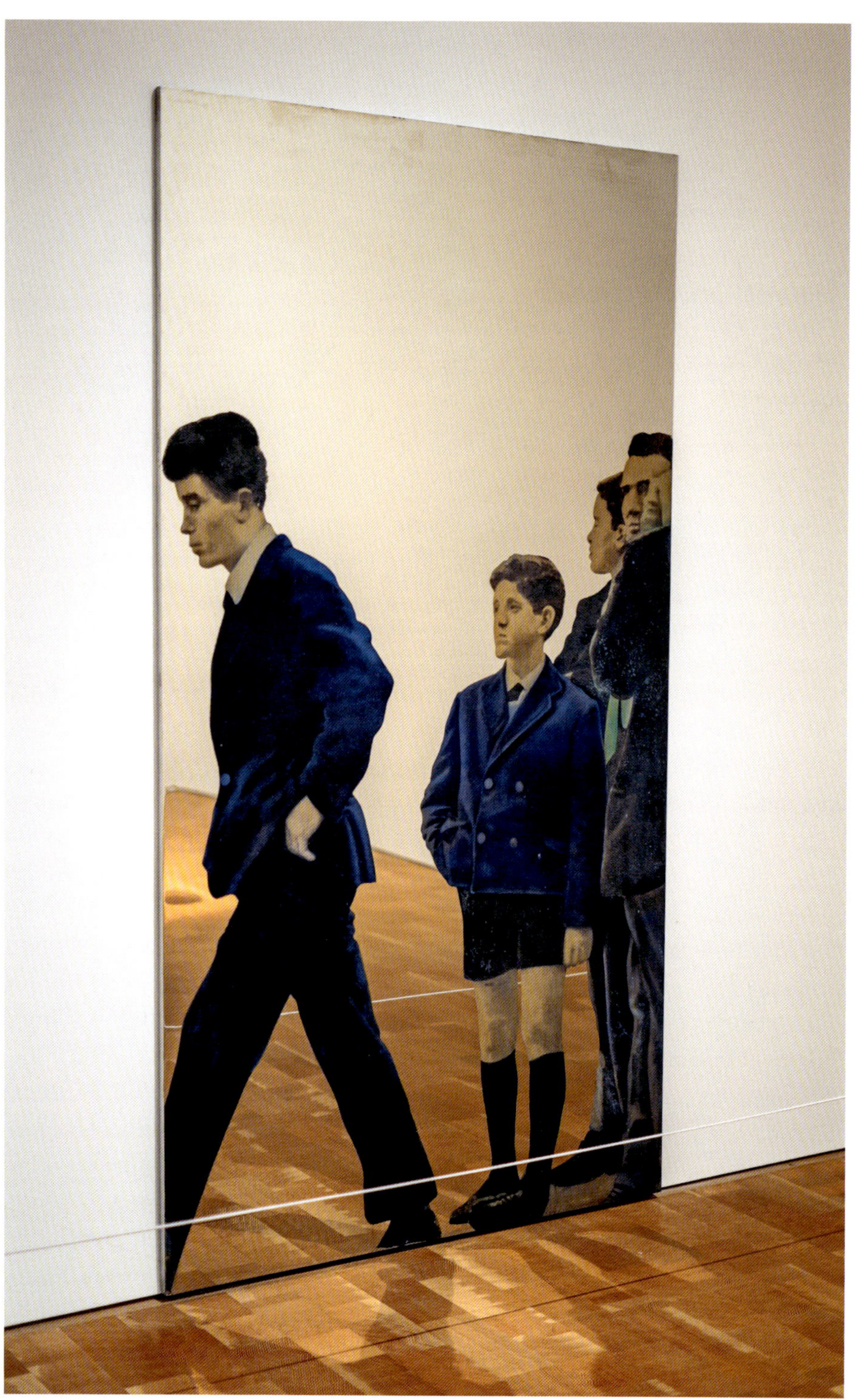

FIG. 52. Michelangelo Pistoletto, *Ragazzo* (Boy), 1965. Painted tissue paper on polished stainless steel, 86⅝ × 47¼ in. (220 × 120 cm). Private collection.

As the Walker exhibition visually telegraphed, the new mirror paintings were distinctive from their precedents in several ways. The works with political subjects were among the first Pistoletto made using photographic source images whose compositions he did not personally stage.[20] The series was therefore the site of two parallel shifts in Pistoletto's practice: first, a move from a directorial model of authorship, to borrow Claire Gilman's term, to a selective, editorial one; and second, a turn away from universally mundane, everyday imagery to political (and politicized) imagery that had become part of the everyday in Italy, united by anticapitalist (and, at times, anti-American) sentiment.[21] Investigation of the convergence of these shifts in these works brings into view a serious negotiation of pop and politics within the context of the works' circulation in the 1960s.[22] Consideration of the Rallies makes us ask: if Pistoletto's mirror paintings are part of the postmodernist enaction and declaration of the end of painting, as held in the existing literature, and the increasingly distracted condition of the postmodern subject, what does their investment in figuration and leftist activity mean for art of the 1960s? Examination of the series' navigation of Italian politics and the broader geopolitical horizon of art in the early years of the Cold War reveals that these works offer a new model of political figuration in the 1960s.

COOL FIGURES

Pistoletto had his US solo debut at the Walker at the moment of international renown of the mirror paintings, on one hand, and the formative years of Arte Povera, on the other. Indeed, not long after Pistoletto's museum debut, more major international opportunities followed, and Pistoletto's mirror paintings were included in exhibitions of contemporary Italian art proliferating in the global context: in Tokyo (with one of the Rallies, in 1967), São Paulo (1967–68), and Mexico City (1971).[23] These exhibitions largely held Pistoletto's mirror paintings apart from the "impoverished" works of Arte Povera. But the cover of the catalog for Pistoletto's Walker show in spring 1966 might have been mistaken for one dedicated to Andy Warhol were it not for the Italian artist's surname, stamped in large black capital letters across the header of the page (fig. 53). Created in-house by then design curator and modernist designer Peter Seitz, without input from Pistoletto, the square cardstock cover, wrapped in reflective silver foil, featured a serigraphic reproduction of photographic figures from one of Pistoletto's latest mirror paintings. Printed in black halftone with accents of pink ink, the figures pop from the page.[24]

The image on the catalog cover, however, was markedly altered from the work of its ostensive reproduction—one of the Rallies, entitled *No all'aumento del tram* (No to the Tram Fare Increase) after the message posted on a sign carried by the figure at the far left of the scene (fig. 54).[25] The figure, one of a group of marching people, wears a red *tessera partito* (or possibly *sindacale*), a party or union membership card, pinned to his lapel. The red color and presence of the card identify him as a member of the Italian Communist Party, who typically wore the cards on Workers' Day or other major party occasions.[26] Another figure in the scenes wears the red kerchief, a popular garment in postwar Italian communist circles worn in homage to those of the historic partigiani, the Italian antifascist resistance. Another still carries a large red flag, while two others carry protest signs held above their heads. On Seitz's cover, however, overtly political figures and protest signs have been abstracted or removed. The first protest sign, bearing the title of the work, has been cropped out, along with the left-hand side of the work, while the second sign is a shadowy object; its halftone printing makes it difficult to place.[27]

On the cover, Pistoletto's figures are a handsome, if somewhat aloof, group. Neatly groomed and well dressed, they are turned away from us in profils perdus, preoccupied with their own thoughts and activities.[28] Their posture lends them a dismissive, "detached," and "impersonal" air in relation to viewer and scene. This affect was not unique to this set of mirror paintings. Martin Friedman described Pistoletto's mirror subjects in his catalog essay as frequently dispassionate. Despite the cover figures' bright pink skin, they still seem "drained," as American art critic Annette Michelson characterized Pistoletto's subjects.[29] The cover in form and subject is paradigmatic of what Friedman called Pistoletto's "cool imagery": images that are recognizably objective—in appearance, if not in fact—in subject matter, media, and production.[30]

Borrowed from the critical lexicon then surrounding American pop and nascent discourse on minimalism, "coolness" accounted for a similarly detached, impersonal, politically apathetic affect of pop art, minimalism, and many of its artists alike. The term summarily

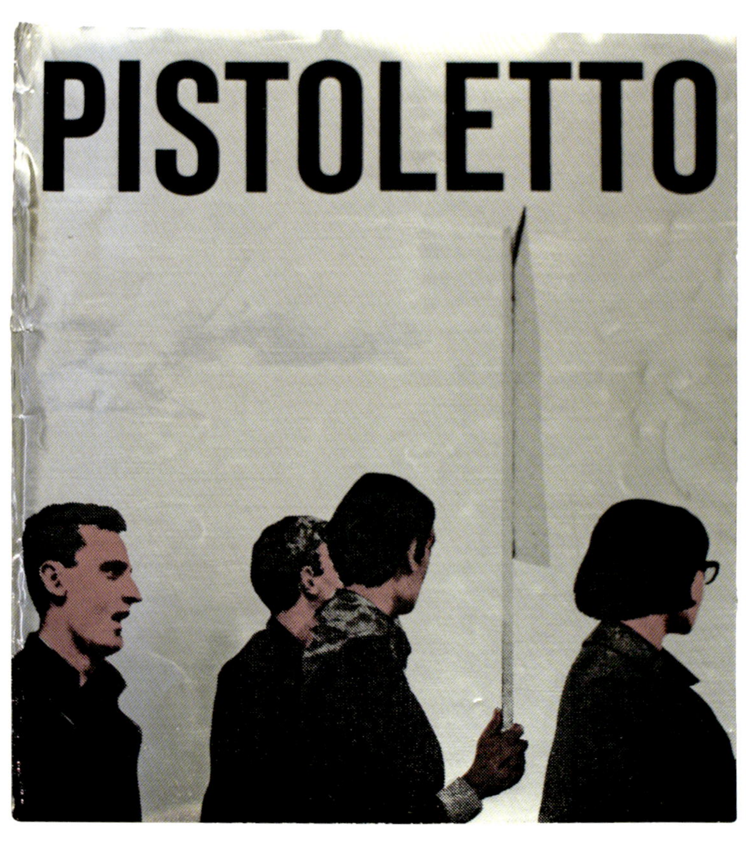

FIG. 53. Cover of the exhibition catalog *Michelangelo Pistoletto: A Reflected World* (Minneapolis: Walker Art Center, 1966), designed by Peter Seitz. Serigraph on silver foil, 8½ × 8½ in. (21.6 × 21.6 cm).

FIG. 54. Michelangelo Pistoletto, *No all'aumento del tram* (No to the Tram Fare Increase), 1965. Paint on paper, mounted on polished stainless steel, 47¼ × 86⅝ in. (120 × 220 cm). Detroit Institute of Arts, Gift of Mr. and Mrs. Richard A. Manoogian, 67.14.

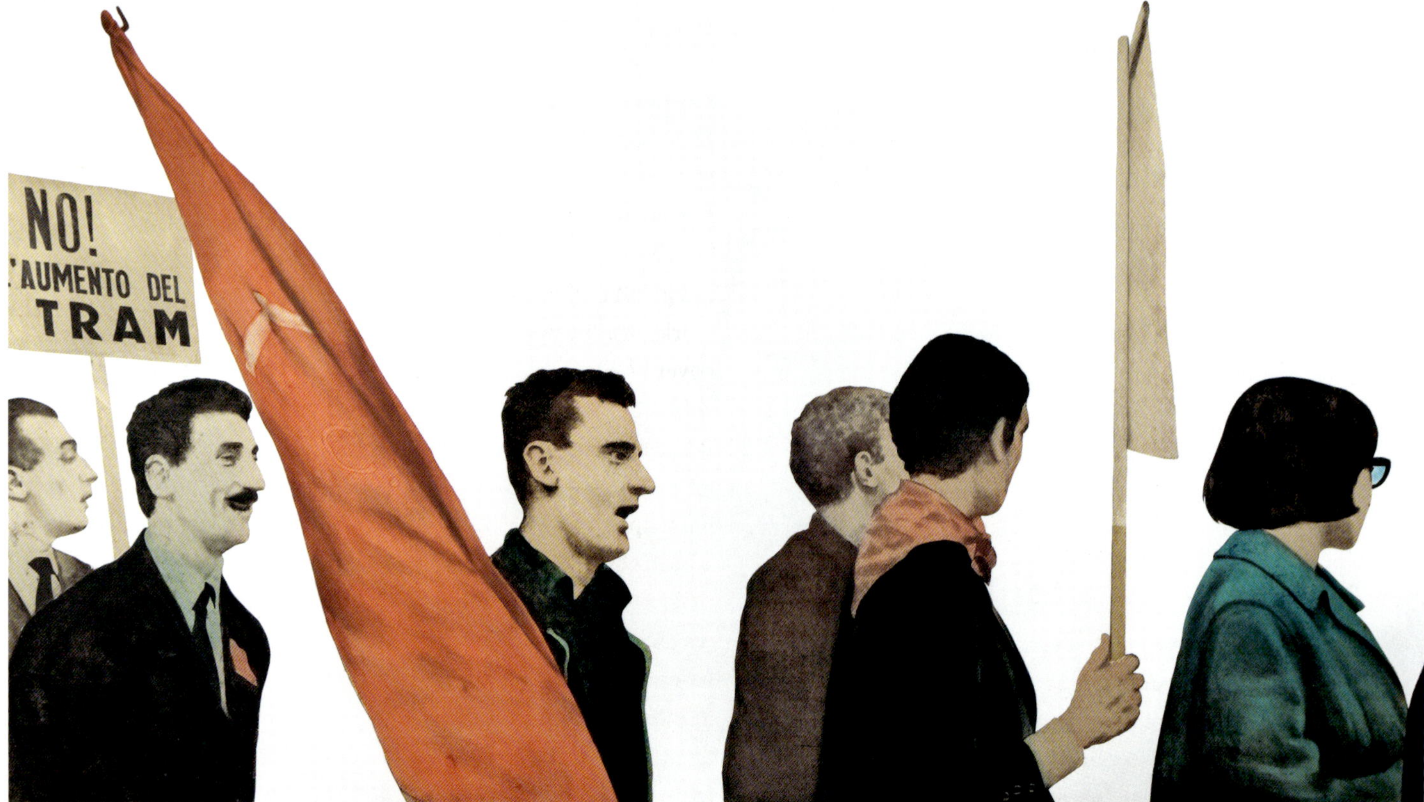

referred to what many observed as a comparably anti-expressionist drive in Pistoletto's mirror paintings and subjects.[31] Given the artist's use of unconventional, mass-produced materials, quasi-photomechanical processes of reproduction (as Tommaso Trini noted in the early 1970s), and everyday subject matter, the term suited the dominant reading of Pistoletto's work in terms of American pop; it was a logical if biased interpretation, as Italian art critic and pop scholar Alberto Boatto later noted.[32] Deployed in writings by Barbara Rose, Thomas Hess, Peter Selz, and Alan Solomon, among other American art critics and curators, coolness by 1966 was a long-established term for sociopolitical passivity and noncommittal, disengaged authorship in pop that was specifically American in character.[33] Its use for Pistoletto's work, along with the Walker's precise manipulation of Pistoletto's political (and more specifically sociocommunist) iconography on the catalog cover, depoliticized the artist's work within the context of his debut in the United States at the height of the Cold War, while also situating it as American in kind.

Indeed, in his catalog essay for the show, Friedman described Pistoletto's mirror paintings with political subjects as "cool" and "American" at the same time:

> In many respects, Pistoletto's artistic ambience is an American one, although he has never lived here. Certain affinities, some admittedly tenuous, exist between his pictures and Pop art, environmental experiments and "happenings." His relationship to current Italian painting and sculpture is negligible. . . . Pistoletto's figures appear either in relaxed, contemplative attitudes or are shown as part of processions frozen in motion. Figures and objects based on actual photographs are shown in mildly distorted "actual" color produced with crayon and other means. Such selective use of the photographic process, frequently used in American Pop art, implies a "cool," detached manner of direct presentation—with immediately recognizable images whose presence in the painting remains enigmatic and rather mysterious.

That concessions were made only for those artists who may have "had some taste of contemporary American life," as Friedman put it, by living in the United States or embracing American culture only reinforces the term's valence as an agent of imperialist nationalism.[34] Indeed, as Hess observed, only "in Italy, where Americanization was met with less resistance from native customers, [was] Pop beginning to flourish."[35] "Coolness" allowed critics to label practices by non-American artists that shared formal qualities with American pop as mimicry. Implicit to such equivocations, however, is the assumption that formal qualities convey the same meaning universally.

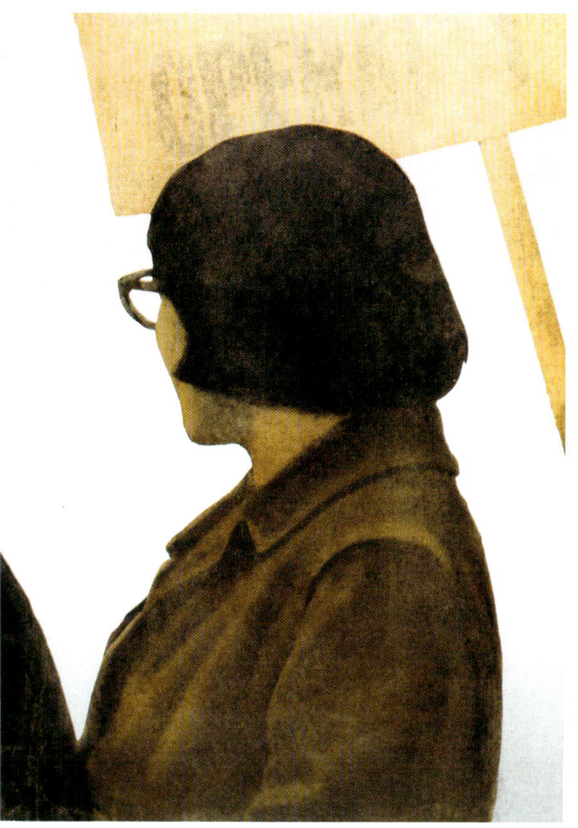

FIG. 55. Michelangelo Pistoletto, *Operai* (Workers), 1965. Previously known as *Person—Back View.* Graphite and oil on tissue paper on stainless steel, 22½ × 16¼ in. (57¼ × 41⅜ cm). Collection of Suzanne Weil.

These changes to the catalog seem especially important given the revelation Pistoletto *did* in fact make a new work for the show specifically intended for the catalog cover or exhibition poster. In February 1965, Pistoletto shipped a small mirror painting to the Walker (fig. 55). Its measurements match those of a work until now known as *Person—Back View.* It featured a young woman participating in a workers' strike.[36] She is framed by a protest sign that reads *Operai*—"Workers"—also the title of the work. Despite arriving in time, the work was not included in the exhibition or in the catalog. The woman's sign was sourced from one of Rinaldi's photographs, the figure from another (fig. 56a–b). Two other documents corroborate these findings: first, a letter from the Walker to US Customs, in which the registrar

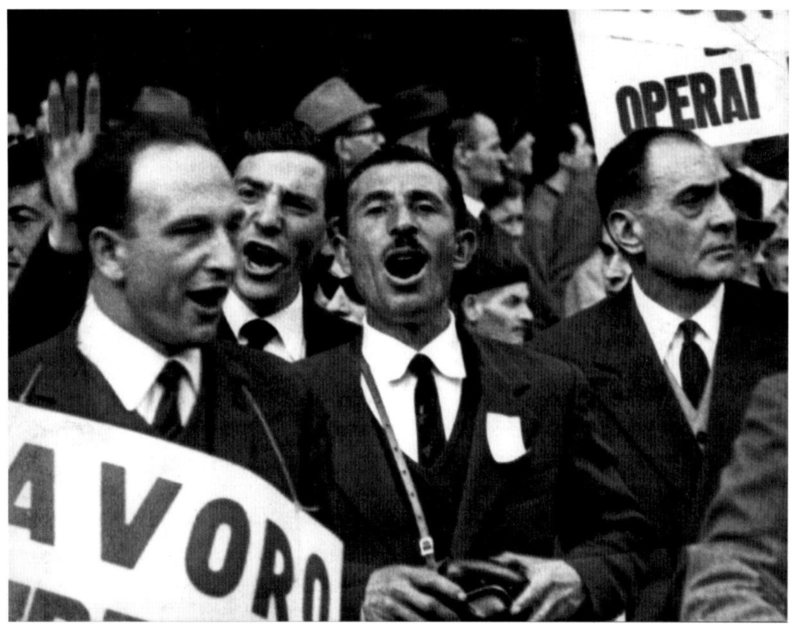

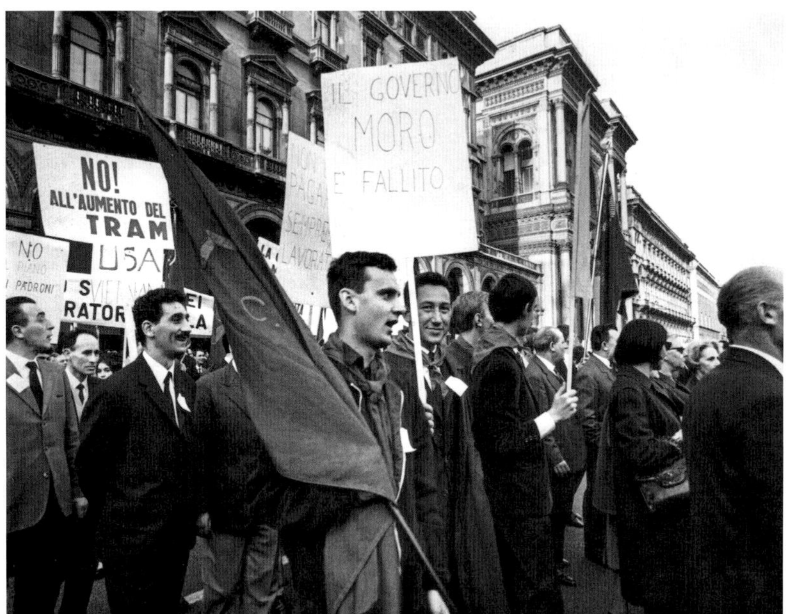

FIG. 56A–B
A–B. Renato Rinaldi, source photographs (top and bottom) for Pistoletto's *Operai*.
B. Renato Rinaldi, source photograph for *No all'aumento del tram.* Both images (top and bottom) were taken in Milan, 1965. Archivio Pistoletto, Biella.

stated that Customs released a painting by Pistoletto, entitled "OPERAI," on March 9 or 10—confirming the Walker's awareness of the work's original title and Customs' release of the painting in time for the catalog printing; second, associate curator Dean Swanson's letter to Leo Castelli, May 17, 1966, regarding an upcoming shipment of works including *Workers,* "which Pistoletto did for possible use as a catalogue cover or poster." The painting was shortly thereafter sold by Castelli. Until now, it has only ever been exhibited and known by the relatively innocuous (and tellingly Anglophone) title of *Person—Back View.*[37]

It is this specifically American depoliticization—by which I mean both the depoliticization of Pistoletto's work (especially with regard to curators' exploration of Marxist ideas of the relation between art and politics) *and* an Americanizing colonization of Pistoletto's mirror paintings—that I am interested in as a historic (and historiographic) problem for his work and the broader field of postwar Italian art. This was the frame for both popular press and art criticism. In a review of Pistoletto's show in 1967 at Detroit's J. L. Hudson Gallery, where Pistoletto's political figures were again depoliticized on the catalog cover, critic William

Tall argued that Pistoletto "strikes a contemporarily universal attitude."[38] By 1968, major exhibitions dedicated to contemporary Italian art characterized it by *internationalism* with, in the case of Pistoletto and the younger postwar generation, a specifically "American" inflection—even though the shows were originally conceived by Italian art historian Eugenio Battisti (Germano Celant's mentor at the University of Genova), then teaching at Pennsylvania State University.[39] In his essay for *Young Italians* at the Institute of Contemporary Art in Boston, Alan Solomon outlined an Italian artistic generational shift from European-influenced to American-influenced practice. Artists over forty made work largely grounded in a Paris-derived, "European tradition," whereas "young Italians" instead were New York focused, "influenced by pop and the new American geometric art."[40] For the paired Jewish Museum exhibition *Recent Italian Painting and Sculpture* (1968), curator Kynaston McShine oppositely repositioned the slightly older generation of postwar Italian artists, distancing them from his idea of a more authentic Italian identity. These were sometimes called "'international' Italians" with a "truly universal" aesthetic that "transcended the possible 'city-state' provincialism" that afflicted the work of regional (and somehow more authentically Italian) Italian artists.[41]

For his part, Pistoletto expressed discomfort, as did many Italian critics, with the categorization of his work in terms of pop, primarily viewed as an American enterprise. Pistoletto shared his view on this conflict in an interview in 1984 with Celant: "Naturally I was thrilled to have found an international platform, which was nowhere to be found in Turin; even still it posed the problem of a misunderstanding: being regarded as one of the American painters. As the only European painter, the idea of becoming part of what was viewed as Pop was an artistic ambiguity that I didn't really love."[42] Pistoletto was neither alone nor extreme in this view. Commenting in the late 1980s on the import of American art to Italy in the 1960s, gallerist Plinio De Martiis of the important Rome-based gallery La Tartaruga (est. 1953), who championed the works of many pop-adjacent artists of the Roman Scuola della Piazza del Popolo, called it an "Americanization ... that colonized and barbarized us, flattening us to the level of a diligent province. More American than the Americans themselves."[43] While American art's presence in mid-1960s Turin was, as Mirella Bandini has argued, formative to Arte Povera, the problem for Pistoletto was more than one of nationality: it hinged on pop's engagement of a specifically capitalist model of mass culture that, he would later note, "seemed to want to be universal."[44] It's important to distinguish that his sentiment—around pop's perceived universal and potentially imperialist capitalism—differed from later arguments by Celant in the late 1960s in *Art Povera* (the English-language edition of his 1969 volume *Arte Povera*), an internationalizing campaign, in part, for the movement. Celant described Arte Povera's "stateless" character, even as he would later curate Arte Povera as an Italian phenomenon in the 1980s—a paradox noted by art historian Raffaele Bedarida in his scholarship on the reception of Italian art in the United States.[45]

One of the most prominent contemporaneous refutations in Italian art criticism of the pop reading of Pistoletto was made by a designer. Ettore Sottsass Jr. argued that differences in commercial culture and everyday life in Italy and America made it impossible for Pistoletto's or any Italian artist's work to be that of pop.[46] Italian art historian Maurizio Fagiolo dell'Arco argued that Pistoletto's works went beyond the "the sweet illusions/tricks of authentic pop," despite the artist's interest in pop characteristics, namely "pop's new objectivity." Instead, Pistoletto was moving toward "symbolic objectivity," achieved through mirroring, while "bringing about a hallucinatory mirroring of mirroring."[47] Other critics found connections to pop to be dangerously attractive. Writing on Pistoletto's exhibition in February 1968 at the Galerie Christian Stein (Turin), *La Stampa* critic Angelo Dragone focused on the Minus Objects on display, now as images on the surface of new mirror paintings, namely *Rosa bruciata* (Burnt Rose), *Mica*, and *Sfera di giornali* (Newspaper Sphere), describing the sphere as "a kind of fun festive gift ... not lacking however an indulgent rekindling of the flame [*gustoso ritorno di fiamma*], more 'pop' than 'op.'"[48] Unpublished photographs of the offices of gallerist Gian Enzo Sperone also reveal Pistoletto's closeness to pop in Italy's artistic context. Behind the dealer and his wife, we see two works of the same size, hanging one above the other: a poster for Pistoletto's group exhibition with Ileana Sonnabend and a Warhol electric-chair print, which had appeared on the poster for the artist's solo show at the Milan location in June 1966 (designed by Clino Trini Castelli, the artist's friend.)

Of course, even "cool" American pop was also political, as most deftly argued in primary American art criticism by Gene Swenson and Gregory Battcock, who saw in pop social realism and a new humanism, respectively.[49] In Pistoletto's view, however, pop's engagement of American commercial culture amounted to a marginalization, if not expulsion, of the human from its social values. Reasons for this view are numerous; key among them are likely the categorization of Italian art in the United States as American and the loaded stakes of figuration in the Italian context, including its closeness to Italian tradition, as I've previously outlined. Echoing these arguments, and bringing them into discussion with figuration, Pistoletto continued:

> American objectification [of the work of art] was achieved through the image of consumption and of distribution; it was through identifying itself with the banal object of the American flag, like Jasper Johns. For me it was [a way] to exit from an abstract crushing [weight] of informalist designs. It's consequential that the American flag becomes Coca-Cola, the seriality of the car accident and Marilyn Monroes [*sic*] and the comic strip—elements referring to American social factors. *On the contrary my work isn't born from an image of local or national involvement, consumerism or public figuration, but derived from the centrality of the human figure.*[50]

In Pistoletto's view, his work categorically differed from American pop because it "derived from the centrality of the human figure."[51] As he wrote to Friedman in February 1966, the only American pop artist who shared his interest was George Segal, whose plaster-cast figures and tableaux suggested that the Italian and American artists had a "common need to consider life through the human figure."[52] Whether Pistoletto regarded this humanist worldview as his alone or as that of Italian culture is less clear. He specified that his work did not stem from "an image of local or national involvement"—a model perhaps too closely aligned with the nationalist rhetoric of fascist culture—while leaving internationalism a possibility. Indeed, Pistoletto's conceptualization also recalled the language of the partisan antifascist resistance and proletarian internationalism it championed, in which the red flag unites the working masses, "superseding national barriers, to unite them [the masses] in internationalism."[53] This wasn't especially distinctive language. Many of the postwar generation, as Antonio Tricomi has written, felt a sense of connection and duty to uphold the achievements and ideals of the partisan resistance before them and sought to create a new Italy by "renewing the traditions of humanism."[54] But Pistoletto's reference to "figurazione pubblica" (public figuration) also distanced him from straightforward attempts to renew humanism through a reprisal of figurative representation. It distanced him, too, from problematic associations with Italian postwar socialist realism. While these disclaimers do not characterize his work in terms of a personal or "private" form of figuration, they distinguish his practice from models of politicized (and political) figuration already in place. Segal aside, Pistoletto's problem with his alignment with pop was one of artistic and geopolitical misidentification.

The Rallies' politicized reception by the Walker Art Center precipitated long-term effects of Cold War culture on the global reception of Pistoletto's work and contemporary Italian art in the 1960s. But this depoliticized and de-Italianized reading of Pistoletto's works—and in some cases, critical ire over their departure from the anonymous, potentially more approachable subjects of his other mirror paintings—has wider ramifications. What is at stake in this interpretation is a destabilization of long-standing models in modern and contemporary art history that have privileged the cultural production of capitalist countries, subordinating postwar Italian art (as well as art of other former Axis powers, sociocommunist nations, and nonaligned states) within historical narratives that identify "progressive" creative practice as the product of democratic, Anglo-European cultures. These images' navigation of Italian labor politics and early Cold War cultural geopolitics consolidate a new model of political figuration in the 1960s.

Further examination of the exhibition and the critical reception of these works within the United States evince the broader dimensions of the problem of their depoliticization within the United States. Michelson had a similar, if more nuanced, view of the works as Friedman. Noting Pistoletto's frequent use of somewhat apathetic figures turned away from the viewer, Michelson wrote: "[They] are involved in somewhat relaxed, casual, and somewhat un-vivacious modes of activity. Even the processions of the protests on

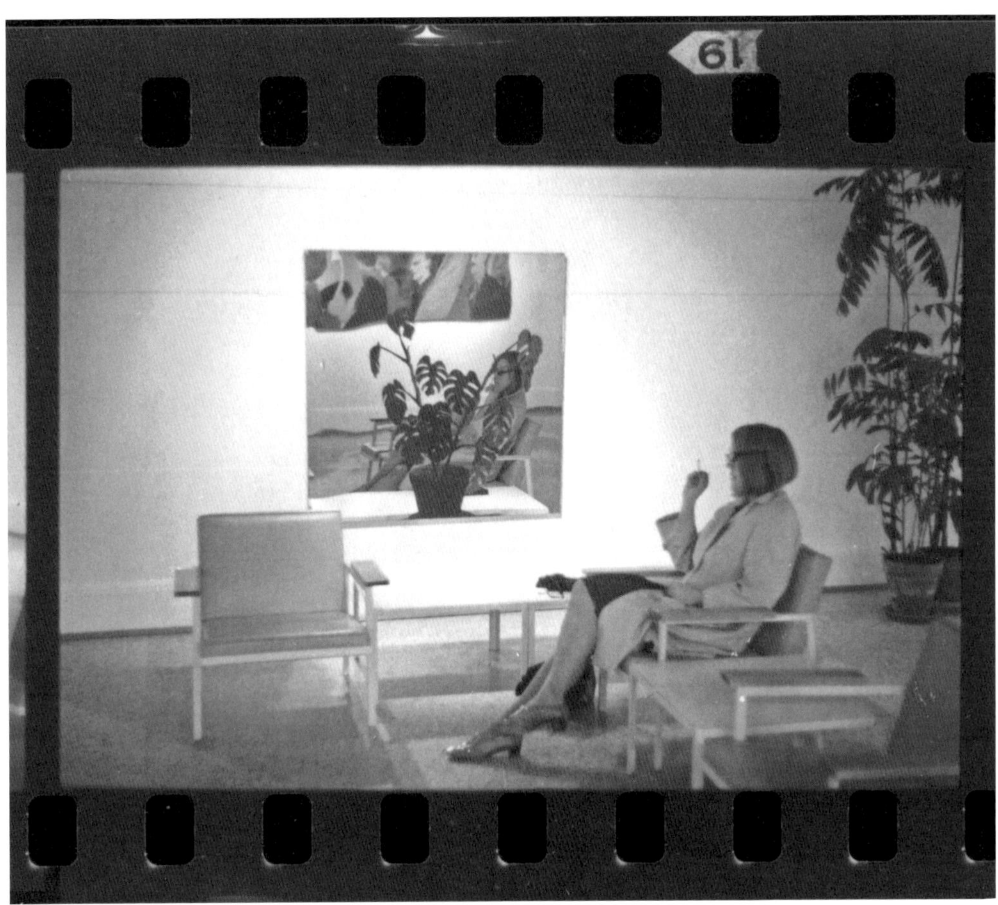

FIG. 57. Enhanced negative, exhibition photography, *Michelangelo Pistoletto: A Reflected World,* Walker Art Center, Minneapolis, April 8–May 4, 1966. Walker Art Center Archives, Minneapolis.

Vietnam, are seen in attitudes of relative passivity or relaxation."[55] In *ARTnews,* American poet and art critic John Ashbery found Pistoletto's political subjects to have a "detached," even "amused" demeanor; referring to *No to the Tram Fare Increase,* he added: "It is true that in this particular one they are merely protesting a rise in trolley fares, so their apathy is perhaps pardonable."[56] Whereas Ashbery found apathy in Pistoletto's protestors if by way of assumption (the hike in public transit fares in Italy was no small matter), Simon for *Art International* flatly rejected the series as "patently ludicrous, plainly without either meaning or focus." Citing the outdoor urban setting of the protest pictures' events as an illogical disruption of the interior environment and even domestic ambient of the exhibition space (and therefore the space also reflected in the mirror paintings), Simon called them "particularly destructive of what one assumed was the desired intent."[57] By contrast, Robert Murdock, in his catalog essay for Pistoletto's solo show in 1969 at the Albright-Knox Gallery in Buffalo, reconciled the Rallies' apparent engagement of "coolness" and "social commentary" by highlighting the works' documentarian formal qualities, likening them to "wirephotos" or "news media images" that have a "sense of instantaneous, disinterested reportage." Murdock assigned the problem to a matter of genre: "Social commentary has never been one of Pistoletto's objectives, but a group of works executed in 1965 might suggest a cool form of that genre."[58]

Study of exhibition photography in the Walker's archives reveals that the third gallery in the exhibition also included two small mirror paintings of plants: *Filodendro* (Philodendron, 1965) staged in a far blind corner of the L-shaped gallery in a seating area, where the installation created the illusion that the potted philodendron in the mirror painting was a real potted plant, arranged on the surface of the actual table pushed up against the wall; and *Vaso rosso* (Red Pot, exhibited as *Plant in a Red Pot*), on a small wall flanking the room's entryway.[59] An exhibition photograph captures a woman lounging in a chair in the gallery, smoking a cigarette. Visitors made themselves at home with the domestic objects in Pistoletto's paintings, even as his political subjects were also reflected in them (fig. 57).

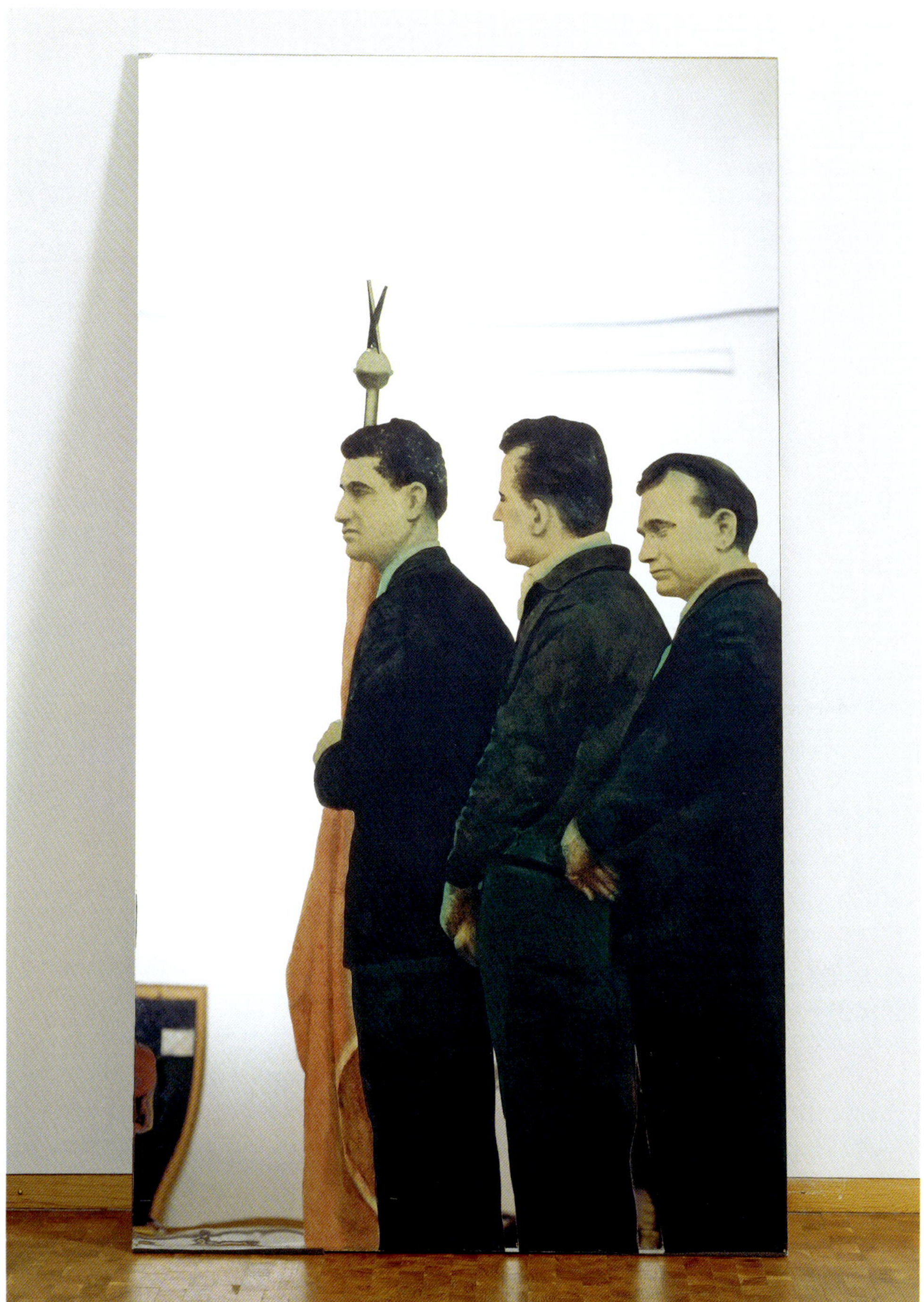

FIG. 58. Michelangelo Pistoletto, *Comizio II* (Rally II), 1965. Oil and graphite on tissue paper on stainless steel, 84½ × 47¼ in. (215 × 120 cm). Museum Ludwig, Cologne.

As in the treatment of *No to the Tram Fare Increase* on the catalog cover, marching figures were similarly reworked in *Comizio II* (Rally II) (fig. 58). Compare the artwork to the exhibition sign on which it was reproduced, prominently displayed on the building exterior at the main entrance (fig. 59).[60] The image is cropped precisely below the flag's star-shaped finial, thereby removing the communist symbol that Pistoletto preserves in the mirror painting. Many other, ostensibly less controversial works in the exhibition did not feature political imagery: a generous twenty-six of the thirty-three displayed. The Walker's decision to select images for the catalog cover and title signage from the works that did include leftist iconography (and potentially anti-American references) seems even more pointed—especially given that Pistoletto did provide a political mirror painting for the cover.

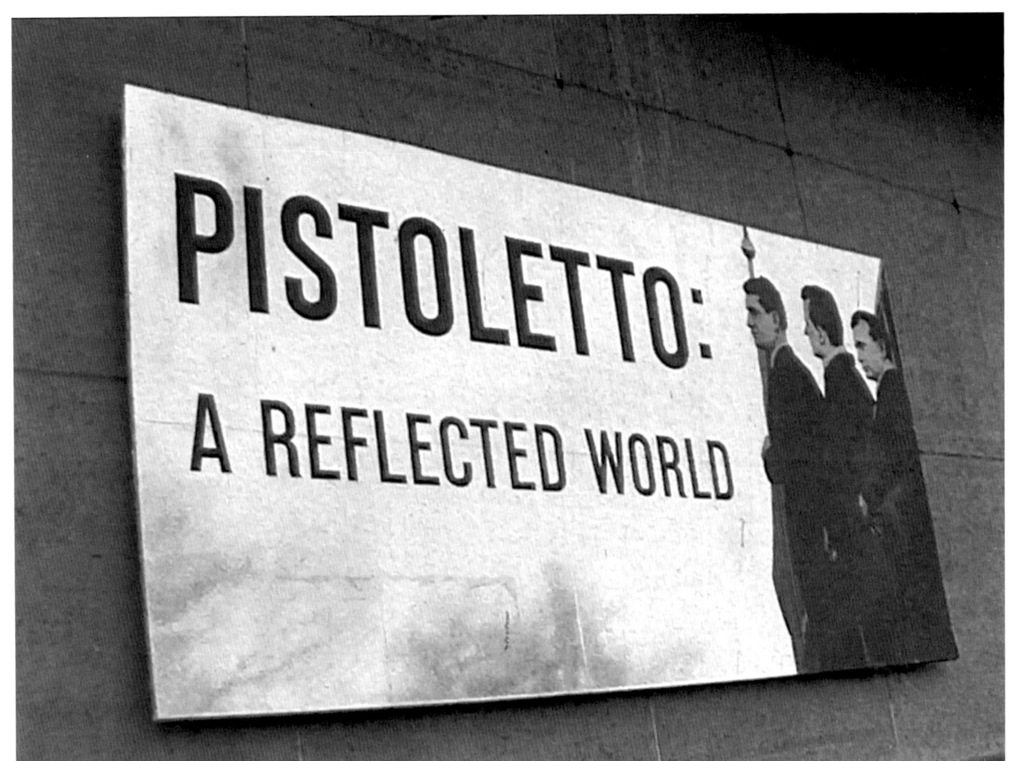

FIG. 59. Exterior exhibition sign, *Michelangelo Pistoletto: A Reflected World,* Walker Art Center, Minneapolis, April 8–May 4, 1966. Excerpted from WCOT-TV, CBS Minneapolis, news report. Walker Art Center Archives, Minneapolis.

POLITICS IN MID-1960S ITALY

In contrast to the neutralized figures on the exhibition signage, contextualization of these works in mid-1960s northern Italy reveals that the Rallies' figures and events are anything but relaxed, passive, and ordinary in subject matter or artistic procedure. Protracted conflicts between metalworkers' trade unions and management at Turin's Fiat, Michelin, and Lancia factories erupted in the largest and most violent riots in city and national history in Piazza Statuto in 1962.[61] By 1963, we recall, the economic miracle was over, precipitated by mounting inflation, capital flight, and an overextended credit system, among other problems.[62] The year 1964 was marked by turmoil within the center-left government and the Italian left. After forming a coalition with the moderate Christian Democrats led by Aldo Moro, the Italian Socialist Party fractured in January 1964. This resulted in the emergence of the left-of-PCI Italian Socialist Party of Proletarian Unity (PSIUP), led by Raniero Panzieri in Turin, which catalyzed the Italian New Left and workers' movement of operaismo.[63] Aldo Moro briefly resigned on June 26, 1964, amid unabated economic decline, increased unemployment, and a reemergence of the coalition a month later.[64] Palmiro Togliatti, leader of the PCI, died on August 21, 1964. The crisis of 1964 set the stage for still more problems in 1965, when public services and workers' rights emerged as two prominent issues. From late 1964 to early 1966, under the leadership of the PCI and PCI-dominated national trade union (Confederazione Generale Italiana del Lavoro, CGIL), mass protests and workers' strikes by industrial labor forces, transit employees, and commuters created major disruptions in city life, sometimes erupting in riots.[65] Conflicts in the Italian left led to additional partisan fracturing; with the formation of the center-left coalitions came conflicts in syndicalism and trade unionism.[66] The mid-1960s in Italy were not, then, as some have held, "characterized by conformity or absence of protest."[67]

The constitution of the Italian left had come under deep questioning when Pistoletto made the Rallies.[68] Pistoletto's many images of PCI members engaged contemporaneous ideas of the Italian left as vanguard and globally minded. From 1959 to 1979, the PCI positioned itself on the front lines of the Italian left; as membership cards stated, the party was the "political organization of the avant-garde of the working class." "In the spirit of the Resistance and of proletarian internationalism," they called for "freedom and valorization of the human character."[69] Pistoletto's figures, however, at times seem less resolute. The figures are often fragmented or cropped.

The contextual scene of the photograph is also replaced by the real scene of the space of display reflected by the steel panel. Perhaps this fragmentation was about an extension out into the world, of staging their own protest in various locales, of making the protests universal.

Within this context of popular unrest and economic uncertainty, debates over public services and workers' rights emerged as prominent issues. Urban population growth during the economic miracle led to policy measures to offset mounting deficits of public transit services. Ticket prices were raised for buses, trams, metros, and state-run trains (Ferrovie dello Stato, for example) and municipal operations (for example, ATAC and STEFER in Rome and ATM in Milan). The majority populace viewed the move as a direct attack on already low-earning urban (and suburban) working classes, the primary demographic affected by the proposed fare hikes. Exacerbating frustrations regarding the poor state of public services and a previous fare increase levied in November 1963, the proposal and eventual implementation of a second fare increase in April 1965 generated widespread agitation and heated conflict in cities nationwide.[70] This was especially the case in the so-called industrial triangle of Turin, Genoa, and Milan, home to large populations of factory laborers. Headlines from national newspapers including *L'Unità*, the official paper of the PCI, and *Corriere della Sera* point to the unrest caused by tram fare increases; illustrative of class tensions was one article from March 1965. It bore the headline "Il tram che mangia oro": "The tram that eats gold."[71]

The relation between the PCI and these unions during the 1960s was critical to the political power of the Italian left and workers' movement, since the PCI was a relatively weak parliamentary minority within the Italian government, then dominated by members of the moderate Christian Democratic Party.[72] The PCI's power came less from party unit presences in the factories, which had halved from 1950 to the mid-1960s, and more from union presence therein.[73] This relation between the PCI and unions, then, was such that workers' strikes organized by the socialist-communist union of the CGIL, such as the one depicted in Pistoletto's work, were synonymous with the (primarily communist) politics of the far Italian left. The strikes were exemplary of the far Italian left's shifting organizational emphasis from factory cell to unions, from workplace to broader social contexts in the 1950s to 1960s.[74]

Beyond these points, the artist's production of the demonstration- and rally-themed paintings were framed by two events that precipitated rampant anti-American sentiment in Italy and broader Europe, and a cataclysmic shift in cultural geopolitics of the 1960s.[75] First was the controversial Thirty-Second Venice Biennale of 1964 (see chapter 2), where Robert Rauschenberg's receipt of the international prize for painting incited public outrage against the award, perceived as a sign of American cultural imperialism. Second was the escalation of the Vietnam War, led by US deployment of combat troops to South Vietnam in February 1965. The American deployment incited Italian protests, primarily led by the Communist Party against the militarized, anticommunist, interventionist foreign policy on the part of the United States. The US invasion of Vietnam was followed shortly thereafter by its invasion of the Dominican Republic in April 1965 to defeat a leftist coup that had aimed to reinstate democratically elected national leadership overthrown shortly before. The Dominican invasion exacerbated leftist anti-American sentiment in Italy.[76] The Italian left organized a protest program, often at syndicalist labor union centers in major Italian cities, which condemned the United States as a new fascist power. Major demonstrations, rallies, and peace marches occurred throughout March, May, and November 1965.[77]

EDITORIAL AUTHORSHIP AND POLITICS OF THE IMAGE

Unlike the early mirror paintings, the Rallies were among the first works Pistoletto made using photographic source images he did not personally compose.[78] The selection of the figure from the full scene of the existing photograph (an image of a real as opposed to studio-constructed scene) inverts, or mirrors, the mirror paintings' completion of the pictorial scene of painting with the plenitude of the real world reflected in its surface. Before the production of the works from 1965, Pistoletto had carefully arranged the photographic subjects that appeared in the mirror paintings. Although he never personally took the photographs from which he traced his cutout figures (a task assigned to the artist's friend, photographer Paolo Bressano), Pistoletto meticulously controlled their production, as Gilman has shown, adjusting lighting and instructing his models to adopt certain poses.[79] The complex process, often confused in the literature on the artist, involved

Pistoletto collaging the highly polished surfaces with hand-painted, tissue-paper cutouts of life-size figures and the occasional object, which he traced in graphite from printed enlargements of Bressano's photographs of scenes Pistoletto meticulously staged in his studio.[80] After creating a template of the photographic image by hand—tracing outlines and fine details in pencil, which he also used for some initial shading—he blocked out any large, dark areas in black paint: the tissue paper sheet would be collaged onto the steel panel (in early works, with a boat varnish adhesive, soon replaced with white enamel paint), front side facing down, so that any sign of the subject's manual production (superficial indentations from the pencil, brushwork, visible facture) would be obscured by the seamless surface of the recto side of the sheet. If we are to regard the mirror paintings as "theatrical tableaux" with "directorial" authorship outlined above, as Gilman describes them, then the Rallies constitute a point of rupture in the artist's practice. That he had only ever made photomontages previously for works with political subjects—in his photomontages of 1962, discussed in chapter 1—underscores the political subject of the Rallies on the level of the artist's practice.

Pistoletto's selection of these subjects from existing images—specifically, works of street photography, a genre aligned with mass media and technologies of reproduction—seemingly contradicts the artist's practice as an example of his relinquishment of directorial control. Contrary to claims that the works resulted from Pistoletto directing Rinaldi to photograph political events in Turin, closer study of the images allows us to date and locate these images to May 1, Workers' Day, in the Piazza del Duomo in Milan, correcting existing misinformation about the works.[81] In source images for Pistoletto's *Vietnam* and *Orange Banner,* we see details of the Duomo and Galleria Vittorio Emanuele II, as well as banners announcing the PCI "Irma Bandiera" chapter of the Young Italian Communist Federation, or FGCI (Federazione Giovanile Comunista Italiana), of the Milanese industrial suburb Sesto San Giovanni (figs. 60, 61). This is an electoral rally, not, as has been stated, a rally for a particular political candidate.[82] By using photographs that he did not stage, by the spring of 1966, when nearly half of these works debuted, Pistoletto in his mirror paintings seems to have moved even closer to the models of decentered authorship, rote objectivity, and "cold literalism" aligned with American pop—or perhaps more with the turn to Arte Povera's anticapitalist authorship, now procedural and iconographic in kind.[83] Tellingly, after the Rallies, Pistoletto used imagery by others, in his mirror paintings or other works of art, in two capacities: either from Dada, using works by Jean Arp and a portrait of Duchamp (sitting on a sculpture by Constantin Brancusi) or from canonical histories of art (as in use of iconic images such as Jean-Auguste-Dominique Ingres's *Turkish Bath* and Vincent van Gogh's sunflowers in his serigraphed mirror-painting multiples). In so doing, he positioned the mirror paintings within the history of avant-gardism and the turn to life through antiauthoritarianism, the invention of the readymade, and mechanical reproducibility; or by drawing on the works of his artist father, most famously by using a sketch of Michelangelo as an infant.[84]

The source photograph of *No to the Tram Fare Increase* depicts a crowd of protestors in Milan's Piazza del Duomo. Their signs protest numerous topics: public transit, workers' rights, national politics, and international issues, all interrelated in the Italian context. Signs called for fair wages for factory labor, decried the failure of the Italian government (following the brief resignation of Prime Minister Aldo Moro in the summer of 1964), and protested the United States' presence in Vietnam. Comparison of the source image to the mirror painting reveals that Pistoletto retained only two of the eight signs that appear in Rinaldi's photograph of the scene, as well as the communist flag, the *bandiera rossa*, that cuts across the mirror painting and source photograph. Adopted by the Italian left in the early twentieth century and canonized in the famous PCI workers' song of the same title and Roman Resistance, which adopted the red flag as their moniker, the bandiera rossa in postwar Italy was most associated with the PCI, labor unions of their support, and red partisanship.[85] David Broder has attended to the use of resistance rhetoric in Italian politics since the postwar period. In his study of the Rome-based resistance group Bandiera Rossa during the German occupation, Broder argues that the conflicts between the PCI and MCd'I (Movimento Comunista d'Italia), which the PCI viewed as sectarian, led to the group's marginalization from histories of the resistance and Italian left after World War II until 1968, with the emergence of leftist extra-parliamentary movements. Pistoletto's works, then, also call to mind the fraught history of red partisanship and interleft conflicts in postfascist Italy during a period of redefinition of Italian communism in relation to ideas of national unity in the emergent republic and Cold War.[86]

In Pistoletto's work, the large swath of fabric announces the leftist politics of the image; swirling around a pole, swollen with gusts of wind, the flag appears to be on the precipice of unfurling across the entirety of the scene and rectangular steel panel of its support. Far from the "becalmed space" Friedman generally found in the mirror paintings in the exhibition, the space of *No to the Tram Fare Increase* is agitated, premonitory.[87] Although the anti-American charge of the Italian protest may have been seemingly defused through Pistoletto's omission of the anti-American protest sign, the artist's change in process for the Rallies embeds the resulting mirror paintings with procedural characteristics best aligned with contemporary American artistic practices, namely in pop art. Rather than think of Pistoletto's works, however, as American in kind, we might consider that *No to the Tram Fare Increase* stages the subject of its own protest through the means of its production.

The overtly political charge of the readymade image also brings up larger questions. The mechanical reproducibility of the work of art that came with the advent of mass printing and expansion of photographic technologies, as theorized by Walter Benjamin in response to the rise of these technologies and of fascism in the mid-1930s, was a watershed moment. The traditional ritual value of the unique work of art, its "aura," "withered" and "decayed" in the age of mechanical reproduction. The function of art also changed; situated in the real world and in the space of the popular, where the work

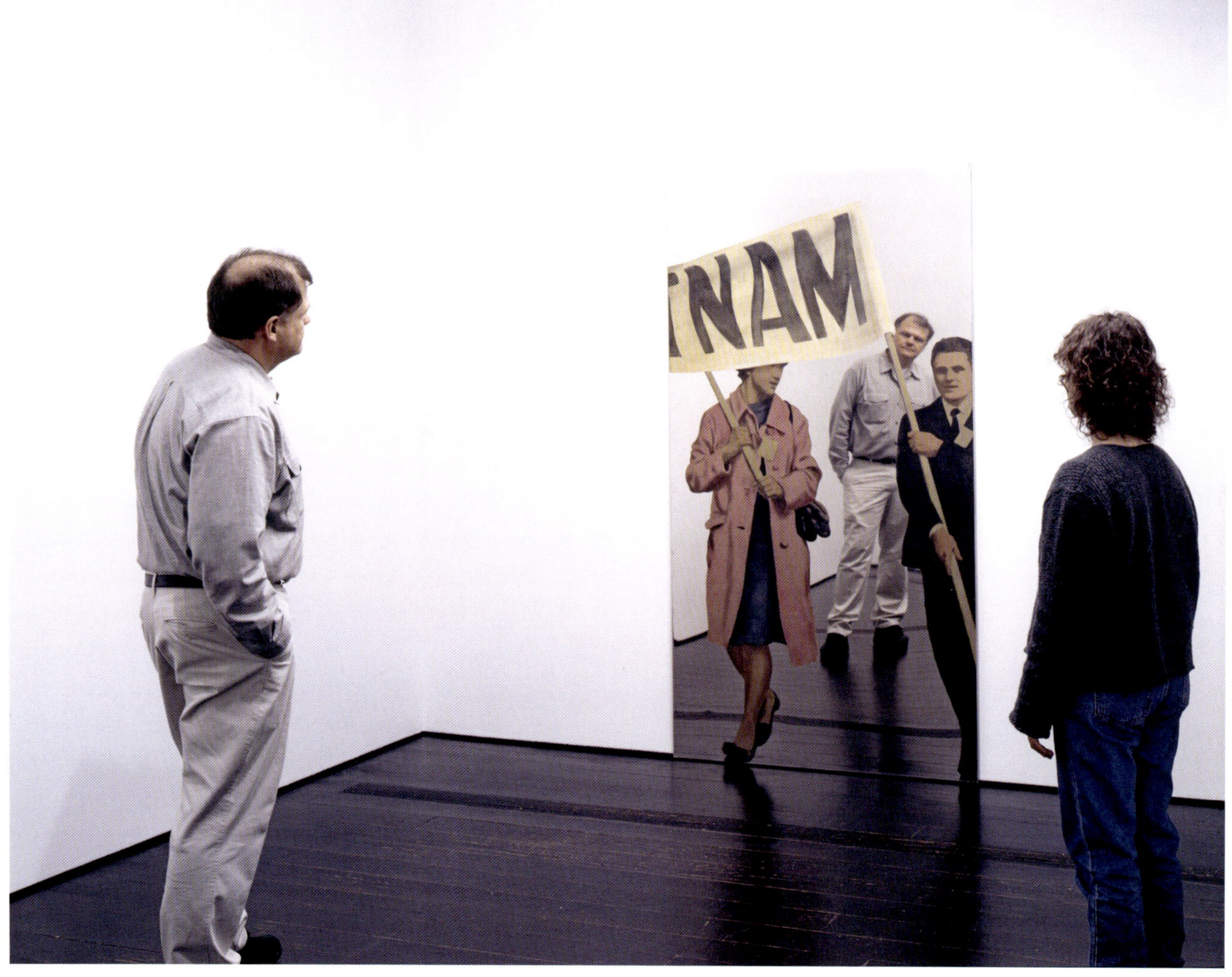

FIG. 60. Michelangelo Pistoletto, *Vietnam,* 1965. Graphite and oil on paper mounted on stainless steel, 86⅝ × 47¼ × ⅞ in. (220 × 120 × 2.2 cm). The Menil Collection, Houston. Photo by George Hixson.

of art was designed for reproducibility as opposed to "authenticity," art was now "based on another practice—politics."[88] Now available to the masses, who in turn rewarded conventional artistic products, the work of art could now be used to aestheticize politics, as in fascism, ultimately culminating in war.[89] Benjamin's deep questioning of the status and function of the work of art and the social stakes of these changes—for humanity, human perception, and society—was attuned to the rise of fascism and the visual propaganda that supported it, and to the growing power of capitalism and its potential triumph over Marxism. Pistoletto's images were made a generation later, after the war but amid new concerns about the renewed rise of fascism. The many connections of the Rallies to antifascist histories (in subject matter, iconography, and theoretical concerns) get to the heart of Marxist concerns regarding art, politics, and society in the 1960s—and even still today—without necessarily offering a neat resolution. Could the work of art still carry ameliorative, socially transformative power for humanity? Was a socialist humanism, facilitated by art, even possible?

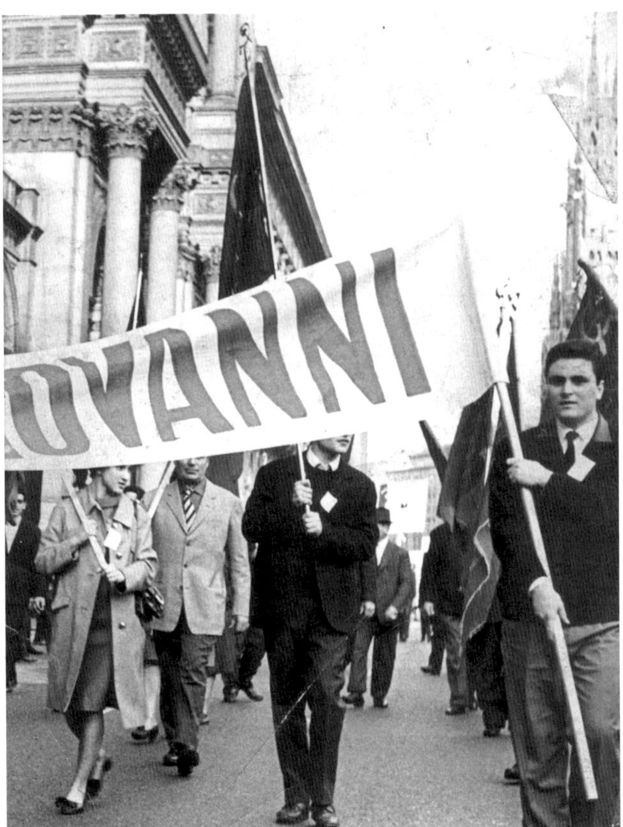

FIG. 61. Renato Rinaldi, source image for *Vietnam*, Milan, 1965. Archivio Pistoletto, Biella.

Examination of these works' production relative to the artist's professional timeline supports this hypothesis regarding the politics of these images. The debut of any work from the series came with the exhibition of *Corteo* (Demonstration, the smaller of two works by this title) in July 1965, at the Fifth Biennial of International European Contemporary Art in San Marino. With the exception of *No to the Tram Fare Increase*, exhibited under its original Italian title (likely because of its appearance in the work of art), all works in the Walker show were exhibited under English titles.[90] Originally intended for the artist's first solo exhibition at an American gallery, to be held in early 1966 at Leo Castelli's prominent outpost of contemporary American art in New York, the works were shipped directly to the Walker from Castelli's gallery when the Castelli show was canceled (see chapter 2). This is an important point: not only were the majority of these works made concurrently with the artist's expanded exhibition opportunities in the United States, but their production coincided with the moment in which Pistoletto began working with a commercial venue known for its prestigious stable of American pop artists.[91] The implication of this context in the 1960s is that the leftist political gambit of the artist was also potentially an anti-American one—not necessarily an expression of explicit anti-American sentiment but a challenge to the ideas of fascism, imperialism, and capitalism then associated with the nation.

Although we might attribute this depoliticization and de-Italianization of Pistoletto's mirror paintings to the Cold War cultural climate of their reception in the transatlantic artistic context of the 1960s, the endurance of this interpretive model today, more than a quarter century after the end of the conflict, is more puzzling. Indeed, in the sixty years since their exhibition at the Walker, Pistoletto's political mirror paintings have been little shown and discussed. They have yet to be the object of rigorous art historical research and have been understudied in the discourses on Pistoletto, postwar Italian art, and postwar art history more broadly—an especially noteworthy absence, given the high volume of literature on the mirror paintings alone. Though some have reappeared in the past ten years in exhibitions of the artist's work, the terms of the primary reception of these works have remained unquestioned.[92] What few mentions they have received in the literature on Pistoletto either assert a lack of ideological viewpoint, arguing that they should be read as belonging to any context (historic or cultural), or continue to uphold Friedman's original argument that these works are strictly apolitical. Others have described them in overly generic terms, as a "series of parade photographs," a problem that seems to have come from their mistranslated titles in English venues.[93] It is not surprising that many have asserted the works' lack of ideological viewpoint, given Pistoletto's own assertion that they "don't have any dramatic function."[94] In one of my interviews with the artist, Pistoletto reflected: "[Peter Seitz] had asked me, simply, what my idea was of the works with the political subjects. And I answered that they didn't have any dramatic function; on the contrary . . . I don't want drama. I want to get out of the drama; rather, the political phenomenon, which is a reality that exists, just as I exist, enters into a temporal dimension that completely changes the drama of the moment. One finds themselves in another situation."[95] Closer analysis of what the works themselves do, as I have outlined above, and of Pistoletto's own interaction with them, however, suggests a more complex narrative.

Pistoletto's mirror paintings of union and workers' strikes, mass protests, and political rallies are leftist, anticapitalist images, many of which were debuted for an American audience. Their politicized reception at the Walker, as I have laid out, precipitated long-term effects of Cold War culture on the global reception of Pistoletto's work and contemporary Italian art in the 1960s. As part of his preparation for the exhibition, Friedman sent Pistoletto a list of questions about his work. One addressed the paintings' subjects outright:

> FRIEDMAN: Some critics might consider that your work represents the social commentary of the 1960s—that is, the "protest paintings" cannot really be considered as detached as are the images of anonymous observers. Can you comment on this?
>
> PISTOLETTO*:* In my most recent paintings I want to show that even the most diverse meanings can live in this demystified dimension; violent or peaceful, they exist with us.
>
> He who makes a protest painting limits his vision to reality [*al fatto*]. I can choose a subject of political protest as a real occurrence in life, precisely to put it in a condition that goes beyond that.[96]

Whereas Friedman interpreted Pistoletto's response as a refutation of the series' political charge, what Pistoletto says is that the Rallies exceed their subjects' initial conditions—that is, as participants in a real event in the real world. Such a view functions as a safeguard against the ascription of Pistoletto's work in the Italian context to neorealism, to which his works have often been compared. But it also hints at some of the formal tactics he used within the series, such as the circulation of the figures across multiple works. Within the context of the artist's remarks, it is this circulation—specifically from those works whose political contexts remain intact to those in which the political context is withdrawn—that gains further valence.

By using photography as his source material, Pistoletto also pushed against the history of figurative representation or, perhaps, allowed it to function in an international context in the guise of the cold "objectivity" of American pop. The Rallies were not unaltered, minimally changed, or "straightforward" selections from source photographs. Figures were selected from a set of fourteen potential source images retained in the artist's archive, seven of which Pistoletto used; one image alone was used for four of the Rallies.[97]

A rare photograph from 1966 sheds further light on Pistoletto's working process in the creation of the Rallies (fig. 62). It is one of three photographs in existence in which we can see the printed enlargements of Rinaldi's photographs that Pistoletto worked with, if not always used, in the series. The scene captures the artist seated on a chair in his studio, surrounded by his works. One of the Rallies hangs on the wall behind him, juxtaposed with one of the enlargements of Rinaldi's source photographs. The enlargement is cropped around the torso of a male figure holding a flagpole, its flag mostly out of view. The enlargement wasn't the source photograph for the finished work that hangs on the wall, nor was it a figure who was ultimately ever used in the series.[98] A second mirror painting—featuring potted plants on a tabletop—is propped up against the wall; its top edge leans against the bottom edge of the paper enlargement. Another mirror painting still, at lower left, shows a reclining female figure. The photograph captures Pistoletto as a subject in the political scene and as one at home, or in the studio, perhaps, among his plants. In the composition, he is also a mirror figure to the man printed on the enlargement.

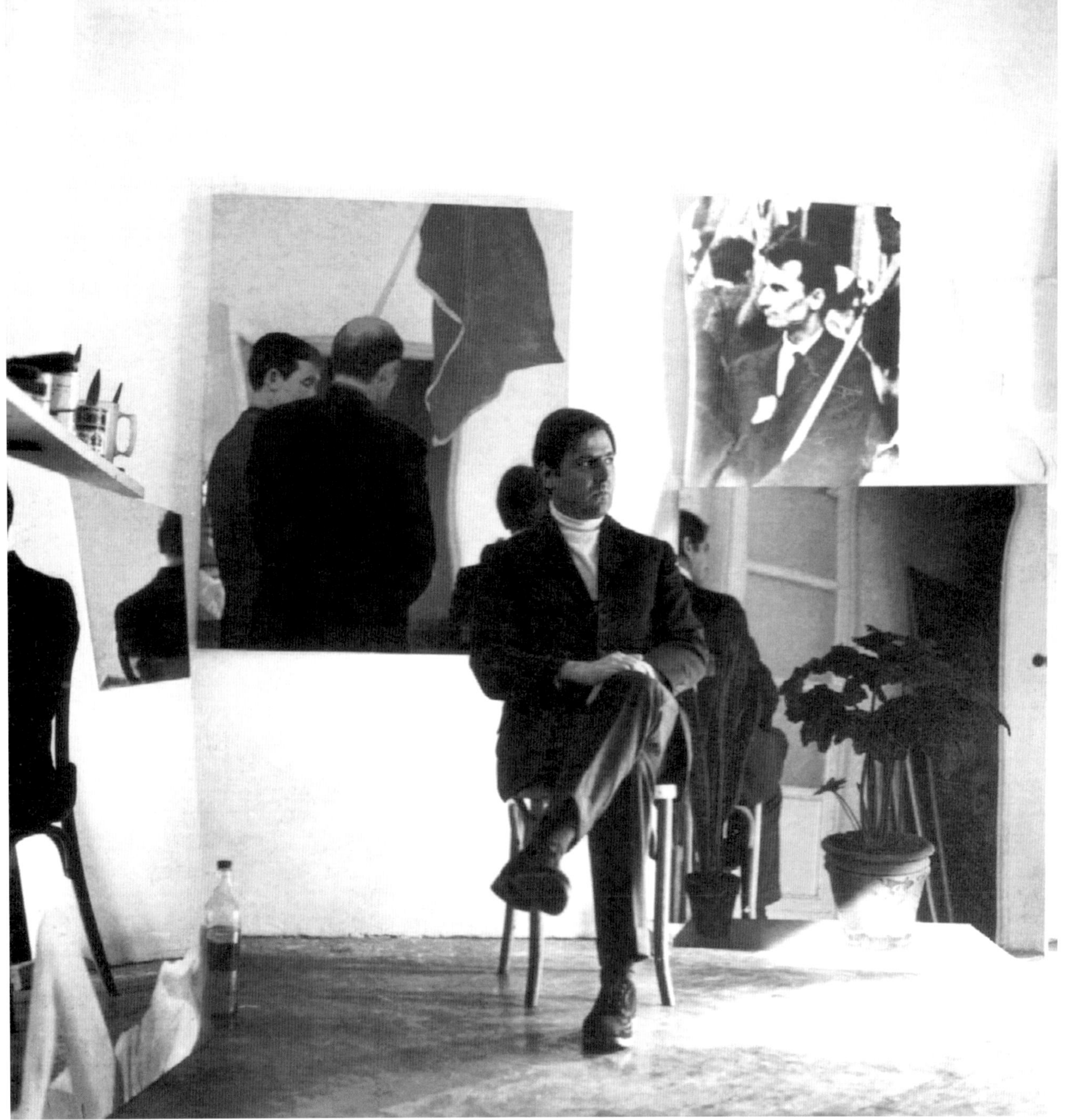

FIG. 62. Photograph of Michelangelo Pistoletto in his studio, Turin, 1966. Archivio Pistoletto, Biella.

When this process of selection (and reselection) is considered in relation to the typical process used for the mirror paintings, we find other steps that distinguish the Rallies from the broader body of work to which they belong. Pistoletto selected figures, flags, and signs, typically from the same source photograph for each work, and rendered them equivalent in scale. This is an important change enacted by the artist's treatment of figures in the source image. The result is that figures appear to march or stand in a more orderly and visually legible fashion; the depth and visual plenitude of the source photograph is removed, which Robert Lumley calls a "reduc[tion of] the sheer quantity of photographic information."[99] What Pistoletto constructs, through his arrangement and editing of selected figures, is also a visual and symbolic equivalency, what me might call an antihieratic scale: previously staggered figures are often selected and repositioned to occupy the same imaginary ground line. In the horizontal format, figures are often cropped at the waist or chest. Our view is as if

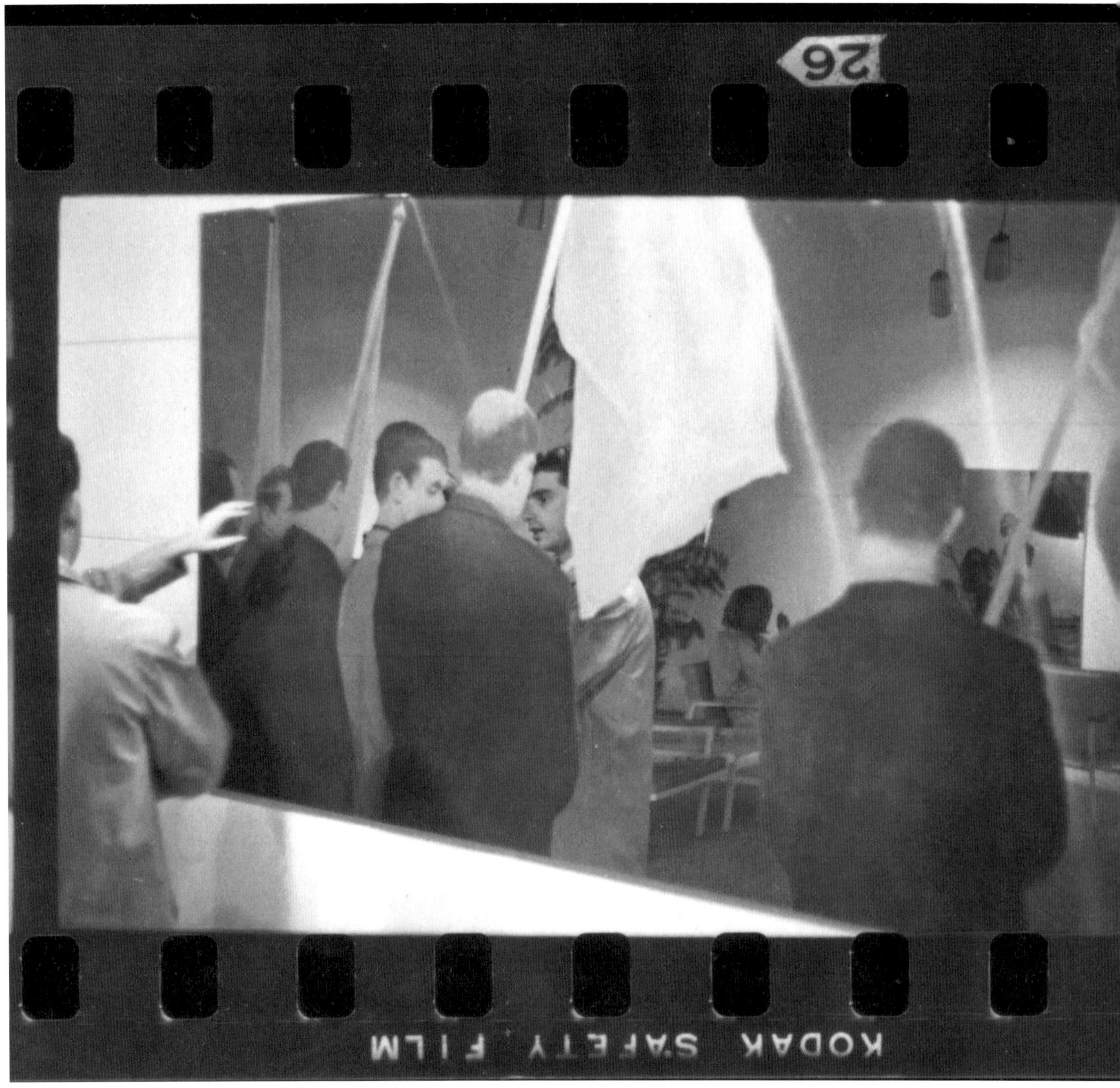

FIG. 63. Visitors look at Pistoletto's *Comizio I* (Rally I, 1965), in *Michelangelo Pistoletto: A Reflected World*, Walker Art Center, Minneapolis, April 8–May 4, 1966. Enhanced negatives, exhibition photography. Walker Art Center Archives, Minneapolis. Collection unknown.

we were peering over the shoulders of others around us, as if we ourselves are in the crowd. Exhibition photographs of visitors at the Walker Art Center demonstrate the interaction and closeness of viewing they invite (fig. 63). Although this antihieratic treatment facilitates the mirror paintings' capacity to position real space (reflected) as perspectival space (pictorial)—diminished scale would be less successful here—it also fosters an atmosphere of socialist humanist equivalency: we are all important, one as much as the other.

Undergirding the political charge of these images are the historical conventions of figuration they engage. Drawing upon histories of realist painting, they positioned the reworking of figuration, specifically as a conceptual and political conceit, as their critical linchpin. More specifically, Pistoletto's

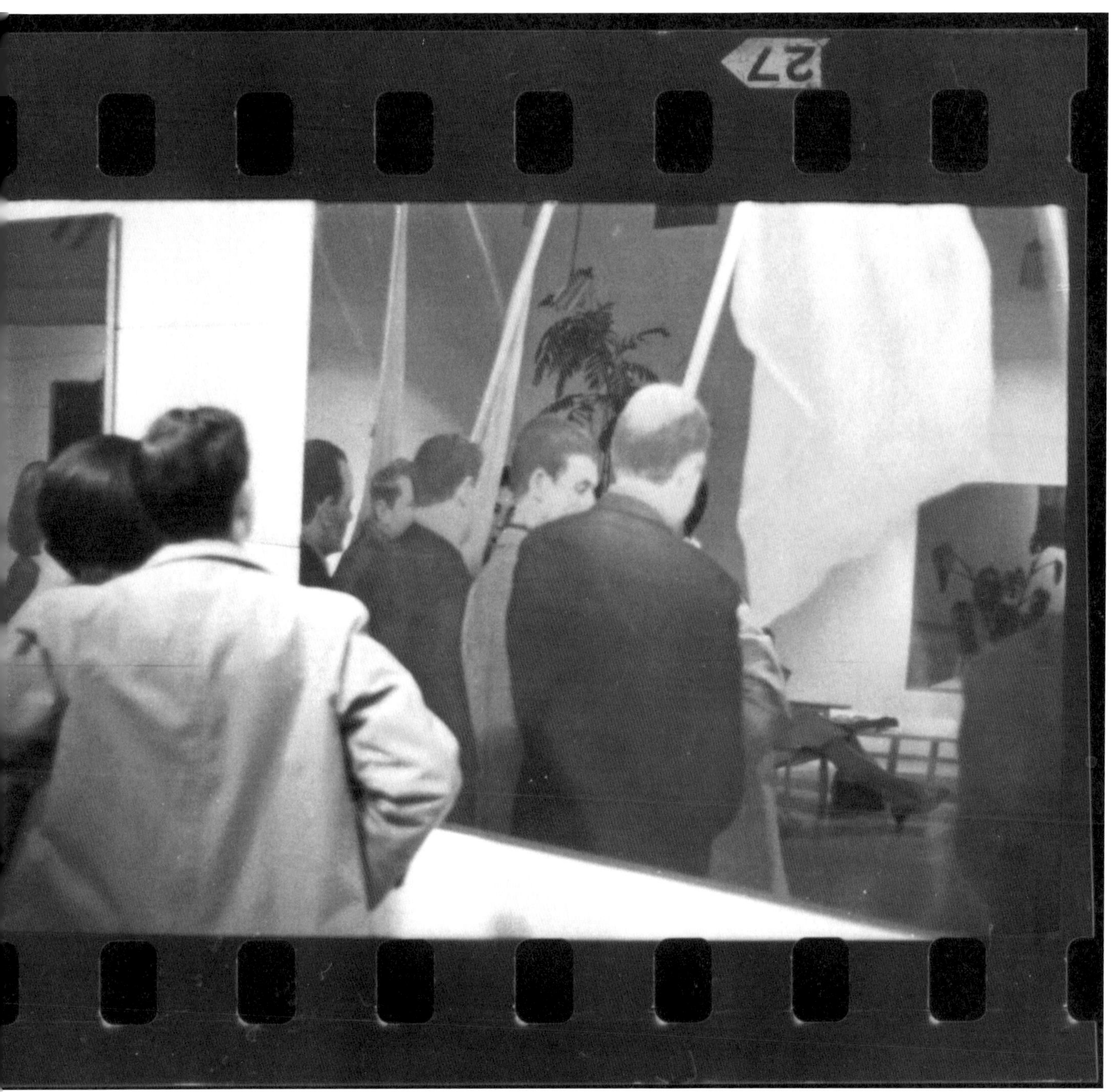

Rallies reflect a nuanced engagement with the figurative conventions and painterly strategies of socialist realist paintings, dating to the Italian Risorgimento and immediate postwar periods. Images of workers have featured prominently within histories of artistic realism; in Italian art, images of laborers were a cornerstone of the mid- to late nineteenth-century realism of the Macchiaioli (1855–1900). Images such as *No to the Tram Fare Increase* echo iconic works within Italian modernist realism, such as Telemaco Signorini's *L'Alzaia* (Towrope, 1864; fig. 64) and Giuseppe Pellizza da Volpedo's *Il quarto stato* (The Fourth Estate, 1899–1901; see fig. 30). The horizontal line of figures, bifurcated pictorial field, compositional cropping of bodies, hand-painted, predominantly ruddy coloring, and dimensions that emphasize the horizontality of the figural group

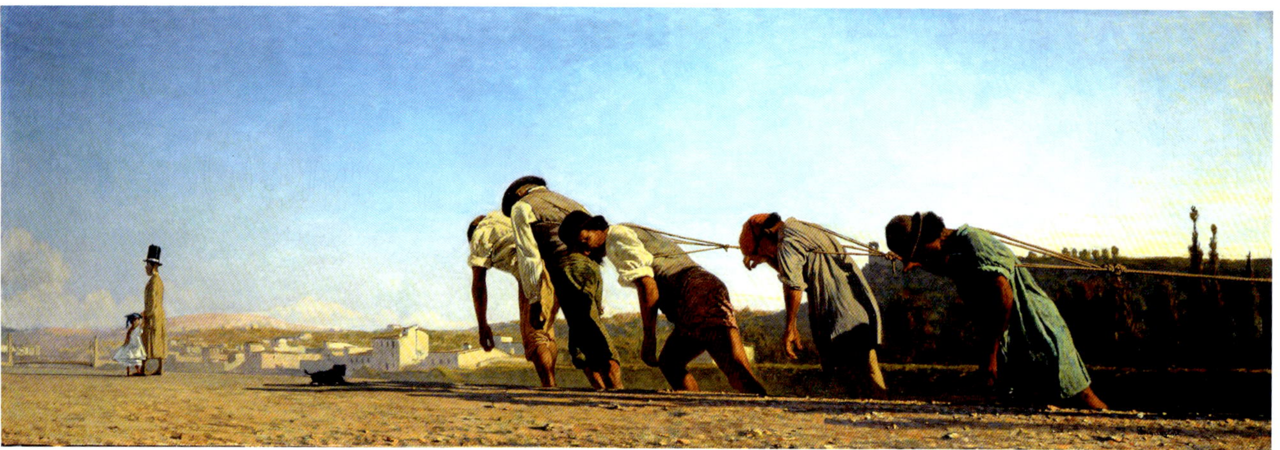

FIG. 64. Telemaco Signorini, *L'Alzaia* (Towrope), 1864. Oil on canvas, 21¼ × 68 in. (54 × 173.2 cm). Private collection.

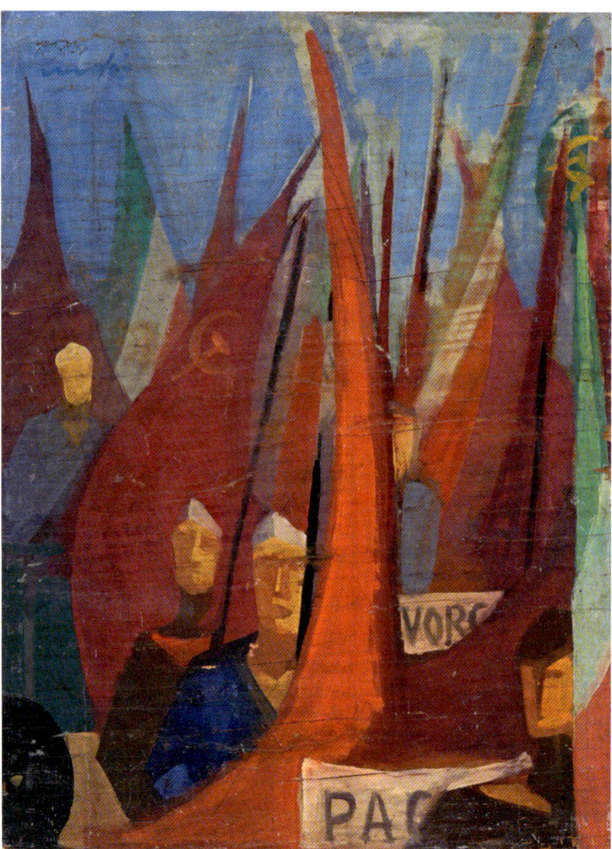

FIG. 65. Mario Mafai, *Il corteo con bandiere* (Demonstration with Flags), 1950. Oil on wood, 25⅝ × 19¾ in. (67.5 × 50 cm). Private collection.

evoke the unity and potential revolutionary power of the working masses telegraphed by these precedents in Italian realist painting. A line of laboring boatmen dominates the foreground of the composition in Signorini's painting. It announces a "more ideologically marked" shift by the Macchiaiolo toward socialism, beyond the Mazzinian liberalism of the Risorgimento; with figures associated with the aristocracy in the periphery of the image, the line of laborers "seem[s] to prefigure," as scholar Marina Camboni has written, "the historical moment forward in which the working classes will conquer the central stage."[100] The iconography of Pistoletto's composition—red flags, marching figures, and figures in single file or bands—also has immediate precedents in Italian socialist realism of the post–World War II period. In the late 1940s and 1950s, and for some into the 1960s and 1970s, Renato Guttuso, Mario Mafai, and Giulio Turcato, among others, produced works featuring imagery of communist rallies, partisan commemorations, and other political events such as those found in Pistoletto's series (fig. 65). As Adrian Duran has demonstrated, these artists—partisans and members of the communist artists' group the Fronte Nuovo delle Arti (New Front of the Arts)—responded to the PCI's postwar policy of artistic realism and mandate to use the arts as a political platform by creating scenes of mass resistance, protest, and partisan pride.[101]

Existing comparisons of Pistoletto's Rallies to socially charged works of Italian realist painting have underscored differences in formal qualities. In one such comparison, Robert Lumley has referred to the plenitude of Guttuso's crowds as "an effect of massing, of which the individual is a part." Unlike the crowded protest and rally scenes depicted by Guttuso, Mafai, and Turcato, in Pistoletto's case the pictorial plenitude is supplied by us, by the space of display, by the world.[102] The effect creates dialogical invitation across space and time and, most important, from representational space to real space. The encounter between reflection and mirror subject provided by Pistoletto is much discussed. Jean Dypréau called the mirror painting "a place of perpetual and infinite confrontations."[103] Henry Martin described this effect as a "dramatic encounter between art and life" in the mirror paintings; within the encounter of art and life they offer us, he wrote, is "the germ of a suggestion as to what to do with both of them."[104]

In the context of 1960s Italian art, the Rallies resonate with other bodies of work, such as Franco Angeli's early 1960s partisan-themed works and later rally images and Mario Schifano's late 1960s *Compagni* (Comrades) series. Angeli and Schifano belonged to the Rome-based Scuola di Piazza del Popolo, known for their "reportage" and as part of a broad strain of neo-avant-garde figuration referred to as *figurazione novissima,* or newest figuration.[105] Despite precedents in each artist's practice, Angeli's and Schifano's overtly political works have been largely framed as responses to 1968. This historical categorization has largely divided political engagement (or *impegno*) in postwar Italian art and subjectivity into two fields (realism and pop); two historical moments (the mid-late 1950s through early 1960s, dominated by leftist debates on what counted as real artistic liberty, and the late 1960s); and two subject types (*apocalittici e integrati,* or apocalyptic and complicit subjects, to borrow Umberto Eco's terminology).[106] Defying such neat categorizations, the Rallies instead compel us to revisit these divisions.

As a forerunner to art of 1968, the Rallies might be aligned with the genre James Meyer has called "the modern vocabulary of revolutionary depiction."[107] Meyer's reading of the "impatient temporality" in the work of West German filmmaker Gerd Conradt's *Die Rote Fahne* (The Red Flag) from 1968 helps us to see some of the peculiarities of Pistoletto's series. What was labeled "coolness" by some may have been a methodological patience in depiction and procedure.[108] Standing figures populate many works in the series.[109] These subjects are not "stilled contemplative forms," "mute specters," or figures of "silent meditation" (the last referring specifically to the figures in the Rallies), as critics and scholars have called Pistoletto's figures.[110] Might these subjects instead configure revolutionary depiction as patient testimony? They articulate protest through figural presence—another vocabulary of revolutionary strategies and depiction recently under revitalization in Italy with the Sardine movement against Italy's far right.

Attention to Pistoletto's work of the mid-1960s, typically left out of these narratives, not only complicates histories of Pistoletto's practice but those of early Arte Povera. Although Pistoletto engaged with current events in Italy as a "political phenomenon" and "reality in which he exist[ed]," his incorporation of these figures into the mirror paintings opened up the specificity of the events in which these figures participated to other situations and scenarios, allowing for expanded protests, rallies, and demonstrations in the politicized cultural transatlantic context of the early Cold War.[111] The result was a diversification, extension, and amplification (spatial, temporal, and semiotic), of the actions the artist fixed on the surfaces of the works.

In 1966, Maurizio Fagiolo dell'Arco referred to the politically themed mirror paintings' "enriched iconography." For him, the works demonstrated a "synthesis of politics" understood by Pistoletto to include "activity and passivity." Fagiolo dell'Arco argued that the series marked a change in Turin's social milieu, away from the social anxiety of the 1920s and early 1930s associated with the Turin of Piero Gobetti, the Italian socialist journalist and antifascist activist assassinated in 1926 by Mussolini's regime: "In a series of recent paintings, man enters in relation, and demonstrations and rallies are born: New 'materialist' Pistoletto is attentive (like the 'novissimo' [Antonio] Porta) to 'human relationships': And yet there is something since the social anxiety of the Turin of [Piero] Gobetti: these characters march, who knows toward what, with a tired and absorbed air, become syntheses of politics intended (says Pistoletto) as 'activity and passivity': even political *vis* can be alienated."[112] What Fagiolo dell'Arco gets to is an inverse relation between outward-looking phenomenology in Pistoletto's works and the enervation of political vigor and socialist activism in 1960s Turin. (Henry Martin would make a similar point in 1967: "His vision is the vision of a world without anguish.")[113] Although these works seem to articulate that the alienated "tired and absorbed air" of the 1960s has subsumed even political force and strength (invoked by the Latin *vis*), Fagiolo dell'Arco also left open the possibility that these works *do* something: they incite demonstrations and rallies. The figures are relational agents of neo-Marxist humanism. Henry Martin would perhaps best get to this point in the mid-1970s, when he wrote: "These works present no invitation to escape beyond the looking glass, but rather a challenge to live and to construct a life in front of it." [114]

In an article for *Konstrevy* from 1965 subsequently published in English in the March 1967 issue of *Métro,* Michael Sonnabend also suggested there may be something Italian or even Turinese about these images. Qualifying the suggestion as a topic for another article, he offered a Catholic reading of Pistoletto's new "ceremonial march[es]," whose ritual drive seems to be descending, for Sonnabend, into an end of criticality: "In these new processional compositions, clear volumes swell and expand in a grave, liturgical rhythm." [115] For Sonnabend, viewing these works amounted to walking through "the artist's mind as we walk into a Bernini chapel or a 'happening' of George Segal's sculpture; or as we move through the vast air-ocean of Rauschenberg's space." In Sonnabend's psychospatial reading of the Rallies, Pistoletto's mind is actually baroque, Catholic and Italian, and then, strikingly, positioned as a comparandum for postwar American art's universal engagement. Indeed, "Like the present generation of Americans from Pollock, Kline and Rothko through Rauschenberg, Rosenquist and Segal, [Pistoletto] senses the universe and life as a total painting." The "passive, expectant masses" articulated by the silhouettes on the steel panels await viewers to be reflected in the scenes, where we become "tourists, visiting the strange country of our own lives." For Sonnabend, the effect was, as for Fagiolo dell'Arco, one of enervation—not of Italian politics but of existentialist ennui and tourist let-down: "But instead of taking part in the event itself as its active pole, waiting and watching ourselves being watched, we are simply there. We fill the piazza as the light fills it and we are a witness to what is happening as detached from his figures as these remain aloof from us." We are, Sonnabend wrote, "immobilized by the formal unity of the rhythmic masses," and our "story content is exhausted at a depth where only plastic meaning remains." [116] Invoking Baudelaire, Sonnabend sees the viewer's fleeting image in front of the Rallies and the vernacular of our lives, "immobilized" and rendered "plastic"—modernity's death knell.

Within the primary literature on Pistoletto, it was ironically Martin, the American art critic living in Italy, who came closest to addressing the cultural politics of these works in relation to this formal quality. A sometime collaborator of Pistoletto's in his experimental theater collective and commune the Zoo (1968–70), Martin had an intimate knowledge of the artist's practice and involvement with international neo-avant-gardes operating in Italy, which uniquely positioned him within the context of art criticism in the late 1960s. In an essay written for the catalog of Pistoletto's exhibition in spring 1969 at Rotterdam's Museum Boijmans Van Beuningen, Martin outlined the subjects featured in the mirror paintings, listing (mistakenly) a protest at an American embassy among them. The critic's distinctive view of the commonality among these works not as ordinary but "unstable" is most compelling: "Pistoletto has taken to using pictures of situations that are unstable, and their stability on the painting has a sense of paradox." [117] For Martin, the common denominator of Pistoletto's mirror subjects was less the banality of the everyday than the *instability* thereof.

In this sense, the Rallies remain connected to figural analogies in the history of painting while opening to the present (and to us) through substitution (and dissimulation) of the canvas ground with reflective panels. As one critic argued in the late 1970s, the mirror paintings captured "the idea of pictorial representation interpenetrated with real phenomenal objectivity." [118] Pistoletto's figures were clearly images, but they visually registered as closer to real figures, insofar as they share the condition of inhabiting a dynamic world. This is a point that Germano Celant captured as well. In a lesser-known passage on Pistoletto's mirror paintings, in 1968, Celant offered: "Reality enters into the mirror and is the first phase for a global relationship between art and life." [119] Although Pistoletto's works engaged with current events in Italy as a "political phenomenon" and "reality in which he exist[ed]," his incorporation of these figures into the mirror paintings opened the specificity of the events in which these figures participated. They opened to other situations and scenarios but were also exemplars of the "global relationship" that Celant ascribed to Arte Povera. They allowed for expanded protests, rallies, and demonstrations in the politicized cultural transatlantic context of the early Cold War and beyond.[120] Might they not have been aligned with broader transnational revolutions in the 1960s? What kind of world was Pistoletto making (or remaking) with these works?

FIGURES OF PROTEST

An examination of the series reveals the complexity of the works' politics and imbrication with the conventions of portraiture. Returning to *Workers* from 1965, we find a closely cropped, portrait-style image of a young woman (see fig. 55). Rather than having her face the camera straight-on or in three-quarters view, or having her stand in profile view, Pistoletto has inverted the logic of the portrait convention; she is turned away from us in profil perdu. Notably, this is a format—a subject compositionally framed and depicted in dimensions common to portraiture but ultimately turned away from us—used previously only in his portrait mirror painting of Roy Lichtenstein's mother.[121] Her features are out of view, through her body remains perpendicular to the viewer. The subject appears to be purposely turning her head away from us. She is framed at left by the dark sloping of a shirtsleeve, belonging to an otherwise out-of-view figure, and at right by a paper sign board mounted on a wooden post, held above her by someone outside the image field. Her dark eyeglasses, bobbed hair, and leather jacket identify her as the same woman in *No to the Tram Fare Increase.* Although some details have been changed—she faces left instead of right—she is decidedly the same figure, situated in the same scene, positioned between the same dark jacket and sign. Whereas the figure carrying the sign in this case remains out of view, by contrast here we can see the text, if partially, posted on his placard. In faded block lettering, it reads "OPERAI" (Workers), followed by a partial letter, after which point the text is cut off by the image frame.

In Italian, *operai*—as opposed to *lavoratori* (workers in any field) or *braccianti* (day laborers or hired hands, generally associated with farm or construction work)—specifically refers to industrial workers and is associated with low- or unskilled labor positions performed by the lower working classes. In 1960s Italy, the term most often referred to the large population of factory workers that had amassed during the economic miracle and the nascent *movimento operaio.* The worker and working-class people were agents of social change in Italian neo- and post-Marxist thought and action. Whereas today "operaio" is often invoked as a classist, derogatory term—someone who is simple-minded, low-class, or utterly average in some capacity is an "operaio" of said task—in the early 1960s it emerged as a position of collective political empowerment. As Robert Lumley has explained, New Left publications led by Antonio Negri, Raniero Panzieri, Mario Tronti, and other key intellectual figures (if often socialist party dissidents), who challenged orthodox Marxist thought and offered "fresh air" to Marxist discourse, were central to this renewed theorization of the power of the worker as an agent of resistance; most important among these publications were *Quaderni Rossi* (Red Notebooks; Turin, 1961–65), *Quaderni Piacentini* (Piacenza Notebooks; Turin, 1962–84), and *Classe Operaia* (Working Class; Milan, 1964–67), which split from *Quaderni Rossi.*[122] Intellectual publications were followed by political organizations broadly grouped within *autonomia operaia* (workers' autonomy) such as Potere Operaio, Lotta Continua, and Autonomia (Workers' Power, the Struggle Continues, and Autonomy, respectively), which also had their own publications, in the late 1960s and 1970s. With regard to its appearance in Pistoletto's work of 1965, the term was enough to place our subject not only in a workers' protest but also within the broader terrain of ideas and actions of a major socialist movement that came to define the 1960s in Italy.[123] The term's articulation on a sign in the picture functions doubly: to underscore the term's indexical function as a sign of the times, and the work's signification of art's potential political function. The sign itself was drawn from another source photograph than that of the girl, from a Workers' Day rally. As a portrait, then—notably, the only one in the series—the image is less one of a "passive" individual than that of a literally and figuratively faceless representative of Italian collective action and a new workers' body politic.

The implication is similar in two aforementioned works in the series, both entitled *Demonstration* (figs. 66, 67). The figure is imperfectly doubled across the works; in both cases, she is turned away from us. As our own reflections register alongside these figures, we find ourselves in scenes of political agitation while wondering what we cannot see; profil perdu here registers an act of refusal. We see similar quasi-repetitions across other works, as figures appear and reappear in different

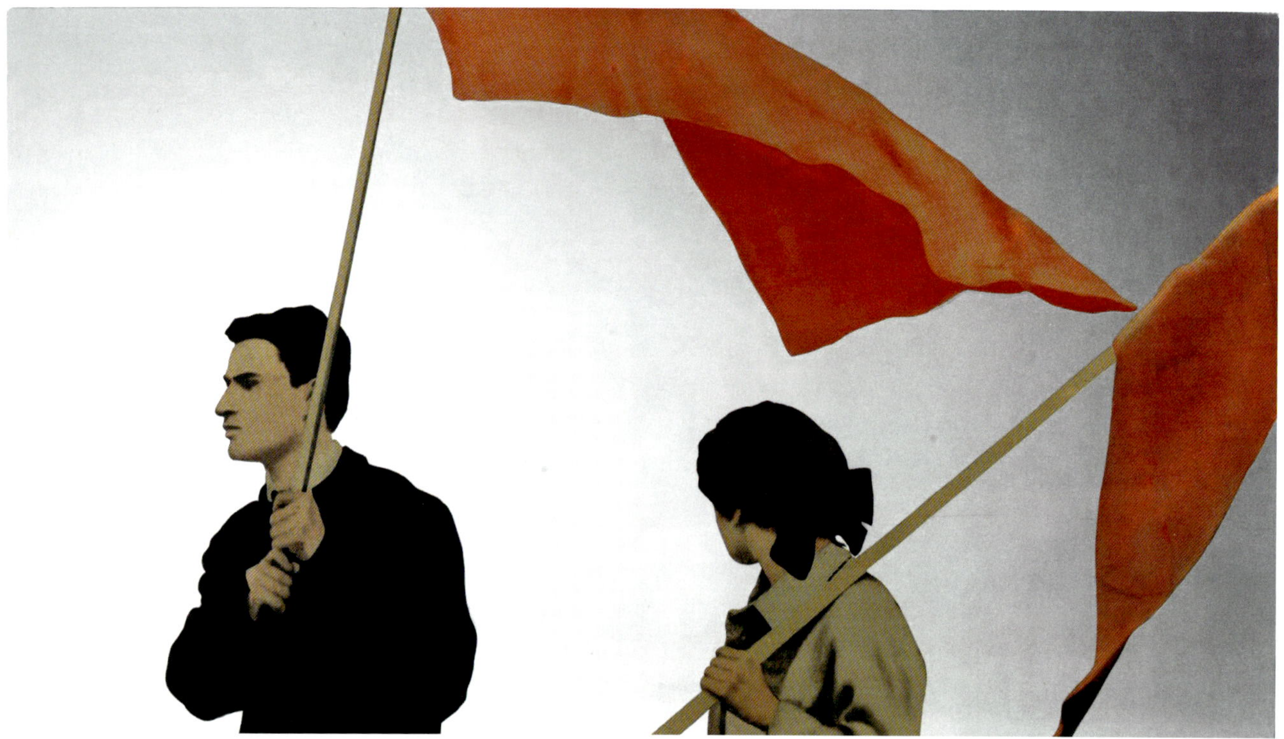

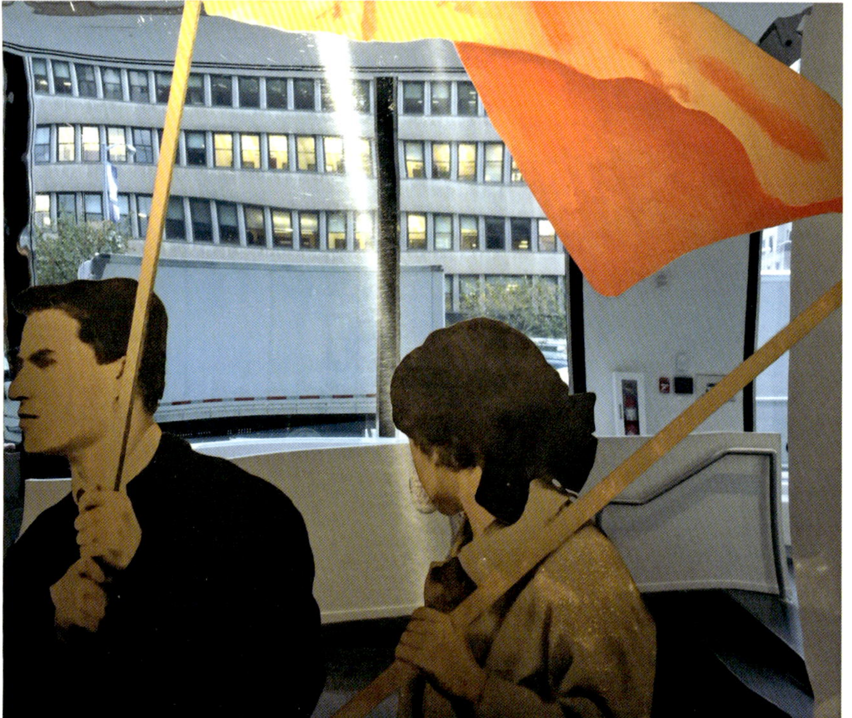

FIG. 66. Michelangelo Pistoletto, *Corteo* (Demonstration), 1965. Oil and graphite on tissue paper on stainless steel, 47¼ × 85 in. (120 × 216 cm). Private collection.

FIG. 67. Michelangelo Pistoletto, *Corteo* (Demonstration), 1965. Oil and graphite on tissue paper on stainless steel, 39⅜ × 47¼ in. (100 × 120 cm). Private collection.

positions within each composition.[124] Germano Celant described this phenomenon in his brief comments on the Rallies in the late 1980s as one that amasses dialogue and collectivity, not only between the photographic figures, but necessarily between figure and world. "Pistoletto's photographed subjects … are walking and leaning, calling or marching (*Meeting* and *Vietnam*, 1965). They are captured unexpectedly and fixed in a surprising instantaneousness that suspends them. But the suspension of an action calls for a *circularity*, the reciprocal movement of a situation which determines it and sustains it. *Seated Man*, 1962, requires an environment, while *Meeting*, 1965, requires the world."[125] What Celant suggests is that the difference between the environment of the mirror paintings and the world *needed* by those with political subjects is not spatial but rather social. The Rallies require socially attuned participation. They don't summon the world (the space of display). They need the World, writ large.

The Rallies also prompt discursive questions that go beyond their immediate subjects. What is the relation between art and politics after fascism, in the age of mass media and advancing capitalism? Can a work of art still transform society? In the late 1960s, Guy Debord echoed Benjamin's concerns, condemning the use of mass media to condition society and, in totalitarian regimes (he wrote on Mao Zedong), to erase individual agency and subjectivity, remaking the populace in the image of the demagogue. The Rallies seem to underscore that the cultural politics of Pistoletto's works get to a major crisis in Marxist thought at the time of their production, debating the possibility of social revolution. The many connections of the Rallies to antifascist histories (in subject matter, iconography, and theoretical concerns) gets to the heart of Marxist concerns regarding art, politics, and society in the 1960s—and still today—without necessarily offering a neat resolution. Could the work of art still offer an ameliorative experience for humanity, for society?

Study of the mirror paintings that feature readily apparent political imagery sheds light on the significance of the supposedly banal imagery in other works. Examination of the series reveals that Pistoletto used the same images in other works that have been displayed together but never explored in relation to the political-themed series. Study of the Rallies reveals that this circularity was also more precise: Pistoletto used the same images across the Rallies, too. Some have been displayed together and briefly addressed, but further analysis of this circulation and effective mirroring of the subject internal to the series has not been pursued.[126] In *Due uomini che camminano* (Two Men Walking, 1965), for example, we recognize the figure on the right-hand side of the image—a man in business dress, with a distinctive mustache and party membership card pinned to his jacket (fig. 68).[127] He is the same figure who appeared in *No to the Tram Fare Increase.* While the subject's communist affiliation and specific cause were made clear in that work, comparison of the works reveals that *Two Men Walking* is more than an image of everyday passersby, of people that seem to have been "plucked en route" from the real world by the photograph, borrowing Sigfried Kracauer's description of photography.[128] Instead, its protagonists were demonstrators.

In *Two Men Walking,* Pistoletto uses a vertically reversed (or mirror) image of the figure (he faces left, in his later appearance) in sepia as opposed to naturalistic coloring. This reversed doubling (or mirroring) of the figure and revision of its coloring plays on conventional chronological, narrative, and technological structures in such a way that the differentiation is not only practical but also symbolic. Although Pistoletto asserted that he used color in the mirror paintings, beginning in 1964, only to heighten the illusion of mass in his mirror subjects, the use of color to differentiate the mustachioed male figure in *No to the Tram Fare Increase* from his iteration in *Two Men Walking* does not enhance the mimetic naturalism of the mirror subjects as the artist has claimed.[129] The shift from full color to sepia emphasizes the historicity of the figure as a photographic subject—what Henry Martin might call "the past tense quality of the image," as he described the temporal aesthetic of Pistoletto's figures—while the redirection of the figure suggests an action of return.[130] As a pair, the works point to the figure's appearance (and reappearance) as a reproduced (and reproducible) image while nevertheless undermining the logic of reproduction itself.

Close attention to the work's production corroborates this point. Even though Pistoletto used Rinaldi's photographs, the resulting mirror subjects were not simply enlarged reproductions of these images. As with his earlier mirror paintings, the process involved several steps that differentiated the ostensive reproduction from its source. First, Pistoletto had Bressano

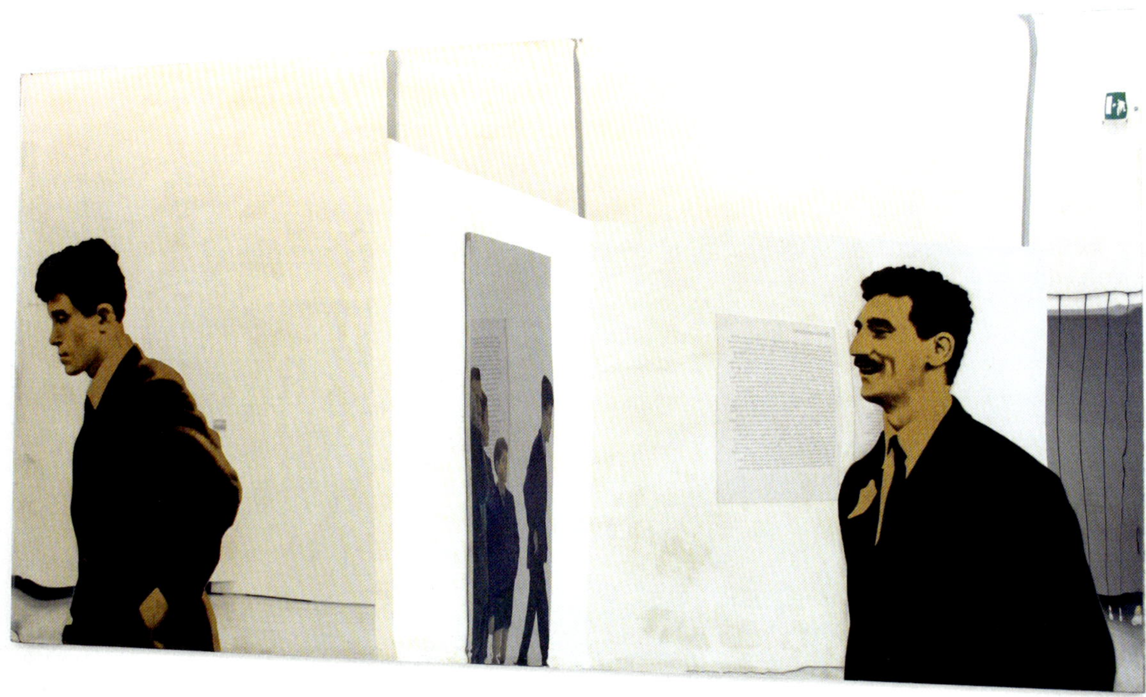

FIG. 68. Michelangelo Pistoletto, *Due uomini che camminano* (Two Men Walking) [also known as *Due persone che passano* (Two People Passing By)], 1965. Painted tissue paper on polished stainless steel, 47¼ × 90½ in. (120 × 230 cm). On view in the artist's retrospective *Michelangelo Pistoletto: Da uno a molti 1956–1974*, MAXXI Museo nazionale delle arti del XXI secolo, March 4–August 15, 2011.

rephotograph Rinaldi's images, so the collaged figure, glued facing down, would be oriented in the same direction as the original photograph (with a few exceptions). Next, he hand-traced a life-size enlargement, which he had printed from Bressano's negative, onto a sheet of tissue paper. This step, however, could be understood as a kind of doubling of the reproduction and distribution of the image. That the figures circulate through several iterations before they are collaged onto the panel makes the works more labor intensive than they first appear, distancing Pistoletto from the "cool" as "lazy" interpretation of pop articulated by some American critics and exemplified by Hess's argument. These are images of workers; the theme suggests that Pistoletto's attention to labor-intensive processes might align him, intentionally or otherwise, with the subjects of his pictures.

Through this lens, Pistoletto's comments on the Rallies seem more logical. In the spring of 1967, Pistoletto downplayed the potential politics of the works. In a review of the artist's "cool work" in his solo exhibition at the Kornblee Gallery, *New York Times* art critic Grace Glueck wrote: "For the arbitrary, pasted-on figures, Pistoletto selects the most banal, anonymous photographic images he can find, often snaps taken by his friends. . . . 'The subject is not important,' he says, dismissing the idea of commitment that might be expressed by the couple carrying Vietnam protest banners. 'I am a political man, but if I wanted to paint political pictures, I'd go much further.'"[131] These sentiments echo broader resistance from some artists associated with Arte Povera to readings of their work as overtly political or driven by *impegno* (duty). Pino Pascali, writing on the protested Venice Biennale of 1968, from which he withdrew his works, cited the historic victimization of artists by politics: "Artists have always been victims of politics. They have been made to serve all kinds of political interests."[132] Pascali would make this salvo not long after making *Le armi* (Weapons) and *Cannoni* (Cannons), both

1965. He seems to echo Pistoletto's own hedging of politicized readings of his works. Pascali's series of trompe l'oeil sculptural objects appear to be life-size military weapons, made of scrap metal and machine parts—"falsi giocattoli" (fake toys), as Vittorio Rubiu called them. Pascali, along with Angeli and Schifano—all based in Rome—invoked partisan rhetoric and iconography in their work of the 1960s as a site of contestation. It is worth noting here that Pistoletto himself facilitated the famous exhibition of Pascali's *Weapons* at the Galleria Gian Enzo Sperone in Turin; the show included the work *Cannone Bella Ciao,* a cannon made of recycled materials, named for the partisan antifascist song "Bella Ciao."

That Pistoletto was able to achieve international career success, specifically in the United States, as an Italian artist in the mid-1960s hinged in large part on such ambiguous statements. This is a view Pistoletto has upheld; in 2013, he reflected: "Some mirror paintings, including *Vietnam,* have images of marches or rallies, but they are memories of events totally devoid of political emphasis, as were all the Zoo's performances." Rather than parrot the artist's dismissal of the works' politics, examination of what the works do (and how Pistoletto interacted with them) compels a different reading.

In the photograph accompanying Glueck's review, attributed to photographers Leo Friedman, Joseph Abeles, and Sy Friedman, Pistoletto poses in front of his mirror painting *Vietnam* (fig. 69). Mimicking the protestors in the scene, he holds his body midstride, one arm forward and one arm back, as if he was swinging them in time with his gait. His gaze is directed forward, slightly lifted; it suggests intention and performance. He leans forward in alignment with the protesting figures, extending the protest to the real scene of the American gallery. The photo reminds us of a passage from Celant's "Notes for a Guerrilla War": "No longer among the ranks of the exploited, the artist becomes a guerrilla fighter, capable of choosing his places of battle and with the advantages conferred by mobility, surprising and striking, rather than the other way around."[133]

Perhaps the mode of figuration Pistoletto employed (or deployed) in the protest mirror paintings were less "cool" images than "cold" ones of the Cold War era: political images that visually recall the tensions between the capitalist United States and communist Soviet bloc but that also undermine and threaten a global economic and cultural hegemonic system. If American pop and its precursor, the British Independent Group, had the potential to tap into the communicative capacities of capitalist popular culture, reaching ever-expansive audiences through mass media, production, and distribution networks, as Lawrence Alloway framed these movements, Pistoletto's mirror paintings with political subjects seemed geared to expose and unseat the structures of power that govern these networks.[134]

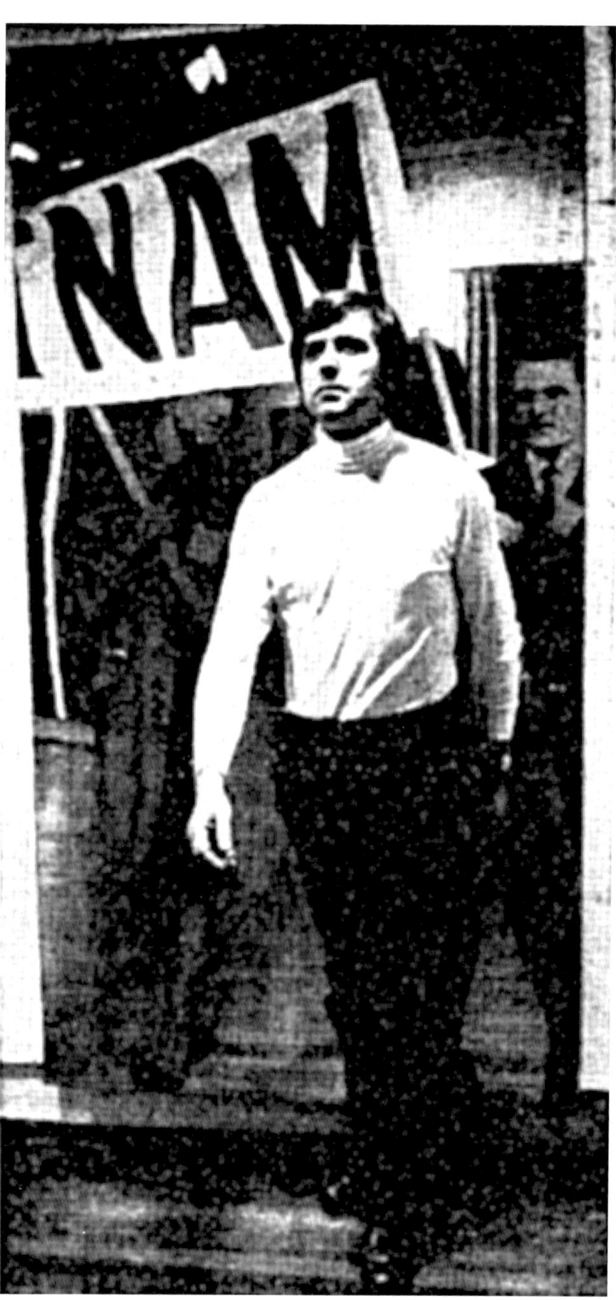

FIG. 69. Photograph of Michelangelo Pistoletto with *Vietnam* (1965), Kornblee Gallery, New York, on occasion of his exhibition (April 22–May 18, 1967). Published in Grace Glueck, "Art Notes: The Hokiest Show on Earth," *New York Times,* April 30, 1967. Photo by Friedman-Abeles.

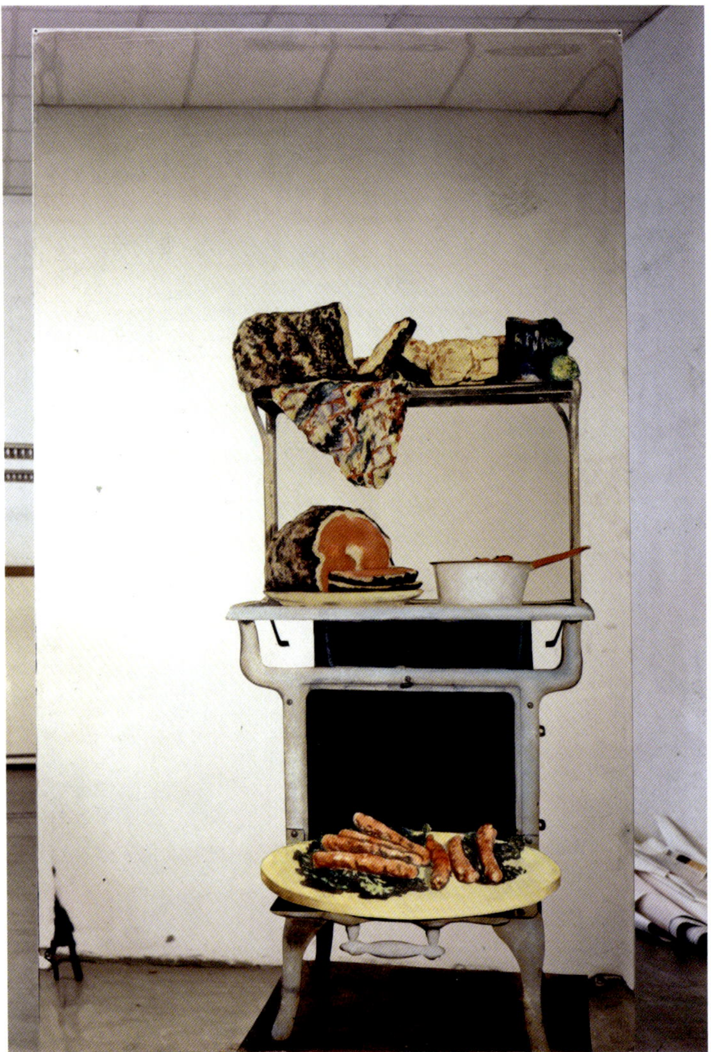

FIG. 70. Michelangelo Pistoletto, *La stufa di Oldenburg* (Oldenburg Stove), 1965. Oil and graphite on tissue paper on polished stainless steel, 86⅝ × 47¼ in. (220 × 120 cm). Private collection.

THE RALLIES AND AMERICAN POP

Excavation of the politics of Pistoletto's Rallies and related works brings a new perspective to other areas of the artist's practice. One of the most pressing revisions they suggest for existing interpretations of the artist's mirror paintings is their relation to a smaller series of mirror paintings that featured full-scale reproductions of works of American pop.[135] Pistoletto made three of these pop-themed works, two of which debuted in the Walker Art Center show.[136]

As in the Rallies, the pop-themed mirror paintings were made with source images drawn from existing photographic images. In this case, however, the images were drawn from mass-media sources, specifically from Italian political publications and cultural reviews. Made alongside the Rallies in 1965, the pop-themed mirror paintings featured life-size cutouts of photographic reproductions of works by Claes Oldenburg and John Chamberlain as installed in the US Pavilion at the controversial Venice Biennale of 1964. Pistoletto's *La stufa di Oldenburg* (Oldenburg Stove) from 1965, for example, featured an enlarged color photograph of Oldenburg's own *Stove* (*Assorted Foods on a Stove*) (1962): the painted, plaster-cast model of the appliance (laden with encrusted, papier-mâché meats) was part of Oldenburg's series of everyday objects, foodstuffs, and bric-a-brac produced as part of his commercial installation *The Store* (1962) (fig. 70). The photograph of Oldenburg's work that Pistoletto used appeared in the July 1964 issue of the Italian weekly *L'Europeo*, dedicated to the Biennale.[137] Pistoletto was not alone in this citation. Artist Claudio Cintoli also referenced details of the same work, among other imagery, including Americana, the Vietnam War, and baroque excess, in a work from 1964, while Pascali and Ettore Innocente made artworks referencing Jasper Johns, though not specific works by the artist, that same year.[138] Although Pistoletto wasn't unique in this engagement, his quotation of American pop was most direct, in content and method.

Two mirror paintings, both *Chamberlain Sculpture*, from 1965, featured a full-scale photographic cutout of one of Chamberlain's abstract welded sculpture made of car parts and beat-up metal siding, painted in a garish palette of bubblegum-pink, carnelian, turquoise, and indigo (fig. 71). Both featured Chamberlain's sculpture as it had appeared on the cover of the Italian art review *La Biennale*: resting on a white plinth, as it was displayed at the Venice Biennale in 1964, marked with a small label bearing Chamberlain's surname in black typeface (fig. 72). Whereas the work was centered on the cover of the magazine, it is shifted to the right or left on Pistoletto's mirror paintings. The smaller example leaves room for the viewer's reflection to occupy the central position, if in dialogue with the opaque image of Chamberlain's work.

One precedent to the *Comizi* and the pop mirror paintings might be found in two works by Pistoletto from 1962 and 1964, both entitled *Alpino* (Alpinist), the latter (and larger) included in the exhibition of American Pop, *Pop* at Galleria Sperone in Turin in the summer of 1965.[139] Pistoletto was the only Italian artist included in the show. As Romy Golan has discussed,

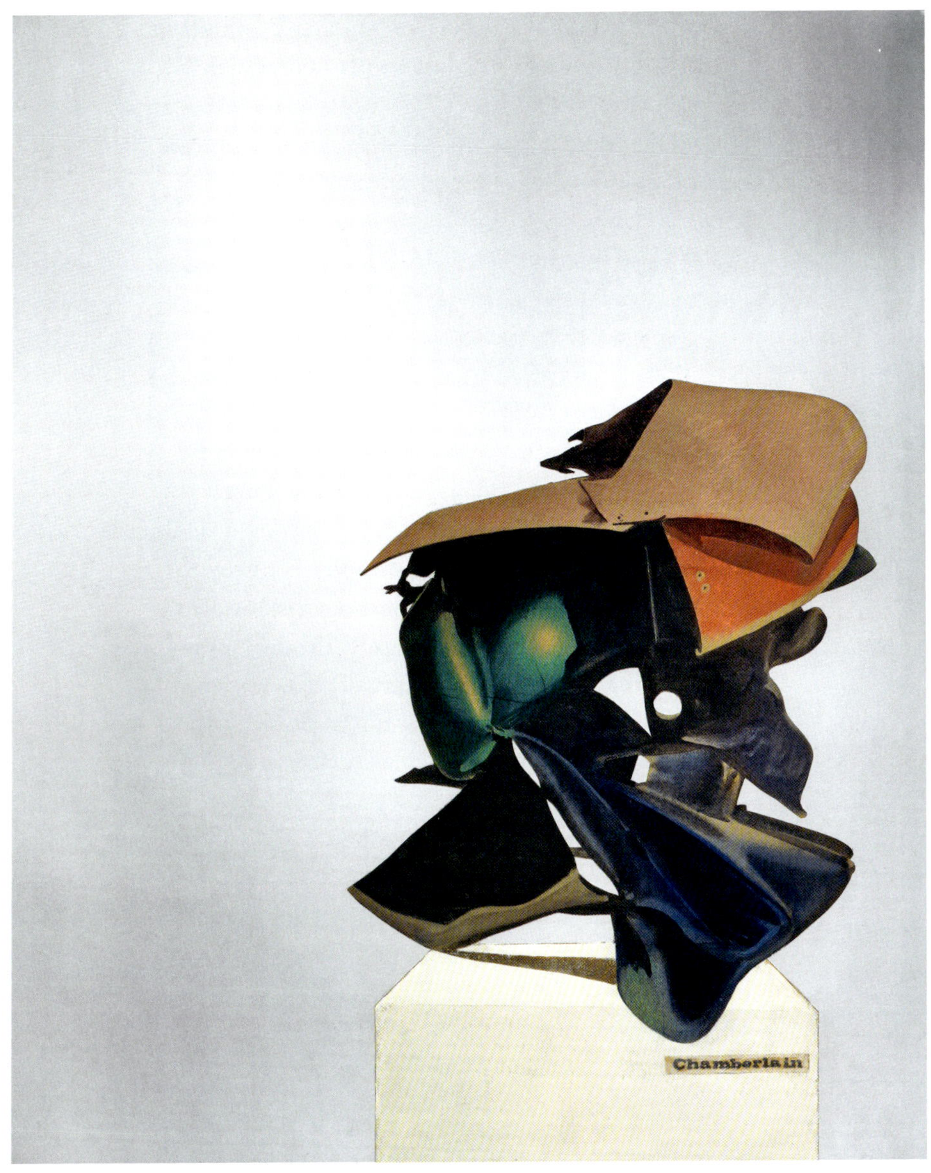

FIG. 71. Michelangelo Pistoletto, *Scultura di Chamberlain* (Chamberlain Sculpture), 1965. Painted tissue paper on polished stainless steel, 47¼ × 39⅜ in. (120 × 100 cm). Private collection.

FIG. 72. Source image for Pistoletto, *Chamberlain Sculpture* (both works), in "La Biennale," *La Biennale di Venezia* 14, no. 54 (December 1964). Archivio Pistoletto, Biella.

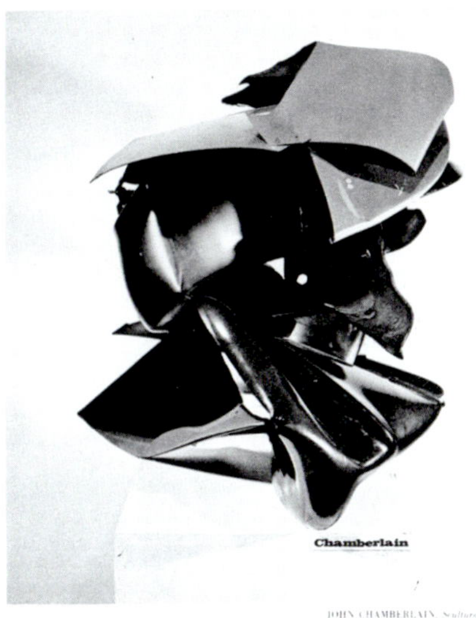

LA BIENNALE

Chamberlain

JOHN CHAMBERLAIN, *Scultura*

Quest'anno la rassegna veneziana ha suscitato polemiche come da tempo il mondo artistico non conosceva. Abbiamo chiesto un giudizio sulla Biennale e sulla pop-art americana a critici e pittori italiani di tutte le tendenze

these mirror paintings positioned a figure of the Alpine regiments, key figures in the Italian antifascist resistance; in *Pop,* one (1962) appeared across from Roy Lichtenstein's *Whaam!* (1963) (fig. 73). In that setting, Pistoletto's *Alpinist* appears positioned against Lichtenstein's fighter jet, drawn from the comic *All-American Men of War* (1962), in which stories on air forces in the world wars and Korean War appeared.[140] What Golan's interest in these exhibition photographs may prompt us to is that the context of the *Pop* exhibition may have informed Pistoletto's production of the pop-themed mirror paintings and subsequent positioning of them in relation to the *Rallies* in subsequent exhibitions.

Indeed, as opposed to regarding the pop and political mirror paintings as arbitrary, one-off themes, their production in 1965 as parallel projects suggests a more intimate connection between them. In a photograph of *Two Men Walking,* taken on the opening of the artist's exhibition at the Galleria Sperone in Milan on November 8, 1966, we see *Chamberlain Sculpture* reflected in the surface of the demonstration mirror painting (fig. 74). A second image, also taken at the Sperone exhibition, captures *Two Men Walking* in the surface of *Chamberlain Sculpture* (fig. 75). Indeed, Pistoletto juxtaposed reproductions of reproductions of American artworks—specifically works selected to represent the United States on a global stage—with anti-American, anticapitalist protest imagery. By strategically placing these works in the same context of display as the Rallies, the pop-themed mirror paintings were often reflected

FIG. 76. Photograph of Michelangelo Pistoletto's *Comizio II* (Rally II, 1965), reflected in the surface of a mirror painting such that the figures face his *La stufa di Oldenburg* (Oldenburg Stove, 1965). Studio Pistoletto, Turin, 1966. Photo by Paolo Bressano. Archivio Pistoletto, Biella.

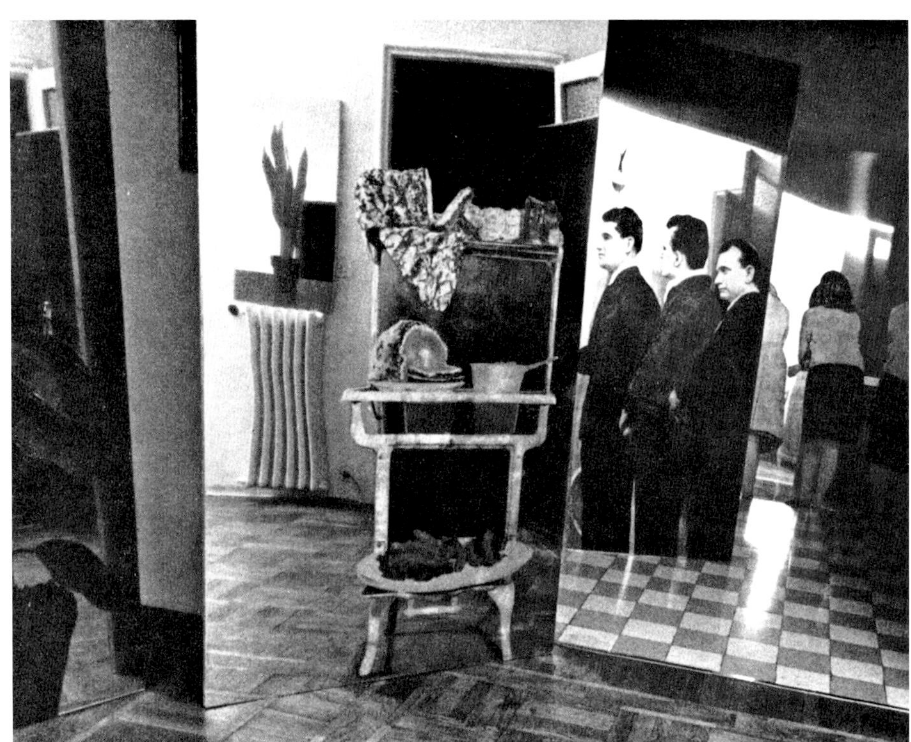

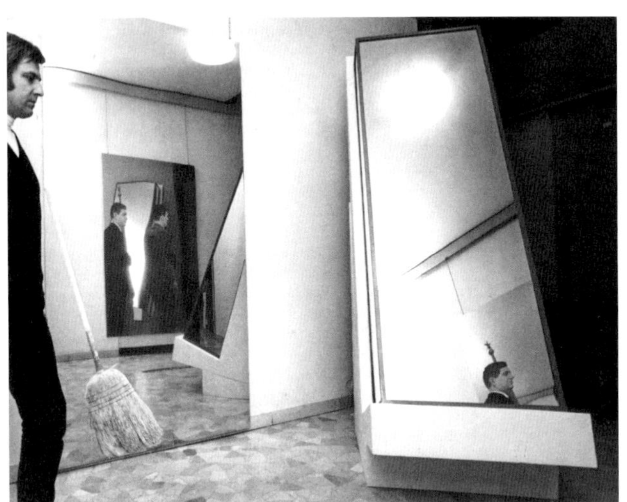

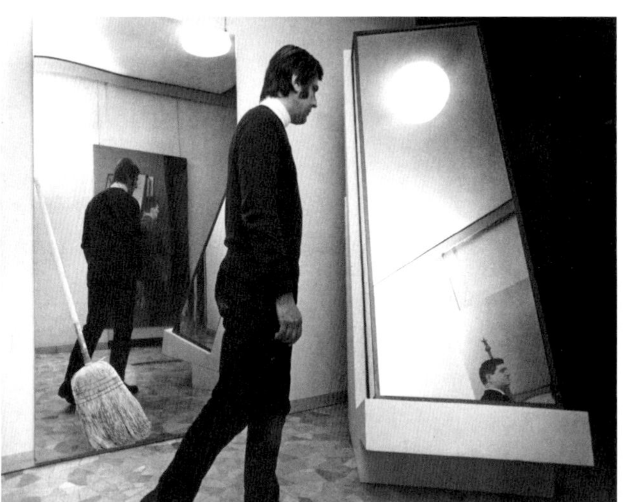

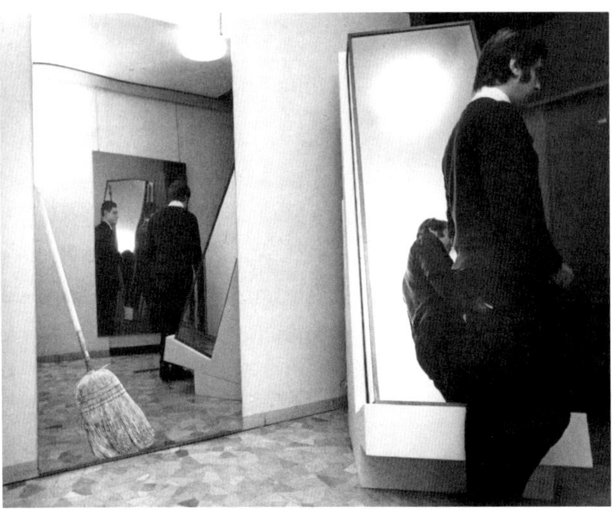

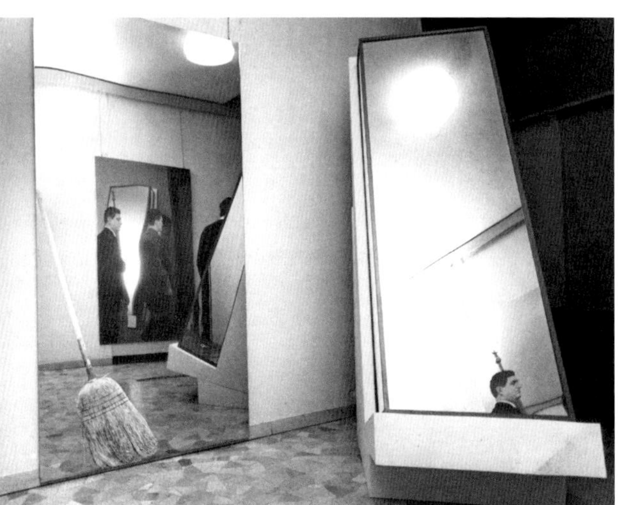

FIG. 77A–D. Photographs of Michelangelo Pistoletto with *Comizio X* (Rally X, 1965) and *Vetrina specchio* (Mirror Display Case, 1966). In *Pistoletto,* Galleria del Naviglio, Milan, February 22–March 7, 1967. Photos by Paolo Bressano. Archivio Pistoletto, Biella.

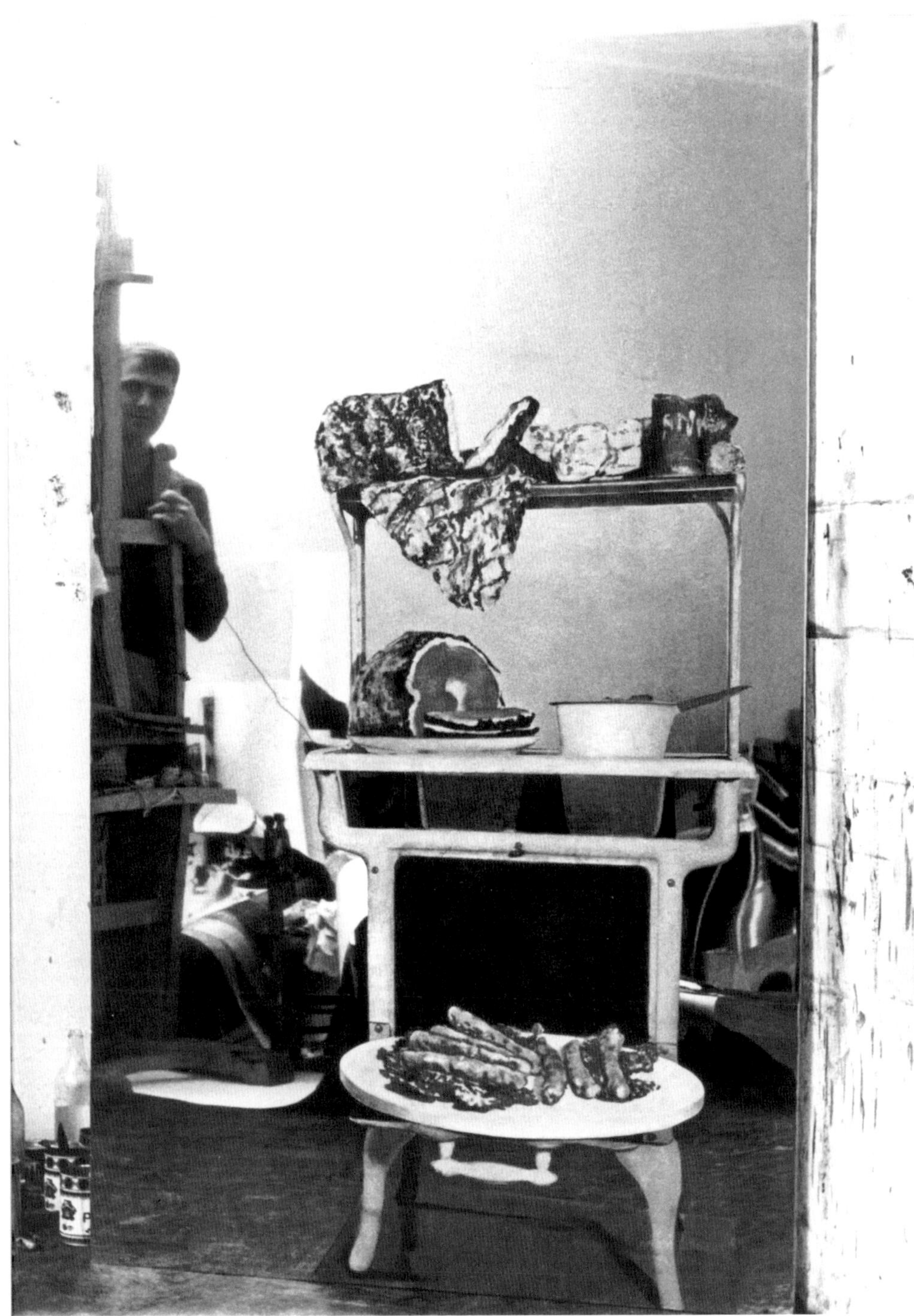

FIG. 78. Michelangelo Pistoletto, photographic self-portrait with *La stufa di Oldenburg* (Oldenburg Stove, 1965), Studio Pistoletto, Turin, 1966. Archivio Pistoletto, Biella.

for the PCI organ *L'Unità,* reported, viewers in the exhibition were filmed while they viewed the mirror paintings (and reflections of themselves on the paintings' surfaces). Pistoletto subsequently projected the footage; viewers could go back a few evenings later and watch themselves originally view the works on display. For Micacchi, the experience invited Marxist self-reflection: "And then they photograph you, they film you, and a few evenings later you can see yourself again on the projector and, depending on how life is going for you, you're either ashamed of yourself or feel like you're a revolutionary. I'm not too vain to say that I felt like a revolutionary who's ashamed of himself."[145]

As if to underscore the fact himself, Pistoletto staged a self-portrait of the artist with his mirror painting *Oldenburg Stove* (fig. 78). We see Pistoletto in the act of taking the picture, reflected in the mirror panel, peeking out from behind an easel. In this kind of protest picture, we see Pistoletto negotiate his position between his mirror paintings and American pop. He reflects on

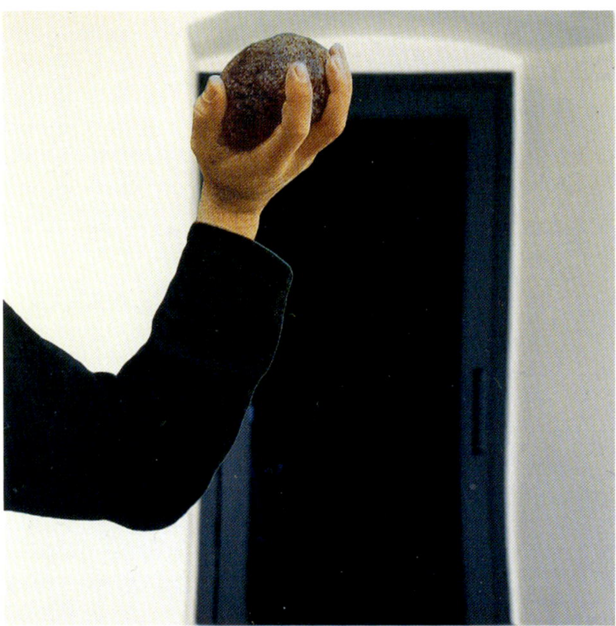

FIG. 79. Michelangelo Pistoletto, *50 azioni: Mano che tira un sasso* (50 Actions: Hand Throwing a Stone), 2004. Silkscreen on stainless steel, 19⅞ × 19⅞ in. (50.4 × 50.4 cm). Edition of 500.

his own reflection in the mirror, and on his position between Italian artist, protest figure, and viewer of the Pistoletto-as-Pop work.

Indeed the Rallies constellated the mirror paintings as a point of action: from our vantage point, they connect the artist's series *50 azioni* (50 Actions), from 1984, a series of smaller mirror paintings, approximating the scale of *Workers,* all cropped around a fragment of the body, the hand, as a sign of action, often signaling the body as worker, the figure as political actor. Hands are poised in protest or shown throwing a stone (*Mano che tira un sasso,* 2004; fig. 79). They are extensions of the Rallies.

THE RED FLAG AS RAG

This study of the Rallies' navigation of Italian labor politics, American pop, and the cultural geopolitics of the 1960s through experiments in figuration uncovers a forgotten history for Pistoletto, a new history within Arte Povera, and a potential new model for a figural history of postmodernism. My investigation into the as-yet-unattended presence of *Man with Red Flag* in that telling photograph (see fig. 1), and how the Rallies came to be, has told this story, as well as another history of Arte Povera entirely. By shedding light on and correcting existing misinformation about the Rallies, we can now introduce them as one point of origin for Arte Povera and Germano Celant's "guerrilla war." Far from the casual object-making understood as Arte Povera's modus operandi, the Rallies were an exercise in precision, involving doublings and returns, an engagement with the figure and with painting, and a site in which Pistoletto's work navigated the cultural geopolitics of the 1960s.

And so we return to *Man with Red Flag,* its flag, composed of sheets of tissue paper, delicately traced, cut, adhered, assembled, collaged, and painted. The Minus Objects that surround it in Bressano's photograph are best known by Pistoletto's own text on the series, first published in December 1966, in the catalog of the artist's exhibition at the Galleria La Bertesca. There, another clue appears: the Sperone exhibition photograph (Milan; November 1966) of *Due uomini che camminano* (Two Men Walking), and the pop-themed mirror painting *Chamberlain Sculpture,* mentioned above, was printed in the Bertesca catalog. The photograph also included one of Pistoletto's Minus Objects, *Struttura per parlare in piedi* (Sculpture for Talking while Standing; also known as *Struttura per chiacchierare in piedi* or Structure for Chatting while Standing; 1965–66), reflected in the surface of *Chamberlain Sculpture.* The photograph seems to present a confrontation between the nonhierarchical relationality of Pistoletto's objects and the rising cultural imperialism of American pop. Pistoletto's Minus Objects now gain new meaning. The liberatory project of the Minus Objects was conceived at a moment of great debate on the social potential of the work of art.

The following year, Pistoletto began making his iconic *stracci,* sculptural works made of rags: his now canonical *Venere degli stracci* (Venus of the Rags; made in several versions), little monuments (of rag-wrapped bricks), and "orchestras" of rag piles, steamed with teakettles. This figural and political connection among the Rallies, Minus Objects, and Rags is concretized in an installation photograph taken in the artist's studio, likely in the early 1980s, when a gilded version of his cement *Venus of the Rags* was positioned, like *Man with Red Flag,* among the Minus Objects, specifically between *Man-Sized House, Burnt Rose,* and *Bath* (fig. 80).[146] These figural and political connections to the Rallies bring additional valence to even the most recent rag artworks; consider the monumental *Venus of the Rags,* installed in Naples's municipal square in the summer of 2023 as a call to confront the tons of waste generated by consumer countries, global inequity, and humanitarian crisis, and also to find the beauty in humanity. In remarking on the visual encounter with the work, Pistoletto explained that you see "this Venus, who is handling [this tragedy], but the Venus is us. It is we who must take better note of ourselves."[147] On July 12, 2023, the work was destroyed by arson, leaving only a bare metal armature, neither Venus nor rags remaining.[148]

When we return to Bressano's photograph of *Man with Red Flag* from 1966 with this trajectory in mind, it is as if the red flag is about to become a rag that only the poorest wave, wealthy in their liberatory impoverishment. It is an image that we still need. The Rags recall poet, filmmaker, and director Pier Paolo Pasolini's lamentation of the partisan symbol and what he saw as the failed legacy of the Resistance in the 1960s. In "Alla bandiera rossa" (To the Red Flag, 1961), Pasolini wrote of laborers becoming beggars, the illiterate becoming buffalos or dogs. He concluded:

> Chi conosceva appena il tuo colore, bandiera rossa,
> sta per non conoscerti più, neanche coi sensi:
> tu che già vanti tante glorie borghesi e operaie,
> ridiventa straccio, e il più povero ti sventoli.
>
> Those who only just got to know your color, red flag,
> Aren't going to know you any further, not even with their senses:
> You who already praised many bourgeois and worker glories,
> become a rag again, and the poorest wave you.[149]

Rather than lament the left and the impoverished populations of postwar Italy, Pistoletto in that photograph made the *red flag* do—and *figure*—more. Perhaps that more was the starting point of Arte Povera itself.

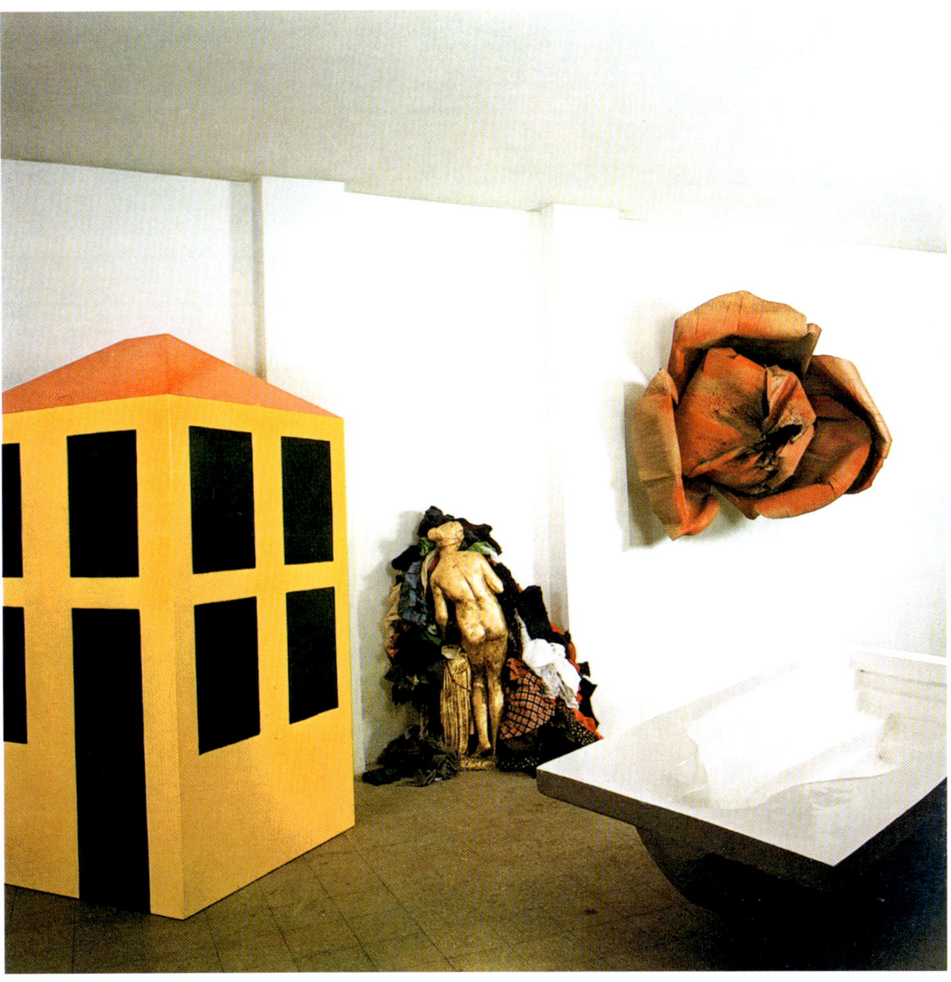

FIG. 80. Michelangelo Pistoletto, *Venere degli stracci dorata* (Golden Venus of the Rags), 1972. Gold-leaf on cement statue with cloth, dimensions variable. Collection of Lia Rumma. Photograph taken in the artist's studio, with *Casa a misura d'uomo* (Man-Sized House, 1965–66), *Rosa bruciata* (Burnt Rose, 1965), and *Bagno* (Bath, ca. 1968). Date of photograph unknown. Archivio Pistoletto, Biella.

4 Extremely Poor Figures

A World Minus Objects, Minus Men

Over two months in the winter of 1965–66, in a live-work space in the basement of an apartment building a few blocks from Fiat's largest factory in the Turinese neighborhood of Lingotto, Pistoletto made twenty-five sculptural objects, each unique in material, process, and form.[1] Made with materials that were ready-at-hand in the studio or easily available at local hardware stores and industrial suppliers, the resulting *Oggetti in meno* (Minus Objects, 1965–66)—a turn of phrase closer in meaning to "fewer," "lesser," or even "minor objects" than the "minus objects" typically used for the English translation—were privately exhibited in two installations for his friends and fellow artists in January and February 1966 (fig. 81a–c). The eclectic series included one-off sculptures, photographs, geometric constructions (some makeshift, others made to order), design objects, and furniture items, all realized (as the artist wrote) as close to the moment of their conceptualization as possible. Unlike the assembly-line products from down the street, or the shared signature style that unified Pistoletto's mirror paintings, none of them were the same.

Indeed among the Minus Objects were such varied works as a set of folding chairs and simple wooden card table with a green-painted pyramidal objet d'art on its tabletop, set up not far from a hanging mercury streetlamp fitted with a green bulb, which cast a lurid glow on visitors; works that integrated Pistoletto's personal possessions, including an iron-framed twin bed, in *Sfera sotto il letto* (Sphere under the Bed, 1965); traditional southern Italian Nativity figurines belonging previously to Pistoletto's father, arranged in (and permanently glued to) a seemingly crudely fashioned, wall-mounted, picture-scaled terrain in *Paesaggio* (Landscape, 1965); and a fifteenth-century wooden statue of the Madonna (*Scultura lignea,* Wooden Sculpture, 1965–66), now partially encased in neon-orange plexiglass. There were also decorative accents: a hand-painted sign that reads "TI AMO" (I LOVE YOU), in bold block lettering; a multicolored grid of store-bought plastic tiles in *Semisfere decorative* (Decorative Semispheres, 1965–66), affixed to the studio wall with Scotch tape; and a waist-high, lopsided, papier-mâché ball, *Sfera di giornali* (Newspaper Sphere, 1966), measuring nearly one meter (about three feet) in diameter. Some works responded to an observed commercial need, like the standing handrail *Struttura per parlare in piedi* (Structure for Talking while Standing, 1965–66) or a new product that had caught Pistoletto's eye, such as the reflective plastic bubble sheets of *Decorative Semispheres* that now festooned one wall with teal, fuchsia, and other eye-catching colors, or the textured glistening surface of *Mica* (1965–66): a square canvas coated in powdered mica. Others were creative solutions for studio clutter or were elicited by childhood memories and personal imaginings. Others still were made simply because they were things the artist liked.[2] Additional works included a terraced fiberglass bathtub; a corrugated paper well, which contained broken-down canvases instead of water; a portrait-scaled blank mirror panel; a trio of twisted canvases and quartet of concrete columns; and a wall-mounted, cardboard sculpture of a giant rose blossom, spray-painted scarlet red: *Rosa bruciata* (Burnt Rose, 1965), whose "petals" the artist had singed with a handheld blowtorch.

The inspirations for the Minus Objects, as described by Pistoletto in writings of the period and later interviews, were as heterogeneous as their formal properties. Though the "anti-stylistic" works, as Bruno Corà later called them, comprised a series, the Minus Objects sought to eschew the trappings of signature style, resembling the pluralist presentation of a group exhibition more than the monographic project of a solo show.[3] For Germano Celant, the objects' visual semblance as works not of individual but rather of multiple authorship, along with their varied material repertoire and seeming refusal of any unifying logic, made them, as noted in this book's introduction, "extremely 'poor' works." They resulted from "a free mode of action, unforeseeable and without restraints" and from an "abolition of all positions couched in terms of categories."[4]

This turn to aesthetics of pluralist authorship was an important one for Pistoletto, who had become wary of gallerist pressures to produce more of his by-then trademark mirror paintings. For him, the Minus Objects constituted a new platform of making that would extend his interest in phenomenology and temporality explored in the mirror paintings while disrupting the interpretation of form and visual language as a representation of the artist himself. As he wrote in 1966: "The works I make shall not be constructions or fabrications of new ideas, as they shall not be objects that represent me, to impose or to impose myself upon others. Rather they are objects through which I free myself from something—they aren't constructions but

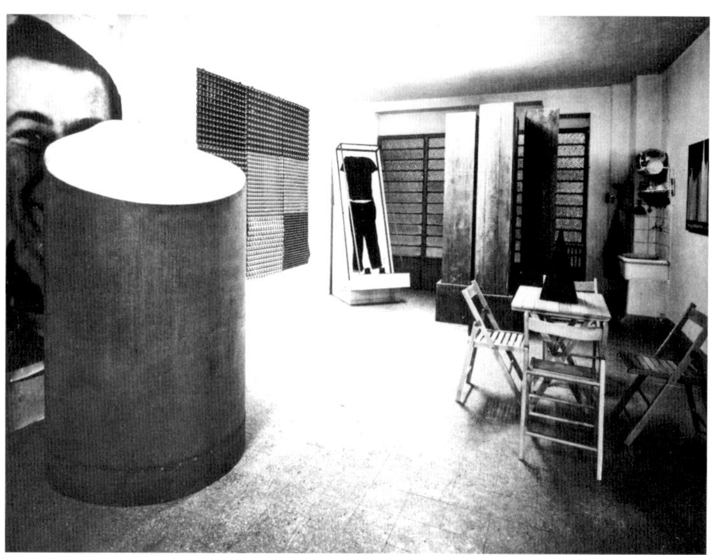

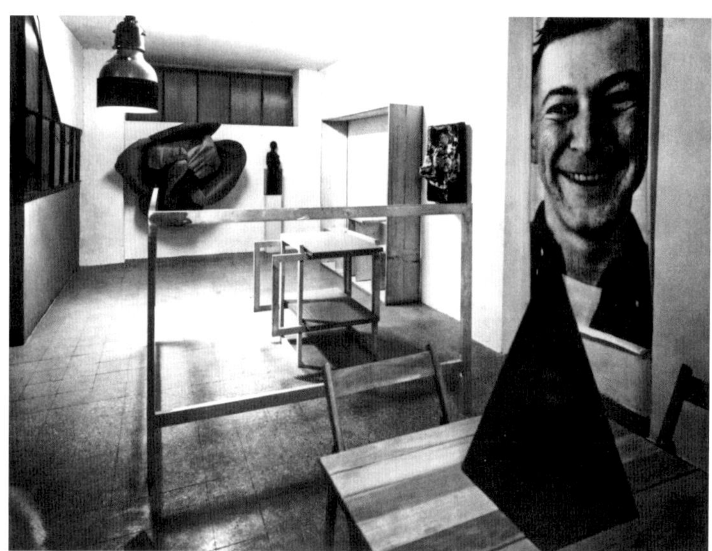

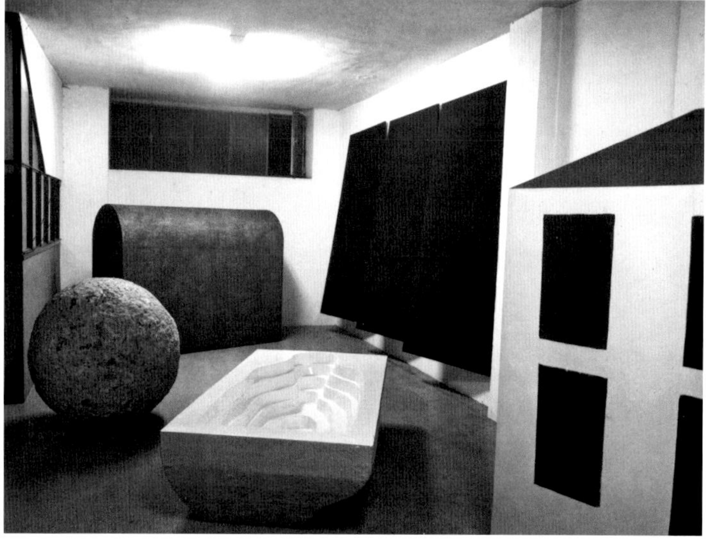

FIG. 81A–C. Three installation views, Michelangelo Pistoletto, *Oggetti in meno* (Minus Objects, 1965–66), two installations, Studio Pistoletto, Turin, January–February 1966. Photos by Paolo Bressano. Archivio Pistoletto, Biella.

liberations—I don't consider them to be extra objects but minus objects, in the sense that they bring with them a perceptual experience that is definitively realized. According to my idea of time, you must learn how to free yourself from a position even while you are engaged in conquering it."[5] One work that resulted from the series—*Mappamondo* (Globe, 1966–68)—when examined closely, is particularly striking. It contained another newspaper "sphere," made of hand-shredded issues of the Turin-based newspapers *La Stampa* and *La Gazzetta del Popolo;* the sphere included a clipping from one of the artist's exhibition reviews, still legible on its surface (though never previously noted in the literature on the work). It is as if the artist had balled them up, as signs of the existing discourse on Pistoletto as Artist writ large. He turned them into throwaway sculpture as opposed to throwing them in the bin.

While the Minus Objects may have seemed mismatched—"incoherent," as Celant described them in the fall of 1967—the series was nevertheless unified by two points: first, its tensile interest between design and impoverished aesthetics unsuitable for commodity production; and second, its connection and disconnection to the artist, by using some items associated with family and others commercially sourced, or some items for personal use and others for use by a group.[6] And yet, despite their frequently worn, makeshift, or cobbled-together material and structural affect, the Minus Objects' geometric lines, vivid colors, synthetic materials, and modular, graphic aesthetic proclaim the works fundamentally as objects of design. Hence, the presentation of the Minus Objects registered less as an exhibition and more as a thoughtfully curated (if rather eclectic) home: personalized interior design that reflected the artist's individual taste and character.

Recent scholarship has drawn attention to the heterogeneous set of sculptural objects as a radical break in the artist's practice based on an anticommercialist effort to free himself from the trappings of (and market demand for) personal style or as a "refusal" of style through a "strategy of subtraction," shared with the collaged mirror paintings.[7] Following consideration of the concurrent production of the Rallies with the Minus Objects, this chapter counters existing histories of the Minus Objects as some of Pistoletto's best-known Arte Povera works. In addition to comparison with the Rallies, I draw attention to Pistoletto's early commercial graphic design work, much of which is shown here for the first time, at the Scuola Armando Testa and as an independent professional graphic designer in 1950s Turin. Situating the Minus Objects in relation to trends in postwar Italian design and advertising, in large part credited as a catalyst of Italy's economic miracle and the associated expansion of its global exports in the 1960s, I examine the works in relation to a shift in Italian advertising design from conventional figurative representation to figural imagery, in which consumer products were depicted as bodily forms. This chapter thereby brings a new perspective to the Minus Objects as what I am naming "figural objects." Consider works as the freestanding *Structure for Talking while Standing*) from 1965–66: a metal structure fitted with railings at elbow and mid-calf height for viewers to lean against while engaging in conversation. Comparably human-scaled is a brightly painted, wooden model of a two-story house, *Casa a misura d'uomo* (Man-Sized House, 1965–66), which stands just a few inches taller than the artist (fig. 82). Flat painted shapes mark the house's windows and door, none of which open. *Man-Sized House* is scaled as sculpture to the body's literal corporeal size—that is, to the human figure—as opposed to being scaled as architecture to shelter a body and accommodate a subject's habitation. I argue that the objects' use of specifically figural languages then taking shape within the landscape of Italian design positions them as figural models that resist capitalist symbolic orders and subject positions. Additional attention is given to Pistoletto's sculptural actions with one Minus Object and experimental films in which two appear as actors. The chapter concludes with the artist's declaration of a performance work, entitled *La fine di Pistoletto* (1967) or "the end of Pistoletto," after which he developed the Zoo and the theatrical role and game of "L'Uomo nero," a mythical figure in Italian culture, translated by the artist as the Minus Man, to be discussed further in chapter 5.

OCCUPATI IN MENO, OGGETTI IN MENO

Scholarship on the Minus Objects has largely upheld tenets of Celant's theorization, but what has gone relatively unnoticed is a troubling neutralization of their politics. Alex Potts, Robert Lumley, Briony Fer, and Anthony White have all emphasized the Minus Objects' formal and semiotic experimentation, citing their

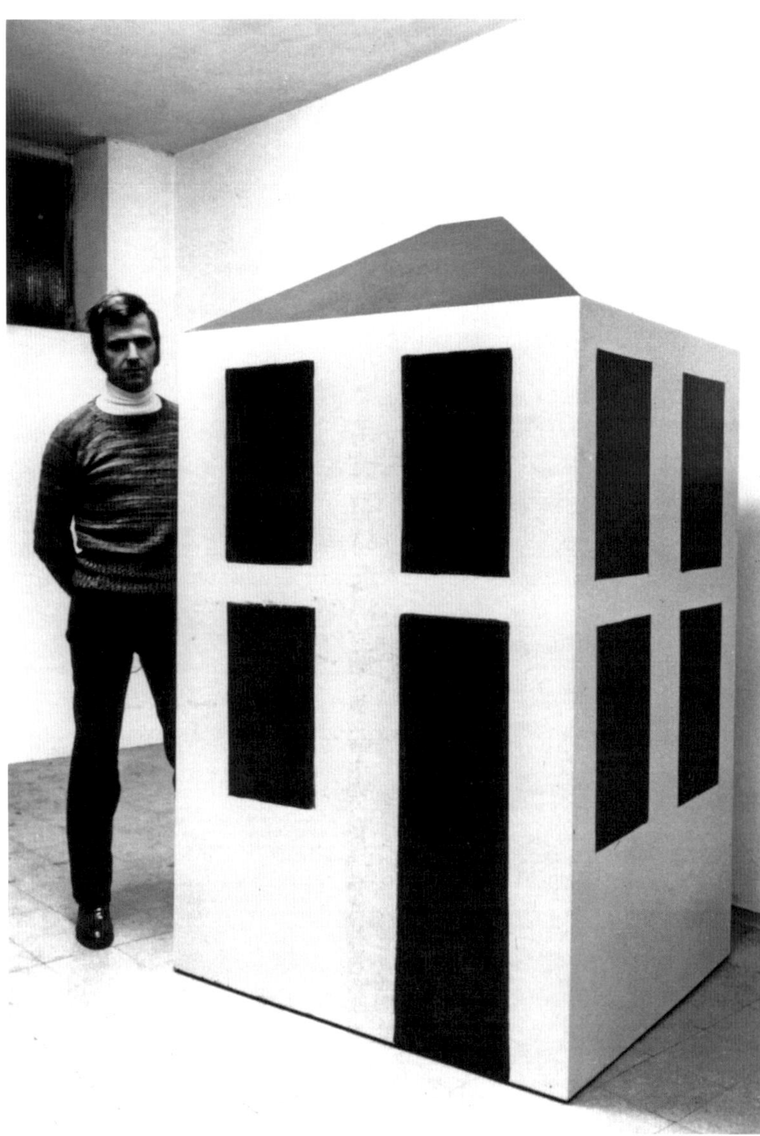

FIG. 82. Photograph of Michelangelo Pistoletto with his *Casa a misura d'uomo* (Man-Sized House, 1965–66), 1966. Object: Wood, paint, 78¾ × 39⅜ × 47¼ in. (200 × 100 × 120 cm). Cittadellarte–Fondazione Pistoletto, Biella. Photo by Paolo Bressano. Archivio Pistoletto, Biella.

de-skilled construction; "simple," "low-fi" stylistics; "cobbled-together affect" and "seemingly casual take-it-or-leave-it manner." Writing on the Minus Objects has been a means to theorize Arte Povera's "casual" strategies—its "do-it-yourself character . . . a degree of casualness."[8] Whereas Celant situated the Minus Objects as formative to Arte Povera in his "Notes on a Guerrilla War," contemporary scholarship has instead rendered them somewhat toothless, ignoring and sometimes outright neutralizing myriad signs of politicized practice while also dismissing Celant's evidently cushy leftist politics, his "easy anarco-libertarianism."[9] More troubling still is the closeness of these secondary readings to neoliberal terminology; disengaged laissez-faire casualness now masks what was not apathy or self-interest but rather methodical, revolutionary artistic practice against capitalism within (and outside of) the context of mid-1960s Italy.

They have not been aligned with Arte Povera's politicized aesthetics yet to come, as Nicholas Cullinan has described some of Arte Povera's works, described as such only through the rearview lens of a post-1968 and post–Cold War world.[10] They also provide us with a precedent to those later politicized aesthetics of Arte Povera, shifting the timeline of anti-American protest and radical aesthetics from the late 1960s to the middle of the decade—before Celant's framework was in place.[11] The closest assertion has been made by Romy Golan, who referred to them as "ambiguous objects, midway between sculpture and mock furniture . . . rooted in a strategy of subtraction that, for Pistoletto, had become something closer to a refusal."[12] Her language recalls the contemporary terminology of withdrawal as a platform for workers' activism, found in the work of operaismo figure Mario Tronti's "strategy of refusal," in which Tronti called on factory workers to refuse to work in protest of poor wages and conditions. What if Pistoletto's process was not a "low-key anarchic approach," as Potts has called it?[13] What do we do with all these claims for lightweight informality and casual object-making when faced with the amount and kind of work many of these works required?

In the preceding chapter I identified new sources for the Minus Objects' conceptualization. The Rallies constitute a repressed political and figural point for Pistoletto's practice and a new framework for the Minus Objects, as well as for Arte Povera. Returning to *Man with Red Flag,* we see Pistoletto's figure cropped at the knees. The figure appears solid, rising from the floor to meet us, or holding his ground, entrenched in the terra firma of the artist's studio. The compositional cropping of the figure signals proletarian strength or demise; his patient yet stalwart expression refuses to give us a singular resolution to this polysemy. In Paolo Bressano's photograph, *Man with Red Flag* is flanked by two Minus Objects: the torched, spray-painted cardboard *Burnt Rose,* at left, and the kitschy reflective, yellow, fuchsia, and teal plastic grid of *Decorative Semispheres,* at right. At first, the mirror painting seems out of place in form, iconography, and politics. It is a recognizably trademark work that disrupts the group-show aesthetic of the installation it occupies; it is labor-intensive and specialized in production, as opposed to makeshift, amateur, and casual. It is also out of place for the mirror paintings: it features specific, overtly politicized subject matter instead of universally banal imagery. Although the photograph was taken later in 1966 than the Minus Objects' initial unveiling, it points us to these works as parallel projects. Closer study of them as such reveals a deep connection.

The series of photographs from which Pistoletto drew the source images for the Rallies, as discussed in the previous chapter, includes photographs of a PCI protest against the United States and Vietnam War held in the Piazza del Duomo in Milan, likely on Workers' Day: May 1, 1965. One of the two photographs, however, cues us to a new source for the Minus Objects' conceptualization. In Italian, the phrase *oggetti in meno* is pointedly strange. Meaning "fewer objects," it also connotes insufficiency; they are "lesser" objects and "less" objects (than something else).[14] A detail from Renato Rinaldi's photograph, however, demonstrates one of the phrase's common usages: employment statistics. "A Milano nel 1964, 75.000 *occupati in meno*" (In Milan in 1964, 75,000 fewer employed), reads the sign of one protestor, at the center of the scene (fig. 83). Other signs warn against political apathy. An image of the Statue of Liberty's crown, covered in blood, accompanies the text: "Don't be indifferent. Think carefully. This is American freedom." Pistoletto was working closely with these images in 1965, on the eve of and through his production of the Minus Objects. This timeline suggests that the Rallies and their source imagery also framed his conceptualization of the Minus Objects and, by extension, the origins of Arte Povera.

The photograph of *Man with Red Flag* installed next to the burnt rose seems to have been preceded by another photograph, also by Bressano, from late 1965. This time, however, we find the artist standing in profile, facing the burnt rose; the image is cropped (fig. 84). The body of the artist extends beyond the image field. The photograph of the figure of the artist with the Minus Object, and the arrangement of his image more specifically with the burnt rose, seems to presage the figure's pose in *Man with Red Flag.* Similar photographs and films would follow.[15] The sculptural blossom recalls Franco Angeli's "partisan flowers" of the early 1960s and Jannis Kounellis's black roses of the period. In their juxtaposition with *Man with Red Flag,* the Minus Objects take on new politicized meaning.

Burnt Rose, for example, resonates more directly with Italian sociocommunist iconography: its visual connotation with *Man with Red Flag* makes it stand out as a political symbol. The red bloom recalls the red carnation of the Italian Socialist Party and hence becomes a reference to the historical Italian left.[16] *Decorative Semispheres* similarly resonates with leftist politics. Its grid form articulates nonhierarchical, decentralized ideology, an association that made the grid a subject of interest for leftist artists in the 1960s; its initial process—stuck to the wall with Scotch tape—reads now as a pointed performance of uncommodifiable work.

The Minus Objects departed from the mirror paintings, abandoning representation, in Pistoletto's view, for existence as such. At the same time, the Minus Objects were also made in tandem with the Rallies.[17] They were part of a shared critical project. To that end, Pistoletto even described the objects as subjects that have their own volition. In the Minus Objects statement, he writes: "The works I make don't intend to be [*non vogliono essere*] constructions or fabrications of new ideas, as they don't intend to be [*non vogliono essere*] objects that represent me, to impose or to impose me on others . . . they aren't constructions but liberations."[18] This discovery gives us a new viewpoint from which to consider the objects. They also staged a kind of rally themselves: a picket or sit-in in the artist's studio, a rally outside of it, a demonstration of collective action. That they would function similarly in public space, where Pistoletto subsequently used two of them, and later appeared on the surfaces of mirror paintings, further supports this reading. Pistoletto rolled and performed the *Newspaper Sphere* and *Burnt Rose* through the streets of Turin, the latter as a figure, running through Piazza C.L.N. and Piazza San Carlo. In Pistoletto's film with Ugo Nespolo, *Buongiorno Michelangelo* (Good Morning Michelangelo, 1968–69), Pistoletto and Maria Pioppi paraded the cardboard rose blossom through the historic arcades and newer parked cars and buses of Piazza San Carlo and the surrounding streets in the heart of Turin (fig. 85). Crossing through Piazza C.L.N., the rose as disruptive figure pauses in front of monumental, modernized neoclassically inflected modernist marble sculptures—allegorical figures of the Po and Dora Riparia Rivers, by Umberto Baglioni. The piazza, designed in the mid-1930s, was originally intended for figurative sculptures dedicated to Mussolini and King Vittorio Emanuele III. In the context of the 1960s, the work underscored the existence of socialist and communist marches (and figures) as practices in everyday life, as a platform for departure.[19] The *Newspaper Sphere,* described by Ulrich Loock as a "history-corpus" "left," in some staged photographs, in

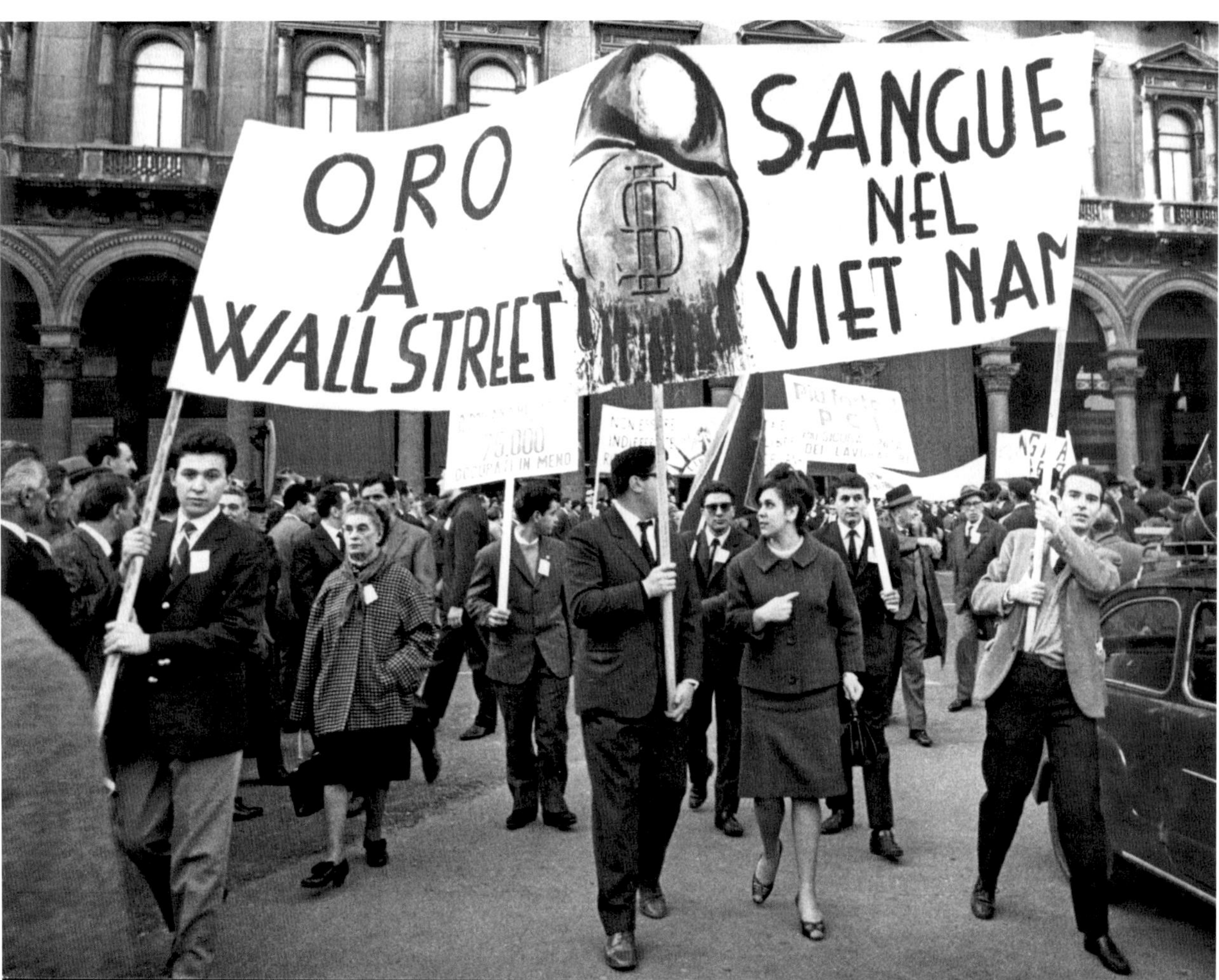

FIG. 83. Renato Rinaldi, unused photograph from the *Comizi* (Rallies) source photos, Piazza del Duomo, Milan, 1965. Archivio Pistoletto, Biella.

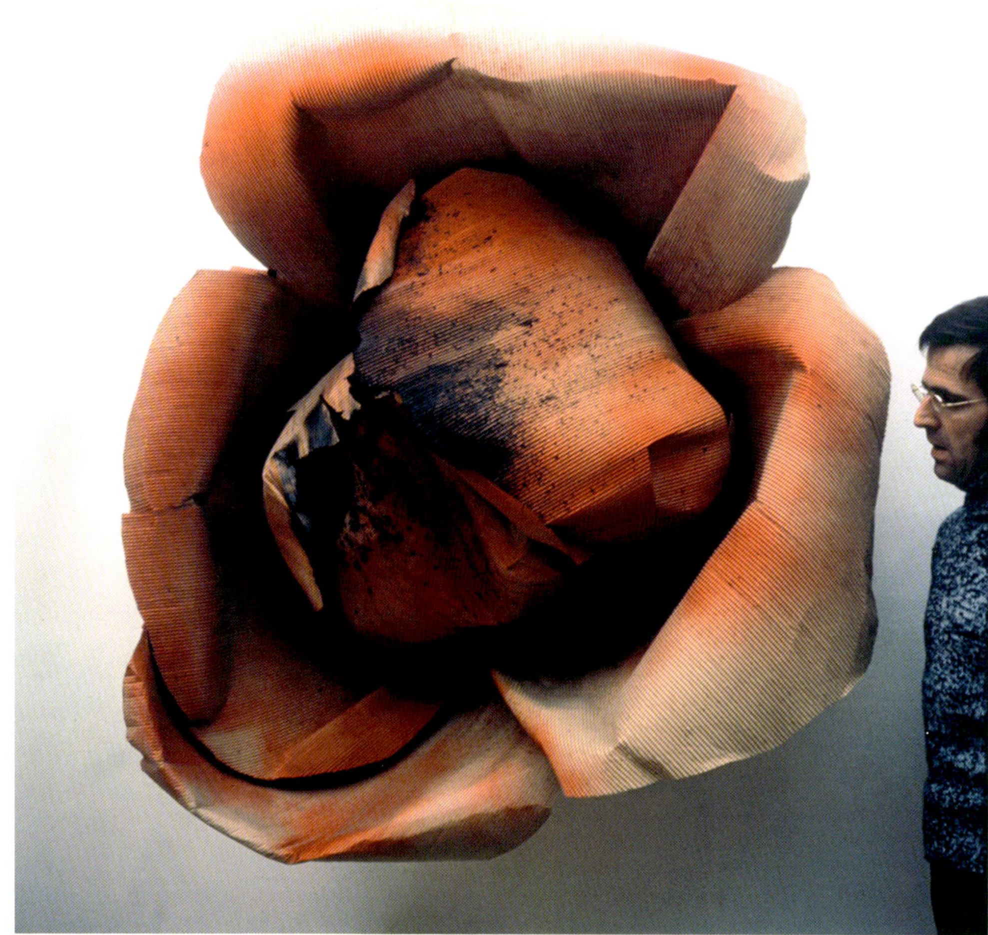

FIG. 84. Michelangelo Pistoletto with his *Rosa bruciata* (Burnt Rose, 1965), in his studio, Turin, late 1965. Corrugated cardboard, paint, spray paint, 55 × 55 × 39⅜ in. (140 × 140 × 100 cm). Photo by Paolo Bressano. Archivio Pistoletto, Biella.

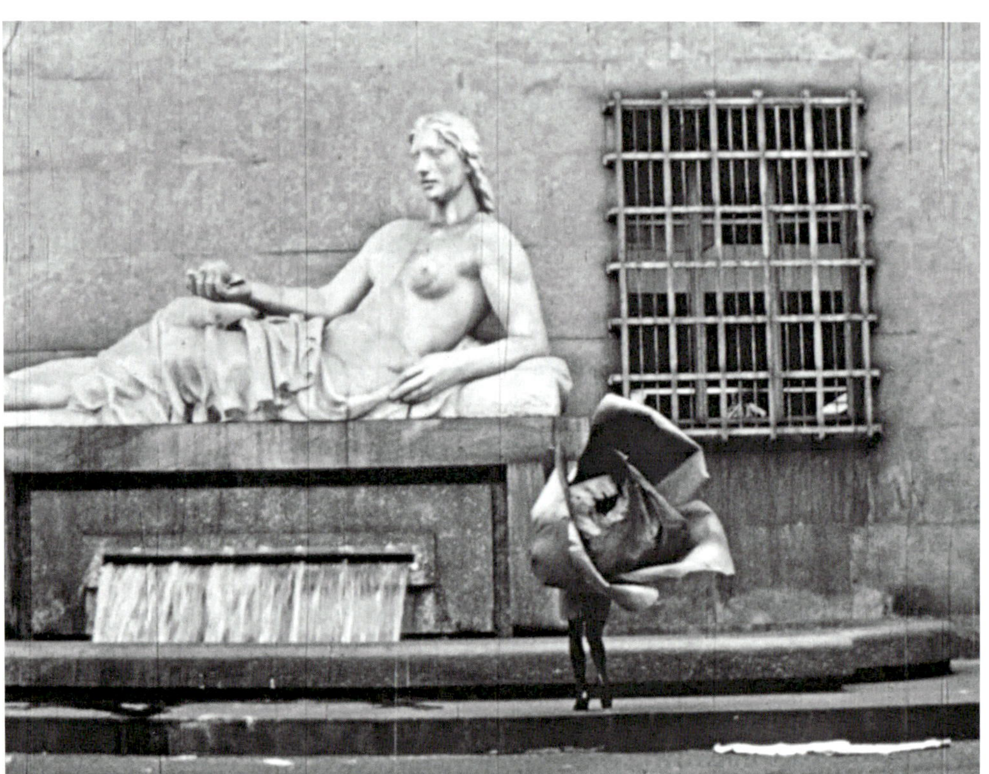

FIG. 85. Film still from Ugo Nespolo, *Buongiorno Michelangelo* (Good Morning Michelangelo), 1968–69. 16mm black-and-white film, sound, 10 min., 40 sec. Direction and photography by Ugo Nespolo, editing by Ugo Nespolo.

the entryway of the Galleria Gian Enzo Sperone in the three-gallery exhibition *Con temp l'azione* ("With Time, Action" and "Contemplation"), also figured history as a blockade (fig. 86).[20] It was a precursor to more overtly political works such as *Trincea* (Trench), a short wall of sandbags later installed in Rome in March 1968. It was a functional parallel to the mirror paintings of brick walls as well as the rag-covered brick walls and structures the artist began making in 1967. The Minus Objects therefore also belong to that other, divergent strand of Arte Povera outlined by Celant a year and a half after he saw them: "a revolutionary way of existence [that] turns into the Reign of Terror." Celant observed that strategy in the comportment and action (*agire*) by all other artists in Celant's original set—except for Pistoletto. If these were "artists whose modes of action pose the problem of this recovery of free self-determination," then the Minus Objects staged their individual liberatory actions as a collective politics, a way of being, *being in,* and *being with* the world.[21]

As is often noted in histories on Pistoletto's work, the artist's decision to make the Minus Objects was catalyzed by a New York visit with art dealer Leo Castelli and curator Alan Solomon, in late 1964 or early 1965, not long after the moment of the Plexiglasses' debut.[22] During a meeting with Castelli and Solomon, who had curated the controversial Rauschenberg-winning Venice Biennale of 1964, the dealer, who had urged the artist to produce more of the mirror paintings for an exhibition at his gallery, insisted that Pistoletto's potential career hinged on increased production of the commercially successful works and relocation to the United States. Put off by Castelli's enterprising agenda and wary of the trappings of signature artistic style, Pistoletto returned home to Turin. While he continued to produce mirror paintings the following year (the Rallies), those works revealed a redirection of the artist's practice away from the everyday, universal thematic for which he had become known toward anticapitalist political imagery. In the fall of 1965, when some of Pistoletto's mirror paintings were vandalized at Castelli's gallery (by an unnamed American artist), he distanced himself from the gallery. He would return to the United States only on brief occasions over the next twenty years.[23]

Potential reasons for Pistoletto's reaction include the pop reception of his work in the United States and the increasingly tense cultural politics of the transatlantic context of 1960s art during the Cold War. Other reasons may have been increased contemplation on pervasive anticapitalist sentiment building in northern Italy with the rise of the workers' movement—a connection to which we see a nod in the photo of *Man with Red Flag* with the Minus Objects, leaning against the wall among them. Likely due to a combination of these reasons, Pistoletto resolved at that point to make work that ignored the art market and its valorization of signature style.[24] One work is notable in this regard: a wall-sized photographic portrait of a grinning Jasper Johns, cropped close to the artist's face. A version of this work, *Le orecchie di Jasper Johns* (The Ears of Jasper Johns, 1966), in which two vertical sections of the mural-scaled portrait (the edges of the portrait photograph) compose

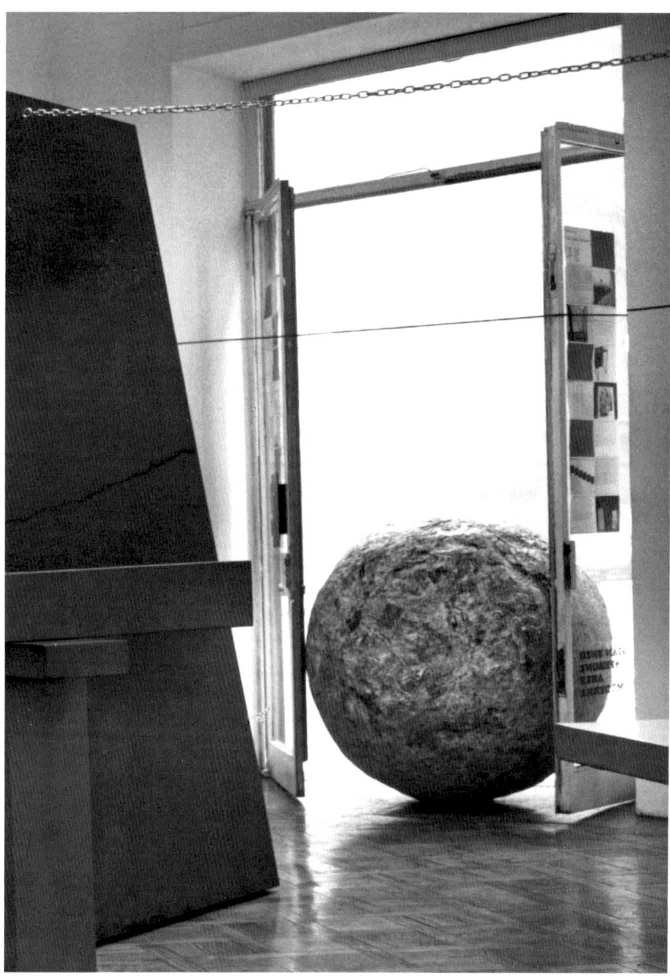

FIG. 86. Installation view of Michelangelo Pistoletto, *Sfera di giornali* (Newspaper Sphere, 1966), 1967. Pressed newspaper, polystyrene core, diameter 39⅜ in. (100 cm). In *Con temp l'azione,* Galleria Gian Enzo Sperone, Turin, opened December 4, 1967. Photo by Paolo Bressano. Archivio Pistoletto, Biella.

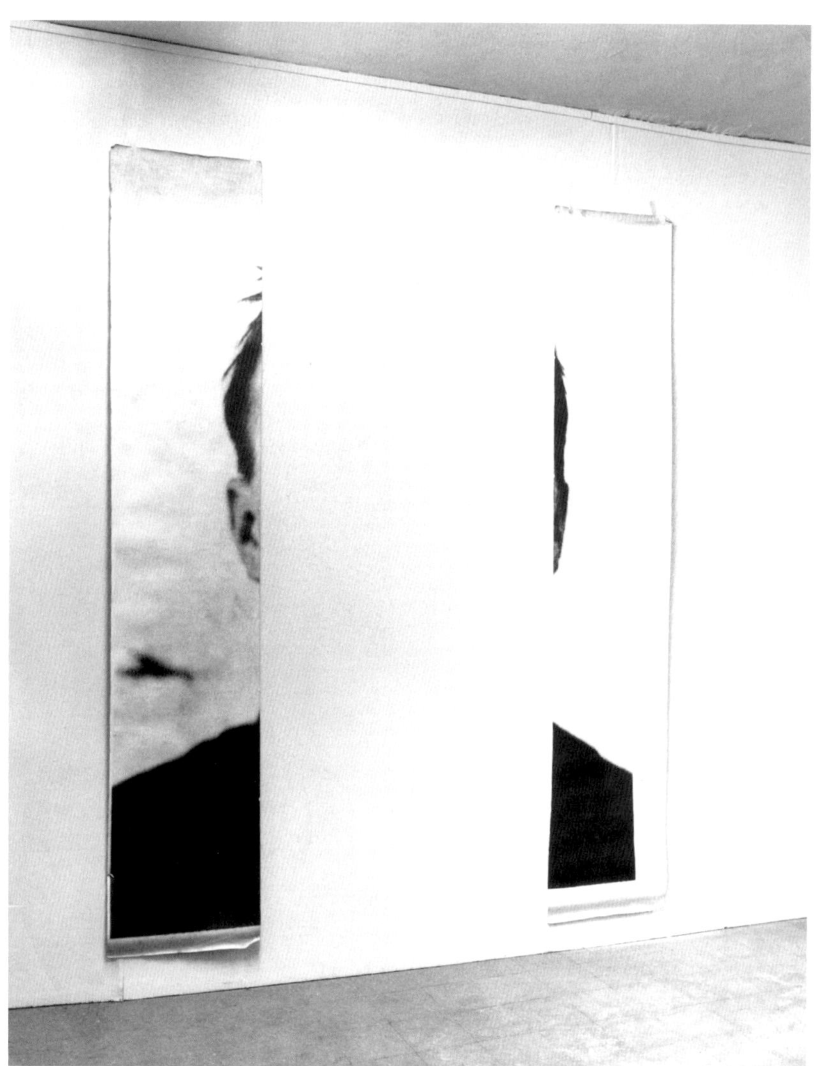

FIG. 87. Michelangelo Pistoletto, *Le orecchie di Jasper Johns* (The Ears of Jasper Johns), 1966. Photograph on paper (2 elements), each 98¼ × 31½ in. (250 × 80 cm). Cittadellarte–Fondazione Pistoletto, Biella.

the work, is seemingly made of the discarded edges of its precedent (fig. 87). (It appeared later in 1966 among adaptations to some of the objects known as the *Versioni*, or "Versions.") The work's image was sourced from a photograph by American photographer Ed Meneeley. The photographic portrait—reformatted by Pistoletto to pop art's sometimes gigantic scale—had appeared in the May 1962 issue of *Métro*, in an article on Johns by Leo Steinberg, where we can deduce Pistoletto saw it. (It was later published in cropped format in 1964 in a catalog for an exhibition of pop in Vienna, in which Johns and Pistoletto participated).[25]

Concurrent with the Minus Objects' production, as with the Plexiglasses, Pistoletto prepared an artist's statement of the same title, in which he situated his new work within the longer trajectory of his recent practice. His narrative begins with his exhibition of his painting, *The Present* (1961), discussed in chapter 1, at Turin's Fine Arts Society in March 1962. The painting depicted a seated figure against a glossy black background that had a peculiar visual effect. Pistoletto stated: "The painted man came forward as if he were alive in the live space of the environment; but the real protagonist was the relationship of instantaneity that was created between the viewer, his reflection, and the painted figure, in an ever-present movement that concentrated the past and the future in itself, as much as to cast their existence into doubt: it was the dimension of time."[26] In this passage, Pistoletto introduces a new term for his work. The relation among viewer, reflection, and figure in the painting—which here he refers to as "the first mirror painting"—was not only spatial but also temporal. If with the Plexiglasses, he continued, he had "aim[ed] to bring the meaning of the mirror into inhabited space," the Minus Objects reflected a subsequent exploration of time. Echoing the narrative of self-introduction articulated in the Plexiglass statement, Pistoletto continued:

> It seems to me with my recent works that I've gone into the mirror, that I've actively entered that dimension of time that was represented in the mirror paintings. My recent works bear witness to the need to live and to act according to this dimension, that is, according to the unrepeatability of each second, of each place and therefore of each present action. . . . What I'm interested in today is to introduce myself, physically, on this line where the four dimensions converge, as if I succeeded in living between the silhouette and the mirroring ground.[27]

The word Pistoletto uses for "living" is *abitare,* in which "to live" means "to dwell" or "reside," as opposed to *vivere,* meaning "to be alive" or "to exist." What logic, if any, may have framed the production of such a series and the kind of living to which they attested? To parse these questions requires situating Pistoletto's work within the historical context of its production, with specific attention to the design-based commodity culture of the series' apparent engagement.

THE POLITICS OF REPRESENTATION AND MODERNITY DURING THE BOOM

The complexity of Italy's economic boom is in some ways best captured by Federico Fellini's iconic film *La dolce vita* (1960). The film depicts a glamorous image of Rome at the time, filled with shiny Alfa Romeos, lux Brioni suits, and other recognizably Italian products that collectively signify the boom of Italian design, marketing, and industry during the economic miracle. As a seductive representation of a thriving, postreconstruction Italy fully recovered from fascism, Fellini's made-in-Italy material excess satirically points to the problematic relation between Italy's prosperous design industry and the "democratic" commodity culture it produced. Indeed, while the rapid industrialization and economic expansion of Italy created a new sense of postfascist national identity, that same identity excluded the majority working classes with low wages and little buying power.[28] As the image of Italy increasingly distanced from fascism became one of *la dolce vita* enjoyed by the bourgeoisie and elite, millions of poorer working-class citizens were increasingly marginalized, socially and geographically. Although consumption among the low to middle classes did change—national consumption from Italy's largest consumer group (middle to low income) was made possible by growing average wages and installment payment plans—class issues persisted.[29] Living in makeshift shelters and *borgate* (shantytowns) that cropped up on the outskirts of Turin, Milan, Rome, and other major cities, Italy's working classes were placed increasingly out of view with the advent of Italy's new urbanism.

As depicted in relatively lesser known films, such as Ermanno Olmi's *Il posto* (The Job, 1961), Italy's popular working classes were largely excluded from a more consumer-friendly model of reality. In Olmi's late neorealist film, the young protagonist Domenico (Sandro Panseri) leaves his dilapidated apartment on the outskirts of Milan in search of employment; while he is ultimately successful, securing work as an errand boy (and later a clerk position, following an employee's death), as is his female counterpart Antonietta (Loredana Detto), the narrative is ultimately not a happy one. His work will be tedious, his pay low. As he walks around the city with Antonietta, his position is inscribed (and reinscribed) as one of spatial and socioeconomic exclusion. The pair stand in the rain outside a well-lit shopwindow, admiring the pristine display of shiny electric appliances, all the latest in Italy's booming *elettrodomestici* industry.[30] Domenico timidly enters a shop selling ready-to-wear men's suiting; unable to afford anything, he nevertheless tries on several jackets. They hang awkwardly on his young, almost gaunt frame. His aspiration is quickly met with failure, absurdity even. Neither jacket nor "suit"—the metonymic symbol of the figure of the white-collar working man—fits.[31]

The conditions of the economic miracle led to a newly globalized, postfascist Italian identity based on the international success of its design and commercial industries but also fueled new internal conflicts and sociopolitical tensions, particularly in the industrial north.[32] Economic and design historians have argued that Italy's new identity was in large part constructed and disseminated by its postwar media, design-based commercial industries, and advertising practices.[33] What it meant to be "Italian" in the 1950s and 1960s was strongly defined by a particular model of bourgeois private consumerism with a taste for *bel disegno,* or "good design."

Consider an advertisement from 1960 for sewing machine company Necchi, a company whose success in

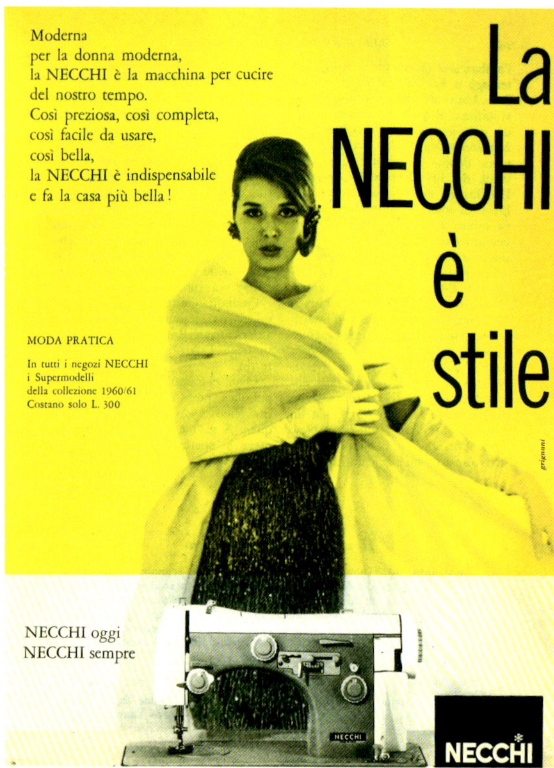

FIG. 88. Print advertisement, *Necchi*, likely by Franco Grignani, 1960.

design and international sales led to the adoption of the tagline "Necchi in tutto il mondo," "Necchi all over the world," reprising earlier success in exports telegraphed in the company's fascist-era advertisements (fig. 88).[34] In the ad, a glamorous young woman stands against a bright-yellow background, balanced by the tagline "La Necchi è stile" (Necchi is style). She is centered in the composition and looks straight out at the viewer. Elegantly dressed in a dark sheath, elbow-length gloves, and formal wrap, which she drapes around her body (and around the object in front of her), she models (and is a model of) confident, alluring style. In front of her is a portable sewing machine, Necchi's latest model, one of its *supermodelli* (supermodels). The name positions the machine as a beautiful woman; the *image* of the sewing machine in front of the woman's body is one of figurative and figural equivalence. This is a sewing machine as beautiful and desirable as the subject to whom it is suited. As the ad tells us, the Necchi is "modern, for the modern woman." The image typified commercial culture during the economic miracle. The subject of the 1960s Necchi advertisements (the sewing machine and the woman who stands behind it) model an idealized picture of postwar Italian modernity, predicated on the private consumption of well-designed Italian products. As the ideal modern Italian woman, the female model is attractive and domestic, stylish and practical—just like the "supermodel" Italian sewing machine.

Such an image illustrates the economically privileged relation between the politics of national identity and those of representation in postwar Italy. This disjunction between popular images of modern bourgeois Italians enjoying democratic economic advancement and the poorer reality many Italians experienced was vast. The boom of Italy's commercial exports shifted the domestic economy to a focus on private consumption.[35] Public institutions and civic services remained relatively unchanged. Housing conditions were poor, especially in working-class neighborhoods, which had developed around city peripheries to accommodate exploding populations of laborers.

In this context, countering common misperceptions of Arte Povera as an engagement of "poor materials" alone, Pistoletto and artists who would come to be associated with Arte Povera also used colored plastics, plexiglass, Lucite, steel, mirrors, fluorescent tubes, fiberglass, and other new synthetic materials associated with Italy's design industries and commercial culture. This work and these tactics make us think more closely about process in relation to the broader series. Other works seemed to visually document their own production but instead highlighted artistic labor that went into the production of other objects in the series. Pistoletto's *Vetrina* (Display Case, 1965) showcased the artist's worn pants, T-shirt, and boots, dirtied from a day's work in the studio, followed by a worn worker's jumpsuit, also belonging to the artist, displacing the goods and fine clothing presented in window displays, as in the Italian department store La Rinascente (fig. 89).[36] (Pistoletto also designed some displays, archival documents reveal, for Turin-based grocer Borello.) We expect to see a men's suit, the ubiquitous symbol of the economic miracle captured in advertisements of the period, as in Armando Testa's iconic campaign for Facis (fig. 90). In a later interview with Celant held in 1971, Pistoletto offered an account for his conceptualization of this work, among others. On *Display Case,* he said:

> The Minus Objects were born from several reasons. . . . [I] imagined another thing of the character of design; that is, I made a small display case; I didn't

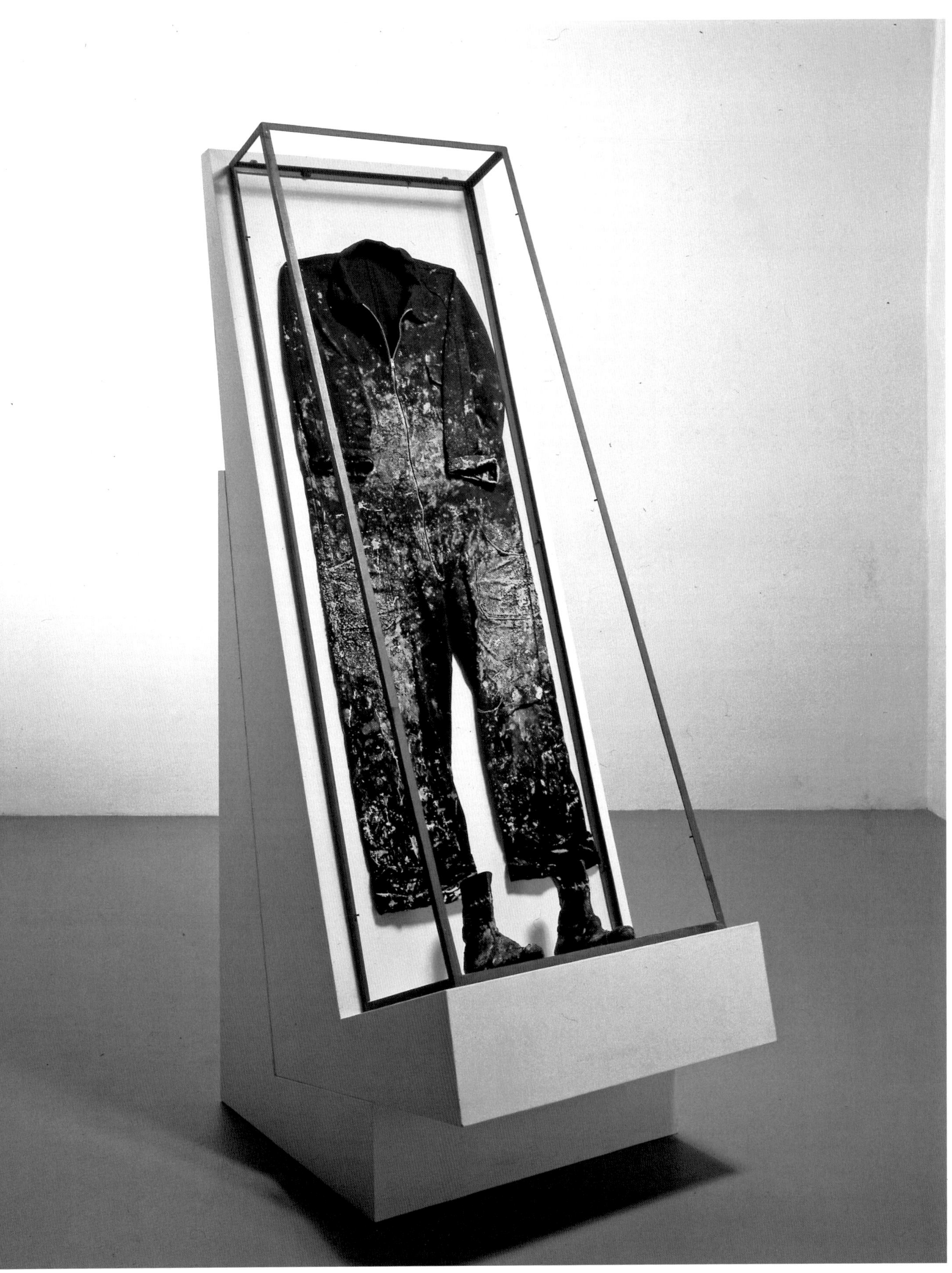

FIG. 89. Michelangelo Pistoletto, *Vetrina* (Display Case), 1965–66. Wood, metal, paint, artist's jumpsuit, boots, 92½ × 39⅜ × 31½ in. (235 × 100 × 80 cm). Cittadellarte–Fondazione Pistoletto, Biella.

> know what I could put in it. I drew it up and had it made by a carpenter. . . . [When] it arrived in the studio, I was looking at it over and over until I had to go out. I took off my dirty work clothes, shoes, jacket, and pants, and instead of putting them on a chair, I put them in the little display case: They became clothes in a vitrine.[37]

Recalling the factory labor that supported more than a third of the population in Turin at the time, Pistoletto's clothes displaced the desirable goods or commodities that display cases are made to present.

ONE FEWER THING, ONE MORE PERSON

This connection between the Minus Objects and labor is amplified when we consider the artist's later comments on the series. To Bruno Corà in the 1980s, Pistoletto remarked: "I called them 'Minus Objects' because in my opinion every action that one does is a liberation from a need. In this sense a thing done is a one less thing [*una cosa di meno*], considering it energy spent, gone out, consumed."[38] In this framing, *Display Case* aligns with the 1960s exploration of the art object in relation to reconceptualizations of artistic labor; it recalls, for example, Leo Steinberg's description of Robert Morris's constructed sculpture of the early 1960s as "a thing done."[39] But Pistoletto's engagement of the figural distinguishes these works from others that would explore labor through neoconstructivist aesthetics or serial production, two common strategies that artists employed to reconsider legitimate artistic labor at the time.[40] The clothes in *Display Case*, by virtue of their proximity to the artist's laboring body, function as a metonym for manual, physical labor, as well as a figural index thereof. The exertion of the artist's body has marked the clothes with sweat and progressive wear on the material. The arrangement of the clothes in the case correlates to the bodily form of the artist they covered. While *Display Case* presents the artist vis-à-vis his body and his work as commodities, it also symbolically displays the human labor that, in Marxist theory, is "secreted" within commodities. (For Marx, when we look at commodities, we do not see the labor expenditure that went into making them; this is a major contributor to the alienating environment of capitalist society.) Rather than articulate what Celant would in 1970 call the "maximum entropy of work in art," Pistoletto's objects by contrast seemed to variably draw attention to and perhaps even exaggerate (given *Display Case*'s origins in outsourced work) the manual and artistic labor exerted in their production.[41]

Mario Merz's *Trucioli* (Shavings, 1967–69) is another such contradictory object: a misshapen bale of wood shavings, haphazardly bound with twine and intersected with a fluorescent neon tube that sticks up from the loosely packed form (fig. 91). In Italian, *trucioli* generally refers to wood shavings or sawdust, with specific emphasis on the material as a byproduct of mechanical woodworking. It is also commonly used to refer to various packaging materials, such as shredded paper (*trucioli di carta*), straw (*di paglia*), and plastic stuffing (*di cellofan*), often used for decorative purposes. Under such a title, the viewer is directed less to the work's formal qualities (to its primarily organic form) and more to its economic ones. In Merz's *Igloo di Giap* (Giap's Igloo, 1968), whose title refers to the North Vietnamese general of the same name, a mound of sandbags is decorated with neon script lettering like that which decorates Italian storefronts in Milan and Turin. In Kounellis's *Cotoniera* (Cotton Container, 1967), shown at Galleria L'Attico in Rome in 1967 and featured in Tommaso Trini's important essay on Arte Povera, "Nuovo alfabeto per corpo e materia" (New Alphabet for Body and Matter), published in *Domus* in January 1969 (also published in the catalog for the now-canonical exhibition *Live in Your Head: When Attitudes Become Form*), a sleek, steel trapezoidal cube seems to have failed (somewhat

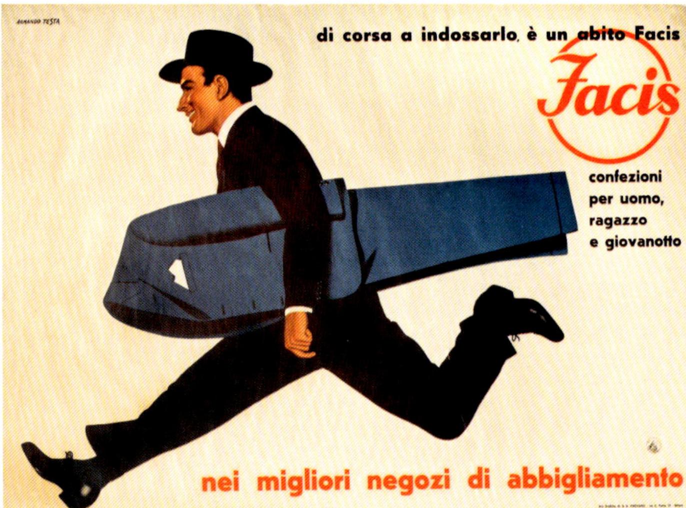

FIG. 90. Armando Testa, Facis, "Di corsa a indossarlo è un abito Facis" (Hurry up and wear it, it's a Facis suit), 1956. Archivio Storico Armando Testa, Turin.

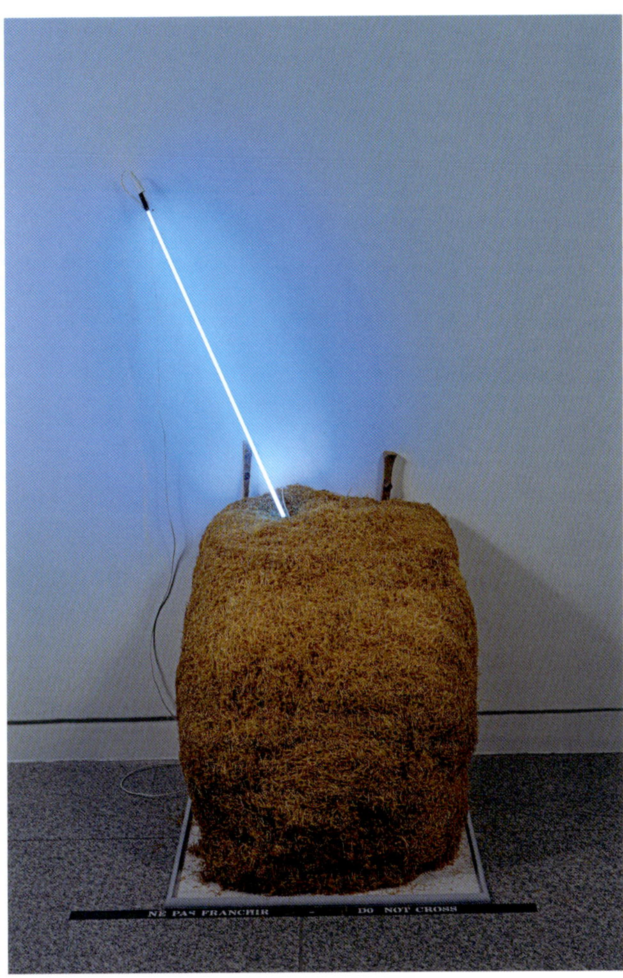

FIG. 91. Mario Merz, *Trucioli* (Shavings), 1967–69. Wood shavings, fluorescent light tube, twine, 59 × 31½ × 27½ in. (150 × 80 × 70 cm). Musée départemental d'art ancien et contemporain, Épinal, France.

impossibly) to contain the white cotton stuffing that pushes through its corners. For Trini, the work exemplified Kounellis's "affirmation" of a "sottonatura" or "subnature," in which "[the] natural and artificial, living and inert, alienated and unalienated" are held in tension. The result, Trini argued, is that "man is both absent and present, man's labor is a toil but also a liberation." Ultimately, this tension "lands on the unification . . . of subject and object."[42] On one hand, then, these objects function as material signs of the economic success of Italian design and advertising, postfascist contemporaneity and renewed nationalism in the *secondo dopoguerra*; on the other, they functioned as artistic signs of the social problems engendered by the economic miracle, some of which were made to seem less real by virtue of the idealized popular imagery of Italy that circulated in support of Italian commerce. Arte Povera's objects were conditioned by what we might call, following Marx, a "material dialectic"—a seemingly contradictory meeting of impoverished and commodity materials—between high- and low-tech, durable and flimsy, popular and passé. Celant attributed this contradiction to an "incoherence."[43] More recent scholarship has resituated Arte Povera less as a literal exercise of impoverished materialism and more as one of experimentation and new processes, theatricality, collaboration, leftist activism, technology, and engagement with artifice.[44] The Minus Objects emerged at a time in which distinctive reworkings of figuration were underway in Italian advertising, constituting what we might call a "figural turn" in postwar Italian commercial culture. The Minus Objects' navigation of those conventions of figuration and associated politics of representation repositions them not only as "lesser" objects but as "lesser" *figural* objects.

For further evidence, we return to *Display Case*'s subversion of the commodity object via this figurative (and figural) presentation of human labor. In the working clothes, we see a nonliteral stand-in for the laboring artist's body and the literal bodily residue of the artist. *Display Case* distinguishes Pistoletto's series from other works in Arte Povera that also explored labor and industrial aesthetics, such as Gianni Piacentino's sculptures of the period. One primary text is particularly elucidating in this regard. Also in "New Alphabet for Body and Matter," Trini described Piacentino's geometric constructions—which, like the Minus Objects, appeared more like furniture items than sculptures—as engaged with "realtà operativa": "working" or "operative reality" (fig. 92).[45] (Indeed, Piacentino and Pistoletto, as well as Piero Gilardi, were close in 1965; they often visited one another's studios.)[46] Piacentino's work did not seek to transform the world, Trini wrote, but rather "utilized . . . a concrete operation on reality." Though not mentioned by Trini, an additional contribution to this effect was Piacentino's practice of spraying his structures with automobile paint—a skill he had gained in his earlier career in this role.[47] Piacentino viewed his work as "closer to that of a furniture maker or builder than an abstract sculptor," as Trini quoted the artist in the essay. Of even greater significance in this comparison is Trini's description of Piacentino's architectural sculpture as a "crisis of the institutionalized object." Trini identified a similar crisis in the produced and institutional object, and the problem of self-removal

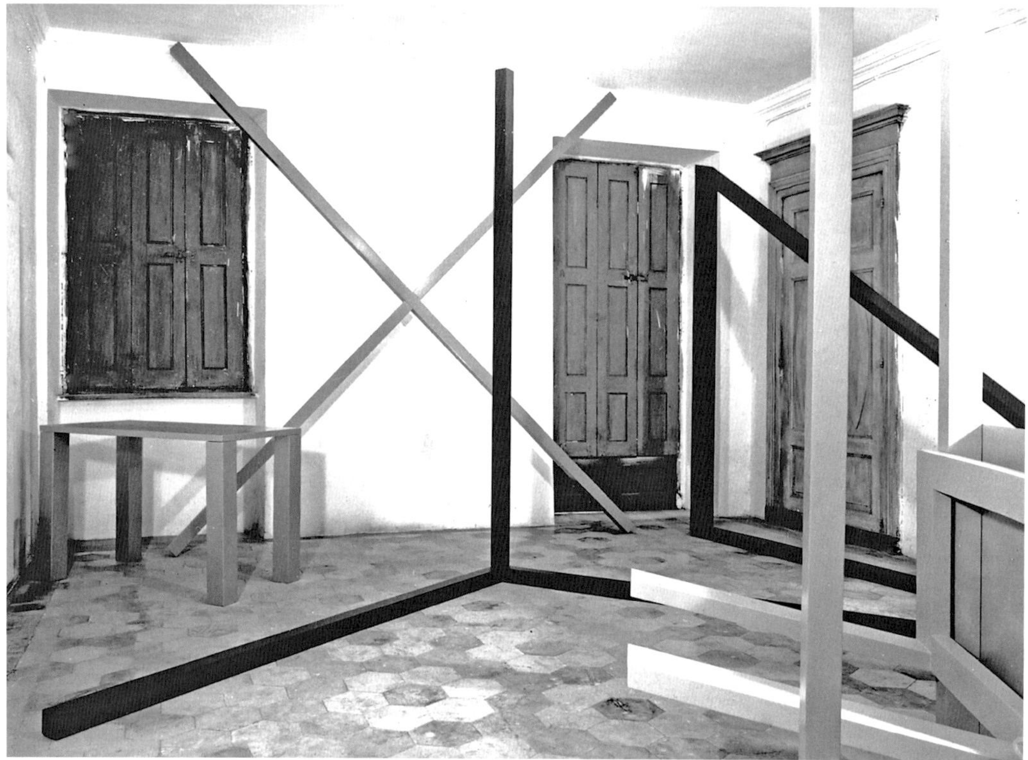

FIG. 92. Gianni Piacentino, works in the artist's studio, Turin, 1966. From left: *Silver-Gray Table Sculpture* (1966), *Dark Dull Pink Large X* (1966), *Dark Purple-Gray Three Dimensions* (1966), *Blue-Purple Rectangle-Triangle* (1966). Photo by Paolo Bressano. Archivio Piacentino, Turin.

that Pistoletto's Minus Objects also underscore: "Piacentino creates sculptures that are 'furniture items' and vice versa: they are the crisis of the institutionalized object. Building posts, tables, windows and doors, wall mirrors are reproposed through a technique and process of recognition that is really the work of young artists who are only trying to distance themselves from operative reality."[48] Piacentino and Pistoletto explored processes and aesthetics of construction, investigated sculpture as a built object for inhabited use, and challenging sculpture as an institutional object, problematizing the work of art as endowed with commodity aesthetics. In contrast to Piacentino, however, Pistoletto homed in on the sociopolitical and artistic conflicts associated with invisible human labor, the commoditized body in Italian design's figural-object trend, and self-valorized subjectivity that surrounded design aesthetics as capitalist aesthetics and the production of the work of art in the neo-Marxist context of Italy in the mid-1960s.

The tendency to categorize Arte Povera, and Pistoletto's work, within the framework of postminimalism can therefore not account for the more complex underpinnings of the Minus Objects' conceptual logic, the diversity of their methods of realization, or the significance of their production in mid-1960s Italy. This historiographic problem can be addressed by examining process in the Minus Objects and in the theatrical works, role-playing exercises, and experiments in communal living that followed. Those experiments were positioned as an extension of the conceptual logic of the project *in meno* but are often held apart from their sculptural precedents. A closing discussion of process in Pistoletto's object-based and theatrical experiments as minor productions, or objects and actions in meno, finds that, unlike the "free unbound act" of Celant's characterization or the makeshift logic offered by later scholarship, these works were bound up with a perpetual performance of new subjectivities, articulated through a methodical experimentation with action and labor that transcends the confines of media and sought to reposition process as a means of self-liberation within a collective framework.

What emerges in these examples above is a series of object-based productions that were the products of conceptual automatism and expedient (or at least expedited) construction, bound up with a serious contemplation and performance of labor in many forms—from the absurdly overwrought and inefficient to the altogether outsourced. Many of the Minus Objects explored and problematized the relations between labor expenditure (how much work goes into making something), labor aesthetics (here, how much work *looks* to have gone into something), and our capacity to see human labor expended within a commodity—a concern thereby connected to alienation, both social and reflexive. Applying pressure to the Marxist theory that labor is secreted within commodities, the Minus Objects by contrast often show us the work (actual or imagined) that went into something (or could have gone into making something) via an aesthetic of poor work (an appearance that suggests sloppy construction or poor quality) or via a figural aesthetic, realized when the artwork presents itself as a bodily object. The latter draws our attention to the embodied human labor that has gone into making something and that the object figures. Though connected to process art, this tactic finds more precise legacies in contemporary artwork such as Lucy Raven's video artwork *Curtains* (2014), that similarly figures the aesthetic commodity (here, 3-D video) as a visibly embodied site of human labor.[49]

PISTOLETTO AND THE FIGURAL TURN IN ITALIAN ADVERTISING

Pistoletto's artistic training included design coursework in the early 1950s at the Scuola Testa in Turin, where he studied under up-and-coming designer Armando Testa. By the mid-1960s, Testa had emerged as an advertising icon, known for his minimal aesthetic, whimsy, and colorful, geometric forms, which had, through his many campaigns, become a defining feature of Italian popular culture. Successful early campaigns for Italian companies—Martini e Rossi (1948), Ciclista Superga (1947), Carpano (1949–51), Pirelli (1954), Borsalino (1954), and ready-to-wear clothier Facis (1954)—earned Testa a succession of national design awards and campaigns for other companies, many of whom adopted Testa's designs in the long term as part of their visual brand. Other campaigns quickly followed across the early 1960s, including Peroni (1960), Punt e Mes (1960), Paulista (Lavazza, 1960), and Sasso olive oil (1964). Testa's success was well publicized in Turin. Newspaper exposés celebrated his work as that of an *artista* or *cartellonista* (poster artist), as opposed to a commercial designer or head of an advertising agency.[50] Although Testa's images were often embraced for their whimsy and irreverence, some of Testa's designs scandalized northern Italians. His iconic campaign for Carpano vermouth included caricatures of historical figures of former Italian nobility and the monarchy, now defunct. In response to criticism, Testa defended the campaign and its anti-authoritarian politics.[51] As his designs became pervasive in Italian commercial culture, they were embraced by Turin for their artistic value, bolstering the city's cultural capital in the postwar period.[52]

Critical to Testa's success was his ability to marry abstraction, which informed his now-iconic geometric style, to more popular figurative design. The result was a new form of design, which often conflated representations of the body with object-forms in such a way as to literalize figurative (symbolic) meaning in figural (bodily and imagistic) form. This strategy was distinctive from the advertising trope in fascist Italy, mapped by Karen Pinkus, of stylized figures or characters such as the Michelin man (notably, a French company), who served to "sell" the product to consumers in the absence of a local salesman.[53] One of the earliest examples of Testa's strategy was his campaign of 1956 for a cold and flu remedy from Algostop (fig. 93). The advertisement depicts the face of a man whose nose has been displaced by a faucet. His eyes are squinted and puffy, and his mouth is open as he strains to breathe. The tagline—"Raffreddore / Algostop! (Fa bene in fretta.)" (Cold / Algostop! [Feel better fast.])—offers a solution to what the figure tells us: the man has a cold and is suffering from a stuffy nose. The image does not represent an actual person suffering from a stuffy nose; rather, it articulates its subject through visual material that literalizes the bodily experience of a cold in *figural* as opposed to conventionally figurative form.

Testa's prolific work quickly concretized a graphic style that would influence Italian design through the 1960s, 1970s, and 1980s and would come to be associated with Italian products on a global scale as commercial exports expanded into foreign markets. Although Pistoletto declined Testa's invitation to join his firm in 1953 in favor of opening his own graphic design business, the Minus Objects' geometric forms, bright color palette, and foregrounded material construction aligned Pistoletto's works with Testa's popular style

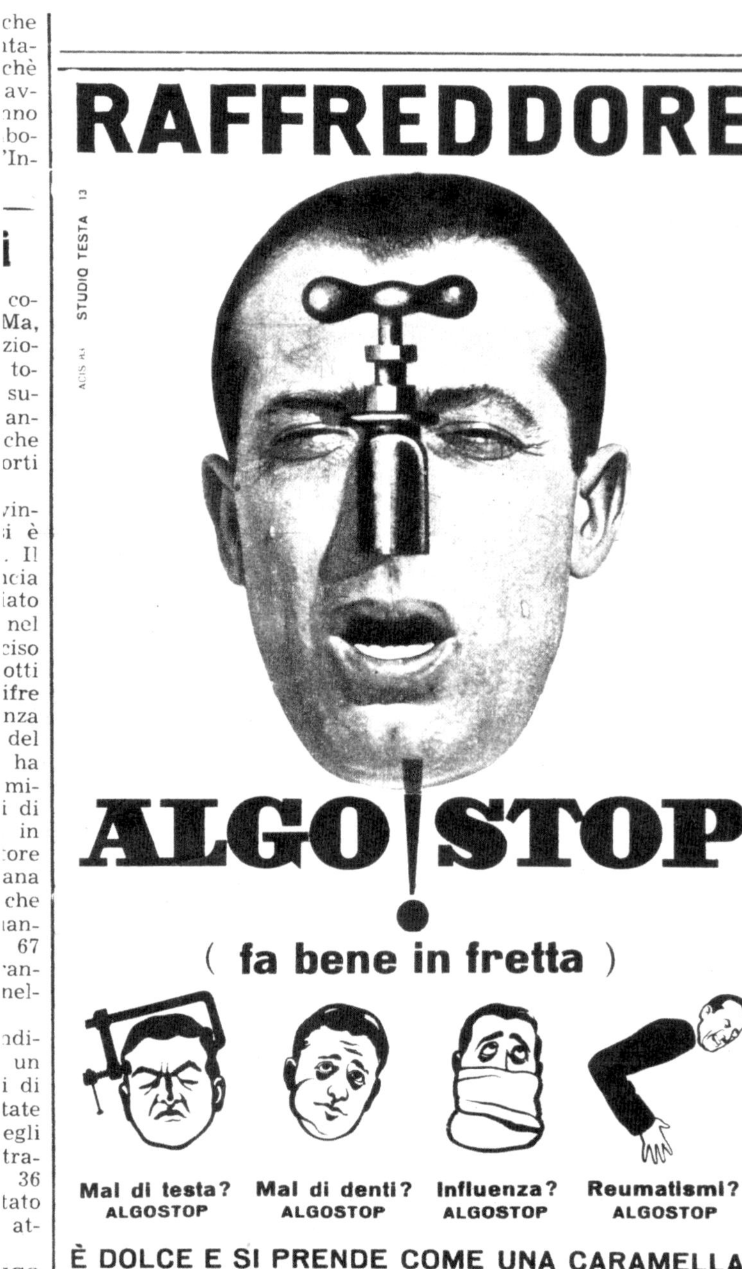

FIG. 93. Studio Testa, print advertisement, Algostop, "Raffeddore / Algostop! (Fa bene in fretta.)" (Cold / Algostop! [Feel better fast.]), 1956. AIAP CDPG Centro di Documentazione sul Progetto Grafico, Collezione Armando Testa. In *Il Tempo,* no. 8 (February 1956).

and the new mode of Italian commercial design it helped initiate.

Although Pistoletto's exploration of design aesthetics is perhaps most pointed with the Minus Objects, this history prompts consideration of the longer trajectory of design in the artist's early practice as well as its significance for Arte Povera. As a professional graphic designer from about 1953 to 1958, he established the Studio Pubblicità Michelangelo Olivero with locations at his parents' home on the Po and on Via Andrea Doria (at the intersection with Via Cavour); his business card featured his self-designed logo: a Harlequin figure. Pistoletto designed ads for Necchi, Singer, Visnova, and Pibigas, among other well-known Italian companies.[54] A number of ads were made for petrol products, underscoring the auto industry boom.[55] Other ads were for Turin-based, well-known Italian consumables.[56] Others still were for personal care.[57] A large number of ads were also produced (or mocked up, for practice) for home furnishing shows and elettrodomestici, including sewing machines, refrigerators, and electric heaters.[58]

In his print advertisement of 1953 for sewing-machine company Visnova, a piece of cloth hangs from the foot of an unmanned, portable electronic sewing machine, where it is tacked in place by the lowered needle (fig. 94).[59] As the cloth drapes down toward the center of the image, the flat textile gains volume and takes the shape of a human figure, nearly the size of the sewing machine above. The figure's arms are outstretched toward the lower register of the page, where they direct our attention by pointing to the company logotype printed below. As a design, Pistoletto's advertisement reflected figurative conventions in postwar Italian advertising: first, the manipulation of scale such that the size of the figure would match that of the advertised product, and second, the more product-specific motif of the figure using the machine to sew the garment they are currently wearing. At the same time, Pistoletto departs from these models. The figure is no longer a distinct entity from the appliance; instead, it is conflated with the cloth that runs through the machine. The suggested message is that the Visnova sewing machine can assemble garments as well as subjects. The appliance is transformative (even transfigurational); while here the image draws upon historical racialized tropes, it presents the machine as capable of producing fashions and identities for the world.

We can find this conflation of figure and object (or user and product) in a wide range of Pistoletto's print-advertising design work from his studies and early professional work. Only recently discovered in a long-forgotten box at the artist's foundation, these works are discussed here for the first time. The discovery gives us a wealth of new information about the artist's formative work in design. A series of mock advertisements for Turin-based Martini, some done as exercises in the Scuola Testa, others as examples for potential clients of the artist's own ad agency, depict the brand's signature bottles and three varieties of vermouths as the bodies of their respective consumers. In one, each of the three Martini-men has a distinctive hat and facial expression; they function as signs of their respective tastes and personas, as do the branded products they literally and figuratively embody. In another version of the same ad, the three bottles (and consumers) are refashioned in historic military garb. White, dry, and red vermouth are aligned in an advancing formation. Each wears a knight's helmet, carries a metal spear, pointed forward, and holds a shield marked with the brand name and product logo. "The avant-garde of vermouths," reads the tagline (fig. 95). In another mock advertisement still, this time for the brand's China Martini (referring not to the country of China but to China root, the plant of the product's derivation), the three bottle-figures are an alpinist (in traditional Piedmontese alpinist dress); a figure in a colonial uniform who carries a life buoy; and an elegant mustachioed figure with a bow tie, walking stick, short top hat, and distinguished expression. Mock advertisements for Superix shoes and *Visto* magazine included other objects-as-figures. For Superix, Pistoletto created a figure out of the company logo (as body), an embroidery hoop (as head), and Superix shoes (as feet) (fig. 96). The tagline reads "La scarpa che prende piede": "The shoe that's taking a foothold." The ad, dominated by a figure with giant shoes, renders the figurative meaning of *prende piede* literally, but in the form of a figure. For *Visto,* a reading chair, with a smiling face, is

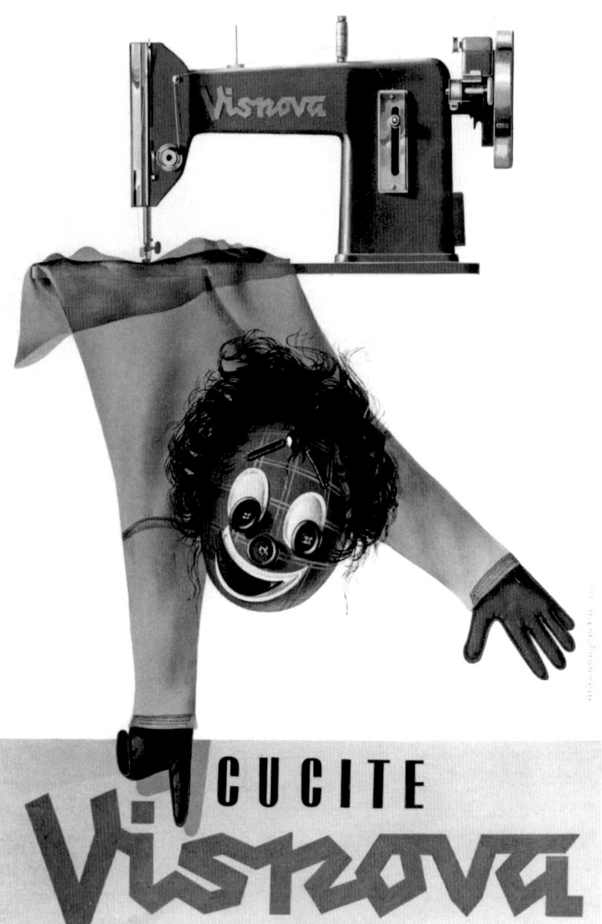

FIG. 94. Michelangelo Pistoletto, photograph of his print advertisement, Visnova, "Cucite Visnova" (Sew Visnova), 1953. Black-and-white photograph, 9 × 6¼ in. (22.8 × 16 cm). Archivio Pistoletto, Biella.

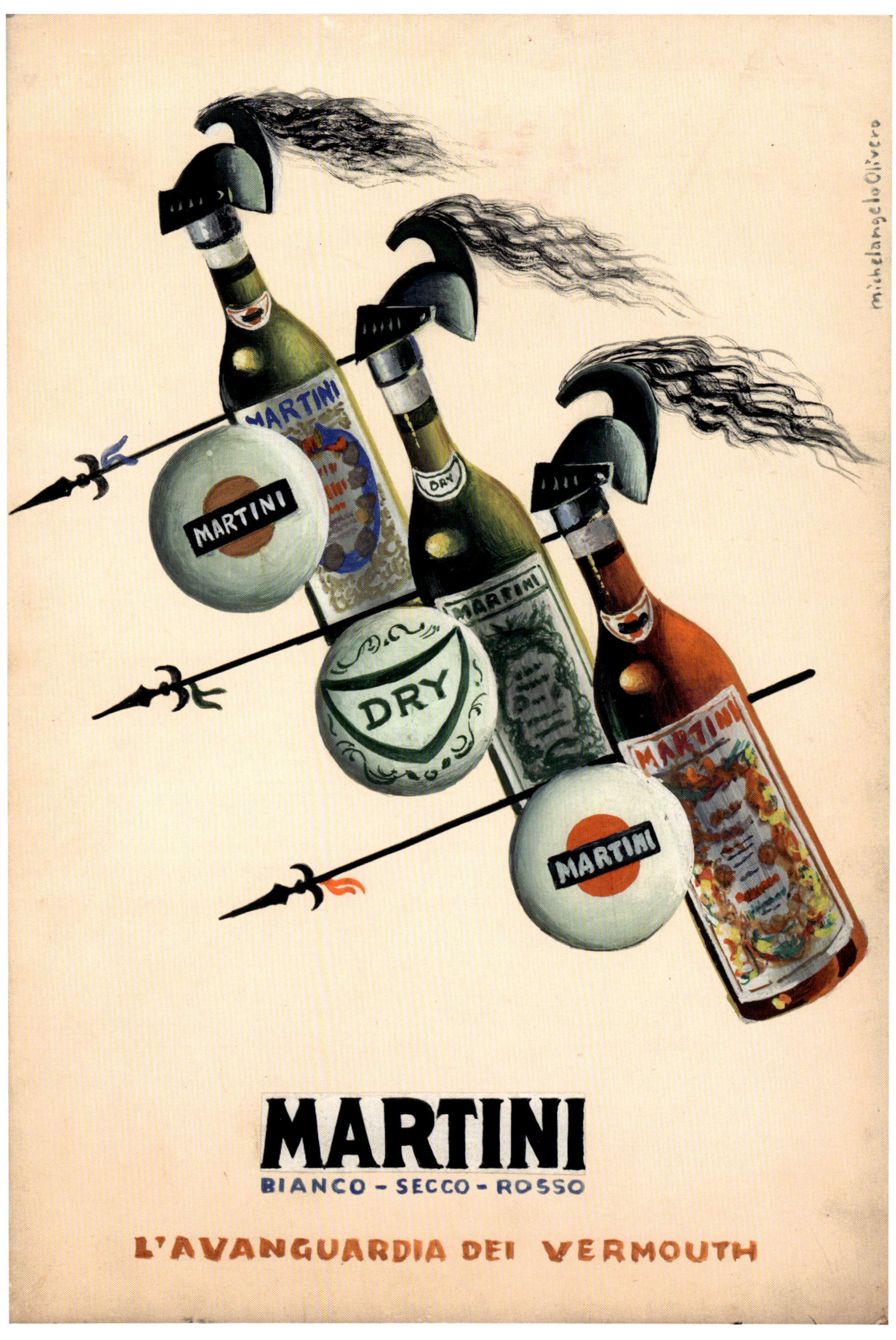

FIG. 95. Michelangelo Pistoletto, unpublished advertisement, Martini, "L'avanguardia dei vermouth" (The avant-garde of vermouths), ca. 1953–55. Acrylic and ink on board, 13⅝ × 9⅝ in. (34.5 × 24.5 cm). Archivio Pistoletto, Biella.

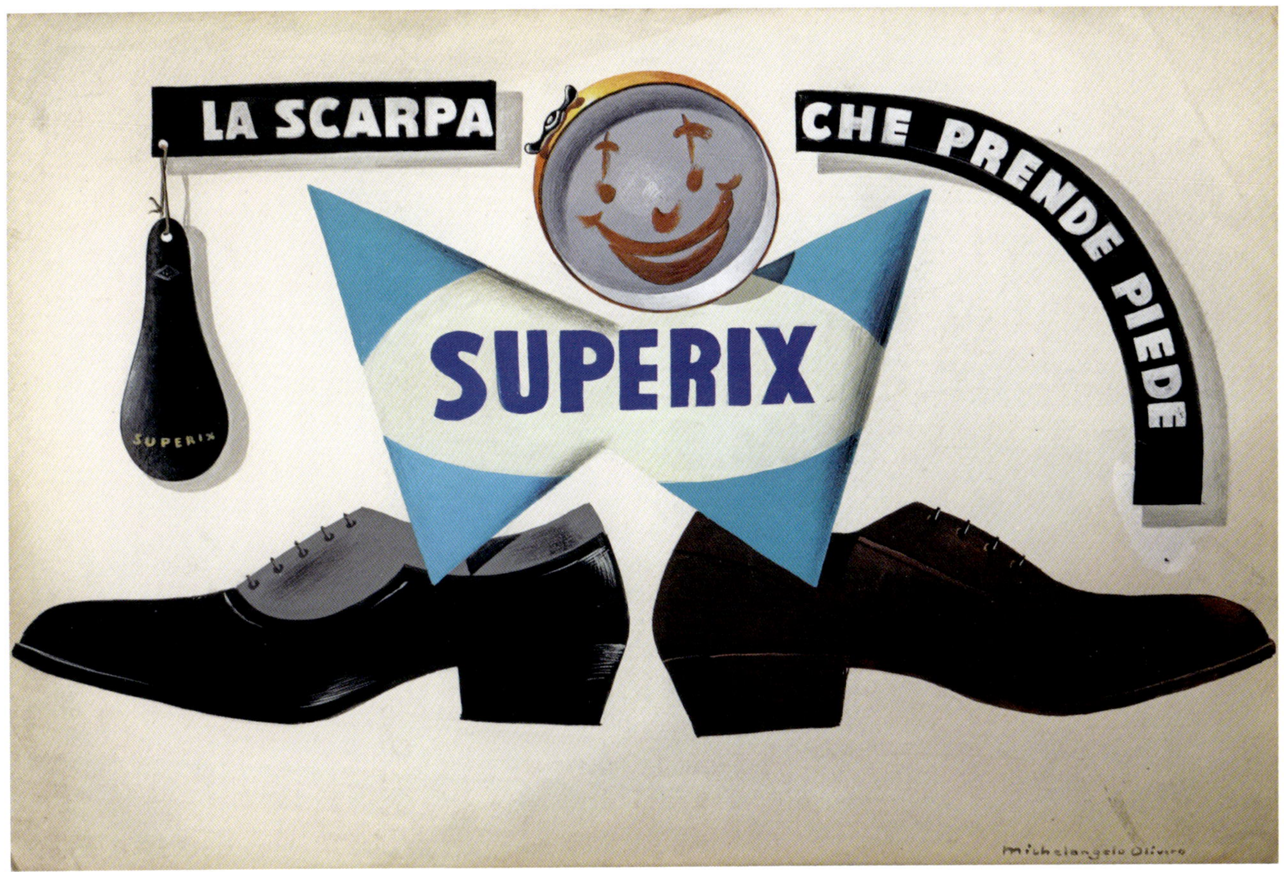

FIG. 96. Michelangelo Pistoletto, advertisement exercise, Superix, "La scarpa che prende piede" (The shoe that's taking a foothold), ca. 1953. Acrylic on board, 13¾ × 19¾ in. (35 × 50 cm). Archivio Pistoletto, Biella.

reading the magazine the advertisement asks us to read. The chair's depiction as a figural object literalizes the activity intended for it.

Sketch sheets of figurative studies might recall similar studies by Renaissance masters; in Pistoletto's sheets, however, figurative studies of parts of bodies are accompanied by typographical studies of product logos. In one sheet, we see an arm raised, forearm pulled back, about to hurl a vague object; a bent leg, knee thrusting forward, as if in midair during a running sprint; and a sketch of the product name, Cinzano vermouth (fig. 97). In another, a seductive pair of lips floats next to a tube of Nivorio toothpaste. Such studies reveal Pistoletto's formative exploration of the body was always in relation to the commodity world it now figuratively represented and, in Pistoletto's images, often also literally embodied.

This conflation of figure and object parallels a similar renegotiation of the figure in other areas of postwar Italian graphic design. In artist and designer Severo Pozzati's campaign from 1959 for clothier Lebole, a yellow measuring tape loops and bends around the page, tracing the form of a human figure. In one version of the ad, Pozzati's now iconic *L'Uomo metro,* or Meter Man figure, carries a smart, orange sport jacket. The jacket hangs neatly in the crook of his left arm, which is a section of the tape measure. The enumerated ticking of his "arm" runs under the fabric, framing it on either side. In his right hand, signified by the rolled end of the tape, he holds a sign of the same color that reads *crociera:* "cruise" (fig. 98). The efficacy of the resort-wear advertisement hinges on the symbolic value of the jacket and tape measure: as opposed to seeing a real person modeling the clothing, we are presented with a symbolic subject—a businessman, with tailored, well-fitting clothes for his vacation—evoked only by the article of the design's advertisement.

A similar reworking of consumer and good can be found in the work of Italian designer Franz Marangolo, most famously in his campaign from 1950 for Campari

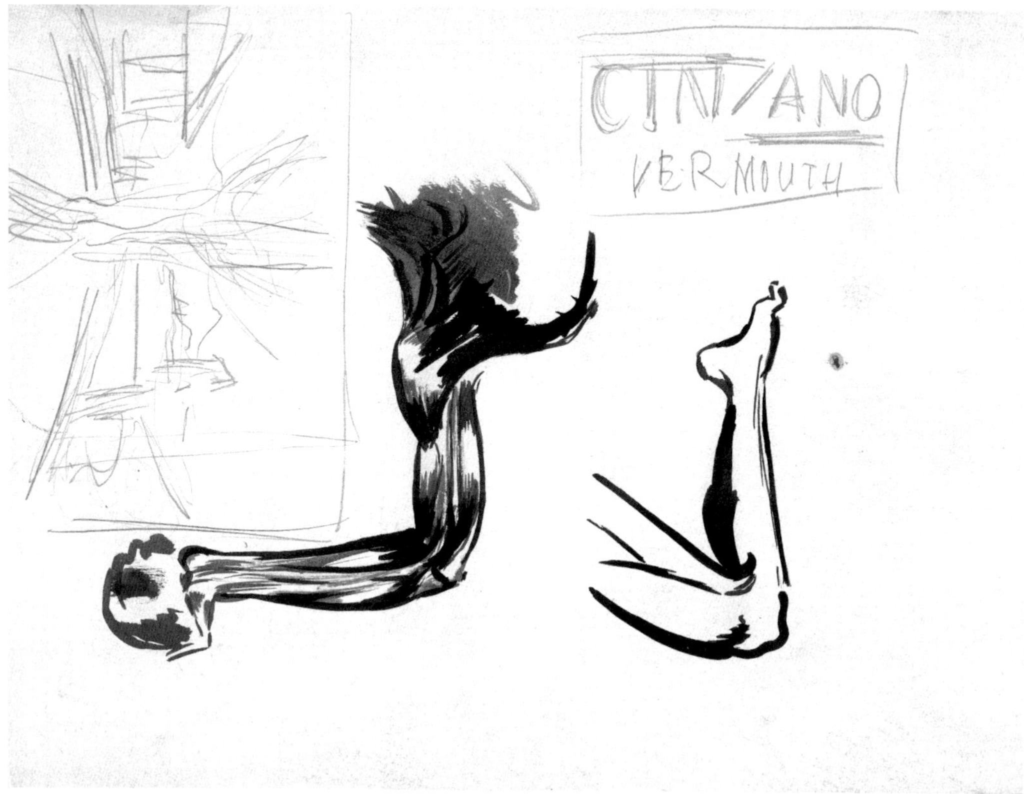

FIG. 97. Michelangelo Pistoletto, sheet with figure sketches and Cinzano vermouth mock-up, mid-1950s. Graphite and ink on newsprint, 9 × 11¼ in. (23 × 31 cm). Archivio Pistoletto, Biella.

(fig. 99). In a print advertisement, we see the iconic Campari soda bottle (itself also designed by an artist, Italian futurist Fortunato Depero, in 1930), filled with the signature red beverage. Centered in the upper register of the image, it tilts slightly forward, against a lime-green background. A pair of shapely legs clad in high heels sprout from the base of the bottle, which in turn doubles as the hemline of a red shift mini dress. With her left foot kicked up behind her, the Campari bottle-as-coquette skips across the page. Her bottle cap, flipped open, doubles as a pillbox hat. She glances over at us with a single well-lined eye; it is just enough to suggest a flirtatious look. Framed by the tagline "per la vostra sete" (for your thirst), the advertisement bears an additional message at the foot of the page: *Campari soda corre col tempo!* The copy has two meanings: literally, "Campari soda runs with time!" and figuratively, "Campari soda keeps up with the times!" The advertisement communicates the figurative meaning of the tagline (Campari is always on trend) through a *literal* depiction of it (Campari is wearing the latest fashions) in the form of the bottle-as-figure—that is, in the form of a *figural* as opposed to figurative representation. Campari quenches the thirst of the on-the-go modern subject in the long run. These images were pervasive. Pistoletto's own advertising designs in the artist's archive include a painted sketch of a similar slogan—"la guerra fredda contro la sete" (the Cold War against thirst)—as well as mock ads for Campari sodas.

Through this reworking of the figure, these designs (as well as Pistoletto's) are examples of a broader figural turn within postwar Italian commercial culture. Like the idealized, Italian bourgeois "model" subject exemplified by the Necchi advertisement, these designs set up, most often, an equivalence between modern Italian subjects and well-designed Italian products. What is distinctive about these designs, however, is equivalence is articulated in the form of the representation of the product (to be consumed), *subsumed* into the representation of the consumer (the figure). They literalize (and literally figure) the process of consumption through this new form of figuration, specifically by engaging a new figural-object convention of Italian design.

FIGURAL OBJECTS

Study of Pistoletto's design work as part of this figural turn in postwar Italian commercial imagery brings a new perspective to the Minus Objects. We become

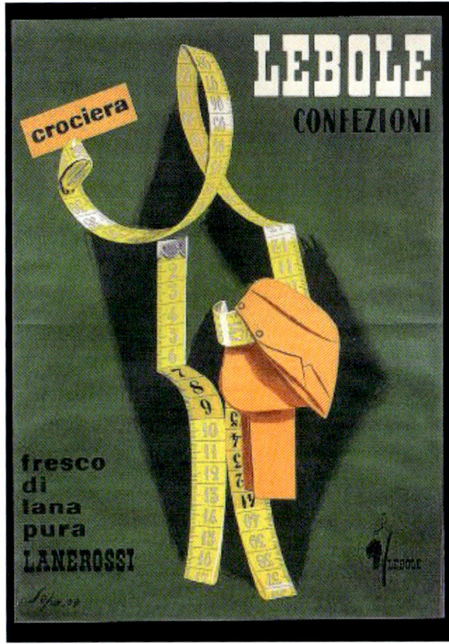

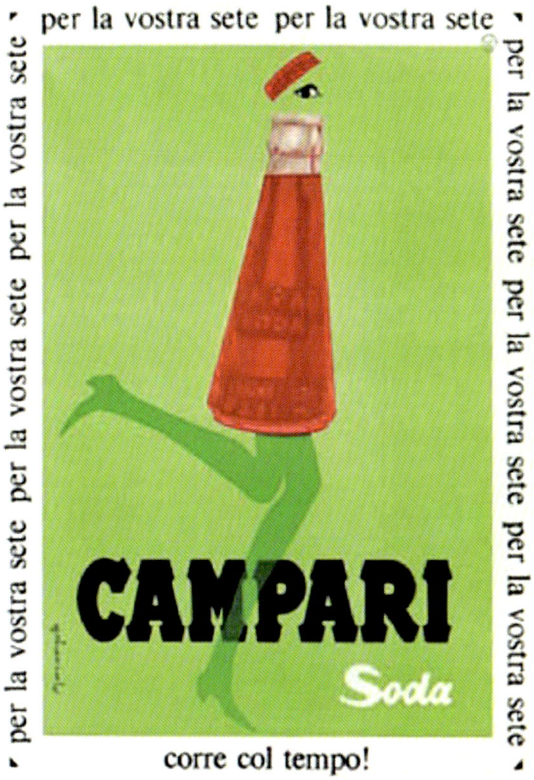

FIG. 98. Sepo (Severo Pozzati), print advertisement, Lebole, featuring *L'Uomo metro* (Meter Man), 1959.

FIG. 99. Franz Marangolo, print advertisement, Campari, "Per la vostra sete, Campari corre col tempo!" (Campari satisfies your thirst for the long run!), 1950.

attuned to the torso-shaped cutout in *Bagno* (Bath, 1965–66), a fiberglass basin, coated in glossy white lacquer paint (see fig. 81; the work appears at bottom center). The sleek lines and flat lip of the basin fake Italian architect and designer Gio Ponti's famous vitreous china bathroom fixtures (made by Italian company Ideal Standard in the mid-1950s) in fiberglass, as does the suggestion of bodily form. Ponti's fixtures were designed to best accommodate the body; they were distinguished by their "physiological form" as opposed to the "geometric [style] of before."[60] As demonstrated by a sketch displayed by Ponti at the Eleventh Triennale di Milano in 1957, the trapezoidal basin of the sink was designed to naturally accommodate the size and shape of your arms while you wash your hands (fig. 100). Pistoletto's tub has a torso-shaped terraced basin that stops short, providing little space for the would-be bather's legs.[61] The ridges of its stepped interior advertise an uncomfortable experience for the viewer as its potential user—a photograph of Gilberto Zorio trying it out confirms its humorous failure in this regard (fig. 101).[62] Examination of its form reveals irregularities and imperfections that belie somewhat sloppy craftsmanship, as opposed to the perfectly smooth and precise form we would expect Ponti's industrially produced object to have. Indeed, the glossy finish of Pistoletto's white basin and the perfect flatness of its upper lip—likely achieved by working on a flat board or table before inverting the fiberglass form—stands in stark contrast to the unfinished semblance of the dark gray exterior—a contrast that suggests that Pistoletto's "bathtub" is not meant to be freestanding but rather is a recessed model that has yet to be installed. We might understand these works on one hand, then, as structurally "poor" designs made with commodity materials or, on the other, as materially "poor" designs with a commodity aesthetic. Either way, they are "lesser," recalling their Italian title, because they are ill-suited, aggressive even, to the body.[63]

We also notice the empty seats in *Quadro da pranzo* (Lunch Painting, 1965)—the first Minus Object—a symmetrical, large geometrical box frame with two built-in chairs and a table surface (fig. 102).[64] *Lunch Painting* seems to be an inviting place, where the viewer and a friend might enjoy a leisurely midday meal. Its shallow seats and material constitution—it is made of discarded, unfinished two-by-fours—however, suggest that lunch might be a precarious, even splintery occasion. It is

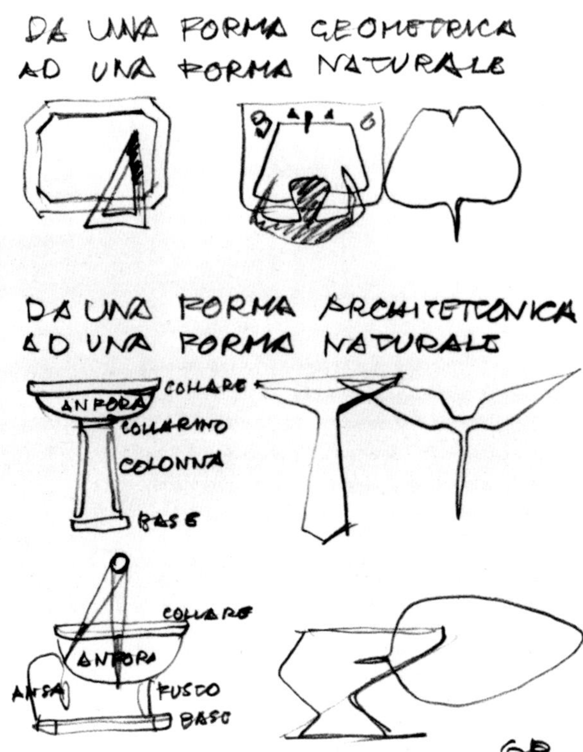

FIG. 100. Gio Ponti, study sheet for the *Serie P* (P Series) bathroom fixtures (1953), designed by George Labalme, Giancarlo Pozzi, and Alberto Rosselli for Ideal Standard, Milan, shown at the Eleventh Triennale di Milano, 1957. Archivio storico di Gio Ponti, Milan.

an example of what Silvia Bottinelli has theorized as modern Italian art's "double-edged comforts," a critical artistic engagement with postwar Italian domestic life that, here, deconstructs its associations with consumption (both capitalist and digestive).[65] We might also notice that the size of *Man-Sized House* invites us to imagine how we might physically inhabit such a confined space if we could access it.[66]

As a photograph of Pistoletto standing next to *Man-Sized House* suggests, the title of the work might be interpreted in two ways. First, we might regard it as a literal construction of its title, modeled after the figure (as body) rather than the subject—a "man-sized house," more logically, would refer to an individual dwelling. After all, the measure of *Man-Sized House* as a material structure—that is, as a geometric form as opposed to a "house"—approximates that of the human body; its width correlates to the span of one's arms if held horizontally in opposite directions. If the structure were outfitted with a physical point of entry as opposed to a representational one (a painted, green rectangle signifies a front door), it could feasibly accommodate one person, if uncomfortably; the person's movement would be greatly limited by its walls and hip roof. Alternatively, we might regard it as a representational structure; if we view the measure of *Man-Sized House* as a symbolic, scaled one, it does not offer the same accommodation for the body. The front door of the architectural model illogically spans two stories: the shorter *piano terra,* or ground floor, and more spacious *piano nobile,* or upper floor. As approximately a one-seventh scale model of a three-story house, the front door of the represented house would stretch over twenty feet high, reminding us less of a classical model designed around the measure of the human body and more of the elongated, looming structures found in Giorgio de Chirico's metaphysical paintings of the 1910s. Rather than function as a feasible architectural model, then, that might be scaled to best accommodate its hypothetical dweller—the symbolic figure the representational structure denotes—*Man-Sized House* instead is dysfunctional, insofar as its form directly corresponds to the human body and physical figure of the viewer rather than being scaled to it. The work sets up a phenomenological experience for the viewer, who becomes aware of

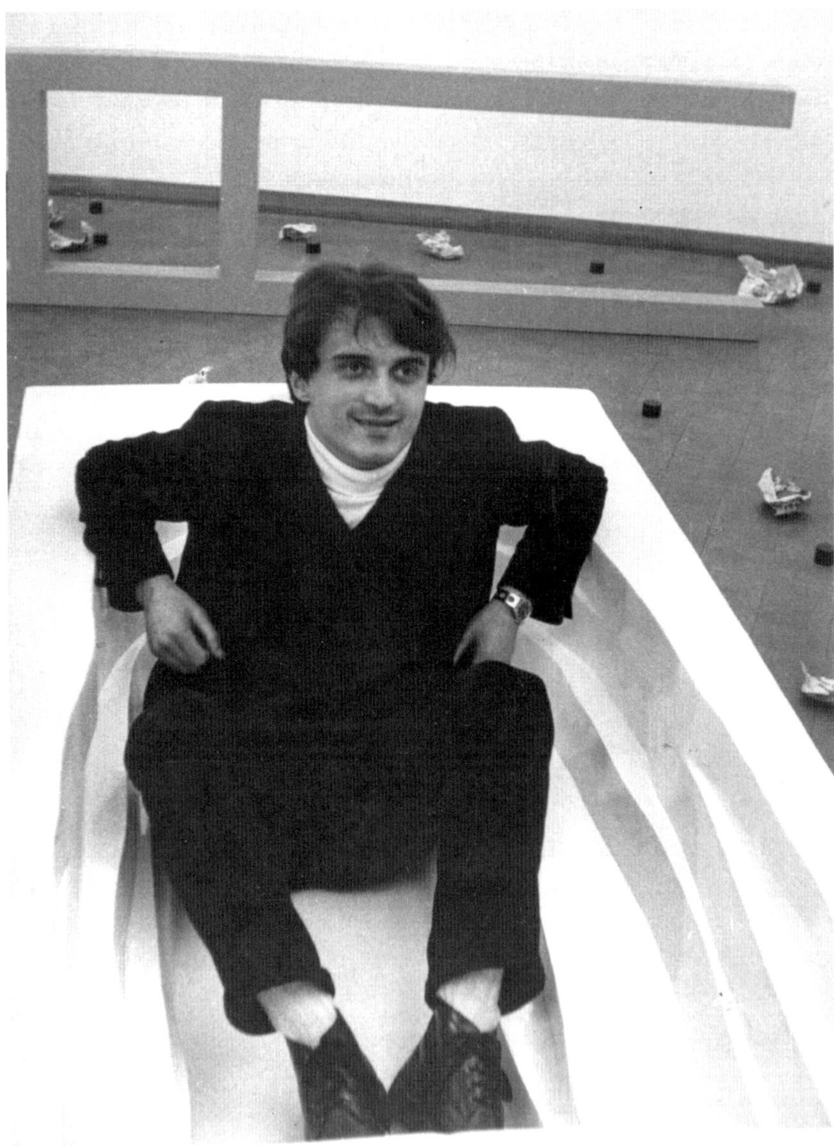

FIG. 101. Gilberto Zorio in Pistoletto's *Bagno* (Bath, 1965–66), ca. 1968, at the Galleria de' Foscherari, Bologna. Archivio De' Foscherari, Bologna.

this correspondence; in so doing, the viewer is made to see the house less as a representational model and more as a rote, material structure—a structure, however, that nevertheless retains its symbolic meaning as a dwelling, if at a diminished level. At that moment, the disjunction between the physical size of the material structure and its symbolic devaluation renders it absurd. After all, fitting in *Man-Sized House* could never amount to living in it.

As with the Plexiglasses, implicit to this paradigmatic shift is a parallel slippage of symbolic meaning and reprioritization of the figure of the viewer. What *Man-Sized House* ultimately presents to the viewer is the absurdity of the fixed, limited subject position denoted to us by physical, material things, as opposed to the self-determined and less restricted positions and pathways we might enjoy as subjects who move away from such structures.

This point is supported by the work's manipulation of classical visual languages of architectural, spatial, and perspectival order from Roman antiquity and the Italian Renaissance, which articulated the world as structured according to the human body and the individual subject as its unit of measure. Often represented by a single, stationary figure positioned within a spatial schema, drawings by Leon Battista Alberti and Filippo Brunelleschi as well as paintings by Piero della Francesca and Masaccio affirmed the subject while nevertheless inscribing him in place. The figural scale of *Man-Sized House* (and the posed photograph, in which the artist stood next to his work) recalls the motif of the points out this misgiving through satire while also offering an alternative. Pistoletto's work was engaged in broader renegotiations of classical humanism then taking place in Italy within the cultural and intellectual left. Many members of the leftist postwar generation, we recall, sought to preserve the humanist ideals of the antifascist partisan resistance in their construction of the Italian Republic.[68] Over the 1960s, however—a decade that bore witness to a series of internal economic, social, and political failures—the prospect of creating a utopian Italian democratic state seemed increasingly impossible. By the point of Pistoletto's production of *Man-Sized House* and the Minus Objects in 1966, the regard for these traditions was one of ambivalence.[69] Rather than see the world as structured according to the human body, Pistoletto's *Man-Sized House* proposes a model of being in the world that prompts a revision of humanist thought; the subject is made to realize how ill-suited, limiting, and parodic such structures might be, and how much freer he might be should he step away from them. In these cases and beyond, the figural in Pistoletto's art was a response to the leftist neohumanism of postwar Italy: it was a way to insist on—to refuse to give up—the core values of humanism while finding a way out of the limiting hegemonic structures that were combatting (and at times offered by) humanism's leftist reprisal in the 1960s and broader postwar period.

Other Minus Objects similarly evoke the image of a physical human body contained within their form. The Minus Objects also present themselves in the space of an embodied, consuming subject—or in some cases, as Véronique Goudinoux has suggested in *Sarcafago* (Sarcophagus), one consumed. In *Sarcophagus* (1965–66), a rectangular volume with an arched top, visible in the installation photographs, we are prompted to imagine that the body is locked inside its form; it is just the right size for its function.[70] Others still have ascribed a reliquary aesthetic to *Display Case*.[71] *Corpo a pera* (Pear-Shaped Body) takes its figurative title literally: the six-foot-tall cylinder is cut around its circumference in the shape of a pear (fig. 104). It is not a figurative sculpture but rather a figural one. It doesn't resemble its referent. It evokes it through literal bodily form.

What distinguishes Pistoletto's Minus Objects from analogous works made by his contemporaries in subsequent years (Alighiero Boetti's dysfunctional furniture objects, say, or Mario Ceroli's human-scaled Vitruvian objects) is that many of his objects stage the dialectic of poor design as a figural problem. Whereas these works are united in their construction of a phenomenological viewing experience, many of Pistoletto's objects are themselves bodily. But unlike other bodily "failed" objects of the Italian and European neo-avant-gardes—Piero Manzoni's *Fiato d'artista* (Artist's Breath) from the *Corpi d'aria* (Bodies of Air) series (1959–60) and *Merda d'artista* (Artist's Shit) multiple (1961), as well as Joseph Beuys's fat sculptures of the early 1960s (for instance, *Fettstuhl* [Fat Chair] 1963)—a large subset of the Minus Objects are bodily insofar as they are figural: they present themselves as figures without representing the body, by evoking the *image* and presence of the body within their material physical form.

This is a point the artist seemed to underline when he created a second set of Minus Objects. Some of these *Versioni,* or Versions, were completely new works (fig. 105). These included *Letto* (Bed, 1965–66), a full-size twin bed, with a blue velvet headboard and mirror in place of a platform, and *Metrocubo d'infinito* (One-Meter Infinity Cube, 1966), a four-foot-square cube made of six mirrors bound together with rope, their reflective surfaces turned inward. Other Versions were less variations on a theme than revisions of the originals. A pear-shaped mirror slab was cut to fit the top of *Pear-Shaped Body,* which, after being repainted in glossy white paint with a royal blue trim became *Corpo a pera specchio* (Pear-Shaped Body Mirror, but also Pear-Mirror-Shaped Body, 1966). A mirror panel (subsequently removed) was added to the front of *Display Case,* which became *Vetrina specchio* (Mirror Display Case, 1966), obscuring its contents from view. The broken-down canvases in *Pozzo* (Well, 1965–66) were replaced with a round mirror. And a mirror was added to span the space between two of the three cement columns, resulting in *Portico* (Portico, 1966).

After completing the versions, Pistoletto rearranged the Minus Objects in his studio. The newly reflective objects, like the mirror paintings before them, invited viewers to move around—to look down into the paper well to see their own reflections on the mirrored disc below, to lean over a mirror-clad bed, to stand on their tiptoes to get glimpse of themselves on the mirrored surface of the whimsical *Pear-Shaped Body Mirror* (fig. 106). With the second set, Pistoletto created an

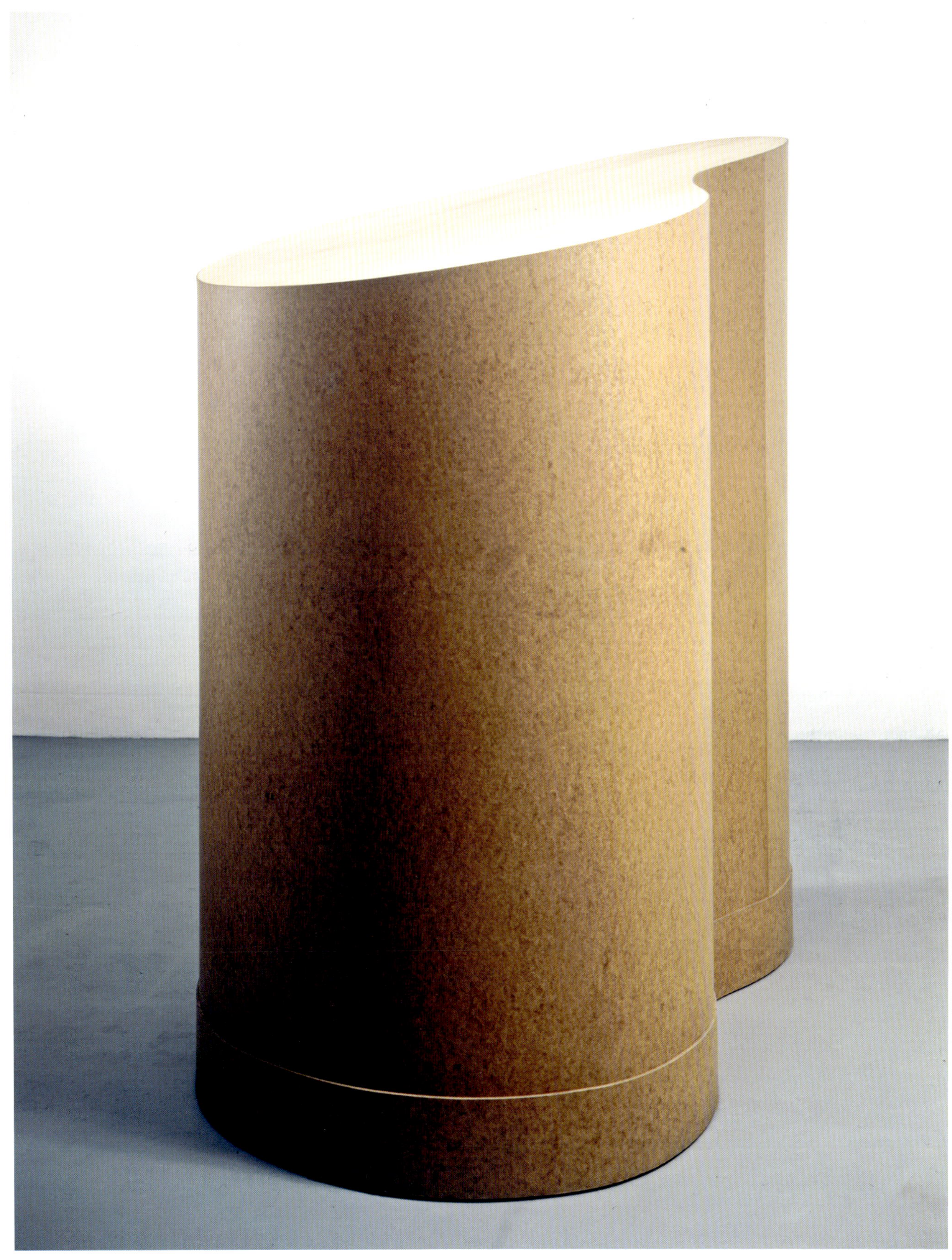

FIG. 104. Michelangelo Pistoletto, *Corpo a pera* (Pear-Shaped Body), 1965–66. Masonite, chipboard, 82⅝ × 69⅝ × 47¼ in. (210 × 177 × 120 cm). Cittadellarte–Fondazione Pistoletto, Biella.

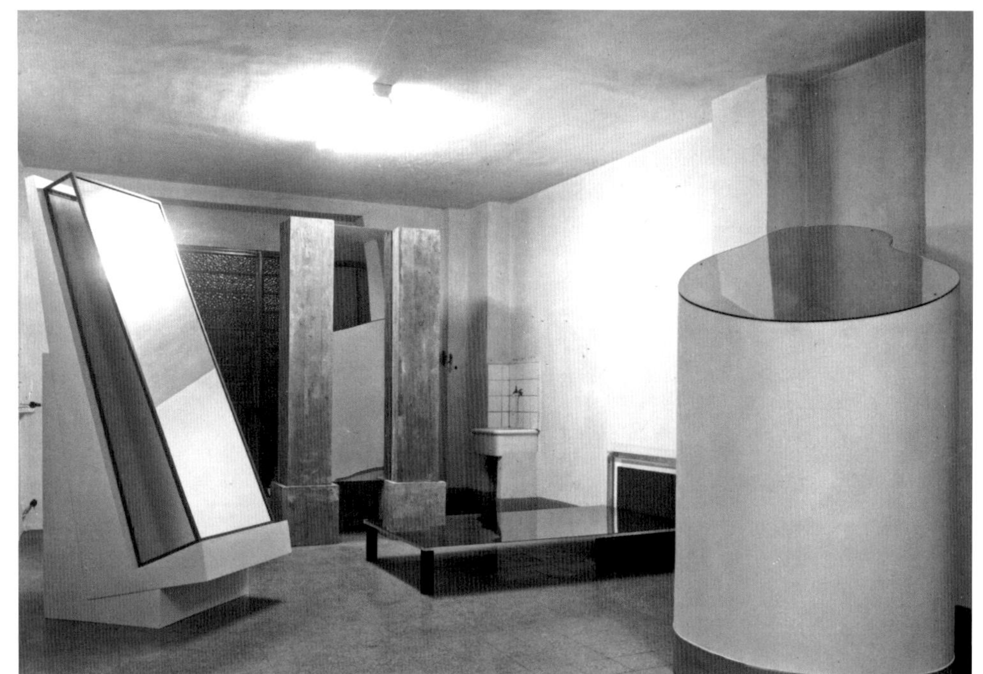

FIG. 105. Exhibition view, *Oggetti in meno (Versioni)* (Minus Objects [Versions]), Studio Pistoletto, 1966. Photo by Paolo Bressano. Archivio Pistoletto, Biella.

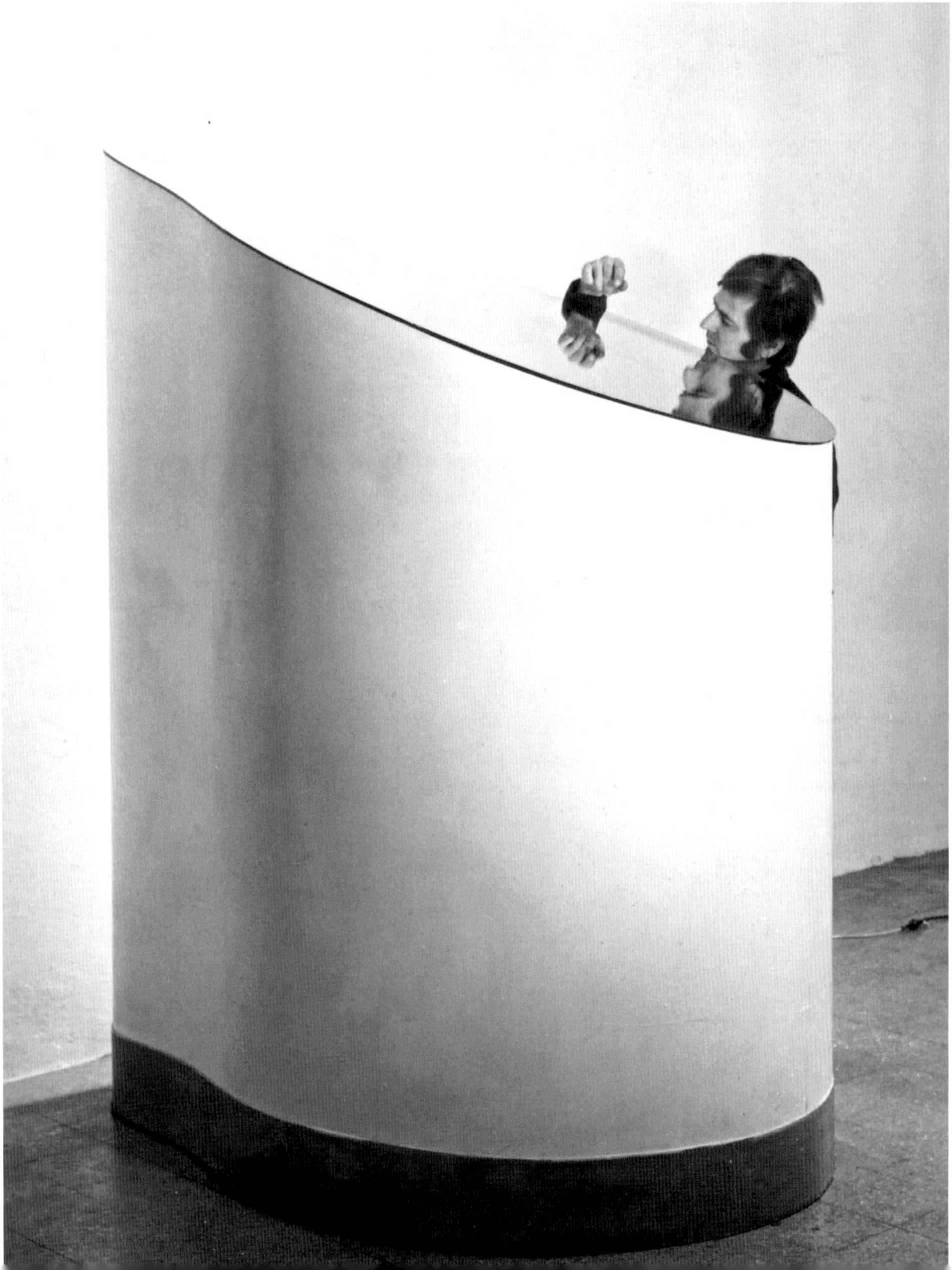

FIG. 106. Michelangelo Pistoletto with *Corpo a pera specchio* (Pear-Shaped Body Mirror and Pear-Mirror-Shaped Body, 1966), 1966. Mirror, Masonite, and chipboard, $82\frac{5}{8} \times 69\frac{5}{8} \times 47\frac{1}{4}$ in. (210 × 177 × 120 cm). Cittadellarte–Fondazione Pistoletto, Biella. Photo by Paolo Bressano.

experience in which viewers saw their own reflections registered on already figural objects.

Several of these works would be showcased the following summer (June–July 1966) at the Galleria Gian Enzo Sperone in Turin in a group exhibition of *arte abitabile,* meaning "live-in" or "habitable art," featuring similarly inspired works by Piero Gilardi and Gianni Piacentino. The central stake of the Minus Objects as objects of design, then, is determined as much (if not more) by the collective installation of the works as by the individual objects themselves. Arranged and rearranged around the studio like things in a home interior, as Briony Fer has suggested, or, as Goudinoux has argued, like things to be encountered and inhabited within a space, perhaps as an editorial arrangement of objects (staged in a furniture showroom, department store, or design pavilion), these works take on a collective affect as commodity objects, design prototypes, or floor models, regardless of their varying media constitutions.[72]

When we think of them as bodily objects, however, the Minus Objects constellate something like a room filled with rather subversive subjects. Consider *Newspaper Sphere,* the aforementioned papier-mâché ball of torn-up newspaper, which rests on the floor like a decorative accent. In the Italian, however, this work is not meant to be a "ball" (*palla*). It is more specifically a "sphere" (*sfera*). As a lumpy (and *lumpen*) misshapen mass, the sculpture is a failed attempt at creating the perfect form conjured by its title. The result of this tension is that the sculpture reads as a recalcitrant, revolutionary object, disrupting the space of the bourgeois, capitalist commodity.

BODIES OF/AT WORK

This dialectic also plays out on the level of process and the perceived quality of the work's fabrication. Some of the works appeared to be the products of slapdash efforts, held together by glue or nails yet, by contrast, were highly labor intensive in their construction, even absurdly so. *Newspaper Sphere* required tearing up newspapers by hand, pressing them together over a polystyrene core until the artist formed a ball with a nearly three-foot diameter, then sealed and smoothed the surface with layers of papier-mâché. By contrast, the pristine, glossy surface and symmetrical form of *Decorative Semispheres* suggest some involvement but was made in a few quick steps: by sticking nine sheets of plastic hemispheres onto the wall with Scotch tape.[73]

It is as a group that the Minus Objects most resemble Italian furniture designs. They recall those found in the pages of such publications as *Domus* (est. 1928), *Casabella* (est. 1928), *Stile industria* (1954–63), and *Abitare* (1961–2014), or other industrial arts and trade show magazines that flourished during the economic miracle. Through this booming design-focused print culture, David Raizman has noted, "Italian industrial design achieved both visibility and national identity in an international market."[74] In the late 1950s and early 1960s, the proliferation of design publications, advertising schools, and commercial design firms led to increasing emphasis on design in Italian production and advertising, leading to huge success in Italian product growth. Smaller companies (among them, Arteluce, est. 1939; Brionvega, est. 1945; Tecno, est. 1952; Gavina, est. 1953; and Zanotta, est. 1954) gained commercial success as their brands became known for a particular "Italian" aesthetic, typically characterized by bold, bright colors, regular, geometric forms, a strong sense of line, and a structure as functional as it is formally pleasing.[75] Advertising campaigns by Olivetti, Fiat, Pirelli, and other larger companies by Italian and non-Italian designers alike further emphasized the distinction of "good" design that came with buying an Italian product. A print advertisement from 1969 for Olivetti, for example, by Swiss graphic designer Walter Ballmer juxtaposes Olivetti's Lettera 32 typewriter (designed by Marcello Nizzoli) with a large ovoid object decorated with swirling colors (fig. 107). The image pairs revered Italian artisanal practices of marbled paper production and glassblowing in the Veneto and Lombardy with modern Italian design. We find similar modeling of the great history, endurance, and italianità of good design in one of Pistoletto's own advertisements (fig. 108). In an undated exercise from the mid-1950s, we find a bottle of Martini dry vermouth on a bare tree—the Martini logos are its only other "fruits"—growing in front of an Ionic column. The suggestion is that the Martini brand is an extension of the cultural achievements of Italy and its connections to the classical world. The tagline affirms the good taste of Martini consumers: "a vermouth that requires a refined palate." The economic miracle was the beginning of Western consumer demand for modern *Italian* cars, washing machines, typewriters, textiles, kitchen

In this sense, these works are rightly *Oggetti in meno,* a phrase that connotes a state of insufficiency; they are "less" objects, we recall, than they are something else. Their title suggests: if the Minus Objects are somewhat "poor" designs and failed objects, they are purposefully so. It is this effort toward failure that Pistoletto and others explored during the peak of Arte Povera from 1967 to 1972. In *Sitin* (Sit-In, 1968), a rectangular tray filled with wax and the words "sit-in" mounted in neon script across its surface, Mario Merz seems to translate Arte Povera's material dialectic into a potentially scarring experience for the viewer (fig. 109). Taken as a practical, if sadistic directive, "sitting in" the wax and on the hot fluorescent tubes would certainly subject the viewer to an exercise of enduring pain. At the same time, if we read the words figuratively, Merz's work becomes a poor example of design—or, perhaps better, a good example of poor design—and a serious call for civil disobedience and political protest. In Giovanni Anselmo's *Senza titolo (Struttura che mangia)* (Untitled [Eating Structure *and* Structure That Eats], 1968)—the more famous of works that also included a "drinking structure" of the same year—a rectangular granite block stands on its end; a smaller block is tied around its top with copper wire, holding a head of lettuce wedged between the two (fig. 110).[81] As the lettuce rots, the tension loosens, and the smaller block falls to the floor. The structure, then, fails. Or, if it has succeeded as an "eating" structure, its success is its self-destruction.

Pistoletto's Minus Objects precipitated a broader revolution in the arts in Italy levied against capitalist consumer culture in the late 1960s and 1970s, including radical *controdisegno* (counterdesign) and architecture movements. In 1968, Pistoletto (with the Zoo), Valerio Adami, and other artists withdrew their work from the Venice Biennale, some as a form of protest (though not Pistoletto, who gave up his space so as to avoid any interpretation of his exhibiting as a desire to occupy the Biennale).[82] Many more turned their paintings toward the wall or refused to open their exhibition rooms.[83] Others still, such as Giangiacomo

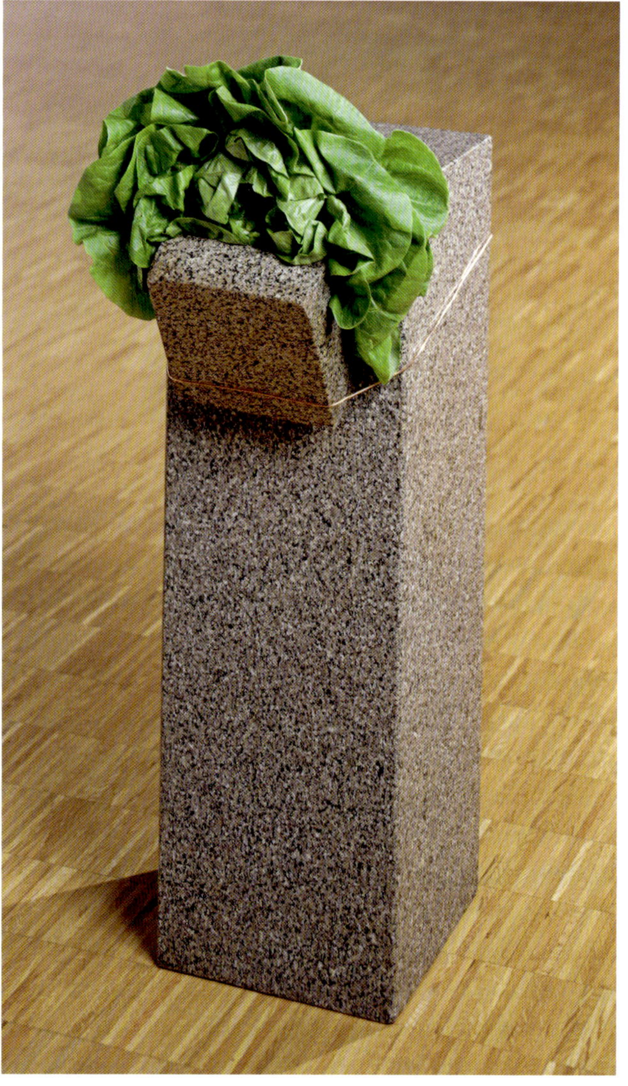

FIG. 109. Mario Merz, *Sitin* (Sit-In), 1968. Wax, neon, metal structure, 7⅛ × 25¼ × 22 in. (18 × 64 × 56 cm). Collezione Merz, Turin.

FIG. 110. Giovanni Anselmo, *Senza titolo (Struttura che mangia)* (Untitled [Eating Structure *and* Structure That Eats]), 1968. Granite pillar, copper, fresh lettuce (regularly substituted), 27½ × 9 × 14⅝ in. (70 × 23 × 37 cm). Musée national d'art moderne/Centre Georges Pompidou, Paris.

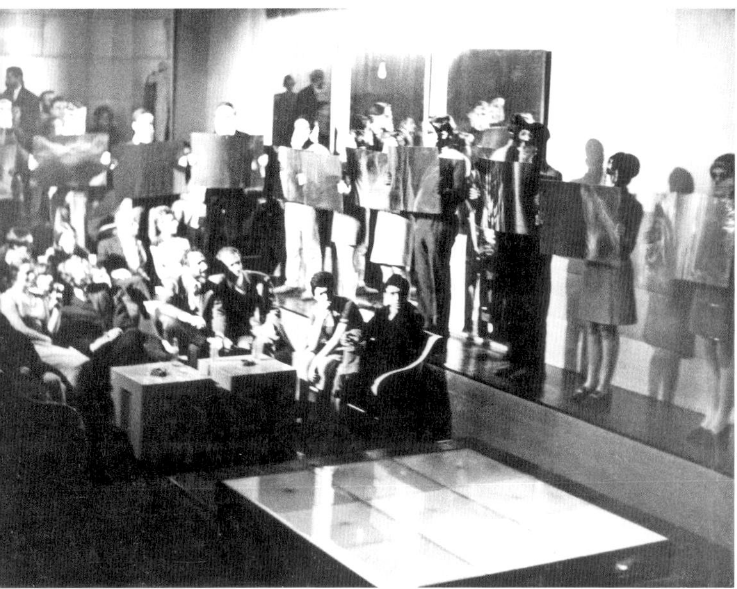

FIG. 111. Michelangelo Pistoletto, *La fine di Pistoletto* (The End of Pistoletto), action, Piper Pluriclub, Turin, March 6, 1967. Photo by Renato Rinaldi. Archivio Pistoletto, Biella.

Spadari, were carried away by police. Young designers at the Fourteenth Milan Triennale of 1968 destroyed washing machines, refrigerators, television sets, and other elettrodomestici for which Italy had become well known in international commercial markets. The appliances were installed in front of images of protestors. Destroying the economic miracle's image of material excess and luxury domesticity pictured in Fellini's Rome and Olmi's Milan, these artists dumped the debris into a pile and presented it as their exhibition, igniting the radical design movement of the late 1960s and early 1970s.

Indeed, Pistoletto soon thereafter distanced himself from individual, product-based practice. In March 1967, he declared *La fine di Pistoletto* (The End of Pistoletto) in a collective action of the same name staged at the Turin location of the Piper Pluriclub, a disco and sometimes alternative arts space (fig. 111).[84] Twenty-five performers among the many other participants wore the same mask: a cardstock life-size photographic cutout of Pistoletto's face.[85] For *The End of Pistoletto,* the artist exhibited his trademark mirror paintings around the club's perimeter. The performers, Pistoletto included, surrounded by mirror paintings that reflected them, played the same role.[86] The masked participants were all "Pistoletto." The actual Pistoletto seemed to have disappeared. The action declared the end of the artist as he had come to be known—the end of the figure of Pistoletto. Now he existed in multiple—but also, not at all.

Advertisements for a show by Pistoletto ran in the theater and happenings announcements of *La Stampa,* beginning on March 9. The subsequent weekend announcement invited local readers to "come and look at yourselves in the mirror in Pistoletto's metal sheets." A poster for the exhibition remixed the title of Pistoletto's action with one source of its inspiration: the apocalyptic tagline of the club ("Piper is the end of the world").[87] Participants shook rectangular sheets of highly polished stainless steel, creating analog wobble sounds that conjured sci-fi sound effects and anarchic discord of the period. Both genre and actual events were evoked, simultaneously.

The same year, Pistoletto published *Le ultime parole famose* (Famous Last Words), a statement in which he again expressed his earlier frustration with the fetishization of the work of art—that is, as a desired symbolic embodiment (if displaced) of the artist himself. Pistoletto would take up this pursuit in the form of experimental performance and collective practice. Echoing the sentiment first articulated in the Minus Objects statement, he wrote:

> Some time ago, I wrote this sentence on the wall of my studio: "One must prepare oneself for being." Every action is in this direction. . . . The way I move now is by stepping to one side. Every piece I make is a liberation and not a construction that is intended to represent me. I am not reflected in them, and the others cannot reflect upon me by means of them. Every piece I make is destined to proceed on its own way by itself without dragging me along behind it, since I am already somewhere else and doing something different. There is no longer any sense in the problem of being up to date in form. The problem is not to change the forms and leave the system intact, but rather to take the forms intact out of the system. In order to do this it's necessary to be absolutely free. And worrying about whether or not the forms are up to date means not being free to consider the forms of the past. And as we do not yet possess the forms of the future, liberty within the system means liberty to do only one thing.[88]

Echoing the theatrical lexicon of Jerzy Grotowski, Pistoletto's apocalyptic manifesto was a platform for the revaluation of forms. It declared his move away from linear models of progress (of "moving forward") even as 1967 proved to be his busiest professional year yet. Perhaps that was the point: to stage his withdrawal at the (then) height of his career. Shows continued through the year, with solo exhibitions in Brussels, Cologne, Detroit, and Paris and Milan. Aligned with the radical sociopolitical climate of the period, the theme of liberation from commercialized "individuality" that we find in Pistoletto's art—in which signature style functioned as a symbol for the artist, eclipsing the value of the human figure of Pistoletto himself—held potential for sociopolitical change. By withdrawing, by staging our own deaths, the idea seemed to be, we might free ourselves to do other things.

At the Biennale of 1968, in place of exhibiting his works as planned, the artist posted a flyer, inviting people to collaborate with him for the exhibition. Dated April 2, 1968, Turin, it explained his view of collaboration: "By collaboration I mean a human relationship that is not competitive but rather sensitive and perceptual in agreement. To cede a part of myself to those who want to cede a part of themselves is the work [of art] that interests me."[89] The manifesto of collaboration, as this document is known, opened the rarified space of legitimate artistic work to others, foreshadowing a longer dismantling of self and reconceptualization of the work (or task) of art as the cultivation of different worlds. In the months preceding the formation of the Zoo, Pistoletto opened his studio to other artists, poets, musicians, and performers. He collaborated with experimental filmmakers, screening a series of experimental shorts at his exhibition at the Galleria L'Attico in February 1968. He brought in props from Cinecittà, creating an exhibition that was at once live theater, film set, and art exhibition.

By May 1968, Pistoletto had given up conventional individual artistic practice and founded his theater group the Zoo (1968–70), addressed in the following chapter. With the Zoo, he created action-based work, conducted living activities as artistic research, and staged theatrical performances until 1970. Tommaso Trini described the emancipatory goals of the group, whose "actions and events" lay "beyond" or after "the objecthood" of Arte Povera: "But what distinguishes the latest experiences is the research of a psychological process of liberation: the audience is not necessarily involved, the acting-out concerns primarily the artist and his surroundings. After the mental theatre of his mirrored paintings, Pistoletto works with the Zoo Group between theatre and visual art; a sort of 'beggars opera' in which they tend to establish a new alphabet for the body."[90] During that time, the Zoo, as Pistoletto described to Celant in 1971, "[were] a group of people living, searching for the why and how rather than doing real work. Every day we would have our so-called rehearsals, which actually were little actions we did on the town square. It was mainly about living together."[91] As the artist wrote, performances would be modest. Each would be "una cosa creativa da poco, senza pretese" (a creative little thing, without any pretenses).[92]

THE MINUS MAN

To that end, rather than make objects, Pistoletto created a set of activities, games, and "research" activities with the Zoo based on the figure of *L'Uomo nero,* discussed in greater detail in the following chapter (fig. 112). Although the phrase literally translates to "the black man," *L'Uomo nero* is a mythical character in popular Italian culture, where he is a quasi-Bogeyman figure invoked to regulate children's behavior. (Pistoletto has therefore translated it as "the Minus Man" since the late 1980s to avoid misinterpretation of the term as one about race, though the character itself was likely informed by historical constructions of race in Italy.) Reconceptualized as an allegorical figure for the artist, the Minus Man was harnessed to enact Pistoletto's evasion—defiance, even—of expectations. He would always be active somewhere other than expected. As if to underscore the unburdened position he occupied, free from the limitations of consumer culture, he carried a small leather suitcase in some actions; it seemed to be full of nothing. On its surface, he wrote, "Questa valigia contiene tutto ciò che non possiedo" (This suitcase contains all that I don't possess).

In the game of the Minus Man, the members of the Zoo enacted this allegory in public, most often, and private spaces. Enacted daily in Corniglia in the summer of 1969 from the hours of 4:00 p.m. to 7:30 p.m., the game provides evidence of more varied activities than the communitarian kind typically ascribed to the group. "In the span of four months in Corniglia, the minus

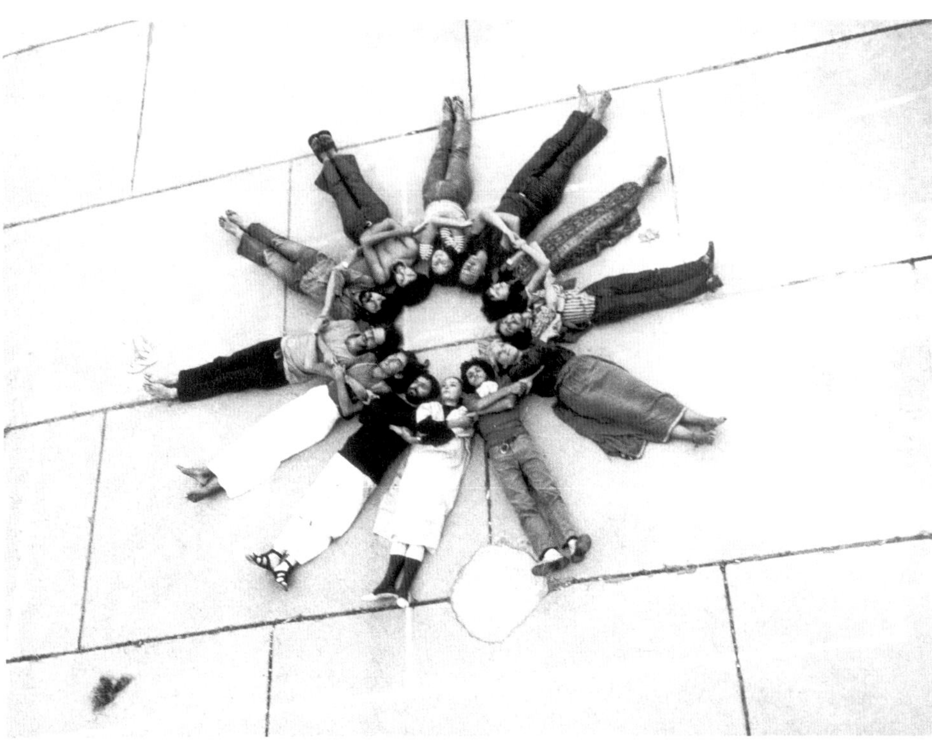

FIG. 112. The Zoo, *La ricerca dell'Uomo nero* (Research of the Minus Man), Corniglia, summer 1969. Photo by Paolo Mussat Sartor. Archivio Pistoletto, Biella.

man game became a circular situation. Each person's freedom enclosed itself in the circle of freedom that was organized for everyone, by turns. What do you do when it's not your turn at freedom? You're not free. And there were twelve of us. Each person got a moment of freedom in every twelve. . . . Then there was the freedom of one's own turn that entered into a circle of repetitive actions, which became the performance of one's own freedom in a possible play."[93] Different than a utopian, communitarian activity, the Minus Man game, while played as a group, was one in which everyone was given the same opportunity to act out their "freedom," in whatever form they desired, in a performance and lived space of repeated, collectively moderated, activity of individual freedom.

The game of the Minus Man was used as a model through which the Zoo created a mode of collaborative practice in their daily lives. The idea was for everyone to do what they wanted to do, alongside one another. Pistoletto would write: "There's more serenity in the air, there are people that do singular things without trying to trounce [*schiacciare*] the others."[94] The result would perhaps be one of supported communal living or the production of new creative forms or nothing at all. Whatever the outcome, the Zoo was an experiment in modeling a new way of living and creating in the world: having full control over oneself while respecting the right of others to have full control over themselves, finding value in the individual and the collective, in the self-regulated community. Like the Minus Objects, the Zoo's dedication to the autonomy of its individual actors—to do or make something or have something made and to be able to step to the side or go make something else—was central to its project. By the 1970s, when the artist pursued the motif of the cage (and electric fence) in the mirror paintings, this mode of living freely together seemed less optimistic. If the mirror paintings after the Zoo, which expanded in size, made us think "of living all together, elbow to elbow," the expanse of the reflective field positioned the viewer as "part of a dissociated chorality" that was the allegory of those darker times.[95]

When we consider this practice within the artistic and sociopolitical contexts of its development in Italy in the late 1960s, the emphasis on individualism within the collective framework of the Zoo gains further valence as a step toward contemporaneous countercultural goals of deconditioning. In the artistic context, primary criticism of work by the Zoo elucidated the importance of individual voluntarism to ideas of radical artistic practice. In the January 1969 issue of *Domus,* Tommaso Trini situated the theatrical activities of the group in relation to the *Oggetti in meno.* In his brief but early text on the Zoo, "Studio chiuso, strada aperta" (Closed Studio, Open Street), he wrote: "After being freed from the objects and the studio for his own sake, Pistoletto did what remained to be done: to create a non-discriminatory space in which individual creativity, the urgency of each person, would be favored by everyone, through collective deconditioning."[96] Trini's words also resonate with other critical viewpoints that addressed the complex importance of individuality in Arte Povera, to move beyond conventional spectatorship. In theorizations of Arte Povera, spectatorship was bound up with mediated (and therefore controlled) subjectivity. Writing in 1969 in the volume *Art Povera* (the title given to the volume in English), Celant famously wrote of the choice of the "artist-alchemist" to experience the world directly. Living the world (as opposed to seeing it) was the goal. Well known is Celant's emphasis on the artist's "discovery . . . of the magic and marvelous value of natural elements," focusing on the artist's material and procedural repertoire. But he also underscored a subject model of immersive individual autonomy for Arte Povera, not in self-reflexive isolation from others but as a site of vitality shared with the natural and social world. Here's Celant: "He has chosen to live within direct experience, no longer the representative—the source of pop artists—he aspires to live, not to see. He immerses himself in individuality because he feels the necessity of leaving intact the value of the existence of things, of plants or animals; he wants to take part in the oneness of every minute in order to possess above all the 'autonomy' both of his own identity and the individuality of things. He wants to feel his vitality in order not to feel that he is a solitary vital individual." By directly experiencing their own vitality, the artist does not impose themselves on the world but inhabits it as one of many. Their work, then, "tend[s] toward . . . an experiment with contingent existence."[97]

Pistoletto and the Zoo's practice of continuously exercising individual freedom within a collective framework echoed ideas that originally circulated in interwar antifascist political theory, namely Carlo Rosselli's theory of liberal socialism, best laid out in his canonical text, *Socialismo liberale* (Liberal Socialism, 1930). Originally published in France, where Rosselli was residing after escaping fascist-era imprisonment, *Liberal Socialism* was a work of intellectual resistance against fascist totalitarianism. It called for personal action against authoritarian rule. As Rosselli wrote: "Liberalism conceives of liberty not as a fact of nature, but as becoming, as development. One is not born free; one becomes free. And one stays free by retaining an active and vigilant sense of one's autonomy, by constantly exercising one's freedoms."[98] For Rosselli, this constant exercise of personal autonomy was the only way to achieve liberal democracy. It also was a way to assert "faith in man" and in our "capacity for self-determination."[99]

By the late 1960s, the Italian New Left had taken renewed interest in Rosselli and his contemporary Piero Gobetti as icons of antiauthoritarianism. Whereas these thinkers of the 1920s and early 1930s—both executed by Mussolini's regime—positioned themselves against fascism, the New Left positioned themselves against capitalism, in which they found many of the same qualities: the regulation of the individual; the primacy of work as the organizational structure of life; and the value of people only insofar as they are productive, measured in terms of individuals' contributions to the state. Rather than think of the Zoo as a communitarian experiment or the Minus Objects as "casual" anticapitalist objects, then, we should more suitably regard them as methodically articulated, liberal, socialist subjects—as embodied activities and practices in meno, through which liberation is repeatedly enacted within a collectively minded environment.[100] They were experiments in modeling a different social order. It also suggests that the categorization of artworks and practices in terms of political ideologies and/or economic models needs more nuance. Variations in economy, politics, and context require further distinction between "socialist" or "capitalist" (for example) practices. This seems especially important (and useful) for practices too often lumped together as "anticapitalist"—a label that tends to reinscribe capitalist-centric structures against which such practices are positioned in the first place. To that end, the Zoo's political and conceptual connection to the Minus Objects suggests that the engagement of the body and undermining of good design were related strategies. The Minus Objects were connected to artistic and political contemplations of liberal autonomy. Because Pistoletto envisioned the Minus Objects as contextually contingent and unrepeatable in form and process, his production of the series amounted to an exercise of individual autonomy, enacted by the artist's action, symbolized by the resulting object, each unique in form.

A NEW SOCIAL ORDER OF "UNDOMESTICATED FORMS OF BEING"

This perspective highlights the Minus Objects and the Zoo's mutual dedication to a humanist, anticapitalist model of form and process in which the individual figure (as image and body, in the Minus Objects, and as allegorical figure and actor, in the Zoo) is the means to a liberated subject, realizing a new model of plurality within the spaces of commercial culture and the counterculture alike. As a collection, the series is a symbolic model of a new social order. This point is further evidenced by work made with the Minus Objects at the end of the Zoo's existence. In January 1970, before the Zoo disbanded, Pistoletto created an installation that concretized the connection between these activities. For *Ufficio dell'Uomo nero* (Office of the Minus Man, 1970), his work for the Third International Biennial of Painting by Young Artists (Bologna, Museo Civico, 1970), Pistoletto installed photomurals on the walls of his installation space—specifically photographs of the installations of the Minus Objects staged in his Turin studio four years earlier (fig. 113). In the same room, Pistoletto set up objects and furniture items that connected to and departed from the subjects (and objects) of their photographed precedents: a generic wooden desk with a chair and a regularly, intermittently ringing telephone; a pedestal with a television that screened the short film *Circolazione* (Circulation), now lost; and a newspaper-sphere sculpture, entitled *La terra e la luna* (The Earth and the Moon, 1966–68). As for the Minus Man—Pistoletto—he was absent. He was, literally and figuratively, out of the office. Out of the symbolic environment of capitalism, he was also out of the role of commoditized artist and of the behavior-conditioned figure at work.[101]

Making "lesser" or minor object-based works and enacting quasi-theatrical productions—productions not of objects but of transgressive being in the world—was not a reflection of failure or act of giving up. It was a mode of resisting commercial culture from within its discourse and of creating a different value for one's work, for oneself, and for others, on one's own terms. On this point, we might recall the work of Jerzy Grotowski, the leading figure of the Polish avant-garde and perhaps defining figure of European experimental theater of the 1960s. In 1965, Grotowski published his concept of a "poor theater." The concept would be fundamental to Celant's subsequent theorization of Arte Povera. In poor theater, actors give themselves wholly to the action, "freeing" themselves in the process: "By a complete stripping down . . . the actor makes a total gift of himself. The result is freedom from the time-lapse between inner impulse and outer reaction. . . . Ours then is a *via negativa*—not a collection of skills but an eradication of blocks."[102] Following Grotowski's *via negativa,* Pistoletto's figural Minus Objects seem to model a similar "stripping down" of the subject. They cast off ideological structures that model the artist, to free the self for a more open, liberated exploration of the world. Perhaps this view—of making Minus Objects (and Minus Men) as a mode of revolution—is what Pistoletto meant when he wrote, as we recall, in 1966: "They are objects through which I free myself from something—they aren't constructions but liberations—I don't consider them extra objects [*oggetti in più*] but minus objects [*oggetti in meno*], in the sense that they bring with them a perceptual experience that is definitively realized. . . . According to the idea I have of time, it is necessary to know how to free oneself from a position while you are conquering it."[103] From this perspective, those works of Pistoletto's (and Arte Povera) that modeled a withdrawal or destruction of the self were positive and productive. Such works—the group show aesthetic of Pistoletto's Minus Objects, the performance enacting the "end" of Pistoletto, the discontinuation of individual work and formation of the Zoo, the rotating theatrical role of the Minus Man—sought to realize a liberation of the self from the overdeterminations and alienation of capitalist culture. They also sought to liberate their own status as special, individual objects, by dint of their belonging to a series, however eclectic in kind.[104]

Like Grotowski's theorization of a "theater of encounter" in the late 1960s, the Zoo's activities in public space were not explicitly intended *for* an audience—for spectators—but were simply done in their presence. Theater, for Grotowski, depended on the actor-spectator relationship, specifically one "of perceptual, direct, 'live' communion."[105] Embodiment of these relations was also of primary concern to Grotowski, who compared the potential spiritual function of an actor in a bright light—not unlike photos of Pistoletto standing, illuminated, under the green light of his mercury lamp Minus

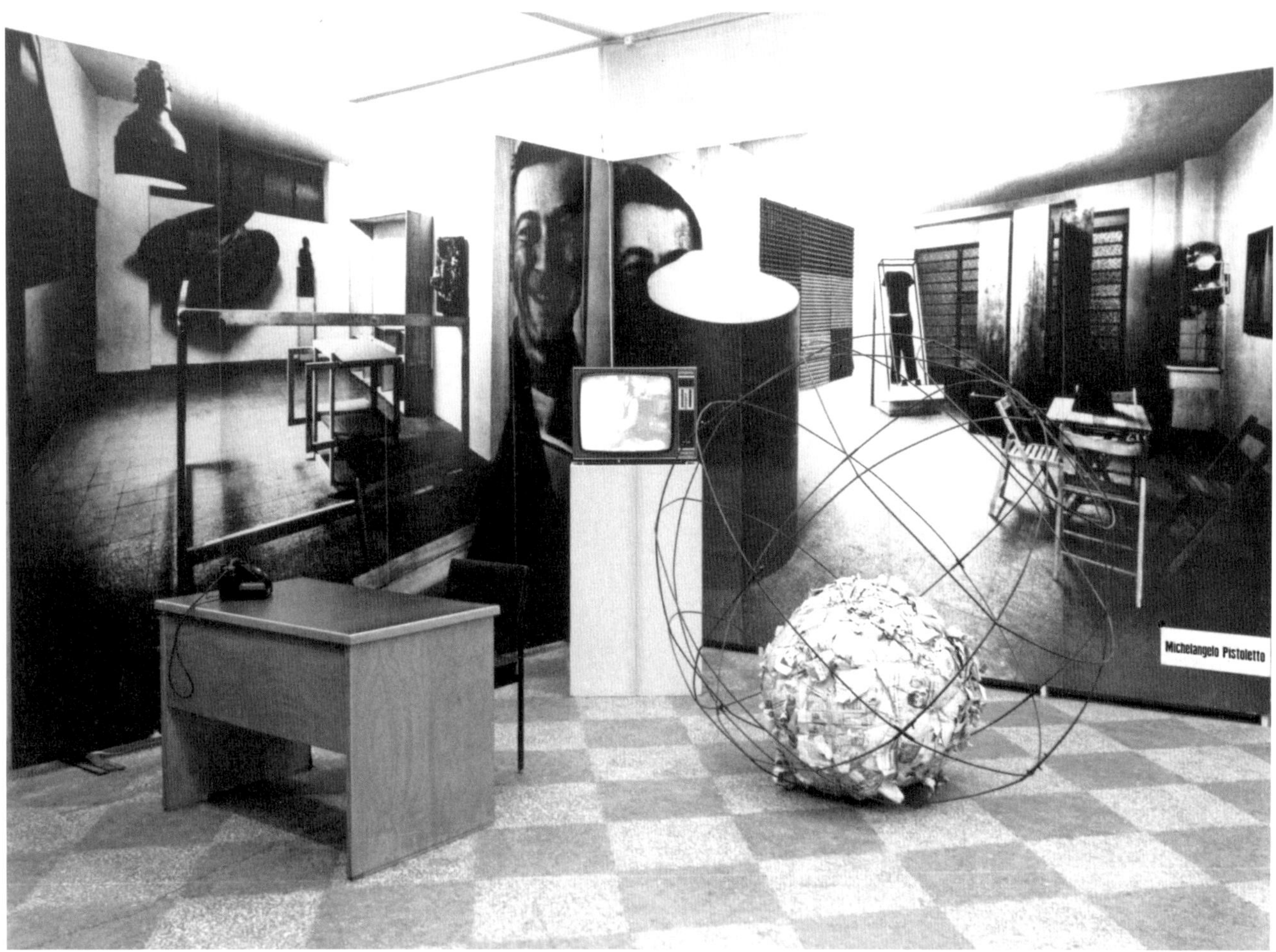

FIG. 113. Michelangelo Pistoletto, *Ufficio dell'Uomo nero* (Office of the Minus Man), 1970. Installation. Exhibition view, III biennale internazionale della giovane pittura, Museo Civico di Bologna, January 31–February 28, 1970. Photomurals, desk with telephone, television with video (*Circolazione* [Circulation]), and Pistoletto's *La terra e la luna* (The Earth and the Moon, 1966–68). Photo by Paolo Mussat Sartor. Archivio Pistoletto, Biella.

Object—to figures in El Greco's paintings.[106] Theater historian Kris Salata has emphasized this understudied distinction in Grotowski's conceptualization of theater, which we also find in the Zoo—perhaps most in the activities of the "Minus Man" staged in open space in Corniglia. As Salata puts it: "The performance is not done *for* the spectator, but merely *facing* the spectator, despite his or her presence, while at the same time that presence remains essential."[107] Acting for Grotowski, as offered in 1971 in his talk "How One Could Live," was "not only practice, but much more a particular kind of living."[108] *Living* was a form of criticality in Grotowski. For Salata, performances by actors working within Grotowski's legacy created a way of doing that didn't compel participation beyond "sharing a living-room space subjected to an undomesticated form of being."[109] It is this *undomesticated* form of being that Pistoletto forged with the Zoo as an embodied, theatrical form of lived criticality. It began perhaps with the Minus Objects, by breaking the domestic and domesticated order of design objects and figures at home.

As a collection made alongside the Rallies, the Minus Objects were an embodied, symbolic model of a new social order. These experiments were a means of creating different value—for one's work, for oneself, and for one another—on one's own set of terms. This was the value, or values, of *extremely poor work*, of *extremely poor figures*. Through a subversion of existing systems of value and meaning, these Minus Objects and Minus Men opened a space for new subject positions and new ways of being, in which value was determined by the subject within a community, which in turn staged different worlds. What happened next was nothing short of revolutionary.

5 The Real and Performed Figure

Lived and Staged Action in and after the Zoo

On May 8, 1968, amid local and global antiauthoritarian occupations and protests, Pistoletto officially established the Zoo with the theatrical action *Cocapicco e vestitorito,* held at the Piper Pluriclub in Turin (fig. 114a–b). As suggested by the title, two worlds were staged in the performance: the low, conjured by *cocapicco* (suggesting "send to the bottom"); and the ideal, captured by *vestitorito,* a compound neologism that evokes the (typically sacred) rite of dressing.[1] Photographs of the event show participants crowded together, seated in a basin. They poured Pepsi cola and threw white talcum powder on one another.[2] Others spilled over the basin's edge and lay sprawled on the floor in front of seated viewers, like human overflow from the evidently uncontainable scene. A second activity drew on Pistoletto's recent collaborations in experimental film (in this case, with Turinese underground filmmaker Tonino De Bernardi). As in the film, participants at the Pluriclub fashioned a transparent plastic dress for Maria Pioppi, who was seated above the crowd on top of a ladder (fig. 115).[3]

The event's staging of "high" and "low" culture was enacted literally (in space: up in the air and down on the floor) and figuratively (in performed behavior) by its participants. The low behavior in the basin, for example, was apropos to the meaning suggested by *cocapicco.* It was also fitting for the cultural and political antiauthoritarianism of the moment. "A picco" is used in a variety of contexts in Italian, most often to describe a boat sinking to the bottom of a body of water. The phrase can denote descent both literal (as in spatial plummeting) and figurative (as in depletion, economic collapse, and failure), in which case it is analogous to the English idiom "to make something go south."[4] For Pistoletto, its meaning was linked to consumerism, via the use of brand-name soda (generally, in Italian, "una Coca"). The action's suggestion therefore was that the subject under consumer culture (and capitalism) existed in a condition of mass social repression. This was the problem with which the Zoo concerned themselves. With a name inspired by Zoo cofounder Carlo Colnaghi, who once said, "I find myself in the same position as the caged lion," the Zoo sought, with such activities, to liberate its participants from the bondage of social order. Acting from "within the bars of the cage," as they theorized their work, the Zoo showed the repressive conditions of consumer culture and simultaneously enacted its desired ruin. *Cocapicco e*

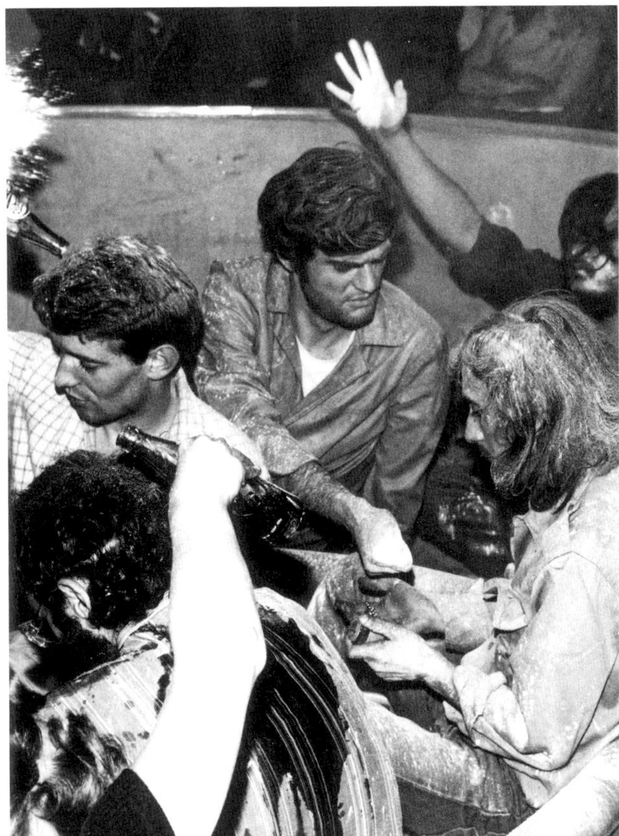
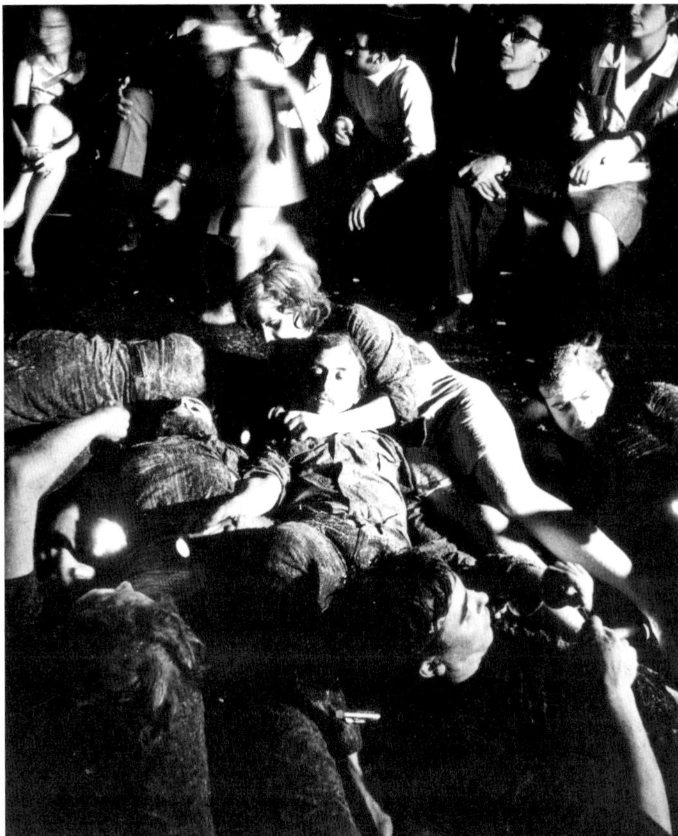

FIG. 114A–B. The Zoo, *Cocapicco e vestitorito,* action, Piper Pluriclub, Turin, May 8, 1968. Photos by Paolo Mussat Sartor. Archivio Pistoletto, Biella.

vestitorito ultimately staged a liberation of the body and subject by exhausting consumerism; participants poured out its products and laid them low.

In and of itself, *Cocapicco e vestitorito* was not especially revolutionary. Such use of embodied debased behavior as a form of resistance and self-emancipation (in psychoanalytic theory, it might be described as "desublimation" of repressed desire) was common in the late 1960s. Comparisons abound in contemporary art and experimental theater in Italy and internationally (as in the work of the anarchic Living Theatre, which had performed in Turin a few years earlier). We can therefore easily position the performance within already codified forms of anticapitalist countercultural practice, such as "carnivalesque agit prop," associated with alternative theater, art, and social action around May 1968.[5] Indeed, many have, as exemplified by common secondary descriptions of the Zoo as a ragtag street theater group and "caravan of itinerant artists—modern minstrels and troubadours."[6] This was also the case in the primary context. Writing in *Data* in 1971, Zoo participant Henry Martin noted the implicit categorization of the group with the global counterculture; summarizing Germano Celant's description of the group, it was a "kind of tribe composed of disparate elements originating in various parts of the world."[7] This categorization of the group as nomadic, countercultural bricoleurs aligned the Zoo with Celant's theorization of the *poveristi* as counterinstitutional actors.[8] In that view, nothing especially remarkable really transpired with *Cocapicco e vestitorito.*

Such ascriptions, however, seem to have precluded closer attention to these theatrical activities that reveals a more complicated story. One point alone merits revisionist study of the work. The event was advertised by formal invitation, often unmentioned in scholarship, which billed *Cocapicco e vestitorito* as a wedding between Pistoletto and Milanese actor Colnaghi. Announced on elegant stationery by Pioppi (presenting Pistoletto) and the Zoo (presenting Colnaghi), the wedding invitation was replete with bourgeois signifiers: family presentations of each spouse, as is tradition; expensive materials

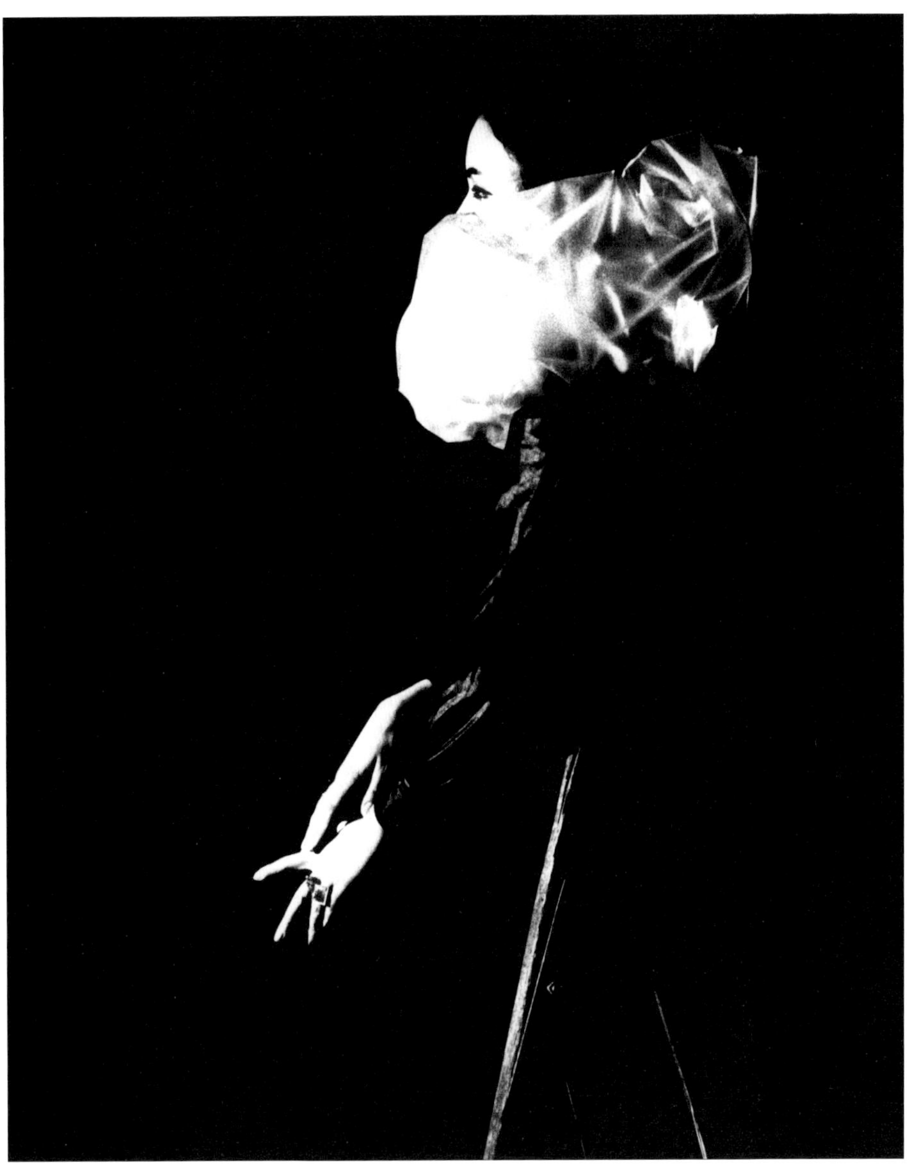

FIG. 115. Maria Pioppi in the Zoo, *Cocapicco e vestitorito,* action, Piper Pluriclub, Turin, May 8, 1968. Photo by Paolo Mussat Sartor. Archivio Pistoletto, Biella.

(heavyweight paper); and ceremonial cursive typeface, printed in deep-purple ink. The invitation set up expectations for a formal affair that didn't come. It also signaled, as would later artistic "marriages" (such as that of feminist artist Tomaso Binga to herself, in 1977), that the action transgressed important social mores.[9] Intended to mark the artistic collaboration between two men and to initiate the birth of the Zoo, the invitation to the Pistoletto-Colnaghi union registered an as-yet unnoted engagement on the part of the artist with the sociopolitical and cultural context of the work. *Cocapicco e vestitorito* coincided more specifically with the reexaminations of Italian identity by the cultural left, the nascent gay rights movement in Turin, and a highly publicized legal case at the forefront of intellectual and cultural debates.[10]

Study of the work in context reveals a trajectory of comparable provocations in Pistoletto's subsequent practice. As with *Man with Red Flag* before it, *Cocapicco e vestitorito* was not a one-off work. Other activities of the period explored structures of power and repressed subjectivity, in which the real and performed figure was used to live and stage radical subject positions. These figures were often situated in the context of themes of mastery, in which they functioned as agents of anti-authoritarian practice and social change. Following Jean-François Lyotard, as well as performance studies on actors' dual positions as themselves and the characters they perform, examination of these figures finds strategies associated with subject positions never before considered in relation to the artist (or Arte Povera).

These positions shift existing understanding of the movement as a largely heterosexual, masculine, and limited entity.[11] These figures and their activities are the subjects of this chapter.

The inquiry undertaken here leads us to see Pistoletto's theater, which sometimes used material props, as more than a purview for sculpture or installation, as it has sometimes been read. Despite the importance of the figure to Pistoletto's theatrical activity and other areas of his work, the small body of art historical scholarship on the Zoo has tended to underscore material elements that more readily connect the group's activities to the visual arts, as opposed to focusing on their "performative traits," to borrow Matthias Dusini's phrase.[12] Such focus has demoted (sometimes explicitly) the figure (as in "the artist's actual body") below "his or her sphere of action."[13] We might attribute this tendency to disciplinary divisions between art history and theater studies or to competing terms in the primary discourse around Arte Povera (for example, its debates on "object" aesthetics versus "actions"). In either case, the result is that Pistoletto's embodied "art actions" within the Zoo's theatrical performances have been subsumed into discussions of "sculptural performance" and "object theater."[14]

Although other scholarship has attended to the Zoo's relation to collectivism, primitivism, and Third Worldism—the last, in discussion on Arte Povera—the reading that has come closest to focusing on the figural nature of Pistoletto's theatrical activities belongs to Bruno Corà.[15] For Corà, the Zoo was one part of Pistoletto's broader exploration of "collaborative activation" executed through "scenic conceptualization" and "choral action," thereby straddling the real and represented worlds.[16] Accompanying Corà in this regard is Claire Gilman; beyond her primary focus on Pistoletto's "objects" in the Zoo, she identifies the group's examination, through theatrical activity, of the construction of discourse—a key interest, I've contended, of figural action.[17] But existing readings still cannot account for Pistoletto's exploration in the figure in performance—of *embodied* theater performance and real-life activities—and its centrality to his investigation of structures of power and subjugation in the cultural contexts of the late 1960s and early 1970s. And so the question remains: where is the figure—both the actual person doing (or living) the action and the character he or she often performs—in all of this?

STAGING A NEW SCENE: THE ZOO AND ITALIAN NEW THEATER AS ANTIAUTHORITARIAN PRACTICE

Pistoletto's theatrical activity had a political charge that was then being theorized, in part by him, in the growing discourse on experimental theater in Italy. Consider the March 1969 issue of the theater journal *Teatro*, dedicated to advancing "political theater." In the issue, critic (and recently appointed art director of Turin's Teatro Stabile) Giuseppe Bartolucci described a crisis in theater. In his introduction to a section on *una diversa scrittura scenica* (meaning "a new or different scene-writing," as opposed to "scenography," or *scenografia*), Bartolucci positioned theater within the revolutionary sociopolitical and artistic context of the late 1960s.[18] He was concerned with new multidisciplinary, nonliterary theatrical work, including that of Pistoletto (who also contributed to the issue). That work, Bartolucci explained, was then taking shape outside of theater and social establishments. For Bartolucci, it was on the frontlines of a creative struggle for authentic theater practice and living.[19] Drawing on established ideas of Jerzy Grotowski's "poor theater," and by extension Celant's Arte Povera (they also contributed to the issue), Bartolucci positioned strategies of new theater, such as theatrical improvisation and spontaneous gesture, as ways of "relating to the world." Any ephemeral action, as Bartolucci cast it in this new scene, is *come catapulta:* theater as catapult.[20]

Pursuant to his metaphor, the new theater (and its unplanned gesture) had the power to disrupt, to irreversibly change established terrain, and to soar, figuratively, over fortified structures of power. By contrast, the theater establishment was mounting "barricades" against this new work, denouncing it as "terrorism" against convention. The new theater's characteristics of impoverishment and "communication of 'alterity'" were the terms of its radicalization.[21] As described by Bartolucci, the new scene-writing also evoked coeval images of actual events. His writing called to mind photographs and actions of students and workers in the bloody protests and occupations of the late 1960s, including the so-called Battle of Valle Giulia in Rome. On March 1, 1968, participants in a student occupation calling for reform at the University of Rome returned to occupy the Department of Architecture after having been ousted by police. Violent armed conflict ensued between students and thousands of police, many in armed cars. Joined by leftist groups, the students fought with stones, found items, and debris. Hundreds were wounded, cars burned.[22] Photographed by Fausto Giaccone and other photojournalists on the scene, the widely mediated events ignited Italy's student movement, distinguished by calls for the right to think, and set off occupations around the country's universities.[23] Now regarded as a watershed moment for 1968 in Italy and the turn toward the violent years of lead in that country, the visibility and valence of the Battle of Valle Giulia haunted Bartolucci's writing, even for readers at that time.

Other contributors to the issue similarly tethered the urgent cultivation of new theater strategies to social upheaval and contemporary social crises.[24] In his text for the issue, Pistoletto focused on actor-spectator relations for theater and society. He declared: "We no longer work for spectators, we are ourselves actors and spectators, manufacturers and consumers."[25] As a "Compagnia di Spettatori" (Company of Spectators), participants in the Zoo would be both actors *and* spectators, as opposed to spectators alone, who would be afflicted by false consciousness. In this regard, the Zoo's theatrical work was a Marxist response to what Pistoletto viewed as the "hobbling" of "so-called civilization," which stifled and controlled humankind's existence, "trapping "every animal in its cage."[26] (The motif of the cage also appeared in his visual artwork of the period, where he similarly used it to explore the theme of society as an agent of dehumanizing incarceration.)

Decrying artists as "trainable monkeys who imitate being men," Pistoletto classified society by degrees of domestication and imprisonment. The "least tamable" were the mad and the criminal, held "in prisons and shackles." The majority were the "least dangerous, more docile and submissive." Until that time, they included students and workers (in his text, the factory-associated operai), who had been relegated to "communal paddocks" of "factories, public housing, sports arenas." Artists in Pistoletto's model were part of an isolated group, between the mad and mainstream majority. They belonged to the elite, "isolated in the Venice Biennales, in theaters, in museums and in organized demonstrations."[27] By contrast, the Zoo would be those "on the other side of the bars" (*al di là delle sbarre*). Though caged, they would refuse domestication from within its system. In this sense, the group's name conjured the trope of prison, freedom, and surveillance, but it also situated their theatrical work as a social service.[28] To that end, activities were often done in official and alternative theaters in Europe, as well as in nontheater spaces of public life and communal living. Seeking to address the state of humanity in a world of intellectual and social imprisonment, the Zoo would create a new theatrical, economic, and social order, free of judgment.

Exemplary of the Zoo's pursuit of this new social and artistic order were explorations of power dynamics and class critique that were fundamental to the Zoo's most frequently enacted theatrical activities, including *L'Uomo ammaestrato* (The Trained Man), *Il principe pazzo* (The Mad Prince), and *L'Uomo nero* (The Minus Man).[29] In late summer and fall of 1968, for example, the Zoo staged *The Trained Man* in various locations in Cinque Terre, Rome, and southern Italy.[30] The title alone engaged discussions in the New Left on the "new forms of control" of capitalism.[31] In the performance in Amalfi in October 1968, for the major exhibition *Arte povera + azioni povere* (Poor Art + Poor Actions), Pistoletto played the role of a *cantastoria nomade*—in Italian culture, a traditional "nomadic storysinger."[32] As in tradition, to illustrate his tales, Pistoletto used a sheet painted with narrative vignettes, depicting biblical figures and animal encounters, as well as scenes of subjugation, enslavement, and forced learned activity (such as reading), showing, as Gilman has argued, the "brutality of the 'civilizing' process.'"[33] Colnaghi joined him; in Rome, he appeared as a theatrical character from the popular tradition of commedia dell'arte (fig. 116). He wore a dark-colored face mask with exaggerated features (reminiscent of several commedia dell'arte characters) and clothing fashioned as a costume (a belted tunic, typical of the popular figure of Pulcinella, but also a cape, associated more with "master" rather than "servant" characters in the genre). Colnaghi conjured commedia dell'arte generally. In concert with the pictorial panel and content of the performance, commedia dell'arte was invoked in the Zoo as a culturally specific tool, employed in a broader theatrical investigation into themes of authoritarianism.

In the performance, Pistoletto introduced the figure of the "trained man" who emerged from the uncivilized linguistic and social space of the vulgar and of wild nature, as depicted on the panel. As Pistoletto described it: "[The trained man] was born out of a donkey's fart. As a baby he's alone in a forest, where he is raised by a snake but he can't read or write and he knows nothing of society. A carriage full of charlatans (played by us) passes by, and then they decide to take the little boy and teach him the basics of civilization."[34] By the end of the action, the trained man could execute many learned skills. The Zoo enacted the socialization of the figure while also positioning themselves as agents who could encounter the boy on the edge of society, on the edge of discourse. In her work on the Zoo, Gilman has argued that the performance therefore narrates how "meaning is acquired" and the artist's longer-term interest in his early career as "a progressive testing of presentational space."[35] To her point we can add another. The figure of the trained man—both the theatrical character and the actual person who played him (in Amalfi, Henry Martin and anarchic Beat poet Gianni Milano)—were modeled in the fringes of society and in fringe theater.[36] Recalling Lyotard, we can also add that the Zoo also staged, through embodied performance as figures, shifting relationships to systems of meaning and society. Using themselves as figures to be encountered in real space, they performed in symbolic roles, testing the limits of discourse and figuring their transgression by acting out liberatory gestures.

In the Italian theater journal *Sipario* the following month, Pistoletto described a new mode of antiauthoritarian, utopian social existence, gained by using theater to kick off "mechanisms of liberation" in the world. As he wrote: "The action must always be *free,* independent and fantastic . . . to act on the freedom (of the public) . . . to make analogous mechanisms of liberation erupt."[37] This work was not traditional thespian theater. It was "creative collaboration," done with and *for* one another—a framework of practice he has pursued for the rest of his career.[38] Although Pistoletto clarified that this new theatrical activity was no different than his earlier work as a painter, he added that the action of the Zoo had the power to agitate public freedom. Improvised action was a method of creative and social liberation, one that would also transgress national borders. In *Sipario,* he used both English and Italian words for being *free,* harnessing the rhetoric of the global counterculture of the late 1960s; he also used *scattare*—the Italian verb meaning "to jerk," as in a sudden movement, or to figuratively erupt or explode, as a protest might. The text positions the Zoo's theatrical activity as not only improvised and

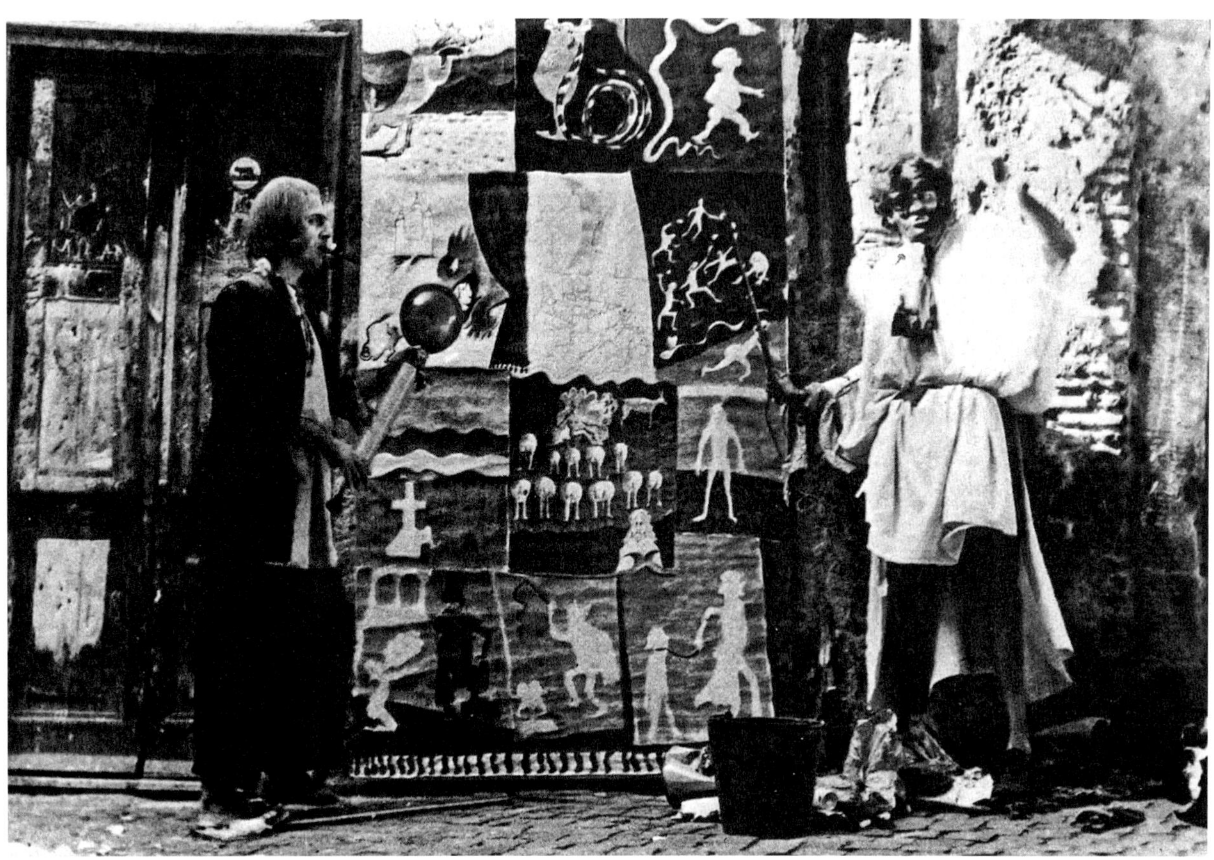

FIG. 116. The Zoo, *L'Uomo ammaestrato* (The Trained Man), Vicolo dell'Atleta, Rome, October 1968. Photo by Claudio Abate.

unexpected but also charged with the emancipatory potential of transnational liberatory action.

The eclectic group included underground poets, actors, experimental musicians, and theater directors, along with Pistoletto and Pioppi.[39] Many had become disillusioned with their individual work: Beppe Bergamasco with photography, Colnaghi with acting, Martin with art criticism.[40] They were all, as Martin later put it, "under the shadow of an anarchic fatigue of living in an anarchy not of their creation: people ready to distance themselves from things that had become too empty or too full for them." In this context, the Zoo's turn to spontaneity, instinct, and an "abandonment of logic" were life-giving, liberatory acts and ways of being.[41]

FIGURES OF POWER: *L'UOMO NERO*

In the summer of 1969, the Zoo shifted from itinerant festival performers in Italy's New Theater scene and Europe's international experimental theater circuit to a relatively isolated commune, whose members did theater as lived actions in the tiny cliffside Ligurian town of Corniglia.[42] Dedicating themselves to enacting *esercizi quotidiani* or "everyday exercises" of liberated behavior and living, they conducted theatrical activities in public, for three and a half hours daily and months on end, typically under the purview of the character of *L'Uomo nero*, introduced in the previous chapter. Pistoletto later described their work as a daily act of invention; whatever they invented was "a work in progress" as opposed to a finished work that we might expect from product-focused artistic labor.[43]

The language of research—as in *La ricerca dell'Uomo nero* (The Research of the Minus Man) and *Lo Zoo scopre l'Uomo nero* (The Zoo Discovers the Minus Man)—was aligned with a range of practices in the 1960s that reconceptualized creative work as social and scientific research. Pistoletto's framing, however, eschewed the technological interests of cybernetic and programmatic art in favor of traditional, humanist ideas from popular Italian culture, specifically associated with fear-based instruction of morals and social conditioning.[44] The result was that the well-known figure of *L'Uomo nero* was used to investigate social relations based on structures of power, including learned behavior as a site of antihumanism.

Photographs of the Zoo's activities in Corniglia show that their actions were often done without material props, which have nevertheless been a major focus in scholarship on this work. Instead they focused on collective configurations of their bodies. One photograph of the Zoo conducting *The Research of the Minus Man* shows the group in a strange arrangement, tethered to one another (fig. 117). They stand, lean, and pose in front of a short wall that protects them from the cliffs behind them. Members pose with their shirtsleeves (emptied of arms) and sections of hair tied together. We see Pistoletto's collaborator and romantic partner, Maria Pioppi, at lower right, wrapped with another member in a bundle on the ground, such that she appears to belong to a conjoined, limbless body. A member at far left sticks his head through another man's legs; his shaggy hair reads now like a gender-bending bush. Occupying the foreground of the scene, Pistoletto lies horizontally on his side, his arms tied behind him. Only Martin stands relatively unencumbered; at the far right of the image, he leans away from the group with his leg outstretched. Only his foot, hooked around the ankle of another participant, remains in contact. The suggestion is that he is still tied to the group.

Close study of this configuration prompts a series of questions. How will they move? If they are hobbled, why does one participant smile? How will they get out of this situation? Do they want to? There is no clear narrative here; this is not a traditional tableau vivant. The Zoo posed as a living collective body, showing the spectator, and themselves, that the limits of an imposed system registered literally on the site of the body, but that bodies and subjects in such conditions might also create new figures, together.

To review, in Italy the mythical figure of *L'Uomo nero* is invoked by parents and in children's games to encourage good behavior (lest *L'Uomo nero* take poorly behaving children away). Typically depicted in silhouette or as a figure cloaked in black, sometimes masked, *L'Uomo nero* is a sinister, frightening figure (akin to the Bogeyman). Sometimes, the Zoo's performances of *L'Uomo nero* invoked these cultural conventions of the figure, such as the use of a black sheet as a hooded cloak. (His appearance in Italian modernism is also not unique to Pistoletto's work. Lucio Fontana, for example, made a ceramic work in the 1930s entitled *L'Uomo nero*, which featured incised figures in silhouette.)[45] For Pistoletto, as Marco Farano has summarized it, *L'Uomo nero* is "the symbol of being alone, of indivisibility in the great game of the double, and of the void understood as container of everything."[46] In this sense, the figure of *L'Uomo nero*

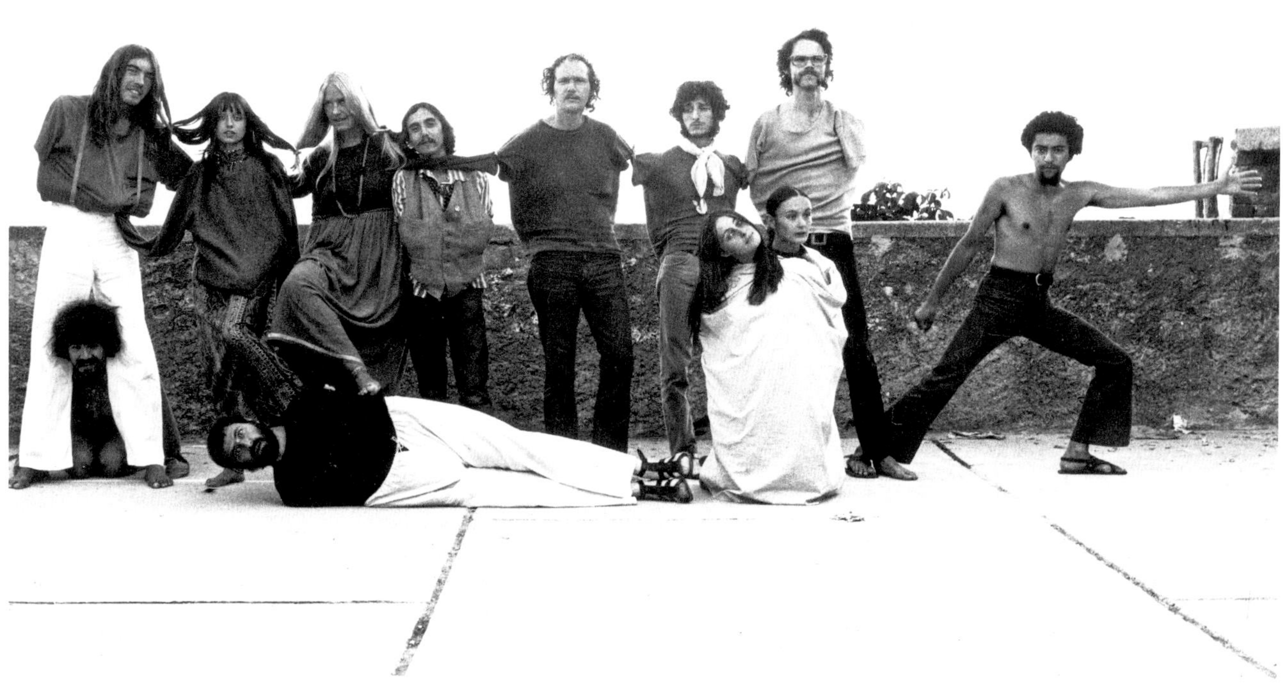

FIG. 117. The Zoo, *La ricerca dell'Uomo nero* (The Research of the Minus Man), Corniglia, May–October 1969, 4:00–7:30 p.m. daily. Photo by Paolo Mussat Sartor. Archivio Pistoletto, Biella.

for Pistoletto is an allegory for the mirror. (As Pistoletto once put it, the mirror is like a void, "null, [but] full of everything.")[47] The figure was chosen to be pursued by the group because it also aligned with methods explored in their earlier works; it optimized participation and avoided individual artistic practice, by then associated with political and artistic pitfalls of capital-motivated creative work.[48]

The performed embodied figure, and theater more broadly, allowed the artist to harness a multiple existence—as figure (human body, Pistoletto) and as character (*L'Uomo nero*). To paraphrase performance theorist and theater director Richard Schechner, Pistoletto wasn't *L'Uomo nero*, but he was also not *not L'Uomo nero*. The result is a linking of "two realms of experience," as Schechner theorizes the actor's embodied position as themselves and as theatrical character: "The world of contingent existence as ordinary objects and persons and the world of transcendent existence as magical implements, gods, demons, characters. It isn't that a performer stops being himself or herself when he or she becomes another—multiple selves coexist in an unresolved dialectical tension."[49] By invoking a recognized figure in Italian culture, Pistoletto also involved cultural memory within tense multiplicity. In performance studies, Marvin Carlson has discussed the relationship between the haunting of theater in its reception, during which time audiences draw on their previous encounters with such performances to navigate the work before them. Critically, Carlson notes: "If a work requires reception techniques outside those provided by an audience's memory, then it falls outside their horizon of expectations, but more commonly it will operate, or can be made to operate, within that horizon, thus adding a new experiential memory for future use."[50] The potential of performance, then, as a site of antiauthoritarian activity and potential social transformation, lies in the figure's prospective excess and departure from what audiences know—a figural transgression, following Lyotard, at the edge of discourse.

Indeed, Pistoletto's conceptualization of *L'Uomo nero* also exceeded its conventional meaning. The Minus Man embodied and enacted—as an allegorical figure and as the real person playing the role—a transgressive figural position, poised to change discourse as a site of social conditioning. "L'Uomo nero" was both victim and conditioner of the group. Consider the "game of the Minus Man," played in private and in public. The activities and objectives of the Zoo explored control, victimization, and psychosocial conditioning. Gameplay went hand in hand with the exploration of power dynamics. Members took turns in the role, which they were to play to the best of their abilities.[51] As he described the work: "This new work had to be entitled 'the black man.' 'The black man' drew its pretext from a game in which participants take turns being put under, that is signed, or better, marked. You could say that he's the victim; these will lead the game until someone else has to take up the position. This 'Black [*sic*] man' is the one who will condition the other participants, drawing attention to himself."[52] Pistoletto also invoked darkness associated with the figure as a void or untenable space.

Pistoletto's written description of the game demonstrates the activity's investment in thinking about power and mob-based, anarchic, extrajudicial violence, as captured by Pistoletto's jarring use of the Italian word *linciaggio,* meaning "lynching": "The opening scene of the minus man marks out the circle and everyone else inside the circle become participants in a competition planned in advance that ends with a revolt and the lynching of the winner and everyone goes to sleep powerless [*impotenti*] because in the game circle there'll be another minus man again, immediately afterward, while everyone sleeps."[53] In Italy, lynching was (and remains) most associated with anti-Black race violence in the United States. The history of lynching in the United States primarily targeted African Americans but also affected Italian immigrants, as in the lynching of eleven Italian Americans and immigrants in New Orleans in 1891.[54]

The role of *L'Uomo nero* was not and did not mean, as Pistoletto later told me, *negro*—the odious racialized Italian term for Black people. Nevertheless, the relation of *L'Uomo nero* to structures of power, as the above passage suggests, had unavoidable racial connotations. Even Pistoletto once remarked on the "extra meaning and provocation" of racial Blackness in the works of the Zoo. In reference to his casting of his friend and collaborator Henry Martin, who was Black, in the Amalfi performance of *The Trained Man,* he said: "The fact that he's black added extra meaning and provocation. On the way from the exhibition to the central piazza where we were going to do *The Trained Man,* each of us carried something for the performance. I had a big straw mattress. . . . Then there was a performer with a whip, lashing the trained man."[55] What Pistoletto gets to in this passage is the added significance and questions that race and ethnicity bring to enacted allegorical inquiries into structures of social power. His work (and the figurality of its exploration) seemed to underscore both the constructedness of race in discourse and the very real lived experiences that discourse structures, thereby evoking more specific histories of subjugation and enslavement through the imagery and staged actions of "the trained man."

On this point, of structural production of racialized bodies and ways of seeing, Pistoletto's own phrasing—the "fact" of Martin's Black identity—evokes theorizations of race in literature of the period. In 1952, Frantz Fanon published his essay "The Fact of Blackness" as a chapter in *Black Skin, White Masks* (originally published in French). Building on the work of W. E. B. Du Bois and Jean-Paul Sartre, while critiquing contemporary anticolonial discourse on race consciousness and Black pride in Négritude, Fanon wrote: "In the white world the man of color encounters difficulties in the development of his bodily schema. Consciousness of the body is solely a negating activity." For Fanon, the experience of coming into being through a bodily schema of race (that is importantly a "definitive structuring" of the self and world rather than an imposition on them) is to experience fixed objectification, ontological negation—a "corporeal malediction," a psychic amputation, a "feeling of nonexistence."[56] If *L'Uomo nero* was not about race, Martin's participation invoked the discourse on it, including ontological negation and the figural model of a bodily schema—in which figures, as images and bodies, can be sites of negation, of the void (as Pistoletto sometimes suggested), and also of transgression.

A poster for the Minus Man performance at Artestudio in Macerata provides additional evidence of the racial connotations this work had for Italian audiences, if not for Pistoletto. Designed by the gallery, without input from the artist, the poster features a racialized primitivist depiction of a profile in silhouette. Such connotations haunt this work and have perhaps contributed to the historiographic inattention to it, despite its prominence in this important period of Pistoletto's practice.

This history suggests that the primary function of this role and activity as invoked by Pistoletto and the Zoo was to examine power. It explored the idea of breaking free from what was perceived as the persecution, bondage, and social control of capitalism. Pistoletto's subsequent discussion touches on the associations between the bureaucratic position and space of the office, invoked in *Office of the Minus Man* (discussed in the previous chapter), and the power of *L'Uomo nero* in the theatrical activity of the Zoo. As he wrote in a rare description of the activity:

> The work had to roughly begin like this: I arrive and draw an enormous circle with chalk on the ground, in order to define the area of the scene. This task was my turn in so far as I was practically "the black man" in office/charge, since it was my project that was chosen. The others arrive after and get in line, bending over like as if on the starting line of a competition, with chalk in hand and on my signal they start to trace their own line on the ground, looking to arrive as quickly as possible at the prearranged finish line. Everything takes place really quickly, as soon as the first to reach it declares himself the winner, all the others pounce on him with such violence that at the end of the struggle, he lies dead on the ground. Then having abandoned his post, everyone lines up on the starting line, but this time lying down to sleep. While everyone is sleeping, the deceased "black man" starts to put on an individual action, followed then by the others who have woken up, having forgotten the past, they collaborate to bring the situation up to the point in which a new "Black man" will improvise the next scene.[57]

Some of what Pistoletto gets to in these activities is the integral function of the figure to social structures of power.

Sometimes the figure was highlighted by the demarcation of their space, which also served to assemble a space of activity and allegorical scene within the real space of the performance. A photograph of this activity staged at the Galleria Sperone (Turin) that fall allows us to imagine the scene (fig. 118). Relating this circularity to the limitation of discovery imposed by the rules and regulations of social and, by extension, cultural systems, Pistoletto and the Zoo sought to harness the frustration of being limited. As Pistoletto wrote in 1969, recalling the spatialists before him: "Man loves to discover new worlds, feeling the need to leave his shell, to fly in this cone of light that expands in his mind. . . . The circularity of the intellectual system that circumscribes every human action in the orbit of a closed vision. . . . But the circle becomes aware of itself and becomes pressing for men who feel in it the intolerableness of every point. For these men the circle becomes centrifugal energy."[58] Pistoletto and the Zoo would use the intolerableness of psychosocial enclosure to launch themselves away from the center. The activity, for Pistoletto, "was symbolic, but so close to reality." The use of chalk aligns with children's games, as well as a range of artistic activities in the 1960s that similarly employed the technique to examine man's place in the world. (In Italy and across the Zoo's European itinerary we can cite Argentine artist Alberto Greco's *Vivo dito* works and Slovenian OHO Group member David Nez's *Cosmology*, from 1969, perhaps known by Pistoletto, since the Zoo performed in Eastern Europe and Arte Povera artists showed in Ljubljana.) The Zoo, however, ultimately realized the "intolerability of the closed system."[59] (They disbanded the following year.)

Later that year, on December 15, 1969, Pistoletto purchased a 365-page journal to be filled over the course of one month, without any predetermined narrative or objective. It was where he considered this intolerability at length. Later titled *L'Uomo nero: Il lato insopportabile* (The Minus Man: The Unbearable Side), published by Rumma Editore in March 1970, the book was both manifesto and stream-of-consciousness account of the group's activities, which included Pistoletto's reflections on collaborative practice. One passage in particular captures the theme of their work: "The economy in our civilization is the most disorganized thing that exists. Ditto the mental economy of one's own individual time. Everyone is a victim of it, industrialists and laborers,

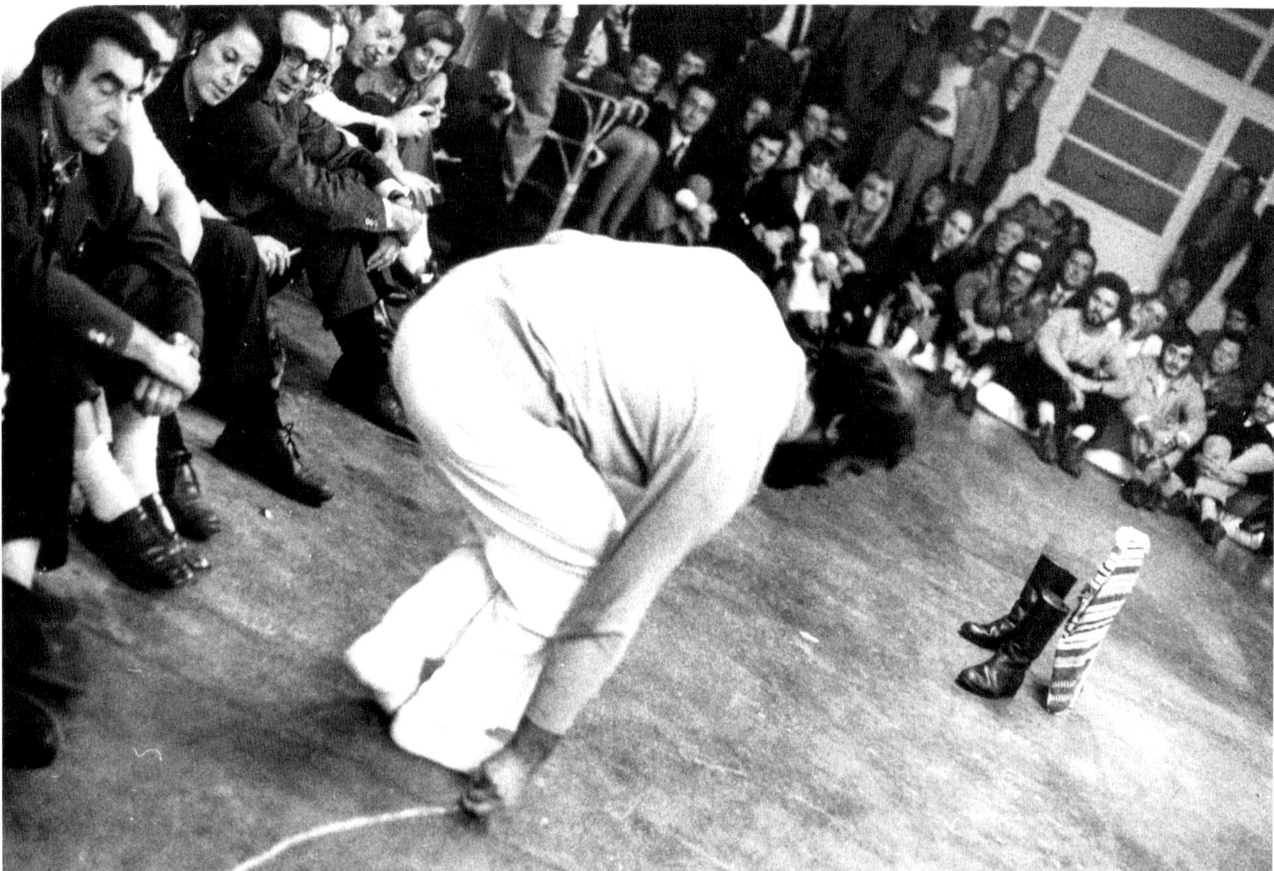

FIG. 118. The Zoo, *Lo Zoo scopre L'Uomo nero* (The Zoo Discovers the Minus Man), Galleria Gian Enzo Sperone, Turin, October 25, 1969. Photo by Paolo Mussat Sartor. Archivio Pistoletto, Biella.

statesmen as policemen and artists. Now I'll tell you one of my almost daydreams. A company of young people gets together to do some theater. But not traditional theater, to do living, directly, creative performances."[60] While the Zoo was dedicated to *living* as a working activity of the group, their activities and rules for group practice also sought to preserve rather than compromise the value and free will of the individual subject. Underscoring the importance of liberal individualism in postfascist Italy, as well as the political significance of assembly within the political and cultural left, this philosophy safeguarded a liberated mode of being or "free open character" for each individual.[61]

Revisitation of structures of liberation and revolutionary movements in recent post-Marxist theory, as Andrea Bellini has suggested, allow us to better account for understudied throughlines in the Zoo—rule-based practices, commitment to regimented activity, and exploration of power dynamics, that complicate or even undermine readings of their work as "spontaneous," "very instinctual, performative, impromptu, and chaotic idea of theater," and "improvisational," and hence unplanned and casual.[62] In *Assembly* (2017), Michael Hardt and Antonio Negri caution against the disavowal of institutional forms made by "horizontal" (as opposed to hierarchical), masterless movements that seek democracy, freedom from authoritarian rule, and liberation from a range of "methods of repression" in modern society. Institutional forms are essential, they argue, to forging a "real democratic alternative" to perpetually fraught representative democracy and to the "double position" of modern liberation movements, which call for vanguard society models without masters while also emphasizing that conditions are not yet right for such models to exist.[63] Through this lens, we can understand the Zoo's exploration of horizontality and institutional forms of power as an expression of their belief that the time was right for real social change.

Although the 1960s were a period of global decolonization and antiauthoritarian sentiment, Italy's avant-gardes, including Arte Povera, frequently experimented with Orientalist and neocolonial motifs that seemed to reinscribe the constructed hierarchies they were working against. Sometimes these experimentations were pursued with language that was being ostensibly repositioned from former racial associations. Fascination with "non-Western" cultures reflected a desire of the cultural left to harness the perceived emancipatory, countercultural potential of those regions; in artistic practice, this often meant that artists imagined solidarity with subjugated elsewheres or deployed constructed tropes of the "non-West" (and the nonwhite) as anti-Occidentalist social critique.[64] Recent scholarship on the subject qualifies these strategies as politicized, creative explorations of "alterity"—geographical (non-Western, provincial, and rural), sociocultural and aesthetic ("tribal"), and historical ("archaic")—through which artists sought to consolidate an aesthetic and political front of resistance to West and to imagine countercultural utopia.[65] Teresa Kittler and Silvia Bottinelli have argued that this work, as in the tent structures of Carla Accardi, explores "modern nomadism" to imagine an anticapitalist utopia, while Ara Merjian, building on the work of Luca Caminati, has argued that Pier Paolo Pasolini's Orientalist films constitute a "heretical" praxis, shared by Arte Povera's sometimes agrarian and archaic interests.[66] Of most relevance to this study is Jacopo Galimberti's discussion of the Zoo as an example of Arte Povera's "humanist poverty" and Third Worldist aesthetics. Discussing Celant's interest in political Third Worldism as aligned with the rise of Mao-Dadaism, Galimberti argues that "Third-Worldist 'art'" of Arte Povera offered a nonfigurative aesthetic and political "metaphor" for guerrilla action, if without result.[67]

In Italy, the tumultuous summer and "hot autumn" of 1969 directly coincided with the Zoo's project of the Minus Man. While the Zoo pursued an often-unmentioned demanding regimen of daily four-hour theatrical activities, riots and protests by workers were erupting across Italy, especially in the industrial north. The Workerist Movement was grounded in frustration on the part of factory workers, many of whom migrated from Italy's south and who contested Italian internal racism in the north, which distinguished Italy's politics at this time from most of its international counterparts. Neo-Marxist organizations and workers' movements—Potere Operaio (1967–73), Lotta Continua (1969–76), and post-Marxist Autonomia Operaia (1973–79), which included a "creative" wing—all called for the refusal of power. Countercultural, reformist, and feminist movements proliferated at this moment and into the 1970s. At the time, as Shelleen Greene has discussed, this engagement with the non-West was seen by the Italian left as a way to resist capitalism and the conditioning of Western modernity: "With the rise of neocolonialism, internal political turmoil and economic downturn, however, the early 1970s were a period of disillusionment for Italian leftist intellectuals as it became evident that the 'non-West' would not serve as a site for resistance to the capitalist system or as a refuge from Western modernity."[68] Italian artists, however, were much slower to respond; for a number of reasons, including delayed migration to Italy from subjects of its former colonies, postcoloniality arrived only in the 1990s and 2000s in Italy. In some ways it is still in development as a post–Cold War phenomenon.[69]

Aligned with widespread artistic interest in Eastern religions and cultures and the personal experiences and tastes of Zoo members, Orientalism in these works aimed to cultivate a worldly countercultural vision. Pioppi had lived in Iran two years before; her Indian garments in *The Trained Man* were also her own—only the veil was added.[70] Costumes were what they wore in their everyday lives, with the exception of having "a bit accentuated the less typical characteristics," as Pioppi would later say.[71] The idea, for the Zoo, was to be "ready to be open to all the different opportunities to meet with a shared interest in many aspects."[72]

Contemporaneous conceptual explorations of darkness and the void were also being forged in Italian and broader European art, sometimes with simultaneous reference to dark bodies. In 1968, Franco Vaccari exhibited *L'ambiente buio* (The Dark Environment) in Piacenza, accompanied by his artist's book of the same year, *La scultura buia* (The Dark Sculpture, as in sculpture made of pitch-black darkness). Whereas Pistoletto explored darkness as a site of absence consolidated in the performed figure, Vaccari seemed to explore darkness as a site of absence to be encountered sensorially in an environment; he described *The Dark Environment* as "a black block, an environment rendered absolutely compact by an absence than by a presence."[73] In Vaccari's related artist book, sixteen pages alternate between stark white pages, with a black text label ("entrance," for example), and pages of black foil. Viewers' reflections are captured in the pages, bringing the viewer into an ambient created by the book. And yet, Vaccari's text reveals a similar interest in the figure: "The dark sculpture is an environment in which every presence, every infiltration of visible radiation, is eliminated; it is a black body [*è un corpo nero*], an environment rendered absolutely solid by an absence instead of a presence."[74] Along with the aforementioned conceptual works of South American and Eastern European–based artists and other artists in the 1960s who were interested in the void (such as Yves Klein), Vaccari's conceptual investigation of darkness in relation to figuration and presence constitutes a key interlocutor for Pistoletto's work.

Of particular and related resonance with the Zoo's interest in breaking with the restrictions of cultural and social convention, as a means to liberate the self, is Germano Celant's frequent discussion of nomadism, primitiveness, and refutation of "slavishness." In *Art Povera,* Celant asserts it is the artist's lack of faith in "cultural control (artistic, intellectual, etc.) that suggests slavishness (spectator, public, etc.) as a pattern of values," as well as the artist's efforts "to live hazardously in an uncertain space."[75] By the text's conclusion, Celant has laid out the stakes of "art, politics, and life 'poveri'": "Today, in life or art or politics one finds in the anarchy and in the continuousness of nomadic behavior the greatest level of liberty for a vital and fantastic expression."[76] To live this impoverished, dynamic, anarchist ontology is to open oneself up to a reality that can be a "stupefying, horrible, poetic entity," to processes of "deculturization, regression, primitiveness and repression," and to a "tendency towards the basic element in nature . . . and in life . . . and in behavior (family, spontaneous action, class struggle, violence, environment)." This "dull absurdity" of reality in which such an artist participates is ultimately "a political deed."[77] Appearing toward the end of his edited volume of artists' entries in *Art Povera,* Celant's text is followed by only one: that of the Zoo.

References and associations to race were under urgent renegotiation in postwar Italy. A few examples from the social and cultural milieux surrounding race further contextualize these issues. First, the establishment of the Italian Republic in 1946 was on the constitutional values of equality regardless of race, human dignity, and prohibition of slavery (instituted in 1948)—values stated in large part as a refutation to the racial laws and persecutions of fascism. The peace treaty of 1947 following World War II also involved Italy's renunciation of colonies and recognition of the independence of areas of former imperial occupation and colonization. By the 1960s, odious racist references such as *negrigura* (negro-ness) were still used by older generations, but had come into association with other "outsides" of class. In literature, as in Natalia Ginzburg's *Lessico famigliare* (Family Sayings) of 1963, which was awarded Italy's prestigious Premio Strega, we find examples of the invocation of negrigura as a generational term for behavior that was inappropriate insofar as it was uninformed or ignorant. Reflecting on some of her father's sayings when she was growing up (in the late 1910s and 1920s in Turin), Ginzburg writes:

> A stage worse than silly men were "negroes." A "negro" for my father was one whose manners were gauche and lacking in assurance; one who dressed inappropriately, who was no good at mountaineering, and was ignorant of foreign languages. Any act or gesture of ours which he thought out of place was classified by him as a "negrigura." Don't be "negroes," don't do those "*negrigure,*" he shouted at us endlessly. The range of such behaviour was wide: wearing town shoes on expeditions in the mountains; getting into conversations with strangers in a train, or in the street; talking out of the window to one's neighbours; taking off one's shoes in the sitting room, or warming one's feet at the stove; complaining on our mountaineering expeditions of thirst, fatigue or sore feet; taking rich food on these walks, and napkins for one's fingers.[78]

These lines in the opening paragraphs of Ginzburg's memoir speak to constructed associations in modern Italian language among race, class, and matters of taste. They also elucidate that this meaning circulated in a specific generation—above Ginzburg (1916–1991) and perhaps two above Pistoletto—in the decades surrounding Italian fascism. Ginzburg's lengthy explanation of her father's use of the term speaks to its idiosyncratic nature, even by 1963. That whiteness was the presumptive corollary in Ginzburg's father's lexicon to "correct," educated behavior also reflects broader historical constructions of racialized nationhood in Italy from the Risorgimento, Italy's period of national unification,

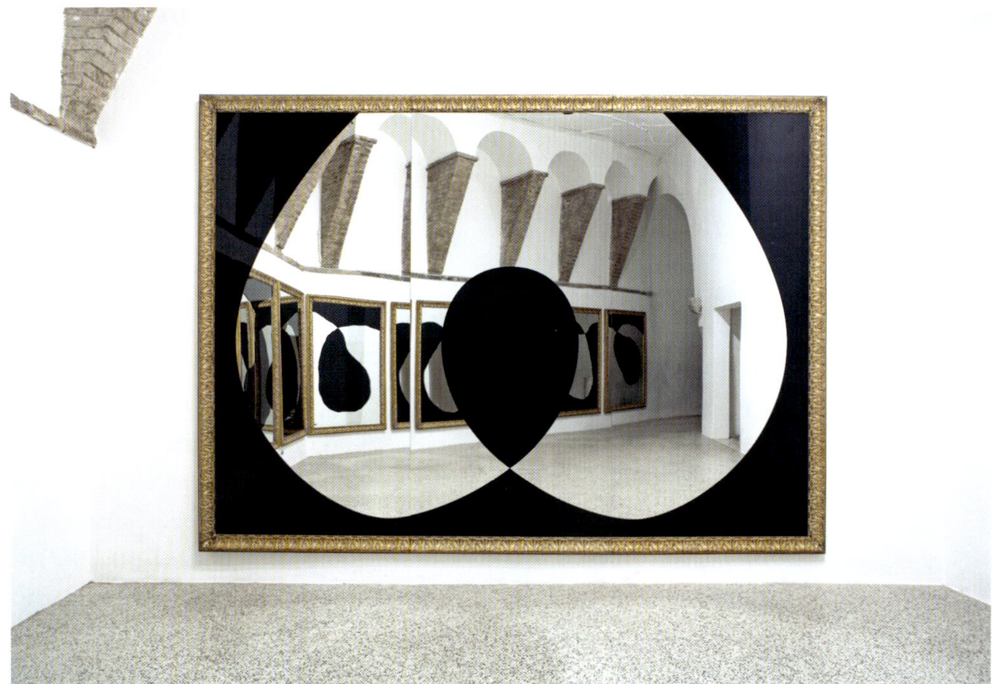

FIG. 120. Michelangelo Pistoletto's *Buco nero* (Black Hole), 2010. Black and silver mirror, gilded wood, 98½ × 141¾ in. (250 × 360 cm). Installation view, Galleria Continua, San Gimignano, September 25, 2010–March 26, 2011.

two-man exhibition at the Galleria Sperone in Turin in May 1971, Pistoletto and his new collaborator, Roman artist Vettor Pisani, displayed a single work of art. Like Pistoletto and Colnaghi before them, the duo had been joined in "matrimony" in a staged wedding witnessed by Achille Bonito Oliva, to mark the beginning of their creative collaboration. The artwork was a composite photographic portrait, entitled *Plagio* (1971).

To make the work, the artists had their individual color photographic portraits taken by Paolo Mussat Sartor and printed them in the format of two 120 medium-format diapositives (or two-inch-square positive slide prints) (fig. 121). They then superimposed the individual portraits on a transparent support and mounted the resulting layered portrait in an iron metal box frame, illuminating them from behind (fig. 122). The resulting work presents the viewer with a single image of a single figure. Both portraits shift between conditions of indiscernibility (we cannot separate one portrait from the other) and recognition (the bearded and mustachioed face, with its strong, furrowed brow, looks more like Pistoletto than the clean-shaven, wide-eyed Pisani, while the ear-length hair is characteristically Pisani).

Certain aspects of the photographic figure and image in *Plagio* catalyze this condition. First, a triangular form on the left-hand side of the image disrupts an otherwise symmetrical slope of the figure's shoulders. Catching the light, this third shoulder, clad in blue-gray fabric, sticks out from behind the black-jacketed form of the figure in front, with which it contrasts sharply in value, color, and shape. Acting as a visual cue, it outs the portrait setting as one occupied by two bodies. Comparison of *Plagio* with its source images, later exhibited as independent works, tells us more. The image of Pisani was placed behind Pistoletto's; it is Pisani's right shoulder that peeks out above Pistoletto's on the left-hand side of the image. Second, the visual density of the figure's coiffure, realized through the layering of two figurative images (and two heads of hair), gives it the appearance of an opaque black helmet. From our perspective, it cuts a sharp edge down the right side of the figure's face. Moving toward the chin, it meets the more textured form of the mustache and beard, realized through the presence of just one mustache and beard, which by contrast is a warm chestnut hue. The result of these "tells" is that the figure in *Plagio* is distinguished by a seemingly paradoxical condition of corporeal plurality and singularity—that is, of having multiple bodies and just one. We know we see more than one body but cannot separate them; the unified figure casts a single shadow. Here is an image and a man—a *figure,* in both senses of the word—made through a layered union of images of masculine bodies that only these two men can make.

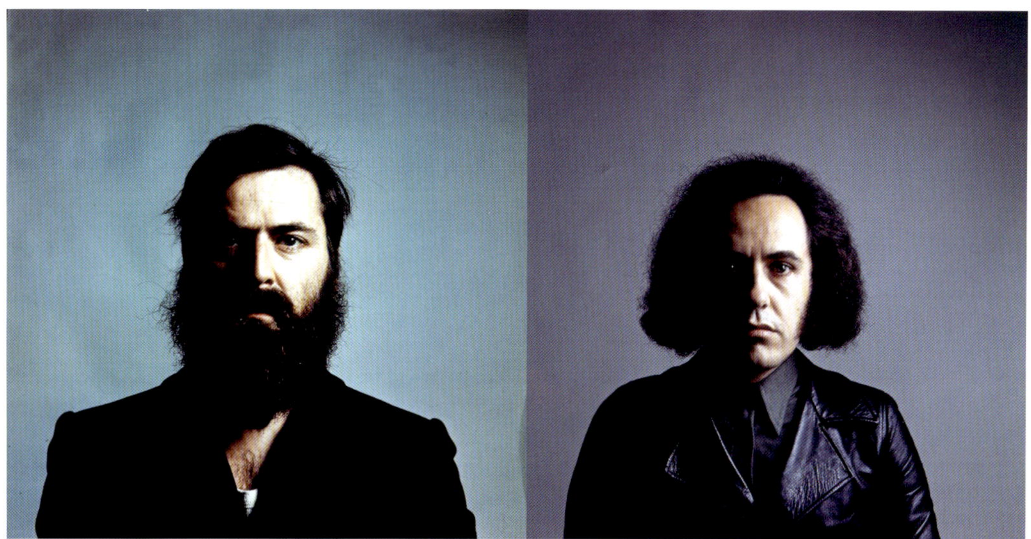

FIG. 121. Photographic portraits of Michelangelo Pistoletto and Vettor Pisani used in *Plagio* (1971). Photos by Paolo Mussat Sartor. Archivio Pistoletto, Biella.

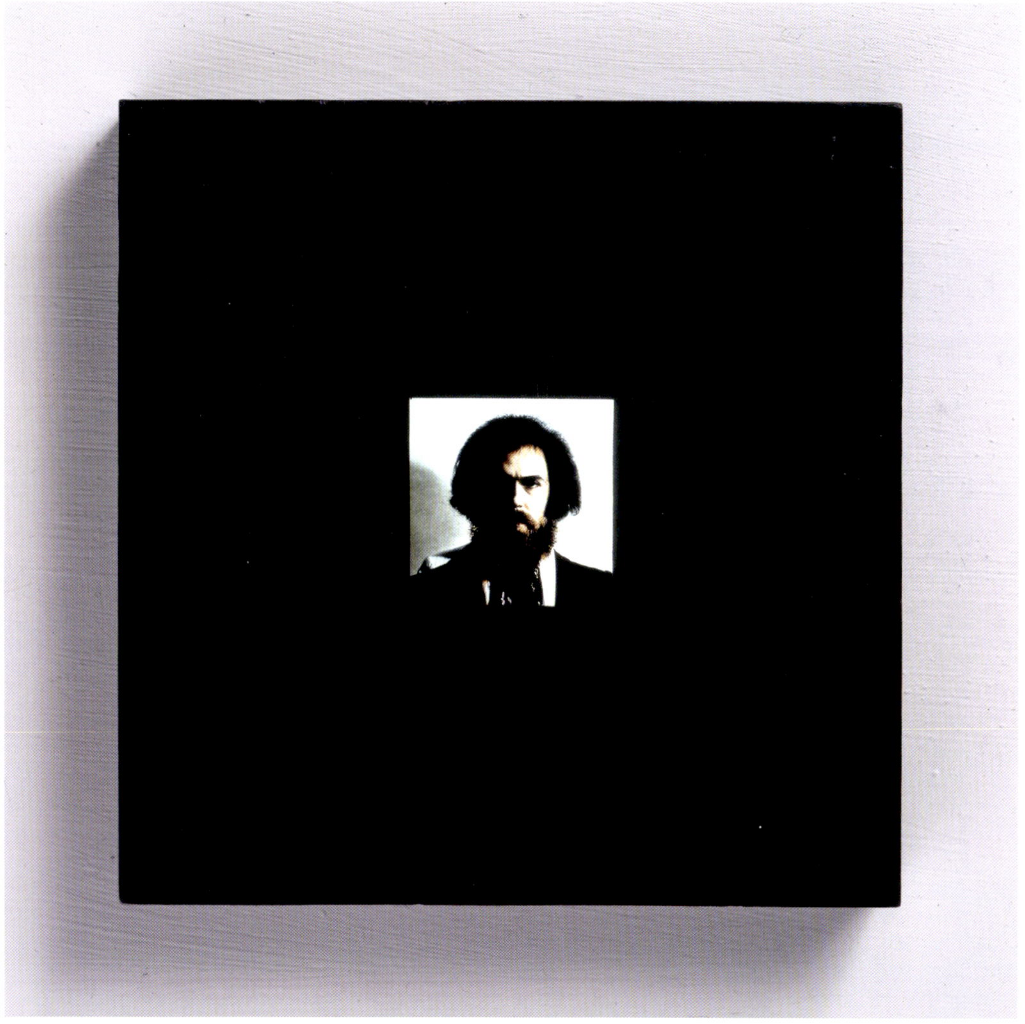

FIG. 122. Michelangelo Pistoletto and Vettor Pisani, *Plagio*, 1971. Two 120 medium-format diapositives (2-inch-square positive slide prints) superimposed on transparent support, retro-illuminated metal box frame. Installation view, Galleria Gian Enzo Sperone, Turin, May 1971. Photo by Paolo Mussat Sartor. Archivio Pistoletto, Biella.

The composite figure produces (or, better, *figures*) a third subject, born of Pisani and Pistoletto's union.

What results is a visual encounter with what we might call a thickened figure, following Alberto Boatto's contemporaneous description of the work. Writing in the Italian arts journal *Data* in September 1971, Boatto described the image, in which two faces become one and two artists become a third, as a "thickening": "They projected their superimposed portraits on the walls, adding their faces together, cancelling and thickening their singular individualities." Boatto described a version of the work in which the artists projected their portraits against the walls of the Galleria Sperone in Turin. For the art historian and critic, this was the practice "of convergence against competition, of choral and public activity against the little asphyxiations of a solitary and private art."[83] This cancellation and thickening, this convergence, resonated with the cultural lexicon surrounding *plagio* in Italy at that time.

The title of the work referenced a famous case and ongoing discussion in Italy in the late 1960s and early 1970s. In December 1967, in the months preceding the Zoo's debut in *Cocapicco e vestitorito,* the Caso Braibanti, as it is now known, convened against Aldo Braibanti (1922–2014)—a gay Communist philosopher, antifascist *partigiano,* experimental dramaturg, and founding member of the important New Left publication *Quaderni Piacentini*—who was charged and imprisoned for the fascist-era crime of plagio, meaning "plagiarism" but also brainwashing and psychological enslavement. Braibanti was charged with the psychological enslavement and indoctrination of two of his male students, one of whom had been his lover. Mainstream Italian newspaper reports emphasized Braibanti's "subjugation" and "annulment of the personalities" of his students, asserting that he had taken away their free will, or *volontà*.[84] (Two months after the Pistoletto-Colnaghi creative union and the Zoo's debut, Braibanti was convicted and sentenced to nine years in prison. He was released after two years, following appeals.)[85] As Braibanti was the only person ever to be charged and indicted for the crime, his imprisonment was viewed by many as a de facto incrimination of Marxist and anarchist ideas, as well as atheism and homosexuality, which, while counter to the Catholic values of the majority Italian public, did not constitute a crime under Italian law.[86] The case incited outrage on the part of the Italian left and galvanized its intelligentsia, including Alberto Moravia and Umberto Eco, who decried it as a thinly veiled attack on leftist politics and homosexuality, as well as a "threat to every free man."[87] The Braibanti case constituted a major civil rights issue and cultural debate in Italy long after the philosopher's release, through the 1970s, until the law's eventual repeal in 1981.

With this context in mind, we can view Pistoletto and Pisani's sustained use of the term in the 1970s as an artistic and political action in dialogue with Italy's culture wars of the period.[88] Indeed, speaking to curator and art historian Andrea Bellini in 2013, Pistoletto noted that the prominence of *plagio* in Italian popular discourse at the time provided the initial spark for his collaboration with Pisani, which they invoked in collaborative action-based and photographic works through 1976 under the title of the crime. As he put it: "If plagiarism was a problem in society, a public problem, we found it just that art would take it on, examine it in depth."[89] But *Plagio*'s specific engagement with these issues has yet to be examined in any depth. Study of these works reveals a different trajectory in Pistoletto's practice of the period: works in which queerness operated as a radical artistic practice and performance of social and discursive transgression—and, perhaps, transformation.

With this context in mind, we might return to the composite portrait. Closer study reveals some inconsistencies in the artists' reported process. One marked difference is evinced by the longer length of Pisani's hair in the alleged source image and the absence of Pisani's left shoulder in the final work; it does not appear on the right side of the image, where we would expect it. Instead, it seems that a slide of another image of Pisani was used for the composite portrait, one that would also appear in Pistoletto's action-based work of the same title. The photographic portraits by Mussat Sartor are to some degree red herrings. The suggestion is that we as viewers seem also to have been "brain-washed."

Instead the source image came from another action, also entitled *Plagio,* executed in the same year. In that work, Pistoletto holds a life-size photographic cutout of Pisani's head, collaged onto a transparent plastic sheet, in front of his face, performing plagio again as a kind of physical, figural transformation of the self (fig. 123). His selection of Pisani's head and use of the image as a kind of mask, which conceals and visually displaces Pistoletto's own visage, also seems to constitute a

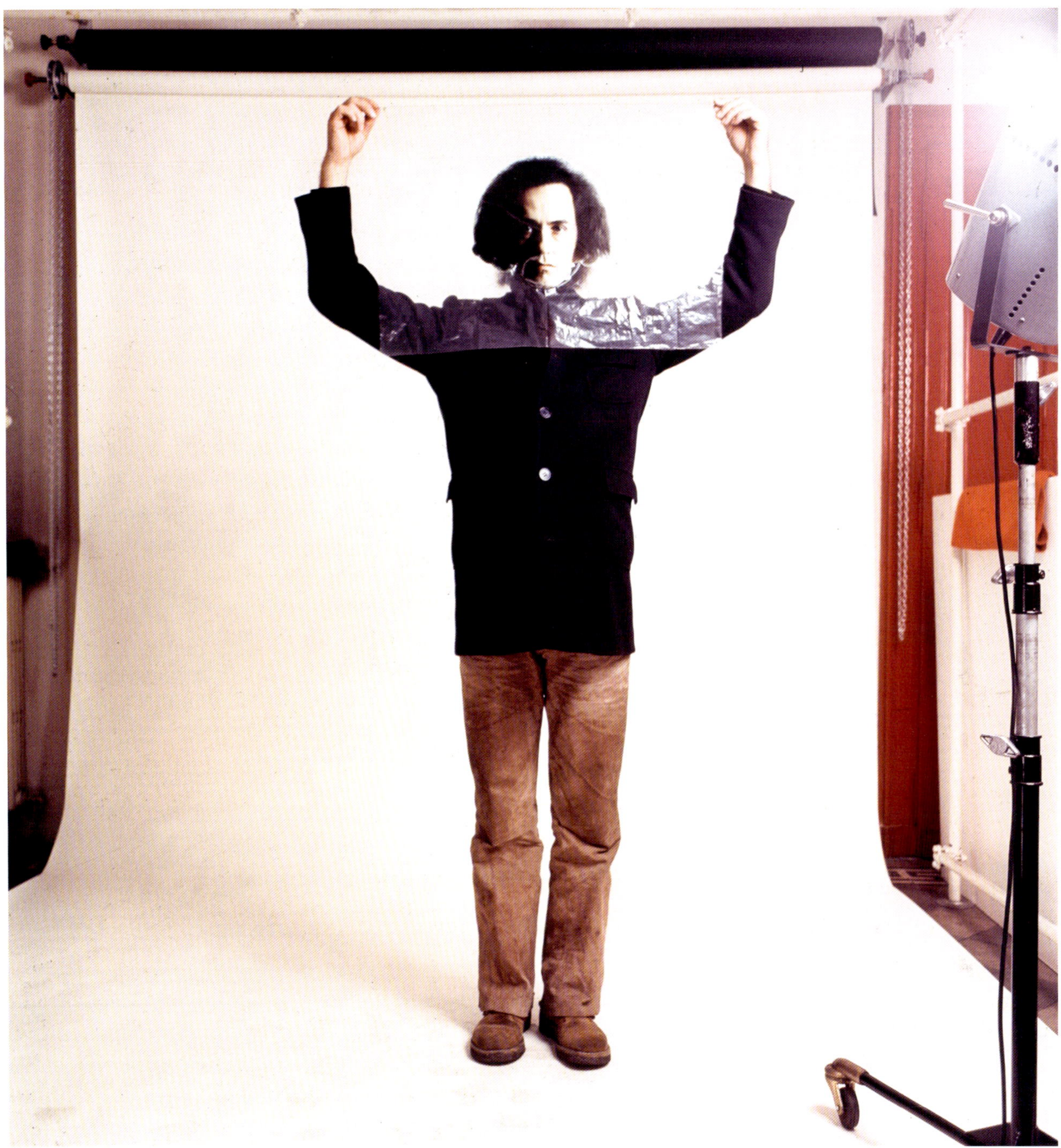

FIG. 123. Michelangelo Pistoletto, *Plagio,* 1971. Action, with portrait of Vettor Pisani. Photo by Paolo Mussat Sartor. Archivio Pistoletto, Biella.

figural allegory of artistic and psychological plagiarism, in which he displaces his own originality and independence with Pisani's own intellectual work. Here, however, Pistoletto describes himself as "plagiarizing Pisani." The use of the image of Pisani is a sign of artistic plagiarism and a performance of queer desire, of making Pisani a part of himself.

This work emerged alongside the formation of Italian feminism and gay rights movements in Italy, in which Turin figured prominently. In December 1971, the collective *Fuori!* (Out!), the leftist gay men's movement and publication of the same name (1971–74), released the "0" [zero] issue of its eponymous journal (fig. 124). The movement's name was also an acronym for Italian United Homosexual Revolutionary Front, which positioned leftist social revolution as the terrain of homosexuals. Subsequent issues frequently included writings by Mario Mieli, the movement's key theorist

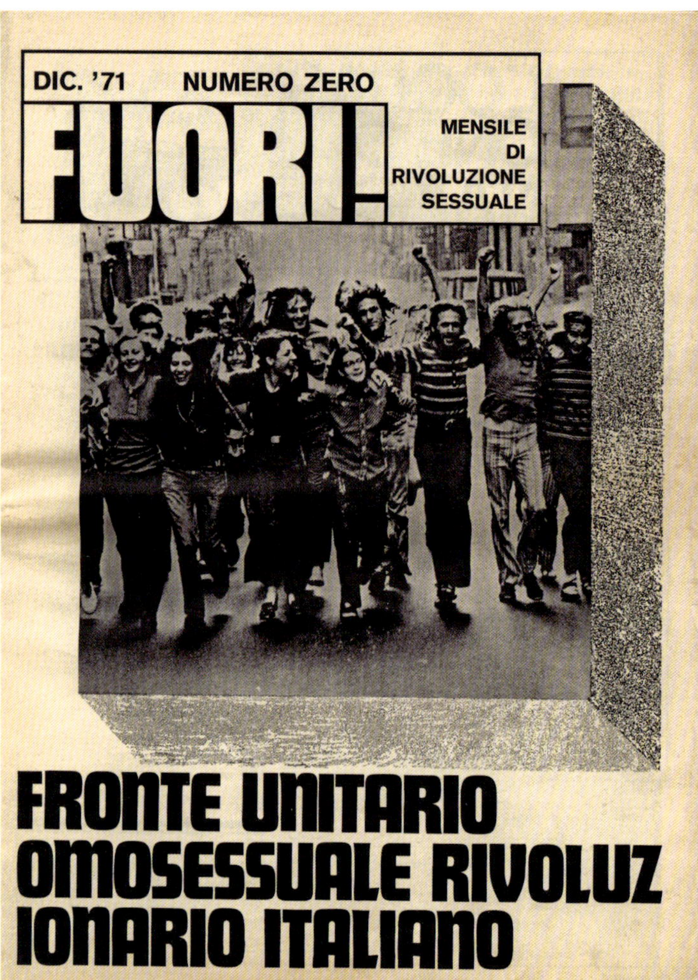

FIG. 124. Cover of *Fuori! Mensile di rivoluzione sessuale,* no. 0 (December 1971). Fondazione Sandro Penna, Turin.

and leading queer Marxist of Italy's homosexual liberation.[90] In his book on gay communism and homosexual critique, published by Einaudi in 1977, Mieli addressed the effort and use of consciousness-raising practices to liberate homosexuals and homosexual desire (held universally) from oppression. Focusing explicitly on male homosexuality, Mieli and the Fuori Movement argued that homosexuality was revolutionary; it was an act of overcoming oppression, achieved through "the process of coming together on the basis of common desire and with the viewpoint of liberation."[91]

In the context of Italy in the 1970s, queerness was a creative and political platform for coming together to stage desired antiauthoritarian worlds of liberation and fantasy. The use of theatrical activities as a kind of *living* was one way to liberate the social subject as it had been and to embody unregulated, freely desiring subjectivity by drawing on forbidden or marginalized social frameworks, such as queer desire. Following queer theorist José Esteban Muñoz, this activity, in which performance is understood as both "theatrical and everyday rituals," can be understood as a "queer worldmaking": a critical modeling of alternative relational worlds as a means of social revolution.[92] This activity has a utopian, social potential; it can have an "encrypted sociality" insofar as it is composed of "quotidian act[s]" with "utopian potentiality."[93]

Returning to the layered portrait, *Plagio,* Pisani and Pistoletto stage plagiarism less as an appropriative or manipulative act than as a mutual, voluntary, *generative* one; less one of individual exchange than one of a desired conjunction and collectivist becoming. This act was made possible through a visual elision of the singular self—represented by the photographic portrait, an image whose indexicality ties it to its subject—into another, specifically multiple and transgressive self, perhaps even a communal one. That is, Pisani-Pistoletto in this image is figured as a *third* artist—neither Pisani nor Pistoletto as individuals but Pisani-Pistoletto, the plural subject of their works' production. This is not a demonstration of the "schizophrenic" or unmoored, postmodern subject position given to us by Gilles Deleuze and Félix Guattari, Fredric Jameson and others—on the contrary, it is what we might think of as a multiple, communal individual: a thickened rather than split, dispersed, or so-called organless subject position. The corporeal veracity of a third subject is underscored by the shadow cast by the figural image itself; by using a box frame and backlighting, the artists situate the composite figure such that it presents itself in real space—that is, in the space of the viewer—for us to encounter.

Pistoletto, of course, wasn't the first artist to approach self-portraiture as a site of artistic intervention. Historical precedents include (again, for Pistoletto) the work of Umberto Boccioni, namely his self-portrait *Io-noi-Boccioni* (I-We-Boccioni, 1907–10): a multiple-exposure photograph, or "multigraph," developed in the late nineteenth century (fig. 125). It captures the artist from five perspectives, such that he appears as five figures, seated in a circle, facing one another.[94] (Following Boccioni, Marcel Duchamp would later deploy his own version.) While in the early twentieth century, Boccioni plumbed the idea of a plural self through new technology, renewed experimentation with self-portraiture in the late

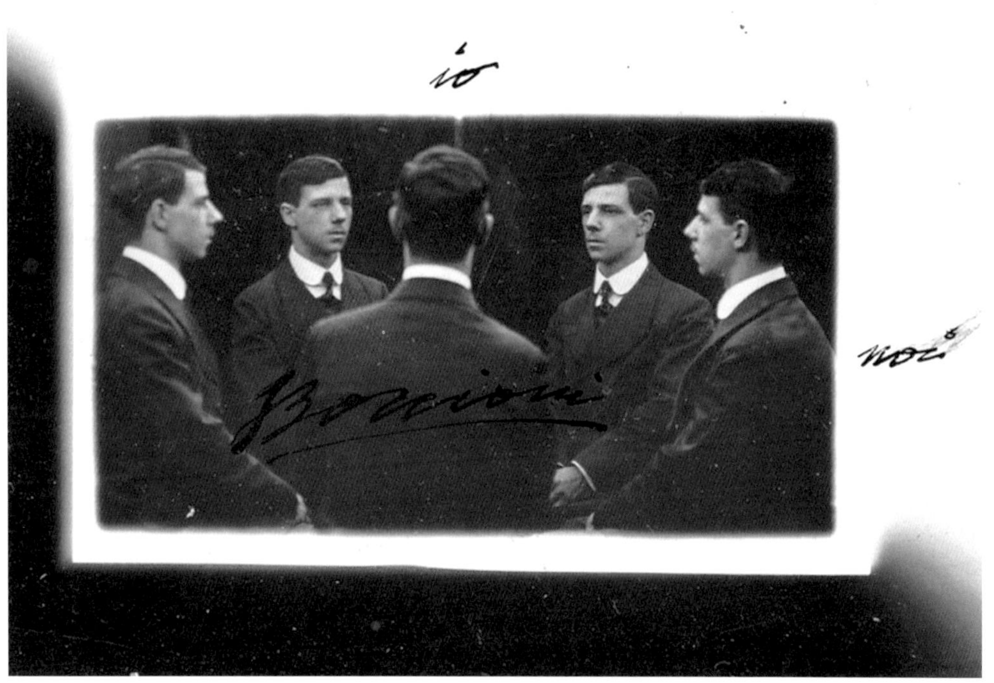

FIG. 125. Umberto Boccioni, *Io-noi-Boccioni* (I-We-Boccioni), 1907–10. Photomontage, 3½ × 5¼ in. (9 × 13.5 cm). Private collection.

1960s was rather aligned with what would later be theorized as the postmodern subject condition noted above—a model Pistoletto's figures at this time defied.[95]

Immediately preceding Pistoletto and Pisani's experiments were a few important works from within or around their artistic circle. In 1969, Carla Lonzi published her important text *Autoritratto* (1969), as noted earlier in this book. Lonzi's "self-portrait" was composed of a series of interviews she held with mostly male artists (and many poveristi, though not Pistoletto), one of whom (Piero Consagra) was her lover. Preceding and appearing in her *Autoritratto* was Giulio Paolini's *Autoritratto* (1968): a photomontage featuring Henri Rousseau (from his self-portrait, *Moi-même, portrait paysage,* or "Myself, Portrait-Landscape," 1890) with photographic cutouts of Paolini and other contemporary artists, both Italian and international. That same year Paolini made a second "autoritratto"; it was composed of a black-and-white photographic reproduction of a self-portrait by Nicolas Poussin from 1650, transferred onto an emulsified canvas, which itself was layered with a smaller emulsified canvas centered on top of it (fig. 126). The smaller section was printed with a detail of the same transfer of the Poussin reproduction (the face), at the same scale as the photographic exposure on the base layer of the portrait, resulting in a portrait in relief. For Paolini, the work spoke to the myth of originality.[96] In theme and composition, however, Paolini's work constitutes a key precedent for Pistoletto's *Plagio* composite portrait with Pisani. *Plagio* is distinguished, however, by the artists' engagement with sociopolitical debates and what were then perceived as radical subject positions in Italy. Hewing closer to Pistoletto and Pisani's *Plagio* work in this regard would be Fabio Mauri's "projection actions." For *Intellettuale* (Intellectual), done in 1975, the artist projected one of Pier Paolo Pasolini's films (*Il Vangelo secondo Matteo,* or "The Gospel According to Saint Matthew," 1964) onto the director's T-shirt-clad body (fig. 127). A gay writer, filmmaker, artist, and radical cultural figure, Pasolini was assassinated later that same year. After Pasolini's (and even Mauri's) death, the work has been re-created by projecting the film onto clothes draped on a chair, in the absence of Pasolini the person and figure. Ara Merjian has eloquently described the work as haunted by the politics of the 1970s—politics that Pistoletto and Pisani's work also addresses: "Evacuated of flesh and breath, the garment became—and remains—the effigy of a body disappeared for its inconvenience."[97]

Although the numerous works completed under the aegis of Pistoletto and Pisani's *Plagio* are diversified in material, form, iconography, and process, they become unified when we consider their engagement of the distinctly Italian meaning of "plagio"—that is, as both an authorial form of appropriation and an *authoritarian,* psychological one. In the fascist penal code, it was a "crime against individual freedom." It referred to subjecting someone to "one's own power in such a way to reduce them to a total state of subjugation." In contrast to the connotations of the term in that context (and adjudication thereof, through which homosexuality was effectively criminalized), in this series, plagiarism was positioned as the unlikely productive platform for nonhierarchical artistic collaboration and reciprocal exchange. Pistoletto and Pisani's distinctive use of plagio—as a reciprocal, transparent, collaborative exercise—ultimately repositioned its defining terms and negative connotations to become the site of collaborative artistic liberation. This practice ultimately functioned as an artistic demonstration of the productive potential of collective work over—but not at the cost of—that of the individual, specifically through an engagement with queerness as a newly positioned leftist revolutionary politics.

The *Plagio* series was the extension of two initial collaborations between Pistoletto and Pisani.[98] The first occurred in June 1970, when Pistoletto invited Pisani to show whatever he liked in his assigned space in Achille Bonito Oliva's group exhibition *Amore mio* (My Love, Montepulciano, 1970). The show encouraged such exchanges, inviting artists to show other artists' works "in which they find a connection to their own formation." The result would be an exhibition focused not on object-dominated or linguistic space but on an "elastically anthropological" one, "where all affective, sentimental, cultural, and psychological instances and preferences that generally remain excluded can merge."[99] Photographic reproductions of Pisani's work,

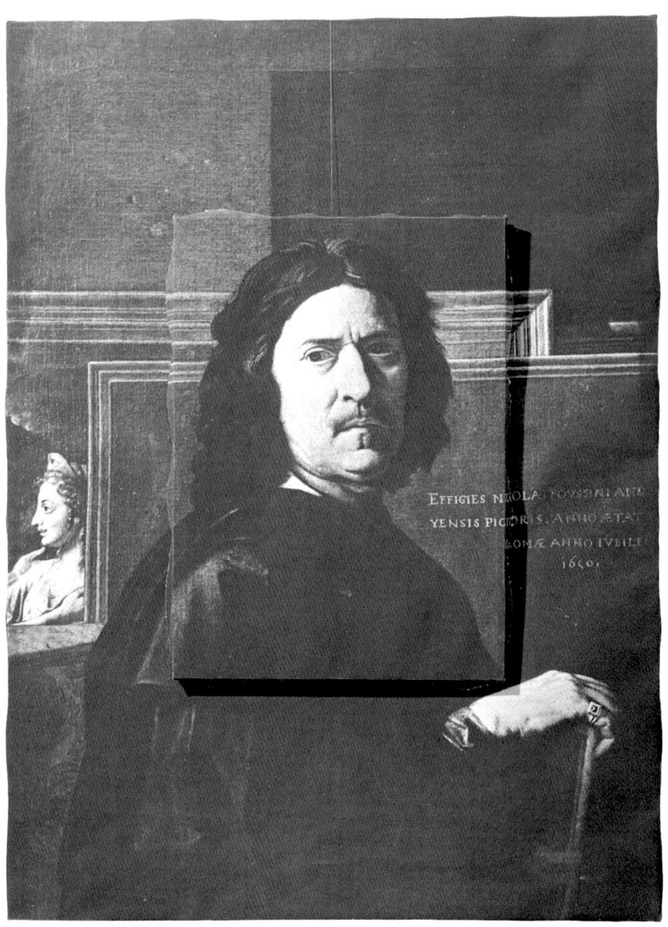

FIG. 126. Giulio Paolini, *Autoritratto* (Self-Portrait), 1968. Photograph on emulsified canvas, nylon thread, 38⅝ × 29⅛ in. (98 × 74 cm). Baldassare Collection.

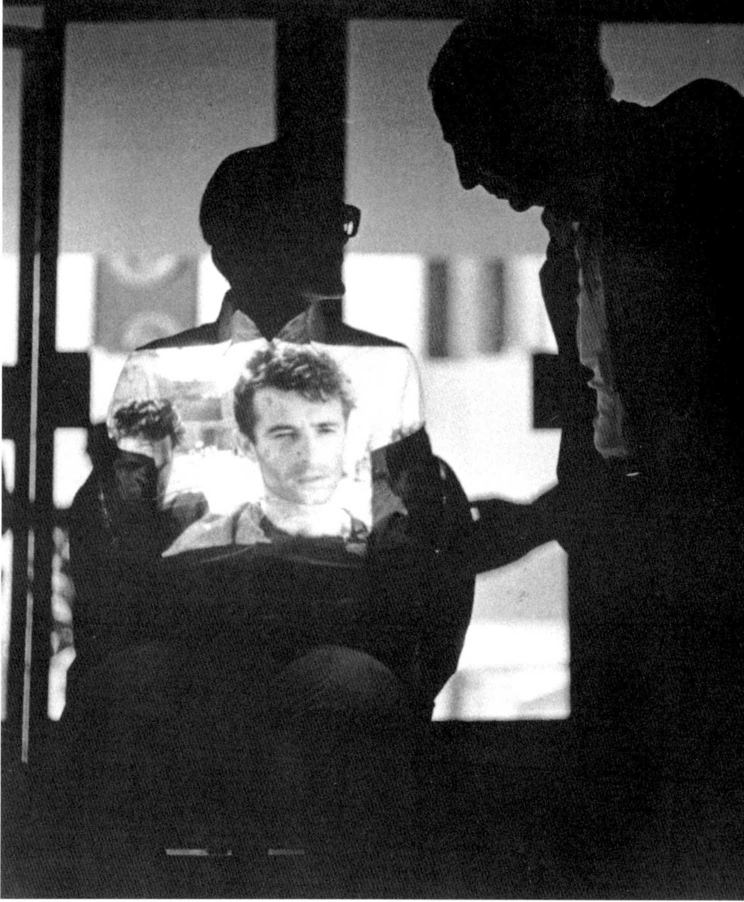

FIG. 127. Fabio Mauri, *Intellettuale* (Intellectual), 1975. Projection-action, with Pier Paolo Pasolini at the Galleria Comunale d'Arte Moderna, Bologna, in 1975. Photo by Antonio Masotti. Studio Mauri.

specifically those that had been exhibited earlier that year at his exhibition *Maschile, femminile e androgino: Incesto e cannibalismo in Marcel Duchamp* (Masculine, Feminine, and Androgyn: Incest and Cannibalism in Marcel Duchamp) at the Galleria La Salita in Rome, were published in the exhibition catalog alongside a handwritten statement from Pistoletto, providing a diaristic account of his encounter with that exhibition.

The second precedent was in the fall of 1971, when Pistoletto had once again been invited, as was Pisani, by Bonito Oliva to join his group exhibition *Persona*, which opened September 10, 1971, at the Bitef (theatrical) Festival in Belgrade. Pisani and Pistoletto created two series of photographs, for which they posed together, joined by their partners. Pisani posed for a series of photographs with Mimma Pisani, as well as Pistoletto and Pioppi, in Rome in June 1971. That August, Pisani met with Pistoletto in Corniglia, where they posed for photographs with their partners and members of the Zoo. They submitted the photographs to Bonito Oliva, who published them in the *Persona* catalog as their representative works for the exhibition. *Plagio* exhibitions began with the Galleria Sperone in Turin in May 1971, followed by another that June at La Salita; two others followed in 1972 and 1973 in Frankfurt and Rome, respectively.

ANTIAUTHORITARIAN GESTURE, SELF-POSSESSION, AND THE DESTRUCTION OF INDIVIDUALISM

In the exhibition at La Salita in May 1971, they exhibited two works: a series of photocollaged glass panels, by Pisani, and one of Pistoletto's trademark mirror paintings: a highly polished steel panel, collaged with a hand-painted figurative cutout, traced from a life-size photographic enlargement. Both works featured the same photograph, drawn from a series of images taken by American Dada and surrealist artist Man Ray in the early 1930s. Entitled *Érotique voilée* (Veiled Erotic), Ray's image captured his fellow artist and surrealist Meret Oppenheim, posing in the nude, save for a thin black necklace around her neck, at the wheel of a press, her hand inked and held up to the viewer.

Pisani's series of collaged glass panels, *Sonata a cinque dita di Meret Oppenheim* (Five-Fingered Sonata for Meret Oppenheim, 1971), and Pistoletto's mirror painting of the same title used appropriation to defuse the authoritarian impulse of plagio in favor of a collaborative, perhaps even "communal" process, as Maurizio Calvesi argued (figs. 128a–d, 129). Pistoletto's work enlarges Oppenheim's figure to life-size, providing a prominent comparative image to the one reproduced in multiple by Pisani. Pisani's work, by contrast, screened a progressive alteration of Oppenheim's figure across its four panels by removing one finger at a time so that her raised hand transforms into a fingerless palm. For his part, Pistoletto viewed Pisani's iteration of the work as a political declaration—specifically one against fascism and authoritarianism. As he put it: "[The] gesture that could suggest a (fascist) salute with an outstretched hand, became a salute with a fist (Communist)."[100]

Alla maniera di Meret Oppenheim (In the Style of Meret Oppenheim, 1972), also known by the alternative title *Maria allo scorrevole* (Sliding Maria), similarly uses appropriation to examine structures of control, in this case, focusing on psychosexual subjugation. Pistoletto uses the image of his partner, Pioppi—staged with Pisani and photographed by yet another artist, Elisabetta Catalano—standing in the pose of Oppenheim, as photographed by Ray (fig. 130a–b). At first glance, the work seems to constitute an artistic demonstration of the Italian concept of plagiarism; the subject is situated in a position of psychosexual vulnerability for a viewer in one of potential domination. But appropriation might also be understood here to evoke and *deconstruct* mechanisms of control. The rapacious nature of plagiarist authorship is repositioned as the accepted technique of artistic appropriation in the history of Duchamp, who inspired Pisani's work. The manipulative, hierarchical structure of plagiarist or coercive relationality is undermined by being shown to be an authoritarian construction (a fiction) of the fascist state and the homophobic antileftist legacies it left behind.[101] Indeed, Pioppi's stance might also be read as a position of voluntary subjugation. The closure of her collar is positioned within easy grasp at the front of her neck; she holds the chain that ties her to the pulley system above. Her bondage from this perspective seems to be voluntary and therefore potentially pleasurable, perhaps even sadomasochistic. Pioppi contributed to these works, in a photograph taken by a female photographer, alongside Pisani, Mimma, and Pistoletto when the Italian feminist movement Rivolta Femminile was also developing.[102] Like the "movimento gay" that followed it, Italian feminism was also a self-described revolutionary movement. This context further underscores

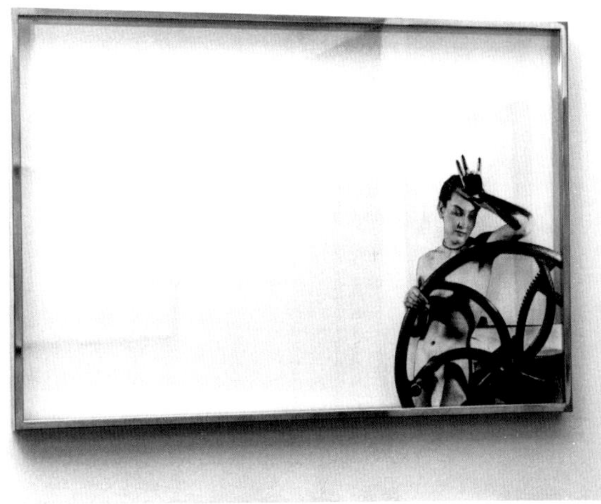
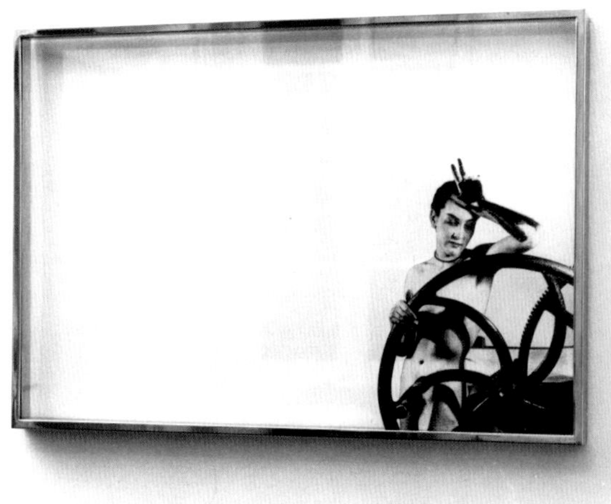
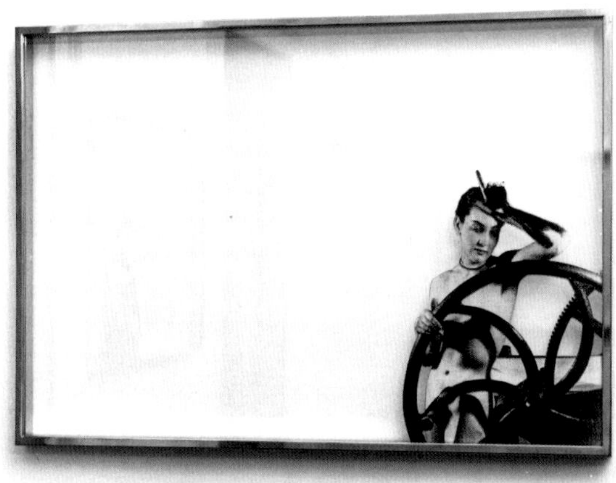
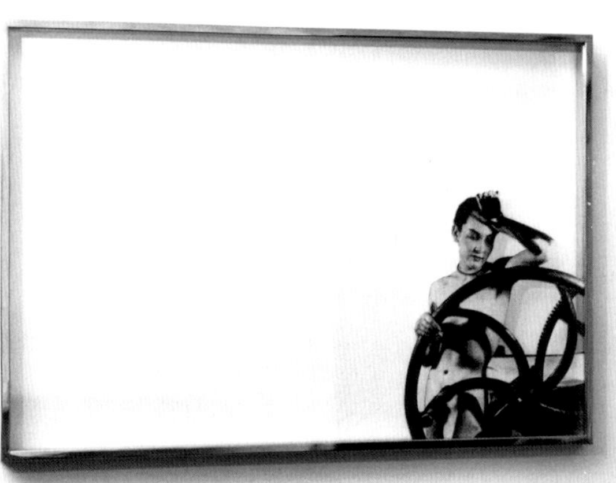

FIG. 128A–D. Vettor Pisani, *Sonata a cinque dita per Meret Oppenheim* (Five-Fingered Sonata for Meret Oppenheim), 1971. Collaged plexiglass, 4 panels, each 31½ × 47¼ in. (80 × 120 cm). In *Plagio,* Galleria La Salita, Rome, June 1971.

the self-possession of Pioppi's action, or at least its complexity, despite the associations that might come with such images.

In a parallel inversion of the authoritarian impetus behind appropriation-as-authorship, Pistoletto and Pisani used this image and variations thereof in both of their practices; simultaneous display of their respective iterations of these works seems not only to diffuse the power structure behind appropriation but to do so in relation to other works—say, Ray's photograph—and especially to each other's. Pistoletto's *Silenzio Vettor Pisani,* an aluminum placard based on Pisani's earlier work *Silenzio Marcel Duchamp,* also uses appropriation as a productive platform; the work can be read in two ways: either as an imperative directive—that is, "Be quiet, Vettor Pisani"—or as a caption, labeling the ostensible immaterial "silence" around the placard as Pisani's work of art, perhaps the silence resulting from the directive to quiet the viewer.

At the exhibition held in Frankfurt, the artists' surnames were printed as a hyphenated conjunction—Pisani-Pistoletto—in the exhibition title. The exhibition showcased the artists' continuation of the Oppenheim series, as discussed above, with the participation of Pistoletto's partner, Pioppi, standing in place of Ray's Oppenheim. On one hand, the hyphen underscores the dialogical form of authorship at work here, in which case the hyphen punctuates a relay and point of connection between the individual artists as equals; on the other, it presents Pisani-Pistoletto as *one* artist—but emphatically not a univocal one.

In his catalog essay for the *Plagio* exhibition at the Marlborough Gallery (Rome) in 1973, Maurizio

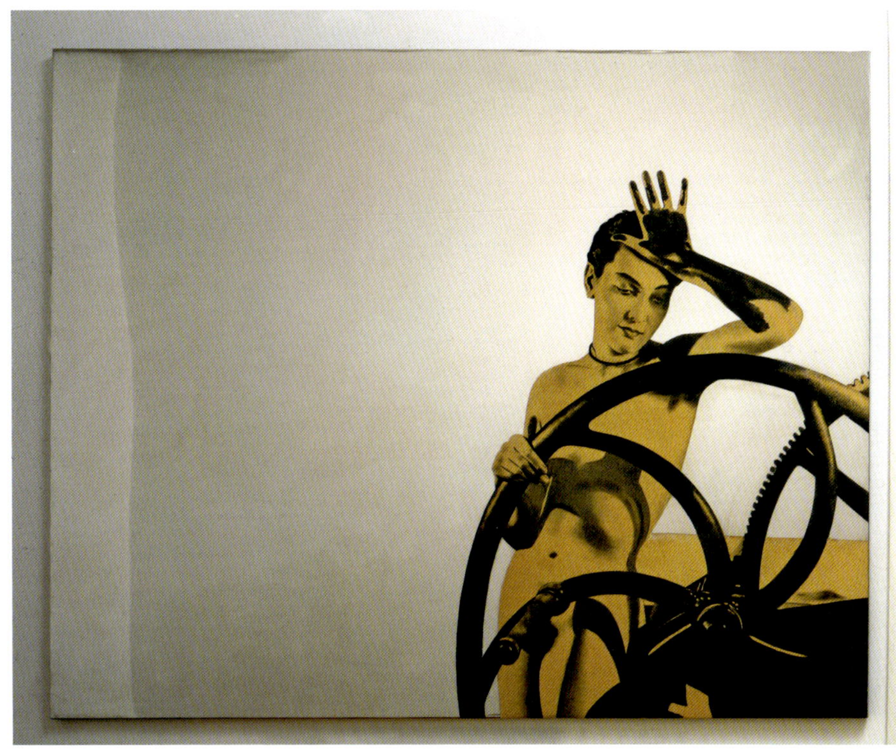

FIG. 129. Michelangelo Pistoletto, *Sonata a cinque dita per Meret Oppenheim* (Five-Fingered Sonata for Meret Oppenheim), 1971. Painted tissue paper on polished stainless steel, 47¼ × 59 in. (120 × 150 cm). In *Plagio,* Galleria La Salita, Rome, June 1971.

Calvesi—perhaps thinking of the Frankfurt exhibition title, *Pisani-Pistoletto*—would write about the "Pisani-Pistoletto" subject as a third individual produced by this specific work. For Calvesi, when we look at "Pisani-Pistoletto" as viewers, we might be inclined to "add ourselves" to the plagiarism at work in front of us—that is, to add ourselves to the person that action produces. Calvesi sees this gesture as a moral act, predicated on the sacrifice of "the satanic myth of individualism" in favor of unity. For Calvesi, "plagio" was grounded in the individual's will not only toward collectivity or "communitarian impulse" but also toward self-sacrifice; he argues that there is even an "ideological violence" to this inclination.[103] By contrast, in a review of the exhibitions at Sperone and La Salita in 1971 for *Domus,* Tommaso Trini offered another reading: "He who remembers the manifesto with which Pistoletto invited [people] in 1968 to display together with him in his room at the Biennale di Venezia finds here confirmation of an operational will that creates convergence, cooperation, and now interaction in the form of plagiarism, as well as tactical moments of attack against individuality, competitor of the work of art as part of a strategy of culture that is oppositely choral and public, choral instead of solitary, public instead of private."[104] Trini positioned what he saw as the collaborative process demonstrated by this work as part of a dialectic with the destruction of individualism.

Departing from Trini's and Calvesi's readings, however, this study of the *Plagio* series (as part of a queer history for Arte Povera and queering of Italian modernism) demonstrates that the work was not a drive toward pain (self-destruction or death) but rather one of pleasure, a logic of conjunction and exchange, an impulse to give of oneself to another—a queer *desire,* which we see played out in these works. This history is paradigmatic of a psychoanalytic turn in Italian art and Italianist art history of the period, alongside tableaux vivants works by Luigi Ontani, who drew on gay icons, as in his invocation of Saint Sebastian.[105] But Pistoletto's work with Colnaghi offers a new precedent in this queer history of Italian avant-gardism. It goes further than what critic Pierbruno Accardi, writing for *Data,* argued amounted to "symbiosis"—a reading that, while invested in theorizing the form of exchange as a form of collectivity, neutralizes the work's insistence, through visual mergers and commingling of these male artists' bodies, on this bond as grounded in queerness as a socially and politically charged union that resonated with contemporary debates on personal freedom in Italy. The authoritarianism associated with the crime of plagio is deconstructed in this work in the form of a radical

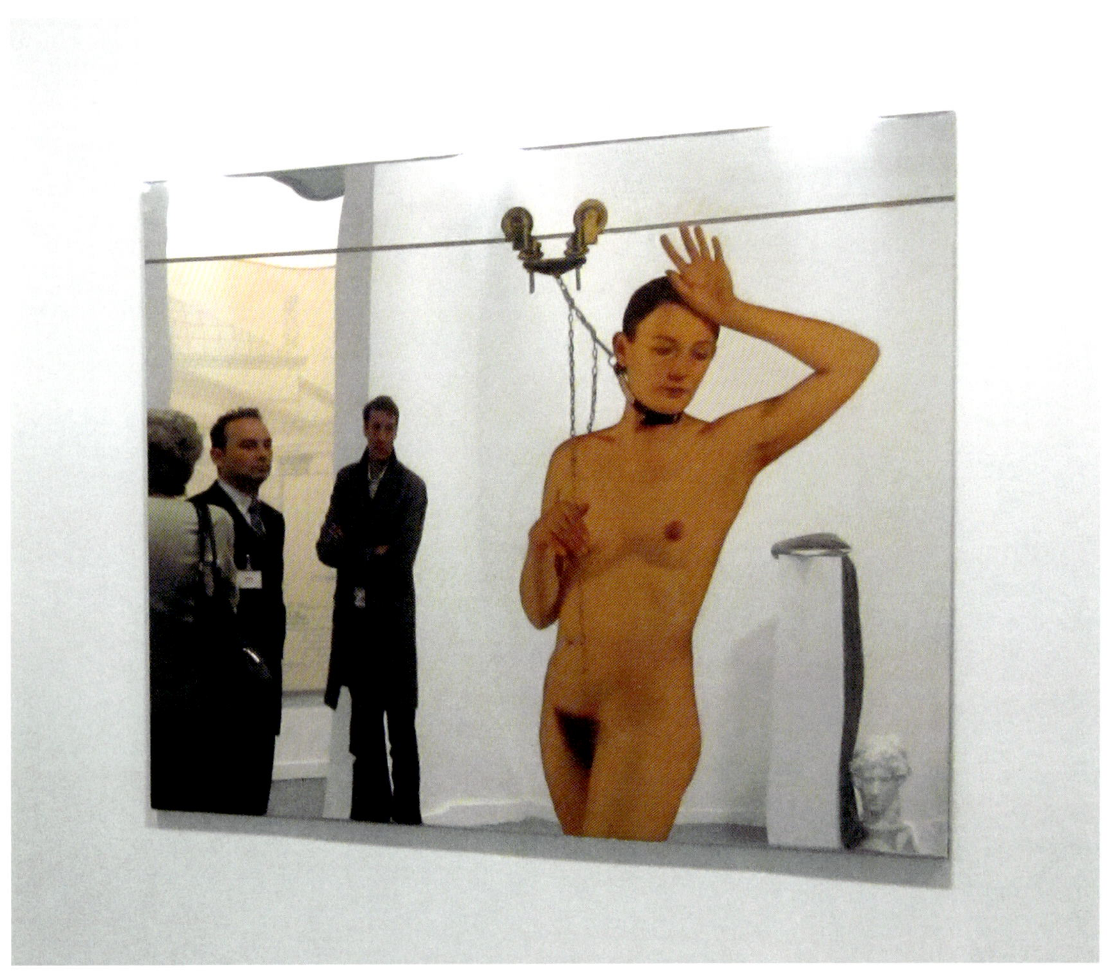

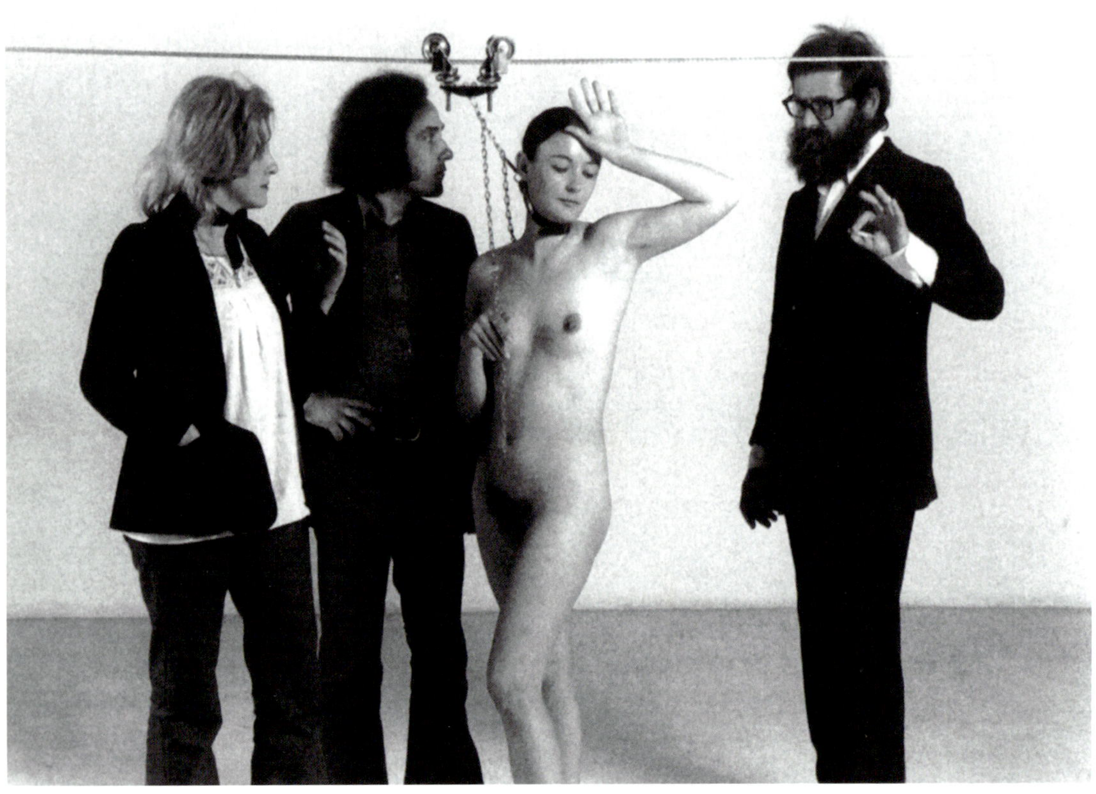

FIG. 130A–B.
A. Michelangelo Pistoletto, *Alla maniera di Meret Oppenheim* [alt. *Maria allo scorrevole* (In the Style of Meret Oppenheim [Sliding Maria])], 1972. Painted tissue paper on polished stainless steel, 47¼ × 59 in. (120 × 150 cm).
B. Photo, ca. 1972, featuring Mimma and Vettor Pisani, Maria (Pioppi), and Michelangelo Pistoletto. Photo by Elisabetta Catalano. Archivio Pistoletto, Biella.

defiance of social rules and restrictions on personal liberties—all captured in the artists' experiment with the figure—as image and as body. Of relevance here are Pistoletto's later remarks about the work: "[We] shot and printed two color photographs, of [Pisani's] and my face, and superimposed them on a transparent support. In that way, the face of a third person appeared, the *fruit of our union,* a person who was different from me and from him, who *didn't exist before our encounter.*"[106] Using the word *frutto,* Pistoletto invokes the word for outcome or result, as well as offspring, as in "fruit of thy womb" or breast, as the traditional Catholic "Hail Mary" prayer or Angelical Salutation goes in Italian. That he articulates the outcome of this work as a subversion of Catholic ideology—a work that engages ideas of queered authorship and a social history of leftist advocacy against the persecution of homosexuality and communist thought—only further registers that Pistoletto's portrait experiments transgressed conventions of artistic media and existing structures of artistic and social identity.

These works engaged both psychological and artistic forms of plagiarism, whether through iconographies of subjugation, through appropriation, or in name only—in which case they might propose a new meaning of the term. Their engagement of both forms urges us to consider their postmodernist critique of artistic concepts of originality, Romantic conceptions of authorship, and centered Cartesian subjectivity as political. It also urges us to consider their critique of politics as an artistic imperative within Italy in the 1970s to confront the use of plagiarism as a fascist-era crime to persecute homosexuality as well as Marxist and anarchist thought.

TO FIGURE SILENCE: *SILENZIO ROSA*

The final iteration of *Plagio* was realized in a series of actions and works at the Thirty-Seventh Venice Biennale in July 1976, where Pistoletto and Pisani opened the project to a third artist: Franco Summa (1938–2020). Summa participated in their work *Silenzio rosa* (Pink Silence, 1976). In that work, Pistoletto and Summa, as well as participants from the public, painted the interior of a large former chapel that had been designated a performance space at the Biennale the same pale pink color that it already was. Preceded by Pisani and Pistoletto's aforementioned text-based works on silence, *Pink Silence* was an extension of postwar explorations of "emptying out" artist-generated artistic content and critiquing original authorship as a myth. As with Duchamp's store-bought readymade, Pistoletto didn't create anything new for *Pink Silence* (fig. 131). The artistic work was perfunctory: painting a pink room pink again. Building on Pistoletto and Pisani's previous exploration of the "silence" in the series, comments from Pistoletto and Summa about the development of

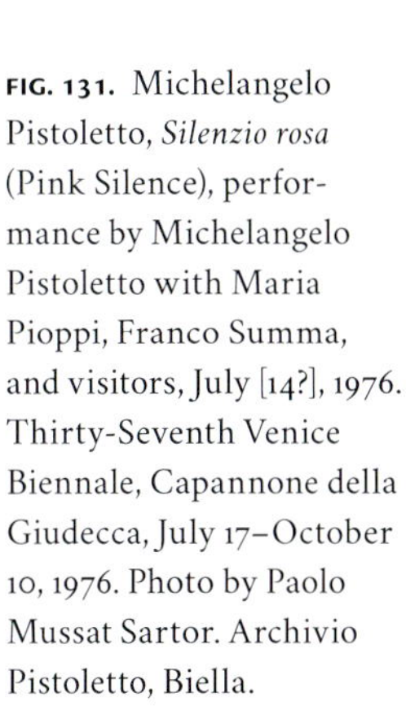
FIG. 131. Michelangelo Pistoletto, *Silenzio rosa* (Pink Silence), performance by Michelangelo Pistoletto with Maria Pioppi, Franco Summa, and visitors, July [14?], 1976. Thirty-Seventh Venice Biennale, Capannone della Giudecca, July 17–October 10, 1976. Photo by Paolo Mussat Sartor. Archivio Pistoletto, Biella.

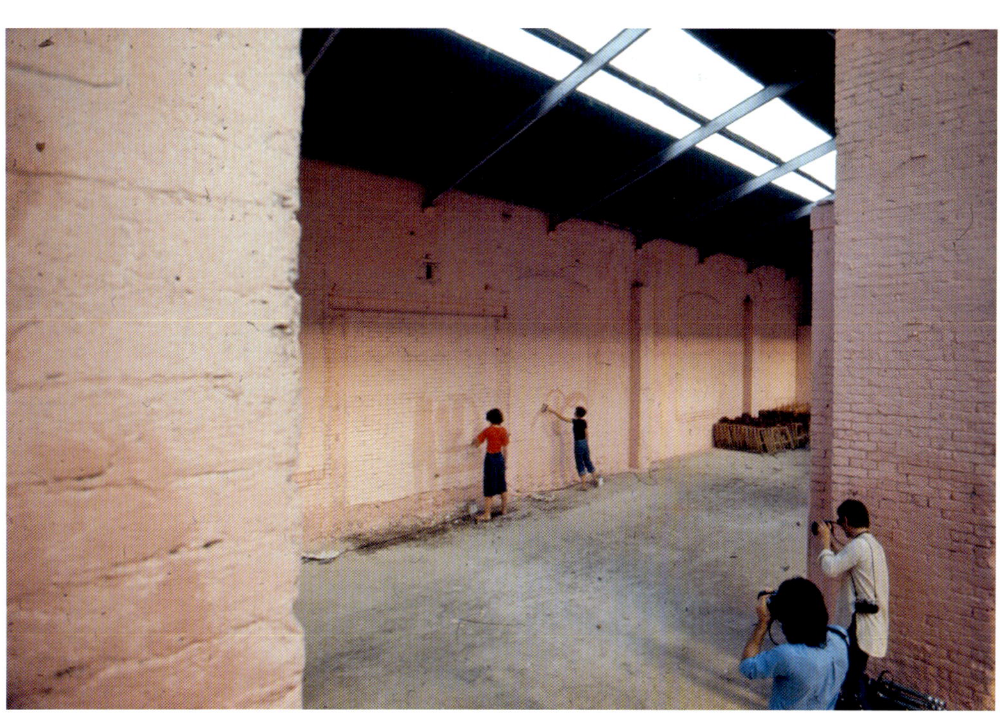

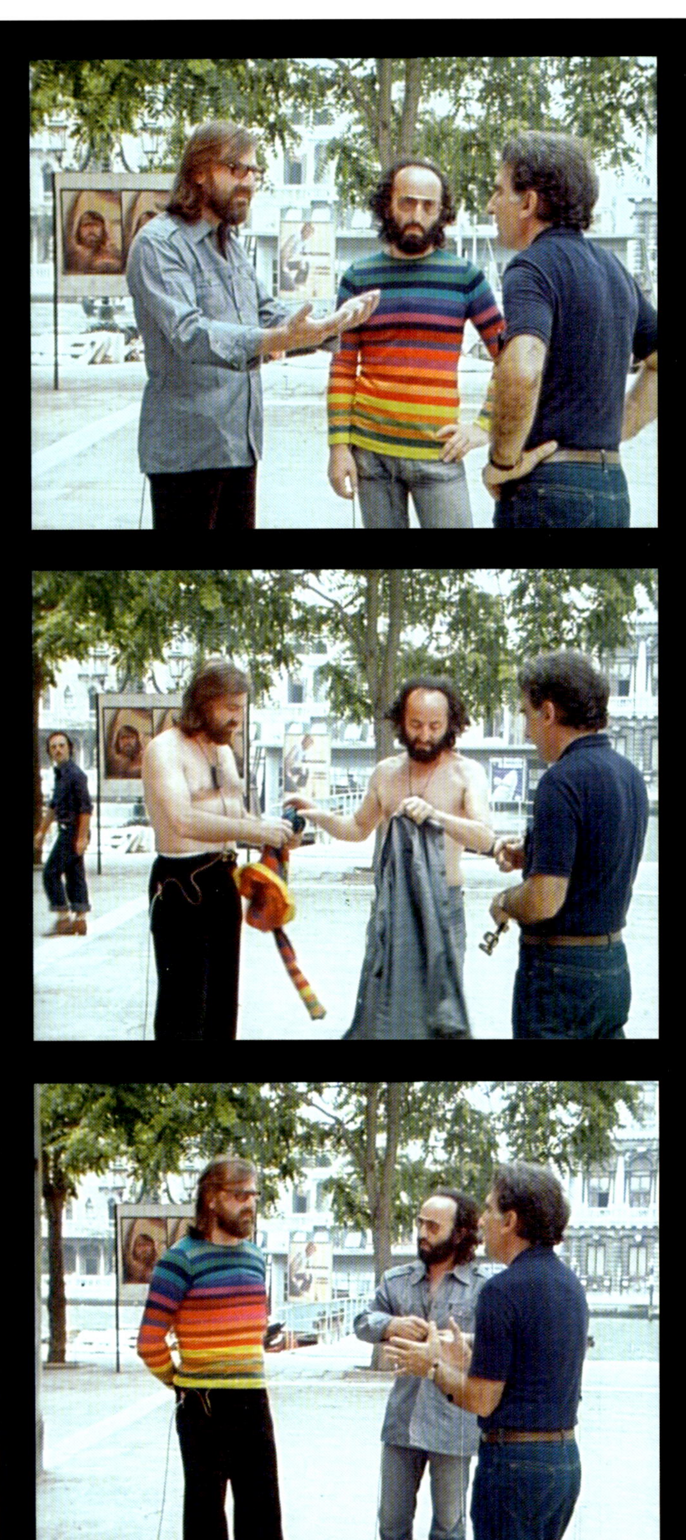

FIG. 132. Stills, footage of Michelangelo Pistoletto and Franco Summa performing *Plagio* (1976), during an interview with Rai television regarding their work of the same title, with Vettor Pisani, on the occasion of the Thirty-Seventh Venice Biennale, July 17–October 10, 1976. Excerpted from a Rai program on the Biennale, *Biennale Rosa,* by Alfredo Di Laura. Archivio Rai, Turin.

the work allow us to situate that work within this history. The aim, according to Summa, was to "figurare il silenzio"—to give a figure to silence.[107] Inviting the public to join them, Pistoletto positioned the monochrome ambient as an action of exclusion; applying the same color to itself excludes the color. "[What] remains is our physical presence," he said. In the context of the *Plagio* project, this work evokes socially transgressive psychosexual resonances as part of its social criticality. Even though Pistoletto didn't select the pink color—it was already in place—the choice to focus on that color, in the context of a project connected to gay liberation as a site of broader social debates in Italy on psychic control, authoritarianism, and free will, recalls state-sanctioned homophobic violence, of labeling gay men in Nazi Germany and fascist Italy with pink triangles. Pink triangles, by the 1970s, were being recalled as part of gay liberation movements.[108]

In this sense, the work conjures ideas cultivated from the early 1970s forward in what is now known as the Movimento del '77. Widely understood as a response to 1968, and aligned with Autonomia, this social movement, no longer holding faith in any existing structure, sought to forge a socialist world order through revolutionary quotidian activity. As Danila Cannamela and Achille Castaldo have written, in response, "a variety of social actors—factory workers, students, feminists, intellectuals, emerging LGBT organizations—engaged in a revolutionary everydayness adverse to any system of exploitation and political order. Less work, better quality of life, self-valorization, re-appropriation of goods, time, and spaces became the key words of [the movement]."[109]

Recalling the manifesto of collaboration, at the same exhibition Pistoletto and Summa exchanged shirts while being interviewed by Rai television as a demonstration of noncompetitive artistic exchange (fig. 132). "The work [Summa's striped sweater] will be on my skin," Pistoletto said. Summa: "A symbol of freedom," transferred from the environment to the body of man. As they exchanged shirts, the Rai interviewer exclaimed that their works would be on each other's skin. "I become him, he becomes me," Summa remarked. Countering the "often alienating" hierarchical structures of society, Pistoletto explained, this exchange modeled a different social structure and way of moving, in which participation and nonhierarchical community were facilitated. Summa's contribution came in the form of one of his trademark multicolored, striped textiles. The textiles figured prominently in Summa's installations, painting-actions (*pittur-azione*), and clothing items starting in the early 1970s (and continuing to his death), all under the framework of the *Arcobaleno* or "Rainbow" (at the time, a sign for peaceful diversity, dating to its use in Italy's peace movement beginning in 1961).[110] Duchampian gesture and antiauthoritarian social expression commingle again here—neither toward the absurd, as in Dada, nor toward liberatory destruction (as in futurism before it), but toward the human body as a real figure of presence against a monochromatic ground (itself a space for images, as Summa put it in the Rai interview). Painting had become atmospheric. The figure of man was an agent of free subjectivity and leftist social transformation in the real world.

THEATER AS CATAPULT, OR FIGURING A NEW WORLD

With and after the Zoo, Pistoletto staged figural activity—with figures of power, and fruits of unions—to pursue new utopian, dystopian, and creative potentials through a giving up of the self to different relational ontologies, to those beyond the bounds of social acceptance, to mutually willed exchanges, to lived contingency, to a subject position whose politics were grounded in emergent frameworks in Italy in the late 1960s and 1970s for revolutionary, fantastic ways of being that continued in subsequent decades in relation to other antiauthoritarian contexts.

Beginning with Pistoletto and Colnaghi's collaborative performance, Pistoletto's lived and performed activities offer a new model of radical practice for the Italian avant-garde that he carried out through the 1970s and into the 1980s. This model counters Celant's theorization of Arte Povera's anarchist tendencies as deculturalization and regression. Pistoletto pursued theater as liberated fantasy enacted by the performing figure to stage and live new antiauthoritarian worlds (in both geographical place and social order).[111] His theatrical activities challenged discourse *figurally,* with embodied and performed subject positions then under persecution as threats to free society. Lived by the artist, most intensively with friends in Corniglia in the summer of 1969 but also through today, theater for Pistoletto is a mode of *lived performance* and *performed living,* through which new worlds are enacted and configured. Pistoletto's new scene writing and, more important, new figures sought to transgress power to change the world—to *figure* different worlds within it.

In the context of Italian New (nonnarrative) Theater and the antiauthoritarian artistic and political contexts of the late 1960s, Pistoletto used theatrical figurality as a challenge to existing cultural and sociopolitical forms, as a means of social and artistic transgression and radical world building that he would pursue through the 1980s. These works engaged the figure in relation to world history, both real and possible.

The radical potential of Pistoletto and the Zoo's experiments in action-based practice, theater, and performance in the 1960s and 1970s found later forms in Pistoletto's "world theater" and *Continenti di tempo* (Continents of Time), realized in multilocational durational works of the late 1980s and 1990s. These include the yearlong project *Anno Bianco* (White Year, 1989), which places the artist's new theater with the Zoo, by way of his own theatrical works from the early 1980s, in dialogue with cataclysmic events of that year. In *Anno Bianco,* Pistoletto revisited his own theatrical works from the early 1980s that seemed to have visually presaged—or, better, prefigured—images of the fall of the Berlin Wall and revolts in Beijing's Tiananmen Square.[112] Twenty years after the founding of the Zoo, he mounted photographs of people celebrating on top of the Berlin Wall on the date of its fall alongside photographs of theatrical work he had gone on to make in Corniglia, building on the *L'Uomo nero* work he initiated in the summer of 1969. Those imagined theatrical worlds and geographical spaces positioned the artist's theatrical activity from the early 1980s, which itself built on the artist's works with the Zoo, as a prescient analogue to the fall of the Berlin Wall in 1989. Pistoletto once again positioned theater to launch, to stage, to engender, and to radically *live* new worlds.

In an exhibition dedicated to the *Continenti,* held at the Musée d'Art Contemporain in Lyon in 2001, visitors encountered two approximately twelve-by-eighteen-foot black-and-white photomurals, spanning two walls of the gallery, respectively, each composed of one enlarged photograph, printed in three vertical sections and collaged onto aluminum on wood (fig. 133a–b). Part of the *Anno Bianco* multiexhibition project of 1989, the images, taken in various places and disparate moments in the 1980s, depict groups of people facing the general direction of the camera. On the left, we see a dozen people in staggered formation on a traditional theater stage. They

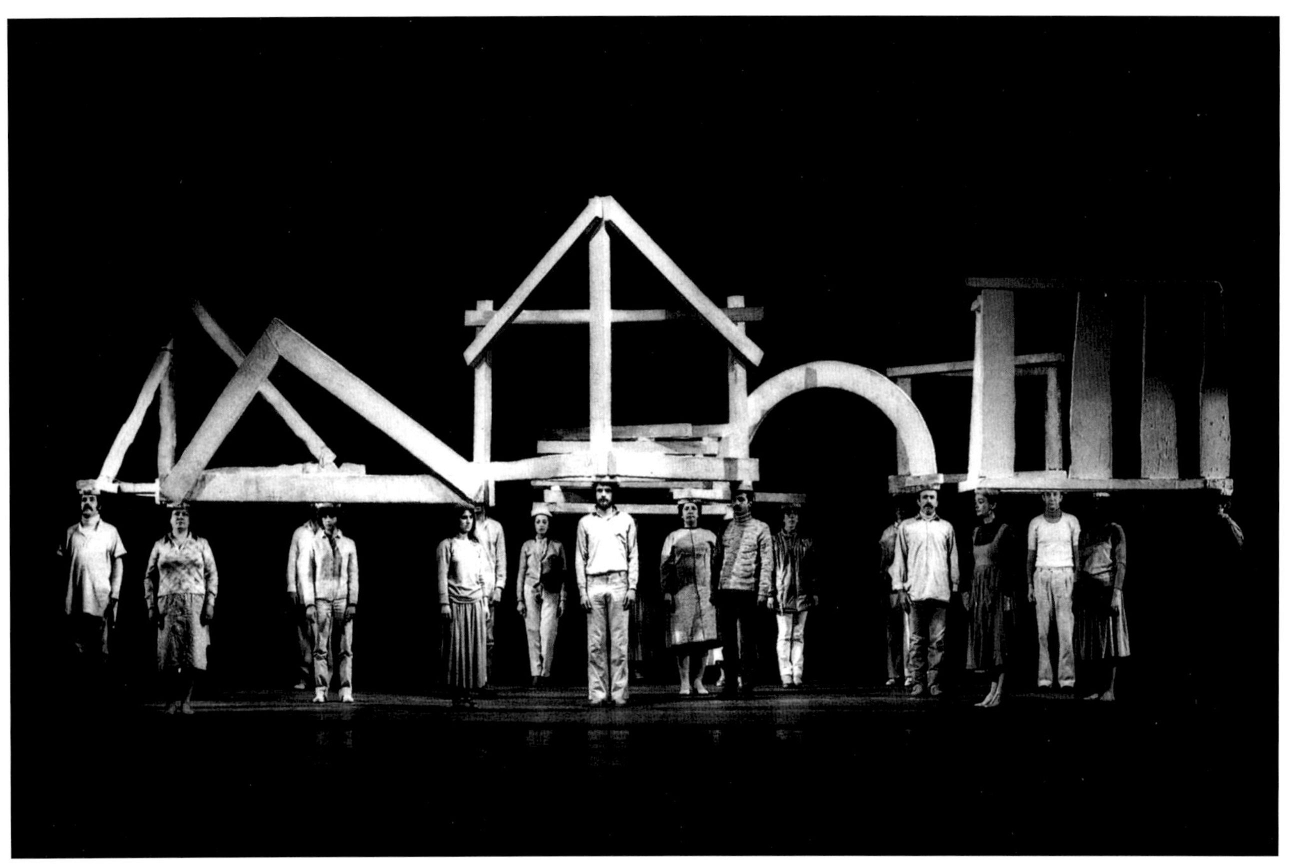

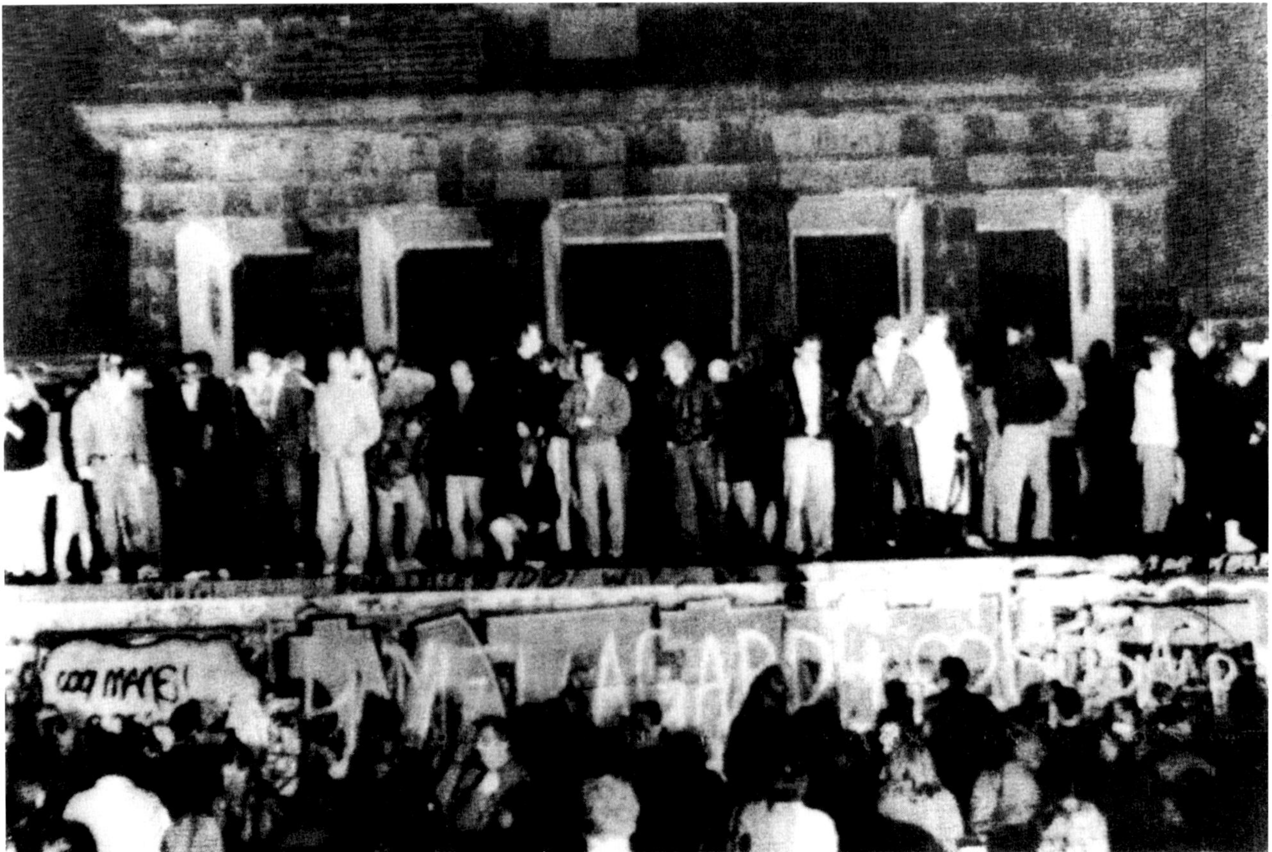

FIG. 133A–B.

A. Michelangelo Pistoletto, *Immagine–Anno bianco* (*Anno Uno, 1981*) (Image–White Year [Year One, 1981]), 1989.

B. *Immagine–Anno bianco* (*La caduta del muro di Berlino, 1989*) (Image–White Year [The Fall of the Berlin Wall, 1989]), 1989. Photographs and wood support, 3 panels, each: 12 ft. 1¾ in. × 17 ft. 8½ in. (370 × 540 cm). Cittadellarte–Fondazione Pistoletto, Biella. Photos by Paolo Mussat Sartor (top); unknown (bottom). Archivio Pistoletto, Biella.

balance large, open, architectonic plywood structures on their heads; as caryatids, they hold up, together, structures including a keystone arch, a simple post-and-lintel portal, pyramidal forms, and a rudimentary portico, reminiscent of Doric structures. On the right, we see a crowded group of people standing on a wall covered in graffiti, overlooking a second crowd gathered below. Behind the crowd on the wall is a large structure (the Brandenburg Gate), with five portals, the side of an arcade. In addition to their material similarities, the images are juxtaposed in a way that encourages apperception of their analogous imagistic form and content: they share three horizontal registers, groups of people, architectonic forms, and horizontal platforms used as spaces of spectacular assembly (where people not only gather but *want to be seen* gathering).

The first photograph captures a performance entitled *Anno Uno* (Year One, 1981), organized by Pistoletto in collaboration with twenty townspeople from Corniglia, with Pioppi, and his daughter Cristina Pistoletto, staged at the Teatro Quirino in Rome. The work addresses "the entire history of mankind," as Andrea Bellini has put it; Pistoletto conceived the work as telegraphing history "from Cain and Abel to Romulus and Remus, the symbols of power and the victories of mankind, Egyptian civilization, Roman civilization, the papal state, the conquest of the moon. *Anno Uno* is the 'eternal city' within which we listen to the rhythms of time up to the present day. The people on the stage, an actual living fragment of society, lead us to face the mirror of our present."[113] Conceived as an extension of Pistoletto's collaborative practice from almost fifteen years earlier with the Zoo, the performance was practiced outside, in a piazza in Corniglia, in front of an entrance to a theater. Corniglia's built environment contains little open space. Study of documentary photographs reveals that the Zoo performed in the open piazza that intersected with the town's main station road. Even there, however, theater-as-living was a kind of disruption.

In the installation from 1989, the photograph of *Anno Uno* is juxtaposed with another photograph, *La caduta del muro del Berlino* (The Fall of the Berlin Wall, 1989), which captures a row of people standing on the Berlin Wall in front of the Brandenburg Gate. Comparison to iconic images of the event tells us that the image dates to November 10, 1989, the day after the fall of the Berlin Wall. Through their shared visual languages, the photomurals invite consideration of other correspondences between the photographs and distinct events of their respective documentation or the historical narratives they both participate in and deliver. In both images, we see people—figures—envisioning new worlds by using their bodies to intervene in architecture as a symbol of a social order. In *Year One,* the people on stage hold up forms that remind us of a built environment; presented as large construction frameworks, they require the actors to remain motionless during the performance. As Pistoletto described the scene: "It is the representation of a city where people are the architecture. It is civilization that immobilizes people under its heavy structures."[114] In *The Fall of the Berlin Wall,* it is the removal (rather than construction) of architecture that is posited as the inauguration of a new world. People have surmounted the architecture (and systems) that have divided them, the civilization that has immobilized them.

This wasn't the last time that Pistoletto revisited *Year One.* In 2009, Pistoletto restaged *Year One* at Turin's Teatro Regio, under the aegis of the Third Paradise (as *Anno Uno–Terzo Paradiso*), updated to include recent events such as the 9/11 attacks on and fall of the Twin Towers.[115] In their tandem installation, the images present gestalts and icons of new democratic worlds and histories in which people, working together, are the literal and figurative (as well as literally figurative) pillars of the communities in which they live. The work of Italian activist and communist philosopher Franco "Bifo" Berardi, a major figure within the 1970s leftist movement Autonomia, is helpful here. In his writings on vision and power, Bifo uses "gestalt" to refer to systems (from empire to commodity aesthetics) that structure vision and power: "Power [is] the temporary condition of implementation of a selection among many possibilities. I call power a regime of visibility and invisibility: the exclusion of different possible concatenations from the space of visibility. A form emerges from many possible forms, then it turns into a gestalt, a format of perception of the surrounding reality. The gestalt is a perceptual code: a form that generates forms. This is power."[116] Bifo's view of capitalism as a "semiotic gestalt" provides a model to consider what happens when we look at Pistoletto's formally and politically analogous images of theater and revolution together. The figure is their shared site of resistance, as image and body.

Conclusion

Figure as Model

Spanning nearly seven decades, the work of Michelangelo Pistoletto has modeled a different narrative for postwar and contemporary art history, one grounded in experiments in figuration as a socially attuned, humanist practice. In the tumultuous aesthetic and social contexts of the post–World War II decades, he perpetually sought new ways to consider the figure and its capacity for artistic and social change. In so doing, he has urged viewers to contemplate the distinctive possibilities offered by figuration, by reconfiguring it into forms that realize actual and imagistic presence, often resulting in a transgression of things as they have been, an opening onto what might be. In this book's introduction, I positioned this figurality as a site of questioning in Pistoletto's practice, through which his works—his figures—asked whether a postwar humanism might be possible. Across these chapters, I mapped Pistoletto's persistent investigation of this question and the many artistic innovations and social proposals that came from it. The answer, I have shown, is a history for postwar art that finds new value in the figure as a major critical strategy within this period. Rather than seeing figuration as something returned to, reactively, as an expression of self, this narrative instead shows how Pistoletto used the figure, as image and body, to reconfigure discourse and the real world—and perhaps ourselves. The figure never went away, as has often been narrated. Instead, as image and body, it has, as Pistoletto has demonstrated, spoken to both art and life and, in his work, revealed its potential to reconfigure both.

One major contribution of this history is that Pistoletto's works realize a new history of avant-gardism based on alternative models of figuration, specifically on an expanded model of the figure as a persistent creative platform in twentieth-century art. With important antecedents in Italian futurism and spatialism, this countermodel stands against politicized narratives of modernism that privileged abstraction as the progressive language of the time. In so doing, it offers a new understanding of Italian modernism and the avant-garde based on these movements' investigation of the figure transitioning from representation to reality, as well as a new model of bringing "art into life," realized through a bodily exploration of space. This figural art history cuts across historical and cultural contexts, opening new narratives and genealogies of twentieth-century

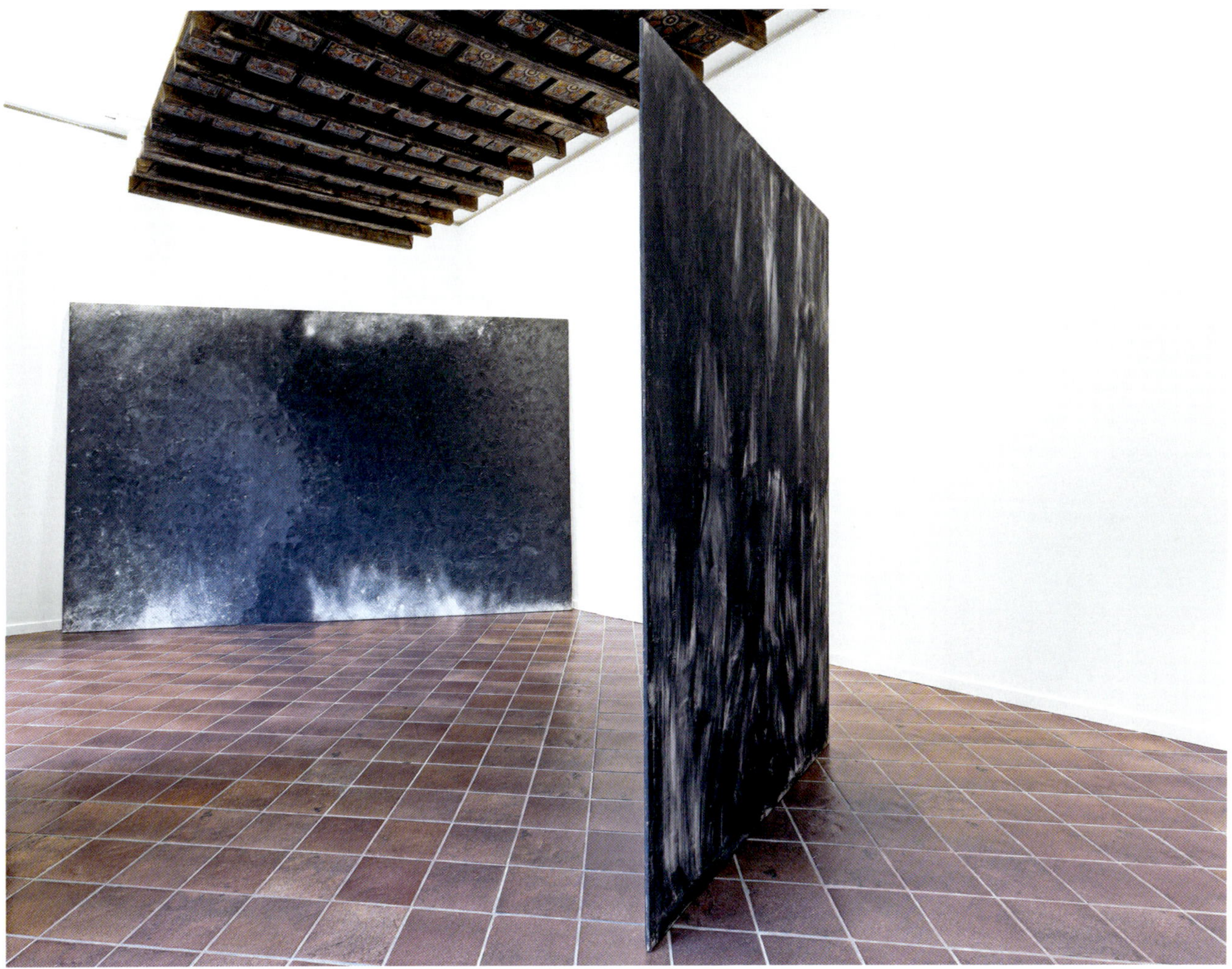

FIG. 134. Installation view, Michelangelo Pistoletto, from the series *Arte dello squallore* (Art of Desolation, Art of Squalor), including *Parallelepipedo dispari-nerume* (Odd-Mold Parallelepiped), 1985, and *Superficie grigia* (Gray Surface), 1985, on exhibition in *Michelangelo Pistoletto: Quarta Generazione*, Galleria Giorgio Persano, Turin, March 2–July 29, 2022.

avant-gardes, expanding the art historical discourse in turn.

Pistoletto continued to ask these questions after the key period of his work that comprises the historical frame of this study. In the 1980s he made large figurative sculpture, "excavating" and destabilizing monumental figures carved in dense polyurethane foam, wood, and marble—materials associated with new synthetics and histories of sculpture across time and place, bridging temporal difference; in those works, he sought the "common spirit" of different sculptural (and cultural) traditions.[1] In the same period, he made large paintings and abstract geometric sculptures, in which he explored gestural abstraction and the monochrome, in *Arte dello squallore* (Art of Desolation or, figuratively, Art of Squalor, 1985; fig. 134). In that understudied series, he imagined dark "surfaces of desolation" of an art that "doesn't represent anything." Describing the series as a "fragmentation" and "pulverization" of the subtractive logic of the Minus Objects, he imagined the works not as an act of destruction but as a dispersal of their sculptural precedents. The idea was that this fragmentation of material might expand the universe. He nevertheless conceived of these abstract, nonreferential works as *figures*, calling them "figures bathed by the black light of billions of shadowy years, leaden in a planet colored by too rich, too creative a nature."[2] By the early 1990s, on the collapse of the Soviet Union, he reimagined his figurative sculptures of the 1980s as toppled monuments, endowing them (as he had with his theatrical activities) with new symbolic meaning as signs of democratic rebellion and agency (fig. 135).

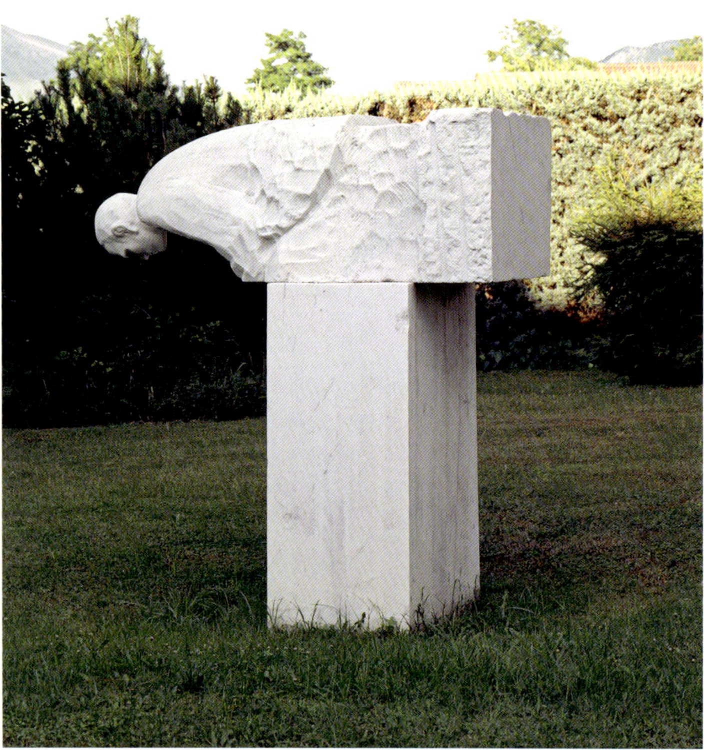

FIG. 135. Michelangelo Pistoletto, *La caduta* (The Fall), 1983–91. Greek marble, 82¾ × 78¾ × 39⅜ in. (210 × 200 × 100 cm). Associazione Longo, Cassino.

In the 1990s and 2000s, with *Segno Arte* (Art Sign) he developed the social practice to which he has dedicated his contemporary work (fig. 136). Dating to early ideas of the mid-1970s, and referencing histories of humanist worldviews in which "man is the measure," as captured by Vitruvius, Art Sign's form corresponds to the fullest extension of the artist's body with which Pistoletto created portals to "inhabitable spaces." Enacting an expansion of the referential capacity of the sign of the artist, Pistoletto envisioned the personal sign as a sign for the cultural figure of the artist ("Pistoletto") and as a sign of the corporeal figure of Pistoletto (his physical body). In so doing, the figurative sign of the artist shifted from a personal sign to a social one. As part of the project, he called on others to deploy their own signs into the world, using art to create openings to "intimate and personal spaces, as well as the space of social meetings."[3]

Pistoletto has devoted his practice in the past twenty years to using art as an agent of social change to address global issues. His recent work is characterized by an often-politicized dedication to this belief, undergirded by a refusal of uniformity, an interest in horizontality, and a rejection of commodifiable artistic practice. Through his work at his foundation, Cittadellarte, and the continued work of the Third Paradise and its "ambassadors," Pistoletto has fostered participatory, community-based art-making all over the world. Installations of the symbol of the Third Paradise have been made to address various sites of significance in global politics and humanitarian crises, including the rise of deaths of migrants amid recent resurgences of cross-Mediterranean migration and climate change, as in his *Third Paradise* works in Ventimiglia and Catania in 2017 and 2019, respectively. In related projects, Pistoletto has positioned his works as spaces for us to imagine global community as a site of individual and collective action, as in his mirror paintings of the mid-1980s for Amnesty International and the Olympics, which prompt self-reflection within the collective spaces of universal humanism these organizations propose, or in more recent work, which includes flags of all countries of the world, arranged in the sign of the Third Paradise.[4]

In December 2014, Pistoletto created the triple-looped symbol of the Third Paradise off the coast of Havana, Cuba, when local fishers traced an ephemeral line with their boats in the Caribbean Sea (fig. 137). Other iterations of the work that followed included an aggregation of stones, arranged in the same form, in Ventimiglia (2017), a northwestern point of border crossing between Italy and France. At the time, Ventimiglia had emerged as a major site of migration advocacy during the twenty-first-century surge in cross-Mediterranean migration, primarily from North and East Africa to southern Europe via Italy, which has incited xenophobic and racist violence in Italy and other European countries. At that point of arbitrary division, Pistoletto created a work, as announced by Cittadellarte, to "superare ogni confine": overcome every boundary. These are ideas that came out of Pistoletto's work and milieu in the 1960s, specifically out of some understudied and misconstrued areas of his practice that get to the heart of difficult intersections among art, labor, and geopolitics addressed in this book.

For Pistoletto, the Third Paradise imagines a new future for society. First realized by the artist in 2003,

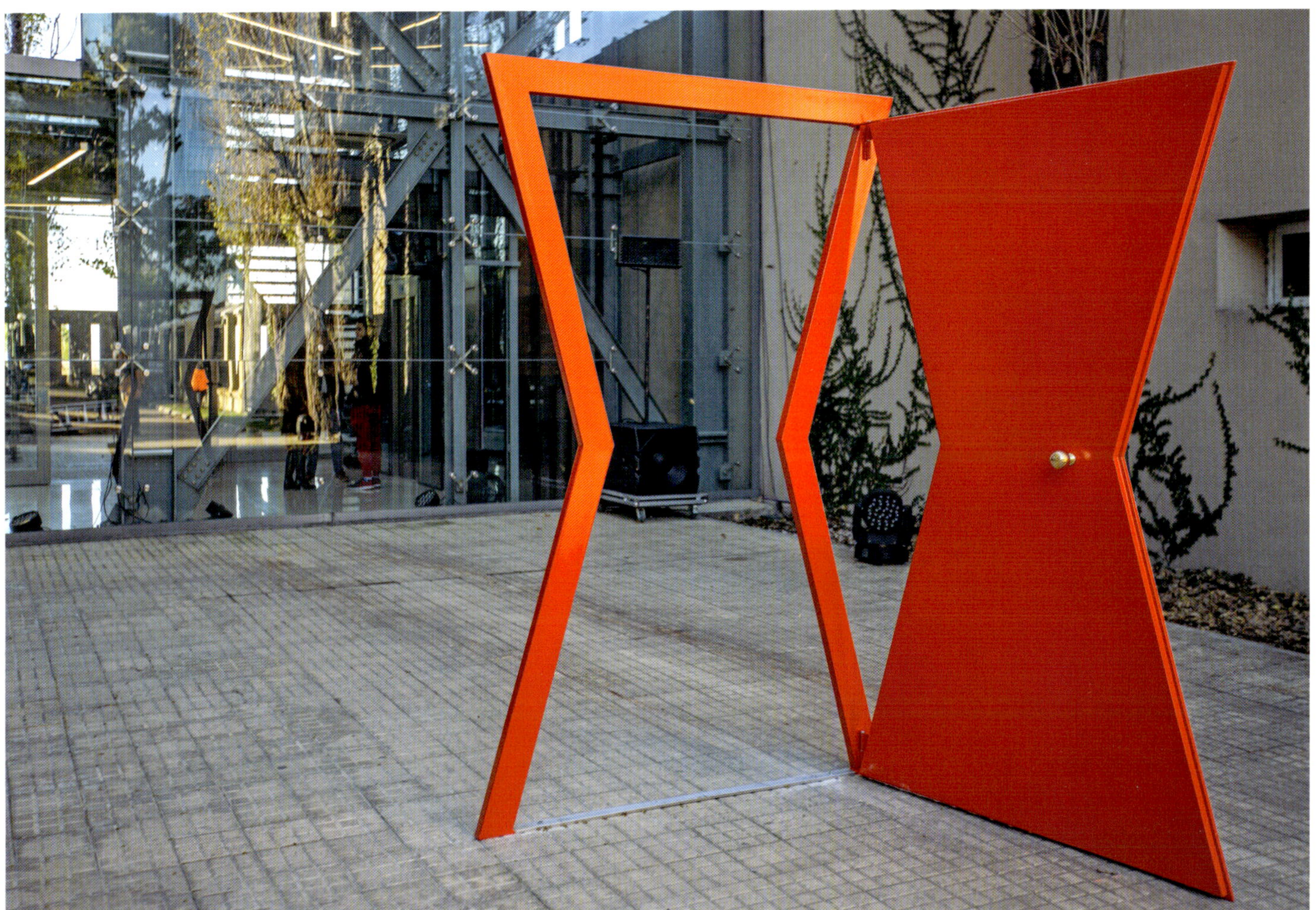

FIG. 136. Michelangelo Pistoletto, *Segno Arte* (Art Sign), 2019. Wood, 86¾ × 55 × 2½ in. (220.4 × 139.7 × 6.4 cm), when closed. In BIENALSUR 2019 Km 3,3 MNAD—Museo Nacional de Arte Decorativo, Buenos Aires.

when he traced the symbol in the sand, and debuted publicly in 2005 with a work at the Venice Biennale, the Third Paradise is the space in which the dialectic between the natural and artificial worlds can bring a sustainable future into existence. That future is defined by individual personal responsibility and a democratic, ethical, interpersonal relativity in which difference is valued and new potentials of that mode of living and working are explored. In his words, as reported on the website of Cittadellarte: "The Third Paradise is the great parable that brings each of us to take *personal* responsibility in the *global* vision. . . . It is a planetary work."[5] Pistoletto's words recall Germano Celant's own language from the late 1960s, which prompted some of this book's primary questions, when the critic called Arte Povera's vision a "global" one—*una visione globale*. And so, in 2019, when asked to speak to the importance of Cuba in the world, Pistoletto responded. He spoke of the twentieth century as one of great polarity: capitalism and communism, East and West, and the island of Cuba as a site of creating a different way to be in the world:

> Cuba is a historical element of our present. It's our history, of everyone, because we lived through the 20th century. . . . [It's] the product of the greatest separations, the greatest contrasts. . . . Cuba created its own autonomy. . . . It remained an island. It remained a small point in the world, as I said before, still on the shoulders of all that the world created in the 20th century. I see there a possibility to depart again, to take off again from this capacity to be free, free in the possibility to understand and to live together in a new way.[6]

The Third Paradise in Cuba, off the coast of Havana, was an event and environmental action, as are many Third Paradises; each participating fisher played their

out ahead of them, first past concrete buildings with vacant commercial spaces, a sign of the post-boom economic downturn, then past grander palazzi (fig. 138). Soon Pistoletto and Pioppi arrive on Via Roma; they cross under illuminated signs advertising Campari and Cinzano in the arcades around the great expanse of Piazza San Carlo. Pistoletto stands outside a Bialetti shop, some distance from us, the sphere next to him. At over half his height but nearly triple the width of his body, from our perspective the sphere has a comparable corporeal presence as the artist.

The film is divided by a raucous nighttime scene; artist friends (Gilberto Zorio), critics (Tommaso Trini), and gallerists (Gian Enzo Sperone) join in. The sphere takes center stage; the sphere is rolled in front of cars and passersby, "refusing" to move until a policeman intervenes. Daylight brings a different cast of characters. We see the *Burnt Rose,* the Minus Object, suspended in midair from the second-story window of the Galerie Christian Stein, as it is lowered to street level. Pioppi hoists the giant cardboard blossom onto her back; nearly twice her size, it overwhelms her small frame. The camera view flips upside down, then right-side up.

Pioppi turns from the camera; the flower hides all but her legs, which from our view appear now to belong to the flower. *Burnt Rose* has become its own subject. It runs across street, like Marangolo's Campari figure, its high-heeled, stockinged legs sticking out from the cardboard blossom that forms "her" body.

The scene constellates reality as one of figurative and figural contrasts: the differences in the figures' bodies resonate with the symbolic differences of the scene. In the shadow of would-be fascist monuments, the antifascist resonances of our red flower—an image that recalls the red carnation of the Italian Socialist Party and the poppy of the partigiani—is brought to the fore. Within

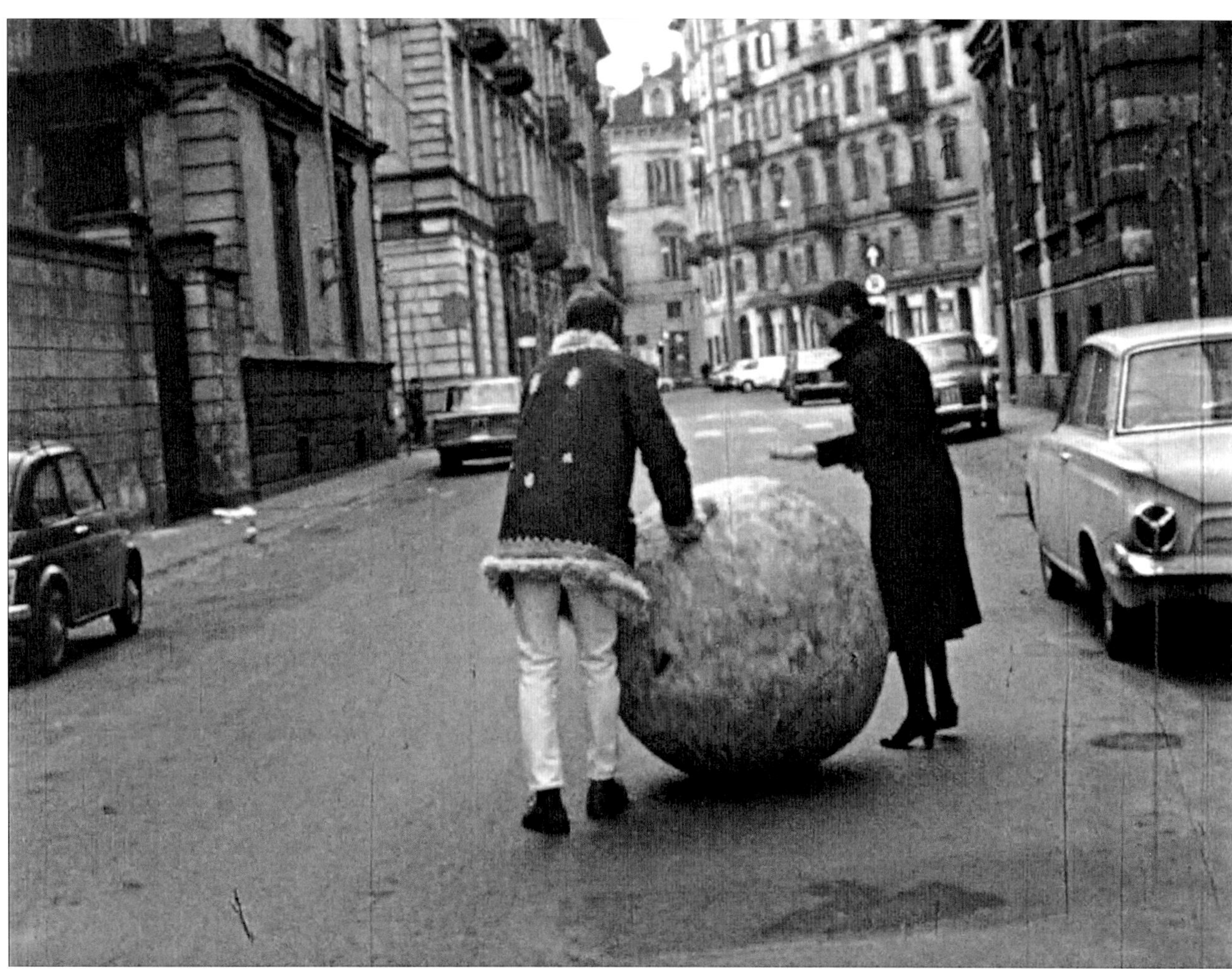

FIG. 138. Film still, Ugo Nespolo, *Buongiorno Michelangelo* (Good Morning Michelangelo), 1968–69. 16mm black-and-white film, sound, 10 min., 40 sec. Direction and photography by Ugo Nespolo, editing by Ugo Nespolo.

the scene, it calls to mind not war but love, evoking contemporary ideas of socialist internationalism and the global counterculture of the 1960s. The frozen, unmoving mass of the statues highlights the sprightly freedom the rose embodies as she runs toward the street that cuts through the square. As she turns to go, the rose has transformed again; it scampers across the street in slacks and dress shoes, traffic whizzing around "him."

In the final moments of the film, we see Pistoletto standing in the great expanse of Piazza San Carlo, surrounded by vehicles and baroque architecture. (The square was then used as a parking lot and bus stop.) He holds the flower up above him in the air. Before he hoists the flower onto his back, the camera view flips upside down for a moment. Pistoletto's work, it seems, has made the world go topsy turvy. Pistoletto stands in the square, smiling at the camera, the rose in his arms. A moment later, the artist steps to one side and disappears. Instead of Pistoletto, we see the rose, dressed in trousers and Chelsea boots, running at full tilt out into the piazza. Like the figural works and guerrilla subjects that preceded him, the rose enacts his own "invasion of the environment." He pauses, turns to the camera, and runs to catch the bus, disappearing among its passengers (fig. 139a–c).

While *Buongiorno Michelangelo* is typically referenced as part of a broader shift in Pistoletto's late 1960s practice away from the studio and the artistic conventions of its association, the positioning of *Walking Sculpture* and *Burnt Rose* as *figures* in the film connects it to a different trajectory for Pistoletto's practice that I have outlined in this book.[13] The film and bodily sculptures within it are another point in the artist's reworking of figuration from the late 1950s through the 1970s and 1980s to the present, into new visual languages of figurality. From the early paintings and Pistoletto's design work to the mirror paintings and Plexiglasses, through the Minus Objects and Rallies to the activities of the Zoo and the *Plagio* series, through his figurative sculptures from the 1980s and his "World Theater" of the 1980s and 1990s into the figures of the Third Paradise and recent mirror paintings of protestors: this was the trajectory, this figure was the model, that fueled one of the most enduring and important bodies of work in postwar and contemporary art.

Looking at the film in this way, Pistoletto's reworking of the figure from the figurative to the figural, in

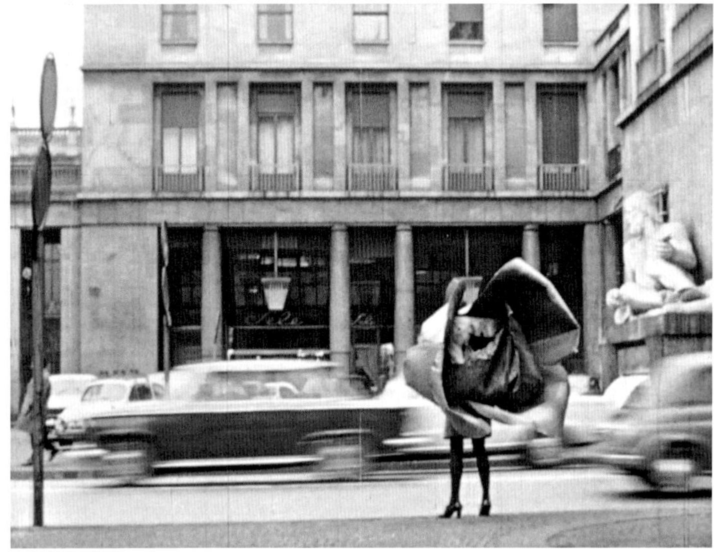

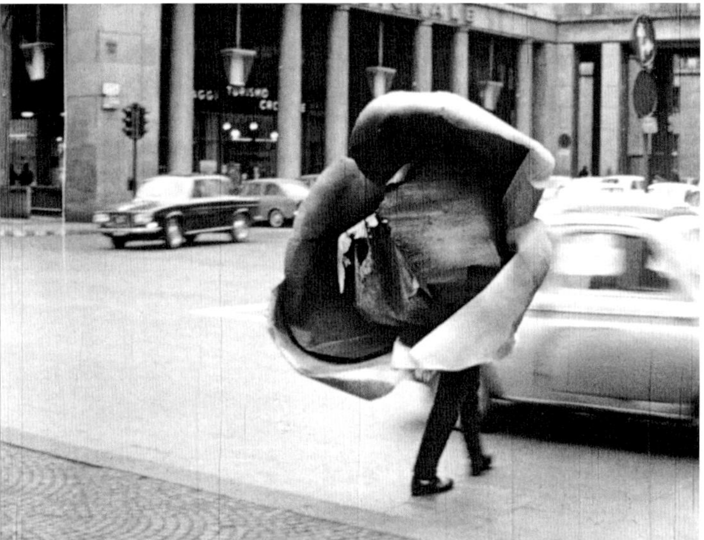

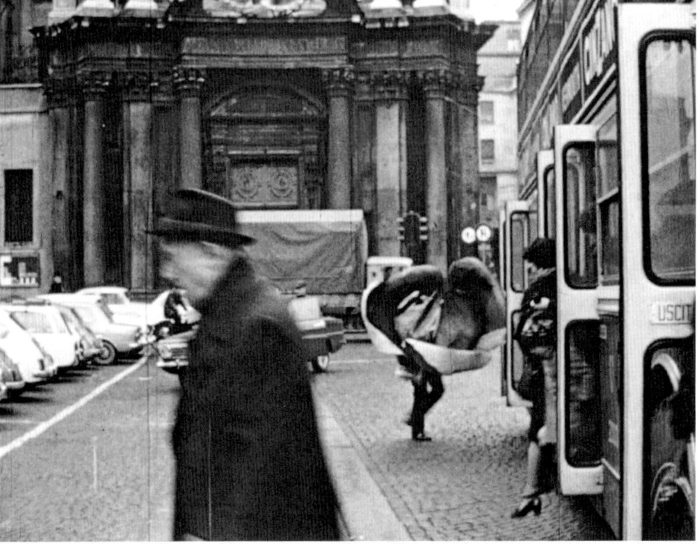

FIG. 139A–C. Film stills, Ugo Nespolo, *Buongiorno Michelangelo* (Good Morning Michelangelo), 1968–69. 16mm black-and-white film, sound, 10 min., 40 sec. Direction and photography by Ugo Nespolo, editing by Ugo Nespolo.

many forms, emerges as the critical conceptual framework for Pistoletto's practice, pursued in relation to the Italian leftist exigency of cultivating a neohumanism after World War II. To regard Pistoletto in this way not only remaps our understanding of postwar Italian art and the Italian historical avant-garde but gives us a new model of progressive artistic practice that may provide new insights into other practices in modern and contemporary art, in Italy and elsewhere.

In that vein, other artistic trajectories might be connected to Pistoletto (and by extension to Arte Povera) than the predominantly process art, "informal" sculpture and actions, and ephemeral, dematerialized practices that have and continue to be linked to Arte Povera. Innumerable contemporary artists who make work using discarded, banal, or inconsequential found objects and detritus materials cite Arte Povera as a major influence. Scholars have also noted this connection. Anthony White, for example, has astutely connected the work of Mike Kelley to the exploration of expenditure in the Minus Objects.[14] The expansion of conventional material repertoires remains one of the movement's major, if overdetermined, legacies. One hope I have for this book is that readers will have found a different, more nuanced history of Arte Povera through close study of the work of one of its major protagonists—if not *the* protagonist of the movement.

Recalling the various figural histories of Italian modernism in these chapters that the study of Pistoletto's art brings into view, this history of the artist's work also connects to the work of other postwar and contemporary artists, Italian and otherwise, in figurative art and social practice. Consider the work of Mimmo Paladino (b. 1948), the Italian artist typically associated with the Transavanguardia and neoexpressionism. The history of Pistoletto's work brings attention to other areas of Paladino's practice: his play with figurative language and systems of representation. The print *Pietra di Pietro* (Peter's Stone, 1980), for example, depicts a scene—a male figure next to a dark, animalistic shadow—associated with the Christian narrative of Christ telling Peter that he would be the "foundational rock" of the church. Paladino used an irregular, stone-shaped plate to make the print; the impression is jagged at one side. The person Peter and symbol of Peter (the stone) are also visually connected in the Italian language; the representation of Peter—the image of the human figure in the print—is also figurally present—in "the figure" of Peter via the stone plate, made present with the impression on the paper. The work includes a red line—an alarm. It seems to call our attention urgently to the "act of becoming" for which Paladino sees this work as a metaphor. Made at the end of the tumultuous years of lead, the figure and meaning here—languages of representation—are in crisis, as relayed by Paladino's figural form.

To this lineage we might also consider adding the work of Gabriel Orozco (b. 1962), an artist most associated with relational aesthetics—Nicolas Bourriaud's term for a proliferation of artistic practices in the 1990s dedicated to experiential, encounter-based practices that explore the "social interstice" of our contemporary world.[15] While Orozco's process-focused sculptural work has already been compared to Pistoletto and to Arte Povera (each is of interest to the artist), we might consider Orozco's photography of the 1990s.[16] In those works, such as *Tortillas y ladrillos* (Tortillas and Bricks, 1990), Orozco remade figurative photography, turning regular objects into figural forms—arrangements of objects that appear to us like people, even as we recognize them as photographic tableaux and images of arranged objects. Within the photograph, the objects of the artist's interventions take on subjective qualities. They are orderly, or "well-behaved," to borrow T. J. Clark's apt description of Orozco's photographic subjects.[17] They are also documents of "tiny revolutions," as Bourriaud put it, figural forms and gestures that share some of the political concerns of Pistoletto's work that I've identified in this book.[18] The juxtaposition of common objects converges into a somewhat figural gestalt: the presence of a human figures coheres for the viewer, even in its absence. Drawing on but exceeding historical languages of social realist photography, Orozco's subject is the process of structural arrangement, often emphasized by the title of the work, it is a residual description of procedure that asserts a language of spatial and human relationality, metonymy, and conjunction grounded in the desire to come together, and in signification.

Or we might consider the work of Marinella Senatore (b. 1977). The Italian artist's figurative collages, sculptures, paintings, drawings, and communal processions, often grounded in the collaborative work of activism and collective authorship, build on the practice of Pistoletto

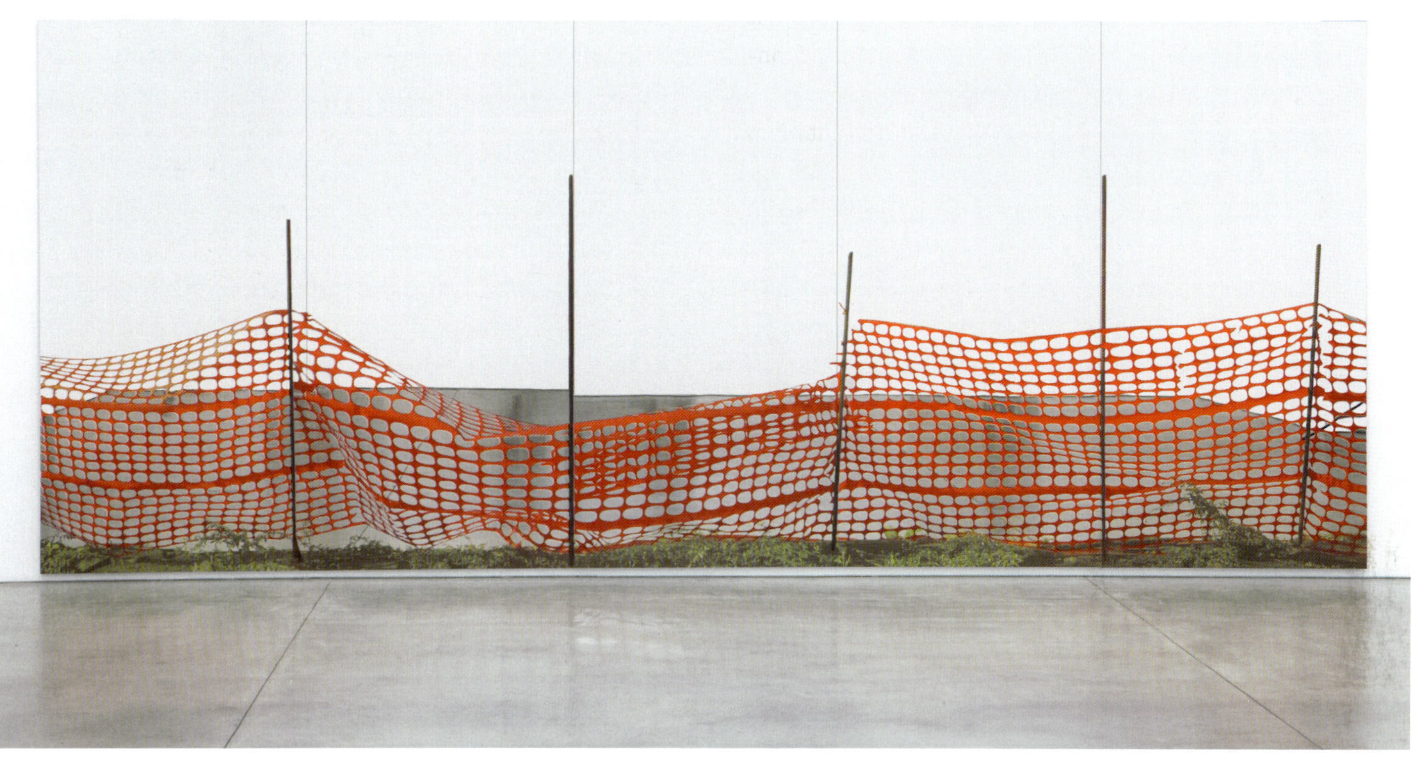

FIG. 140. Michelangelo Pistoletto, *Lavori in corso* (Work in Progress), 2008. Serigraph on mirrorized stainless steel, 98½ in. × 20 ft. 10 in. (250 × 625 cm).

in which depicted and embodied figures—in which figural forms—function as a means of resistance, of reimagining the world and how we live in it. In her *Autoritratto* (Self-Portrait) sculptures of the early 2020s, made in a range of materials including cast bronze and glass, we find a pair of life-size hands, reaching down to us from reflective metal tiles, suspended from the ceiling, or up to us from a pedestal. The molds for the hands were made from the body of the artist (for one hand) and a collaborator (for the other): they are both representations and bodily presences in the gallery. Along with references to Carla Lonzi's book of the same title, the presence of the body and the representation of it make Senatore's work a figural sculpture in the vein of Pistoletto's work of the early 1970s. As with the steel panels of the mirror paintings, Senatore's use of reflective material doubles the sculptural dimensional forms with their imagistic reflection, which seems to reach up to the ceiling. Visualizing the dual subject of the real hands, the suggestion transgresses ideas of self-constitution and mastery associated with gazing into our own reflections, following Jacques Lacan, and reconfigures discourse such that the personal is the common.

Or we might consider the work of the wide range of contemporary artists who have experimented with figural objects, as theorized in this book's chapter on the Minus Objects. Gordon Hall (they/them, b. 1983) makes sculptural, furniture-inspired objects that explore the body and anticapitalist symbolic orders. Hall explores a range of materials that evoke the body as a presence, even as the works do not literally depict one; they seek to "imagin[e] more expansive forms of embodied life," as the artist has written.[19] Hall describes the concrete ribbed plank *Leaning Back* (2021) as a "leaner and his orange shadow."[20] The top section (the seeming "head" of the work that lies vertically, flush against the wall), human proportions, and figural language for the work, positions the leaning back—the literal description of the form of the work, which leans away from freestanding to propped form—into a figural one that suggests a body. Hall's work recalls postminimalist performed sculptures, such as Charles Ray's *Plank Pieces* (1973), whose photographic sculptural actions we might also add to this history.

What these brief examples offer is a trajectory that positions exploration of the figure, at its intersections with images, language, and humanism, as a major strategy for figuring creative revolutions in postwar and contemporary art. Long overlooked, like *Man with Red Flag,* the exploration of figuration as a concept that I have theorized in this book, which intersects with art, meaning, and humanity, gives us a different critical model for postwar and contemporary art history. This is the history Pistoletto's work has brought into view. The figure and figural in Pistoletto's works of art envisioned new ways of being in the world at a time of immense sociopolitical and cultural upheaval.

There is still more to say on Pistoletto and the challenges he poses to us as viewers. For large parts of the world, the early 2020s have been a moment of reckoning for humankind, in the face of a global pandemic, persistent racist and gendered violence, far-right nationalism, and climate change; more people are feeling renewed urgency for social justice and reform. As he publicly shared during the pandemic, Pistoletto himself nearly died from the coronavirus. Thereafter he immediately resumed his practice and continues to work today. During this tumultuous time, many are considering, as is Pistoletto, the potential democratic and transformative power of *assembly,* to borrow from the work of Michael Hardt and Antonio Negri.[21] While the crises of our globalized contemporary world have been regarded by some as entirely distinct from the international crises of the 1960s, they nevertheless comprise a similar moment. We are still trying to figure out who we are in the world, to potentially reconfigure *how* we are in the world with one another. This is, as one of Pistoletto's contemporary mirror paintings suggests, work in progress (fig. 140). In that painting, which lacks collaged figures, Pistoletto situates us as real people and figurative images simultaneously. As figural subjects, we find ourselves in the position, like that of *Man with Red Flag,* to potentially transgress and change systems of meaning and the world as it is. The scale of work—at more than ten feet in length—also urges us to contemplate the scale of such a task. How might we come together to make a better world? It is this art historical and sociopolitical inquiry and connection that makes this study of Pistoletto's work particularly pressing and potentially generative for us today. This is how Pistoletto's work figures, we might say, in view and valence, for art history and for humanity at large.

Notes

Author's note: I have included the original Italian in notes for quotations of Pistoletto when the original carries nuance pertinent to the evidentiary role of the quotation as well as for all quotations from my unpublished interviews with the artist. Unless otherwise noted, all translations are mine.

INTRODUCTION

1. Germano Celant, "Arte Povera: Appunti per una guerriglia," *Flash Art*, no. 5 (November–December 1967): 3. Celant later describes this stripping down of Arte Povera (using the verb *spogliare*, "to disrobe, to strip") in his essay "Arte Povera" in *Arte Povera* (Bologna: Galleria de' Foscherari, 1968), n.p., catalog published in conjunction with the exhibition of the same title, held February 24–March 15, 1968.
2. Anthony George White, "Michelangelo Pistoletto's *Minus Objects*," in *The Minus Objects, 1965–1966* (New York: Luhring Augustine; Munich: DelMonico Books, Prestel, 2017), 84. White also notes (on this page) that the works do not fit with the many areas of their engagement in postwar art. Although we have different readings, on that point we are firmly in agreement.
3. The title of the work is descriptive; because its location is unknown, it is also unknown if a title was written on the back. I use the title given in the caption of the image in the catalog for Pistoletto's exhibit in 1966 at the Galleria La Bertesca.
4. Germano Celant, "Arte Povera: Notes for a Guerrilla War," trans. Henry Martin, in *Flash Art: Two Decades of History: XXI Years*, ed. Giancarlo Politi and Helen Kontova (Cambridge, MA: MIT Press, 1990), 190. Celant seems to draw on the concept of the "real man" from volume 2 of Karl Marx and Friedrich Engels's *German Ideology*. Originally published in 1846, *The German Ideology* was finding new readership around the time of Celant's essay, having been first translated into Italian in its entirety in 1958 by Fausto Codini (Rome: Edizioni Riuniti).
5. Peter Bürger, *Theory of the Avant-Garde*, trans. Michael Shaw (Minneapolis: University of Minnesota, 1984).
6. See *Michelangelo Pistoletto* (Genoa: Galleria La Bertesca, 1966).
7. Pistoletto, interview by Germano Celant, in *Pistoletto*, ed. Germano Celant and Ida Gianelli (Milan: Electa, 1984), 31.
8. The precise date of the photograph is unknown. Because other photos in the series show some of the artist's variations on the Minus Objects, called "Versions," this photo can be dated to later in 1966 than the initial installations.
9. This point, that Pistoletto doesn't always fit into the framing of Arte Povera, has been noted elsewhere, most recently in White, "Michelangelo Pistoletto's *Minus Objects*," 84.
10. Pistoletto participated in the Venice Biennale in 1966; 1968, with a personal room, canceled due to protests at the Biennale; 1972; 1976; 1978; 1984; 1986; 1993; 2003, when he was awarded the career-long Golden Lion; 2005; 2009; and 2011. He participated in the São Paulo Bienal in 1967, 1971, 1975, and 1979.
11. See, e.g., Clement Greenberg, "Abstract, Representational, and So Forth" (1954), in *Art and Culture: Critical Essays* (Boston: Beacon, 1971), 135–36. Greenberg famously argued that figuration was extraneous to the "characteristic" concerns of painting that should be the focus of modernism's task: to examine the discipline and to "entrench it more firmly in its area of competence." Clement Greenberg, "Modernist Painting" (1965), reprinted in Francis Frascina and Charles Harrison, eds., *Modern Art and Modernism: A Critical Anthology* (New York: Harper and Row, 1982), 5–10, at 5.
12. See Benjamin H. D. Buchloh, "Memory Lessons and History Tableaux: James Coleman's Archaeology of Spectacle," in *Neo-Avantgarde and Culture Industry: Essays on European and American Art from 1955 to 1975* (Cambridge, MA: MIT Press, 2000), 144.
13. Identifying similar strategies in the work of Giulio Paolini and Pistoletto, on whom Claire Gilman offered a key study in the issue of *October* that she edited in 2008, Gilman has argued that these artists' works share a "theatrical sensibility," which emerged in response to the Romantic conceptions of authenticity and self-possession heralded by stymied gestural abstract painting of the 1950s and early 1960s. This sensibility, for Gilman, was defined by a self-conscious engagement with conventions—of perception, of human behavior, of spatial relations—that counters the reading of Arte Povera's ideology of unmediated presence, elemental form, and materiality. Claire Gilman, "Figuring Boetti," in *Alighiero Boetti: Game Plan*, ed. Christian Rattemeyer, Lynne Cooke, and Mark Godfrey (London: Tate Modern, 2012), 133–42, at 133–34, catalog published in conjunction with the exhibition of the same title held at the Tate Modern, February 28–May 27, 2012. See also Claire Gilman, "Pascali's Consumer Creatures," in "Arte Povera's Theater: Artifice and Anti-Modernism in Italian Art of the 1960s" (PhD diss., Columbia University, 2006), 158–219.
14. Gilman, "Figuring Boetti," 134.
15. Mark Godfrey, "The Artist According to Alighiero e Boetti," in *Alighiero e Boetti* (New Haven: Yale University Press, 2011), 73–117.
16. Max Horkheimer and Theodor W. Adorno, *The Dialectic of Enlightenment: Philosophical Fragments* (1947), ed. Gunzelin Schmid Noerr, trans. Edmund Jephcott (Stanford, CA: Stanford University Press, 2003), 1.
17. Horkheimer and Adorno, *Dialectic of Enlightenment*, 13.
18. Theodor W. Adorno, "Cultural Criticism and Society" (1949), in *Prisms*, trans. Samuel Weber and Shierry Weber Nicholsen (Cambridge, MA: MIT Press, 1997), 33.
19. Theodor W. Adorno, *Negative Dialectics* (1966), trans. E. B. Ashton (New York: Continuum, 2007), 365.
20. Adorno, *Negative Dialectics*, 365.
21. Many texts have discussed the debates between abstraction and figuration in postwar Italy and the polarizing effect they had on what was initially a more pluralist artistic field. For a key primary text, see Tristan Sauvage [Arturo Schwarz], *Pittura italiana del dopoguerra (1945–1957)* (Milan: Schwarz, 1957), esp. part 2, "Dalla figurazione all'astrazione, e viceversa," 49–90. Key secondary sources include Paola Barocchi, "Tra realismo e astrattismo: 1943–48," in *Storia moderna dell'arte in Italia: Manifesti polemiche documenti*, ed. Paola Barocchi, vol. 3:2, *Tra realismo ed anni novanta, 1945–1990* (Turin: Einaudi, 1990), 3–7; Mario De Micheli, "Realism and the Postwar

Debate," in *Italian Art in the 20th Century: Painting and Sculpture, 1900–1988,* ed. Emily Braun (Munich: Prestel, 1989), 187–92; Nancy Jachec, "The Abstraction-Realism Debate and Its Background, 1938–1948," in *Politics and Painting at the Venice Biennale, 1948–1964: Italy and the Idea of Europe* (Manchester: Manchester University Press, 2007), 18–35; and Marcia E. Vetrocq, "Painting and Beyond: Recovery and Regeneration, 1943–1952," in *The Italian Metamorphosis, 1943–1968,* ed. Germano Celant (New York: Guggenheim Museum, 1994), 20–31.

22. As artist Mario Ballocco asserted for the Rome-based Gruppo Origine (Origin Group, 1950–51). Mario Ballocco, "Origine," *AZ arte d'oggi* 2, no. 6 (1950): 1.
23. Palmiro Togliatti, who had a Zhdanovist perspective, already positioned party policy above culture in the immediate postwar years. See Fabio Guidali, "Cultural and Political Commitment in the Non-Orthodox Marxist Left: The Case of *Quaderni piacentini* in Pre-1968 Italy," *History of European Ideas* 46, no. 6 (2020): 862–75, at 863. In his review of the important *Prima mostra nazionale d'arte contemporanea* (First National Exhibition of Contemporary Art, Bologna, 1948), as Adrian Duran has discussed, Togliatti wrote under a pseudonym and ridiculed abstraction as mere "scribblings." See Roderigo di Castiglia, "Segnalazioni," *Rinascità: Rassegna di politica e cultura italiana* 5, no. 11 (1948): 424, reprinted in Barocchi, *Storia moderna dell'arte in Italia,* 77. See also PCI Leadership, *Per la salvezza della cultura italiana* (March 1, 1948) (Rome: *VII Congresso del Partito Comunista Italiano—Documenti politici del Comitato Centrale, della direzione, della segreteria,* July 6–7, 1949), reprinted in Nicoletta Misler, *La via italiana al realismo* (Milan: Gabriele Mazzotta, 1973), 133–35. See also Adrian R. Duran, "Abstract Expressionism's Italian Reception: Questions of Influence," in *Abstract Expressionism: The International Context,* ed. Joan Marter (New Brunswick, NJ: Rutgers University Press, 2007), 145–46; and Adrian R. Duran, "The Communist Politics of Abstraction and the Onset of the Cold War," in *Painting, Politics, and the New Front of Cold War Italy* (Farnham, UK: Ashgate, 2014), 99–118.
24. On Italian modernism, the Italian Communist Party, and *europeismo,* see Vetrocq, "Painting and Beyond," 22–24.
25. On the Informale and Europeanism, see Nancy Jachec, "The 1958 Biennale: The Collapse of the *Ente* and the Rise of Gesture Painting as the 'European Idea,'" in *Politics and Painting,* 86–105. See also Duran, "Abstract Expressionism's Italian Reception," 138–51.
26. Vetrocq, "Painting and Beyond," 20–22. For Forma's manifesto, see Carla Accardi et al., *Manifesto* (Rome, March 15, 1947), reprinted in Sauvage, *Pittura italiana del dopoguerra,* 248–49.
27. Lionello Venturi, *Otto pittori italiani,* in Luciano Caramel, *Arte in Italia: 1945–1960* (Milan: Vita e Pensiero, 1994), 167–69, at 168.
28. Ballocco, "Origine," 1; Mario Ballocco, *Origine: Ballocco, Burri, Capogrossi, Colla* (Rome: Fondazione Origine, 1951), n.p.
29. Primary among these movements were: Gruppo Origine (1950–51); Forma I (Rome, 1947–52); Gruppo MAC (Milan, Movimento arte concreta, or Concrete Art Movement, 1947–58), with later outposts in Turin and other Italian cities. The late 1950s included the short-lived but impactful movement Azimuth (Milan, 1959–60) and Continuità (Rome, 1961).
30. Renato Guttuso, for example, was given a mini-retrospective at the Venice Biennale of 1960, suggesting the historicity of realist painting. Artists who had been associated with realism but tended toward abstract stylistics, such as Lionello Venturi's Group of Eight, were repositioned as part of European informalist movements. See Duran, "Abstract Expressionism's Italian Reception," 150. See also Ruth Ben-Ghiat, "The Politics of Realism: *Corrente di Vita Giovanile* and the Youth Culture of the 1930s," *Stanford Italian Review* 8, nos. 1–2 (1990): 139–64. On the exhaustion of realism by the mid-1950s, see Ben-Ghiat, "Politics of Realism," 162–63.
31. Pistoletto, interview with the author, Cittadellarte–Fondazione Pistoletto, July 16, 2018. (Original Italian: "Ma effettivamente, quello che era chiaro in quel momento, era questa tensione tra astrazione e figurazione. C'era chi considerava che se era un'opera astratta era moderna, se era raffigurativa non era moderna. E c'era chi non sopportava l'astrazione e chi non sopportava la figurazione.")
32. Additional bibliography supports this point, including major exhibitions and exhibition catalogs (Alberto Burri at the Guggenheim, New York, 2016; Lucio Fontana at the Pompidou, 1987, the Musée d'Art Moderne de la Ville, Paris, in 2014, and the Met Breuer, 2019; Piero Manzoni at the Museu de Arte Moderna in Rio de Janeiro, 2015), catalogues raisonnés (Bruno Corà for Burri, 2016; Freddy Battino and Luca Palazzoli for Manzoni, 1991; Enrico Crispolti for Fontana's sculpture, 2006; Luca Massimo Barbero for Fontana's works on paper, 2014), edited volumes (Barbero on Manzoni and Azimut, 2014), peer-reviewed articles by Italianists (Katie Larson on Burri, 2019 and 2022; Jaleh Mansoor on Manzoni, 2008) and non-Italianists (Yve-Alain Bois on Fontana, 1989; Jaimey Hamilton on Burri, 2008), and their obligatory presence in modern and contemporary art survey texts.
33. See Achille Bonito Oliva, "La Trans-avanguardia italiana," *Flash Art,* no. 92–93 (October–November 1979): 17–20; Benjamin H. D. Buchloh, "Figures of Authority, Ciphers of Regression: Notes on the Return of Representation in European Painting," *October,* no. 16 (Spring 1981): 39–68.
34. Robert Slifkin, "Figuration circa 1970," in *Out of Time: Philip Guston and the Refiguration of Postwar American Art* (Berkeley: University of California Press, 2013), 6.
35. Slifkin, "Figuration circa 1970," 5.
36. Pistoletto noted this connection in his most recent text, *La formula della creazione* (2022), translated into English by Huw Evans in 2023: a book on his biography and work, the history of art, science, and philosophy, and his vision for art as a platform for social transformation and for the "genesi dell'Universo," genesis of the Universe, using his term for the "genesis of a new society." See Pistoletto, *La formula della creazione* (Biella: Cittadellarte Edizioni, 2022), 29.
37. Pistoletto, "Michelangelo on Pistoletto: Michelangelo Pistoletto in Conversation with Andrea Bellini," in *Facing Pistoletto,* ed. Andrea Bellini, trans. Barbara McGilvray and Simon Turner (Zurich: JRP Ringier, 2009), 17. The original Italian of Pistoletto's interview with Bellini can be found on pages 212–25. I refer to the translation for all subsequent references, unless otherwise noted.
38. For a dense but brief discussion of New Left actors and "anti-authoritarian and anti-dogmatic" factions in relation to culture in the context of Italy's pre-1968 left, see Guidali, "Cultural and Political Commitment," 863, 865.
39. Anthony L. Cardoza and Geoffrey W. Symcox, *A History of Turin* (Turin: Einaudi, 2006), 248.
40. The Piazza Statuto riots were incited by protracted conflicts between Italy's metalworkers' trade unions and management at Turin's Fiat, Michelin, and Lancia factories regarding poor work conditions and contract negotiations. See Stefano Musso, *Storia del lavoro in Italia: Dall'Unità a oggi* (Venice: Marsilio, 2002), 225–26; Marco Scavino, "Sviluppo economico e culture del conflitto: Grande industria e sindacati negli anni del boom economico," in *La città e lo sviluppo: Crescita e disordine a Torino, 1945–1970,* ed. Fabio Levi and Bruno Maida (Milan: Franco Angeli, 2002), 474–78; Dario Lanzardo, *La rivolta di piazza Statuto: Torino, luglio 1962* (Milan: Feltrinelli, 1979); and Paul Ginsborg, *A History of Contemporary Italy: 1945–1988,* 2nd exp. ed. (New York: St. Martin's, 2003), 250–53.

41. In the mid-1960s, literary critic and workerist Alberto Asor Rosa criticized the fallacy of "revolutionary culture." The only means of resistance in capitalist culture was for workers to assert the particularity of their contradictory position to it. See Alberto Asor Rosa, "La fine della battaglia della cultura," *Classe operaia* 1, no. 2 (1964): 17–19. For a summary of this position within leftist cultural politics of mid-1960s Italy, see Guidali, "Culture and Political Commitment," 869.
42. Although the official name of the Gruppo d'Arte "l'Arlecchino" included quotation marks, they are omitted hereafter for improved readability.
43. Jean-François Lyotard, *Discours, figure* (Paris: Klincksieck, 1971), 13.
44. Jean-François Lyotard, *Discourse, Figure,* trans. Antony Hudek and Mary Lydon (Minneapolis: University of Minnesota, 2011), at 7. Therein see also esp. "The Bias of the Figural" (3–19); "Dialectics, Index, Form" (23–50); "The Line and the Letter" (205–32); and "Desire in Discourse" (277–326).
45. See Gilles Deleuze, *Francis Bacon: The Logic of Sensation* (1981), trans. Daniel W. Smith (London: Continuum, 2003), 1.
46. Deleuze, *Francis Bacon.*
47. Writing on late medieval and early modern Europe, for example, Alexander Nagel and Christopher S. Wood have proposed a "figural" art history, in which the figural is engaged as a historical subject of study and art historical method. Nagel and Wood argue that figuration was often used to create imagistic forms (visual and plastic) that were both figurative (representational) as well as figural (bodily). Icons and religious statuary, for example, were figures that *embodied* their own signifieds. This tendency for images of the body to be perceived as embodiments of their own referents gave them reflexivity and a *figural* function that superseded their figurative one. Nagel and Wood's key contribution is that the condition of *figurality*—of being imagistic or bodily—means that images in the history of art can constellate alternative, nonchronological models of history and time for the viewer. See Alexander Nagel and Christopher S. Wood, "Interventions: Toward a New Model of Renaissance Anachronism," *Art Bulletin* 87, no. 3 (2005): 406, 408–9; and Alexander Nagel and Christopher S. Wood, *Anachronic Renaissance* (Princeton, NJ: Princeton University Press, 2020), 29–34.
48. See Erich Auerbach, "Figura" (1944), trans. Ralph Mannheim, in *Scenes from the Drama of European Literature* (Minneapolis: University of Minnesota Press, 1984), 11–76; and Erich Auerbach, *Mimesis: The Representation of Reality in Western Literature* (1946), trans. Willard R. Trask, 50th anniversary ed. (Princeton, NJ: Princeton University Press, 2003), 73, 156–57, 195–96.
49. Auerbach, *Mimesis,* 73.
50. See Mark Godfrey, *Alighiero e Boetti* (New Haven: Yale University Press, 2011); and Elizabeth Mangini, *Seeing through Closed Eyelids: Giuseppe Penone and the Nature of Sculpture* (Toronto: University of Toronto Press, 2021).
51. Pistoletto, *Cento mostre nel mese d'ottobre* (Turin: Galleria Giorgio Persano, 1976), n.p. [no. 12].
52. On Arte Povera actions as "intentionally weak" in contrast to the "heroic terms" of performance in the United States, see Mangini, *Seeing through Closed Eyelids,* 22.
53. Herbert Marcuse, *An Essay on Liberation* (Boston: Beacon, 1969), 26.
54. See Kristin Ross, *May '68 and Its Afterlives* (Chicago: University of Chicago Press, 2002); and James Meyer, *The Art of Return: The Sixties and Contemporary Culture* (Chicago: University of Chicago Press, 2019).
55. Marshall McLuhan, *Understanding Media: The Extensions of Man* (London: McGraw-Hill, 1964), 6–7.
56. Celant, "Arte Povera," in *Arte Povera,* n.p. Celant revisited these ideas in 2011 in his edited volume *Arte Povera,* which asked scholars to "revisit" the movement on occasion of Italy's 150th anniversary of national unification.
57. See *Fuoco Immagine Acqua Terra* (Fire Image Water Earth), Galleria L'Attico (Rome: June 1967).
58. Umberto Eco, *Opera aperta: Forma e indeterminazione nelle poetiche contemporanee* (Milan: Bompiani, 1962); Roland Barthes, "The Death of the Author" (1968), in *Image-Music-Text,* ed. and trans. Stephen Heath (London: Fontana, 1977), 142–48.
59. In 1943, Pistoletto and his family moved to his paternal grandmother's farm in the Susa Valley surrounding Turin, following Allied bombings and increased military attacks on the city during German occupation. When he was nine years old, a bomb entered the family home in Turin; although it did not go off, the moment remains with him, even now, eighty years later. He also recalls seeing a *partigiano,* a member of Italy's antifascist resistance, murder a German soldier in the streets, and witnessing the retaliation of German forces. See Michelangelo Pistoletto and Alain Elkann, *La voce di Pistoletto* (Milan: Bompiani, 2013), 16–17.
60. Pistoletto, interview with the author, Cittadellarte–Fondazione Pistoletto, October 25, 2021.
61. Pistoletto and Elkann, *La voce di Pistoletto,* 23, 59–60.
62. See Pistoletto's latest text, *La formula della creazione* (Biella: Edizioni Cittadellarte, 2022).

CHAPTER 1. FORMATIVE FIGURES

1. The Galatea was established in 1957 by Mario Tazzoli, a banker and art dealer who contracted Pistoletto into his stable in 1958. Pistoletto showed under his full family name (Olivero Pistoletto) until 1962, at which point he changed to "Pistoletto."
2. At the Galatea, Pistoletto showed seventeen paintings and three works on paper. Luigi Carluccio, *Pistoletto* (Turin: Galleria Galatea, 1960), n.p., catalog published in conjunction with the exhibition of the same title, held March 30–April 15, 1960. Carluccio had previously directed the Galleria La Bussola, also in Turin, and was the principal art critic for the Turin-based daily newspaper *La Gazzetta del Popolo.* He had introduced Mario Tazzoli to Pistoletto following the young artist's receipt in 1958 of the prestigious Milan-based Premio San Fedele for young artists. On Carluccio and the Premio, see Michelangelo Pistoletto and Alain Elkann, *La voce di Pistoletto* (Milan: Bompiani, 2013), 66.
3. An arts writer since the 1930s, curator, and champion of neonaturalism and figuration in exhibitions in Piedmont and beyond, Carluccio also participated in broader national exhibitions that had led him to encounter Pistoletto's work. See, e.g., *Premio Repubblica di San Marino: Biennale per la pittura* (Turin: Ente Governativo per il Turismo, lo Sport e lo Spettacolo, 1959), which Carluccio juried. Carluccio also co-organized the six editions of *Pittori d'Oggi.*
4. Carluccio, *Pistoletto,* n.p.
5. This is true both generally and specifically. Aerial artists were common scenes in circuses of the period, newsreel footage of which was transmitted in Italian cinemas and increasingly on television, as the medium was popularized in the 1950s.
6. RAI (Radio Audizioni Italiane), e.g., changed its name to include television in 1954; it added a second channel in 1961. Turin received its first private television station in the same month as Pistoletto's solo debut. "Torino—la prima stazione televisiva privata," *SETTIMANALE CIAC / SC586* (March 3, 1960), 00:00:56, b/w, sound, codice filmato KB058606, Archivio Luce, https://patrimonio.archivioluce.com/.
7. See, e.g., the exhibition *Italy at Work: Her Renaissance in Design Today* (1950–53), which traveled from the Brooklyn Museum to eleven

other US institutions. See Antje Gamble, *Cold War American Exhibitions of Italian Art and Design* (Abingdon, UK: Routledge, 2023); and Kate Devine, "Selling Italy: Craft and Italianness in Italy at Work: Her Renaissance in Design Today (1950–53)," *Journal of Modern Craft* 15, no. 3 (2022): 259–73.

8. Guy Debord, *The Society of the Spectacle* (1967), trans. Donald Nicholson-Smith (Cambridge, MA: MIT Press, 1994), 12. On spectacle and commodities, see Debord, *Society of the Spectacle,* 42.
9. In semiotics, an index is a type of sign that points to that which it refers through connection; an index might be a physical trace. (The adage "where there's smoke, there's fire" works because we know that smoke is an index for fire.) The relation is not one of analogy or resemblance but a connection that is also recognized, through the senses or memory, by the person who sees it as such. Theories of photography have long commented on the photograph as a physical trace of the photographic subject; it is an image trace, a sign of "that-has-been." See Charles Sanders Peirce, *Philosophical Writings of Peirce,* ed. Justus Buchler (New York: Dover, 1955), 104, 107; and Roland Barthes, *Camera Lucida: Reflections on Photography,* trans. Richard Howard (New York: Hill and Wang, 1981), 77.
10. See Barthes, *Camera Lucida,* 77.
11. The precondition of absence for the sign comes from structuralist semiotics. See Ferdinand de Saussure, *Course in General Linguistics,* trans. Wade Baskin (New York: McGraw-Hill, 1959). See also Rosalind Krauss, "In the Name of Picasso," *October* 16 (Spring 1981): 15–16.
12. Simonetta Falasca-Zamponi, *Fascist Spectacle: The Aesthetics of Power* (Berkeley: University of California Press, 1997), 13.
13. Falasca-Zamponi, *Fascist Spectacle,* 13.
14. This is not to say that the Novecento was uniformly fascist or that the tendency toward neoclassicism in the interwar period should be understood as a wholesale investment in the regime. Indeed, the Novecento has since been read as a stabilizing response to the historical avant-gardes and revolutionary movements that preceded it. See Emily Braun, *Mario Sironi and Italian Modernism* (Cambridge: Cambridge University Press, 2000), 108.
15. This reading of Felice Casorati aligns with Francesco Poli's assessment of postwar figurative art in Turin, in which Casorati is representative of Italy's "old" artistic guard. See Francesco Poli, "Le arti figurative," in *Storia di Torino,* vol. 9, *Gli anni della Repubblica,* ed. Nicola Tranfaglia (Turin: Giulio Einaudi, 1999), 481–531. For a primary source from the postwar period that underscores the importance of Casorati's presence in Turin, see "Artisti nuovi dopo l'anno 1920," in *50 anni d'arte a Torino,* ed. Adalberto Campagnoli (Turin: Fratelli Pozzo, 1959), n.p. Casorati, Gigi Chessa, and Francesco Menzio of the Gruppo di Sei all had young artist sons who were contemporaries of Pistoletto's in 1950s and 1960s Turin. Especially noteworthy is Paolo Menzio, with whom Pistoletto collaborated on an experimental film, *Frankenstein prossimamente* (Frankenstein: Coming Soon), now lost, for Pistoletto's solo exhibition of 1968 at the Galleria l'Attico, Rome.
16. He was, for example, peers with the prominent socialist political theorist and activist Piero Gobetti. On Casorati and Piero Gobetti, see Fernando Mazzocca, "Arti e vita: Miti e protagonisti del Novecento," in *Novecento: Arte e vita in Italia tra le due guerre,* ed. Fernando Mazzocca (Milan: Silvana, 2013), 37. See also Piero Gobetti, "Un artista moderno: Felice Casorati," *L'Ordine Nuovo,* June 19, 1921, cited in Mazzocca, "Arti e vita," 37.
17. Tristan Sauvage's *Pittura italiana del dopoguerra (1945–1957)* (Milan: Schwarz, 1957) remains a key survey text on postwar Italian art that also sheds light on postwar perspectives of early twentieth-century and interwar Italian art. Sauvage devoted a large portion of his discussion of abstraction and concrete art in Turin from 1920 through the 1950s to Casorati and the *scuola casoratiana,* indicating the historical importance Casorati had accrued within Italian art history before his death in 1964. See Tristan Sauvage, "Astrattisti e concretisti a Torino," in *Pittura italiana del dopoguerra,* 123–32, esp. 123–28. For a review of the characteristics and development of the Novecento in relation to Italian modernism, see Emily Braun, "Sironi and the Novecento," in *Mario Sironi,* 90–112, esp. 95–105. Guido Armellini, *Le immagini del fascismo nelle arti figurative* (Milan: Gruppo Editoriale Fabbri, 1980), 130. See also Silvia Regonelli, "Giovinezza, Giovinezza . . . Il culto del corpo e l'ideologia dello sport," in Mazzocca, *Novecento,* 294.
18. Casorati influenced artists both before and after World War II. In the postwar years, at the Accademia Albertina di Belle Arti, Turin's school of fine arts, he trained many Italian artists of the younger postwar generation from 1952 to his death in 1963. For a survey of Casorati's work from this period, see Francesco Poli with Giorgina Bertolini, eds., *Felice Casorati: Dagli anni venti agli anni quaranta* (Milan: Electa, 1996).
19. For a study of Pistoletto in relation to Casorati as connected by antifascist resistance and "returns" to the figure, see Romy Golan, "Magic Realism Redux: Pistoletto and Felice Casorati," in *Flashback, Eclipse: The Political Imaginary of Italian Art in the 1960s* (Princeton, NJ: Princeton University Press, 2021), 89–103, esp. 93, 103.
20. See Angelo Dragone et al., *Arte nuova: Esposizione internazionale di pittura e scultura; Ikebana di Sofu Teshigahara* (Turin: Circolo degli artisti, 1959), catalog published in conjunction with the exhibition of the same title, held May 5–June 15, 1959. See also Ming Tiampo, "Turin, 1959," in *Gutai: Decentering Modernism* (Chicago: University of Chicago Press, 2011), 113–18.
21. The exhibition was held at Turin's Artists' Circle club in collaboration with the Figurative Arts Association.
22. The quotation about the congress comes from the event program and from Asger Jorn's opening speech there. Pistoletto wrote about Gallizio's importance for Italian art on Gallizio's death. Pistoletto was interested in the avant-garde circle in Alba as early as 1956, when he participated in a collective performance at Gallizio's studio. Pistoletto, in response to the author in the Q&A session for "Session Two: Pistoletto and Arte Povera," *Three Conversations with Michelangelo Pistoletto, Germano Celant, and Carlos Basualdo* (Philadelphia: Philadelphia Museum of Art, October 31, 2010), program associated with the exhibition of the same title. The Gallizio Archives are unaware of any documentation of Pistoletto's participation.
23. For the reframing of futurism, see James Thrall Soby and Alfred H. Barr Jr., "Early Futurism," in *Twentieth-Century Italian Art* (New York: Museum of Modern Art, 1949), 7–16. Calling for new attention to Italy after fascism, the exhibition focused on the futurism of Boccioni rather than that of Marinetti.
24. See Keala Jewell, *The Art of Enigma: The de Chirico Brothers and the Politics of Modernism* (University Park: Pennsylvania State University Press, 2004). The exhibition at MoMA in 1949 referenced in the previous note, for example, explicitly named the "vital contributions" of futurism and metaphysical painting "to the international mainstream of art in our time" as the reason for renewed study of these movements. See Thrall Soby and Barr, *Twentieth-Century Italian Art,* 5.
25. Adrian R. Duran, *Painting, Politics, and the New Front of Cold War Italy* (Farnham, UK: Ashgate, 2014), 103.
26. Corrente developed around an antifascist youth journal on politics and culture, *Vita Giovanile* (Youth Life, est. 1938). See Bette L. Talvacchia, "Politics Considered as a Category of Culture: The Anti-Fascist *Corrente* Group," *Art History* 8, no. 3 (1985): 337, 340, 350–51;

and Adrian R. Duran, "*Corrente,* Italian Art under Fascism and the Resistance," in *Painting, Politics, and the New Front of Cold War Italy,* 14–15.

27. Marcia E. Vetrocq, "Painting and Beyond: Recovery and Regeneration, 1943–1952," in *The Italian Metamorphosis, 1943–1968,* ed. Germano Celant (New York: Guggenheim Museum, 1994), 21, 23. See Ennio Morlotti and Emilio Vedova, "Manifesto del realismo di pittori e scultori," better known as *Oltre Guernica,* Milan, February 1946, reprinted in Sauvage, *Pittura italiana del dopoguerra,* 232–33.
28. Morlotti and Vedova, "Manifesto del realismo," n.p. This idea was echoed by the Nuova Secessione Artistica Italiana (New Italian Artistic Secession) later that year in their manifesto on realism. See Renato Birolli, *Manifesto di Fondazione della "Nuova Secessione Artistica Italiana,"* Venice, October 1, 1946, reprinted in Sauvage, *Pittura italiana del dopoguerra,* 234.
29. Birolli, Manifesto, n.p. See also Duran, *Painting, Politics, and the New Front of Cold War Italy,* 49.
30. This date corresponds to Bèrgomi's exhibition of work by Antonio Bueno, Silvio Loffredo, and Alberto Moretti, after which the movement was named. See Mario Bèrgomi, *La nuova figurazione: Mostra internazionale di pittura sotto gli auspici del Comune di Firenze* (Florence: La Strozzina, 1963).
31. Bèrgomi, "La nuova figurazione," introduction to *La Nuova figurazione,* n.p.
32. Bèrgomi, "La nuova figurazione," n.p.
33. On the relation between Nuova Figurazione and the Informale, see Bèrgomi, "La nuova figurazione," n.p. Broader coeval theorizations of new figuration with exhibitions that were international in scope include *New Images of Man* (1959), curated by Peter Selz. Selz defined the "new images of man" in contemporary art as a "human protest" against the "transformed, distorted, disrupted," and eventually absent figure in recent art. Peter Selz, "Introduction," in *New Images of Man* (New York: Museum of Modern Art, 1959), 11–12.
34. *Corriere dei Piccoli,* the comics supplement to *Corriere della Sera,* was one reference for the artist.
35. In one of our later interviews (October 25, 2021), Pistoletto underscored the importance of arte nucleare to the context of his early work.
36. For Pistoletto's discussion of the importance of Notizie, the Galleria Civica d'Arte Moderna (GAM), and the Galatea's role in the internationalization of Turin's art scene, see Pistoletto, "Michelangelo on Pistoletto: Michelangelo Pistoletto in Conversation with Andrea Bellini," in *Facing Pistoletto,* ed. Andrea Bellini, trans. Barbara McGilvray and Simon Turner (Zurich: JRP Ringier, 2009), 17.
37. For this timeline on Michel Tapié's collaboration with Luciano Pistoi, see Bruno Corà, *Michelangelo Pistoletto: Lo spazio della riflessione nell'arte* (Ravenna: Essegi, 1986), 10.
38. Francis Bacon would continue to receive a platform in Turin with Luigi Carluccio's assistance, as in his solo exhibition (1962) at the city's modern and contemporary art museum. See Luigi Carluccio, *Francis Bacon* (Torino: Galleria Galatea, 1958); and *Bacon* (Torino: Galleria civica d'arte moderna, 1962). See also group shows *Selezione I* (Turin: Galleria Galatea, 1960), *Selezione 2* (Turin: Galleria Galatea, 1960–61), and *Selezione 4* (Turin: Galleria Galatea, 1962). For Bacon at Notizie, see *Opere scelte di Tobey, Fautrier, Hartung, Riopelle, Bacon, Fontana, Appel, Sam Francis, Burri, Tal Coat, Hultberg, Jorn, Bram van Velde, Salles* (Turin: Notizie, 1961).
39. Francis Bacon's singular figures were themselves based on the British artist's study of Eadweard Muybridge's movement photographs—images that Pistoletto later excerpted for one of his mirror paintings. For information on Muybridge and Bacon, see *Bacon,* 68.
40. See Giorgio Vasari, *Le vite degli più eccellenti pittori, scultori e architettori,* enlarged ed. (Florence: Giunti, 1568), 566. See also Erwin Panofsky, *Renaissance and Renascences in Western Art* (1960) (reprint, New York: Routledge, 2018), 35.
41. Pistoletto, "Per Armando Testa," in *Armando Testa: Before Punt e Mes* (Pistoia: Gli ori, 2019), 6, English translation at 7.
42. Pistoletto set up his *studio pubblicità* following his training with Testa. He worked from the family home on Lungo Po Cadorna and from a studio on Via Andrea Doria and Via Pomba, addresses found on surviving business labels.
43. On the synesthetic experience with icons in Byzantium, see Bissera V. Pentcheva, "The Performative Icon," *Art Bulletin* 8, no. 4 (2006): 631–55.
44. Luigi Carluccio, untitled catalog text, in *Pistoletto* (Turin: Galleria Galatea, 1960), n.p. [1].
45. Carluccio, *Pistoletto* (1960), n.p. [1].
46. Carluccio, *Pistoletto* (1960), n.p. [2].
47. Marziano Bernardi, "Ritorna l'immagine umana," *La Stampa,* March 31, 1960.
48. Bernardi, "Ritorna l'immagine umana."
49. Germano Celant, "Intervista a Pistoletto," in *Pistoletto,* ed. Germano Celant and Ida Gianelli (Milan: Electa, 1984), 23. On "impasse," see Germano Celant and Pistoletto, "Continuum: Painting as Event," in *Pistoletto: Division and Multiplication of the Mirror,* ed. Germano Celant and Ida Gianelli (New York: Institute for Contemporary Art, P.S. 1 Museum, 1988), 33. He underscored his desire to rid himself of the drama in order to "gain his freedom" (*acquistare la mia libertà*) in an interview with me, Casa Pistoletto, November 6, 2017.
50. Pistoletto, "Michelangelo on Pistoletto," 18.
51. Some of the following discussion was first published in Bick, "Where There's Everything: Pistoletto, the Gruppo d'Arte 'l'Arlecchino,' and Localist Internationalism in *Presenze,*" *Word and Image* 38, no. 2 (2022): 132–64.
52. The first issue (May–June 1957) was published as *Presenze: Foglio del Gruppo d'Arte "L'Arlecchino."* After two issues, the journal became a bimonthly periodical entitled *Presenze: Bimestrale d'Arte e Cultura* (nos. 3–4, nos. 5–6, nos. 7–10). The final issue (July–August 1960) was published as a "new series" (vol. 3, no. 1). Six printed issues were published; they included a double, triple, and quadruple issue, for eleven conceptualized issues in total. Never longer than thirteen pages, issues were typically eight pages in length.
53. The artist destroyed the two works shortly after their reproduction in *Presenze.* Pistoletto, interview with the author, July 16, 2018. Pistoletto, "Astrattismo," *Presenze,* nos. 3–4 (December 1957–January 1958), n.p. Farano mentions the exploration of religious architecture and figures in his chronologies for the PMA/MAXXI catalogs. See Farano, "Chronology of Michelangelo Pistoletto, 1956–74," 352; and "Michelangelo Pistoletto, 1956–1974," 368.
54. Pistoletto, interview with the author, July 16, 2018.
55. Pistoletto's then wife, Marzia Olivero Pistoletto (née Calleri), also contributed texts to the review for the duration of the pair's activity with the group, from its inception in May 1957 through issue of September 1958. Work by Pistoletto and/or Calleri was included in the first four of the review's six publications. Whether they chose not to contribute to the last two issues, had departed the group, or were excluded is unclear; given the pair's consistent participation in the preceding issues, however, changes in the review's leadership and editorial direction after the fourth issue suggest that Pistoletto and Calleri likely moved on between September and October 1958.
56. Olivero-Pistoletto, "Astrattismo," *Presenze* 1, nos. 3–4 (December 1957–January 1958): n.p.
57. Olivero-Pistoletto, "Astrattismo," n.p.

58. John Picchione, *The New Avant-Garde in Italy: Theoretical Debate and Poetic Practices* (Toronto: University of Toronto Press, 2004).
59. Indeed, primary scholarship on Pistoletto's work of the mid-1960s would describe his interest in human relationships as shared terrain with one of the Novissimi, as I note in chapter 3. See Maurizio Fagiolo dell'Arco, *Rapporto 60: Le arti oggi in Italia* (Rome: Bulzoni, 1966), 211.
60. See Pistoletto, "I plexiglass," September 1964, text published in association with the artist's exhibition of the same title at the Galleria Gian Enzo Sperone in Turin.
61. See Matteo D'Ambrosio, "Documento Sud (1959–1961), rivista dell'avanguardia europea," *Forum Italicum* 52, no. 2 (2018): 430–45, at 431; Mark Nicholls and Anthony White, "*Il Gesto:* Global Art and Italian Gesture Painting in the 1950s," *Humanities Research* 19, no. 2 (2013): 81–97; Luca Massimo Barbero, "Azimut/h: Continuity and Newness," in *Azimut/h: Continuity and Newness,* ed. Barbero (Venice: Marsilio, 2015), 18–41; Silvia Bottinelli, *«seleArte» (1952–1966), una finestra sul mondo: Ragghianti, Olivetti e la divulgazione dell'arte internazionale all'indomani del Fascismo* (Lucca: Edizioni Fondazione Ragghianti Studi sull'arte, and Maria Pacini Fazzi, 2010); Jaleh Mansoor, "Lucio Fontana and the Politics of the Gesture," in *Marshall Plan Modernism: Italian Postwar Abstraction and the Beginnings of Autonomia* (Durham, NC: Duke University Press, 2016), 74–76. This emphasis parallels the interest in broader scholarship in art history and literary studies on internationalism in artist publications and literary magazines in wider historical and geographical contexts. My thoughts on internationalism in postwar Italy as a historiographic problem are also informed by the expansion of global art history in studies of art of the 1960s. See Reiko Tomii, *Radicalism in the Wilderness: International Contemporaneity and 1960s Art in Japan* (Cambridge, MA: MIT Press, 2016); and Armin Medosch, *New Tendencies: Art at the Threshold of the Information Revolution (1961–1978)* (Cambridge, MA: MIT Press, 2016). See, e.g., Ming Tiampo, "Lines of Flight: The Gutai Journal," chap. 3 in *Gutai,* esp. section 1, "Yoshihara's Postwar Internationalism and the *Gutai* Journal"; Eric White, *Transatlantic Avant-Gardes: Little Magazines and Localist Modernism* (Edinburgh: Edinburgh University Press, 2013); and Lori Cole, *Surveying the Avant-Garde: Questions on Modernism, Art, and the Americas in Transatlantic Magazines* (University Park: Penn State University Press, 2018).
62. Elisabetta Mondello, *Gli anni delle riviste: Le riviste letterarie dal 1945 agli anni ottanta* (Lecce: Milella, 1985), 7; Luisa Perlo, "Sperimentare al plurale: Le esperienze e le ricerche dei gruppi," in *Torino Sperimentale: Una storia della cronaca: Il sistema delle arti come avanguardia,* ed. Luca Massimo Barbero (Turin: Umberto Allemandi and Regione Piemonte, 2010), 310–35. Talvacchia, "Politics Considered," 336–55, at 337–40, 350–51. See also Duran, *Painting, Politics, and the New Front of Cold War Italy,* 11–15.
63. See, e.g., *Il Contemporaneo* (The Contemporary, est. 1924) and *Cosmopolis: Arti, Lettere, Spettacoli* (Cosmopolis: Arts, Letters, Plays; est. 1926), which appeared in the early years of the *ventennio* and situated Turin as a cosmopolitan center. See the digital database for periodicals from Piemonte and Valle d'Aosta (Banca dati periodici Piemonte e Valle d'Aosta): http://periodicipiemonte.it. See, e.g., *Fucine* (a monthly on art criticism and set design; est. 1947), whose title literally means "hotbeds" from the phrase "fucina di idee" or "hotbed of ideas"; the poetry journal *Momenti* (Moments; 1951–54); *La Città dell'Uomo: Organo del Movimento Umanistico Rinascimentale Italico* (The City of Man: Agency of the Humanist Movement for Italian Renewal; est. 1953); Gino Simonetti's *Critica Anticritica: Microrivista Polemica delle Arti Figurative (Critique Countercritique: Polemical Microjournal on the Figurative Arts;* est. 1956); and the literary journal *Il Menabò* (1959–67), published by Einaudi and directed by Italo Calvino and Elio Vittorini. Journal details retrieved from Banca dati periodici Piemonte e Valle d'Aosta. On *Il Menabò,* see Mondello, *Gli anni delle riviste,* 137.
64. See Alberto Cesare Ambesi and Guido Raccone, untitled editorial statement, *Presenze* 1, no. 1 (May–June 1957): n.p.; and Ambesi and Raccone, "Una nuova dimensione," *Presenze* 3, no. 1 (July–August 1960): n.p.
65. Silvia Bottinelli has discussed a related engagement of the international in her book-length study on the journal *«seleArte»* (1952–66). The journal looked to certain aspects of contemporary art and culture in countries outside of Italy, she argues, not as signs of nationalism (in their respective contexts) but as "reference points in the international landscape," fashioning contemporary identity in part on shared reactions to the experience of war. See Bottinelli, *«seleArte» (1952–1966), una finestra sul mondo,* chap. 4, esp. quotation at 121. Translation mine.
66. The image was *Uomo seduto* (Seated Man, 1958), a painting on canvas shown at the Premio San Fedele, also in 1958, now in a private collection. For reproductions of *Presenze*'s pages and in-depth discussion of these correspondences, see Bick, "Where There's Everything," 132–64.
67. On the "tabular image" and spaces of recombination in post–World War II art, see Hal Foster, *The First Pop Age: Painting and Subjectivity in the Art of Hamilton, Lichtenstein, Warhol, Richter, and Ruscha* (Princeton, NJ: Princeton University Press, 2014); and Leo Steinberg, "Other Criteria," 55–91.
68. Whether the group dropped the name entirely from usage is unclear. Pistoletto continues to refer to the group today as "Arlecchino."
69. Susanna Arangio, "La fortuna dell'iconografia di Pulcinella all'inizio degli anni Venti del Novecento: Pablo Picasso e Gino Severini," *Babel* 35 (2017): 195–223.
70. See, e.g., the text for Arlecchino in the commedia dell'arte exhibition at the Museo Nazionale delle Arti Popolari e Tradizioni in Rome.
71. See Sharon Hecker, "'Servant of Two Masters': Lucio Fontana's Sculptures in Milan's Cinema Arlecchino," *Oxford Art Journal* 35, no. 3 (2012): 346–47. At the time of the group's activity, Arlecchino was also emerging as a popular topic within international scholarship on commedia dell'arte. See, e.g., Fausto Nicolini, *Vita di Arlecchino* (Milan: R. Ricciardi, 1958); Allardyce Nicoll, *The World of Harlequin: A Critical Study of the Commedia dell'Arte* (Cambridge: Cambridge University Press, 1963); and Michele Bottini, "You Must Have Heard of Harlequin . . . ," trans. Samuel Angus McGehee and Michael J. Grady, in *The Routledge Companion to Commedia dell'Arte,* ed. Judith Chaffee and Olly Crick (London: Routledge, 2015), 56.
72. See Ambesi and Raccone, untitled editorial statement, *Presenze* 1, no. 1 (May–June 1957), n.p.
73. Pistoletto, interview with the author, July 16, 2018. (Original Italian: "una piccola rivista, un piccolo giornale di fatto creato proprio per condensare le nostre voci, per connettere le nostre voci.")
74. Pistoletto, interview with the author, July 16, 2018. (Original Italian: "L'abbiamo chiamato 'l'Arlecchino' proprio perché sapevamo che non c'era nessuna relazione pratica all'Arlecchino—vuol dire tutti i colori. Facciamo una cosa dove c'è tutto, *tutto* è possibile, *tutti* possono dire qualcosa. Questa cosa era basata sull'incontro, attraverso anche differenti opinioni, differenti provenienze, perché poi, a quell'età lì, avevamo ciascuno già delle provenienze diverse." Emphasis in original.)
75. Indeed, Pistoletto later related the creative can-do attitude of the Harlequin Art Group to the formation of the now canonical

exhibition *Arte abitabile* (Inhabitable Art), a key precedent for Arte Povera, held at the Galleria Gian Enzo Sperone in 1965. Pistoletto, interview with the author, July 16, 2018.

76. Local fascination with the faraway was exemplified in late 1950s Turin, for example, by the exhibition of Italian photographer Domenico Riccardo Peretti Griva's photographs *di tutto il mondo*—"of the whole world"—in 1959. See Carluccio, "Fotografie di tutto il mondo nella mostra di Peretti Griva," *La Gazzetta del Popolo*, April 27, 1959.
77. In Turin, we can also add Savoyard expeditions for economic and archaeological research (forming the basis of the city's extensive Egyptian Museum). See Angela Scattolin Morecroft, "The Vitaliano Donati Collection at the Turin Egyptian Museum," *Journal of Egyptian Archaeology* 92, no. 1 (2006): 278–82.
78. Pistoletto has written about Armando Testa's work as icons. See Pistoletto, "Per Armando Testa," 6.
79. Pistoletto's father was also involved in graphic design, in advertising for Ermenegildo Zegna. He long served as a portraitist and artist for the Zegna family, painting large-scale murals for the Zegna home in Trivero. See Pistoletto and Elkann, *La voce di Pistoletto*, 14–15. For images of Facis ads in situ, which show the extent of advertising that papered Turin's piazzas, see *La Settimana Incom*, "Italia: Torino si prepara alla celebrazione del Centenario dell'Unità d'Italia," July 7, 1960, 00:01:12, b/w, sound, I194303, Archivio Luce.
80. These comments draw inspiration from T. J. Clark, *The Painting of Modern Life: Paris in the Art of Manet and His Followers*, rev. ed. (Princeton, NJ: Princeton University Press, 1984).
81. I thank Erika Loic for her suggestion to consider fictive marbles here.
82. Robert Mills, "Back to Front: Abstraction and Figuration in Bosch's *Visions of the Hereafter*," in *Abstraction in Medieval Art: Beyond the Ornament*, ed. Elina Gertsman (Amsterdam: Amsterdam University Press, 2021), 120.
83. Herbert L. Kessler, *Seeing Medieval Art* (Peterborough, ON: Broadview, 2004), 34.
84. See, e.g., *Uomo seduto* (Seated Man, 1958), *Uomo che dorme* (Sleeping Man, 1958), the somnolent *Uomo coricato* (Reclining Man, 1960, drawing), *Uomo sul divano* (Man on Sofa, 1960, drawing), and the sedentary *Uomo sul sofà* (Man on Sofa, 1958).
85. See, e.g., *Figura di professionista* (1958), shown at the painting biennial, the Premio Repubblica di San Marino, in 1959.
86. This quotation comes from Bruno Corà's interviews with the artist in the 1980s, excerpted throughout his book. For this quotation, see Corà, *Pistoletto: Lo spazio della riflessione nell'arte*, 16.
87. Pistoletto, *The Formula of Creation*, trans. Huw Evans (Biella: Cittadellarte Edizioni, 2023), 37. The original Italian, which uses *ritagliate* ("cut out") to describe the position of icon figures on the gold ground, further underscores a connection between them and Pistoletto's later works, as in the mirror paintings.
88. Throughout his childhood, Pistoletto visited the Galleria Sabauda and the Museo Egizio with his father on Sundays. Pistoletto and Elkann, *La voce di Pistoletto*, 21; Pistoletto, *La formula della creazione*, 37.
89. Pistoletto, interview with the author, July 16, 2018.
90. Pistoletto and Mila Pistoi, "Intervista a Michelangelo Pistoletto," *Marcatrè* 4, nos. 26–29 (1966): 411. (Original Italian: "togliere il senso dell'azione e dell'espressione alle mie figure . . . scoprire uno spazio nuovo per le mie figure, non di raccontare le loro vicende.")
91. See Andreina Griseri, "Pistoletto Olivero Michelangelo," in *Disegni e parole*, ed. Luigi Carluccio, Ezio Gribaudo, and Edoardo Sanguineti (Turin: Edizioni d'arte fratelli rosso, 1963), n.p., catalog published in conjunction with the exhibition of the same title held at Galleria Il Punto, Turin, 1963.
92. Bruno Corà has aptly suggested that aspects of advertising design—editorial layouts, window displays—then practiced by the artist in his professional work may have also encouraged the artist's technical skill in image production and amplified his attention to ways of capturing the attention of a viewer. See Corà, *Pistoletto: Lo spazio della riflessione nell'arte*, 12–13.
93. For a different reading of 1950s European figurative artists' use of framing motifs, see Yves Bonnefoy, *Giacometti* (Paris: Flammarion, 1993), 393.
94. Pistoletto shared this detail regarding the still life with me in an interview, Casa Pistoletto, June 6, 2022. Dates of the contract come from the artist's chronology, by Marco Farano.
95. Jacques Derrida, "The Parergon," trans. Craig Owens, *October* 9 (Summer 1979): 3–41, esp. 18–29, at 21, 20, emphasis in original. Translated from the original essay "Parergon," in Derrida, *La verité en peinture* (Paris: Flammarion, 1978).
96. Derrida, "Parergon," 21.
97. When sold at auction, this work was identified as a self-portrait. The artist notes it was only a portrait. Communication with Marco Farano, December 6, 2023.
98. See Victor I. Stoichita, *The Self-Aware Image: An Insight into Early Modern Meta-Painting*, new, improved, and updated ed., trans. Anne-Marie Glasheen, intro. Lorenzo Pericolo (London: Harvey Miller, 2015); Lorenzo Pericolo, "What Is Metapainting? *The Self-Aware Image* Twenty Years Later," in Stoichita, *Self-Aware Image*, 11–31; and James Meyer, "The Double: Identity and Difference in Art since 1900," in *The Double: Identity and Difference in Art since 1900*, ed. Meyer (Washington, DC: National Gallery of Art, 2022), 14.
99. Importantly, this metapictorial work developed before the "metapictorial logic" described for the artist's mirror paintings by Corà. See Corà, *Pistoletto: Lo spazio della riflessione nell'arte*, 43.
100. Corà documents that Pistoletto was looking at Pollock in the early period of his work. Corà, *Pistoletto: Lo spazio della riflessione nell'arte*, 14.
101. The photomontages preceded two anomalous mirror paintings in 1963 in which the artist seems to have continued technical experimentation: *Bottiglia per terra* (Bottle on the Ground, 1963), in which the artist applied a life-size material photograph of the bottle to the stainless-steel panel, and *Tavolino con bicchieri e occhiali* (Table with Drinking Glasses and Eyeglasses, 1963), in which a transfer of a gelatin photograph was made on stainless steel.
102. Montella's "Compito in classe" was published September 16, 1962.
103. Renato Rinaldi, "Racconto con chiesa," *Presenze* 1, no. 2 (July–August 1957): n.p.
104. Rinaldi, "Le nostre speranze al cinema," *Presenze* 1, no. 3–4 (December 1957–January 1958): n.p.
105. On the "humanitarian," realist strain of Italian divisionism, see Dario Del Puppo, "Il Quarto Stato," *Science and Society* 58, no. 2 (1994): 141.
106. For this reading and more on the crowd in futurism, see Christine Poggi, "*Folla/Follia:* Futurism and the Crowd," *Critical Inquiry* 28, no. 3 (2002): 709–48.
107. Del Puppo, "Il Quarto Stato," 144.
108. Judith Butler, "Bodies in Alliance and the Politics of the Street," in *Notes toward a Performative Theory of Assembly* (Cambridge, MA: Harvard University Press, 2015), 66–98, quotation at 88.
109. Martina Caruso, *Italian Humanist Photography: From Fascism to the Cold War* (London: Routledge, 2016).
110. Michelangelo Pistoletto, "Oggetti in meno" (1966), in *Michelangelo Pistoletto* (Genoa: Galleria La Bertesca, 1966), 13–16, catalog

published in conjunction with the exhibition of the same title held December 1966–January 1967.

111. Pistoletto, "Michelangelo on Pistoletto," 21.
112. Piet Mondrian, for example, wrote of the aesthetically purified language of neo-plasticism, whose elementary forms, to the Dutch artist, reflected man's turn inward to the mind.

CHAPTER 2. FRAGMENTS OF FIGURATION

1. See Luigi Carluccio, *Michelangelo Pistoletto: Opere recenti* (Turin: Galleria Galatea, 1963), catalog published in conjunction with the exhibition of the same title, held April 27–May 14, 1963.
2. For a different reading, which finds that these photographs render the reflections fixed rather than dynamic as they are in real life, see Romy Golan's article on Pistoletto. I share Golan's interest in these images but also find that the series demonstrates the dynamism of the work. Pistoletto tended in later years to have the mirror paintings photographed from different positions in different settings, perhaps supporting the idea of the original series of photographs in the Galatea catalog. See Romy Golan, "Flashbacks and Eclipses in Italian Art in the 1960s," *Grey Room,* no. 49 (Fall 2012): 103.
3. Marziano Bernardi, "Pitture sperimentali di giovani: Quadri con l'aiuto della fotografia," *La Stampa,* May 8, 1963.
4. Luigi Carluccio, untitled essay, in *Michelangelo Pistoletto: Opere recenti* (Turin: Galleria Galatea, 1963), n.p.
5. Henry Martin, "Mirror, Mirror," *Art and Artists* 2, no. 5 (1967): 21. Also published in *Michelangelo Pistoletto* (Brussels: Palais des Beaux Arts, 1967) as "Mirror, Mirror . . . ," and in Italian as "Specchio, bello specchio," trans. Milli Graffi, *Marcatrè* 5, nos. 30–33 (July 1967): 274.
6. Pistoletto and Mila Pistoi, "Intervista a Michelangelo Pistoletto," *Marcatrè* 4, nos. 26–29 (1966): 411.
7. Ileana Sonnabend subsequently contracted other protagonists of Arte Povera, including in the mid-1960s Piero Gilardi, followed by Giovanni Anselmo, Gilberto Zorio, and Mario Merz by 1968. For contract timelines, see Corinne Criticos, "La Galerie Gian Enzo Sperone: Notes pour une historique," *Ligeia,* nos. 25–28 (1998): 152.
8. Denys Zacharopoulos, "Liberations: The Minus Works of Michelangelo Pistoletto," *Artforum* 24, no. 7 (1986): 80.
9. Laurie Schneider Adams, *The Methodologies of Art: An Introduction* (Boulder, CO: Westview, 1996), 141.
10. Revisions to painting through an opening onto its environment were already underway, if by strategies of assemblage, as in the work of Robert Rauschenberg. Douglas Crimp, "The End of Painting," *October* 16 (Spring 1981): 73. Kaja Silverman unpacks Richter's description of his practice as "photography by other means" to offer a theory of photography as analogy. See Silverman, "Photography by Other Means," in *Flesh of My Flesh* (Stanford, CA: Stanford University Press, 2009), 168–221.
11. Annette Michelson nevertheless found in Pistoletto's figures, however, a deathlike quality; their draining of color made them seem somewhat drained of life, to her, a point to which I return in chapter 3. See Michelson, "Paris Letter," *Art International* 8, no. 3 (1964): 66–70, at 70, emphasis added.
12. I translate the title as "the Plexiglasses" in English, using the generic name of the material as used by the artist. This translation retains the plurality of the Italian title, which we also find in the *Oggetti in meno* (Minus Objects) that followed. It is also faithful to the original as any series of works named after a material denoted in Italian (e.g., *i rami*) would pluralize the material to underscore the plurality of discrete works. While that is not possible with the Italian treatment of "plexiglass" as an English word, it is nevertheless implied.
13. There has been some confusion about these works in the existing literature. Celant, one of the few who have discussed the plexiglass works, stated they "were done in transparent resin, on which the artist painted or photographically reproduced an electric wire hanging on a wall or staircase." They were not painted, except for the red circle on *Tavolino,* discussed later in this chapter. See Germano Celant in *Pistoletto: Division and Multiplication of the Mirror,* ed. Celant and Ida Gianelli (New York: Institute for Contemporary Art, P.S. 1 Museum, 1988), 23.
14. Pistoletto, interview with the author, Cittadellarte–Fondazione Pistoletto, October 25, 2021.
15. Roland Barthes, "The Reality Effect" (1969), in *The Rustle of Language,* trans. Richard Howard, ed. François Wahl (Berkeley: University of California Press, 1989), 141–48, at 143.
16. See Yve-Alain Bois, "Kahnweiler's Lesson," in *Painting as Model* (Cambridge, MA: MIT Press, 1990), 75, 91.
17. Pistoletto, "I plexiglass," September 1964, n.p., text published in conjunction with the artist's exhibition of the same title at the Galleria Gian Enzo Sperone in Turin. (Original Italian: "Una 'cosa' non è arte. L'idea espressa della stessa 'cosa' può esserlo. . . . In questo momento per me la 'cosa' è la struttura dell'espressione figurativa, che ho accettato come realtà. L'invadenza fisica del quadro nell'ambiente reale, portando con sé le rappresentazioni dello specchio, mi permette di introdurmi tra gli elementi scomposti della figurazione." Underlining original.)
18. *The Large Glass* was notably circulating art journals of the period. It was reproduced in a full-page illustration in *Art International*'s December 1963–January 1964 issue, in an article on Duchamp's Pasadena retrospective. See Richard Hamilton, "Duchamp," *Art International* 7, no. 10 (1964): 27.
19. Pistoletto, interview by Germano Celant (Genoa: February 1971), in *Pistoletto,* ed. Celant (Milan: Electa, 1976), 8.
20. Artist Gualtiero Schönenberger has also compared Pistoletto's work to animation, albeit in relation to the mirror paintings. See Schönenberger, "Scheda su Pistoletto: 4," *L'Uomo e l'arte* 7 (December 1971): 39.
21. See the work of Harry Smith, who used direct-to-film techniques, and Stan Vanderbeek. I sincerely thank Maureen Furniss and Celia Mercer for discussion on these points.
22. This effect is enriched by the material changes to the photograph, likely catalyzed by chemical interactions with adhesive. The photograph (a black-and-white print) has yellowed over time and browned at its edges, as a real newspaper might.
23. The term "antimediation" has previously been offered by Henry Louis Gates Jr. as a term for the kind of signatory "trickery" and "play on language use" that seem to remove referentiality from sites and systems of meaning. Antimediation might, for example, reposition allegory as literal fact. See Henry Louis Gates Jr., "The Signifying Monkey and the Language of Signifyin(g): Rhetorical Difference and Orders of Meaning," in *The Signifying Monkey: A Theory of African-American Literary Criticism* (1988), 25th anniversary ed. (Oxford: Oxford University Press, 2014), 49–96.
24. Front-page headlines, *Stampa Sera,* July 20–21, 1964.
25. For the first and second quotations, see Leonard, "Des dollars chez les Doges," *France Observateur,* June 25, 1964, available online as "Cartoon Satirizing Robert Rauschenberg Winning First Prize at the Venice Biennale Art Exhibition, 25 June 1964," Alan R. Solomon Papers, 1930–72, Archives of American Art, Smithsonian Institution, https://www.aaa.si.edu/collections/items/detail/cartoon-satirizing-robert-rauschenberg-winning-first-prize-venice-biennale-art-exhibition-9051. For the third, see Marziano Bernardi, "Vecchia di 80 anni l'arte 'moderna' degli americani trionfanti alla Biennale," *La Stampa,* June 25, 1964.

26. Bernardi, "Vecchia di 80 anni."
27. Tullia Zevi, "The Biennale: How Evil Is Pop Art?," *New Republic,* September 19, 1964, 33, emphasis in original.
28. Giulio Carlo Argan is reported to have had this view by Giorgio De Marchis in De Marchis, "The Significance of the 1964 Venice Biennale," trans. Donatella Andalo, *Art International* 8, no. 8 (1964): 21–23. Argan's views were reported, De Marchis notes, by R. Leyde in "La Biennale," *L'Europeo,* July 19, 1964.
29. Annette Michelson, "The 1964 Venice Biennale," *Art International* 8, no. 7 (1965): 38.
30. Laurie J. Monahan, "Cultural Cartography: American Designs at the 1964 Venice Biennale," in *Reconstructing Modernism: Art in New York, Paris, and Montreal, 1945–1964,* ed. Serge Guilbaut (Cambridge, MA: MIT Press, 1990), 372.
31. Monahan, "Cultural Cartography," 372–73.
32. Annie Cohen-Solal, *Leo and His Circle: The Life of Leo Castelli,* trans. Mark Polizzotti with Cohen-Solal (New York: Alfred A. Knopf, 2010), 296–97. Cohen-Solol gives a detailed account of the events and tactics that preceded the award (June 14–19). Solomon, Castelli and Sonnabend were there as the artists' gallerists. See Cohen-Solal, *Leo and His Circle,* 294–98. Monahan, "Cultural Cartography," 371.
33. Cohen-Solal, *Leo and His Circle,* 296–97. For rumors, see Monahan, "Cultural Cartography," 371.
34. Cohen-Solal, *Leo and His Circle,* 298; Monahan, "Cultural Cartography," 373. Romy Golan has emphasized the importance of images of artworks that circulated in magazines for contemplating geopolitics of pop in Italy. She notes Mulas's spread for *Domus,* in particular. See Romy Golan, *Flashback, Eclipse: The Political Imaginary of Italian Art in the 1960s* (Princeton, NJ: Princeton University Press, 2021), 60.
35. Uncited critic quoted by Zevi, "Biennale," 34.
36. Renata Pisu, "Tutto è perduto, anche il pudore," *ABC,* June 28, 1964, 8–11.
37. Cardinal Giovanni Urbani (then patriarch of Venice), as quoted by Zevi, "Biennale," 33.
38. Pistoletto told me he was likely sent the record from Ileana Sonnabend; she worked with artists included in the show. Alice Denney curated the show with Leo Castelli, Richard Bellamy, and Ivan Karp as advisers. See Denney, *The Popular Image,* with a text by Alan Solomon (Washington, DC: Washington Gallery of Modern Art, 1963), catalog published in conjunction with the exhibition of the same title, held April 18–June 2, 1963.
39. Other exhibitions in the early 1960s similarly claimed these movements, especially pop art, as an American product. See *Pop Art, U.S.A.* (Oakland, CA: Oakland Museum of Art, 1963); and *Amerikansk Pop-Konst,* ed. Carlo Derkert, with texts by Billy Klüver, Alan Solomon, and Öyvind Fahlström (Stockholm: Moderna Museet, 1964).
40. Robert Rauschenberg, in Billy Klüver, "Interviews with Artists Participating in the *Popular Image* Exhibition, Washington Gallery of Modern Art, 1963," Washington Gallery of Modern Art records, 1959–1992, Archives of American Art, Smithsonian Institution, Digital ID 19362.
41. Clarification of when Friedman first saw Pistoletto's works was provided by Jill Vuchetich, head archivist, WAC Archives. Email correspondence, April 22, 2015.
42. On the development of the Castelli Gallery as a stronghold for American pop, see Hiroko Ikegami, "Dislocations: Robert Rauschenberg and the Americanization of Modern Art, circa 1964" (PhD diss., Yale University, 2007); and Hiroko Ikegami, "A Spectacle in Venice," chap. 2 in *The Great Migrator: Robert Rauschenberg and the Global Rise of American Art* (Cambridge, MA: MIT Press, 2010).
43. Recently Pistoletto's discussion of pop has shifted to embrace different artistic interests in pop, namely the creation of visual forms that captured the phenomenology of image production in the age of mass media. In one of my interviews with him (October 25, 2021), he shared his interest in Lichtenstein, never previously documented, including a purchase he made of one of the American artist's works through Sperone, likely from Panza di Biumo.
44. Dates of these exhibitions, see Ikegami, "Dislocations," 55.
45. Ikegami, "Dislocations," 72.
46. Pierre Cabanne, "À Venise, l'Amérique proclame la fin de l'École de Paris et lance le pop art pour coloniser l'Europe," *Arts,* June 24–30, 1964. For discussion of reactions by the French press, see Ikegami, "Dislocations," 60–61.
47. Publications included *L'Ordine nuovo* (The New Order, 1919–22, Turin), of which Antonio Gramsci was cofounder, *Avanti!* (Forward!, 1911–93, Milan), *La rivoluzione liberale* (The Liberal Revolution, 1922–25, Turin), founded by Piero Gobetti, and *L'Unità* (Unity, est. 1924, Milan), established by Gramsci, among others. *Avanti!*'s early years (1911–14) are associated with irredentist politics and Mussolini, an editor at the paper; I refer here to the paper's activity from 1914 onward, following Mussolini's expulsion.
48. See Paul Ginsborg, *A History of Contemporary Italy: 1945–1988,* 2nd exp. ed. (New York: St. Martin's, 2003), 115–16; and Kaeten Mistry, *The United States, Italy and the Origins of Cold War: Waging Political Warfare, 1945–1950* (Cambridge: Cambridge University Press, 2014), esp. "Means Short of War (1946–1948)," 95–126, and "Organising Political Warfare (1948–1950)," 176–99.
49. Mistry, *United States, Italy and the Origins of Cold War,* 19, 95–126. These loans constituted approximately 20 percent of the $1.4 billion in Marshall Plan aid that was distributed to Italy from 1948 to 1952. See also Ginsborg, *History of Contemporary Italy,* 158.
50. On Fiat and the Marshall Plan, see Ginsborg, *History of Contemporary Italy,* 214. On changes in management, infrastructure, labor organization, and performance, see Stefano Musso, *Storia del lavoro in Italia: Dall'Unità a oggi* (Venice: Marsilio, 2002), 209–10, 216.
51. Musso, *Storia del lavoro,* 209–10, 216.
52. Although the title of the film translates to "Bicycle Thieves" in English, it was released for Anglophone distribution as *The Bicycle Thief,* as it remains best known in these contexts.
53. Compelling work is being done on the futility of the "rat race" as expressed by other practices of 1960s European art. See Cynthia Evans's work on the Effekt Gruppe and on *Mausbild* (1964) in particular.
54. Pistoletto's metal ladder specifies an urban worker, perhaps one engaged in construction. Other works of Arte Povera, made later in the 1960s, also invoked the ladder, but with agrarian imagery and rustic ladders, as used by Pino Pascali and Alighiero Boetti, respectively.
55. Some areas of the New Left, such as the major publication *Quaderni piacentini,* criticized progressive intellectuals in Italy as ineffective and compromised by their position within the bourgeoisie. See Fabio Guidali, "Cultural and Political Commitment in the Non-Orthodox Marxist Left: The Case of *Quaderni piacentini* in Pre-1968 Italy," *History of European Ideas* 46, no. 6 (2020): 867.
56. Rhodiatoce, *Caio Gregorio er [sic] guardiano der [sic] Pretorio,* carosello, dir. Gino and Roberto Gavioli, episodes *Montgolfier* (1960), *Parcheggio* (1960), *Penelope* (1960), and *Lucrezia Borgia* (1964).
57. Italy's textile industry had produced synthetic fabrics on a large scale since the 1920s. Interwar production was limited to artificial cellulose-fiber fabrics; postwar production introduced synthetic resin-based fabrics including nylon and polyester, invented in the late 1930s and early 1940s, respectively. See Vera Zamagni, *The*

Economic History of Italy, 1860–1990: Recovery after Decline (Oxford: Clarendon, 1993), 276–77.

58. Jacques Lacan, "The Dream of Irma's Injection," in *The Seminar of Jacques Lacan: Book 2, The Ego in Freud's Theory and in the Technique of Psychoanalysis, 1954–1955,* ed. Jacques-Alain Miller, trans. Sylvana Tomaselli (New York: W. W. Norton, 1991), 169.
59. Lacan, "The Topic of the Imaginary," in *The Seminar of Jacques Lacan, Book 1, Freud's Papers on Technique, 1953–54,* ed. Jacques-Alain Miller, trans. John Forrester (New York: W. W. Norton, 1988), 76.
60. Lacan, "Topic of the Imaginary," 78.
61. This is different than the model of the expansive body offered by Henri Lefebvre, in which everyday objects "extend [the body] into the surrounding networks of relationships and pathways." See Lefebvre, *The Production of Space,* trans. Donald Nicholson-Smith (Oxford: Blackwell, 1991), 211.
62. See Antonio Negri, *The Politics of Subversion: A Manifesto for the Twenty-First Century,* trans. James Newell (Cambridge: Polity, 1989). See also Karl Marx, *Capital: A Critique of Political Economy,* vol. 1, trans. Ben Fowkes (London: Penguin, 1982), 255. This is not to be confused with new contemporaneous theories of the individual, such as Hans Blumenberg's concept of "self-assertion" (*Selbstbehauptung*). For Blumenberg, modern man is defined by his drive to systematically expand his skill set and knowledge to facilitate his adaptation to the world around him and "assert" himself therein. Recent scholarship on Italian modernity has tied Blumenberg's and other theories of the individual to new social subject positions that emerged with capitalist economic development, finding a connection between "self-assertion" and Italian literary modernism. See Hans Blumenberg, *The Legitimacy of the Modern Age* (1966), trans. Robert M. Wallace (Cambridge, MA: MIT Press, 1985); and Remo Ceserani, "Italy and Modernity: Peculiarities and Contradictions," in *Italian Modernism,* ed. Luca Somigli and Mario Moroni (Toronto: University of Toronto Press, 2004), 44–46.
63. Milan-based art dealer Arturo Schwarz's advertised comparable disdain for pop. In a postscript to an advertisement in the October 1964 issue of *Art International,* he wrote, "We do *not* handle 'pop art,' we are interested in *individuals* (not in schools or schoolboys)." Arturo Schwarz, gallery advertisement, *Art International* 8, no. 8 (1964): 14.
64. See Jean-François Lyotard, *Discourse, Figure* (1971), trans. Antony Hudek and Mary Lydon (Minneapolis: University of Minnesota, 2011), esp. "The Bias of the Figural" (3–19); "Dialectics, Index, Form" (23–50); "The Line and the Letter" (205–32); and "Desire in Discourse" (277–326).
65. For a clear review of that conflict and an outline of the historicity of experience espoused in phenomenology, see Silvia Stoller, "Phenomenology and the Poststructural Critique of Experience," *International Journal of Philosophical Studies* 17, no. 5 (2009): 707–37.
66. W. J. T. Mitchell, *Iconology: Image, Text, Ideology* (Chicago: University of Chicago Press, 1986), 9, 46.
67. Mark Godfrey, "The Artist According to Alighiero e Boetti," in *Alighiero e Boetti* (New Haven: Yale University Press, 2011), 73–117.
68. Godfrey, *Alighiero e Boetti,* 73–74, 79.
69. Godfrey, *Alighiero e Boetti,* 76.
70. Godfrey, *Alighiero e Boetti,* 108.
71. See Marcus Vitruvius Pollio, *De architectura,* trans. Luciano Migotto (Pordenone: Studio Tesi, 1990), chap. 1, bk. 3.
72. Elizabeth Mangini, *Seeing through Closed Eyelids: Giuseppe Penone and the Nature of Sculpture* (Toronto: University of Toronto Press, 2021), 85–87.
73. Alexander Nagel and Christopher S. Wood, "Interventions: Toward a New Model of Renaissance Anachronism," *Art Bulletin* 87, no. 3 (2005): 403–13; Alexander Nagel and Christopher S. Wood, *Anachronic Renaissance* (Princeton, NJ: Princeton University Press, 2020), 7–20, 29–34; Christopher S. Wood, *Forgery, Replica, Fiction: Temporalities of German Renaissance Art* (Chicago: University of Chicago Press, 2010).
74. Umberto Boccioni, *Manifesto tecnico della scultura futurista* (Milan: Governing Group of the Futurist Movement, 1912), n.p.
75. Boccioni, *Manifesto tecnico,* n.p.
76. Boccioni, *Manifesto tecnico,* n.p.
77. The original Italian imperative *spalanchiamo* calls for an action of extreme degree. The verb *spalancare* is used in a variety of contexts: to open your arms wide for an embrace or, more commonly, to fling open a door. In proper usage, the action is limited to parts of the body or sensory organs (e.g., to open your eyes or mouth as far as possible). Boccioni's directive was to open the sculptural figure to its sensorial, corporeal, and subjective limits. Boccioni, *Manifesto tecnico,* n.p., emphasis in original.
78. These thoughts respond in part to Hal Foster's mapping of the technological body in early twentieth-century modernisms, and discussion of the "fetishistic logic" underpinning the creation of what he calls the machinic figure. See Hal Foster, "Prosthetic Gods," in *Prosthetic Gods* (Cambridge, MA: MIT Press, 2006), 109–49.
79. The futurist exploration of ugliness as a thematic can be traced to Marinetti's *Manifesto tecnico della letteratura futurista* (May 11, 1912), reprinted in Filippo Marinetti, *Teoria e invenzione futurista,* ed. Luciano De Maria (Milan: Arnoldo Mondadori, 1983), 179.
80. On CoBrA and the creaturely, see Foster, "Creaturely CoBrA," *October* 141 (Summer 2012): 4–21.
81. Artists involved with spatialism declared themselves as "Artisti Spaziali" in a text regarded as the group's third manifesto: Lucio Fontana et al., *Proposta di un regolamento del movimento spaziale* (Milan, April 2, 1950), in *Lucio Fontana,* ed. Enrico Crispolti and Rosella Siligato (Milan: Electa, 1998), 174.
82. Lucio Fontana et al., "Secondo manifesto dello spazialismo" (Milan, March 1948), in *Lucio Fontana: Concetti spaziali,* ed. Paolo Fossati (Turin: Giulio Einaudi, 1970), 127. My translation seeks to preserve the meaning of *esca* (from the verb *uscire,* "to go out"). Translations typically use "escape" or "leave"—better suited to different Italian verbs (*scappare* and *fuggire*)—that change the emphasis in the original *to which* the movement is oriented rather than the point *from which* it left.
83. On Argentine interests, see Andrea Giunta, *Avant-Garde, Internationalism, and Politics: Argentine Art in the Sixties* (Durham, NC: Duke University Press, 2007), 36–39.
84. Movimento Spaziale, "Proposta di un regolamento" (April 2, 1950).
85. Anthony White, *Lucio Fontana: Between Utopia and Kitsch* (Cambridge, MA: MIT Press, 2011); Yve-Alain Bois, "Fontana's Base Materialism," *Art in America* 77, no. 4 (1989): 238–48.
86. My reference to an "expanded field" of figuration makes use of Rosalind Krauss's term, which refers to the postmodern expansion of the medium. George Baker expanded the term thereafter to offer a theoretical mapping of new directions in contemporary photography. See Rosalind E. Krauss, *Passages in Modern Sculpture* (Cambridge, MA: MIT Press, 1981); and George Baker, "Photography's Expanded Field," *October* 114 (Fall 2005): 120–40.
87. (Original Italian: "[Devo] far uscire il quadro nella realtà, creando la finzione di trovarmi oltre lo specchio. . . . L'invasione fisica del quadro nella realtà mi permette di introdurmi tra gli elementi scomposti della figurazione." Underlining original.)
88. Bernardo Arias, Horacio Cazeneuve, and Marcos Fridman,

Manifiesto blanco (Buenos Aires: October–November 1946). Fontana participated as an author but did not sign the manifesto. Reprinted in Crispolti and Siligati, *Lucio Fontana*, 115–17.

89. Arias, Cazeneuve, and Fridman, *Manifiesto blanco*, n.p.
90. See Benjamin H. D. Buchloh, "Memory Lessons and History Tableaux: James Coleman's Archaeology of Spectacle" (1995), in *Neo-Avantgarde and Culture Industry: Essays on European and American Art from 1955 to 1975* (Cambridge, MA: MIT Press, 2000), 141–78.

CHAPTER 3. FIGURES OF PROTEST

1. Sidney Simon, "Michelangelo Pistoletto," *Art International* 10, no. 6 (1966): 70.
2. Comparison of this photograph by Hiro with images of the two known mirror paintings (*Figura umana*, 1962; *Un uomo*, 1964) that include this figure reveals that the artwork included in this photograph must be a third, unknown work. The Hiro archive verified that the image was a "straight" photograph, confirming that the artwork must be another work than one currently known. I thank Gregory Wakabayashi and Marco Farano for their assistance in our effort to identify the work.
3. They include: *Nieuwe Realisten* (New Realists) at The Hague's Gemeentemuseum (June 24–August 30, 1964), *Mythologies quotidiennes* (Everyday Mythologies) at the Musée d'Art Moderne de la Ville in Paris (July–October 1964), and *POP, Etc.*, at the Museum des 20 Jahrhunderts in Vienna (September 19–October 31, 1964).
4. The Museum of Modern Art purchased *Man with Yellow Pants*, in which Gian Enzo Sperone appears.
5. "Now You Can Put Yourself . . . in the Picture," *Minneapolis Tribune Picture Magazine*, April 3, 1966, 12–13.
6. Exhibition layout was culled from my study of photography, local news footage, and blueprints of the original Walker building. See also Simon, "Michelangelo Pistoletto," 69, 71.
7. See, e.g., Tommaso Trini, "Scheda su Michelangelo Pistoletto: 1," *L'Uomo e l'arte* 7 (December 1971): 28; Luigi Carluccio, *Michelangelo Pistoletto: Opere recenti* (Turin: Galleria Galatea, 1963), n.p.; and Alain Jouffroy, untitled essay, in *Pistoletto* (Paris: Galerie Sonnabend, 1964), n.p.
8. The films include *L'Avventura* (The Adventure, 1960), *L'Eclisse* (The Eclipse, 1962), and *Red Desert* (1964). See Bruno Corà, *Michelangelo Pistoletto: Lo spazio della riflessione nell'arte* (Ravenna: Essegi, 1986), 19; Carlos Basualdo, "Michelangelo Pistoletto: From One to Many, 1956–1974," in *Michelangelo Pistoletto: From One to Many, 1956–1974*, ed. Basualdo (Philadelphia: Philadelphia Museum of Art, 2010), 5; and Romy Golan, "Flashbacks and Eclipses in Italian Art of the 1960s," *Grey Room*, no. 49 (Fall 2012): 102–27. For a primary source, see the following interview with fellow Turinese artist and friend Piero Gilardi, who also shares this view. See Piero Gilardi, "An Interview with Piero Gilardi," interview by LeGrace G. Benson with Gabriele Muresu, *Leonardo* 1, no. 4 (1968): 431.
9. Romy Golan, for example, has argued that the photographs of the mirror paintings offer us insights into the artist's position, "transiting out of the politically *engagement* of the immediate postwar decade to the psychological disaffection of the economic miracle." See Golan, "Flashbacks and Eclipses," 104. In her book, the figures are "those of anomie," during the conjuncture, or decline of the economic miracle. See Romy Golan, *Flashback, Eclipse: The Political Imaginary of Italian Art in the 1960s* (Princeton, NJ: Princeton University Press, 2021), 18.
10. See Nicholas Cullinan, "From Vietnam to Fiat-Nam: The Politics of Arte Povera," *October* 128 (Spring 2008): 14.
11. Jouffroy, untitled essay, n.p.
12. Claire Gilman, "Figuring Boetti," in *Alighiero Boetti: Game Plan*, ed. Christian Rattemeyer, Lynne Cooke, and Mark Godfrey (London: Tate Modern, 2012), 136; Claire Gilman, "Pistoletto's Staged Subjects," *October* 124 (Spring 2008): 73.
13. Pistoletto and Mila Pistoi, "Intervista a Michelangelo Pistoletto," *Marcatrè* 4, no. 26–29 (1966): 411.
14. Existing literature incorrectly states that the entire series was shown at the exhibition. See Germano Celant and Ida Gianelli, eds., *Pistoletto* (Milan: Electa, 1984), 16. Other works in the series debuted later that year at the artist's solo exhibitions at the Galleria del Leone in Venice and Galleria Gian Enzo Sperone in Milan in 1966. Others still were sold in the United States without exhibition by Leo Castelli.
15. Robert Murdock, *Pistoletto* (Buffalo, NY: Albright-Knox Gallery, 1969), n.p.
16. Until now, *Striscione arancio*, the title written by the artist on the verso of the panel, has been known by its secondary title, *Corteo n. 3*, or "Demonstration n. 3." It was exhibited at the Walker as *Demonstration III*. It is now in the collection of the Herbert F. Johnson Museum of Art at Cornell University, as *Parade n. 3*.
17. In 1965 the Lombardy seat of the ANPI was bombed in Milan, three days after the celebration of the twentieth anniversary of Italy's liberation during World War II.
18. In more recent writing on the "*Comizzi*" [*sic*], Romy Golan notes difficulty in dating the photographs, suggesting that the photograph of *Boy* looks just as much like images of the days following Armistice in September 1943 as they do the 1960s and that the boy could therefore be a young Pistoletto; for her, the Rallies have in this case a "temporal oscillation." ANPI, whose flag is clearly visible in the painting, was not founded until April 1945. See Golan, *Flashback, Eclipse*, 103.
19. They are not from an "award-winning film shown at the 1966 biennale," as one essay has held. See "Michelangelo Pistoletto (b. 1933), Biennale 66" (lot essay), for *Works from the Collection of Ileana Sonnabend and the Estate of Nina Castelli Sundell* (New York: Christie's, 2015), www.christies.com/en/lot/lot-5946580.
20. The first was *Donne nude che ballano* (Nude Women Dancing, 1964), with source images by Scottish photographer Eadweard Muybridge, famed in the history of photography for his contributions to chronophotography and movement studies. See Gilman, "Pistoletto's Staged Subjects," 58.
21. Suzanne Penn, conservator at the Philadelphia Museum of Art, also invokes Claire Gilman's term in her discussion of Pistoletto's authorship. See Suzanne Penn, "'The Complicity of the Materials' in Pistoletto's Paintings and Mirror Paintings," in Basualdo, *Pistoletto: From One to Many*, 142–67, at 153.
22. This finding does not position Pistoletto as a pop artist, as some other Pistoletto scholars have done in discussions of the mirror paintings and pop. Romy Golan distinguishes Pistoletto's pop from that of Italian pop of the Piazza del Popolo. See Golan, *Flashback, Eclipse*, 19, 58–72.
23. *Comizio IX* (Rally IX) appeared in the fall 1967 *Exhibition of Contemporary Italian Art* (National Museum of Modern Art, Tokyo; co-organized with the National Gallery of Modern Art, Rome). Additional support was provided by Japanese and Italian cultural and diplomatic institutes. Mirror paintings were also included in an exhibition of contemporary Italian art at the São Paulo Bienal (winter 1967–68) and Museo de Arte Moderno Mexico City (spring 1971). Other poveristi would exhibit at that time on an international stage. See Corinne Criticos, "La Galerie Gian Enzo Sperone: Notes pour une historique," *Ligeia*, nos. 25–28 (1998): 156.

24. The Walker Art Center employed Seitz, a German-born American designer who trained with Max Bill and Paul Rand, as design curator and sole employee of the design department from 1964 to 1968. During that time, Seitz was responsible for the design of all museum publications and publicity materials; he also edited the in-house periodical *Design Quarterly*. For in-house design projects, Seitz would consult with Martin Friedman, to whom he reported. Consultation of other examples of Seitz's work at the Walker suggests that the creative direction of the catalog cover for Pistoletto's exhibition may have incorporated Friedman's input, since it is somewhat of an anomaly in the designer's work from the period, which were typically geometric or text-based designs. No other files relating to the cover design (such as budget or art direction) remain extant. On Seitz's reporting to Friedman, see Ryan Gerald Nelson, "From Ulm to Minneapolis: Tracing Peter Seitz's Modernist Traditions," *The Gradient*, WAC blog, October 31, 2007, http://blogs.walkerart.org/design/2007/10/31/ulm-minneapolis-tracing-peter. For more on Seitz, see *Peter Seitz: Designing a Life*, ed. Andrew Blauvelt and Pamela Johnson (Minneapolis, MN: Minneapolis College of Art and Design, 2007). Pistoletto confirmed to me that Seitz did not consult him on the cover. Pistoletto, interview with the author, National Gallery of Art, Washington, DC, November 6, 2017.
25. I am using my own translation of the title to capture the efficiency of the Italian title. Galleries in the United States in the 1960s used *No to the Increase of the Tram Fare*, as does the Detroit Institute of Arts today.
26. The *tessere* are most often worn, as study of photographs of mid-1960s demonstrations, strikes, and workers' parades illustrate, by card-carrying members of the PCI typically during the May Day Festa dei lavoratori or Festa de l'Unità, the celebratory day of the founding of the PCI newspaper, not to be confused with the celebration of national unification, the Festa dell'Unità. See, e.g., photographs by Silvestre Loconsolo, Archivio del Lavoro, Milan (Sesto San Giovanni).
27. Pistoletto interview with the author, November 6, 2017.
28. This description draws on Michael Fried's discussion of absorption in eighteenth-century figurative painting and Maurizio Fagiolo dell'Arco's discussion of the mirror paintings' figures as having an absorbed air. See Fried, *Absorption and Theatricality: Painting and Beholder in the Age of Diderot* (Chicago: University of Chicago Press, 1980); and Fagiolo dell'Arco, "Il dramma fisico di Pistoletto," in *Rapporto 60: Le arti oggi in Italia* (Rome: Bulzoni, 1966), 211.
29. See Martin Friedman and Annette Michelson, "Michelangelo Pistoletto: A Reflected World; Members' Preview with Art Critic Annette Michelson," April 4, 1966, QuickTime audio, track 2 of 5, WAC Archives, digital audio of reel-to-reel original from the WAC Collections and Resources Database, previously available at http://collections.walkerart.org/item/archive/110.
30. Martin Friedman, *Michelangelo Pistoletto: A Reflected World* (Minneapolis, MN: Walker Art Center, 1965), n.p.
31. Irving Sandler, "The New Cool Art," *Art in America* 53, no. 1 (1965): 96–101.
32. See Tommaso Trini, "Scheda su Michelangelo Pistoletto," *L'Uomo e l'arte* 7 (December 1971): 29; and Alberto Boatto, *Dentro/fuori lo specchio* (Roma: Fantini, 1969), 7.
33. Characterizations of pop's practitioners and artworks as "cool" can be found across the literature. See esp. Sidney Janis, "On the Theme of the Exhibition," in *The New Realists* (New York: Sidney Janis Gallery, 1962), n.p.; Barbara Rose, "Dada, Then and Now," *Art International* 7, no. 1 (1963): 23; Peter Selz, "Pop Goes the Artist," *Partisan Review* 30, no. 2 (1963): 315; John Coplans, "Pop Art, USA," *Artforum* 2, no. 4 (1963): 28; Thomas Hess, "Pop and Public," *ARTnews* 62, no. 7 (1963): 23; and Alan Solomon, "Jim Dine and the Psychology of the New Art," *Art International* 8, no. 8 (1964): 52. Solomon describes Roy Lichtenstein, James Rosenquist, Andy Warhol, and Tom Wesselmann, specifically, as "cool"; descriptions of pop's practitioners as "cool" tended otherwise to refer to the general "pop artist." In related usage, Claes Oldenburg referred to Warhol's indifference to his subject matter as his "cold attitude." See "Oldenburg, Lichtenstein, Warhol: A Discussion," moderated by Bruce Glaser, *Artforum* 4, no. 6 (1966): 24. Pop artists also used the term to describe their own work. See Roy Lichtenstein in conversation with Gene Swenson, in "What Is Pop Art? Answers from 8 Painters, Part I," *ARTnews* 62, no. 7 (1963): 27. In late 1966, Martin Friedman described "cool" as a "current term" in art discourse for artistic disengagement and detachment. Friedman, "Introduction," in *Eight Sculptors: The Ambiguous Image* (Minneapolis, MN: Walker Art Center, 1966), n.p.
34. Friedman, *Reflected World*, n.p.
35. Hess, "Pop and Public," 59–60.
36. The title and potential role of the work for the catalog cover are documented in an artist's letter, correspondence with Gian Enzo Sperone, and shipping correspondence from the Walker's then registrar, Linda Merritt. A letter of March 7, 1966, from Merritt to the Galleria Sperone includes the following: "The small painting by Michelangelo Pistoletto, which you sent for our use in the Pistoletto Exhibition and to photograph for the exhibition catalogue cover, is being held up at customs . . . as we need the painting for the catalogue lay-out in three or four days." Pistoletto's letter of March 10, 1966, to Merritt confirms the title of the small painting in question. In that letter, Pistoletto confirmed that he is the artist of the painting entitled "Operai" (57 × 41.5 cm), shipped by airmail on February 17, 1966. Walker Art Center Exhibition Archives, Pistoletto, Lenders files.
37. The work does not have an inscription on its verso. Although the owner of the work declined my requests to examine the work in person, the lack of inscription is based on data from the Archivio Pistoletto and from the appendix of the catalog for the Philadelphia Museum of Art retrospective in 2010.
38. William Tall, "This Mirror-Art Seems . . . Alive!," *Detroit Free Press*, September 24, 1967.
39. On the roles of Eugenio Battisti, Alan Solomon, and Kynaston McShine, see Raffaele Bedarida, "Export/Import: The Promotion of Contemporary Italian Art in the United States, 1935–1969" (PhD diss., CUNY, 2016), 24, 204–15.
40. Alan Solomon, *Young Italians* (Boston: Institute of Contemporary Art, 1968), 5.
41. McShine, Foreword to *Recent Italian Painting and Sculpture* (New York: Jewish Museum, with the Istituto Italiano di Cultura of New York, 1968), n.p.
42. Pistoletto, interview by Celant, in Celant and Gianelli, *Pistoletto*, 29. Translation mine.
43. Plinio De Martiis, "Gli anni originali," *La Tartaruga: Quaderni d'arte e letteratura*, nos. 5–6 (March 1989): 3. See also Valentina Valentini, *New Theater in Italy, 1963–2013*, trans. Thomas Haskell Simpson (London: Routledge, 2018), 4.
44. Mirella Bandini, "Turin in the 1970s: Fiat, Arte Povera, and Other Heroes," *Flash Art*, no. 160 (October 1991): 104–9; Pistoletto, "Michelangelo on Pistoletto," in *Facing Pistoletto*, ed. Andrea Bellini, trans. Barbara McGilvray and Simon Turner (Zurich: JRP Ringier, 2009), 28.
45. Bedarida, "Export/Import," 195–96.
46. Ettore Sottsass Jr., "Pop e non-pop: A proposito di Michelangelo Pistoletto," *Domus*, May 1964, 35.

47. Fagiolo dell'Arco, "Il dramma fisico di Pistoletto," 210. Translations mine.
48. Angelo Dragone, "Una gigantesca rosa di cartoni ondulati," *Stampa Sera,* February 6, 1968.
49. See G. R. Swenson, "Social Realism in Blue: An Interview with James Rosenquist," *Studio International,* February 1968, 76, 79–80, 83; and Gregory Battcock, "Humanism and Realism: Thek and Warhol," in *The New Art: A Critical Anthology,* ed. Gregory Battcock (New York: E. P. Dutton, 1966), 235–42. Attention to pop and politics is extensive in the secondary literature. See especially, on the reception of pop as political in Europe, Andreas Huyssen, "The Cultural Politics of Pop," *New German Critique* 4 (1975): 77–98; and, for major secondary readings of American pop (namely Warhol) as political, Thomas Crow, "Saturday Disasters: Trace and Reference in Early Warhol," *Art in America* 75, no. 5 (1987): 129–36; and Hal Foster, "Death in America," *October* 75 (Winter 1996): 36–59. Huyssen deftly demonstrated that the reception of American pop in West Germany in the late 1960s as critical art, even an art of protest, coincided with the student movements and an interest in cultural forms as tools of social critique and change, following Herbert Marcuse. See Huyssen, "Cultural Politics of Pop," 78, 82.
50. Pistoletto, interview by Celant, 31. (Original Italian of the passage with added emphasis: "Al contrario il mio lavoro non nasce da un'immagine di coinvolgimento locale o nazionale, di consumismo e di figurazione pubblica, ma deriva dalla centralità della figura umana.")
51. Pistoletto, interview by Celant, 31.
52. Martin Friedman, "Questions for Pistoletto," no. 3, Pistoletto response, WAC Archives. Aldo Mondino, Pistoletto's friend since his student days, had saved photographic reproductions of George Segal's plaster-cast figures from *Métro,* where they had been published in May 1962. Criticos, "La Galerie Gian Enzo Sperone," 150. Data from unpublished interview with Aldo Mondino in 1996.
53. See, e.g., Bandiera Rossa, front-page statement, *Bandiera Rossa,* no. 1 (October 5, 1943): n.p. Broder underscores similar language elsewhere in Bandiera Rossa's texts. On Bandiera Rossa and postwar formations of "Resistance mythology," see David Broder, "Red Partisans: *Bandiera Rossa* in Occupied Rome, 1943–44," *Historical Materialism* 25, no. 2 (2017): 63–95.
54. Antonio Tricomi, "Killing the Father: Politics and Intellectuals, Utopia and Disillusion," in *Imagining Terrorism: The Rhetoric and Representation of Political Violence in Italy, 1969–2009,* ed. Pierpaolo Antonello and Alan O'Leary (London: Routledge, 2009), 17–18.
55. Friedman and Michelson, "Michelangelo Pistoletto: A Reflected World," track 2.
56. Ashbery, "Talking of Pistoletto," *ARTnews* 65, no. 4 (1966): 64.
57. Simon, "Michelangelo Pistoletto," 70.
58. Murdock, *Pistoletto,* n.p.
59. Another work, *Cane* (Dog), was adjacent to the gallery entrance.
60. Color photography of the exhibition sign does not exist. Although the reproduction of *Rally II* preserves the flags from the original image, they were likely printed on the steel sign in grayscale, neutralizing their political associations.
61. For discussion of Turin's central position within the national trade union conflicts of 1962, see Stefano Musso, *Storia del lavoro in Italia: Dall'Unità a oggi* (Venice: Marsilio, 2002), 225–26; Marco Scavino, "Sviluppo economico e culture del conflitto: Grande industria e sindacati negli anni del boom economico," in *La città e lo sviluppo: Crescita e disordine a Torino, 1945–1970,* ed. Fabio Levi and Bruno Maida (Milan: Franco Angeli, 2002), 474–78; and Paul Ginsborg, *A History of Contemporary Italy: 1945–1988,* 2nd exp. ed. (New York: St. Martin's, 2003), 250–53.
62. Ginsborg, *History of Contemporary Italy,* 274.
63. Ginsborg, *History of Contemporary Italy,* 274–75; John Foot, *The Archipelago: Italy since 1945* (London: Bloomsbury, 2018), 135–36; see also Valdo Spini, "The New Left in Italy," *Journal of Contemporary History* 7, nos. 1–2 (1972): 57.
64. Ginsborg, *History of Contemporary Italy,* 274.
65. See, e.g., "Tram: Le cifre dello sciopero," *Corriere della Sera,* March 3–4, 1965; "Contro l'aumento bloccati i tram," *L'Unità,* February 23, 1964; "Caos per la taglia sulle tariffe: La città protesta contro l'aumento," *L'Unità,* May 4, 1965; "Il Paese paralizzato dallo sciopero ferroviario," *Il Messaggero,* April 15, 1965; and Arturo Barone, "Tram e pullman fermi per ventiquattro ore: Lo sciopero dei trasporti pubblici ha paralizzato ieri Roma e Lazio," *La Stampa,* July 16, 1965.
66. Main strike issues in the mid-1960s included better hours, contractual salary, layoffs, transit fare hikes, the right to work, and worker solidarity, all called for by—in Milan alone—CGE (Compagnia Generale di Elettricità; General Electric Company), Ceruti, Fargas, ATM (Azienda Trasporti Milanesi, Milan's public transport company), FIOM (Federazione Impiegati Operai Metallurgici; Italian Federation of Metalworkers), and CISL (Italian Confederation of Trade Unions). Issues summarized from examination of protest photographs in the Archivio del Lavoro. See also, e.g., the following reports: "Domattina i tram fermi per lo sciopero," *Stampa Sera,* February 22–23, 1965; "Tram: Le cifre dello sciopero"; Barone, "Tram e pullman fermi per ventiquattro ore"; "Contro l'aumento bloccati i tram"; "Milano: Fallito l'attacco alla CGIL"; "Caos per la taglia sulle tariffe"; "Ritirare il progetto per il 'caro-tariffe,'" *L'Unità,* May 23, 1964; "Il Paese paralizzato dallo sciopero ferroviario"; and "Lo sciopero dei trasporti pubblici ha paralizzato ieri Roma e il Lazio," *La Stampa,* July 16, 1965. On the constitution of CGIL, see Spini, "New Left in Italy," 66. On conflicts between center-left coalitions and trade unions, see Vittorio Foa, "Il sindacato e la programmazione" (1965), in *Sindacati e lotte operaie, 1943–1973: Documenti della Storia,* ed. Massimo L. Salvadori (Turin: Loescher, 1975), 143–44. Known as a "critical minority" within the Italian Socialist Party (PSI), Foa addresses the conflict between the CGIL's advocacy for workers and confrontation of the PSI's association with the Moro government. On Foa as dissident, see Robert Lumley, *States of Emergency: Cultures of Revolt in Italy from 1968 to 1972* (London: Verso Books, 1990) 35.
67. See Robert Lumley, "Michelangelo Pistoletto: Stepping Sideways, Changing Direction," in *Pistoletto Politico: Works by Michelangelo Pistoletto* (London: Luxembourg & Dayan, 2013), 11, catalog published in conjunction with the exhibition of the same title, February 12–April 12, 2013.
68. Spini, "New Left in Italy," 56–57.
69. PCI membership card text, 1959–79.
70. See the following news reports on workers' strikes and mass protests against new public transit fares in 1965: "Milano: Fallito l'attacco alla CGIL: L'80% dei tramvieri partecipa allo sciopero," *L'Unità,* March 3, 1965; "Caos per la taglia sulle tariffe"; and Giancarlo Galli, "Il tram che mangia oro" [Milan], *Corriere della Sera,* March 6–7, 1965.
71. Galli, "Il tram che mangia oro."
72. For more on this relationship, see Musso, *Storia del lavoro,* 227–28.
73. Miriam Golden, *Labor Divided: Austerity and Working-Class Politics in Contemporary Italy* (Ithaca, NY: Cornell University Press, 1988), 34–35.
74. Musso, *Storia del lavoro,* 227–28; Golden, *Labor Divided,* 34–35.
75. Nicholas Cullinan has also discussed the import of these events for Arte Povera. See Cullinan, "From Vietnam to Fiat-Nam," 13–14.
76. Protests were held in the Piazza del Duomo in Milan on May 22,

1965. See *Corriere della Sera,* "Scontri in centro tra polizia e comunisti," May 23, 1965.

77. For reports on these protests, see, e.g.: "Oggi a Roma: Un'assurda 'marcia della pace,'" *Corriere della Sera,* May 20–21, 1965; M. B., "La 'marcia' antiamericana organizzata dai comunisti," *Corriere della Sera,* May 21, 1965; "Dopo il comizio per il Vietnam: Scontri in centro tra polizia e comunisti," *Corriere della Sera,* May 23, 1965; "Le manifestazioni antiamericane: Violenti scontri a Genova tra polizia e dimostranti," *Corriere della Sera,* May 25, 1965; "Manifestazione comunista contro la guerra nel Vietnam," *Corriere della Sera,* November 27, 1965; and "Sotto la pioggia a Roma, le dimostrazioni per il Vietnam," *Corriere della Sera,* March 28, 1966.
78. The precedent to this turn was one mirror painting, featuring two nude women dancing, inspired by a photograph from Scottish photographer Eadweard Muybridge's *Human Figure in Motion* (1907). The relation of the mirror painting (*Nude donne che ballano* or "Nude Women Dancing," 1964) to Muybridge's work has been variously framed as having used the Muybridge image or being based on it; closer examination reveals that Pistoletto's work was staged with a contemporary model in a Muybridge-inspired position. As in Muybridge's compositions, Pistoletto centered the figures in his mirror painting. For descriptions of the Muybridge-Pistoletto relationship, see Tommaso T. [Trini] Castelli, untitled essay (August 1966), in Germano Celant, ed., *Michelangelo Pistoletto: Edizioni di arte contemporanea* (Genoa: Galleria La Bertesca, 1966), 48; Penn, "'Complicity of the Materials,'" 157, 160; and Gilman, "Pistoletto's Staged Subjects," 58. Gilman notes that the difference between the figures, who have similar hairstyles and physiques, is only one of position. I suspect that the figures are also, in fact, the same model.
79. Gilman, "Pistoletto's Staged Subjects," 57–58.
80. Accounts of this process abound in the literature on Pistoletto. The best account in terms of accuracy and thoroughness belongs to Suzanne Penn. I draw on her account here and in the following paragraphs. See Penn, "'Complicity of the Materials,'" 147–60. See also Gilman, "Pistoletto's Staged Subjects," 73.
81. The exhibition text for the Rallies in the retrospective on Pistoletto at the Philadelphia Museum of Art in 2010 claimed, for example, that the images were taken in Turin. I am indebted to this exhibition for having allowed me to see so much of Pistoletto's work early in this research.
82. Consultation of additional source photographs found by the archive between 2018 and 2019 confirm this finding.
83. Friedman, *Reflected World,* n.p. Although many comparisons were made between Pistoletto and pop within the primary reception of his work, notable descriptions of Pistoletto's mirror paintings in the Walker Art Center exhibition as "cool" were also offered by Michelson and an unattributed exhibition review in *Picture Magazine,* a Sunday magazine associated with the *Minneapolis Tribune.* See Friedman and Michelson, track 2 of 5; and "Now You Can Put Yourself . . . in the Picture," *Picture Magazine,* April 3, 1966, 12–13.
84. On Duchamp's portrait in Pistoletto's mirror painting, see Marcia E. Vetrocq, "Michelangelo and Ugo Eye to Eye," *Art in America* 98, no. 10 (2010): 16.
85. I refer here to the song "Bandiera Rossa" (1908) and the group within the left-communist Movimento Comunista d'Italia. These unions include the CGIL and FIOM, both dominated by the PCI. See Broder, "Red Partisans," 63–95, esp. 64–67, 88–91.
86. Broder, "Red Partisans."
87. Friedman, *Reflected World,* n.p.
88. Walter Benjamin, "The Work of Art in the Age of Mechanical Reproduction," in *Illuminations,* trans. Harry Zohn, ed. Hannah Arendt (New York: Schocken Books, 1968), 217–224, at 224.
89. Benjamin, "Work of Art," 241.
90. These titles correspond to the provided translations, unless otherwise noted.
91. For information on the Castelli Gallery and Walker Art Center exhibition plans, see Ileana Sonnabend to Martin Friedman, November 3, 1965, WAC Archives.
92. See the retrospective curated by Carlos Basualdo (PMA/MAXXI) in 2010 as well as the exhibition *Pistoletto Politico: Works by Michelangelo Pistoletto,* February 12–April 12, 2013, Luxembourg & Dayan gallery, London, curated by Daniella Luxembourg, Amalia Dayan, and Alma Luxembourg.
93. See Penn, "'Complicity of the Materials,'" 157.
94. Pistoletto interview with the author.
95. Pistoletto interview with the author. (Original Italian [in its entirety]: "Lui mi ha chiesto, semplicemente, qual era la mia idea delle opere, con il soggetto politico. E io gli ho risposto che non avevano nessuna funzione drammatica, anzi—proprio rispetto a quello che ho detto prima che non voglio il dramma—voglio uscire dal dramma, anzi, il fenomeno politico, che è una realtà esistente, così come io esisto, però, entra in una dimensione temporale, che cambia completamente il dramma del momento. Si trova in una altra situazione.")
96. Pistoletto, "Questions for Pistoletto," no. 13. (Original Italian: "Voglio mostrare nei quadri più recenti che anche i più diversi significati possono vivere in questa dimensione demistificata; siano violenti o pacifici, essi esistono con noi. Uno chi fa un quadro di protesta limita la sua visione al fatto. Io posso scegliere un soggetto di protesta politica come un avvenimento reale della vita, proprio per metterlo in una condizione che va oltre." An unattributed English translation of this document ostensibly used by Friedman during his preparation of the catalog essay is held in the WAC Archives. Because the translation takes some liberty with Pistoletto's language—though not enough to misconstrue its content—I use my translation for accuracy.)
97. Murdock, *Pistoletto,* n.p. The four are *Rally II, Rally X, Man with Red Flag,* and *Uomini che ascoltano* (*Una manifestazione*) (Men Listening [A Demonstration])—a work more often mistakenly shown as *Persone che guardano* (People Watching).
98. The source photograph posted on the wall of the studio doesn't correspond to any of the ten known photographs by Rinaldi associated with the series and retained by the archive. This suggests that there may have been another source photograph, now lost, but it also demonstrates that Pistoletto worked closely with images from Rinaldi's series, even if they didn't make it into his eventual *Comizi.*
99. Lumley, "Michelangelo Pistoletto," 9. I thank Adam Jolles for his observation regarding the plenitude of Rinaldi's images.
100. Marina Camboni, "William Wetmore Story, Walt Whitman, and Enrico Nencioni," in *Republics and Empires: Italian and American Art in Transnational Perspective, 1840–1970,* ed. Melissa Dabakis and Paul H. D. Kaplan (Manchester: Manchester University Press, 2021), 117; on Signorini and Mazzinian republicanism, see 106.
101. Adrian R. Duran, *Painting, Politics, and the New Front of Cold War Italy* (Farnham, UK: Ashgate, 2014), 2014. See, e.g., Turcato's *Comizio* (Rally, 1950) and Guttuso's *Il comizio* (*Omaggio a Giuseppe Di Vittorio*) (Rally [Homage to Giuseppe Di Vittorio], 1962).
102. Lumley, "Michelangelo Pistoletto," 9. Lumley has also differentiated Arte Povera (specifically Boetti and Pistoletto) from politicized artists such as Guttuso. On Pistoletto, he offered: "[The] relationship of [Pistoletto's] work to social and political realities is often oblique, never documentary or polemical" (8). Lumley discusses Guttuso's famous painting of Togliatti's funeral. Notably, Pistoletto's own *Rally I* (1965) was shown as *RALLY I* (*Togliatti's Funeral*) in Pistoletto's

solo show at the Albright-Knox Art Gallery (Buffalo, NY, 1969), held in a double billing with a solo Mario Ceroli show. See Robert M. Murdock, *Pistoletto: May 13–June 15, 1969, Albright-Knox Art Gallery, Buffalo, New York* (Buffalo, NY: The Gallery, 1969), n.p. The whereabouts of *Rally I* are unknown. Its last traceable owner was Emily McFadden Harrison. I have found one extant color photograph of the work, in the archives of the Albright-Knox Art Gallery. The center figure's jacket was blue. Documents in the Albright-Knox archives suggest that the alternate title was given after discussion with McFadden Harrison. See Murdock, *Pistoletto*, n.p. On Pistoletto's reaction to the exhibition plan, see Pistoletto to Jill Kornblee, Turin, April 11, 1969, Albright-Knox Archive.

103. Jean Dypréau, "Pistoletto ou le peintre devant et derrière le miroir," in *Pistoletto* (Brussels: Palais de Beaux Arts, 1967), n.p. Translation mine.
104. Martin, "Mirror, Mirror," 21.
105. See, e.g., Luca Massimo Barbero, *Nascità di una nazione: Tra Guttuso, Fontana, e Schifano* (Florence: Fondazione Palazzo Strozzi, 2018). On other framings of the school, see Adachiara Zevi, *Peripezie del dopoguerra nell'arte italiana* (Turin: Einaudi, 2005), 229.
106. The key text for the former is Norberto Bobbio, *Politica e cultura* (Turin: Einaudi, 1955), esp. chap. 6, "Libertà dell'arte e politica culturale." see Umberto Eco, *Apocalittici e integrati: Comunicazione di massa e teorie della cultura di massa* (Milan: Bompiani, 1964). Historians of the fomentation of 1968 in Italy have also positioned 1956 as a watershed year, citing major world events but also renewed Italianization of the Communist Party in Italy. See Angelo d'Orsi, "L'odore della rivoluzione," in *Aspettando il Sessantotto: Continuità e fratture nelle culture politiche italiane dal 1956 al 1968*, ed. Francesco Chiarotto (Turin: Accademia University Press, 2017), 1–3.
107. James Meyer, *The Art of Return: The Sixties and Contemporary Culture* (Chicago: University of Chicago Press, 2019), 101–2.
108. See, e.g., Gilman, "Pistoletto's Staged Subjects," 64.
109. See *Boy, Rally I, Rally II, Rally X, Man with Red Flag,* and *Uomini che ascoltano* (*Una manifestazione*) (Men Listening [A Demonstration], 1965), often discussed and shown as *Persone che guardano* (People Watching).
110. These remarks belong to Michael Sonnabend, Robert Lumley, and Claire Gilman. Michael Sonnabend, "A Strange Shock: Notes on Pistoletto," *Métro* 7, no. 12 (1967): 92, originally published in Swedish in *Konstrevy*, no. 6 (1965): 184–89; Lumley, "Michelangelo Pistoletto," 9; Gilman, "Pistoletto's Staged Subjects," 58.
111. Pistoletto interview with the author.
112. Fagiolo dell'Arco, "Il dramma fisico di Pistoletto," 209–13, at 211.
113. Henry Martin, "Mirror, Mirror," 21.
114. Martin, "Mirror, Mirror," 21.
115. Sonnabend, "Strange Shock," 92.
116. Sonnabend, "Strange Shock," 91–92.
117. Henry Martin, "Michelangelo Pistoletto," in *Pistoletto*, ed. Renilde Hammacher-van den Brande (Rotterdam: Museum Boijmans Van Beuningen, 1969), n.p. Martin specifies *Comizio II* (Rally II, 1965).
118. Rosa Maria Rinaldi, "Michelangelo Pistoletto," *Data* 7, no. 6 (1978): 34. Rinaldi is also a painter.
119. Germano Celant, "Arte Povera," in *Arte Povera* (Bologna: Galleria de' Foscherari, 1968), n.p.
120. Pistoletto interview with the author.
121. The mirror painting of Roy Lichtenstein's mother was based on a photo taken by Ettore Sottsass Jr. in late 1962, published in *Domus* in February 1963. Pistoletto also made a portrait mirror painting of Leo Castelli, shown at the Sonnabend exhibition in 1964. That work framed the subject's face but captured the sitter head on.
122. Lumley, *States of Emergency*, 34–41.
123. As Robert Lumley has explained, workers themselves were not frequently in touch with ideas of the intellectual left until 1968. The ideas of the intellectual left and the actions of workers, found in factory strikes, before 1968 would have been of influence rather than of an explicit connection between workers and intellectuals. Lumley, *States of Emergency*, 41.
124. The central figure in *Rally I* and *Bandiera Rossa* (Red Flag) and the central figure in *Man with Red Flag, Rally II,* and *Rally X,* variously staged at far right and center.
125. Germano Celant, "Reflections on Lava" in *Michelangelo Pistoletto: Division and Multiplication of the Mirror*, ed. Germano Celant and Ida Gianelli (New York: Institute for Contemporary Art, P.S. 1 Museum, 1988). Also see "Riflessi di lava," in *Pistoletto* (Milan: Fabbri, 1992), 14.
126. They were shown together at the Philadelphia Museum of Art and briefly addressed by Suzanne Penn.
127. This is the title written on the verso of the work, though it is also known as *Due uomini che passano*.
128. Siegfried Kracauer, *History: The Last Things before the Last* (Princeton, NJ: Markus Wiener, 1995), 58.
129. See Friedman, "Questions for Pistoletto," no. 11, Pistoletto response. Fagiolo dell'Arco also positioned Pistoletto's treatment of his human figures and objects in the mirror paintings as "drawn from a life-size photographic enlargement, repainted in some parts" (translation mine). Fagiolo dell'Arco, "Il dramma fisico di Pistoletto," 209. Unlike the early mirror paintings, rendered only in black paint and pencil, mirror paintings beginning in 1964 (including some Rallies) had a naturalistic color palette. He added color to his subject in the form of thinned oil paint after trimming excess tissue from the silhouettes, to stain the tissue paper than apply paint to its surface, which may detract from its smooth, "untouched" quality. On process, see Penn, "'Complicity of the Materials,'" 149–52.
130. Martin, "Mirror, Mirror," 21.
131. Grace Glueck, "Art Notes: The Hokiest Show in New York," *New York Times*, April 30, 1967. For the subsection on Pistoletto within this multishow review, see "Done with Mirrors."
132. Pino Pascali, "Io la contestazione la vedo così" (1968). (Original Italian: "L'artista è sempre stato una vittima della politica ed è stato usato ora da questo ora da quello.") Translation from *Arte Povera*, reprinted in Germano Celant, *Arte Povera: Storia e storie* (Milan: Mondadori Electa, 2011), 75.
133. Germano Celant, "Arte Povera: Notes for a Guerrilla War," trans. Henry Martin, in *Flash Art: Two Decades of History: XXI Years*, ed. Giancarlo Politi and Helen Kontova (Cambridge, MA: MIT Press, 1990), 190.
134. See Lawrence Alloway, "The Arts and Mass Media," *Architectural Design* 28, no. 2 (1958): 84–85; and Lawrence Alloway, *American Pop Art* (New York: Macmillan, 1974), 1, published in conjunction with the exhibition of the same title held at the Whitney Museum of American Art.
135. Fagiolo dell'Arco discusses both series in his short entry on Pistoletto but doesn't connect them beyond the fact that they were both made recently and are positioned in his reading as examples of Pistoletto as a "materialist." See Fagiolo dell'Arco, "Il dramma fisico di Pistoletto," 209–13.
136. This corrects existing misinformation about the pop-related series. They have previously been cited as fewer in number. See Golan, *Flashback, Eclipse*, 117.
137. See *L'Europeo* 20, no. 29, La Biennale (July 19, 1964), n.p. Laura Iamurri's "Il pennello nell'occhio: La pop art sui rotocalchi, prima

e dopo la Biennale del 1964," brought the source of this image to my attention. See Iamurri in *Studi di Memofonte* (November 2013): 135, http://www.memofonte.it/contenuti-rivista-n.11/l.-iamurri-il-pennello-nell-occhio.-la-pop-art-sui-rotocalchi-prima-e-dopo-la-biennale-del-1964.html.

138. Carlotta Sylos Calò, *Corpo a corpo: Estetica e politica nell'arte italiana degli anni Sessanta* (Macerata: Quodlibet, 2018), 120.
139. The second of the pair has been published with various dates. Pistoletto's archive stipulated 1964, which I use here.
140. Golan, "Flashbacks and Eclipses," 118–19; Golan, *Flashback, Eclipse,* 72–79. Golan suggests that the unchanged uniforms of alpinists across the world wars makes Pistoletto's *Alpini* simultaneous referents to futurists' participation in World War I, where many were enlisted in the regiments, and to antifascist resistance in World War II, specifically recalling partisan strikes in Turin just before liberation, at a moment of Italian commitment to resistance. See Golan, *Flashback, Eclipse,* 76, 79.
141. Anthony George White, "Michelangelo Pistoletto's *Minus Objects,*" in *The Minus Objects, 1965–1966* (New York: Luhring Augustine; Munich: DelMonico Books, Prestel, 2017), 88. Pistoletto made this statement in Germano Celant, "Intervista con Pistoletto, San Sicario, 1983," in Celant and Gianelli, *Pistoletto,* 159–60.
142. Pistoletto, "I plexiglass," September 1964, n.p., text published in conjunction with the artist's exhibition of the same title at the Galleria Gian Enzo Sperone in Turin.
143. See Giulio Carlo Argan, "La nuova figurazione," *Il Messaggero,* April 17, 1962.
144. Rosenquist and Warhol followed in November 1964 and late February and early March 1965; Rauschenberg's Dante series was exhibited in April of 1965. For dates of shows and timeline of exhibitions at Sperone, see Criticos, "La Galerie Gian Enzo Sperone," 158.
145. Dario Micacchi, "Per una volta dentro il quadro," *L'Unità,* March 19, 1968, 8.
146. While this photograph was published in the catalog for the artist's exhibition at the Palacio Cristal in Madrid in 1983, neither the gilded *Venus of the Rags* nor *Man-Sized House* was shown in the Madrid exhibition. Photographs published in a *Domus* report in 1981 on *Identité italienne* show some of these same works, though a plain instead of a gilded *Venus of the Rags.* The photograph I discuss here was therefore likely taken of the works in preparation for the artist's works to be shown at the Pompidou exhibition. I thank Marco Farano for finding the *Domus* photographs and providing a provisional date of the photo.
147. Pistoletto, interview with *Web Comune di Napoli,* "La Venere degli stracci di Pistoletto in piazza Municipio," June 29, 2023, https://youtu.be/nnNklqusYZU. (Original Italian: "Questa venere, che se ne occupi, ma la venere siamo noi. Siamo noi che devono prendere atto migliore di noi stessi.")
148. The work was remade and reinstalled in March 2024.
149. Pier Paolo Pasolini, "Alla bandiera rossa" (1961), in *La religione del mio tempo* (Milan: Garzanti, 1995), 118.

CHAPTER 4. EXTREMELY POOR FIGURES

1. The complete list, revised from Bruno Corà's, includes twenty-five objects in the first installations: *Rosa bruciata* (1965), *Colonne di cemento* (1965–66), *Statua lignea* (1965), *Il letto* (1965–66), *Quadro da pranzo* (1965–66), *Pozzo* (1966), *Paesaggio* (1966), *Ti amo* (1966), *La vetrina* (1966), *Lampada a mercurio* (1966), *Letto* (1965–66), *Tele-torte* (1966), *Foto di Jasper Johns* (1966), *Struttura per parlare in piedi* (1966), *Corpo a pera* (1966), *Piramide verde* (1966), *Semisfere decorative* (1965–66), *Mobile* (1966), *Fontana luminosa* (1966), *Mica* (1966), *Bagno* (1966), *Casa a misura d'uomo* (1966), *Metrocubo d'infinito* (1966), *Piccola sfera sotto il letto* (1966), *Sarcafago* (1966), and *Sfera di giornali* (Newspaper Sphere, 1966). Pistoletto ultimately made two roses, bringing the final count to twenty-six.

   These were followed by the thirteen "versions" of the Minus Objects, including three that were not produced until 1968: *Le orecchie di Jasper Johns* (1966), *Pozzo cartone e specchio* (1966), *Pozzo specchio* (1966), *Corpo a pera specchio* (1966), *Vetrina specchio* (1966), *Portico* (1966), *Mappamondo* (1966–68), *Grande sfera di giornali* (*progetto per un museo*) (1966), *Cinque pozzi* (1966), *Pozzo nero* (1966), *Pozzo culla* (1966–68), *La terra e la luna* (1966–68), and *Bagno barca* (1966–68).
2. On commercial need, see Michelangelo Pistoletto, "Oggetti in meno" (1966), in *Michelangelo Pistoletto* (Genoa: Galleria La Bertesca, 1966), 16. On new products, studio clutter, and childhood memories, see Pistoletto, conversation with Carlos Basualdo, Germano Celant, and Christine Poggi, "Session Two: Pistoletto and Arte Povera," in *Three Conversations with Michelangelo Pistoletto, Germano Celant, and Carlos Basualdo* (Philadelphia: Philadelphia Museum of Art, October 31, 2010), program held in conjunction with the exhibition *Michelangelo Pistoletto: From One to Many, 1956–1974* at the Philadelphia Museum of Art, October 30, 2010–January 16, 2011. On childhood memories and things he liked, see Pistoletto, "Interview with Germano Celant" (1971), in *Pistoletto,* ed. Germano Celant and Ida Gianelli (Milan: Electa, 1984), 50–52.
3. Bruno Corà, *Michelangelo Pistoletto: Lo spazio della riflessione nell'arte* (Ravenna: Essegi, 1986), 76.
4. Germano Celant, "Arte Povera: Notes for a Guerrilla War," trans. Henry Martin, *Flash Art,* no. 5 (November–December 1967): 190.
5. For the original, see Pistoletto, "Oggetti in meno," 5. The existing translation of this text makes some changes to the original. I use my own translation here and throughout this book.
6. Germano Celant, *Arte povera* (Bologna: Galleria De Foscherari, 1968), n.p., catalog published in conjunction with the exhibition of the same title held at the Galleria de' Foscherari, February 24–March 15, 1968. Corà, *Pistoletto: Lo spazio della riflessione nell'arte,* 76.
7. Romy Golan, *Flashback, Eclipse: The Political Imaginary of Italian Art in the 1960s* (Princeton, NJ: Princeton University Press, 2021), 87.
8. See Robert Lumley, *Arte Povera* (London: Tate, 2004), 50; Alex Potts, "Disencumbered Objects," *October* 124 (Spring 2008): 169–70; Anthony George White, "Michelangelo Pistoletto's *Minus Objects,*" in *The Minus Objects, 1965–1966* (New York: Luhring Augustine; Munich: DelMonico Books, Prestel, 2017), 93; and Briony Fer, *The Infinite Line: Remaking Art after Modernism* (New Haven: Yale University Press, 2004), 167.
9. See Potts, "Disencumbered Objects," 171.
10. See Nicholas Cullinan, "From Vietnam to Fiat-Nam: The Politics of Arte Povera," *October* 124 (Spring 2008): 24. I thank Denis Viva for his encouragement to further underscore my focus on this earlier moment in Italian history in relation to framings of politics more commonly focused on 1968, as might be suited to more overtly political works such as *Trincea* (Trench), noted later in this chapter.
11. Raffaele Bedarida argues that Arte Povera both rejected Americanization and expressed "newly Americanized Italian culture." See Bedarida, *Exhibiting Italian Art in the United States from Futurism to Arte Povera: "Like a Giant Screen"* (London: Routledge, 2022), intro. and chap. 5.
12. Golan, *Flashback, Eclipse,* 87.
13. Potts, "Disencumbered Objects," 173.
14. Indeed, the better translation of "less objects" appeared in the English version of Tommaso Trini's essay "Nuovo alfabeto per corpo e materia" (1969). See Trini, "New Alphabet for Body and Matter," *Domus,* January 1969, 46.

15. A photograph published in Alberto Boatto's *Dentro/fuori lo specchio* (1969) of a mirror painting of a young couple embracing shows the rose reflected in its surface. The photo was taken at the artist's exhibition at Galleria Naviglio in 1967.
16. Pistoletto later offered two mirror paintings in exchange for the return of *Burnt Rose* from gallerist Margherita Stein. My thanks to Gianfranco Benedetti for sharing this history with me. Pistoletto confirmed for me in November 2021 that he destroyed the first rose because he was dissatisfied with it. This is the first study to document two burnt roses in his oeuvre. Pistoletto also made more than one *Mica* painting. The first, a square canvas, was made in 1966 with the Minus Objects. The artist made other *Mica* paintings, among them some with a circular shape, in 1970, to be shown in his exhibition at Galleria Gian Enzo Sperone, Turin. Germano Celant, ed., *Pistoletto* (Milan: Electa, 1976), 22.
17. Many have addressed the tendency to hold the mirror paintings apart from the Minus Objects. For an early example, see Claire Gilman, "Reconsidering Arte Povera" in *Arte Povera: Selections from the Sonnabend Collection* (New York: Miriam and Ira D. Wallach Art Gallery, Columbia University, 2001), 11.
18. Pistoletto, "Oggetti in meno," 15.
19. See Tenley Bick, "Figure as Model: The Early Work of Michelangelo Pistoletto, 1956–1966" (PhD diss., UCLA, 2016); and Marin Sullivan, *Sculptural Materiality in the Age of Conceptualism: International Experiments in Italy* (London: Routledge, 2017), 56–89.
20. Ulrich Loock, "Michelangelo Pistoletto's 'Oggetti in meno' heute," in *Michelangelo Pistoletto: Oggetti in meno, 1965–1966* (Bern: Kunsthalle Bern and Wiener Secession, 1989), 13.
21. Celant, "Arte Povera: Notes for a Guerrilla War," 190.
22. Claire Gilman has also noted this tendency in narratives on Pistoletto's work. Gilman, "Reconsidering Arte Povera," 11. My study is, beyond that, emphasizing the conflict's timing, which coincided with the Plexiglasses. The precise timeline of this conversation remains unclear. Pistoletto has variously recalled the date of first travel to New York as 1964 (Marco Farano, "Chronology," in Basualdo, *Pistoletto: From One to Many*, 356), with the conversation taking place in late 1964 (interview with Celant, in Celant and Gianelli, *Pistoletto*, 29–32) and 1965 (interview with Giovanni Lista, in *Arte Povera: Interviste curate e raccolte da Giovanni Lista* [Milan: Abscondita, 2011], 62–63). Photographs of Pistoletto in James Rosenquist's studio (with Rauschenberg, Sonnabend, Castelli, Solomon, and others), where *F-111* (1964–65) was on display, document that he was, at the very least, present in New York, with these individuals, in 1965.
23. Pistoletto interview by Lista, in *Arte Povera: Interviste curate e raccolte da Giovanni Lista*. With Alain Elkann, Pistoletto said the works were damaged at Castelli's gallery, but in preparation for his show at the Kornblee. See Pistoletto and Elkann, *La voce di Pistoletto* (Milan: Bompiani, 2013), 90–95.
24. Pistoletto expressed this perspective in his discussion of the production of the *Minus Objects*. See Pistoletto, untitled [on the production of the Minus Objects], excerpted from an unpublished interview by Germano Celant (1971), in Celant, *Pistoletto*, 50–58.
25. Pistoletto later told Germano Celant that he had selected the photograph from a book on Johns (likely mistaken for the spread in *Métro*) because he liked the smile. The *Métro* spread must be the source because it included the full image required for Pistoletto to enlarge it. See his interview with Celant, in Celant and Gianelli, *Pistoletto*, 52. Flavio Fergonzi identified the Meneeley photograph in his *Una nuova superficie: Jasper Johns e gli artisti italiani, 1958–1966* (Milan: Electa, 2019), 16–17. See also Leo Steinberg, "Jasper Johns," *Métro* 3, no. 4–5 (1962): 86–109 (photo, 86). The Vienna catalog was *POP, Etc.*, held at the Museum des 20. Jahrhunderts in Vienna, September 19–October 31, 1964.
26. Pistoletto, "Oggetti in meno," 13. Translation mine.
27. Pistoletto, "Oggetti in meno," 13. Translation mine.
28. For more statistics on industrialization in Italy, see David Carson, "Marketing in Italy Today," *Journal of Marketing* 30, no. 1 (1966): 10–16; Adam Arvidsson, *Marketing Modernity: Italian Advertising from Fascism to Postmodernity* (New York: Routledge, 2003); and Paul Ginsborg, *A History of Contemporary Italy: 1945–1988*, 2nd exp. ed. (New York: St. Martin's, 2003).
29. See Ginsborg, *History of Contemporary Italy*, 216.
30. By the mid-1960s, following the establishment of the European Common Market in 1958, Italy would be the largest producer and exporter in Europe. Ivan Paris, "Domestic Appliances and Industrial Design: The Italian White-Goods Industry during the 1950s and 1960s," *Technology and Culture* 57, no. 3 (2016): 617; and Ivan Paris, "L'industria italiana degli elettrodomestici bianchi e la conquista del mercato nazionale," *Impresa e storia* 38, no. 2 (2009): 79–120.
31. Christopher Bennett and I have both been interested in *Il posto* in relation to Italian art and class politics during and after the boom. His work on Jannis Kounellis, in conference format and subsequent publication, drew my attention to the suit-shopping scene. See Christopher Bennett, "1968—Past, Present, Future: Models of Art and Activism in Jannis Kounellis's *Senza titolo* (Untitled)," in *Global Revolutionary Aesthetics and Politics after Paris '68*, ed. Martin Munro, William J. Cloonan, Barry J. Faulk, and Christian P. Weber (Lanham, MD: Lexington Books, 2020), 15.
32. On national identity and the success of Italy's design industries, see Adam Arvidsson, "The Economic Miracle: Mass Consumption and Modernization," in *Marketing Modernity*, 67–89.
33. See Arvidsson, "Economic Miracle," 67–89; Carson, "Marketing in Italy Today," 10–13; David Raizman, *History of Modern Design: Graphics and Products since the Industrial Revolution* (London: Lawrence King, 2003), 275; and Penny Sparke, *Design in Italy: 1870 to the Present* (New York: Abbeville, 1988). Antje Gamble has also discussed American exhibitions of Italian design; Marshall Plan support of Italian craft and design during the Cold War further supported the global association between Italian design and identity in the postwar period. See Antje Gamble, *Cold War American Exhibitions of Italian Art and Design* (Abingdon, UK: Routledge, 2024). My thanks to the author for sharing her book with me in advance of its arrival in print.
34. Necchi's Mirella model (by Marcello Nizzoli), from 1957, won design accolades in Italy and the United States. By 1960, Necchi was the number-one Italian sewing machine company in international sales. Efforts to confirm the designer of this ad were unsuccessful; it can likely be attributed to Franco Grignani, perhaps with Jeanne Grignani, his wife and frequent collaborator; Franco designed award-winning campaigns for Necchi in the late 1950s, some of which featured similar imagery. On the company's fascist-era ads, see Bianca Gaudenzi, *Fascismi in vetrina: Pubblicità e modelli di consumo nel Ventennio e nel Terzo Reich* (Roma: Viella, 2023), 230.
35. Ginsborg, *History of Contemporary Italy*, 216.
36. Design historian Jonathan Woodham has noted the role of La Rinascente in promoting design culture in Italy. The department store hired prominent Italian designers Franco Albini and Gio Ponti to produce lower-cost items for the mass market. See Jonatham Woodham, *Twentieth-Century Design* (Oxford: Oxford University Press, 1997), 126.
37. Pistoletto, interview by Celant (1971), in Celant and Gianelli, *Pistoletto*, 50–52.

38. Pistoletto, quoted by Bruno Corà, in Corà, *Pistoletto: Lo spazio della riflessione nell'arte,* 76. (Original Italian: "Li ho chiamati 'Oggetti in meno' perché secondo me ogni azione che uno fa è una liberazione da una necessità. In questo senso una cosa fatta è una cosa in meno, considerandola energia spesa, uscita, consumata.")
39. Leo Steinberg, "Other Criteria," in *Other Criteria: Confrontations with Twentieth-Century Art* (Oxford: Oxford University Press, 1972), 60.
40. On art and artistic labor in the 1960s, see especially Caroline Jones, *Machine in the Studio: Constructing the Postwar American Artist* (Cambridge, MA: MIT Press, 1998); and Helen Molesworth, ed., *Work Ethic* (University Park: Penn State University Press, 2003).
41. See Germano Celant, *Conceptual Art, Arte Povera, Land Art* (Turin: Galleria Civica d'Arte Moderna, 1970).
42. Trini, "New Alphabet for Body and Matter," 51.
43. Germano Celant, *Art Povera* (New York: Praeger, 1969).
44. On Arte Povera and experimentation, see Richard Flood and Frances Morris, "Introduction," in *Zero to Infinity: Arte Povera: 1962–1972,* ed. Flood and Morris (Minneapolis, MN: Walker Art Center, 2001), 9–21, esp. 16–20, catalog published in conjunction with the exhibition of the same title, October 13, 2001–January 13, 2002 (Tate Modern: May 31–August 19, 2001); theatricality, Claire Gilman, "Arte Povera's Theater: Artifice and Anti-Modernism in Italian Art of the 1960s" (PhD diss., Columbia University, 2006); and Gilman, "Pistoletto's Staged Subjects," *October* 124 (Spring 2008): 53–74; political activism, Cullinan, "From Vietnam to Fiat-Nam," 8–30; technology, Mirella Bandini, "Turin in the 1970s: FIAT, Arte Povera, and Other Heroes," *Flash Art,* no. 160 (October 1991): 105; and artifice and Potts, Christopher G. Bennett, "Boetti and Pascali: Revisiting Arte Povera through Two Case Studies" (PhD diss., University of Michigan, 2008).
45. Trini, "New Alphabet for Body and Matter," 49.
46. Pistoletto, "Interview with Germano Celant" (1971), in Celant and Gianelli, *Pistoletto,* 52.
47. My sincerest thanks to Gianni Piacentino for discussing his early career in applying specialized lacquer paint to automobiles with me in Turin in the spring of 2013.
48. Trini, "New Alphabet for Body and Matter," 49. Although part of Trini's essay is available in the same issue in English translation, this section is not. Translation mine.
49. On Lucy Raven's work as one that "reveal[s]" labor, see Alex Kitnick, "No Resolution: Video Art in and around the Contemporary," *Artforum* 61, no. 9 (2023): 136.
50. See, e.g., *La Stampa,* "Notizie" [Armando Testa Awarded First National Prize in Advertising for his campaign *Re Carpano*], November 7, 1953; *Stampa Sera,* "Artisti torinesi premiati a Bologna," March 30–31, 1955; L.A., "La tecnica della suggestione: Un cartellonista torinese illustra i segreti della sua professione," *Stampa Sera,* February 26, 1956; and *Stampa Sera,* "Vinto un torinese il concorso per le Olimpiadi: Un manifesto chiama la gioventù del mondo," June 3–4, 1958.
51. See Armando Testa's response to a reader in *La Stampa,* who had criticized his figurative designs as a smear campaign of Italian (and specifically Piedmontese) history, as Turin was the home of Italy's monarchy and government post-Unification. Testa, reader's letter, "Specchio dei tempi: Il re e la pubblicità," *La Stampa,* June 23, 1956.
52. The erection of a monument in 2015 dedicated to Armando Testa's Punt e Mes campaign of 1961 is indicative of how iconic his work was and remains in Italian popular culture.
53. Karen Pinkus, *Bodily Regimes: Italian Advertising under Fascism* (Minneapolis: University of Minnesota Press, 1995), 12–13.
54. On Necchi, Singer, and Pibigas, see Pistoletto and Elkann, *La voce di Pistoletto,* 60. The first reproduction of the Visnova ad was in the catalog of the retrospective of 1984 at the Forte Belvedere in Florence; see "M. Pistoletto, bozzetto pubblicitario, 1953," in Celant and Gianelli, *Pistoletto,* 24.
55. They included Domogas, Gastine (likely one of the few he made before his training at the Scuola Testa), Esso motor oil, the Turin-based industrial magazine *Arco e Gas,* and industrial products, such as Rivoira gases and chemical products.
56. They included Campari cordial, Martini and Rossi vermouths, Superga amaro, and Elan caramels (from nearby Genoa).
57. They included Rumianca soap, Beta laundry detergent, Linetti hair polish, Paglieri talcum powder, Knapp vitamin tablets, and Vel cream cosmetics, for which he executed a design for a box and a print advertisement, both on commission, as was an advertisement for Italy's Federation of Barbers and Hairstylists in 1953.
58. They include Chëlvinator and Triplex.
59. The catalog for Pistoletto's retrospective at the Forte Belvedere in Florence in 1984 dates this image to 1953. The date may be slightly later. See Celant and Gianelli, *Pistoletto,* 24.
60. *Aria d'Italia,* vol. 8, *Espressione di Gio Ponti* (Milan: Daria Guarnati, 1954), 1994.
61. See Claudio Piersanti and Rita Rava, "Ceramica e architettura," in *Gio Ponti: Ceramica e architettura,* ed. Gian Carlo Bojani, Claudio Piersanti, and Rita Rava (Florence: Centro Di, 1987), 68.
62. His presence and the clear discomfort of the tub add nuance to existing readings of the interior shape of *Bagno* as that of a human figure. See Corà, *Pistoletto: Lo spazio della riflessione nell'arte,* 78.
63. In a different reading, Silvia Bottinelli has interpreted the stepped interior of *Bagno* as that of a map or lake, seeing a melding between habitat and inhabitant in the work. The work's revision into a *Bagno barca* (Bathtub Boat) links the reference to nature, for Bottinelli, to nomadism. See Bottinelli, *Double-Edged Comforts: Domestic Life in Modern Italian Art and Visual Culture* (Montreal: McGill-Queen's University Press, 2021), 157–58.
64. On being the first, see Carlos Basualdo and Michelangelo Pistoletto, "Conversations," in *The Minus Objects, 1965–1966* (New York: Luhring Augustine; Munich: DelMonico Books, Prestel, 2017), 135.
65. Bottinelli sees this work as engaging with the home and lunch as a space of conviviality. See Bottinelli, *Double-Edged Comforts,* 226–27.
66. For a different reading, which addresses the childlike discrepancy between Pistoletto's work and "man-based architecture" such as Le Corbusier's *Modular,* see Anthony George White, "Michelangelo Pistoletto's *Minus Objects,*" in *The Minus Objects, 1965–1966,* 103. Véronique Goudinoux also discusses wordplay and scale in *Casa,* as well as the humanist tropes it evokes. See Goudinoux, "*Oggetti in meno:* Redefining the Work," in *Michelangelo Pistoletto* (Barcelona: Museu d'art Contemporani de Barcelona, 2000), 66. See also Goudinoux, "Pratique du divers la forme, l'atelier, le spectateur et l'exposition autour des *Oggetti in meno* (1965–1966) de Michelangelo Pistoletto et de leurs constructions critiques" (PhD diss., Université de Lille III, 1996).
67. Studio Testa, carosello Facis "Ogni uomo corre contento" (Every Man Runs Happily), 1965, Archivio G. F. T. (Gruppo Finanziario Tessile), Archivio di Stato di Torino and Archivio Nazionale Cinema d'Impresa, 131/166: YouTube.
68 Antonio Tricomi, "Killing the Father: Politics and Intellectuals, Utopia and Disillusion," in *Imagining Terrorism: The Rhetoric and Representation of Political Violence in Italy, 1969–2009,* ed. Pierpaolo Antonello and Alan O'Leary (London: Routledge, 2009), 17–18.
69. See Antonio Tricomi, "Killing the Father: Politics and Intellectuals, Utopia and Disillusion," in *Imagining Terrorism: The Rhetoric and Representation of Violence in Italy, 1969–2009,* ed. Pierpaolo Antonello and Alan O'Leary (London: Legenda, 2009), 17.
70. Goudinoux, "*Oggetti in meno,*" 66.

71. Carlotta Sylos Calò, *Corpo a corpo: Estetica e politica nell'arte italiana degli anni Sessanta* (Macerata: Quodlibet, 2018), 102.
72. Briony Fer, *The Infinite Line: Re-Making Art after Modernism* (New Haven: Yale University Press, 2004), 174; Goudinoux, "*Oggetti in meno*," 66.
73. Michelangelo Pistoletto, "Sur la création des 'Objets en moins,'" in interview with Celant (1971), in *Pistoletto*, ed. Germano Celant and Ida Gianelli (Milan: Electa, 1984), 96.
74. Raizman, *History of Modern Design*, 275.
75. Woodham, *Twentieth-Century Design*, 127.
76. See Roland Barthes, "Rhetoric of the Image," in *Image—Music—Text*, trans. Stephen Heath (New York: Hill and Wang, 1977), 34–35.
77. For more on Lucio Fontana's use of kitsch, see Anthony White, "Lucio Fontana: Between Utopia and Kitsch," *Grey Room* 5 (Fall 2001): 54–77; and White, *Lucio Fontana: Between Utopia and Kitsch* (Cambridge, MA: MIT Press, 2011). See also Yve-Alain Bois, "Fontana's Base Materialism," *Art in America* 77, no. 4 (1989): 238–48.
78. See White, *Lucio Fontana*.
79. Cullinan, "From Vietnam to Fiat-Nam," 8–10.
80. Woodham, *Twentieth-Century Design*, 191.
81. For a different reading of this work, which has been read as "performative sculpture," in relation to Arte Povera's interest in artistic action, see Nike Bätzner, "Sculptural Performance—Performative Sculpture," in *Entrare nell'opera: Processes and Performative Attitudes in Arte Povera*, ed. Nike Bätzner, Maddalena Disch, Christiane Meyer-Stoll, and Valentina Pero (Cologne: Buchhandlung Walther König, 2019), 75–86, at 86, catalog published in conjunction with the exhibition held at the Kunstmuseum Liechtenstein, June 7–September 1, 2019.
82. See Pistoletto, *L'uomo nero: Il lato insopportabile* (1970), in Pistoletto, *Un artista in meno* (Florence: Hopefulmonster, 1988), 77.
83. For an account of artists' protests at the Bienniale, see Chiara Di Stefano, "The 1968 Biennale: Boycotting the Exhibition," in *Starting from Venice: Studies on the Biennale*, ed. Clarissa Ricci (Milan: Et al., 2010), 131.
84. For an excellent overview of the Piper as "habitat" for avant-garde theater and art, see Francesco Guzzetti, "Piper Pluriclub, Turin, 1966–1969," in Bätzner, Disch, Meyer-Stoll, and Pero, *Entrare nell'opera*, 268–69.
85. The number of participants comes from Corà, *Pistoletto: Lo spazio della riflessione nell'arte*, 84.
86. "La fine di Pistoletto," in Celant, *Pistoletto*, 29. A photograph of the event, appearing in Celant's *Art Povera* compendium published two years later, shows participants unmasked and gathered in a less organized manner.
87. On Piper's inspiration for the title, see "La fine di Pistoletto," 29. The poster was designed by Clino Trini Castelli.
88. Pistoletto, *Le ultime parole famose* (Turin: Published by the author, 1967), n.p. Translation mine.
89. Pistoletto, *Manifesto della collaborazione* (Turin, April 2, 1968), printed flyer made from handwritten original, reproduced in Marco Farano, Maria Cristina Mundici, and Maria Teresa Roberto, *Michelangelo Pistoletto: Il varco dello specchio: Azioni e collaborazioni, 1967–2004* (Turin: Fondazione Torino musei, 2005), 79. Translation mine.
90. Trini, "New Alphabet for Body and Matter, 46.
91. Pistoletto, in conversation with Celant (Genoa, 1971), in *Michelangelo Pistoletto: Azioni materiali*, ed. Matthias Dusini (Cologne: Buchhandlung Walther König, 1999), 39, catalog published in association with the exhibition of the same title, Galerie im Taxispalais, Innsbruck, August 11–October 10, 1999.
92. Pistoletto, *L'Uomo nero*, 115.
93. Pistoletto, *L'Uomo nero*, 44. Some of my translation draws on the existing translation of this text. See Pistoletto, "The Minus Man: The Unbearable Side," trans. Paul Blanchard, in Pistoletto, *A Minus Artist* (Florence: Hopefulmonster, 1988), 45.
94. Pistoletto, *L'Uomo nero*, 112.
95. Lorenza Trucchi, "Pistoletto alla Sperone," *Momento-Sera*, January 29, 1975.
96. Tommaso Trini, "Studio chiuso, strada aperta," *Domus*, January 1969, 52.
97. Celant, untitled text, in *Art Povera*, 225, 226.
98. Carlo Rosselli, *Liberal Socialism*, ed. Nadia Urbinati, trans. William McCuaig (Princeton, NJ: Princeton University Press, 1994), 85.
99. Carlo Rosselli, *Socialismo liberale* (1930) (reprint, Turin: Einaudi, 1973), 435.
100. This reading builds on art historian Christina Kiaer's description of works of Russian Constructivism as "socialist objects." See Kiaer, *Imagine No Possessions: The Socialist Objects of Russian Constructivism* (Cambridge, MA: MIT Press, 2008).
101. The work overlapped with contemporaneous work in Arte Povera that likewise explored office life. See Emilio Prini's *Azioni di comportamento: Alzarsi e andare al lavoro* (Behavior Actions: Get Up and Go to Work), 1969–74, Genoa.
102. Jerzy Grotowski's writings were published in Italy in 1965 owing to the efforts of an Italian student, Eugenio Barba, who smuggled his work out of communist Poland and translated the essays for publication. See Jerzy Grotowski, "Towards a Poor Theatre," trans. T. K. Wiewiorowski, in Jerzy Grotowski, *Towards a Poor Theatre*, ed. Eugenio Barba (New York: Simon and Schuster, 1968), 16–17. Originally published in Polish as "Ku teatrowi ubogiemu," in *Odra*, no. 9 (1965): 21–27.
103. Pistoletto, "Oggetti in meno," n.p.
104. I am thinking here of Mark Godfrey's description of Boetti's *Autoritratto in negativo*, discussed in chap. 1. See Godfrey, *Alighiero e Boetti* (New Haven: Yale University Press, 2011), 73–74.
105. Grotowski, "Towards a Poor Theatre," 19.
106. Grotowski, "Towards a Poor Theatre," 20–21.
107. Kris Salata, *The Unwritten Grotowski: Theory and Practice of the Encounter* (London: Routledge, 2013), 27.
108. Jerzy Grotowski, "How One Could Live" (abridged translation of original), *Le Théâtre en Pologne/The Theatre in Poland*, nos. 4–5 (1975): 33–34. Originally published as "Jak żyć by można" (How One Could Live), *Odra*, no. 4 (1972): 33–38. I am indebted to Kris Salata's work for drawing my attention to this passage.
109. Salata, *Unwritten Grotowski*, 11.

CHAPTER 5. THE REAL AND PERFORMED FIGURE

1. On these suggestions of the title, see Pistoletto, "Michelangelo on Pistoletto: Michelangelo Pistoletto in Conversation with Andrea Bellini," in *Facing Pistoletto*, ed. Andrea Bellini, trans. Barbara McGilvray and Simon Turner (Zurich: JRP Ringier, 2009), 54 (original Italian, 217). The phrase resists translation. Italian scholars have described it as composed of nonsense words. See Francesco Guzzetti, "Piper Pluriclub, Turin, 1966–1969," in *Entrare nell'opera: Processes and Performative Attitudes in Arte Povera*, ed. Nike Bätzner, Maddalena Disch, Christiane Meyer-Stoll, and Valentina Pero (Cologne: Buchhandlung Walther König, 2019), 269.
2. Description of materials, Marco Farano, ed., "Dai quadri specchianti all'Anno Uno: Una cronologia" (July 1999, Biella), in *Michelangelo Pistoletto: Azioni materiali*, ed. Matthias Dusini (Cologne: Buchhandlung Walther König, 1999), 226. Participants included artist Vasco Are, Antonio (Tato) Russo, and Gianni Milano, who had performed in a poetry evening held as part of the opening of Pistoletto's studio the previous month. They met at the Folk Club in Turin. See Maria Teresa Roberto, "Davanti allo specchio, al di qua delle sbarre: Lo Zoo dagli antifatti a *L'uomo nero*, 1966–1970," in Marco Farano, Maria Cristina Mundici, and Maria Teresa Roberto,

Michelangelo Pistoletto: Il varco dello specchio: Azioni e collaborazioni, 1967–2004 (Turin: Fondazioni Torino musei, 2005), 26.

3. The collaboration was *La vestizione* (Dressing; color, 25 mins., 8mm, 1968), made for Pistoletto's exhibition at the Galleria L'Attico. Farano, Mundici, and Roberto, *Pistoletto: Il varco dello specchio*, 93. Note: The *La Stampa* theater listing states that the performance "tells the story of the birth of a future, imaginary city." Pistoletto rejects that information and does not know from where it came.
4. S.v. "picco," in *Grande dizionario della lingua italiana*, vol. 13, ed. Salvatore Battaglia (Turin: UTET, 1995), 356.
5. See, e.g., Baz Kershaw's work on alternative theater in 1960s Britain: *The Politics of Performance: Radical Theatre as Cultural Intervention* (London: Routledge, 1992), 212.
6. See Bellini, in Pistoletto, "Michelangelo on Pistoletto," interview by Bellini, in *Facing Pistoletto*, ed. Andrea Bellini, trans. Barbara McGilvray and Simon Turner (Zurich: JRP Ringier, 2009), 63. Others have called this work "ambivalent" toward actual radical activity of 1968, insofar as it is "directed chaos," with starts and stops. See Claire Gilman, "Pistoletto's 'Object Theater,'" in *Michelangelo Pistoletto: From One to Many, 1956–1974*, ed. Carlos Basualdo (Philadelphia: Philadelphia Museum of Art, 2010), 101.
7. Henry Martin, "The Zoo non è una badia," *Data* 1, no. 1 (September 1971): 61. Here, in his own words, Martin recalls Germano Celant's description of the group. The Zoo worked with international members. Pistoletto would later emphasize the distinctive composition of the Zoo's community, recounting the deportation of American members who did not have their residency papers. Pistoletto, *L'Uomo nero: Il lato insopportabile* (1970), reprinted in his *Un artista in meno* (Florence: Hopefulmonster, 1988), 27–132, at 28–29. Originally published as *L'Uomo nero: Il lato insopportabile* (Salerno: Rumma, 1970).
8. In the late 1960s, he wrote: "[The artist] comes from the closed spaces of the galleries and the museums (at times, notwithstanding all, he goes back there); he goes down to the public places, crosses forests, deserts, fields of snow, to appraise a participating intervention." See Germano Celant, *Art Povera* (New York: Praeger, 1969), n.p.
9. I thank Andrea Maglio for noting the overtly bourgeois aesthetics of the invitation. The size of the edition and dissemination is unknown. An example of it is available for study in the Archivio Pistoletto. I thank Silvia Bottinelli for the prompt to consider this work's relationship to Binga's.
10. On this intention, see Farano, "Dai quadri specchianti," 226.
11. The literature on women artists in Arte Povera—namely on Marisa Merz, but also on female collaborators such as Pioppi—and on Italian women artists, critics, and feminism in the 1960s and 1970s more broadly, has proliferated in recent years. Key texts include Rafallea Perna, *Altra misura: Arte, fotografia e femminismo in Italia negli anni '70* (Poggibonsi: Carlo Cambi, 2016); Cornelia Butler, ed., *Marisa Merz: The Sky Is a Great Space* (Munich: DelMonico Books, Prestel, 2017); Francesca Ventrella and Giovanni Zapperi, eds., *Feminism and Art in Postwar Italy: The Legacy of Carla Lonzi* (London: Bloomsbury, 2020); and the journal *Palinsesti*'s double issue, *"Yet Who Is the Genius?" Women's Art and Criticism in Postwar Italy*, edited by Silvia Bottinelli and Giorgia Gastaldon, nos. 8 (2019) and 9 (2020). Teresa Kittler drew attention to women collaborators in Arte Povera in an online conference at Magazzino Italian Art in 2020.
12. Matthias Dusini, "Theatre, Art, Politics and the Zoo—The Performative Traits in Michelangelo Pistoletto's Work," in *Michelangelo Pistoletto: Azioni materiali*, ed. Dusini, 115–26.
13. See Nike Bätzner, "Sculptural Performance—Performative Sculpture," in *Entrare nell'opera: Processes and Performative Attitudes in Arte Povera*, ed. Nike Bätzner, Maddalena Disch, Christiane Meyer-Stoll, and Valentina Pero (Cologne: Buchhandlung Walther König, 2019), 75.
14. On "object" aesthetics versus "actions," exemplified by *Arte povera + azioni povere* and its catalog, edited by Germano Celant, see Alessandra Acocella, *Avanguardia diffusa: Luoghi di sperimentazione artistica in Italia, 1967–1970* (Macerata: Quodlibet and Fondazione Passaré, 2016), 126–27. Bätzner, "Sculptural Performance—Performative Sculpture," 75–86; Gilman, "Pistoletto's 'Object Theater,'" 89. Gilman emphasizes Pistoletto's construction of little sculptures as part of some of the Zoo's actions as an interest in the Zoo's "production of things" (even as this scholarship notes that these "things" were images) for Pistoletto. We might also note the title of one of the volumes documenting the Zoo's actions: Dusini, *Pistoletto: Azioni materiali*.
15. See esp. Gabriele Guercio, "A Community of the Non-All," in Basualdo, *Pistoletto: From One to Many*, 109–42; Dusini, "Theatre, Art, Politics and the Zoo"; Maria Teresa Roberto, "Davanti allo specchio, al di qua delle sbarre," in Farano, Mundici, and Roberto, *Pistoletto: Il varco dello specchio*, 840; and Jacopo Galimberti, "A Third-Worldist Art? Germano Celant's Invention of Arte Povera," *Art History* 36, no. 2 (2013): 418–41. Others still have compiled invaluable documentary chronologies and descriptions of the Zoo's activities. Key volumes of primary material include Dusini, *Pistoletto: Azioni materiali;* Farano, Mundici, and Roberto, *Pistoletto: Il varco dello specchio;* and Bellini, *Facing Pistoletto*.
16. Bruno Corà, *Michelangelo Pistoletto: Lo spazio della riflessione nell'arte* (Ravenna: Essegi, 1986), 103.
17. While Claire Gilman focuses on Pistoletto's sculptural installations in the Zoo, of relevance to my concern with the figure is her discussion of discourse and systems of meaning as topics in some of the Zoo's activity, namely in *The Trained Man* (1968). See Gilman, "Pistoletto's 'Object Theater,'" 82–89.
18. Giuseppe Bartolucci, "Introduzione" [to section "Testimonianze: Strategia di una 'diversa' scrittura scenica"], *Teatro* 2, no. 1 (March 1969): 11. Curran underscored the importance of Bartolucci to the organization of *PLAY*, and for theater in Turin and the Teatro Argentina in Rome. Alvin Curran, e-mail to the author, January 18, 2022. In a separate conversation with the author in 2022, Pistoletto also underscored Bartolucci's importance.
19. Other artists cited included Mario Ceroli and Jannis Kounellis in Arte Povera, who, Bartolucci contended, most pursued theater. Bartolucci also included American expanded cinema and experimental music.
20. Bartolucci, "Introduzione," 11.
21. Bartolucci, "Introduzione," 11–12.
22. On *scrittura scenica* as the major contribution of experimental theater in the second half of the twentieth century, see Lorenzo Mango, *La scrittura scenica: Un codice e le sue pratiche nel teatro del Novecento* (Roma: Bulzoni, 2003), 33. The Gruppo 63 is now widely accepted as the origins of Italian New Theater. See Valentina Valentini, *New Theater in Italy: 1963–2013*, trans. Thomas Haskell Simpson (London: Routledge, 2018), x–xi, 1. For a brief overview of Valle Giulia in relation to transnational events of May 1968, see Arthur Marwick, "'1968' and the Cultural Revolution of the Long Sixties," in *Transnational Moments of Change: Europe, 1945, 1968, 1989*, ed. Gerd-Rainer Horn and Padraic Kenney (Lanham, MD: Rowman and Littlefield, 2004), 84–85. On Italian New Theater generally, see Daniela Visone, *La nascita del nuovo teatro in Italia, 1959–1967* (Corrazono [Pisa]: Titivillus, 2010); and Gianluca Rizzo, *Poetry on Stage: The Theatre of the Italian Neo-Avant-Garde* (Toronto: University of Toronto Press, 2020).

23. See Nanni Balestrini and Primo Moroni, "L'esplosione del '68," chapter 5 in *L'Orda d'oro, 1968–1977: La grande ondata rivoluzionaria e creativa, politica ed esistenziale* (Milan: Feltrinelli, 1988), esp. "'Non siam scappati più': La battaglia di Valle Giulia."
24. Writing on masked comedic acting in Jerzy Grotowski, for example, French writer Marc Fumaroli declared a crisis in world theater that he connected to civilization's state of self-deception. Self-described "anarchic composer" Frederic Rzewski, a cofounder of the Rome-based American music collective (and Zoo collaborators) Musica Elettronica Viva, called for improvisation-as-dialogue in response to states of emergency. See Marc Fumaroli, "L'attore comico o il commediante mascherato: In margine a Towards a Poor Theatre di Jerzy Grotowski," trans. Olimpia Saletti, *Teatro* 2, no. 1 (March 1969): 37; and Frederic Rzewski, "L'improvvisazione, forma di dialogo perduta," in the same issue, 18–23. Musica Elettronica Viva and the Zoo's first official collaboration was *Zuppa,* held at the Galleria L'Attico, in Rome, October 25–26, 1968. Per Alvin Curran, they also executed collaborative little actions in the streets of Trastevere. Alvin Curran, Zoom interview with the author, January 24, 2022.
25. Pistoletto, "Lo Zoo," *Teatro* 2, no. 1 (March 1969): 17. (Original Italian: "Noi non lavoriamo piú [*sic*] per gli spettatori, siamo noi stessi attori e spettatori, fabbricanti e consumatori.")
26. Pistoletto, "Lo Zoo," 16.
27. Pistoletto, "Lo Zoo," 16.
28. Farano, Mundici, and Roberto, *Pistoletto: Il varco dello specchio,* 46.
29. In 2015, the Galleria Continua attributed a painting by Pistoletto from 1959 as *L'Uomo nero,* under which title it has also come up for auction. That painting, however, has no title on its verso; one fragmentary label that remains on a stretcher bar from its exhibition at the Premio Alfieri in 1962 suggests the title was *Uomo in grigio* (Man in Gray), which may have simply been descriptive. Pistoletto's archivist does not know why the work was given that attribution. In the absence of evidence, it cannot be included in the history of *L'Uomo nero* in Pistoletto's practice.
30. The group performed *The Trained Man* in Manarola and Levanto the same month. In early October 1968, at the now-canonical exhibition *Arte povera + azioni povere* (Poor Art + Poor Actions) organized by Marcello Rumma in Amalfi, they performed it once again, this time with Henry Martin, the American art critic and frequent participant in the Zoo's activities, in the role of "the trained man."
31. Herbert Marcuse, *One-Dimensional Man: Studies in the Ideology of Advanced Industrial Society* (Boston: Beacon, 1964).
32. Tommaso Trini noted this role in an early text on the Zoo. See Tommaso Trini, "Studio chiuso, strada aperta," *Domus,* January 1969, 52. Pistoletto also acted as street entertainer, inflating balloons and blowing a bird whistle.
33. Gilman, "Pistoletto's 'Object Theater,'" 90.
34. Pistoletto, "Michelangelo on Pistoletto," 54.
35. Gilman, "Pistoletto's 'Object Theater,'" 90, 101.
36. Gianni Milano (b. 1938), a member of the literary underground, gained national attention for his book *Guru* (Turin: Pitecantropus, 1967), denounced for indecency. Both Milano and Pistoletto contributed to the important short-lived countercultural psychedelic magazine *Pianeta Fresco* (Cool Planet), founded in Turin in 1967 by Fernanda Pivano and Ettore Sottsass, in which Pistoletto published a letter that same winter.
37. Pistoletto, "Michelangelo on Pistoletto," 54, emphasis in original.
38. On "creative collaboration" as opposed to conventional "thespian" work of theater, see Pistoletto, "Michelangelo on Pistoletto," 61. See also Marco Farano, "Michelangelo Pistoletto and Creative Collaboration," in Bätzner, Disch, Meyer-Stoll, and Pero, *Entrare nell'opera,* 224–33.
39. They included Guido Scategni, Denis Kaufmann, Gianni Milano, Claudia Fiorelli, Carol, Bill Higgins, Carlo Colnaghi, Lionello Gennero, Jimmy, Mike Wotell, photographer Beppe Bergamasco, and Anna MacArthur.
40. Martin, "The Zoo non è una badia," 60.
41. Martin, "The Zoo non è una badia," 60.
42. They performed in experimental theater and performance festivals and at vanguard galleries in Turin, Naples, Amsterdam, Belgrade, Novi Sad, and other cities.
43. Pistoletto, "Il tempo del Giudizio," Radio Papesse Intervista, February 16, 2009, available at https://archive.org/details/MichelangeloPistoletto-IlTempoDelGiudizio-RadioPapesseIntervista (these quotations). Pistoletto stated "a work in progress" in English in this otherwise Italian interview. The *L'Uomo nero* works included *La ricerca dell'Uomo nero* (Summer 1969); *The Zoo scopre L'Uomo nero* (Turin, Galleria Sperone, September 1969); *L'Uomo nero* (Macerata, Artestudio, November 1969, March 1970); and the installation *Ufficio dell'uomo nero* (Bologna 1970). Marco Farano, Chronology, "The Zoo," http://www.pistoletto.it/eng/crono07b.htm. Pistoletto also shares the address in a letter to curator Jean-Christophe Ammann, published in the catalog for Ammann's exhibition in Luzern.
44. This exploration might be contemplated further in broader studies on the poveristi's exploration of cybernetics in tension with humanism. See, e.g., LeGrace Benson with Gabriele Mureau, "An Interview with Piero Gilardi," trans. Alan Nagel (November 1967, Fischbach Gallery, New York), 3. Fischbach Gallery records, 1937–2015, bulk 1963–1977, Archives of American Art, Smithsonian Institution, series 1, box 6, folder 39. See also Pamela M. Lee and Fred Turner, "The Cybernetic Vision in Postwar Art," in *Postwar: Art between the Pacific and the Atlantic, 1945–1965,* ed. Okwui Enwezor, Katy Siegel, and Ulrich Wilmes (Munich: Prestel, Haus der Kunst, 2017), 696–703. See also Armin Medosch, *New Tendencies: Art at the Threshold of the Information Revolution (1961–1978)* (Cambridge, MA: MIT Press, 2016).
45. Art historian Aja Martin is exploring race and themes of darkness in the work of Fontana in her PhD dissertation in development: "Dark Matters: Lucio Fontana's Grotesque World" (Rice University).
46. Marco Farano, "L'Uomo nero," artist's website, http://www.pistoletto.it/it/crono08.htm.
47. Pistoletto, interview by Corà (late December 1985, Turin), in Corà, *Pistoletto: Lo spazio della riflessione nell'arte,* 210. (Original Italian: "nulla, pieno di tutto.")
48. Pistoletto, "In piazza a Corniglia sei mesi di spettacolo ogni giorno dalle 16 alle 19.30" (unpublished working notes), in Celant, *Pistoletto,* 43–44. These notes are undated; we can speculate that they were made contemporaneous to the work discussed, in 1969.
49. Richard Schechner, *Between Theater and Anthropology* (Philadelphia: University of Pennsylvania Press, 1985), 17.
50. Marvin Carlson, *The Haunted Stage: The Theatre as Memory Machine* (Ann Arbor: University of Michigan Press, 2001), 5–6.
51. See Pistoletto, *L'Uomo nero,* in *Un artista in meno,* 112.
52. Pistoletto, "In piazza a Corniglia sei mesi di spettacolo ogni giorno dalle 16 alle 19.30," in Celant, *Pistoletto,* 43. (Original Italian: "Questo nuovo lavoro doveva intitolarsi 'l'uomo nero.' 'L'uomo nero' traeva pretesto da un gioco in cui a turno un partecipante viene messo sotto, cioè segnato, o meglio marcato. Si potrebbe dire che è la vittima; questi condurrà il gioco finché qualcun altro dovrà prenderne il posto. Questo 'Uomo nero' è colui che condizionerà gli altri partecipanti attraendo su di sé l'attenzione.")
53. Pistoletto, *L'Uomo nero,* in *Un artista in meno,* 44–45. (Original Italian: "La scenetta iniziale dell'uomo nero che traccia il cerchio e

tutti gli altri all'interno diventano concorrenti in una gara già predisposta che finisce con la rivolta e il linciaggio del vincitore e poi tutti vanno a dormire impotenti perché nel cerchio del gioco, un altro uomo nero ci sarà di nuovo, subito dopo mentre si dorme.")

54. In New Orleans in 1891, eleven Italian Americans and immigrants were lynched by a mob who accused them of murder of a police chief. (Some had already been acquitted.)
55. Pistoletto, "Michelangelo on Pistoletto," 63. (Original Italian: "Un uomo nero ammaestrato portava un significato a una provocazione ulteriore. Durante il percorso dal luogo dell'esposizione alla piazza centrale dove avremmo fatto *L'Uomo ammaestrato,* ognuno portava con sé qualcosa per lo spettacolo. Io avevo un grande saccone con dentro tutti i miei arnesi . . . poi c'era il capo comico con la frusta che sferzava l'uomo ammaestrato.")
56. Frantz Fanon, "The Fact of Blackness," in *Black Skin, White Masks* (1952), trans. Charles Lam Markmann (London: Pluto, 1986), 109–40, at 110, 111, 139.
57. Pistoletto, *L'Uomo nero,* in his *Un artista in meno,* 45.
58. Pistoletto, *L'Uomo nero,* in his *Un artista in meno,* 45.
59. Pistoletto, *L'Uomo nero,* in his *Un artista in meno,* 45.
60. See Pistoletto, *L'Uomo nero,* in his *Un artista in meno,* 60–61. Translation by Paul Blanchard, in Pistoletto, *A Minus Artist* (Florence: Hopefulmonster, 1988), 61. (Original Italian: "L'economia nella nostra civiltà è la cosa più disorganizzata che esista. La stessa economia mentale del proprio tempo individuale. Ne sono vittime tutti, gli industriali come gli operai, gli statisti come i gendarmi e gli artisti. Ora ti racconto uno dei miei occhi semiaperti. Una compagnia di giovani si compone per fare del teatro. Ma non del teatro tradizionale, per fare degli spettacoli vivi, direttamente, creativi.")
61. Pistoletto, *L'Uomo nero,* in *Un artista in meno,* 112.
62. These are terms also used by the artist, who in 2009 said to Andrea Bellini, "Our work method was open, free, and spontaneous." See Pistoletto, "Michelangelo on Pistoletto," 53. The quotation on "very instinctual" belongs to Bellini, *Facing Pistoletto,* 57.
63. Michael Hardt and Antonio Negri, *Assembly* (Oxford: Oxford University Press, 2017), 4–9.
64. A more reinscriptive example of Eurocentric racialized fantasies in Arte Povera can be found in Pino Pascali's *Tribute to Billie Holiday* (1964): a black sculptural monochrome painting with bright red lips.
65. On "geographical alterity," see Luca Caminati, *Il cinema come happening: Il primitivismo pasoliniano e la scena artistica italiana degli anni Sessanta* (Milan: Postmedia, 2010). Focused on the critical value of neoprimitivism in 1960s Italy, Caminati argues that this work posited resistance to modernity that recoded the economic boom and those marginalized by capitalism. See also Giovanna Trento, "From Marinetti to Pasolini: Massawa, the Red Sea, and the Construction of 'Mediterranean Africa' in Italian Literature and Cinema," *Northeast African Studies* 12, no. 1 (2012): 273–307.
66. Teresa Kittler, "Living Differently, Seeing Differently: Carla Accardi's Temporary Structures: 1965–1972," *Oxford Art Journal* 40, no. 1 (2017): 85–107; Silvia Bottinelli, "The Discourse of Modern Nomadism: The Tent in Italian Art and Architecture of the 1960s and 1970s," *Art Journal* 74, no. 2 (2015): 62–80. Bottinelli uses "modern nomadism," drawing on the early 1960s work of Georges-Hubert de Radkowski. Ara Merjian, "Arte Povera: Prehistory and the Aesthetics of Contamination," chap. 3 in *Against the Avant-garde: Pier Paolo Pasolini, Contemporary Art, and Neocapitalism* (Chicago: University of Chicago Press, 2020). See also Valérie Da Costa, *Pino Pascali—Retour à la Méditerranée* (Paris: Les presses du réel, 2015). I have also discussed this trajectory elsewhere; see my essay "Ghosts for the Present: Countercultural Aesthetics and Postcoloniality for Contemporary Italy; The Work of Wu Ming 2 and Fare Ala," in *Global Revolutionary Aesthetics and Politics after Paris '68,* ed. William Cloonan, Barry Faulk, Martin Munro, and Christian Weber (Lanham, MD: Lexington Books, 2021), 56–57.
67. Galimberti, "A Third-Worldist Art?," 419–41, esp. 424.
68. Shelleen Greene, *Equivocal Subjects: Between Italy and Africa—Constructions of Racial Identity in the Italian Cinema* (London: Bloomsbury, 2012), 54.
69. Cristina Lombardi-Diop and Caterina Romeo, "Introduction: Paradigms of Postcoloniality in Contemporary Italy," in *Postcolonial Italy, Challenging National Homogeneity,* ed. Lombardi-Diop and Romeo (New York: Palgrave Macmillan, 2012), 20.
70. Maria Pioppi, interview with Silvia Eiblmayr, in Dusini, *Azioni materiali,* 181.
71. Pioppi interview with Eiblmayr, 181.
72. Pioppi interview with Eiblmayr, 180.
73. Franco Vaccari, "Note di Franco Vaccari" (March 28, 1968), *Data* 2, no. 5 (1972): 28–32 (original Italian for this quotation at 28; translation from *Data,* 29).
74. Franco Vaccari, text, in *La scultura buia* (Piacenza: Centro di Documentazione Visiva, 1968), n.p.
75. Celant, *Art Povera,* 226.
76. Celant, *Art Povera,* 229.
77. Celant, *Art Povera,* 230.
78. Natalia Ginzburg, *Family Sayings,* trans. D. M. Low (New York: Arcade, 1967), 9. I thank Saskia Ziolkowski for this reference.
79. This discussion draws on my essay "Un sentimento di libertà: Toward a Transnational Italian Art History," *Forum Italicum* 57, no. 2 (2023): 431–42. It first appeared in short form as Tenley Bick, "Towards a Transnational Italian Art History: A User's Guide," *Italian Art Society Newsletter* 33, no. 2 (Spring 2022): 11–13. See also Fabrizio De Donno, "La Razza Ario-Mediterranea: Ideas of Race and Citizenship in Colonial and Fascist Italy, 1885–1941," *Interventions: International Journal of Postcolonial Studies* 8, no. 3 (2006): 396; and Silvana Patriarca, "Italian Uses of Orientalism from the Risorgimento to Fascism," *Journal of Modern Italian Studies* 26, no. 2 (2021): 220–26.
80. Annamaria Sapienza, "Oltre il testo: La sperimentazione teatrale napoletana negli anni Sessanta e Settanta," *Forum Italicum* 52, no. 2 (2018): 631–48.
81. My thanks to Marco Farano for these identifications.
82. See "Michelangelo Pistoletto—Pascale Marthine Tayou," Galleria Continua (2012), www.youtube.com/watch?v=e5uHfgdldfo. Translation mine.
83. On the "third," see Pistoletto, "Intervista a Michelangelo Pistoletto attorno alla collaborazione con Vettor Pisani," interview by Andrea Bellini, in *Vettor Pisani—Eroica/antieroica: Una monografia,* ed. Laura Cherubini, Andrea Viliani, and Eugenio Viola (Milan: Electa, 2016), 95. Alberto Boatto, "Plagio," *Data* 1, no. 1 (September 1971): 77.
84. See, e.g., "Professore di filosofia arrestato per plagio a danno di due studenti," *La Stampa,* December 6, 1967; "Annullato la personalità," *Stampa Sera,* July 15–16, 1968, 4; and "Alla sbarra un professore di filosofia per 'plagio' di due studenti," *Corriere della Sera,* July 12, 1968.
85. Guido Guidi, "Quattro anni al Braibanti," *La Stampa,* October 1, 1971.
86. Guidi, "Quattro anni."
87. Alberto Moravia, "La cultura sotto accusa," in *Sotto il nome di plagio: Studi e interventi sul caso Braibanti* (Milan: Bompiani, 1969), 7; Umberto Eco, "Le parole magiche: Analisi semiologica dell'istruttoria, del processo e della sentenza Braibanti," in *Sotto il nome di plagio,* 22.

88. Pistoletto, "Intervista a Michelangelo Pistoletto attorno alla collaborazione con Vettor Pisani," 95.
89. Pistoletto, "Intervista a Michelangelo Pistoletto attorno alla collaborazione con Vettor Pisani," 95.
90. Andrea Pini, *Quando eravamo froci: Gli omosessuali nell'Italia di una volta* (Milan: Il Saggiatore, 2011), 64.
91. Mario Mieli, *Towards a Gay Communism: Elements of a Homosexual Critique* (1977), trans. David Fernbach and Evan Calder Williams (London: Pluto, 2018), 2.
92. José Esteban Muñoz, *Disidentifications: Queers of Color and the Performance of Politics* (Minneapolis: University of Minnesota Press, 1999), 195; José Esteban Muñoz, *Cruising Utopia: The Then and There of Queer Futurity* (New York: New York University Press, 2004), 6. A study day I participated in, with a presentation on this work ("Productive Plagiarism: Michelangelo Pistoletto and Vettor Pisani's *Plagio* [1970–1976]"), at the Center for Italian Modern Art (CIMA) was formative to my early thinking on this topic; Maria Bremer's presentation ("A Relational Self: Epigonism and Pathos in Vettor Pisani's Performance: 'L'Eroe da camera,' 1972") on anthropological relationality in the work of Vettor Pisani was especially helpful, as was Stefano Chiodi's "Lo Scorrevole: Vettor Pisani's 'Theatre of Cruelty." See *Post-It: Reconsidering the Postmodern in Italian Art and Performance,* organized by Emily Braun (New York: Center for Italian Modern Art, February 13–14, 2017).
93. Muñoz, *Cruising Utopia,* 6.
94. Elke Reinhuber, *Counterfactualism in the Fine Arts* (London: Routledge, 2023), 143.
95. Gilles Deleuze and Félix Guattari, *A Thousand Plateaus: Capitalism and Schizophrenia* (1980), trans. Brian Massumi (Minneapolis: University of Minnesota Press, 1987).
96. See Giluio Paolini, interview with Achille Bonito Oliva (1973), republished in *Giulio Paolini: La voce del pittore—Scritti e interviste, 1965–1995,* ed. Maddelena Disch (Lugano: ADV, 1995), 154. See also Paolini's website, which offers this and other bibliography on all works by the artist.
97. Ara H. Merjian, *Against the Avant-Garde: Pier Paolo Pasolini, Contemporary Art, and Neo-Capitalism* (Chicago: University of Chicago Press, 2020), 210.
98. These precedents are outlined and underscored in importance by Marco Farano, "Amore mio—Persona—Plagio," in Farano, Mundici, and Roberto, *Pistoletto: Il varco dello specchio,* 131.
99. See Achille Bonito Oliva, untitled introduction, in *Amore mio* (Montepulciano: Centro Di, 1970), n.p.
100. Pistoletto, "Intervista a Michelangelo Pistoletto attorno alla collaborazione con Vettor Pisani," 95.
101. Andrea Bellini has noted Marcel Duchamp's *Large Glass* and *Étant donnés* as sources for Pisani's own *Lo scorrevole,* an installation and performance shown on several occasions in different versions. See Bellini in Pistoletto, "Intervista a Michelangelo Pistoletto attorno alla collaborazione con Vettor Pisani," 96.
102. The Rivolta Femminile was established in Rome in 1970 by former art critic Carla Lonzi, journalist Elvira Banotti, and artist Carla Accardi.
103. Maurizio Calvesi, *Plagio: "Sonata a cinque dita per Meret Oppenheim" (1° quintetto)* (Rome: Galleria La Salita, 1971), 3, 1.
104. Tommaso Trini, "Mostre," *Domus,* June 1971, 53.
105. This passage builds on existing work on queerness in Italian modernism—namely, that of art historian Denis Viva, who has situated Pisani's work, particularly a show from 1970, *Maschile, femminile, e androgino: Incesto e cannibalismo di Marcel Duchamp* (Masculine, Feminine, and Androgyn: Incest and Cannibalism in Marcel Duchamp), as an important forerunner to this history. See Denis Viva, "Learning from Artists: Methodological Notes on Postwar Italian Art History," in *Postwar Italian Art History Today: Untying "the Knot,"* ed. Sharon Hecker and Marin Sullivan (London: Bloomsbury, 2018), 43–44.
106. Pistoletto, "Intervista a Michelangelo Pistoletto attorno alla collaborazione con Vettor Pisani," 96.
107. Franco Summa, "Silenzio Rosa 1976," https://francosumma.it/Silenzio-Rosa-1976.
108. On the 1970s and memories of homosexual persecution, see Erik N. Jensen, "The Pink Triangle and Political Consciousness: Gays, Lesbians, and the Memory of Nazi Persecution," *Journal of the History of Sexuality* 11, no. 1/2 (2022): 321.
109. Danila Cannamela and Achille Castaldo, "Neither Utopia nor Juvenile Transgression: Retracing the Link between the Movimento del '77, Autonomy, and Literature," *Italian Studies* 76, no. 1 (2021): 96.
110. Pistoletto would make a mirror painting featuring the flag in 2007.
111. Celant, *Art Povera,* 230.
112. Marco Farano, "Anno Bianco," in "Michelangelo Pistoletto: Opere," *Michelangelo Pistoletto,* http://pistoletto.it/it/crono19.htm.
113. Pistoletto, "Michelangelo on Pistoletto," 118–22.
114. Pistoletto, "Anno Uno" (1981), 1, http://pistoletto.it/it/testi/anno_uno.pdf. For an English translation, see Pistoletto, "Year One" (1981), 1, http://www.pistoletto.it/eng/testi/year_one.pdf.
115. In 2009, art historian and curator Andrea Bellini revisited the history of the Zoo on occasion of Pistoletto's restaging of *Year One.* See Pistoletto, "Michelangelo on Pistoletto," 122.
116. Franco "Bifo" Berardi, *Futurability: The Age of Impotence and the Horizon of Possibility* (London: Verso Books, 2019), 103–4.

CONCLUSION

1. For Pistoletto on these figurative sculptures in polyurethane, see his interview with Germano Celant, in Celant, *Pistoletto* (New York: Institute for Contemporary Art [P.S. 1 Museum], 1988), 186–87, catalog published in conjunction with the exhibition of the same title; on this "common spirit," see Pistoletto, in Bruno Corà, "Sulla scultura, dialogo con Michelangelo Pistoletto," in *Costellazione,* text by D. Paparoni (Turin: Galleria Giorgio Persano, 1983).
2. For his description of this fragmentation, see Pistoletto, "Dialogo tra Bruno Corà e Michelangelo Pistoletto," in Bruno Corà, *Michelangelo Pistoletto: Lo spazio della riflessione nell'arte* (Ravenna: Essegi, 1986), 209. See also Pistoletto, "Hard Poetry," in *Arte dello squallore: Michelangelo Pistoletto: Quarta generazione,* trans. Joachim Neugroschel (Turin: Giorgio Persano, 1985), 13, text published in conjunction with the exhibition *Quarta generazione,* (Fourth Generation) at the Galleria Giorgio Persano, Turin, May 1985. Pagination in the catalog is irregular. Pages provided are approximations. For a different reading, which upheld these works as an effort to cast off the "image or object," see Denys Zacharopoulos, "Liberations: The Minus Works of Pistoletto," *Artforum* 24, no. 7 (1986): 80–84.
3. See Pistoletto, in *Michelangelo Pistoletto: La porta dello specchio* (Sarajevo: Ars Aevi, 2001), 78. See also Marco Farano, "Segno Arte," in "Michelangelo Pistoletto: Opere," Michelangelo Pistoletto: http://pistoletto.it/it/crono19.htm.
4. See *La bandiera del mondo, 1+1=3* (2019), in collaboration with artist Angelo Savarese, for Macro Asilo, Rome.
5. Translation mine.
6. Pistoletto, interview, "Giornate della cultura cubana in Italia," *TeleAmbiente,* Oct. 18, 2019, YouTube. (Original Italian: "Cuba è un elemento storico del nostro presente. È la storia nostra di tutti, perché l'abbiamo vissuta attraverso il ventesimo secolo, che ha sentito vissuto e anche prodotto le più grandi separazioni, più grandi

contrasti. . . . Cuba ha creato una sua autonomia. . . . È rimasta un'isola. È rimasto un punto piccolo nel mondo che, come ho detto prima, ancora sulle spalle a tutto quello che il mondo ha creato nel ventesimo secolo. Io vedo lì ancora una possibilità di ripartire, di ripartire da questa capacità di essere liberi nella possibilità di intendersi e di convivere in maniera nuova.")

7. Terry Smith, "Picturing Planetarity," chap. 8 in *Art to Come: Histories of Contemporary Art* (Durham, NC: Duke University Press, 2019).
8. The opening for *Con temp l'azione* was held on December 4, 1967. The precise date of *Scultura da passeggio* is unknown. For more on the exhibition, see Daniela Palazzoli, ed., *Con temp l'azione* (Turin: Christian Stein, Gian Enzo Sperone, and Il Punto, 1967), catalog published in conjunction with the exhibition of the same title, December 4, 1967–February 1968.
9. Pistoletto, *Le ultime parole famose* (Turin: Published by the author, 1967), n.p., emphasis added.
10. The date of the film is typically listed as 1968–69. It was, however, made in January 1968 and shown at Pistoletto's solo exhibition at L'Attico in February 1968 in Rome; the music track includes songs that weren't released until 1969. Whether Ugo Nespolo included different audio in the original is unclear.
11. Ugo Nespolo, in "Michelangelo e il suo doppio," symposium, Circolo degli Lettori, Turin, November 13, 2012.
12. The song is "Strangely Strange but Oddly Normal" (1969), by Dr. Strangely Strange.
13. See, e.g., Marin Sullivan, *Sculptural Materiality in the Age of Conceptualism: International Experiments in Italy* (Abingdon, UK: Routledge, 2017), 56–89; and Anthony George White, "Michelangelo Pistoletto's *Minus Objects*," in *The Minus Objects, 1965–1966* (New York: Luhring Augustine; Munich: DelMonico Books, Prestel, 2017), 109.
14. White, "Michelangelo Pistoletto's *Minus Objects*," 100.
15. Nicolas Bourriaud, *Relational Aesthetics* (1998), trans. Simon Pleasance, Fronza Woods, and Mathieu Copeland (Paris: Les presses du réel, 2002), 18.
16. See, e.g., Benjamin H. D. Buchloh, "Gabriel Orozco: The Sculpture of Everyday Life" (1996), in *Gabriel Orozco*, ed. Yve-Alain Bois (Cambridge, MA: MIT Press, 2009), 35.
17. T. J. Clark, review of *Gabriel Orozco*, edited by Yve-Alain Bois, *London Review of Books*, February 17, 2011, 33.
18. Bourriaud, *Relational Aesthetics*, 17.
19. Gordon Hall, quoted in Sarah Workneh, foreword to Gordon Hall, *Over-Beliefs: Collected Writing, 2011–2018* (Portland, OR: Portland Institute for Contemporary Art, 2018), 5.
20. Gordon Hall, "Leaning Back," Instagram photo, May 8, 2023, https://gordonhall.net/?q=ProjectImage&ID=833.
21. Michael Hardt and Antonio Negri, *Assembly* (Oxford: Oxford University Press, 2017).

Credits

All works by Michelangelo Pistoletto are reproduced courtesy of the artist. Photography of the artist's works and actions by Damiano Andreotti, Paolo Bressano, Alessandro Lacirasella, R. Morichetti, and P. Pellion are provided courtesy of the Archivio Pistoletto (Cittadellarte–Fondazione Pistoletto), as are photographs by Renato Rinaldi.

Figs. 1, 2, 22, 35, 36, 37, 38, 39, 40, 41, 73, 74, 75, 76, 77a–d, 81a–c, 82, 84, 86, 87, 92 (Courtesy of Gianni Piacentino), 105, 106. Photos: © Paolo Bressano
Fig. 3. Photographer unknown. Courtesy of Fondazione Istituto piemontese Antonio Gramsci—Archivio Storico, cat. no. R0166257 008.001
Figs. 4, 34. Getty Research Institute, Los Angeles (2014.R.20), Harry Shunk and Shunk-Kender photographs, 1957–1987 © J. Paul Getty Trust
Figs. 5, 12, 14, 18, 29, 53. Photos: © Tenley Bick
Figs. 6, 7, 11, 28, 55, 62, 66, 70, 72, 79, 80, 89, 94, 95, 96, 97, 108, 128a–d, 129, 133, 135. Archivio Pistoletto, Biella
Figs. 8, 9, 10, 13, 17, 20, 32, 33, 102, 104. Photos: P. Pellion
Figs. 15, 19, 68. Photos: Alessandro Lacirasella
Fig. 16. Courtesy of Mic-Musei Reali
Fig. 21. Photo: Damiano Andreotti
Figs. 23, 24. Courtesy of Aste Bolaffi, Turin
Figs. 25, 120. Photos: © Ela Bialkowska. Fig. 25: In *Prima dello* Specchio, May 2–September 5, 2015. Fig. 120: In *Michelangelo Pistoletto: Buco nero,* September 25, 2010–March 26, 2011. Galleria Continua, San Gimignano. Courtesy of Galleria Continua
Fig. 26. Photo: Oscar Giacomini, Courtesy of Sotheby's Milan
Fig. 27. Photo: © Dorotheum Vienna
Fig. 30. Photo: © Comune di Milano (all rights reserved), Milan, Galleria d'Arte Moderna. Photo: Luca Carrà
Figs. 31, 125. Photos: Luca Carrà. Fig. 31. Courtesy of the photographer. Fig. 125. Source: Ester Coen, *Umberto Boccioni* (New York: Metropolitan Museum of Art; Harry N. Abrams, 1988), 256.
Fig. 42. CSC Archivio Nazionale Cinema Impresa, Turin, courtesy of Edison
Fig. 43. © 2023 Artists Rights Society (ARS), New York / SIAE, Rome. B/w photograph. Photo: © Paolo Bressano, as directed by Boetti
Fig. 44. © 2023 Artists Rights Society (ARS), New York / SIAE, Rome. Kunstmuseum Wolfsburg, Germany. Photo: © Renato Ghiazza. Courtesy of the Fondazione Merz, Turin
Fig. 45. Silvia Fabro (Archivio Luciano e Carla Fabro). Photo: © Giovanni Ricci © Photographic Archive A. Guidetti and G. Ricci
Fig. 46. Photo: © Archivio Penone
Fig. 47. Photo: Paul Maenz. Courtesy of the Fondazione Giulio e Anna Paolini, Turin
Fig. 48. © Victoria and Albert Museum, London
Figs. 49, 51. Photos: © Eric Sutherland. Fig. 49: Archivio Pistoletto, Biella. Fig. 51. Walker Art Center Archives, Courtesy of the Walker Art Center. Fig. 50. © 2025 Estate of Y. Hiro Wakabayashi (Hiro)
Fig. 52. Photo: Will Knight © Tenley Bick
Fig. 54. Detroit Institute of Arts
Figs. 56a–b, 61, 83, 111. © Renato Rinaldi
Figs. 57, 63. Walker Art Center Archives. Courtesy of the Walker Art Center
Fig. 58. Photo: © Rheinisches Bildarchiv Cologne, rba_c010748
Fig. 59. Reproduction permission courtesy of the Walker Art Center Archives and WCOT-TV, CBS Minneapolis
Fig. 60. Photo: George Hixson. Courtesy of the Menil Collection
Fig. 64. Wikimedia Commons
Fig. 65. Courtesy of Farsettiarte, Prato
Fig. 67. Photo: Phillips. Courtesy of Phillips
Fig. 69. Photo by Friedman-Abeles © The New York Public Library for the Performing Arts
Fig. 71. Photograph Courtesy of Sotheby's, Inc. © 2024
Fig. 78. © Michelangelo Pistoletto
Fig. 85. © Ugo Nespolo. Courtesy of Studio Nespolo
Fig. 90. Archivio Storico Armando Testa, Turin. Reproduced with permission of the heirs of Armando Testa
Fig. 91. © 2023 Artists Rights Society (ARS), New York / SIAE, Rome. © Musée départemental d'art ancient et contemporain, Epinal (France). Photo: Claude Philippot
Fig. 93. AIAP CDPG Centro di Documentazione sul Progetto Grafico, Collezione Armando Testa. In: *Il Tempo,* no. 8 (February 1956). Codice AIAP: CAT-Puri010. Reproduced with permission of the heirs of Armando Testa
Fig. 100. Courtesy Gio Ponti Archives—Archivio storico di Gio Ponti—Photo: Giorgio Casali
Fig. 101. Archivio De' Foscherari, Bologna
Fig. 103a–b. Archivio G. F. T. (Gruppo Finanziario Tessile). From Archivio Nazionale Cinema Impresa, courtesy of the l'Archivio dello Stato di Torino. Reproduced with permission of the heirs of Armando Testa
Fig. 107. Associazione Archivio Storico Olivetti, Ivrea, Italy
Fig. 109. © 2023 Artists Rights Society (ARS), New York / SIAE, Rome. Photo: P. Pellion. Archivio Merz
Fig. 110. Photo: Phillipe Migeat, via CNAC/MNAM, Dist. RMN-Grand Palais, via Art Resource
Figs. 112, 113, 114a–b, 115, 117, 118, 121, 122, 123, 131, 133 (left). Photos: © Paolo Mussat Sartor
Fig. 116. © Claudio Abate, courtesy of the Archivio Abate, Rome
Fig. 119. © R. Morichetti
Fig. 124. Courtesy of the Fondazione Sandro Penna, Turin
Fig. 126. © Giulio Paolini. Photo: Mario Sarotto. Courtesy Fondazione Giulio e Anna Paolini, Turin
Fig. 127. Photo: Antonio Masotti. Courtesy of Studio Mauri
Fig. 130b. Photo: © Elisabetta Catalano. Archivio Pistoletto, Biella. Courtesy Archivio Elisabetta Catalano.
Fig. 132. Archivio Rai, Turin
Fig. 134. Photo: Nicola Morittu / Courtesy Galleria Giorgio Persano, Turin
Fig. 136. Photo: Jimena Salvatierra. Courtesy Galleria Continua, San Gimignano/Beijing/Les Moulins/Habana/Roma/Sau Paolo/Paris
Fig. 137. Photo: © Paola Martínez Fiterre & Alejandro Mesa Crespo. Archivio Pistoletto, Biella.
Figs. 138, 139a–c. Photos: © Ugo Nespolo. Courtesy of Studio Nespolo, Turin
Fig. 140. Photo: Luhring Augustine, New York. Archivio Pistoletto, Biella.

INDEX

Illustrations are indicated by page numbers in *italics*.